THE COMPLETE DOC UNKNOWN

THE COMPLETE DOC
UNKN

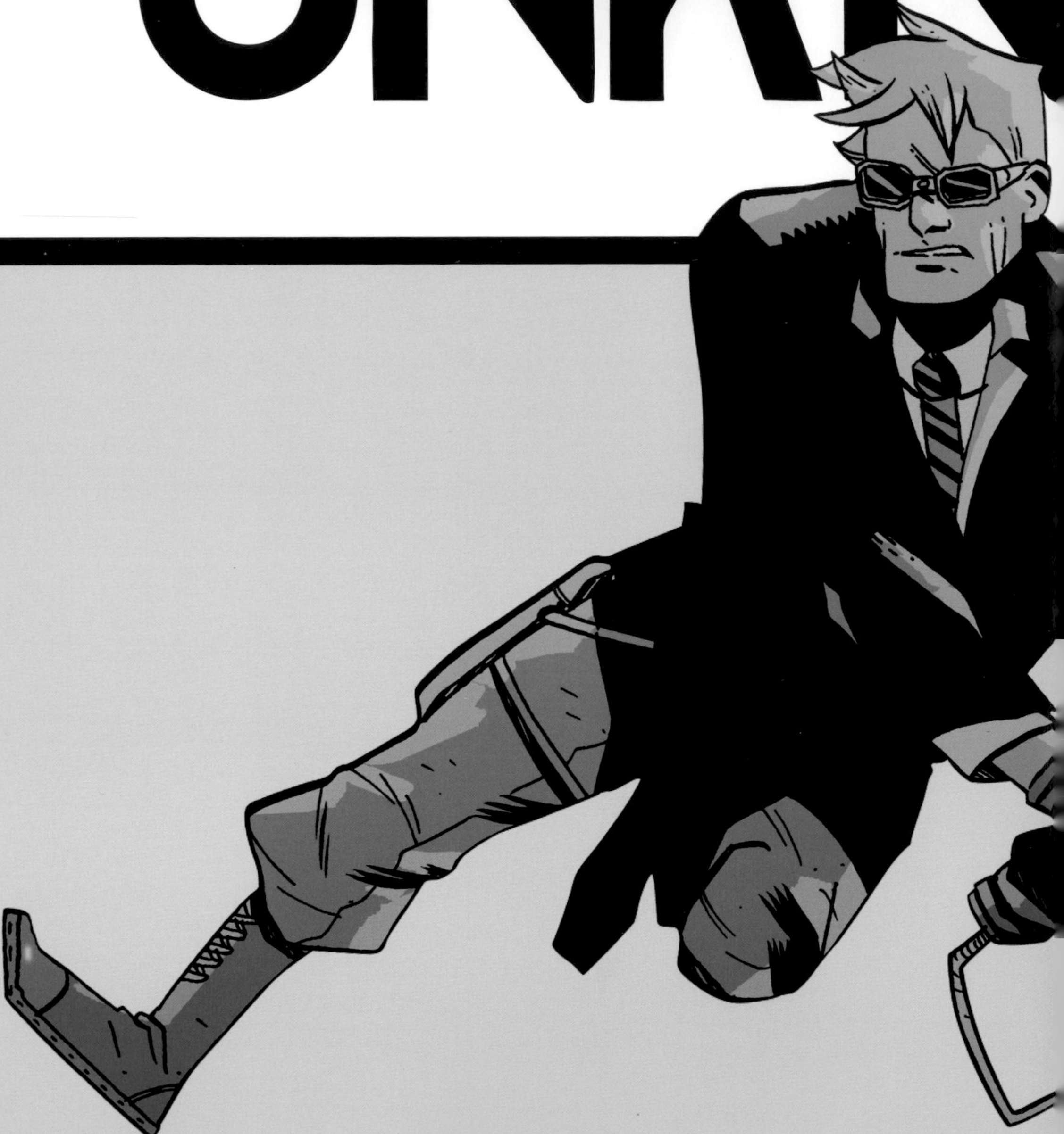

OWN

CREATED BY
FABIAN RANGEL JR. and **RYAN CODY**

WRITERS
FABIAN RANGEL JR. and **RYAN CODY**

ARTISTS
RYAN CODY, PHIL SLOAN,
JIM McMUNN, and **JOHN BROGLIA**

LETTERERS
ED BRISSON, NIC SHAW, FRANK BARBIERE,
RACHEL DEERING, EVELYN RANGEL, and **RYAN CODY**

DARK HORSE BOOKS

PRESIDENT & PUBLISHER **MIKE RICHARDSON**
COLLECTION EDITOR **SPENCER CUSHING**
COLLECTION ASSISTANT EDITOR **KEVIN BURKHALTER**
DESIGNER **SARAH TERRY**
DIGITAL ART TECHNICIAN **ADAM PRUETT**

Published by Dark Horse Books
A division of Dark Horse Comics, Inc.
10956 SE Main Street, Milwaukie, OR 97222

First edition: July 2017
ISBN 978-1-50670-288-9

10 9 8 7 6 5 4 3 2 1
Printed in China

International Licensing: (503) 905-2377
Comic Shop Locator Service: (888) 266-4226

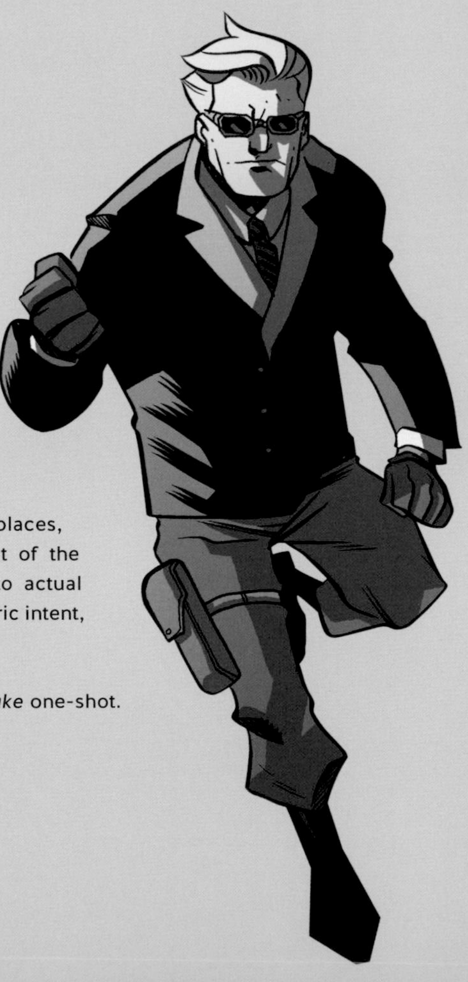

This volume collects *Doc Unknown* Volumes 1–3, and the *Boss Snake* one-shot.

TABLE OF CONTENTS

THE MUSEUM
OF MADNESS

SCRIPT BY **FABIAN RANGEL JR.**

ART BY **RYAN CODY**

LETTERS BY **ED BRISSON**

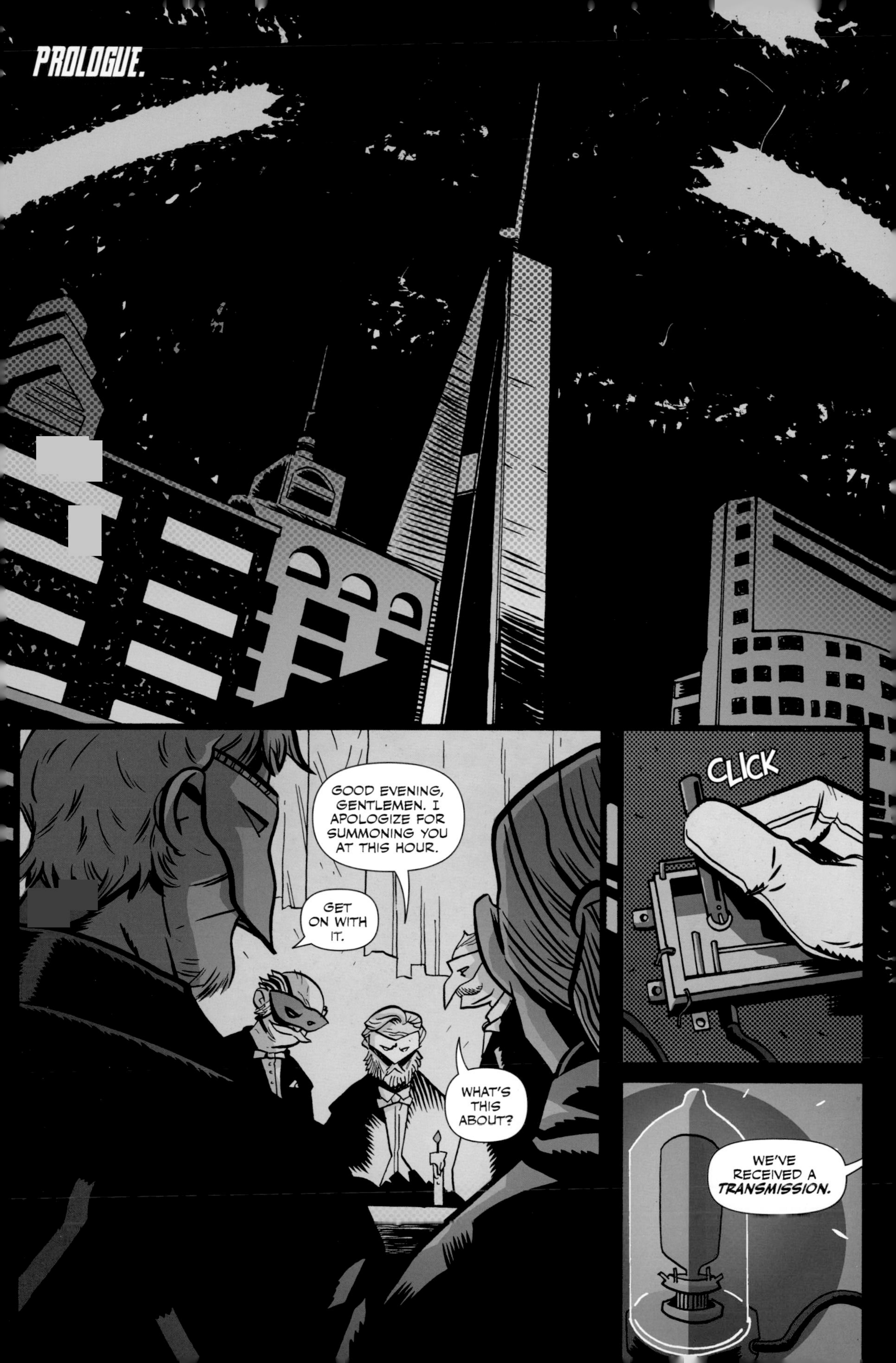
PROLOGUE.
GOOD EVENING, GENTLEMEN. I APOLOGIZE FOR SUMMONING YOU AT THIS HOUR.
GET ON WITH IT.
WHAT'S THIS ABOUT?
CLICK
WE'VE RECEIVED A TRANSMISSION.

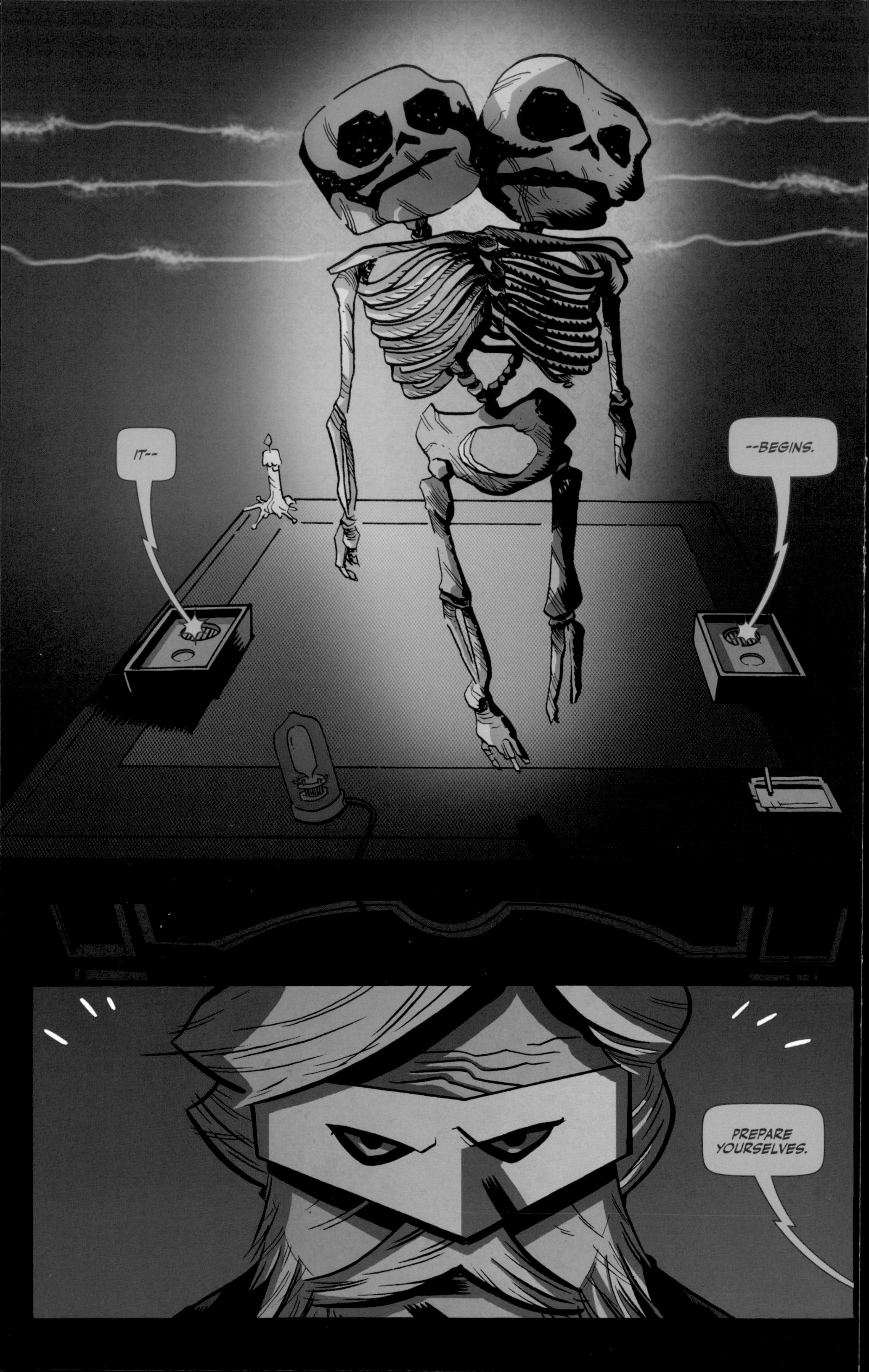
IT--
--BEGINS.
PREPARE YOURSELVES.

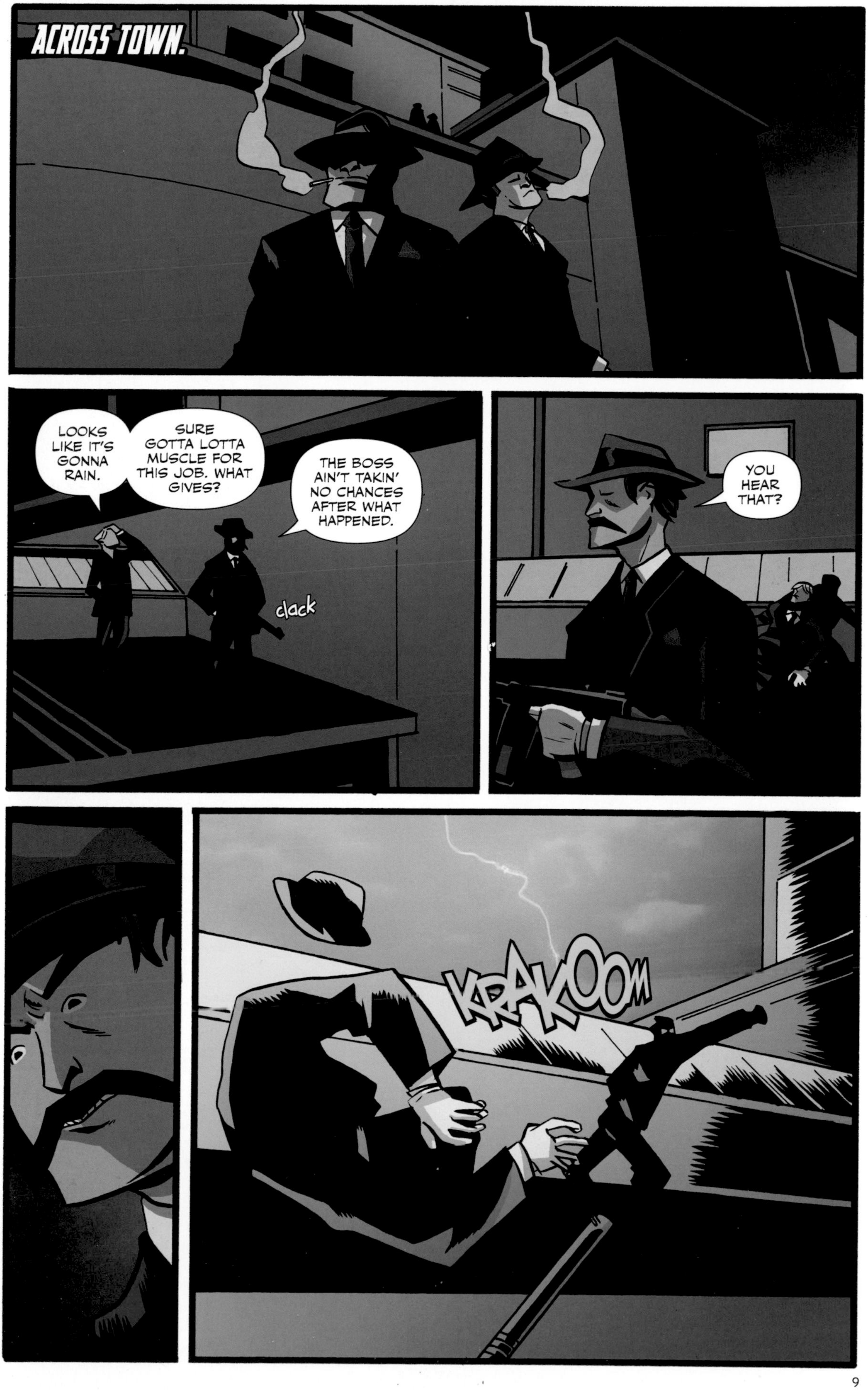
ACROSS TOWN.
LOOKS LIKE IT'S GONNA RAIN.
SURE GOTTA LOTTA MUSCLE FOR THIS JOB. WHAT GIVES?
THE BOSS AIN'T TAKIN' NO CHANCES AFTER WHAT HAPPENED.
clack
YOU HEAR THAT?
KRAKOOM

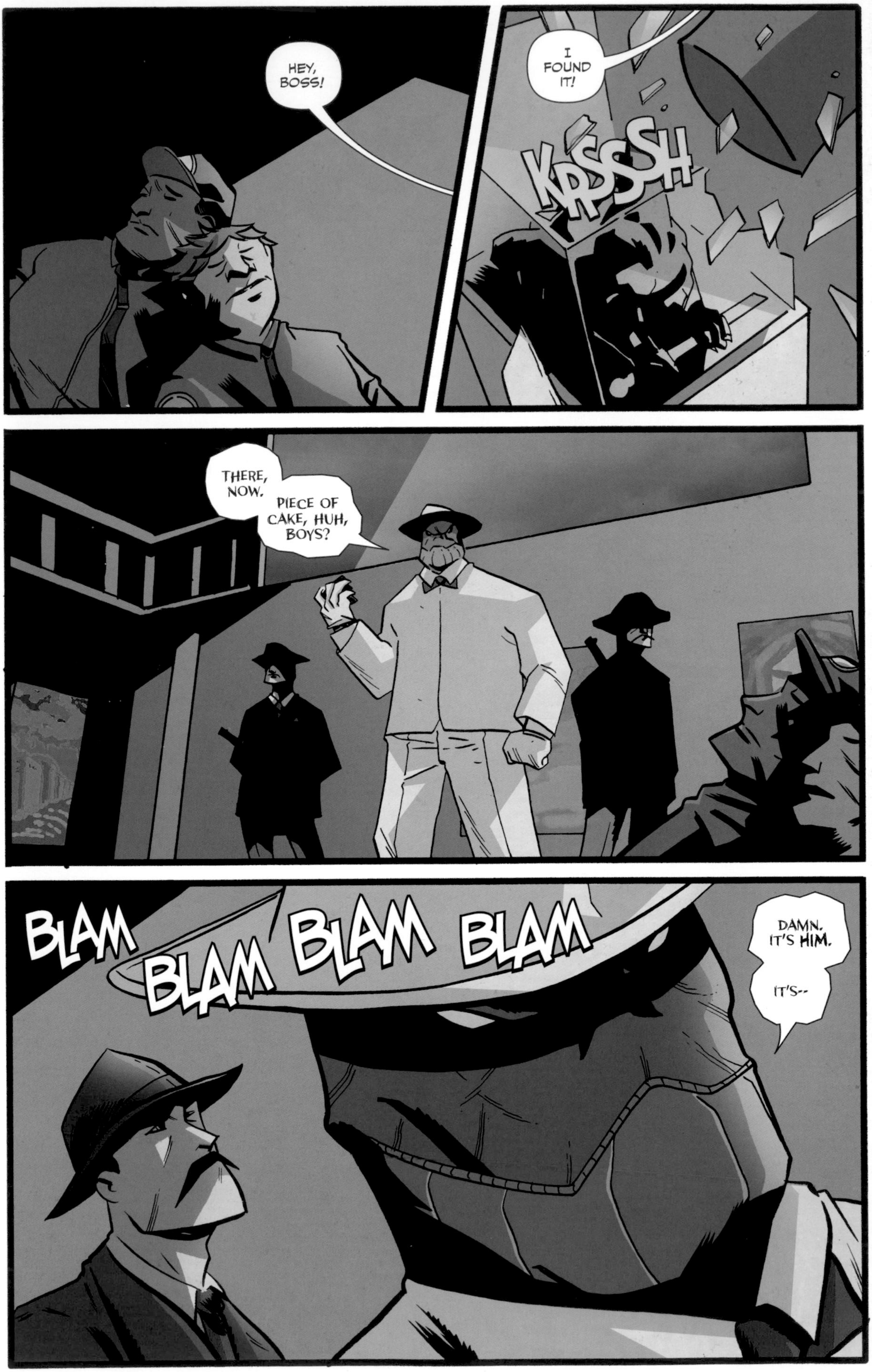
HEY, BOSS!
I FOUND IT!
KRSSSH
THERE, NOW.
PIECE OF CAKE, HUH, BOYS?
BLAM
BLAM BLAM BLAM
DAMN. IT'S HIM.
IT'S--

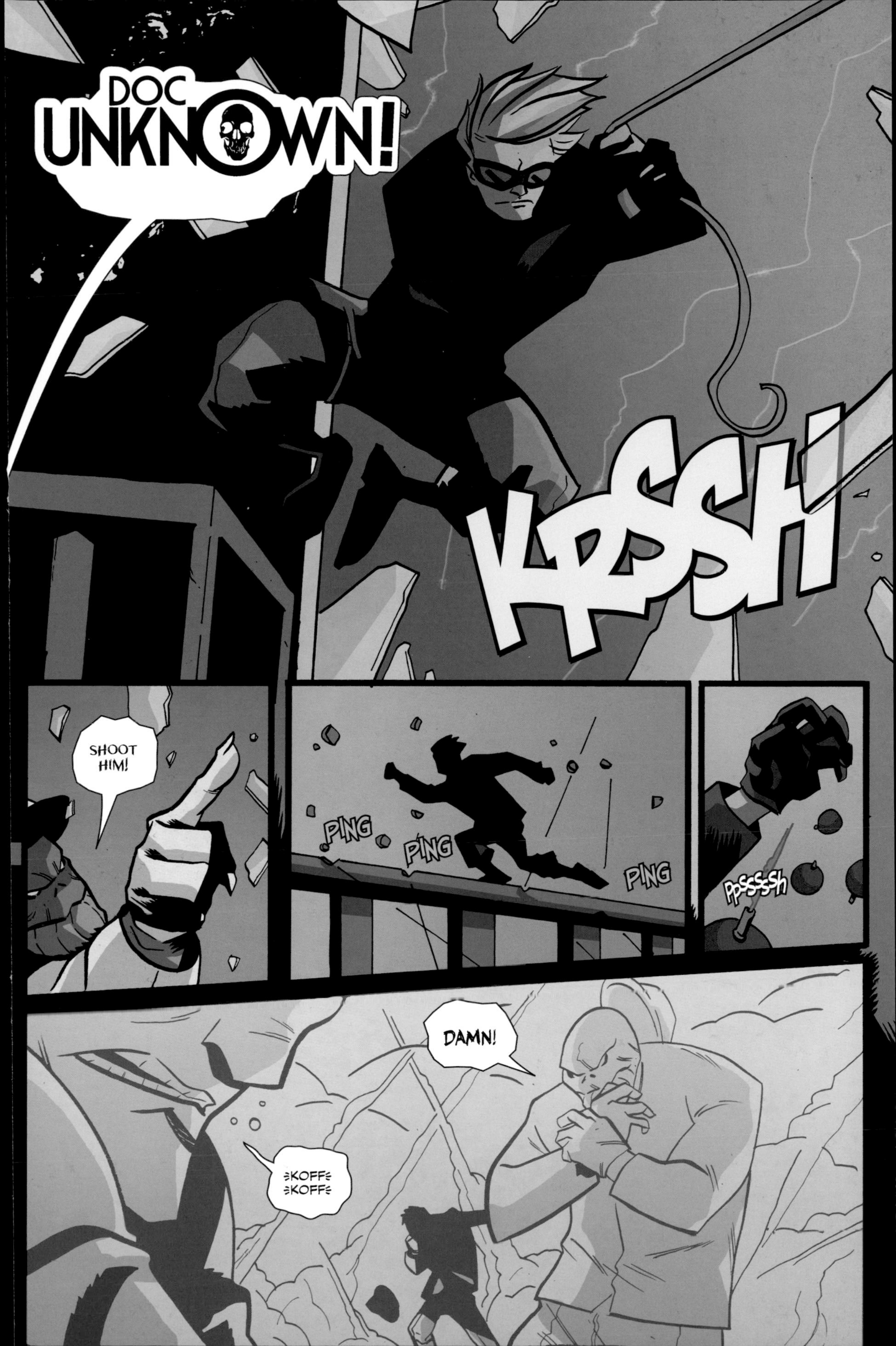
DOC UNKNOWN!
KRSSH
SHOOT HIM!
PING
PING
PING
PPSSSSH
DAMN!
KOFF KOFF

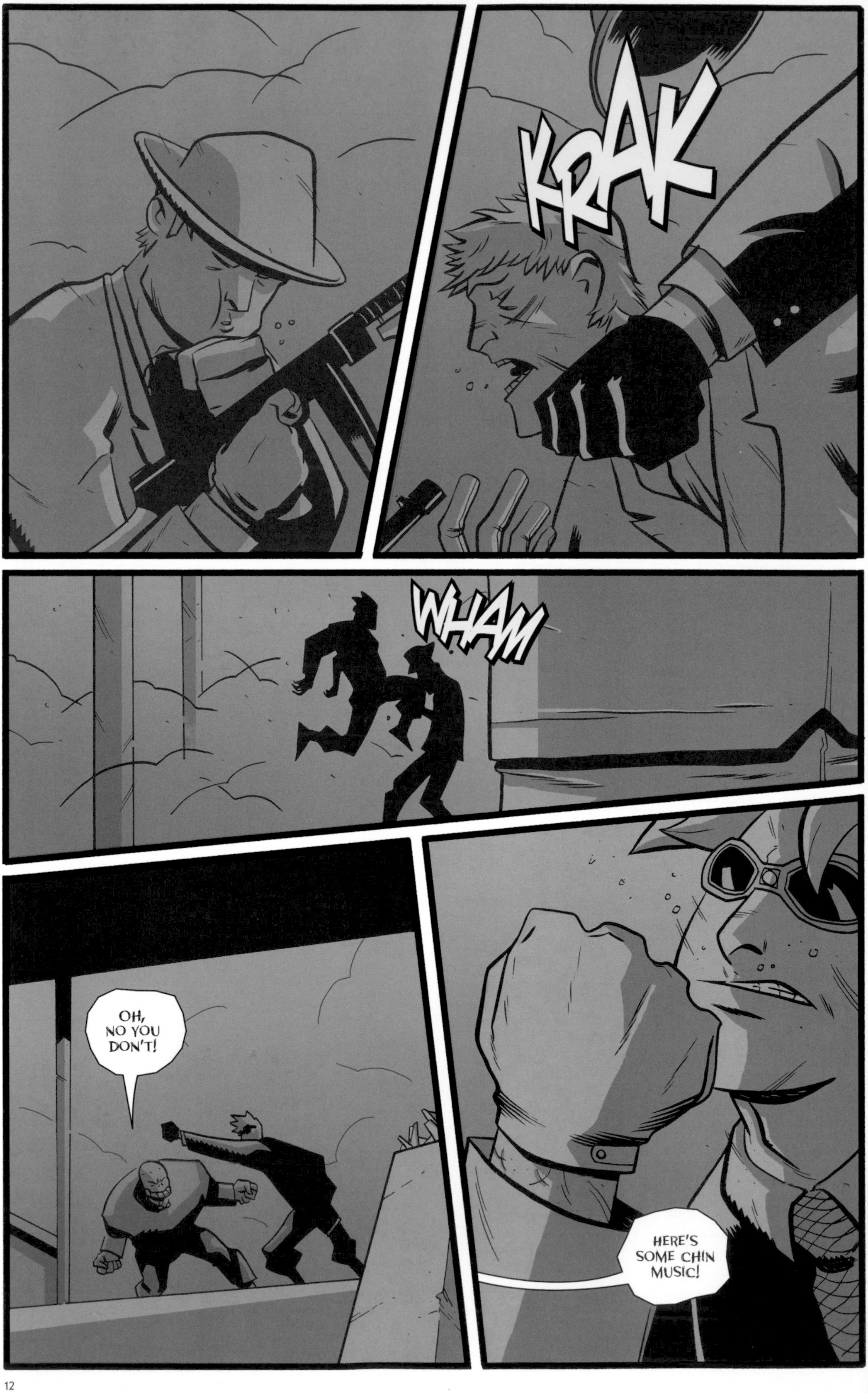
KRAK
WHAM
OH, NO YOU DON'T!
HERE'S SOME CHIN MUSIC!

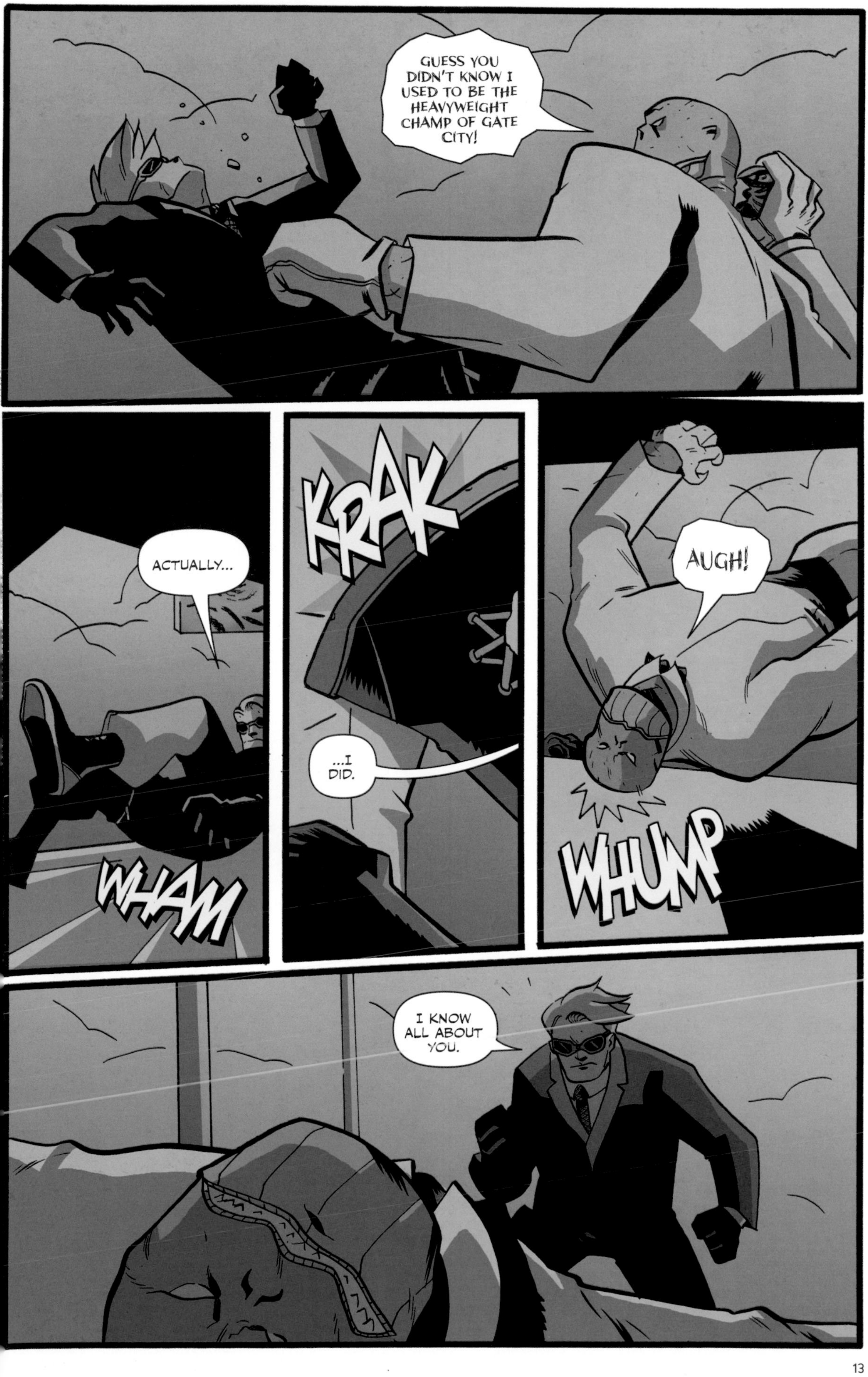
GUESS YOU DIDN'T KNOW I USED TO BE THE HEAVYWEIGHT CHAMP OF GATE CITY!
ACTUALLY...
WHAM
KRAK
...I DID.
AUGH!
WHUMP
I KNOW ALL ABOUT YOU.

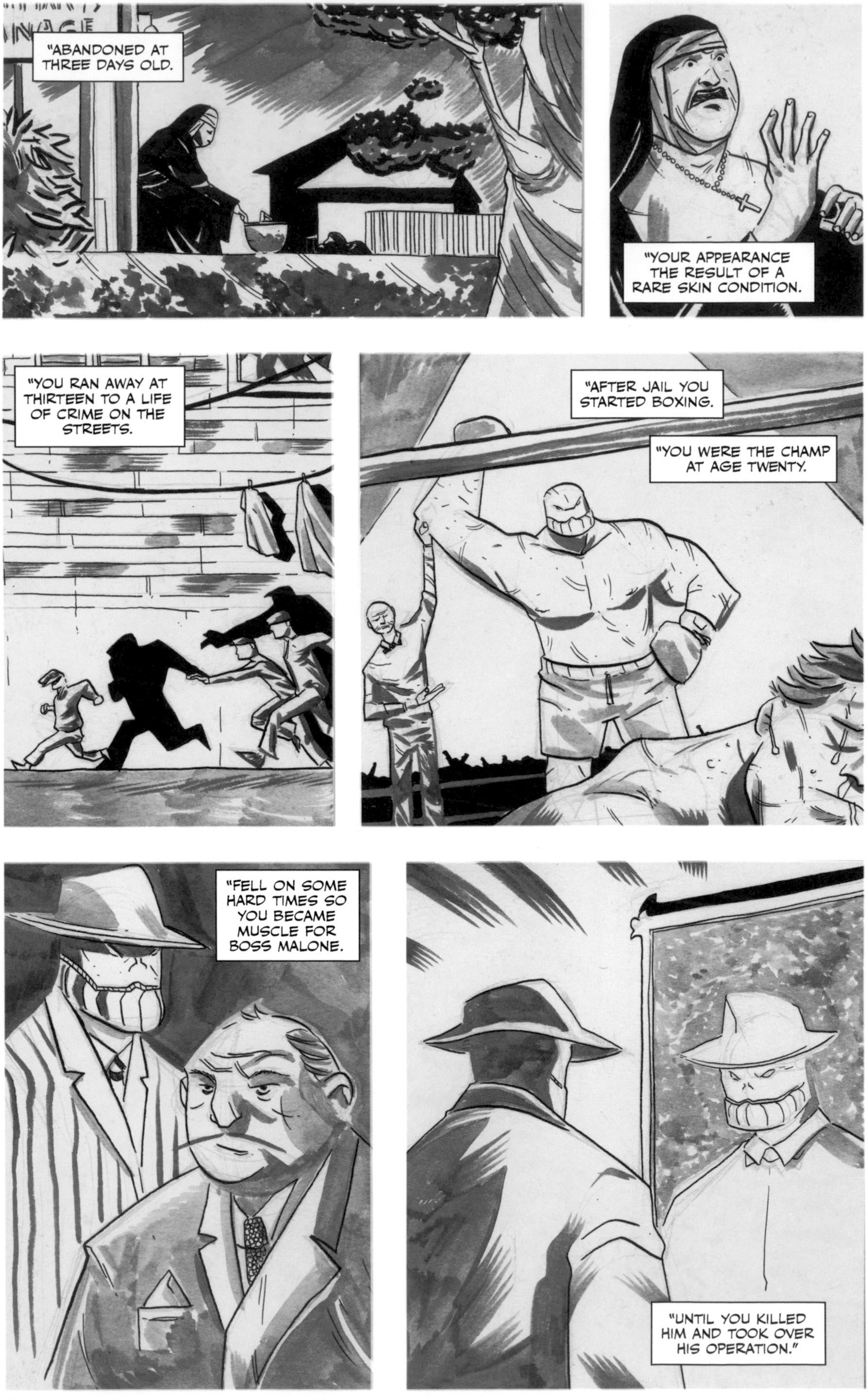
"ABANDONED AT THREE DAYS OLD.
"YOUR APPEARANCE THE RESULT OF A RARE SKIN CONDITION.
"YOU RAN AWAY AT THIRTEEN TO A LIFE OF CRIME ON THE STREETS.
"AFTER JAIL YOU STARTED BOXING.
"YOU WERE THE CHAMP AT AGE TWENTY.
"FELL ON SOME HARD TIMES SO YOU BECAME MUSCLE FOR BOSS MALONE.
"UNTIL YOU KILLED HIM AND TOOK OVER HIS OPERATION."

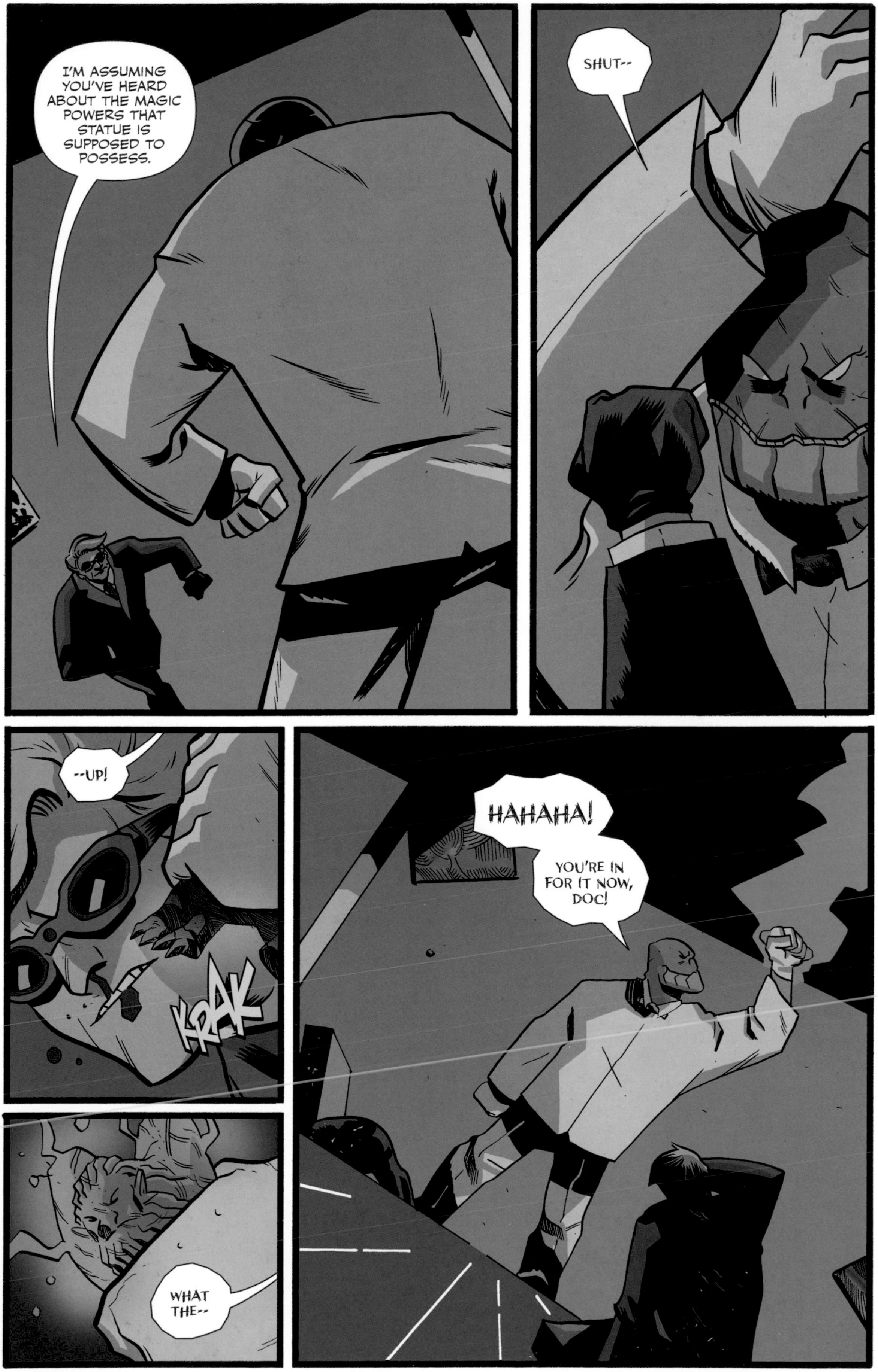
I'M ASSUMING YOU'VE HEARD ABOUT THE MAGIC POWERS THAT STATUE IS SUPPOSED TO POSSESS.
SHUT--
--UP!
KRAK
HAHAHA!
YOU'RE IN FOR IT NOW, DOC!
WHAT THE--

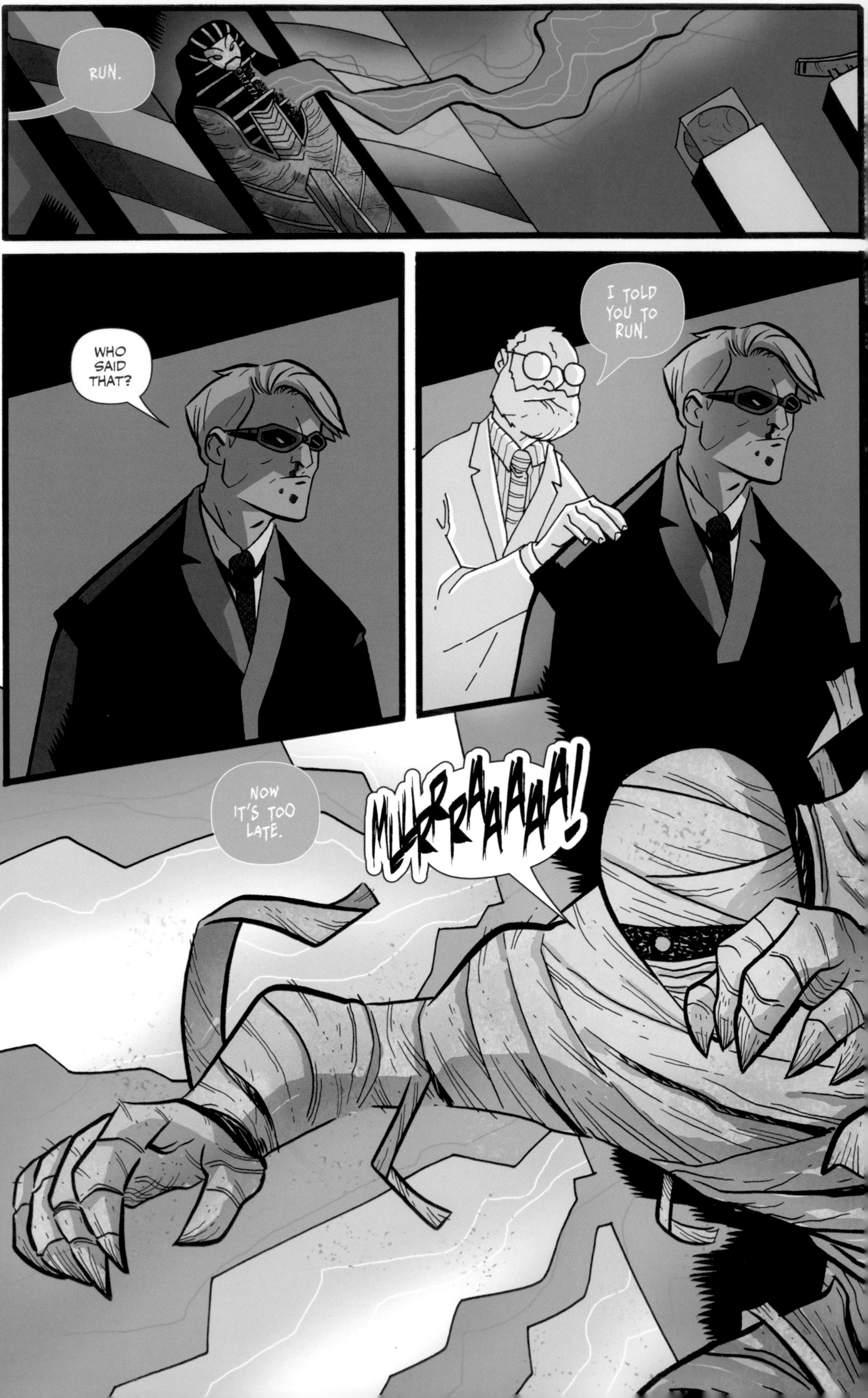
RUN.
WHO SAID THAT?
I TOLD YOU TO RUN.
NOW IT'S TOO LATE.
MURRRAAAAA!

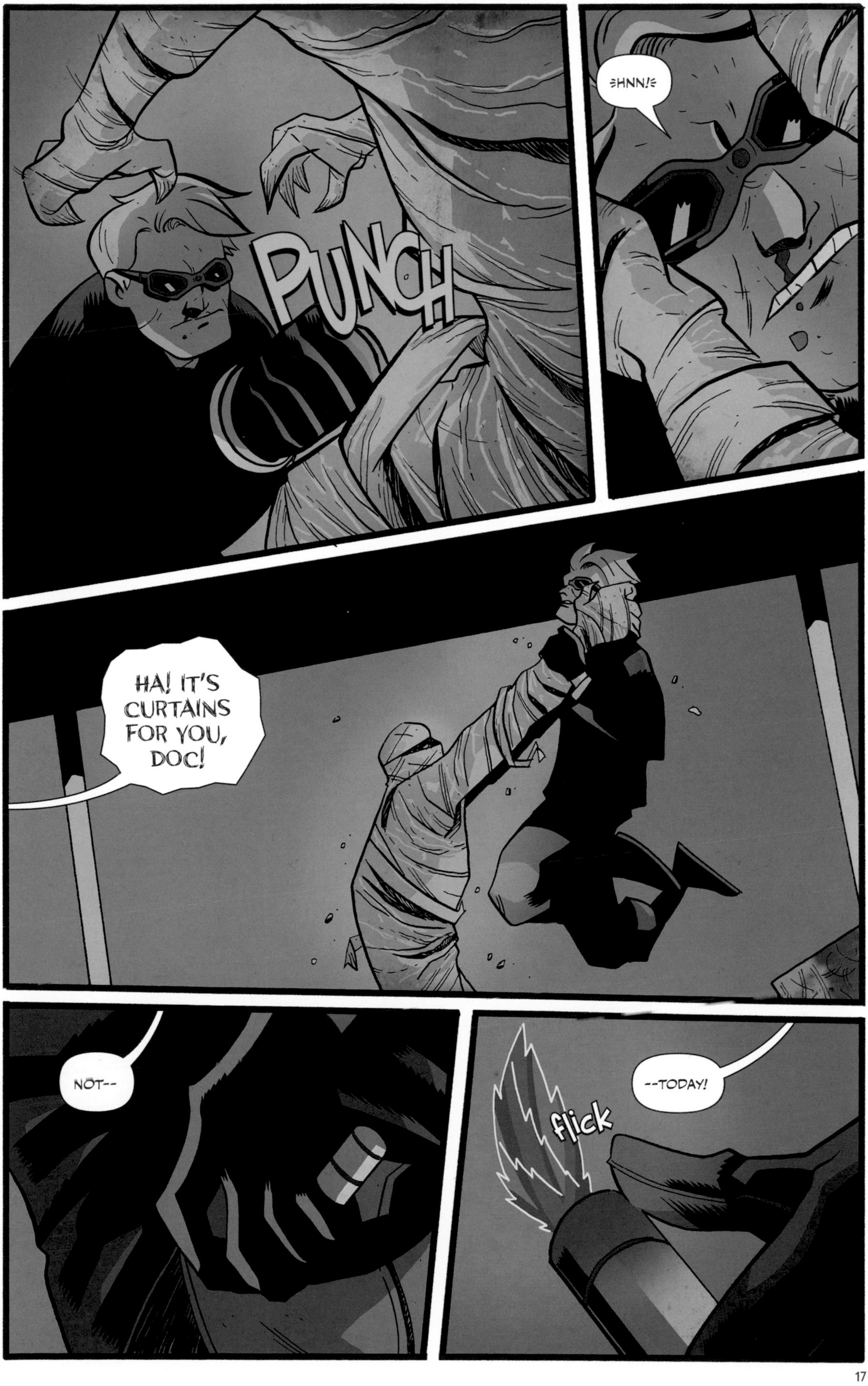
PUNCH
HNN!
HA! IT'S CURTAINS FOR YOU, DOC!
NOT--
--TODAY!
flick

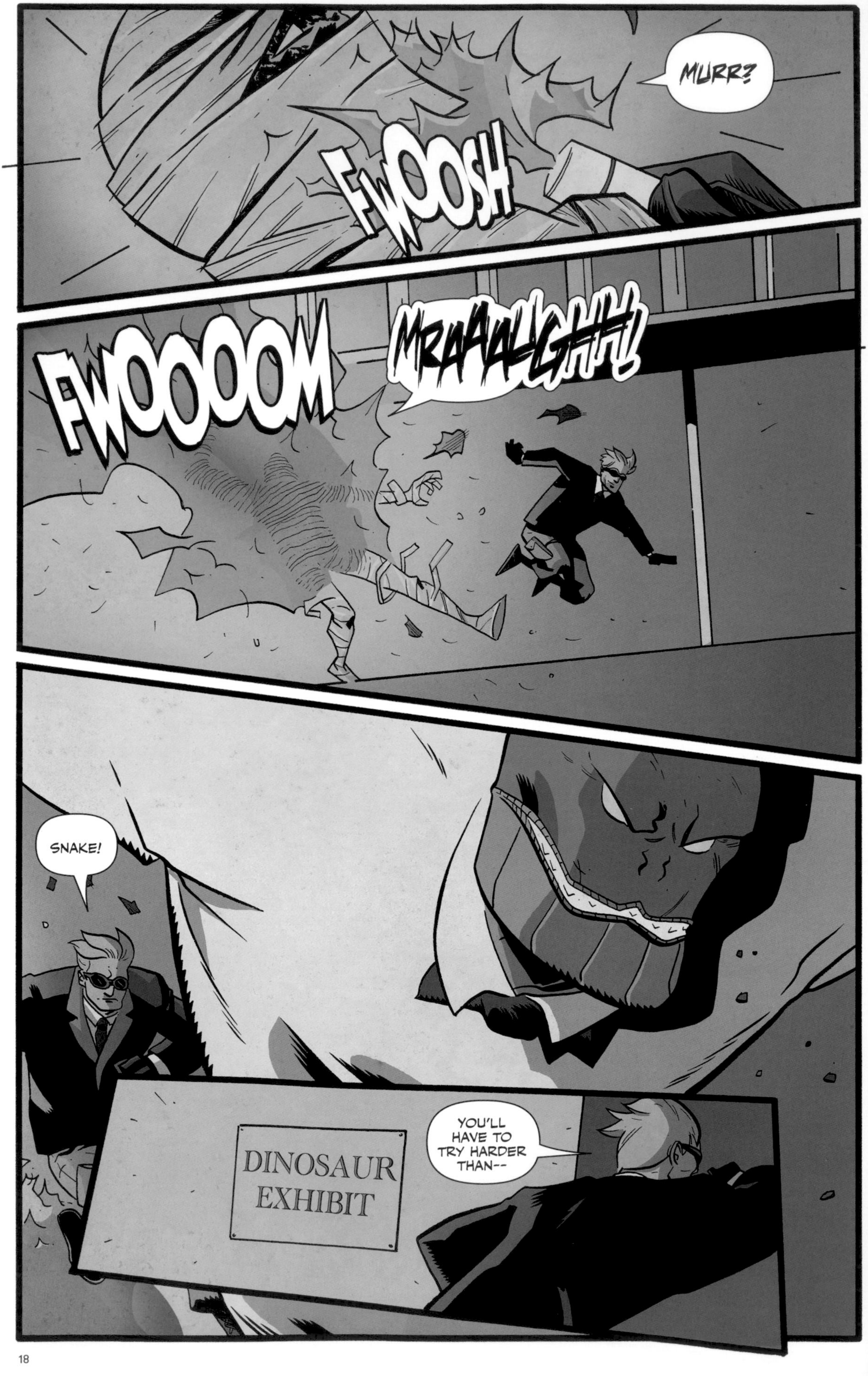
MURR?
FWOOSH
FWOOOOM
MRAAAUGHH!
SNAKE!
DINOSAUR EXHIBIT
YOU'LL HAVE TO TRY HARDER THAN--

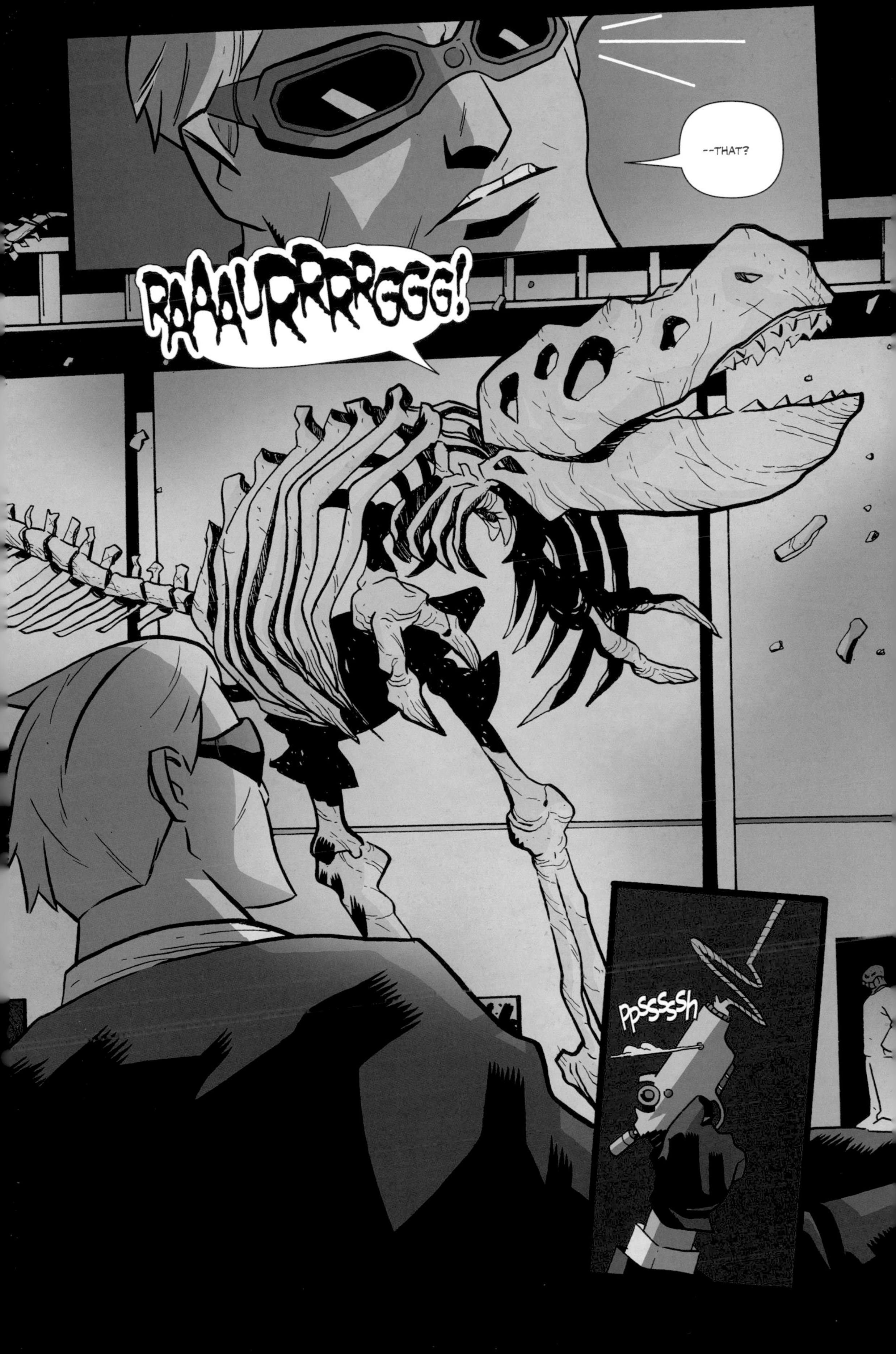
--THAT?
RAAAURRRRGGG!
Ppssssh

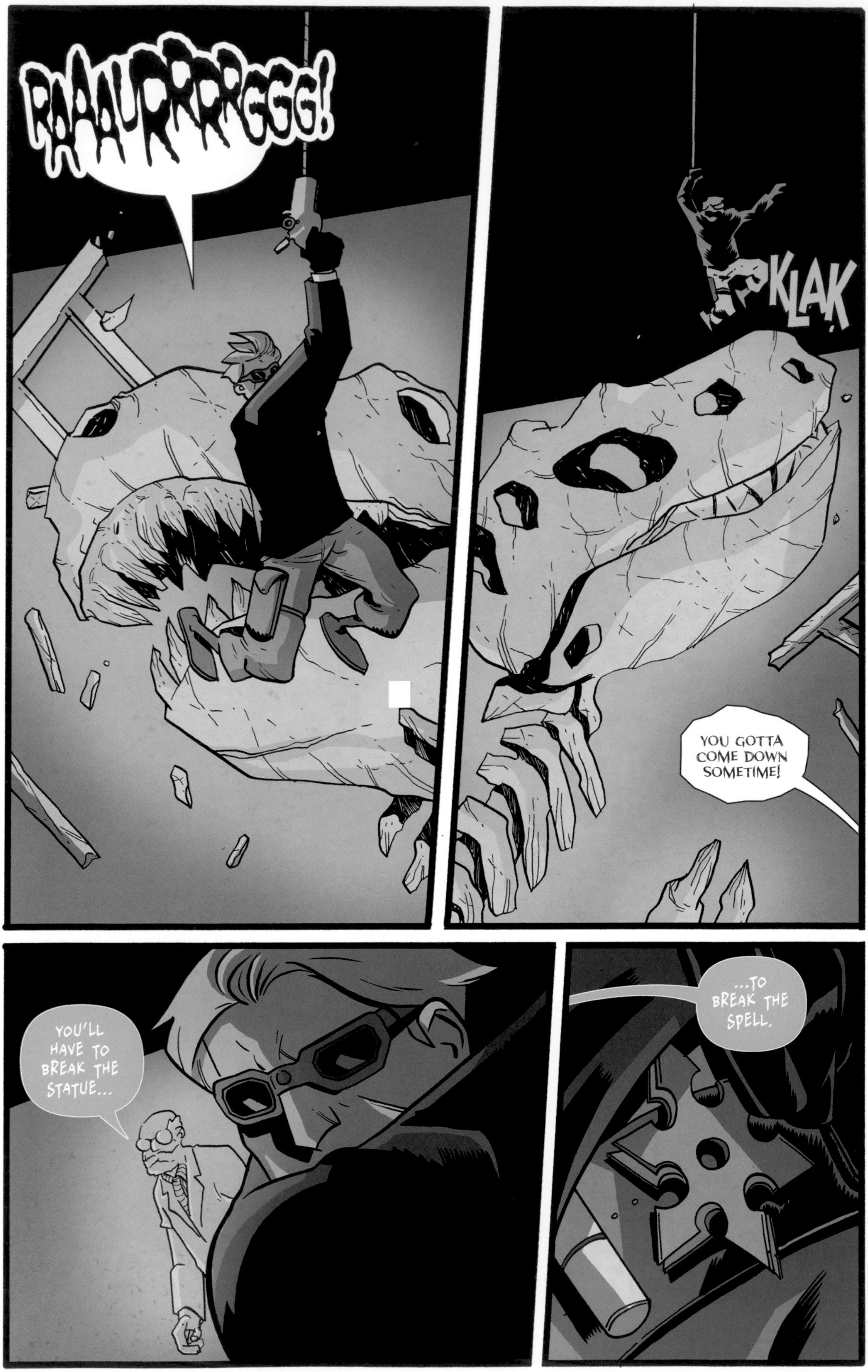
RAAAURRRRGGG!
KLAK
YOU GOTTA COME DOWN SOMETIME!
YOU'LL HAVE TO BREAK THE STATUE...
...TO BREAK THE SPELL.

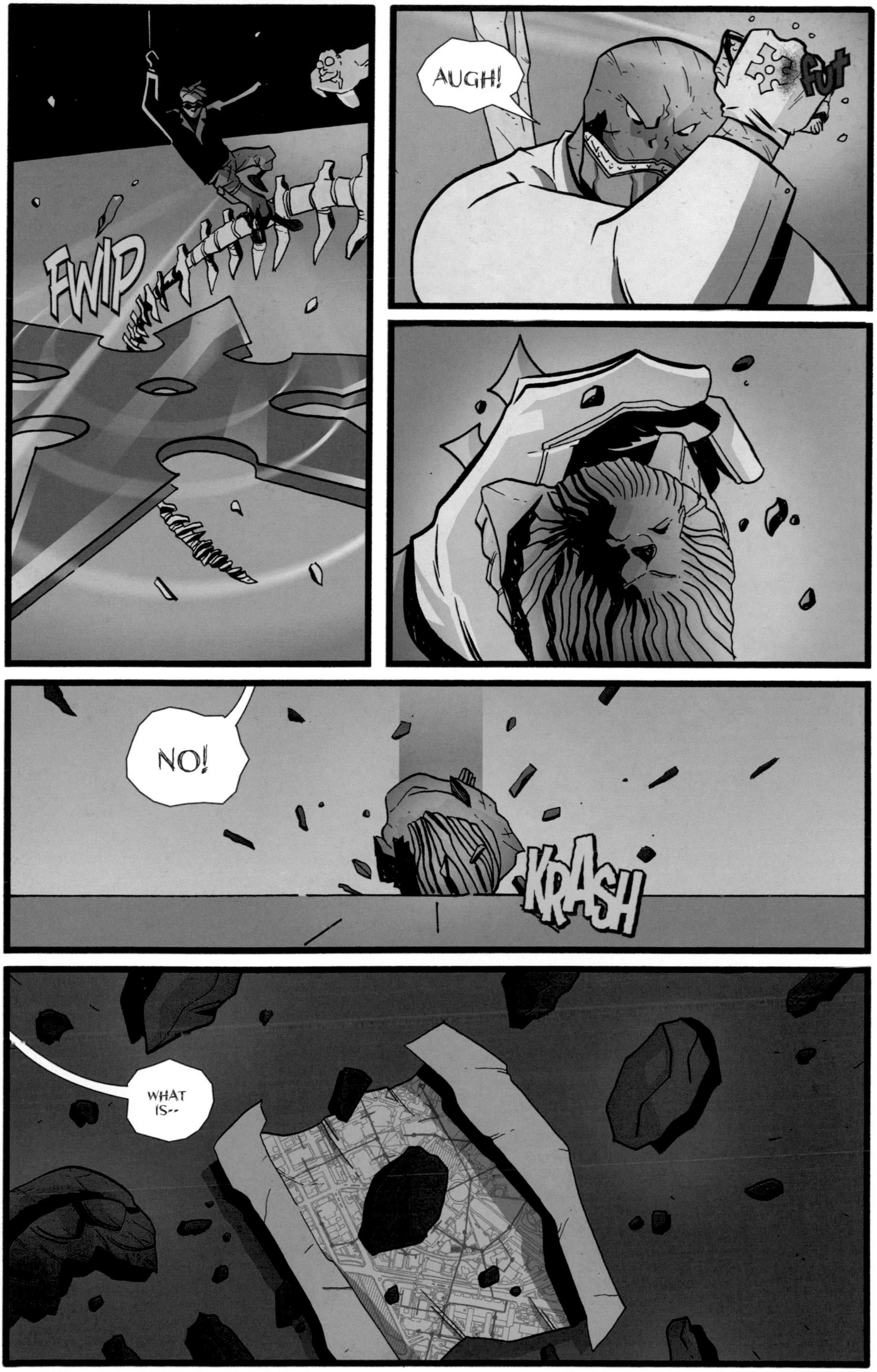
FWIP
AUGH!
FUT
NO!
KRASH
WHAT IS--

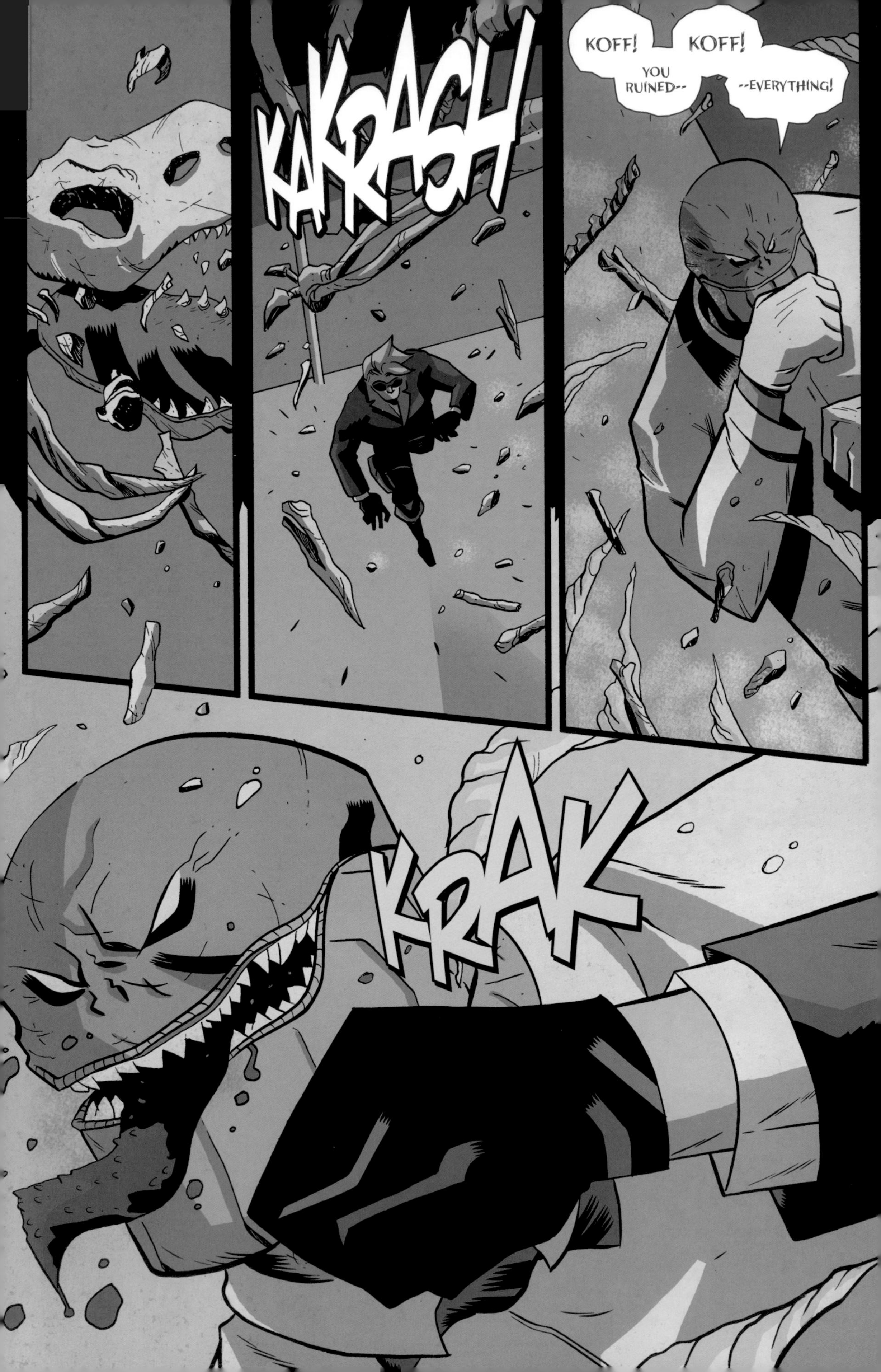
KAKRASH
KOFF! KOFF!
YOU RUINED--
--EVERYTHING!
KRAK

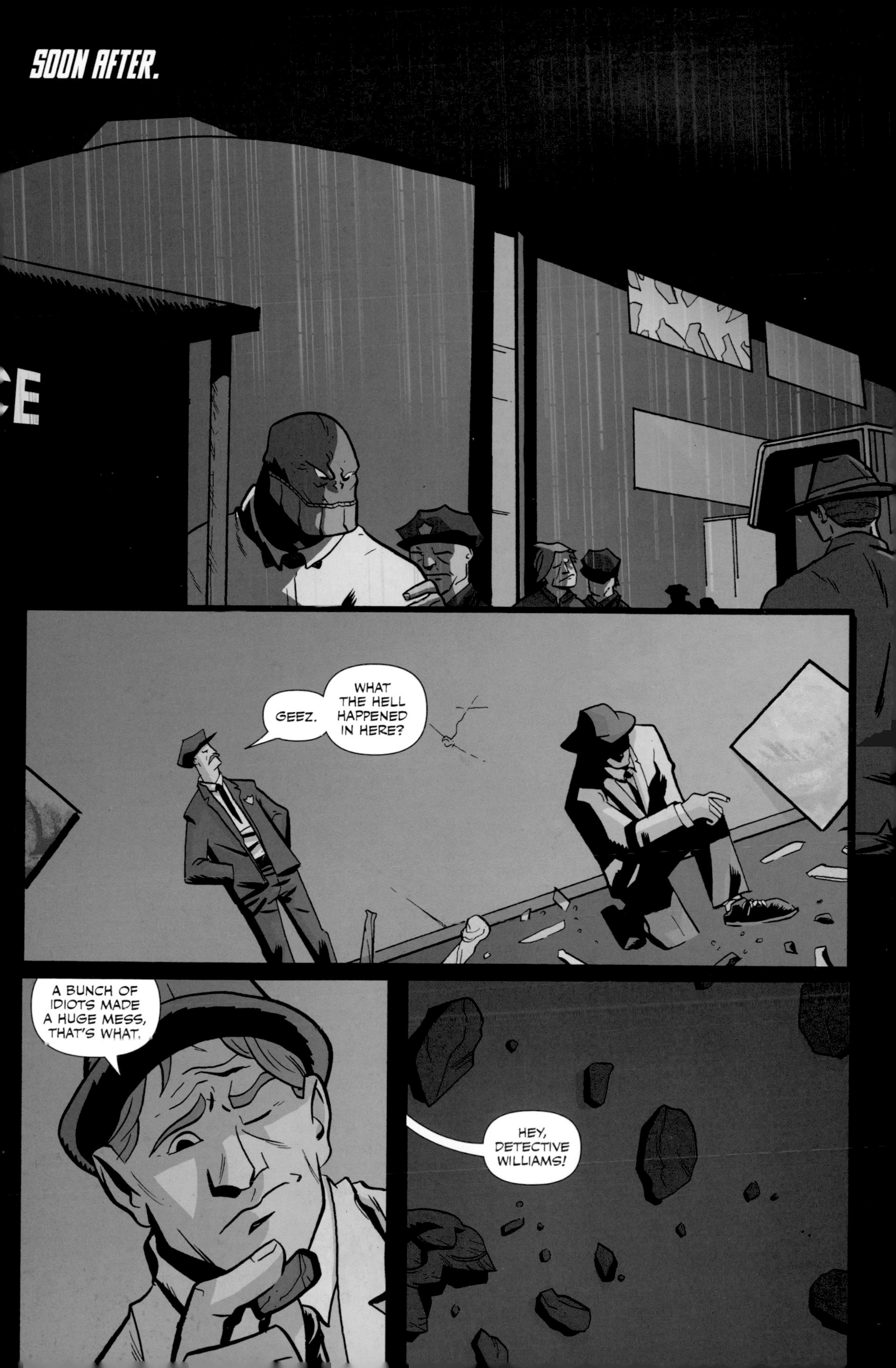
SOON AFTER.
GEEZ.
WHAT THE HELL HAPPENED IN HERE?
A BUNCH OF IDIOTS MADE A HUGE MESS, THAT'S WHAT.
HEY, DETECTIVE WILLIAMS!

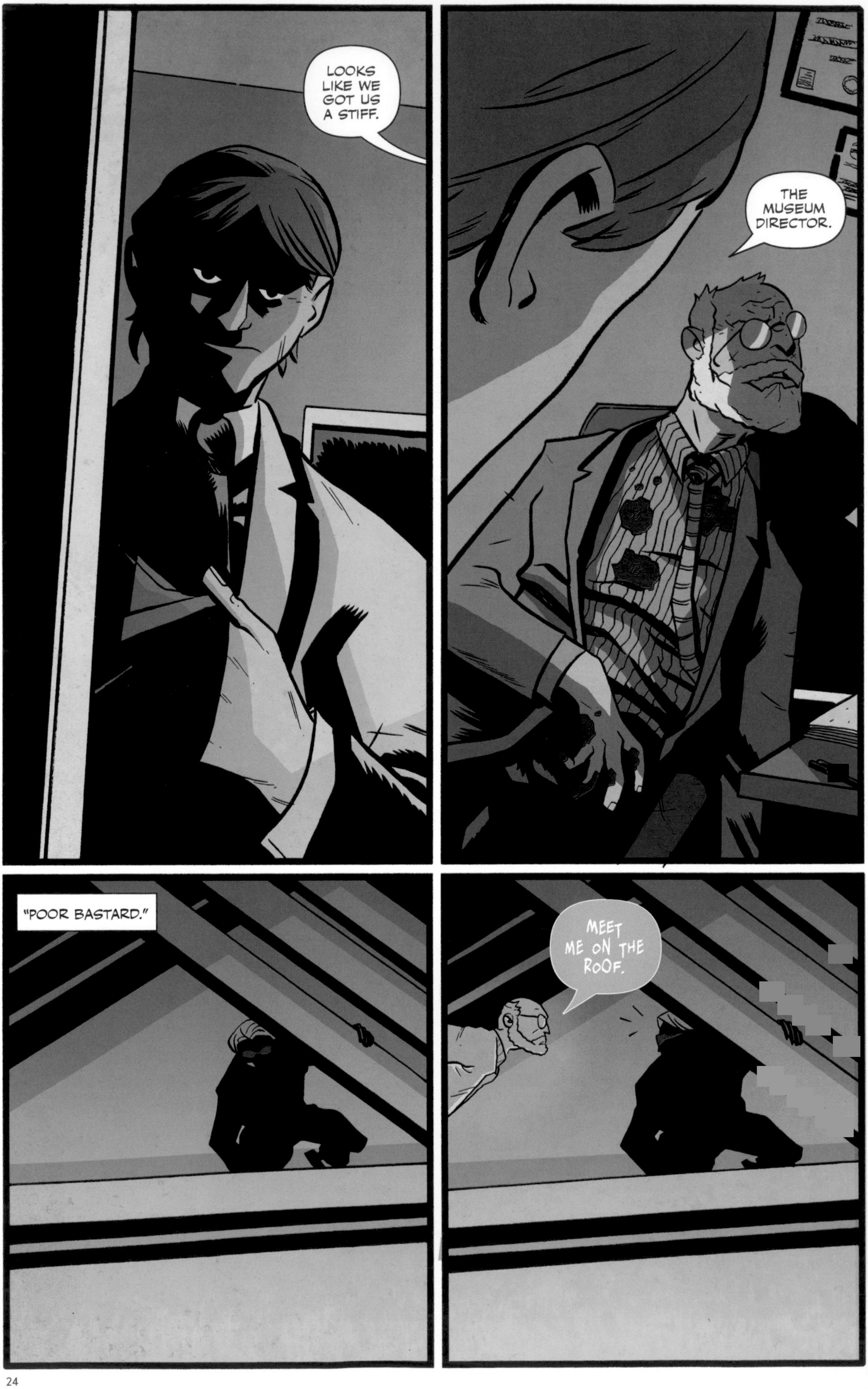
LOOKS LIKE WE GOT US A STIFF.
THE MUSEUM DIRECTOR.
"POOR BASTARD."
MEET ME ON THE ROOF.

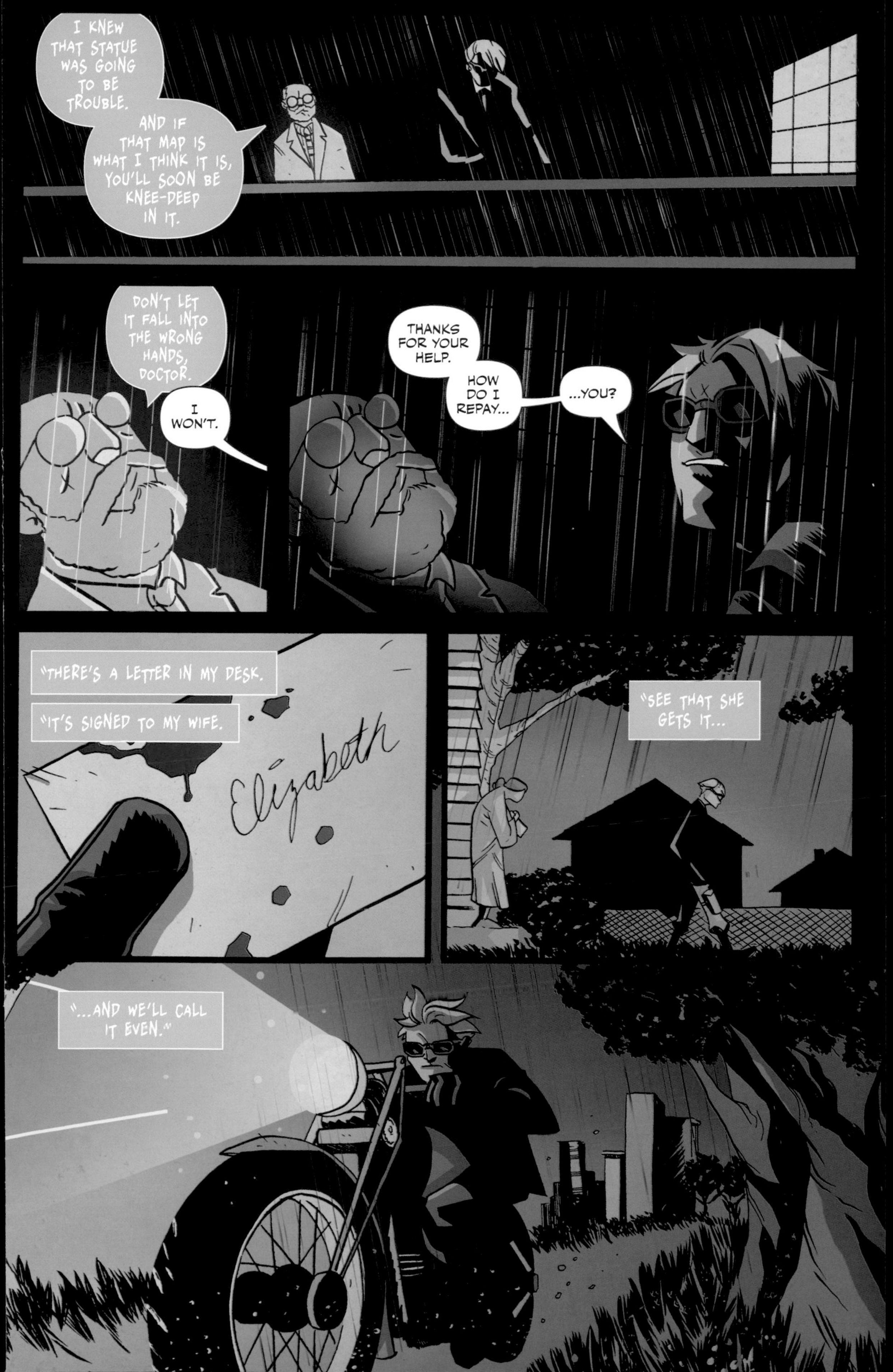
I KNEW THAT STATUE WAS GOING TO BE TROUBLE.
AND IF THAT MAP IS WHAT I THINK IT IS, YOU'LL SOON BE KNEE-DEEP IN IT.
DON'T LET IT FALL INTO THE WRONG HANDS, DOCTOR.
I WON'T.
THANKS FOR YOUR HELP.
HOW DO I REPAY...
...YOU?
"THERE'S A LETTER IN MY DESK.
"IT'S SIGNED TO MY WIFE.
Elizabeth
"SEE THAT SHE GETS IT...
"...AND WE'LL CALL IT EVEN."

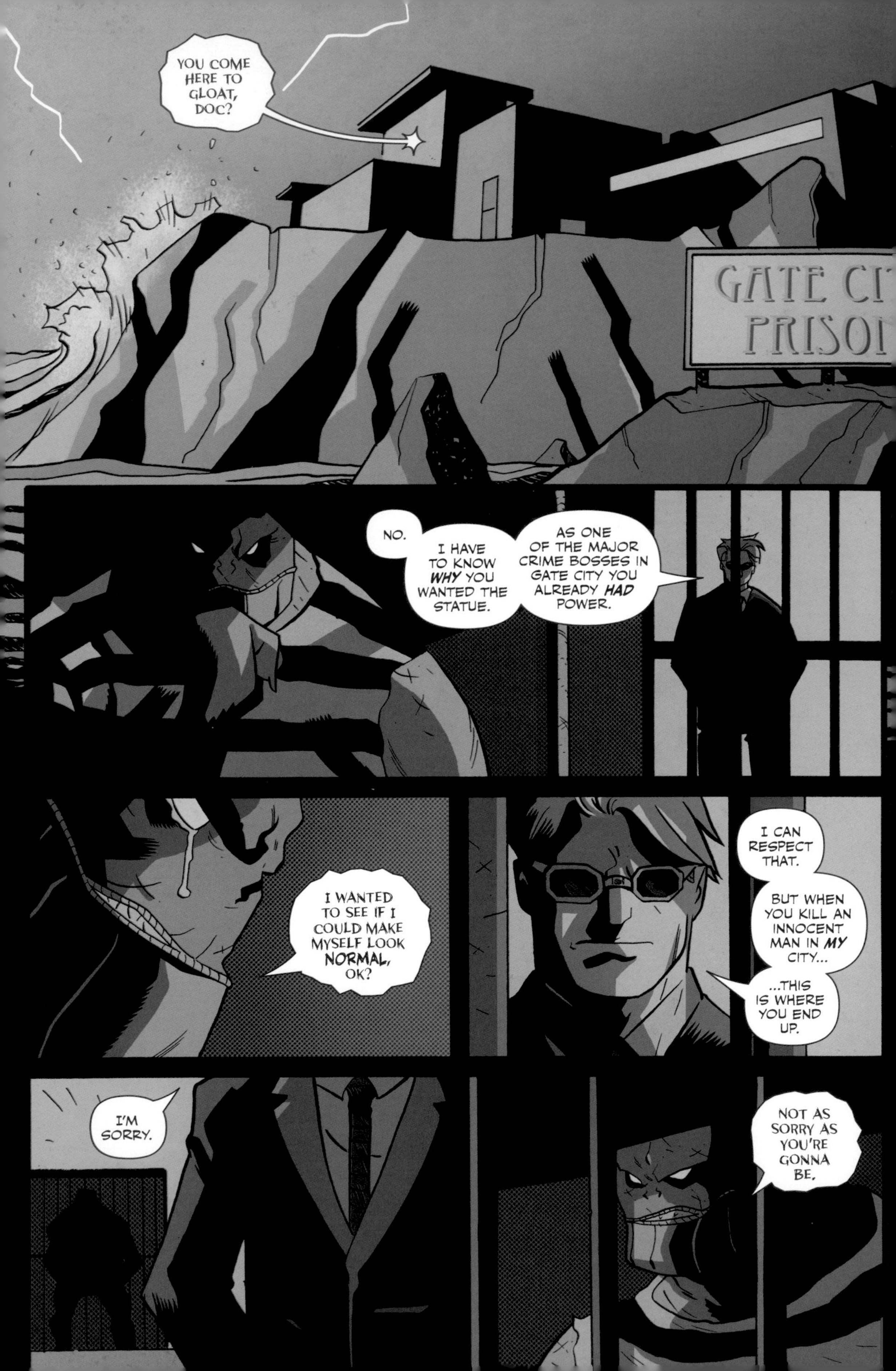
YOU COME HERE TO GLOAT, DOC?
GATE CIT
PRISO
NO.
I HAVE TO KNOW WHY YOU WANTED THE STATUE.
AS ONE OF THE MAJOR CRIME BOSSES IN GATE CITY YOU ALREADY HAD POWER.
I WANTED TO SEE IF I COULD MAKE MYSELF LOOK NORMAL, OK?
I CAN RESPECT THAT.
BUT WHEN YOU KILL AN INNOCENT MAN IN MY CITY...
...THIS IS WHERE YOU END UP.
I'M SORRY.
NOT AS SORRY AS YOU'RE GONNA BE.

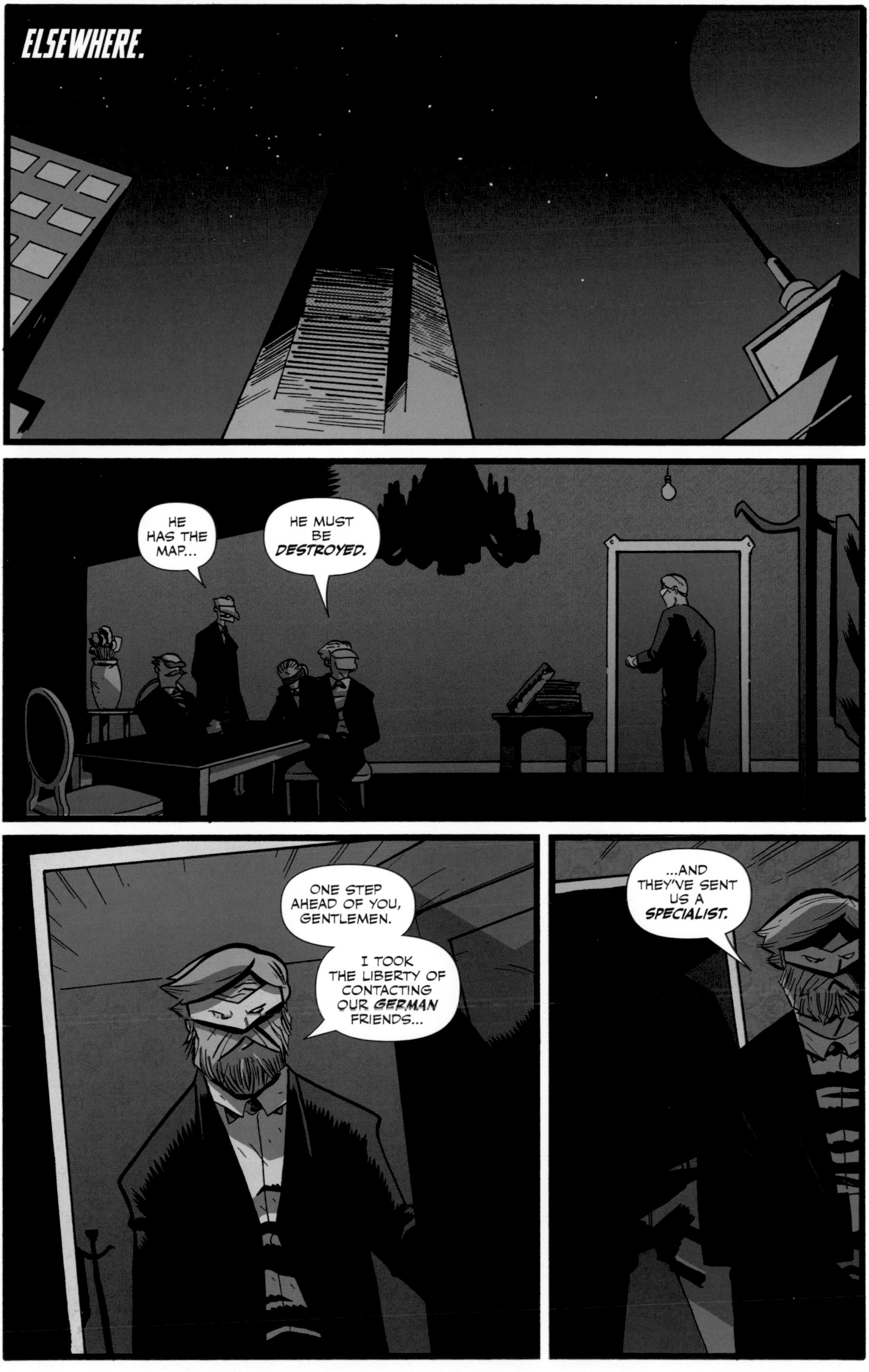
ELSEWHERE.
HE HAS THE MAP...
HE MUST BE DESTROYED.
ONE STEP AHEAD OF YOU, GENTLEMEN.
I TOOK THE LIBERTY OF CONTACTING OUR GERMAN FRIENDS...
...AND THEY'VE SENT US A SPECIALIST.

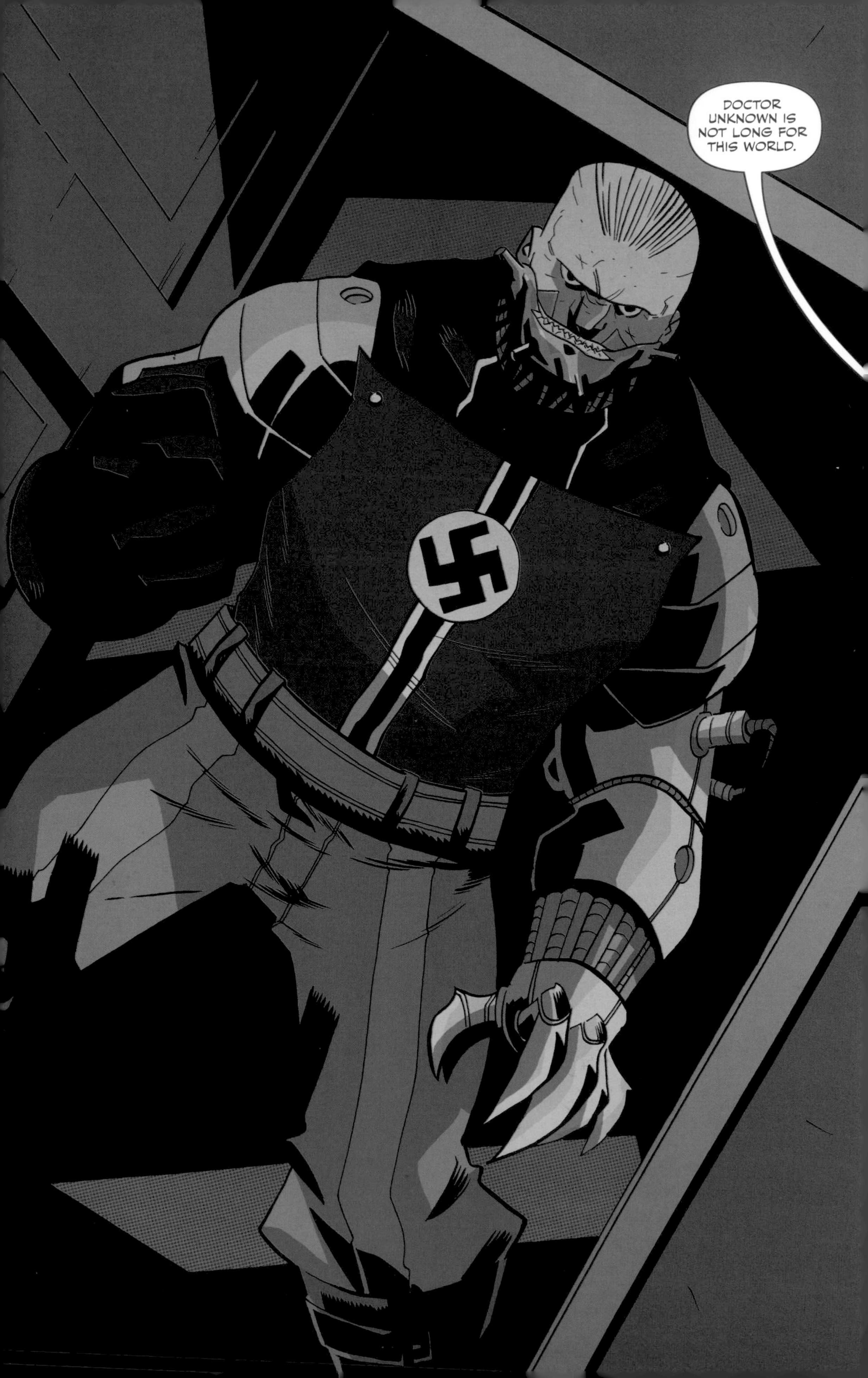
DOCTOR UNKNOWN IS NOT LONG FOR THIS WORLD.

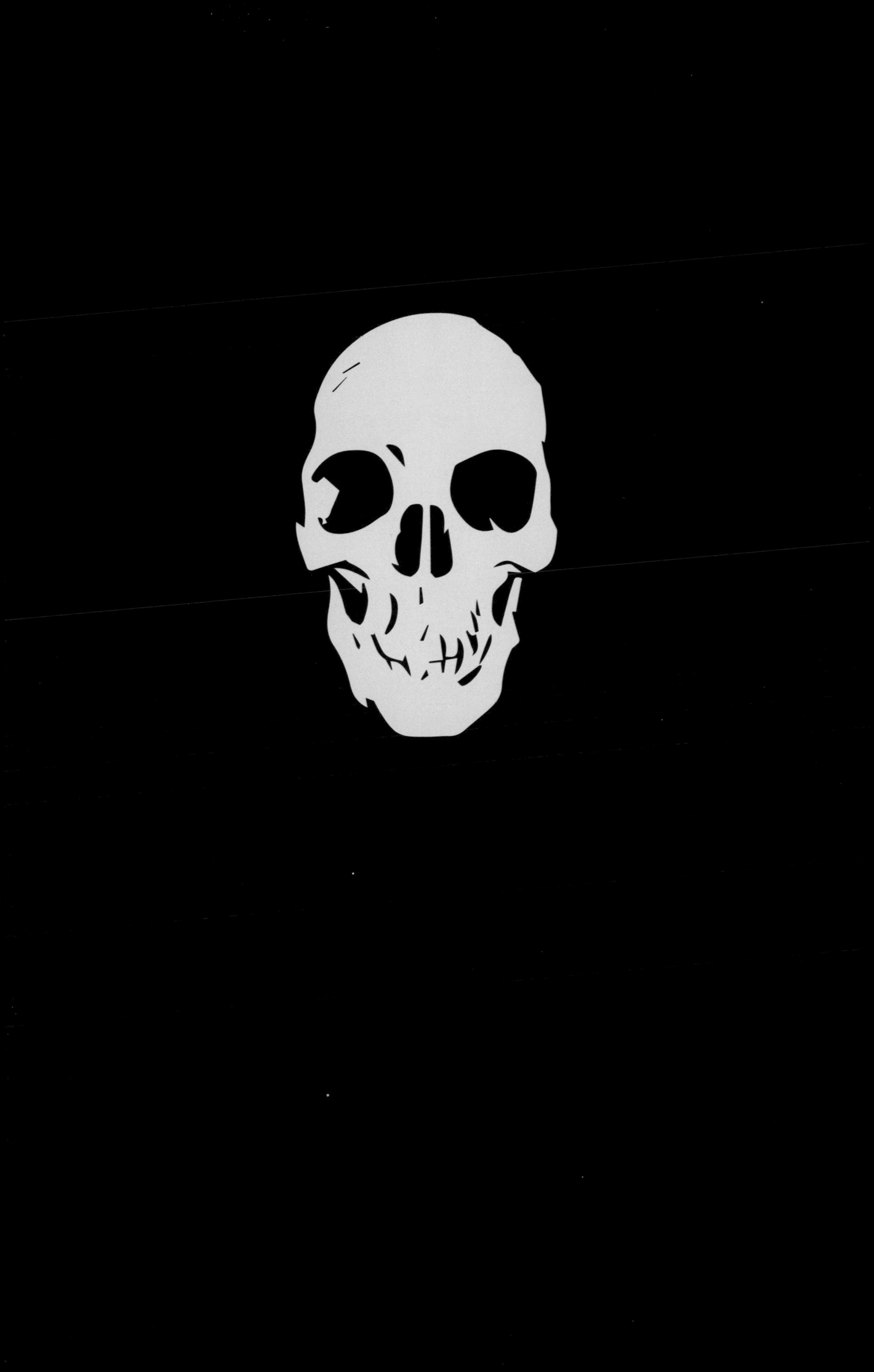

THE SHADOW OF EVIL

SCRIPT BY **FABIAN RANGEL JR.**

ART BY **RYAN CODY**

LETTERS BY **ED BRISSON**

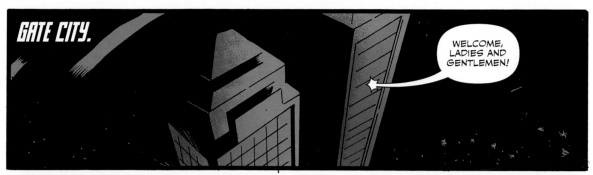

GATE CITY.

WELCOME, LADIES AND GENTLEMEN!

I'D LIKE TO THANK YOU ALL FOR SHOWING UP TO OUR LITTLE FUNDRAISER.

HOPEFULLY YOU'RE FEELING GENEROUS AND WE CAN--

VVVMMMMMM

WHAT THE DEVIL?!

KRASH

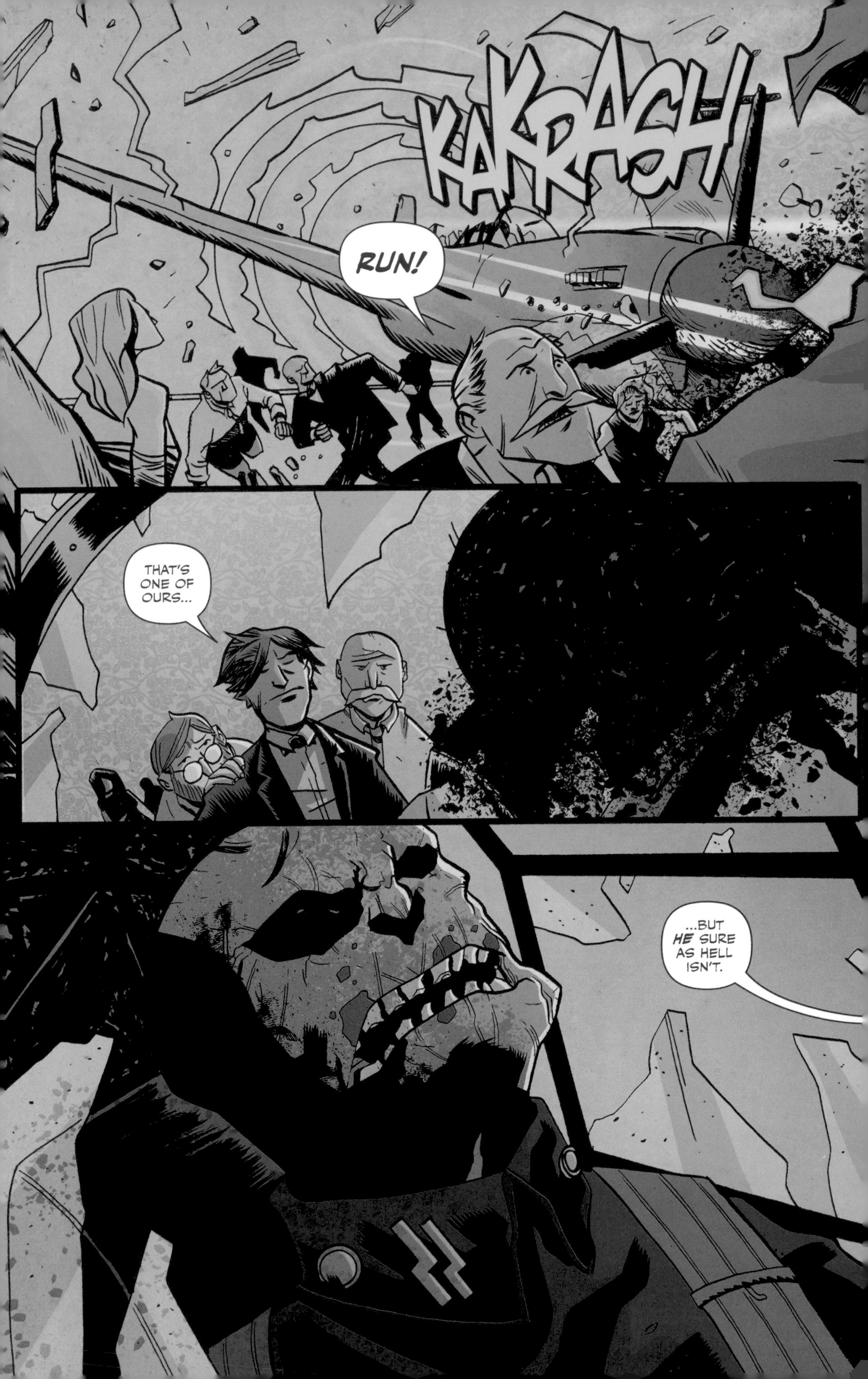
KAKRACH
RUN!
THAT'S ONE OF OURS...
...BUT HE SURE AS HELL ISN'T.

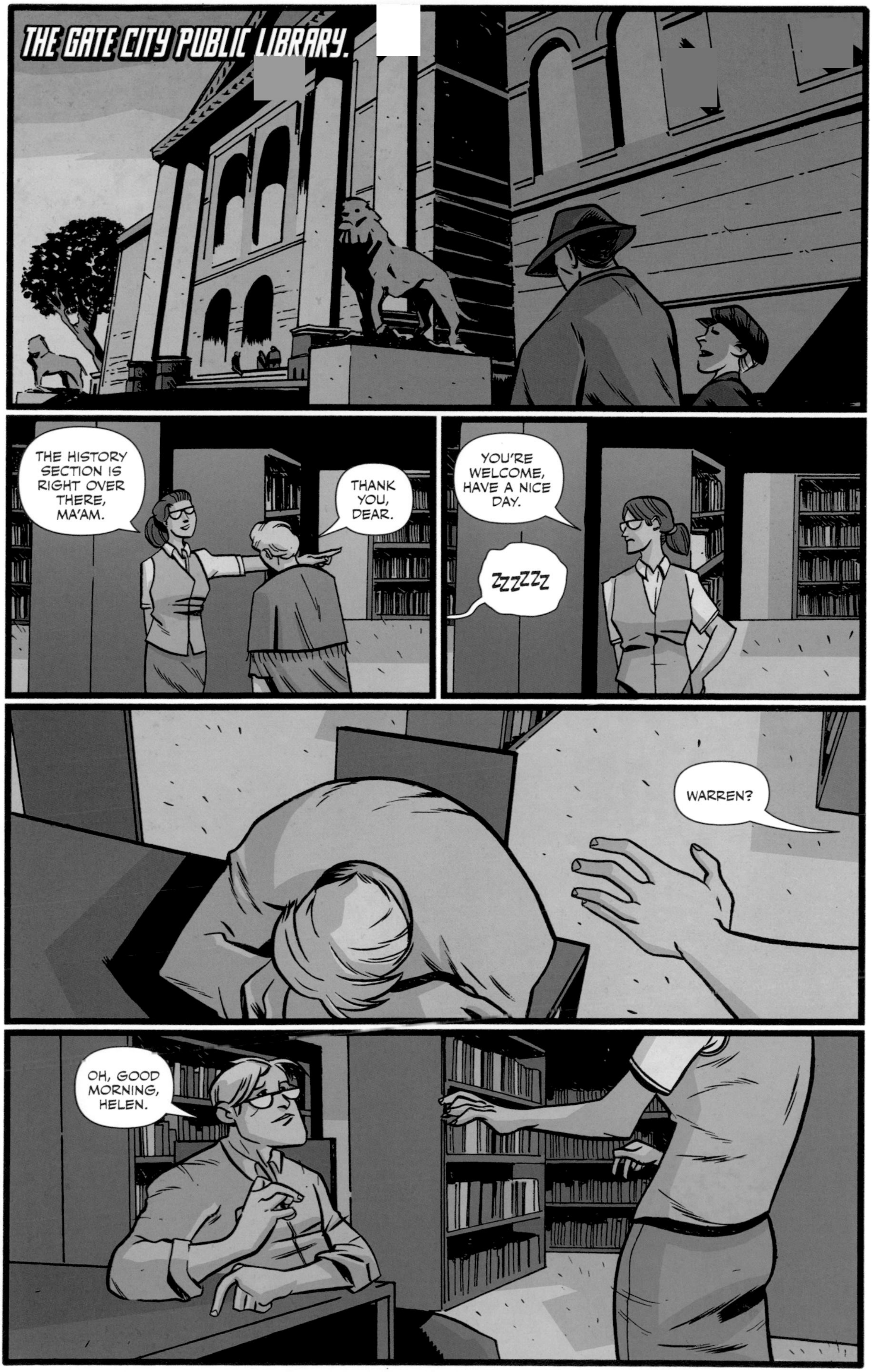
THE GATE CITY PUBLIC LIBRARY.
THE HISTORY SECTION IS RIGHT OVER THERE, MA'AM.
THANK YOU, DEAR.
YOU'RE WELCOME, HAVE A NICE DAY.
ZZZZZZ
WARREN?
OH, GOOD MORNING, HELEN.

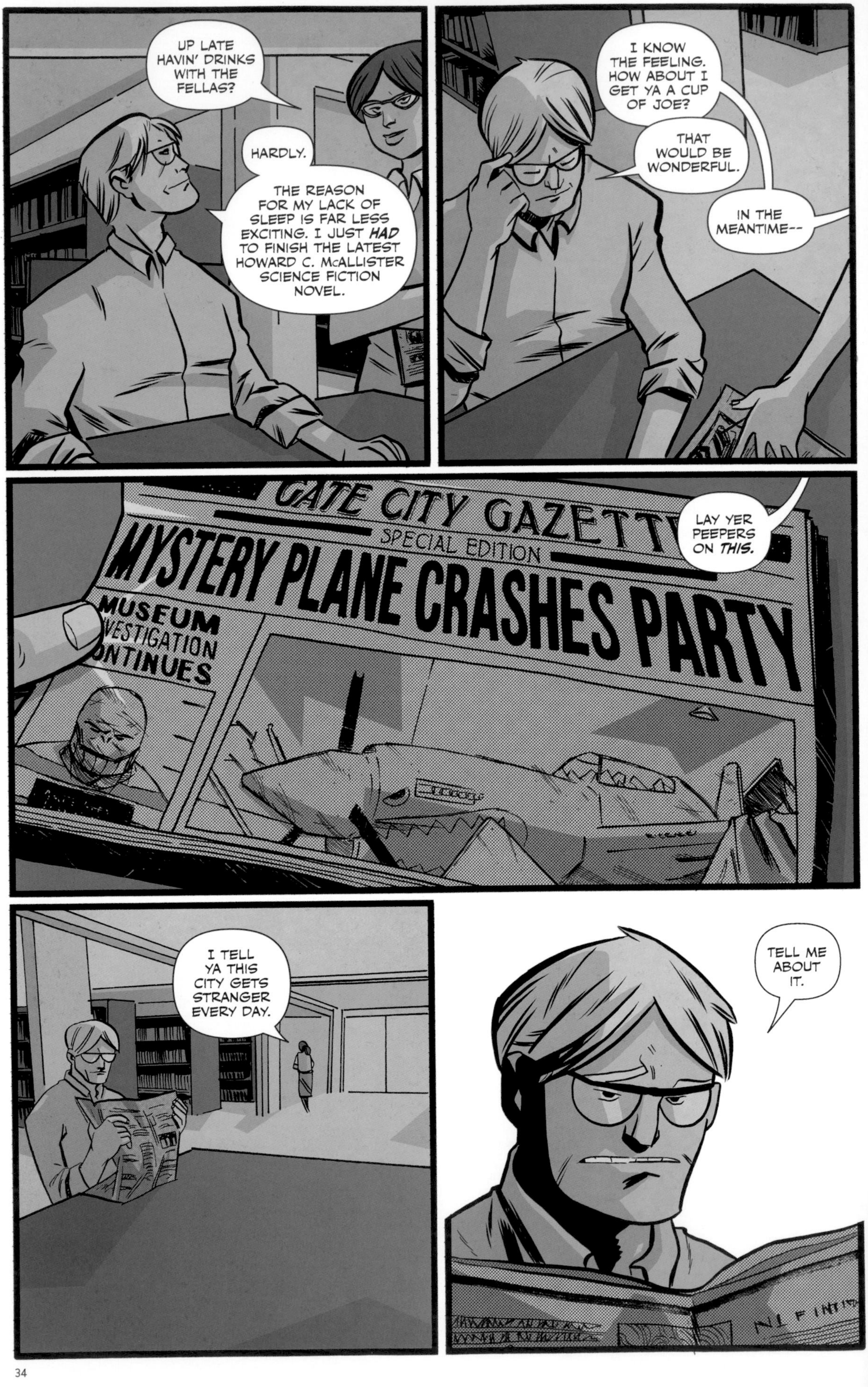
UP LATE HAVIN' DRINKS WITH THE FELLAS?
HARDLY.
THE REASON FOR MY LACK OF SLEEP IS FAR LESS EXCITING. I JUST *HAD* TO FINISH THE LATEST HOWARD C. McALLISTER SCIENCE FICTION NOVEL.
I KNOW THE FEELING. HOW ABOUT I GET YA A CUP OF JOE?
THAT WOULD BE WONDERFUL.
IN THE MEANTIME--
GATE CITY GAZETT
SPECIAL EDITION
MYSTERY PLANE CRASHES PARTY
MUSEUM
VESTIGATION
ONTINUES
LAY YER PEEPERS ON *THIS.*
I TELL YA THIS CITY GETS STRANGER EVERY DAY.
TELL ME ABOUT IT.

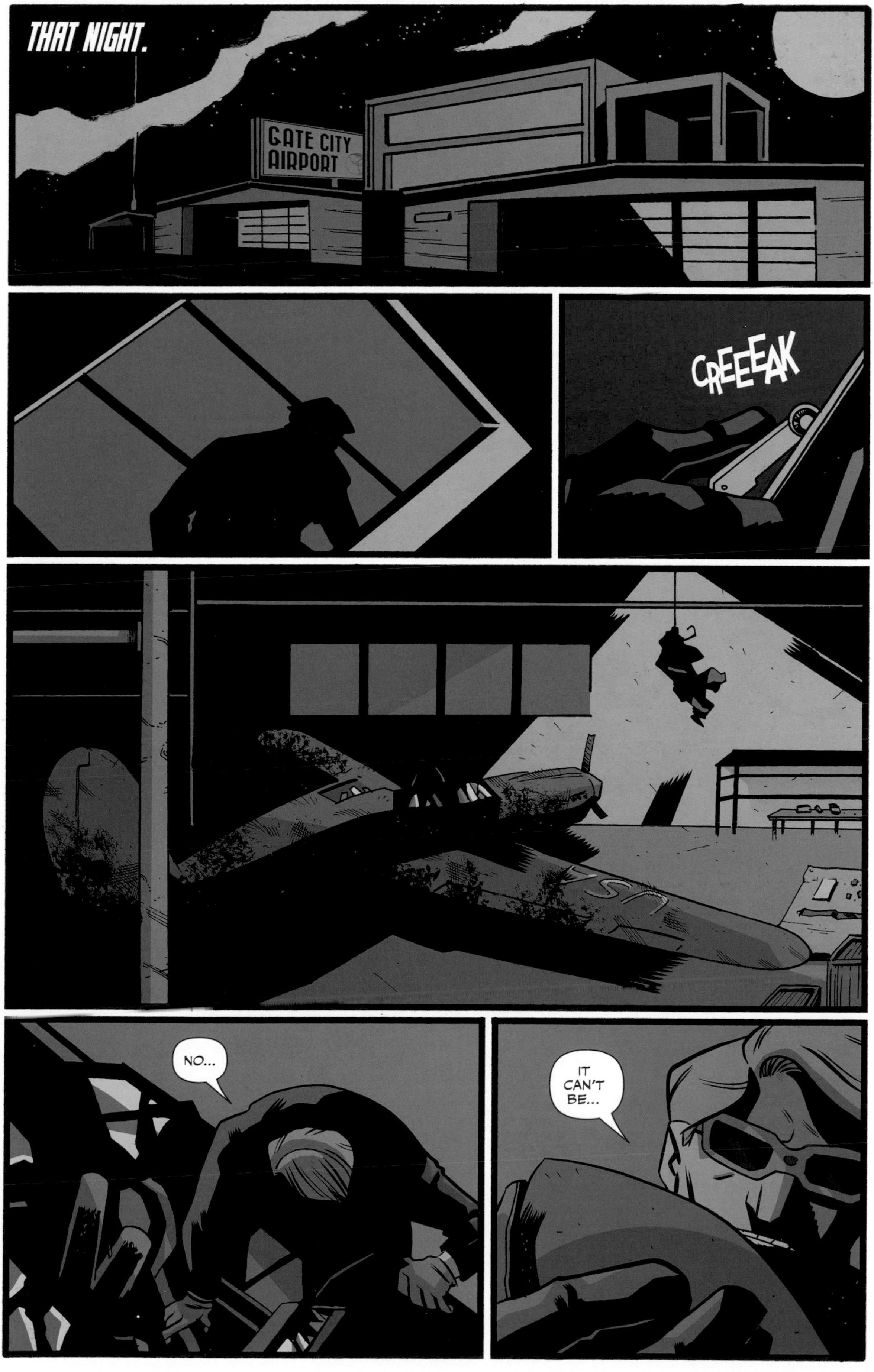
THAT NIGHT.
GATE CITY AIRPORT
CREEEAK
NO...
IT CAN'T BE...

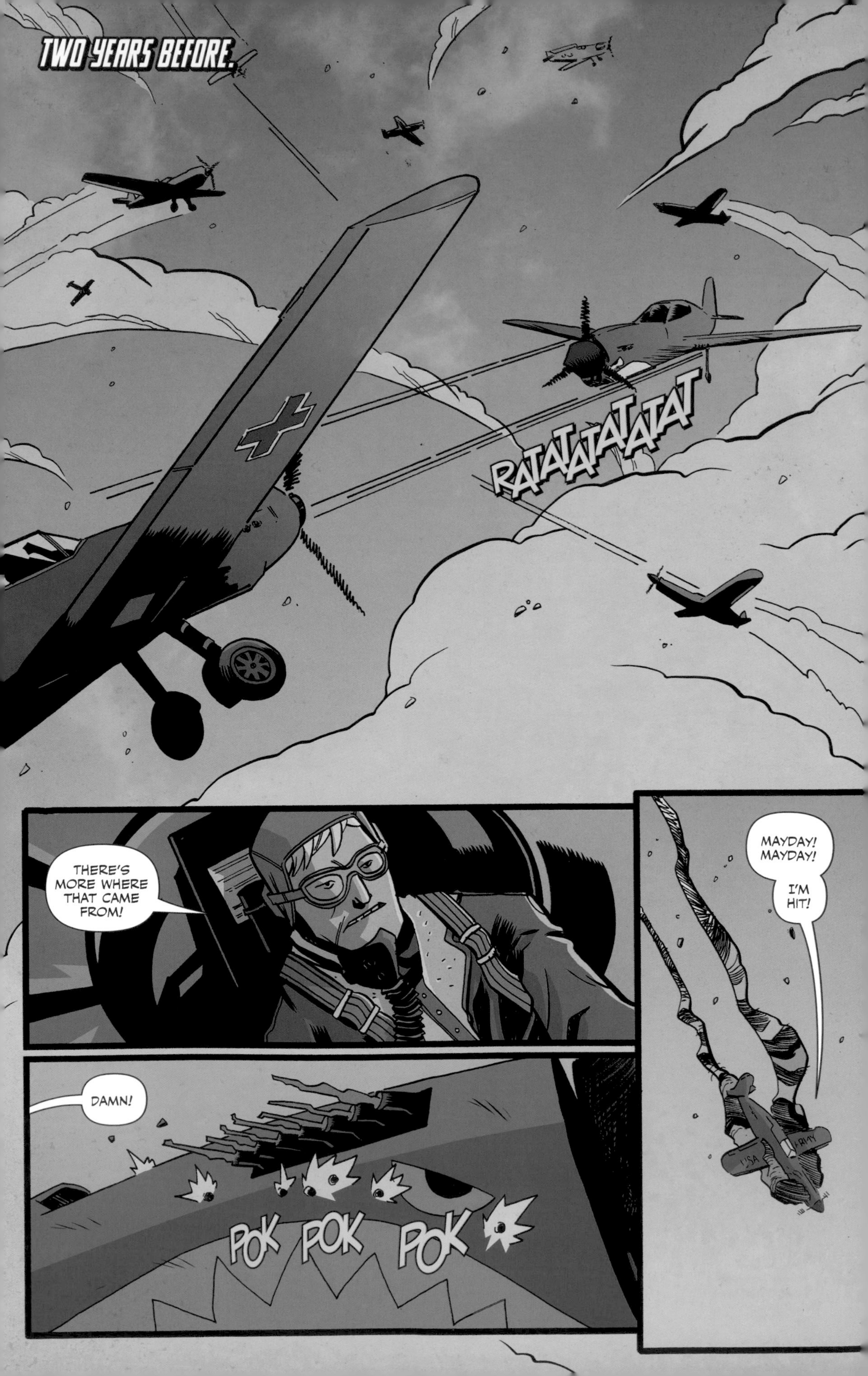
TWO YEARS BEFORE.
RATATATATATAT
THERE'S MORE WHERE THAT CAME FROM!
DAMN!
POK POK POK
MAYDAY! MAYDAY!
I'M HIT!

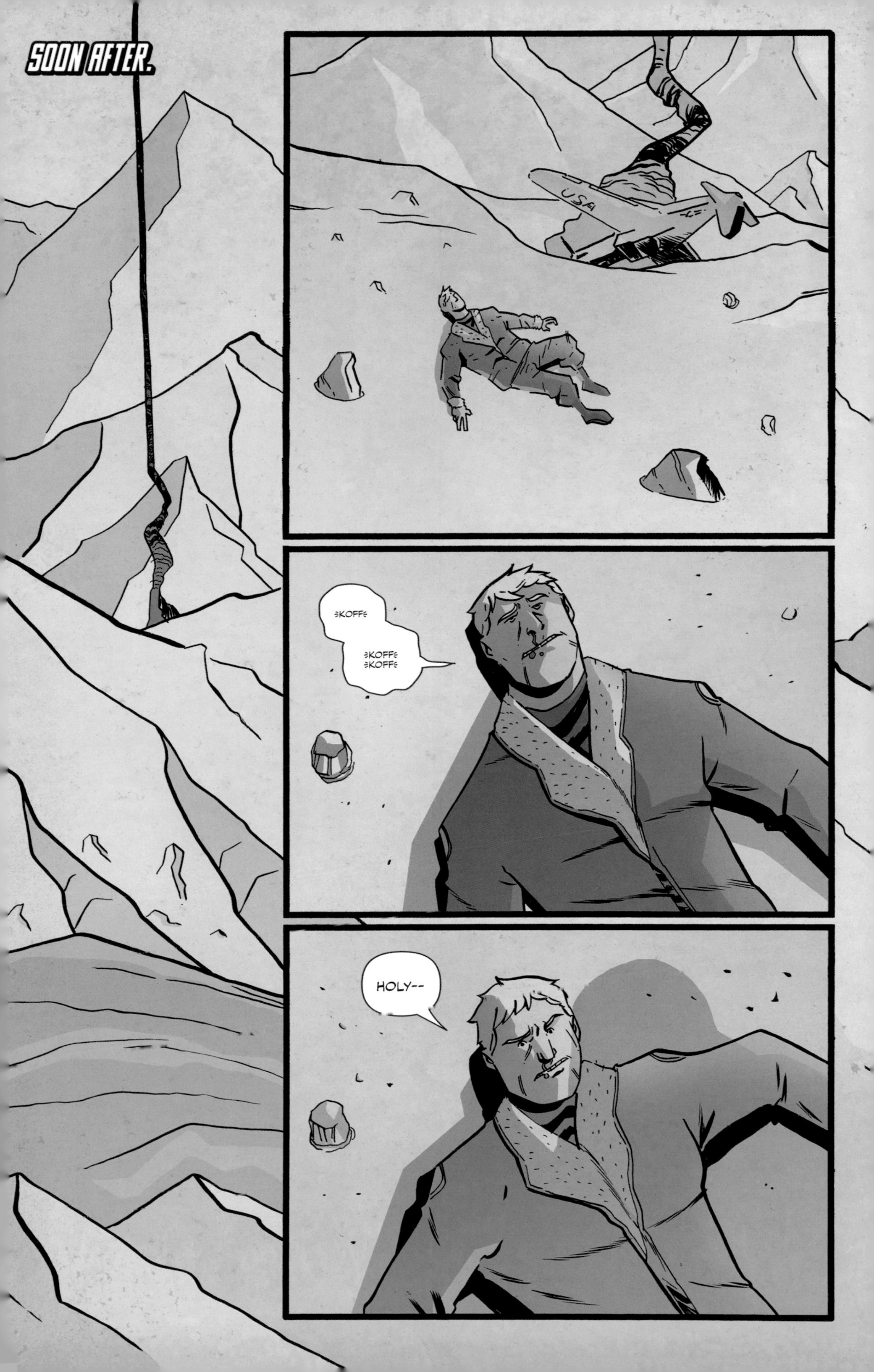
SOON AFTER.
KOFF
KOFF
KOFF
HOLY--

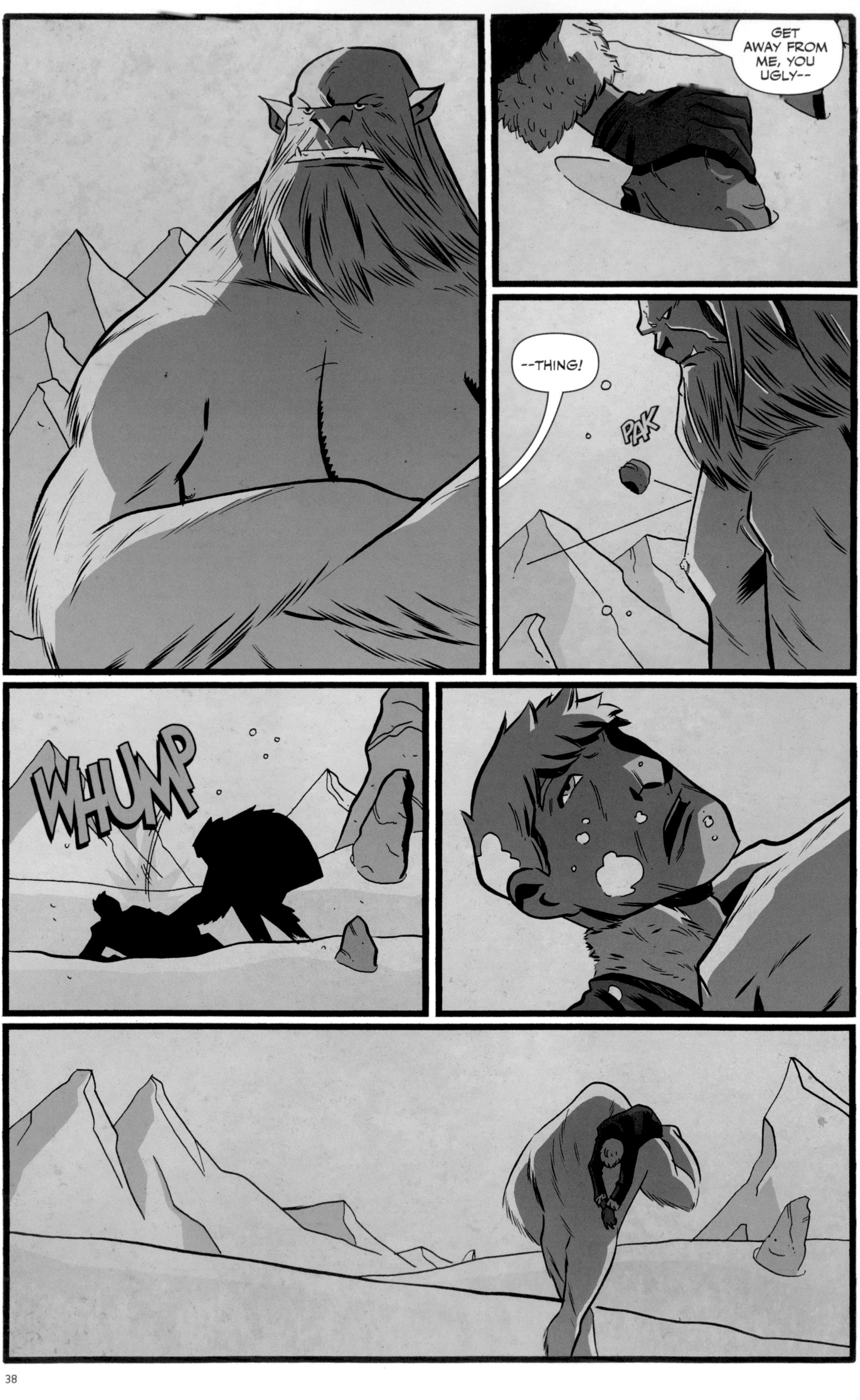
GET AWAY FROM ME, YOU UGLY--
--THING!
PAK
WHUMP

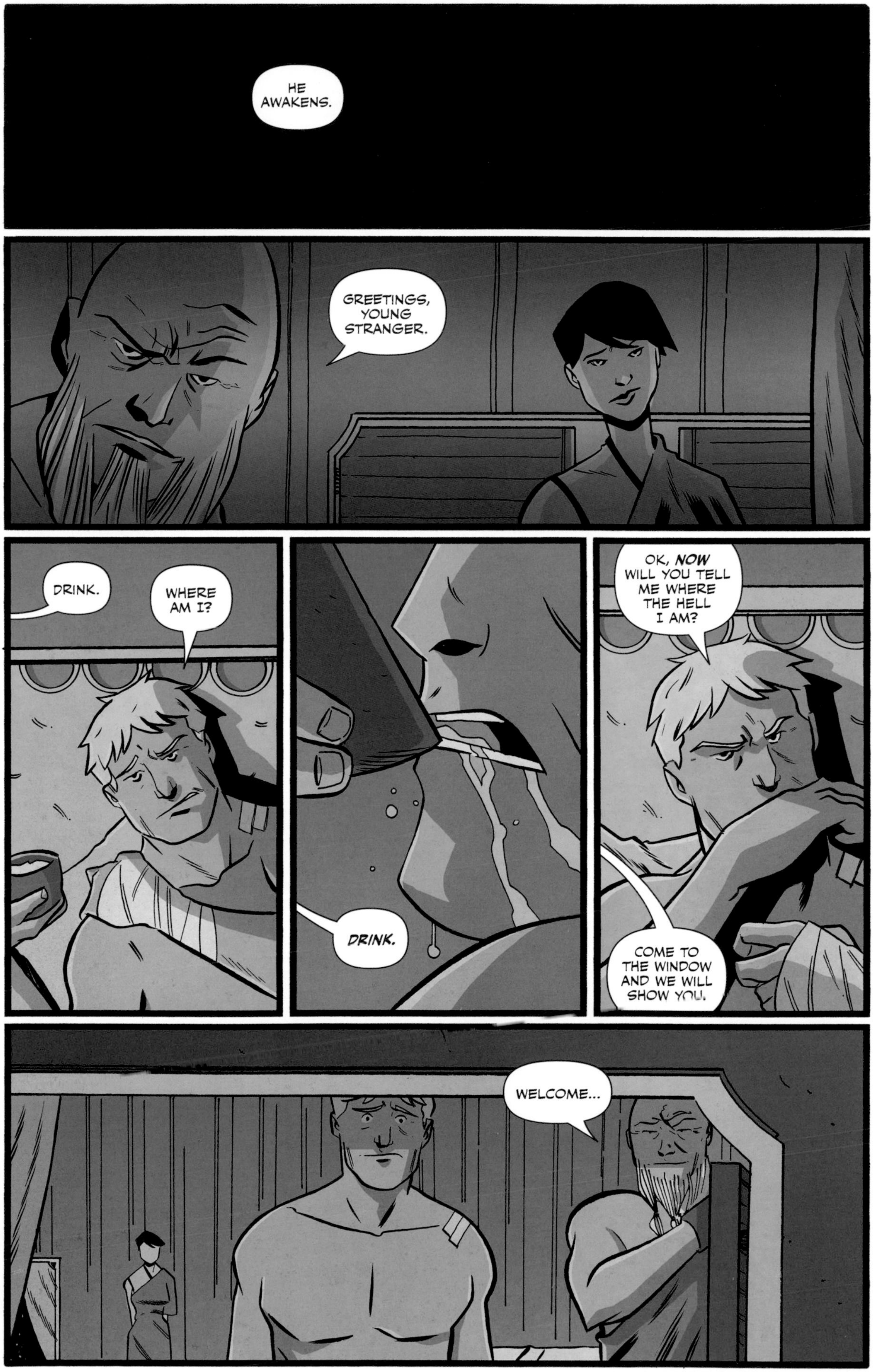
HE AWAKENS.
GREETINGS, YOUNG STRANGER.
DRINK.
WHERE AM I?
DRINK.
OK, NOW WILL YOU TELL ME WHERE THE HELL I AM?
COME TO THE WINDOW AND WE WILL SHOW YOU.
WELCOME...

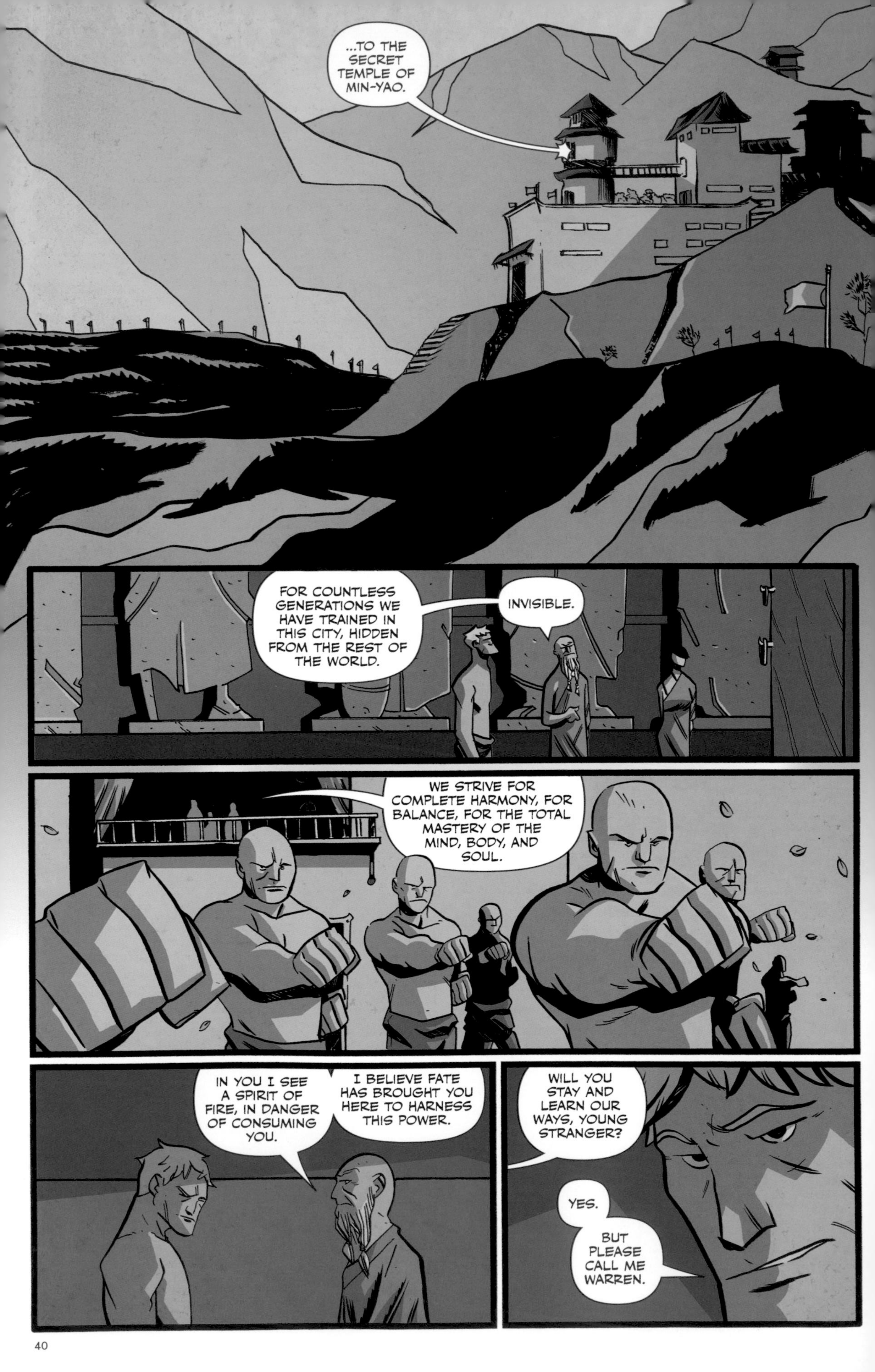
...TO THE SECRET TEMPLE OF MIN-YAO.
FOR COUNTLESS GENERATIONS WE HAVE TRAINED IN THIS CITY, HIDDEN FROM THE REST OF THE WORLD.
INVISIBLE.
WE STRIVE FOR COMPLETE HARMONY, FOR BALANCE, FOR THE TOTAL MASTERY OF THE MIND, BODY, AND SOUL.
IN YOU I SEE A SPIRIT OF FIRE, IN DANGER OF CONSUMING YOU.
I BELIEVE FATE HAS BROUGHT YOU HERE TO HARNESS THIS POWER.
WILL YOU STAY AND LEARN OUR WAYS, YOUNG STRANGER?
YES.
BUT PLEASE CALL ME WARREN.

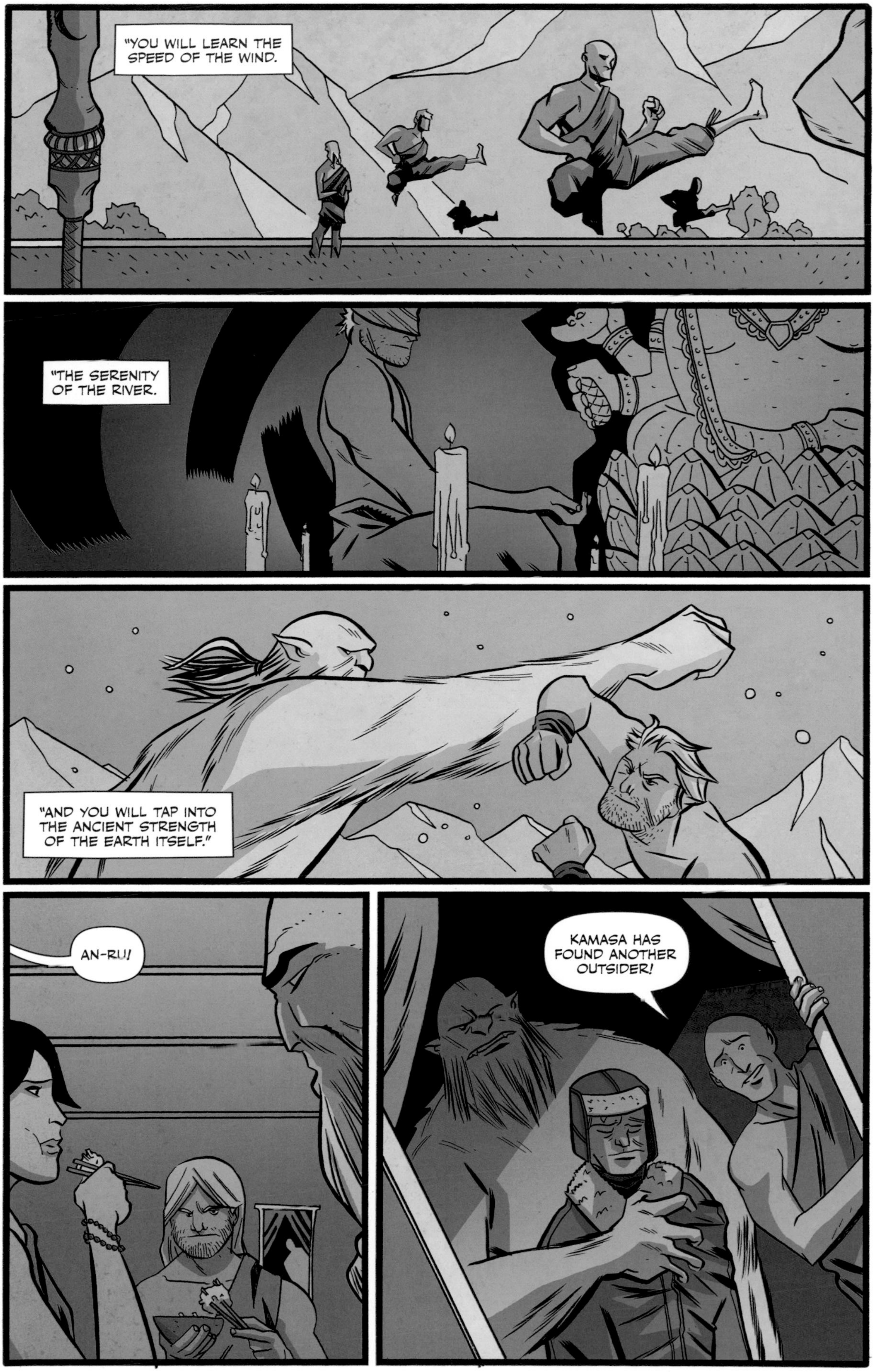
"YOU WILL LEARN THE SPEED OF THE WIND.
"THE SERENITY OF THE RIVER.
"AND YOU WILL TAP INTO THE ANCIENT STRENGTH OF THE EARTH ITSELF."
AN-RU!
KAMASA HAS FOUND ANOTHER OUTSIDER!

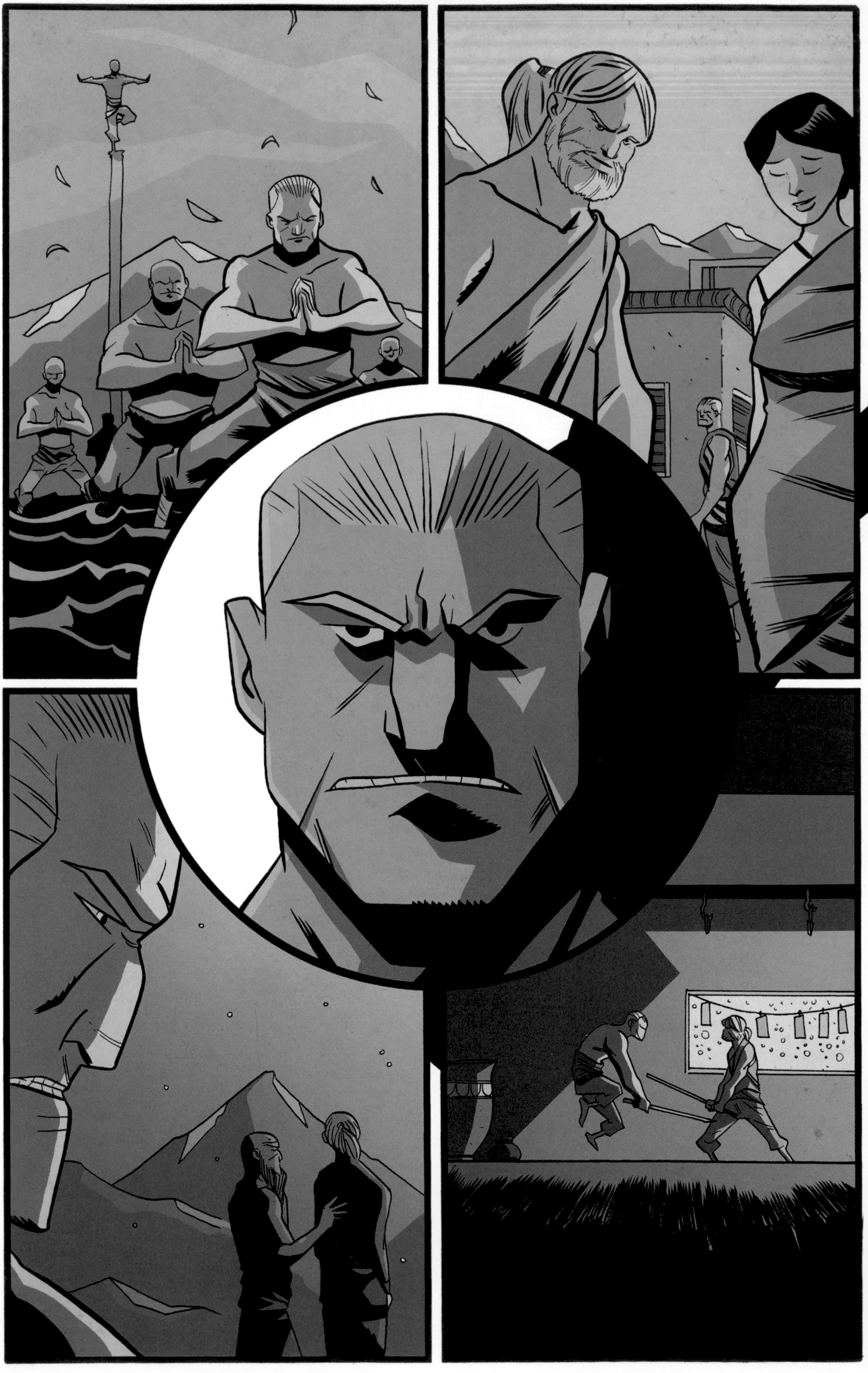

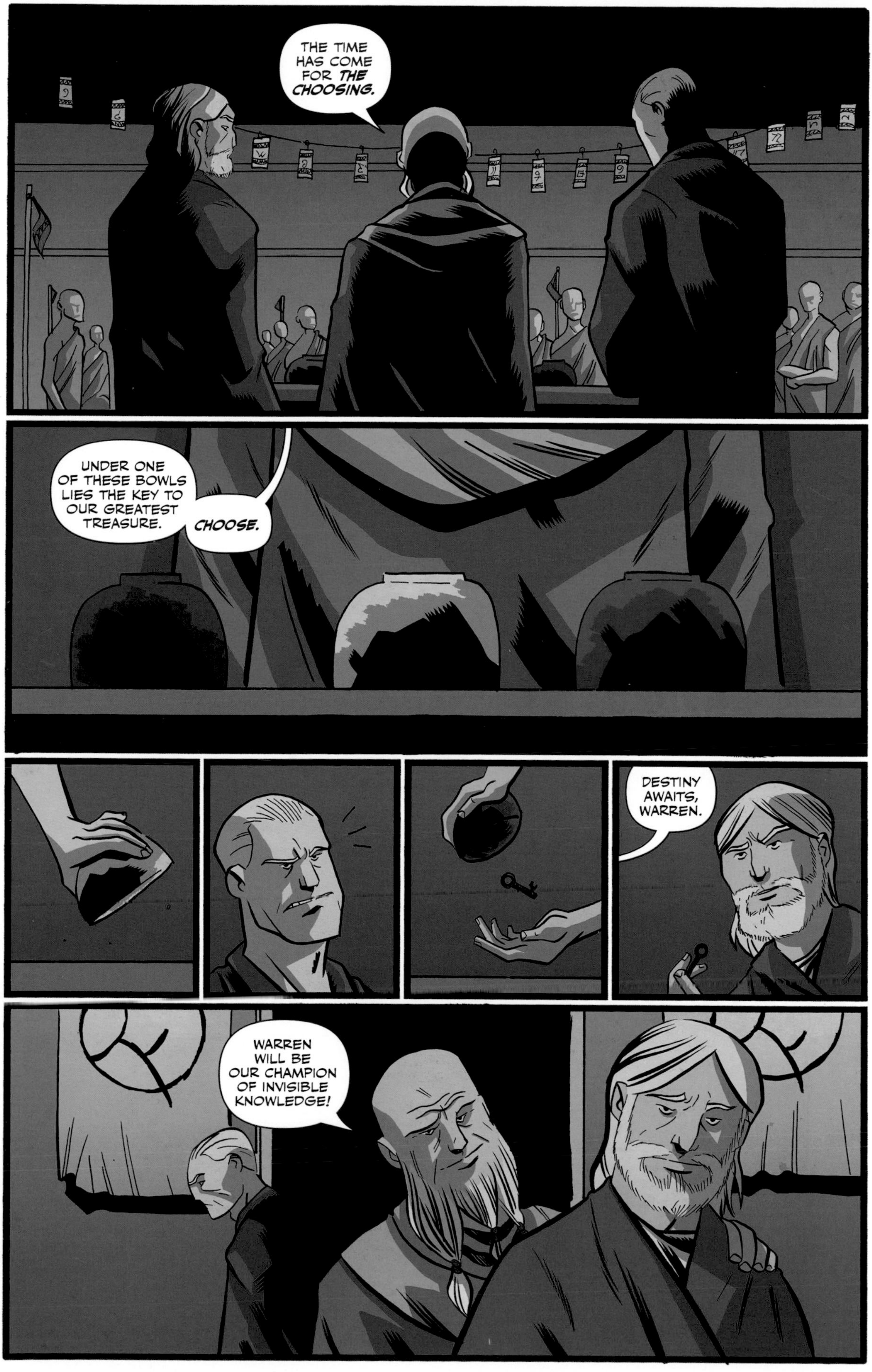
THE TIME HAS COME FOR THE CHOOSING.
UNDER ONE OF THESE BOWLS LIES THE KEY TO OUR GREATEST TREASURE.
CHOOSE.
DESTINY AWAITS, WARREN.
WARREN WILL BE OUR CHAMPION OF INVISIBLE KNOWLEDGE!

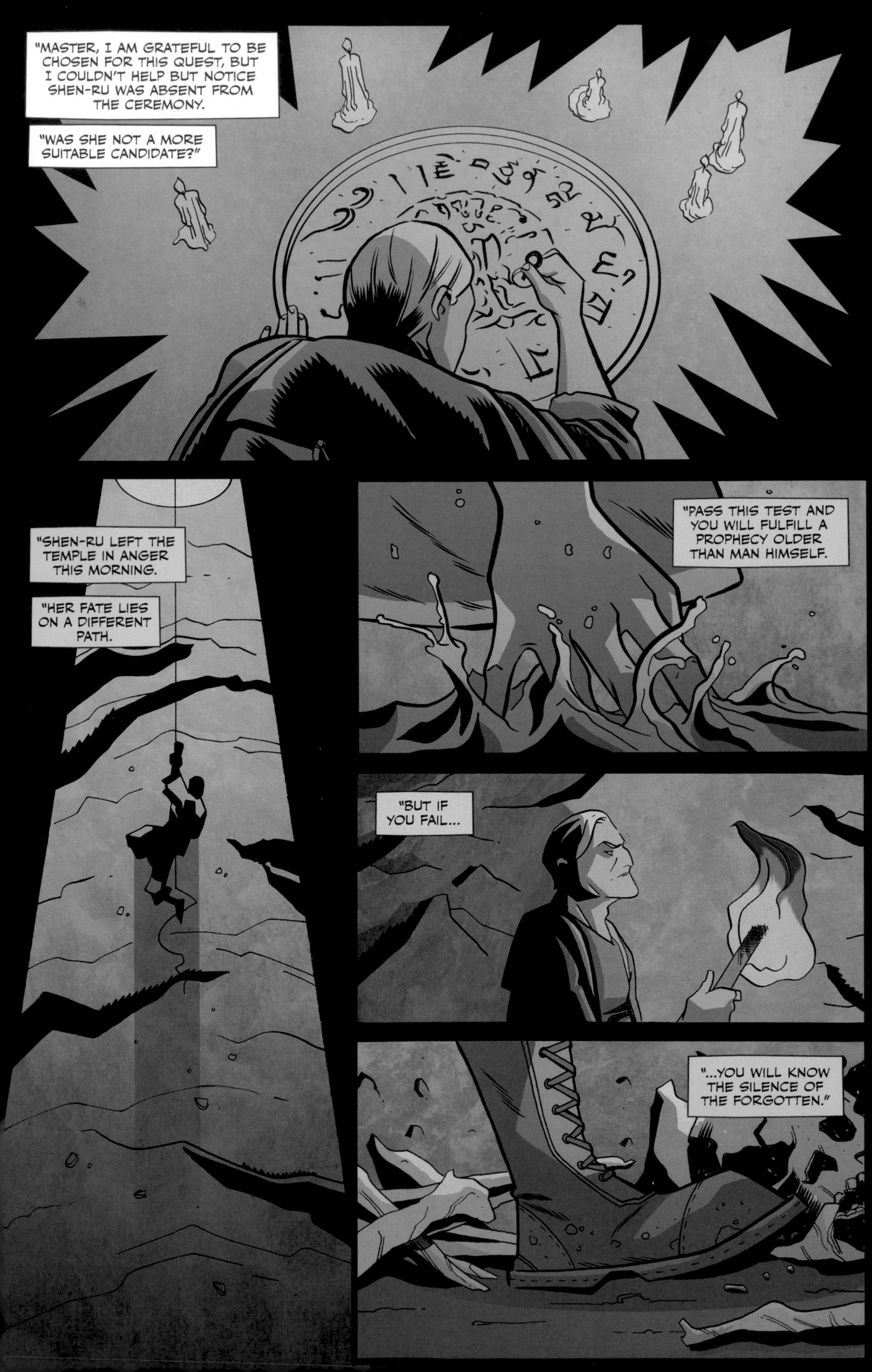
"MASTER, I AM GRATEFUL TO BE CHOSEN FOR THIS QUEST, BUT I COULDN'T HELP BUT NOTICE SHEN-RU WAS ABSENT FROM THE CEREMONY.
"WAS SHE NOT A MORE SUITABLE CANDIDATE?"
"SHEN-RU LEFT THE TEMPLE IN ANGER THIS MORNING.
"HER FATE LIES ON A DIFFERENT PATH.
"PASS THIS TEST AND YOU WILL FULFILL A PROPHECY OLDER THAN MAN HIMSELF.
"BUT IF YOU FAIL...
"...YOU WILL KNOW THE SILENCE OF THE FORGOTTEN."

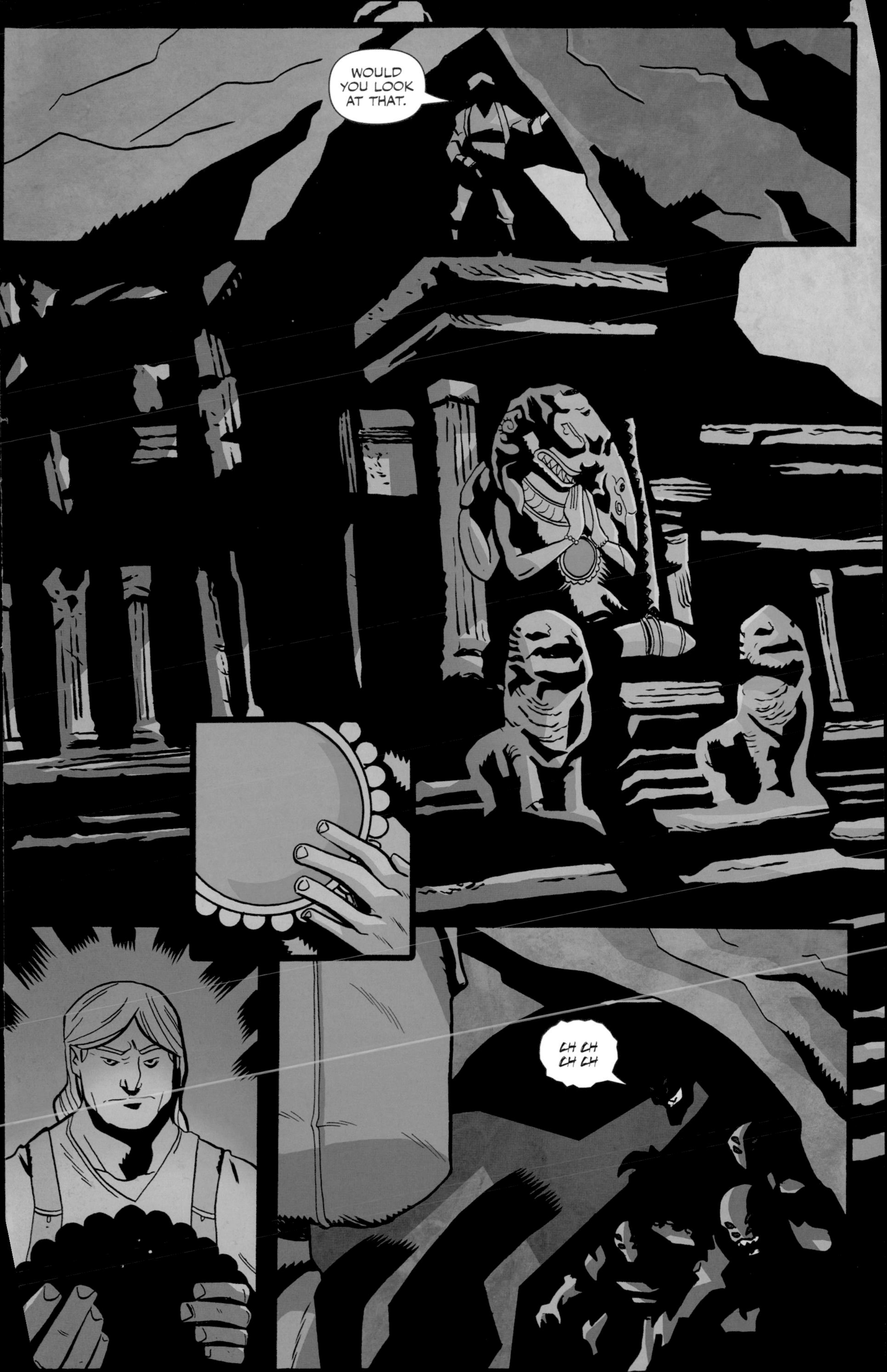
WOULD YOU LOOK AT THAT.
CH CH
CH CH

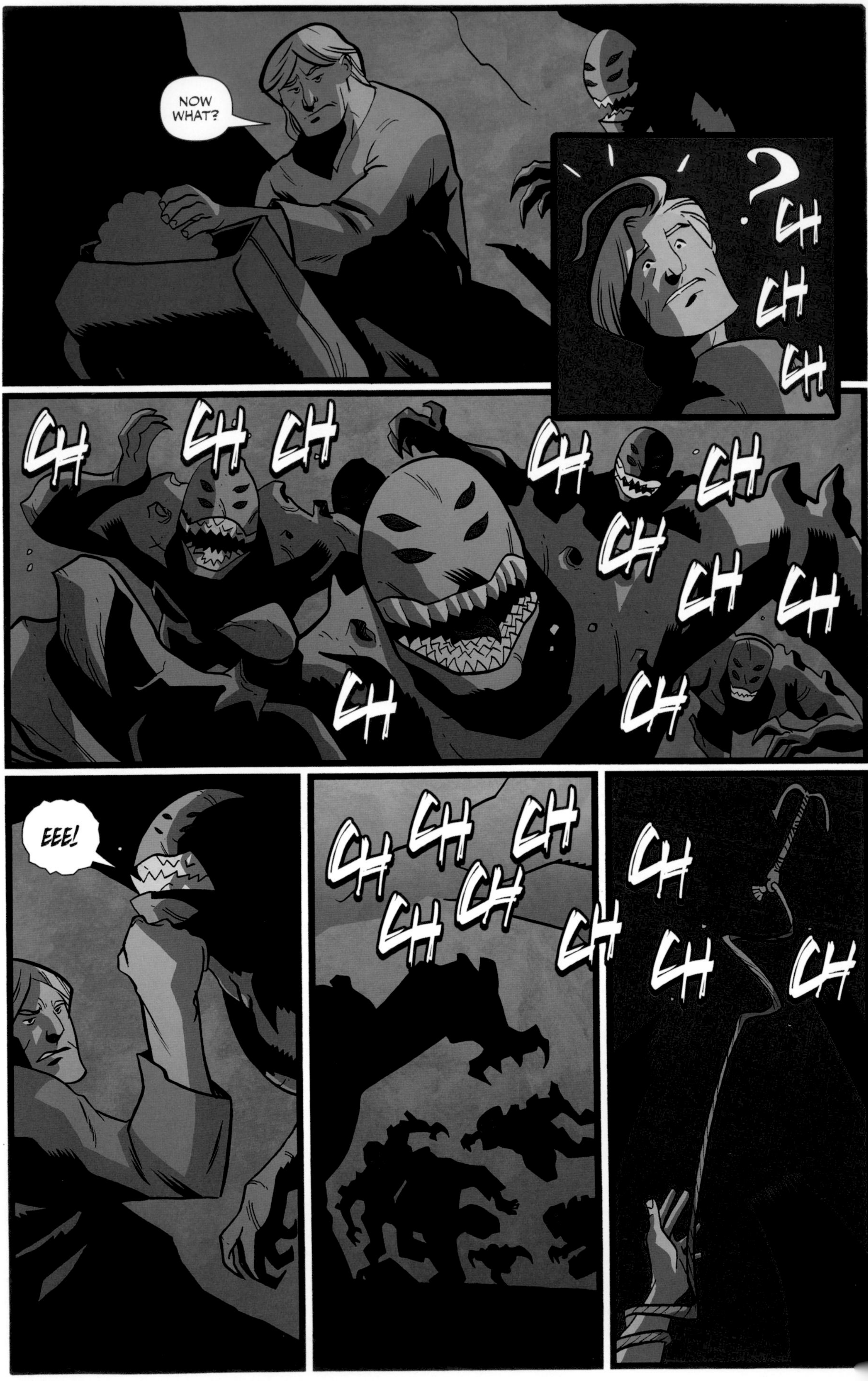

NOW WHAT?
?
CH CH CH
CH CH CH CH CH CH CH CH CH CH
EEE!
CH CH CH CH CH CH
CH CH CH

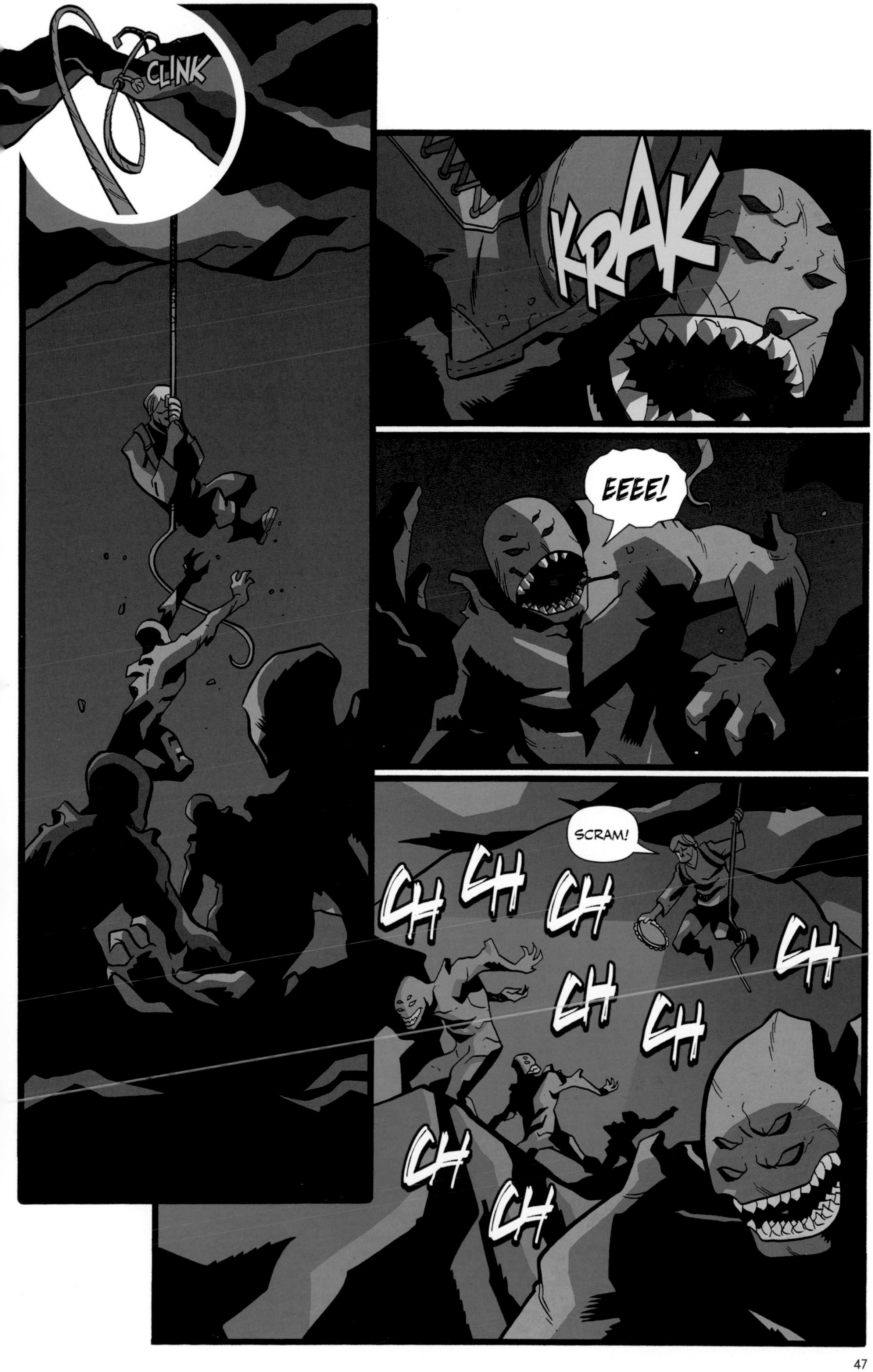
CLINK
KRAK
EEEE!
SCRAM!
CH CH CH
CH
CH CH
CH CH

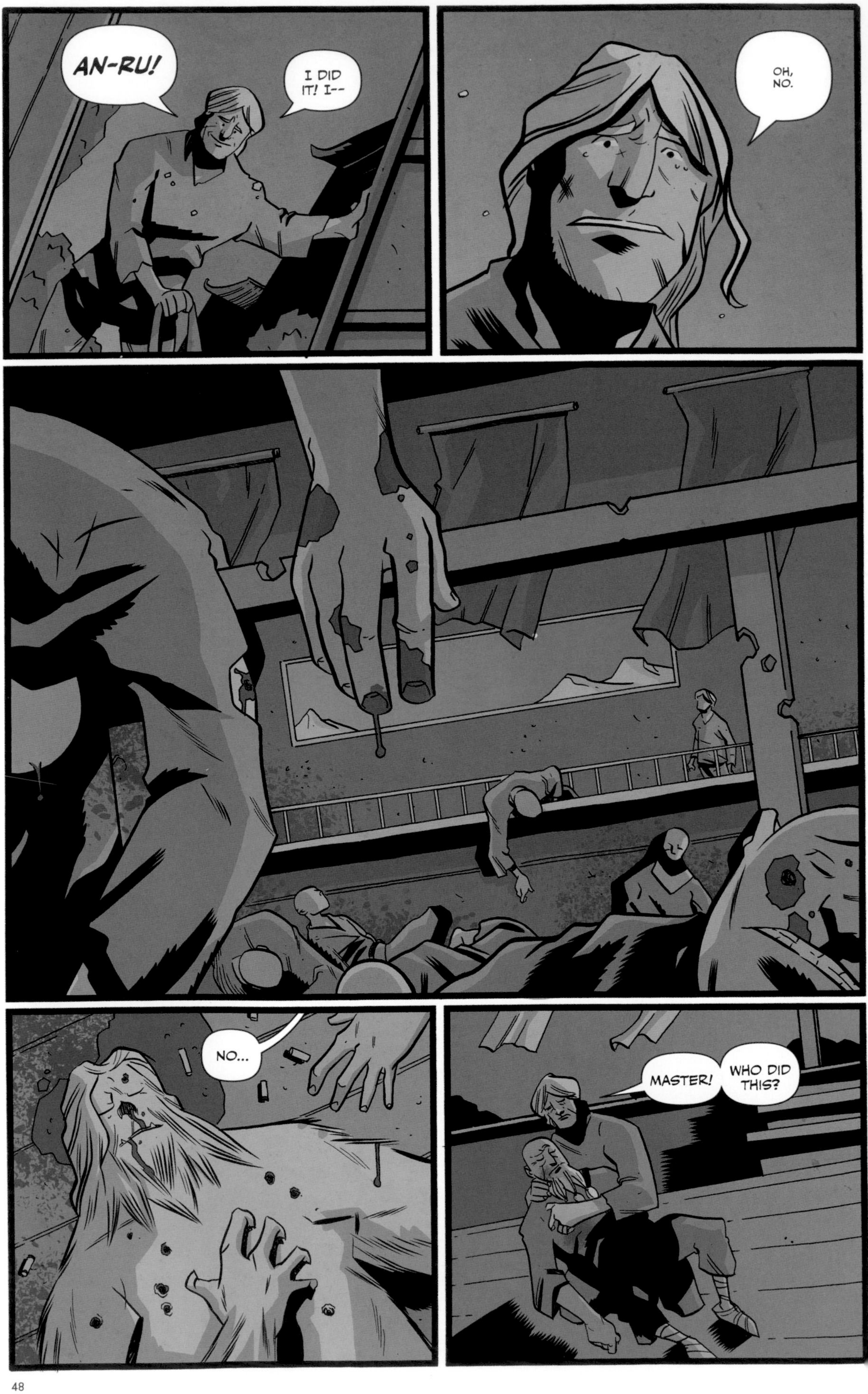
AN-RU!
I DID IT! I--
OH, NO.
NO...
MASTER!
WHO DID THIS?

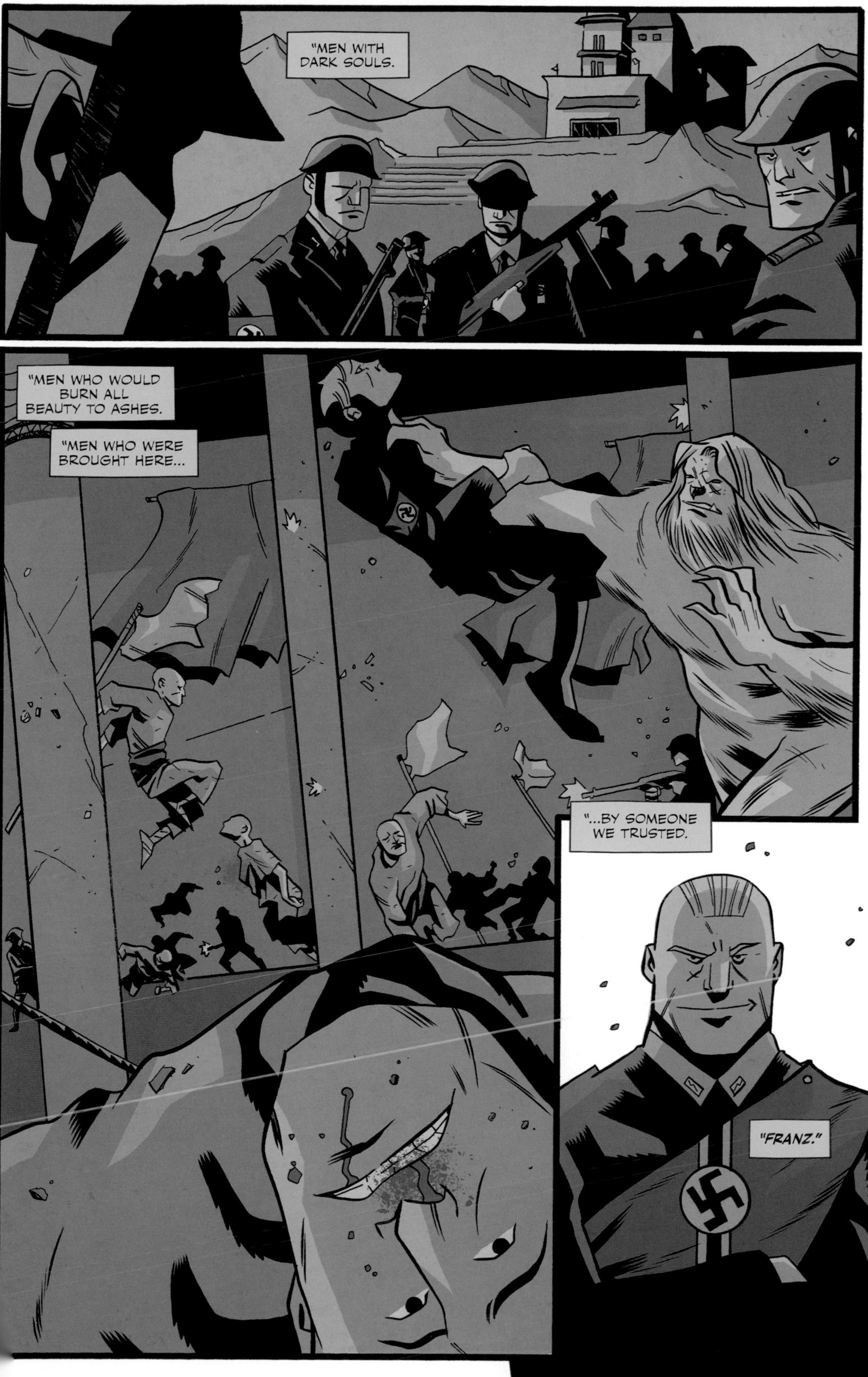
"MEN WITH DARK SOULS.
"MEN WHO WOULD BURN ALL BEAUTY TO ASHES.
"MEN WHO WERE BROUGHT HERE...
"...BY SOMEONE WE TRUSTED.
"FRANZ."

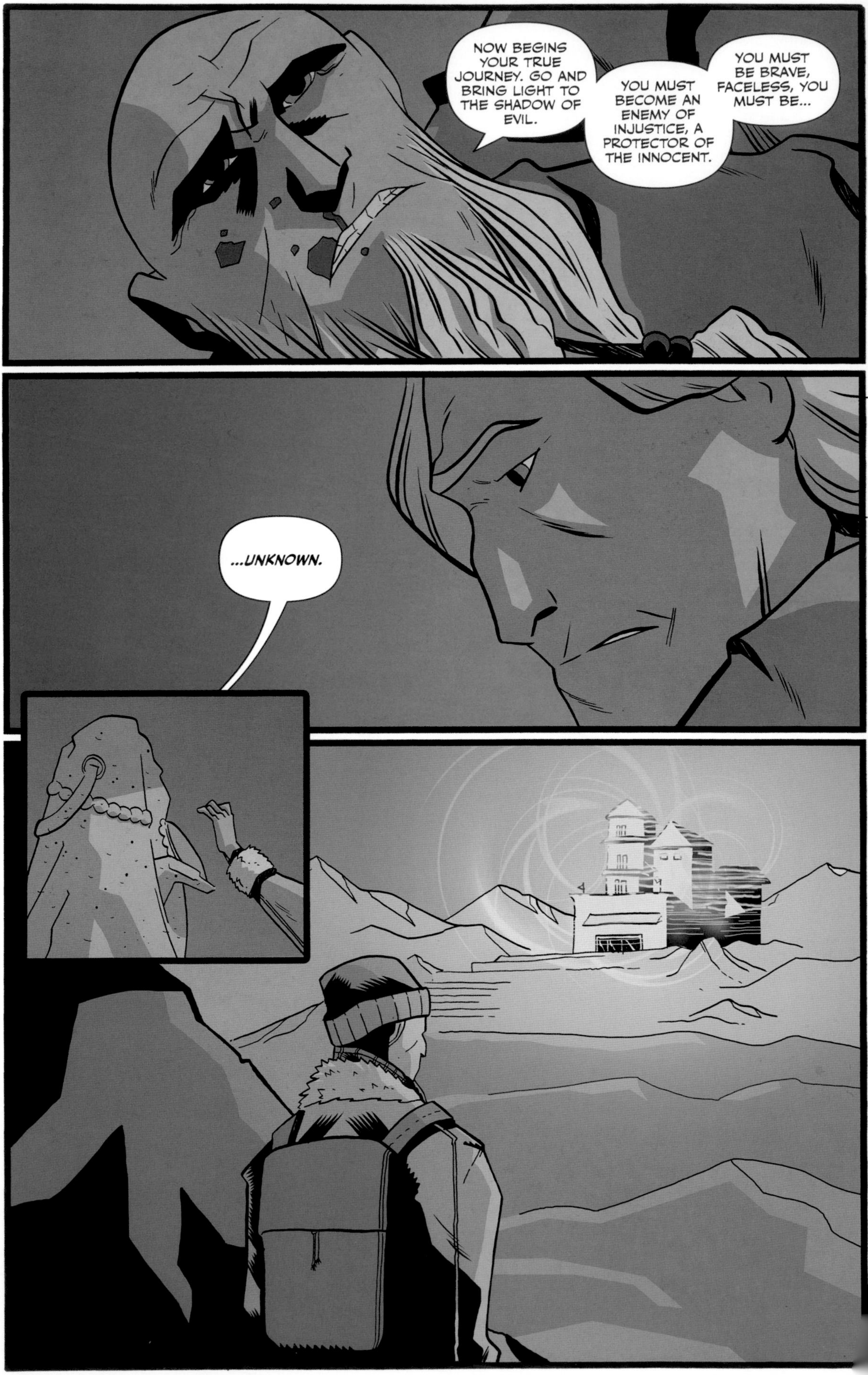
NOW BEGINS YOUR TRUE JOURNEY. GO AND BRING LIGHT TO THE SHADOW OF EVIL.
YOU MUST BECOME AN ENEMY OF INJUSTICE, A PROTECTOR OF THE INNOCENT.
YOU MUST BE BRAVE, FACELESS, YOU MUST BE...
...UNKNOWN.

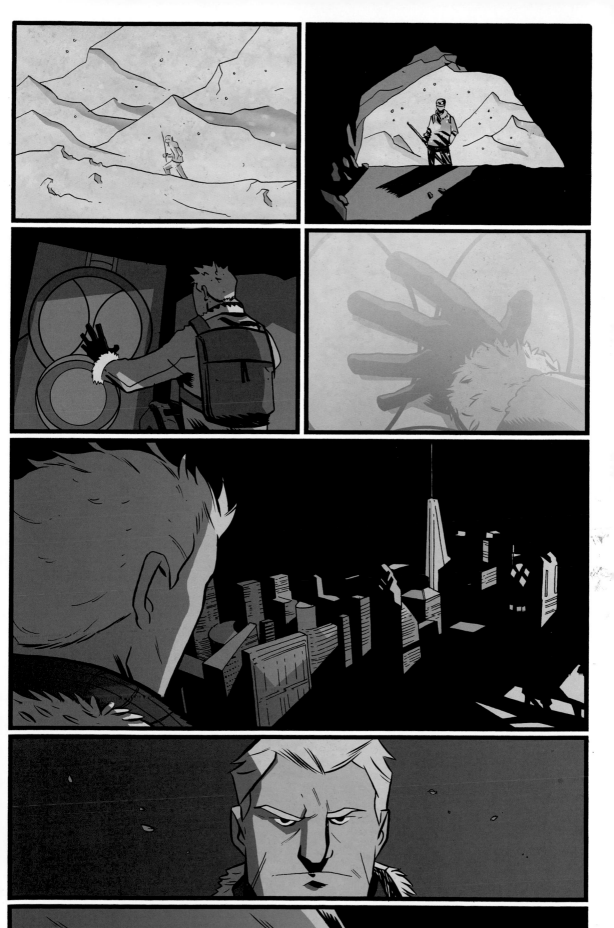

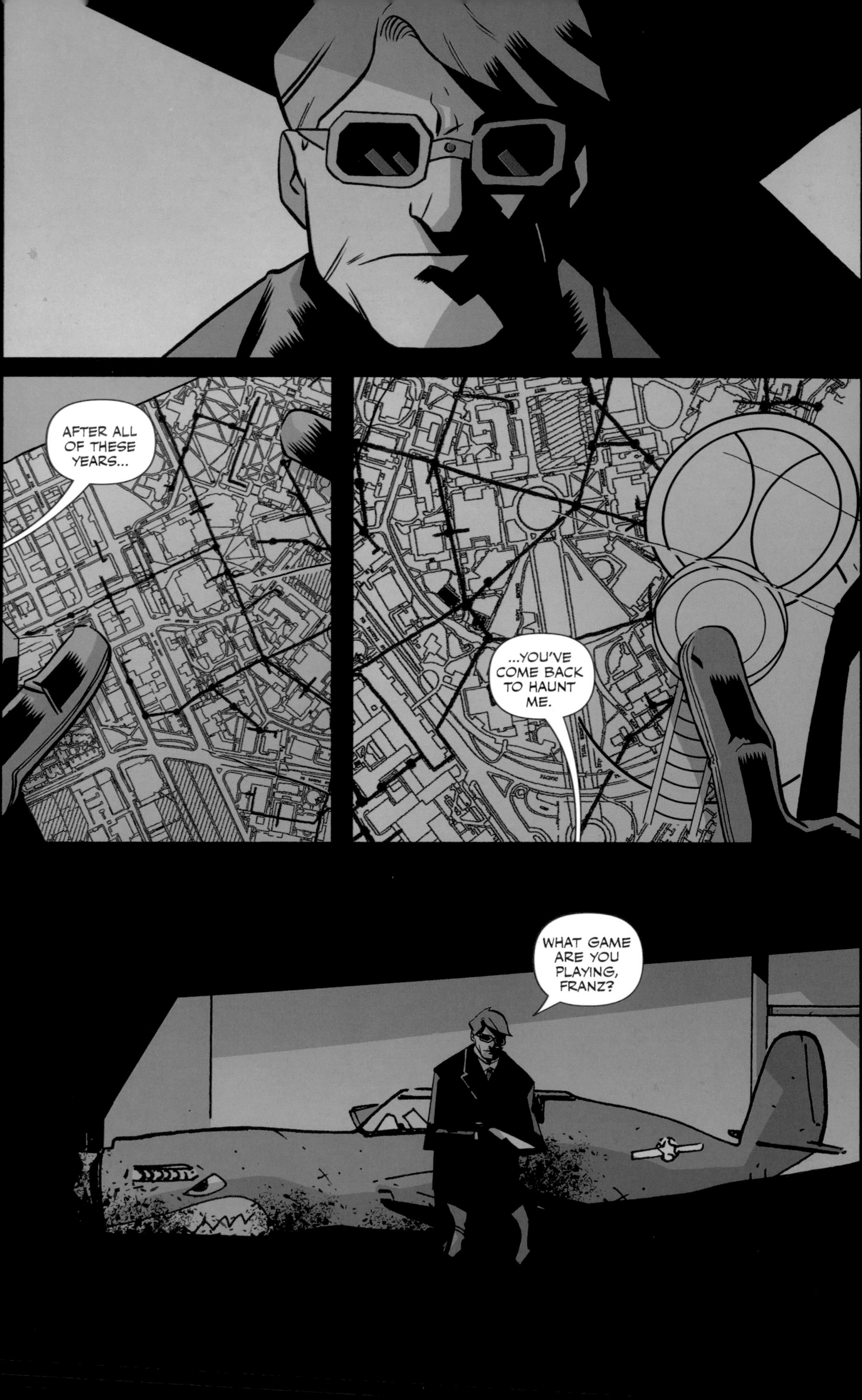
AFTER ALL OF THESE YEARS...
...YOU'VE COME BACK TO HAUNT ME.
WHAT GAME ARE YOU PLAYING, FRANZ?

THE MASK OF THE CRIMSON DRAGON

SCRIPT BY **FABIAN RANGEL JR.**

ART BY **RYAN CODY**

LETTERS BY **ED BRISSON**

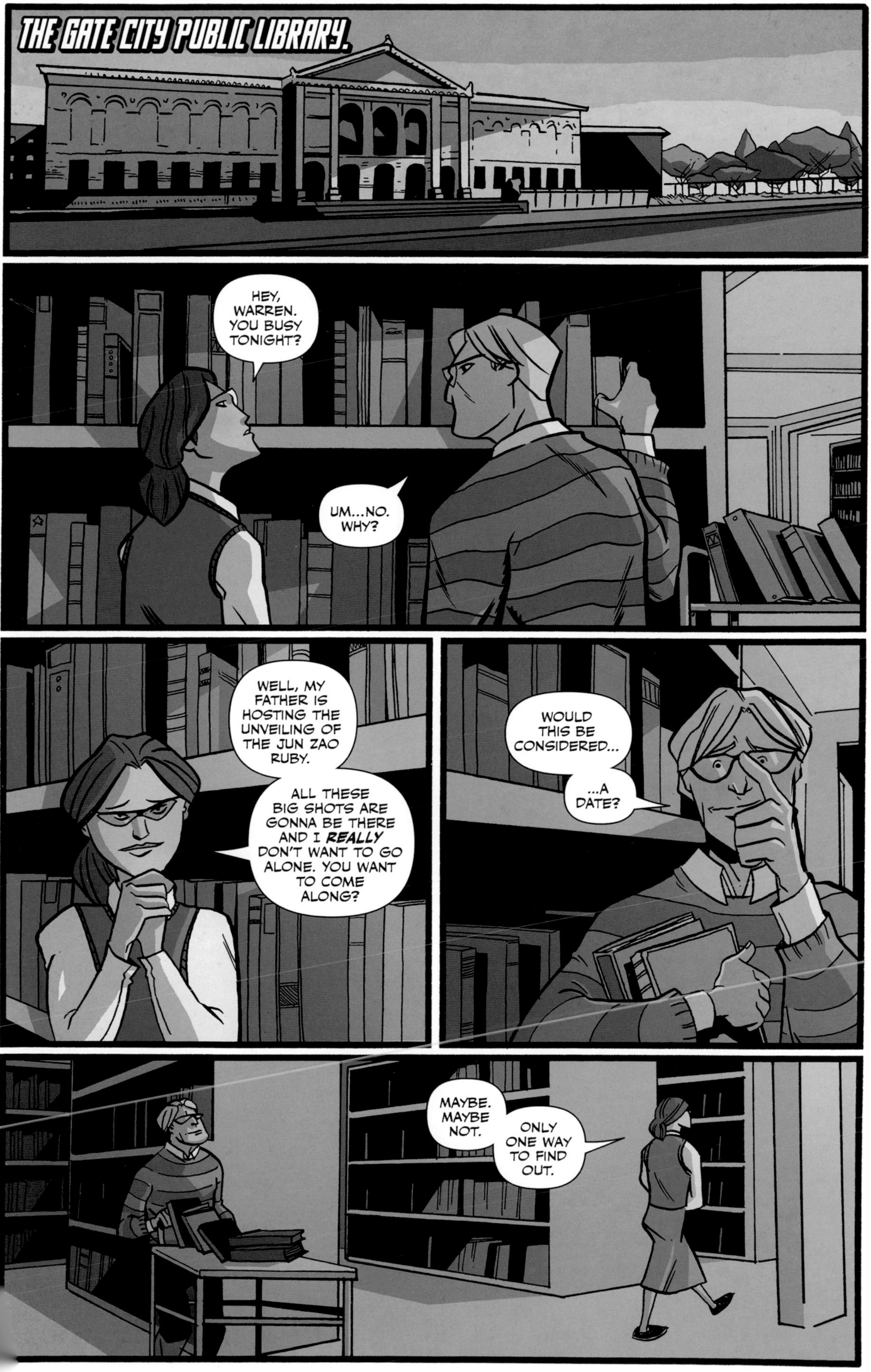
THE GATE CITY PUBLIC LIBRARY.
HEY, WARREN. YOU BUSY TONIGHT?
UM...NO. WHY?
WELL, MY FATHER IS HOSTING THE UNVEILING OF THE JUN ZAO RUBY.
ALL THESE BIG SHOTS ARE GONNA BE THERE AND I *REALLY* DON'T WANT TO GO ALONE. YOU WANT TO COME ALONG?
WOULD THIS BE CONSIDERED...
...A DATE?
MAYBE. MAYBE NOT.
ONLY ONE WAY TO FIND OUT.

YOU SURE DO CLEAN UP WELL, WARREN. YOU SHOULD WEAR A SUIT MORE OFTEN.

I'LL TAKE THAT INTO CONSIDERATION.

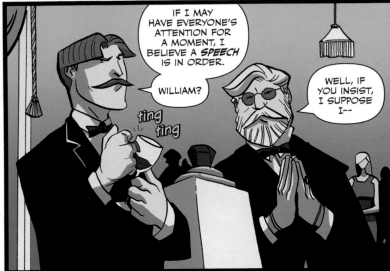

IF I MAY HAVE EVERYONE'S ATTENTION FOR A MOMENT, I BELIEVE A *SPEECH* IS IN ORDER.

WILLIAM?

WELL, IF YOU INSIST, I SUPPOSE I--

ting ting

KSSHH

OH MY GOD!

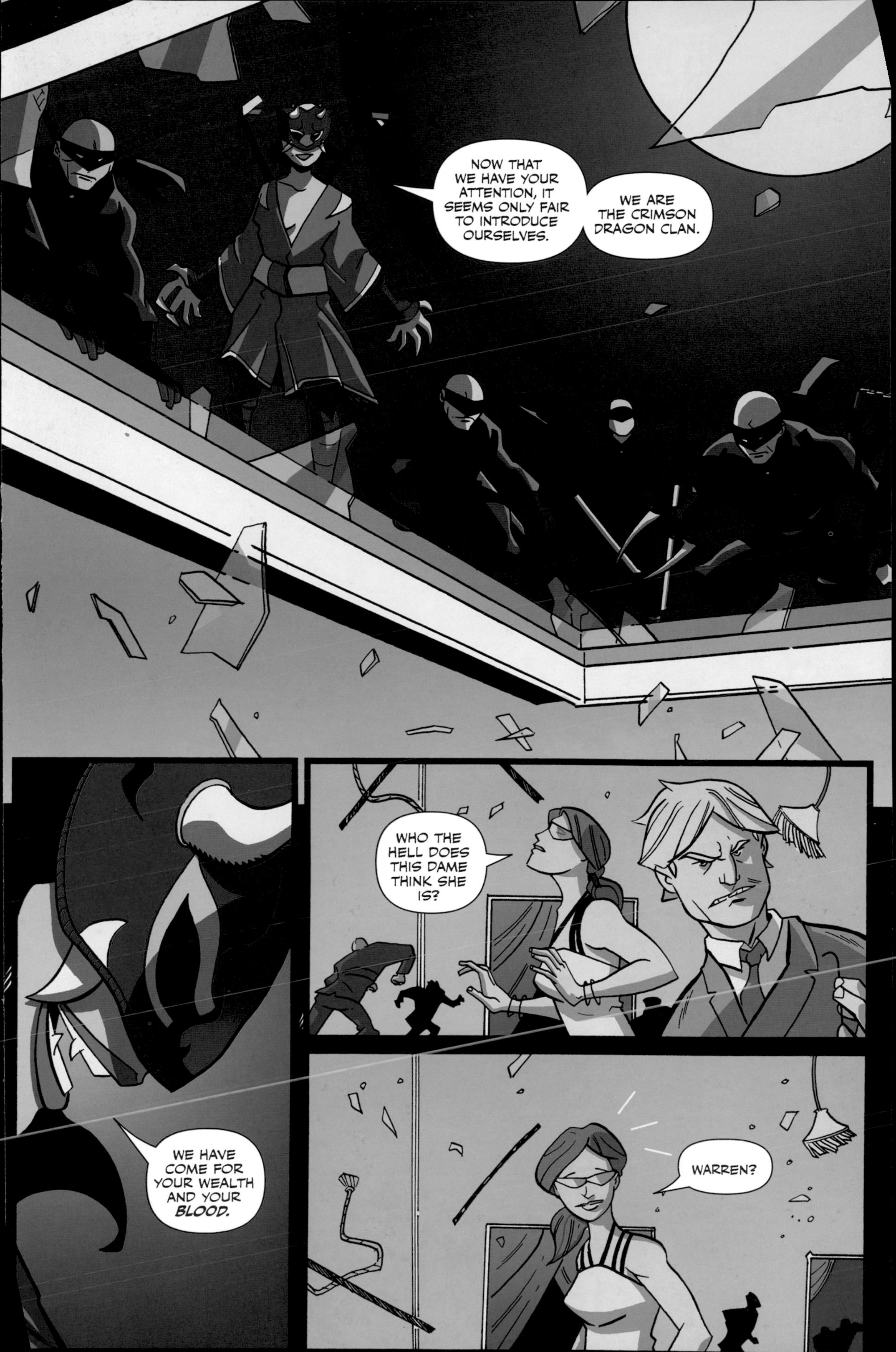
NOW THAT WE HAVE YOUR ATTENTION, IT SEEMS ONLY FAIR TO INTRODUCE OURSELVES.
WE ARE THE CRIMSON DRAGON CLAN.
WE HAVE COME FOR YOUR WEALTH AND YOUR *BLOOD.*
WHO THE HELL DOES THIS DAME THINK SHE IS?
WARREN?

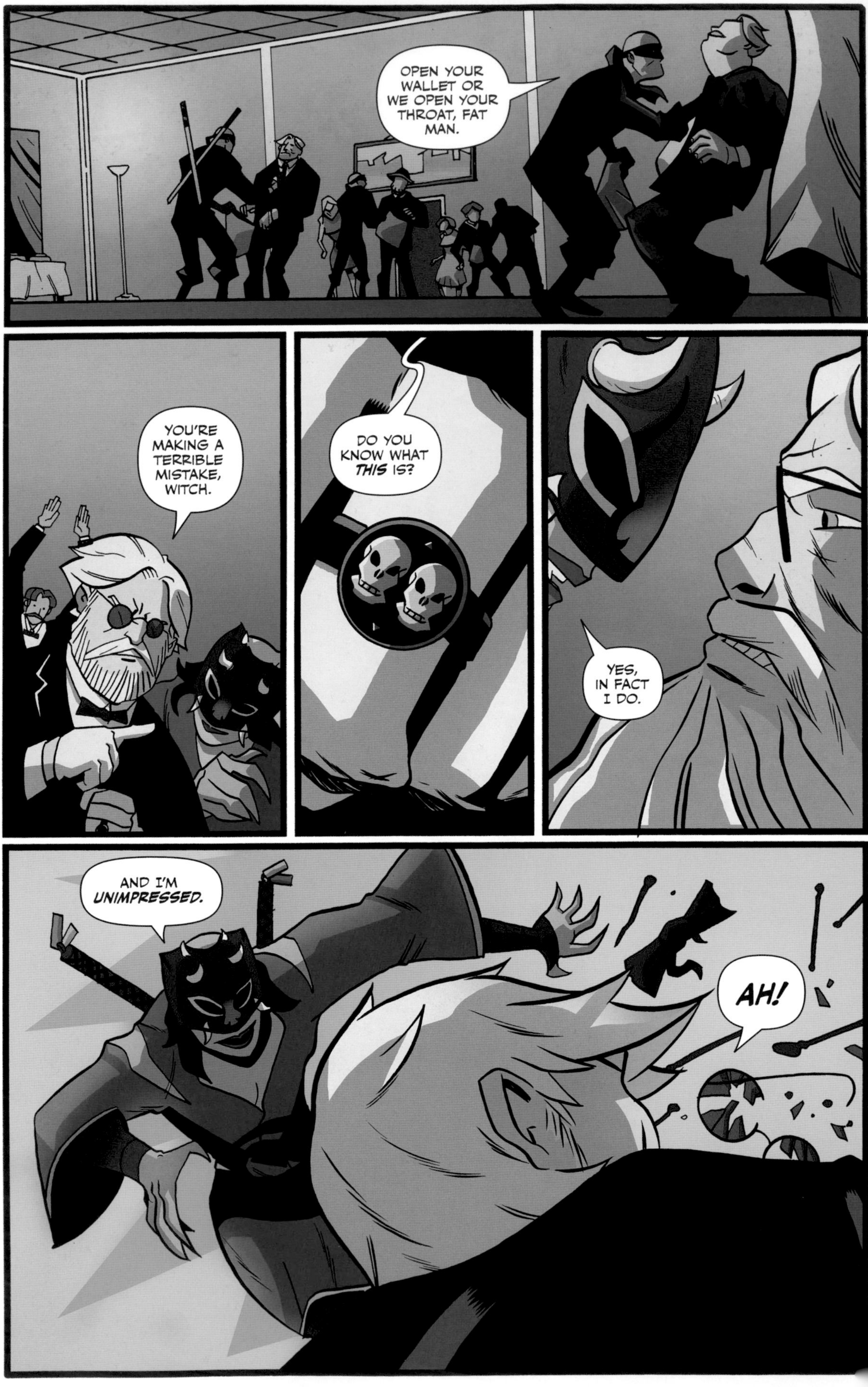
OPEN YOUR WALLET OR WE OPEN YOUR THROAT, FAT MAN.
YOU'RE MAKING A TERRIBLE MISTAKE, WITCH.
DO YOU KNOW WHAT *THIS* IS?
YES, IN FACT I DO.
AND I'M *UNIMPRESSED.*
AH!

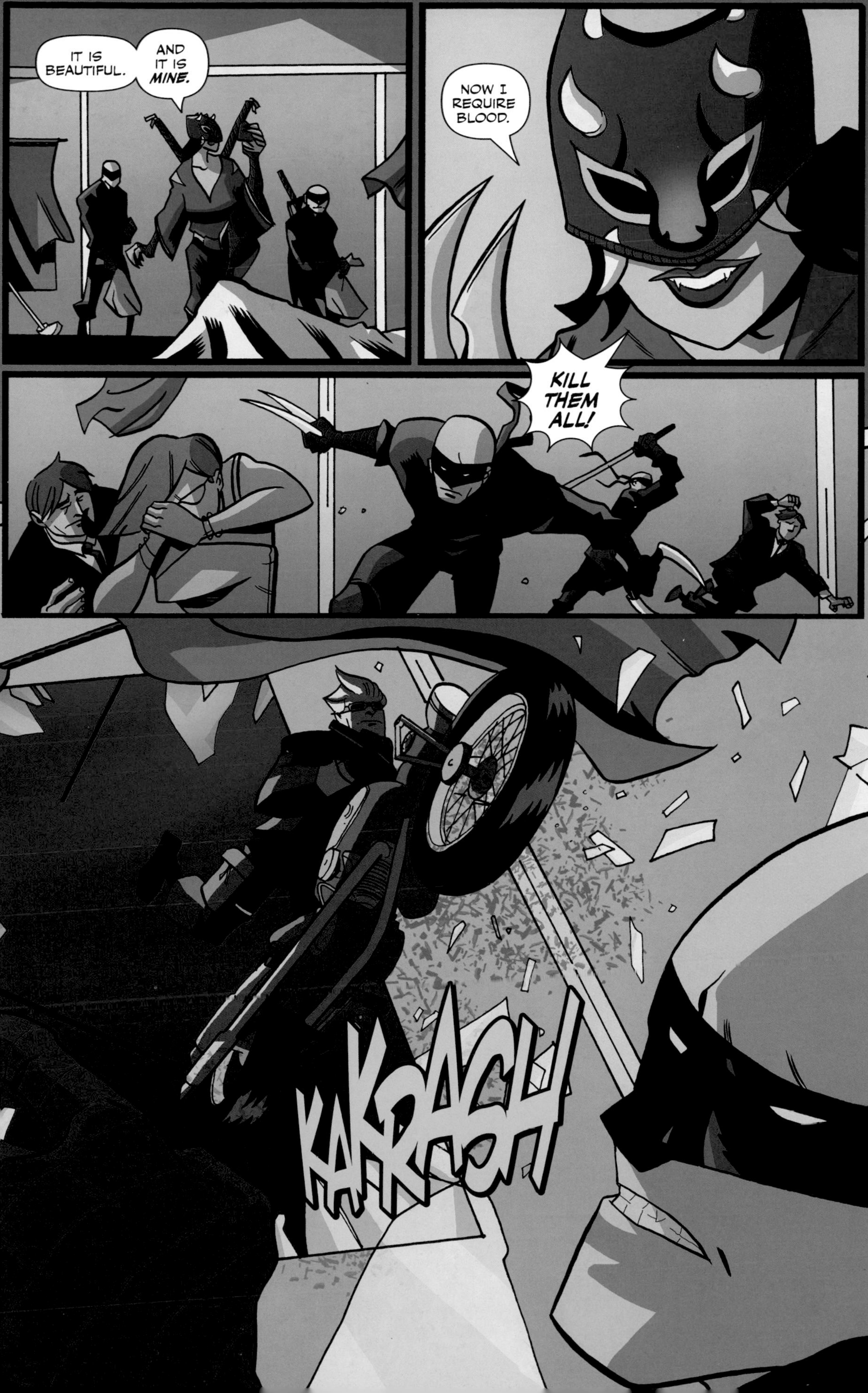

IT IS BEAUTIFUL.
AND IT IS *MINE.*
NOW I REQUIRE BLOOD.
KILL THEM ALL!
KAKRACH

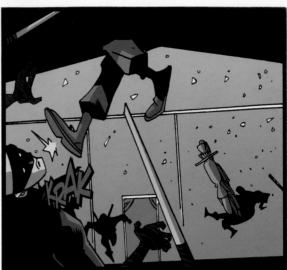

RETURN WHAT WAS STOLEN OR ELSE.

ATTACK!

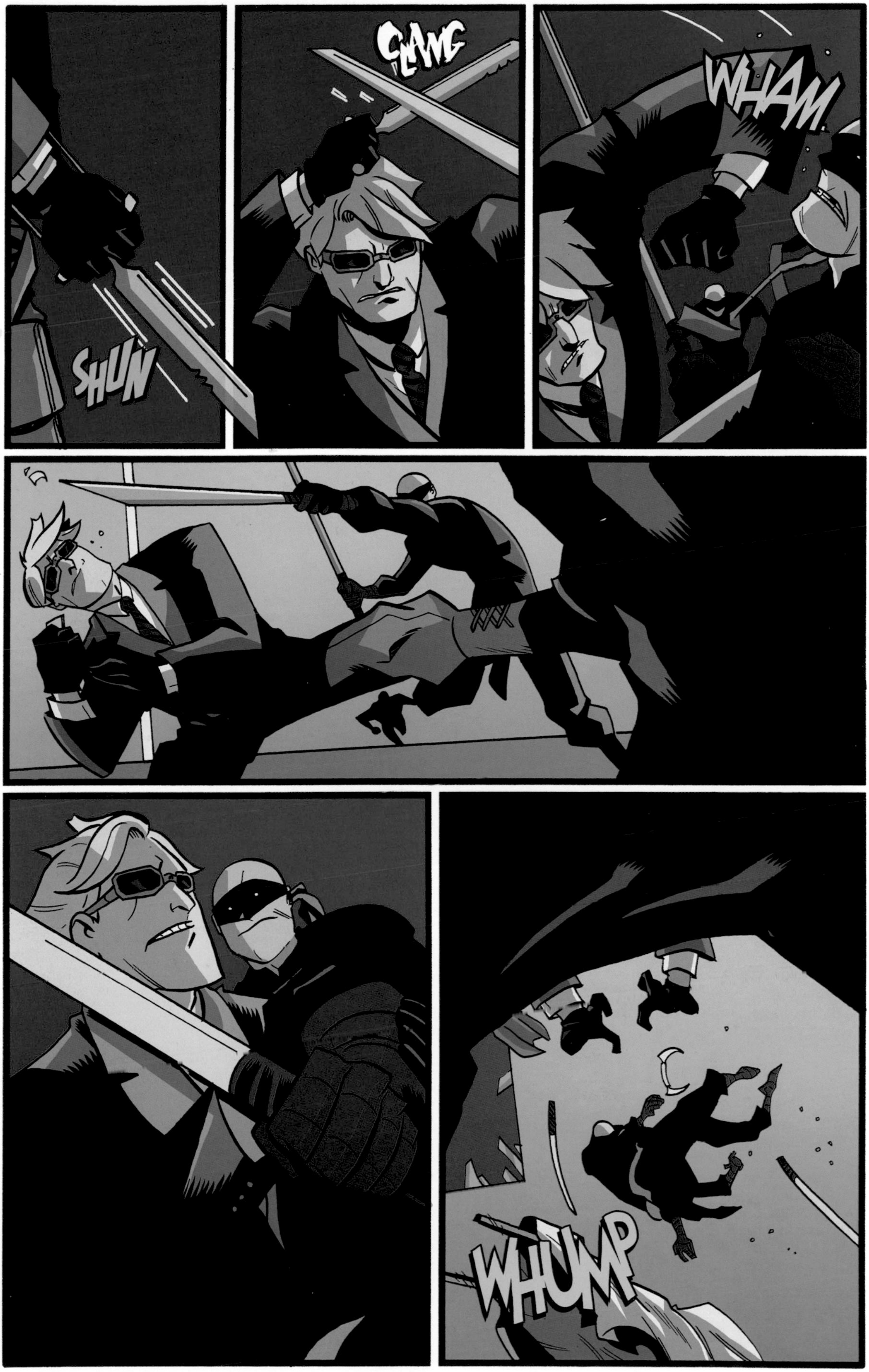
SHUN
CLANG
WHAM
WHUMP

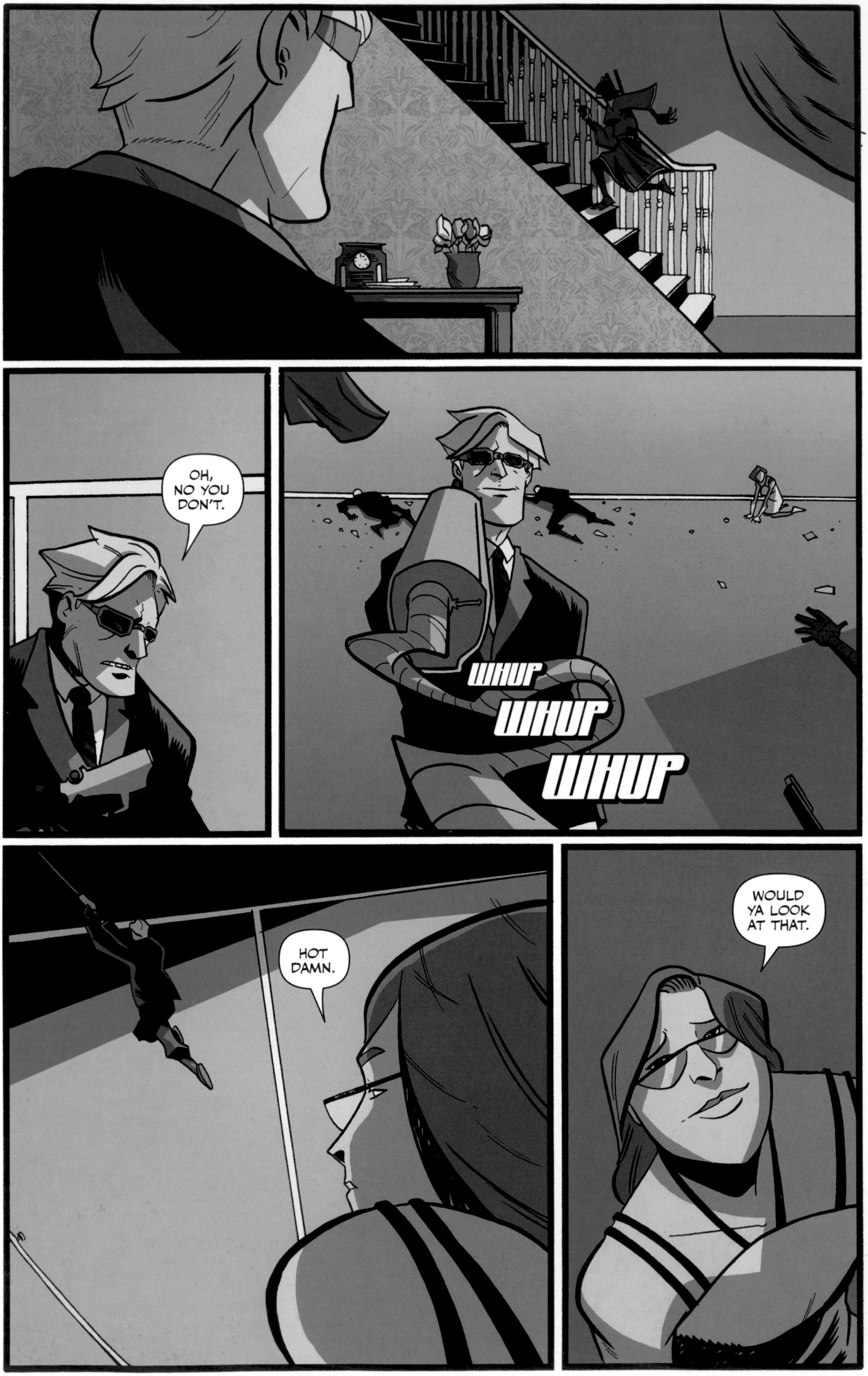
OH, NO YOU DON'T.
WHUP
WHUP
WHUP
HOT DAMN.
WOULD YA LOOK AT THAT.

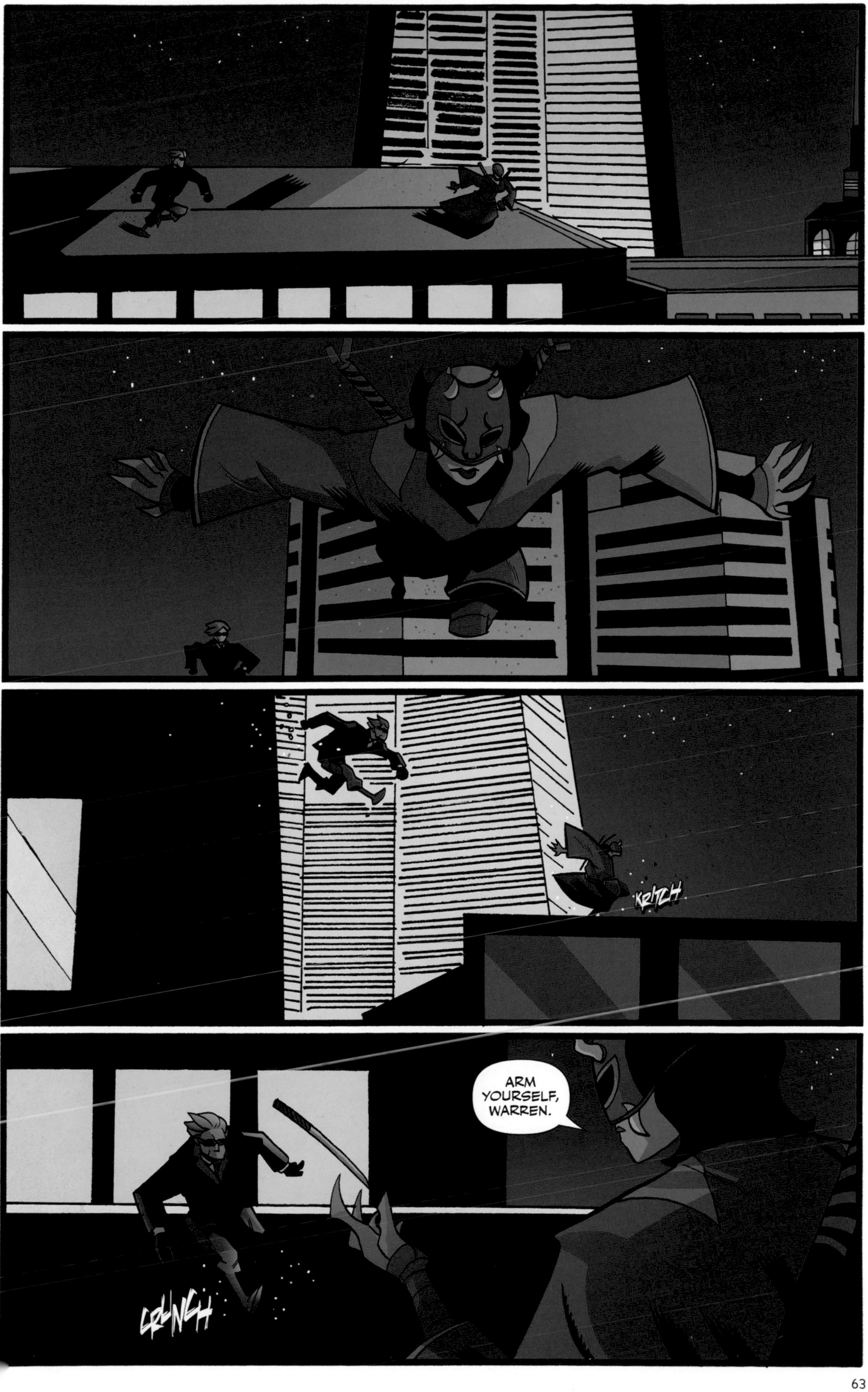
KRITCH
ARM YOURSELF, WARREN.
CRUNCH

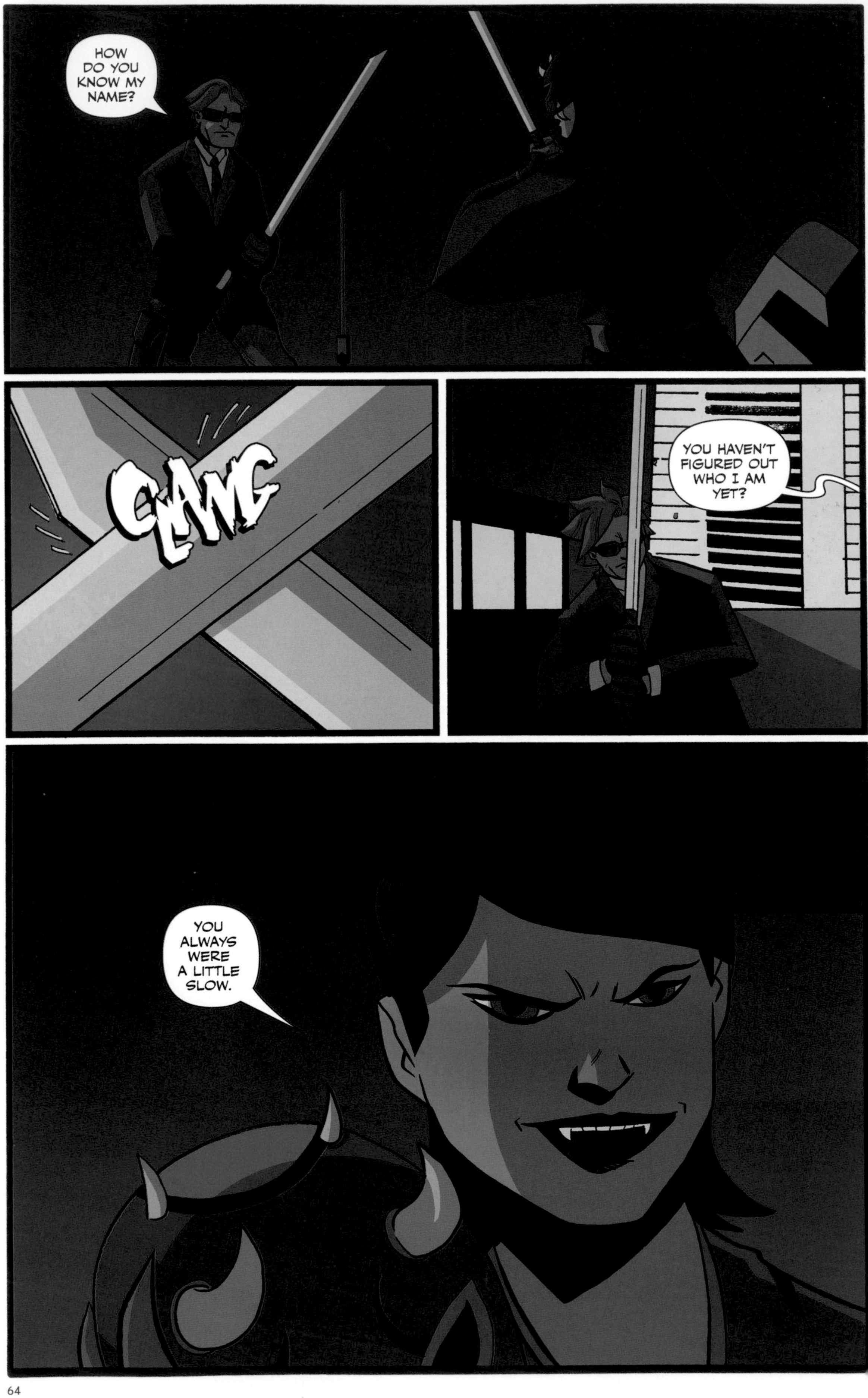
HOW DO YOU KNOW MY NAME?
CLANG
YOU HAVEN'T FIGURED OUT WHO I AM YET?
YOU ALWAYS WERE A LITTLE SLOW.

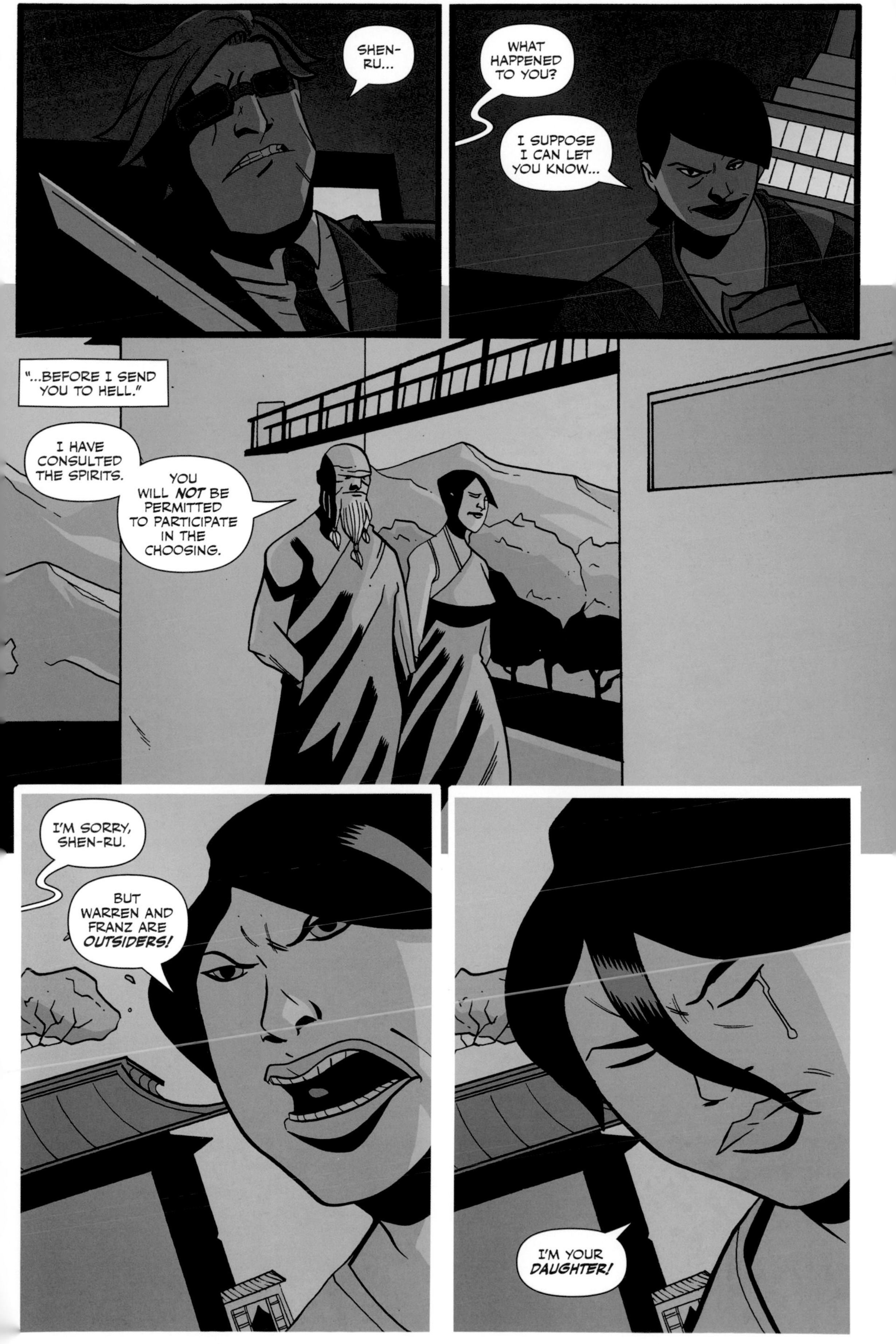
SHEN-RU...
WHAT HAPPENED TO YOU?
I SUPPOSE I CAN LET YOU KNOW...
"...BEFORE I SEND YOU TO HELL."
I HAVE CONSULTED THE SPIRITS.
YOU WILL NOT BE PERMITTED TO PARTICIPATE IN THE CHOOSING.
I'M SORRY, SHEN-RU.
BUT WARREN AND FRANZ ARE OUTSIDERS!
I'M YOUR DAUGHTER!

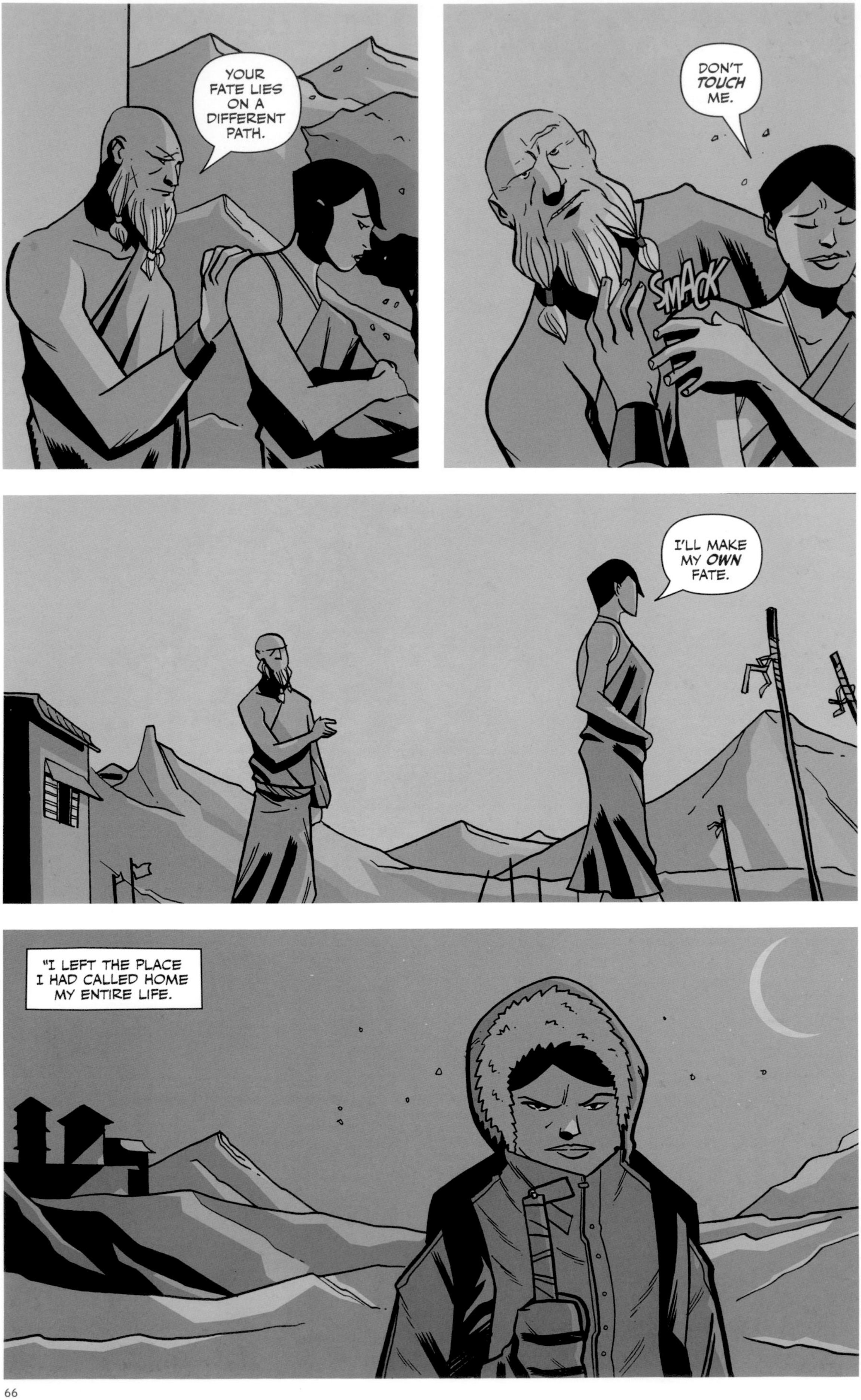
YOUR FATE LIES ON A DIFFERENT PATH.
DON'T *TOUCH* ME.
SMACK
I'LL MAKE MY *OWN* FATE.
"I LEFT THE PLACE I HAD CALLED HOME MY ENTIRE LIFE.

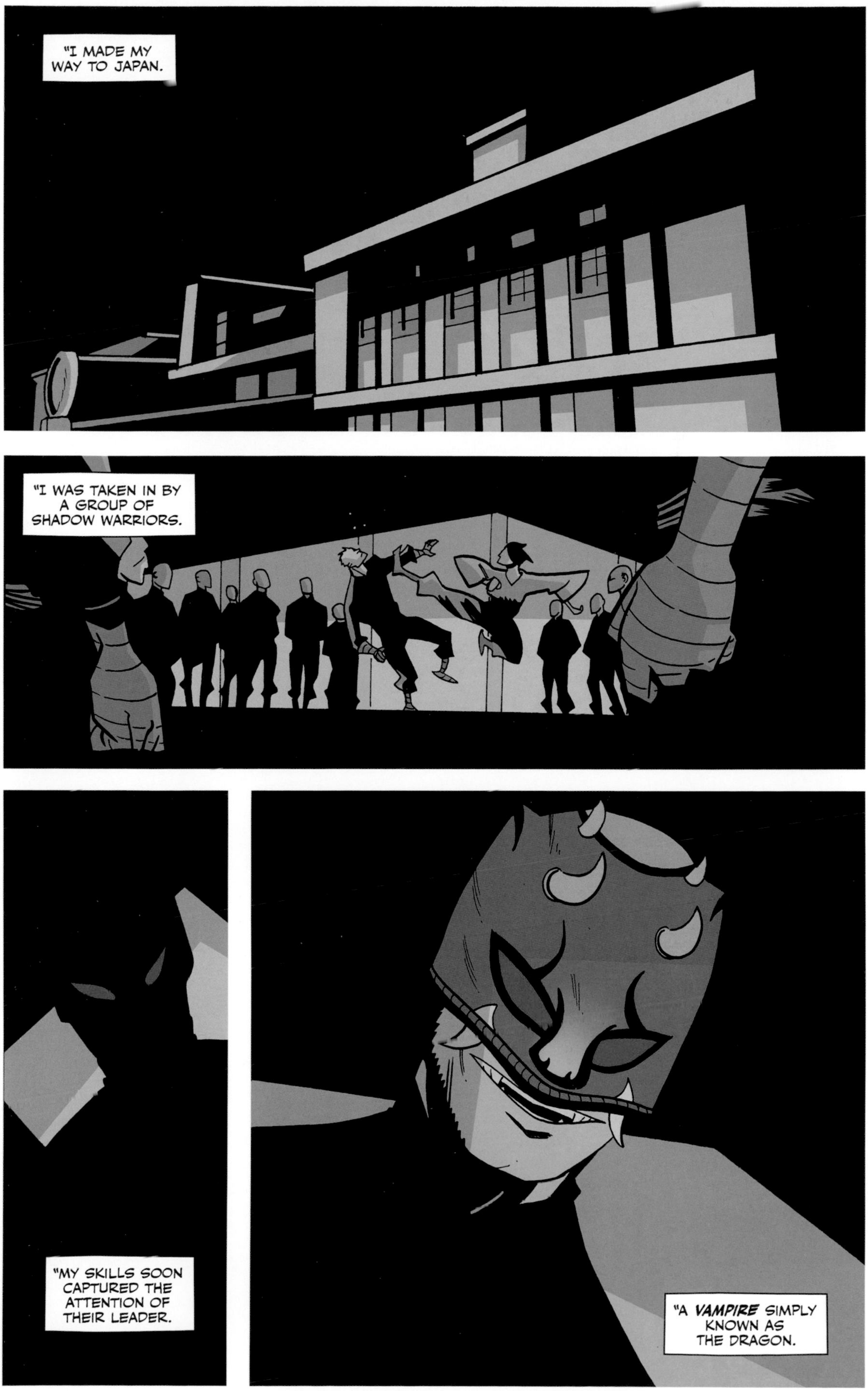
"I MADE MY WAY TO JAPAN.
"I WAS TAKEN IN BY A GROUP OF SHADOW WARRIORS.
"MY SKILLS SOON CAPTURED THE ATTENTION OF THEIR LEADER.
"A *VAMPIRE* SIMPLY KNOWN AS THE DRAGON.

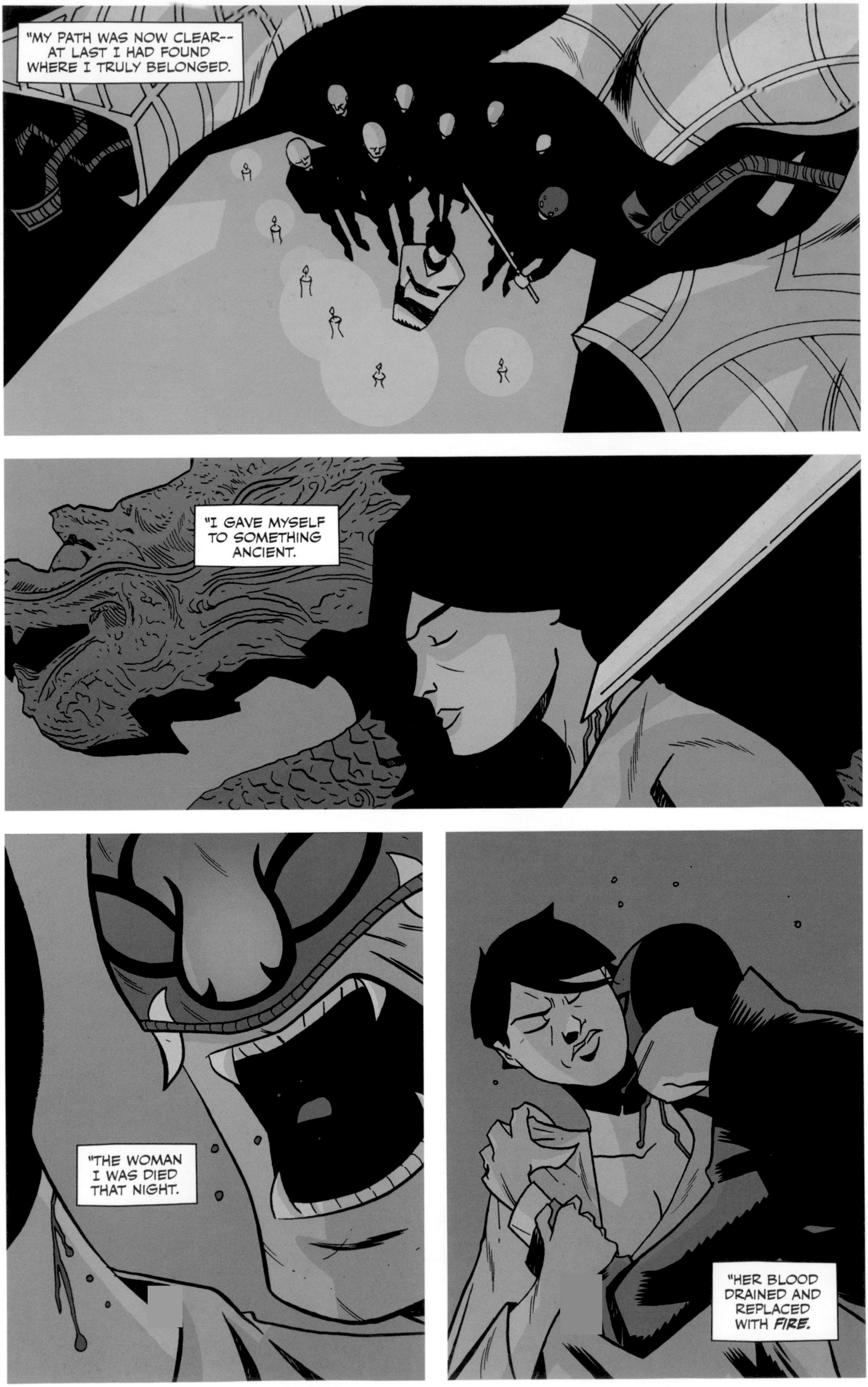
"MY PATH WAS NOW CLEAR-- AT LAST I HAD FOUND WHERE I TRULY BELONGED.
"I GAVE MYSELF TO SOMETHING ANCIENT.
"THE WOMAN I WAS DIED THAT NIGHT.
"HER BLOOD DRAINED AND REPLACED WITH *FIRE.*

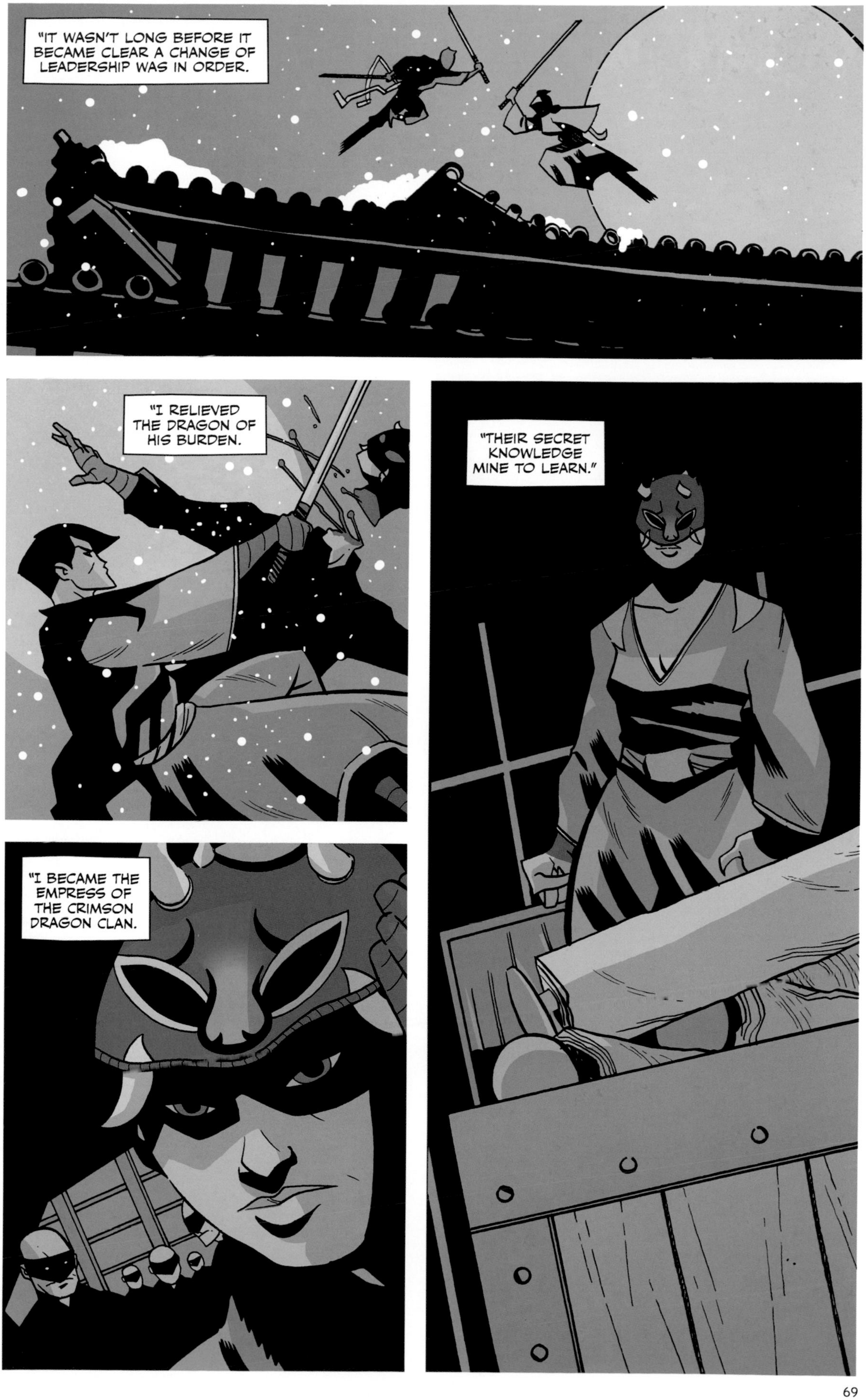
"IT WASN'T LONG BEFORE IT BECAME CLEAR A CHANGE OF LEADERSHIP WAS IN ORDER.
"I RELIEVED THE DRAGON OF HIS BURDEN.
"I BECAME THE EMPRESS OF THE CRIMSON DRAGON CLAN.
"THEIR SECRET KNOWLEDGE MINE TO LEARN."

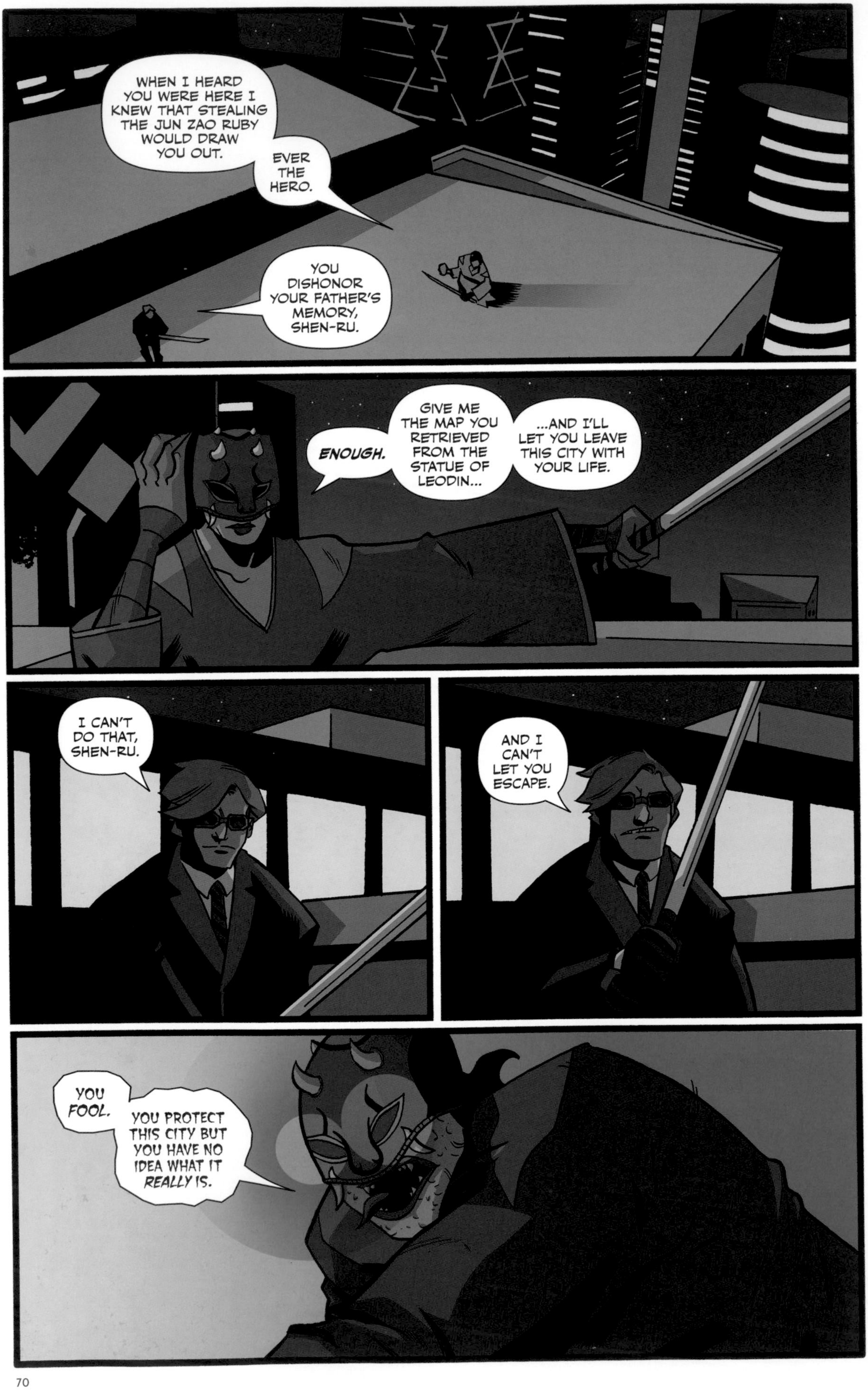
WHEN I HEARD YOU WERE HERE I KNEW THAT STEALING THE JUN ZAO RUBY WOULD DRAW YOU OUT.
EVER THE HERO.
YOU DISHONOR YOUR FATHER'S MEMORY, SHEN-RU.
ENOUGH.
GIVE ME THE MAP YOU RETRIEVED FROM THE STATUE OF LEODIN...
...AND I'LL LET YOU LEAVE THIS CITY WITH YOUR LIFE.
I CAN'T DO THAT, SHEN-RU.
AND I CAN'T LET YOU ESCAPE.
YOU FOOL.
YOU PROTECT THIS CITY BUT YOU HAVE NO IDEA WHAT IT REALLY IS.

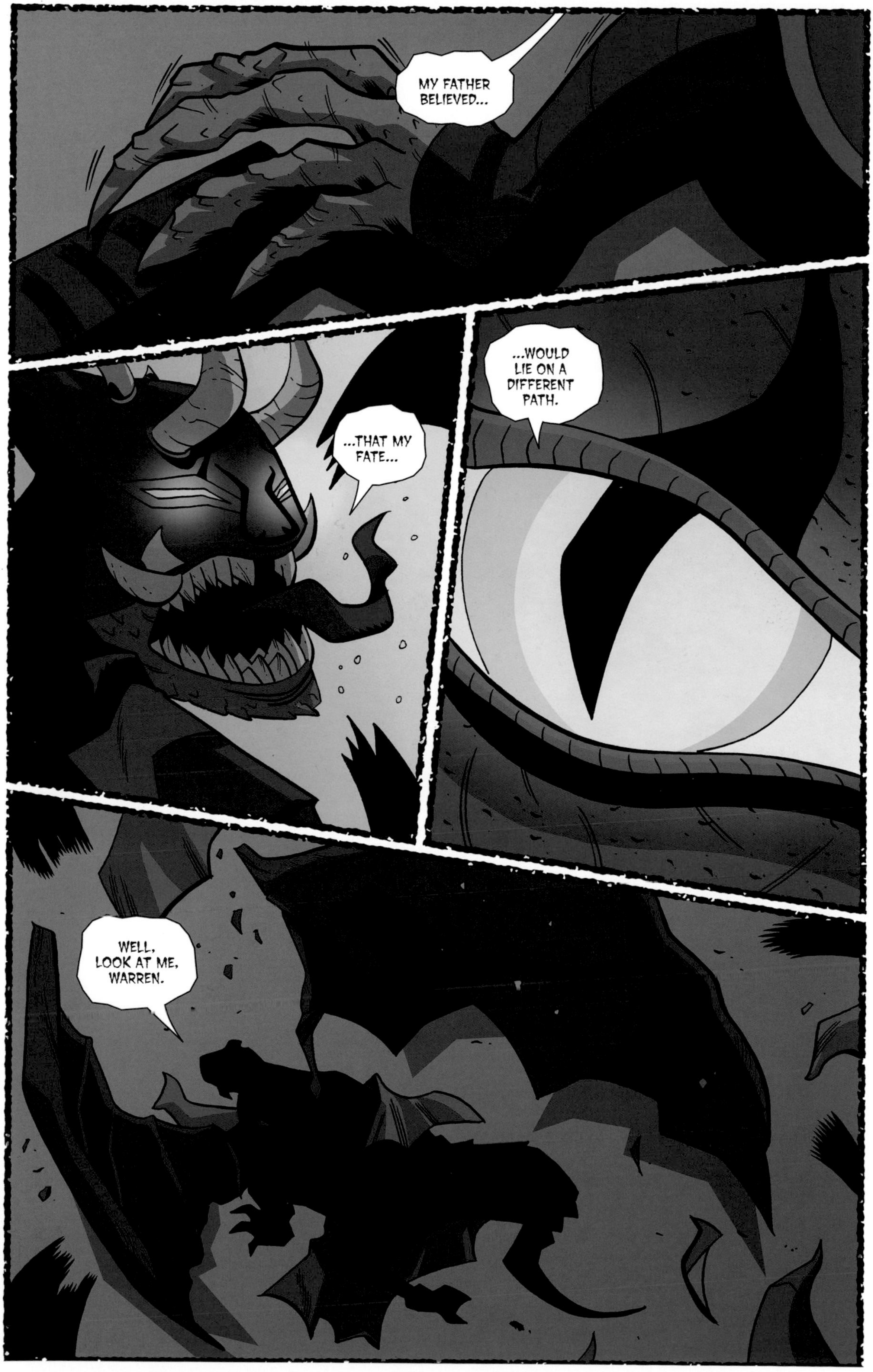
MY FATHER BELIEVED...
...THAT MY FATE...
...WOULD LIE ON A DIFFERENT PATH.
WELL, LOOK AT ME, WARREN.

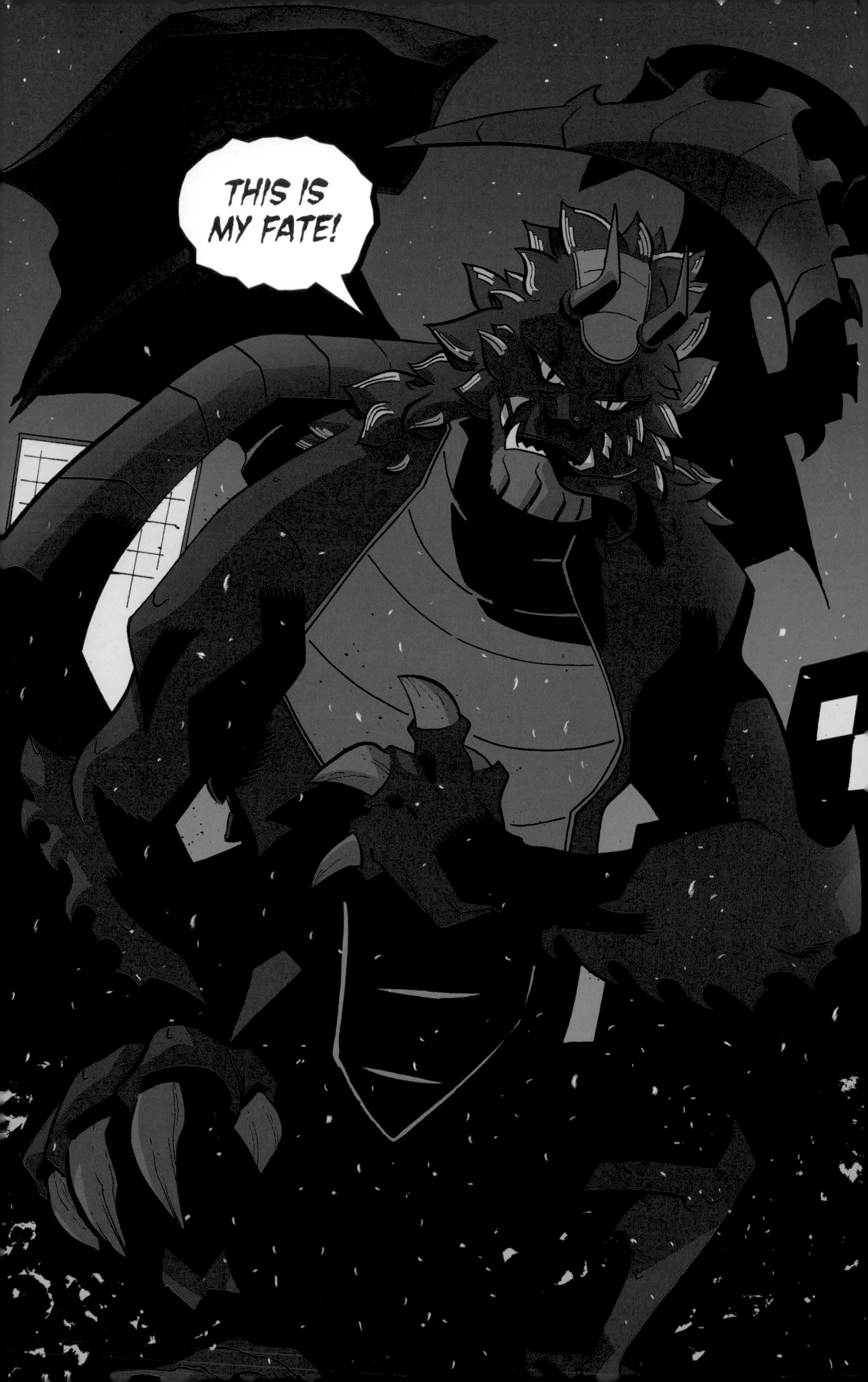
THIS IS MY FATE!

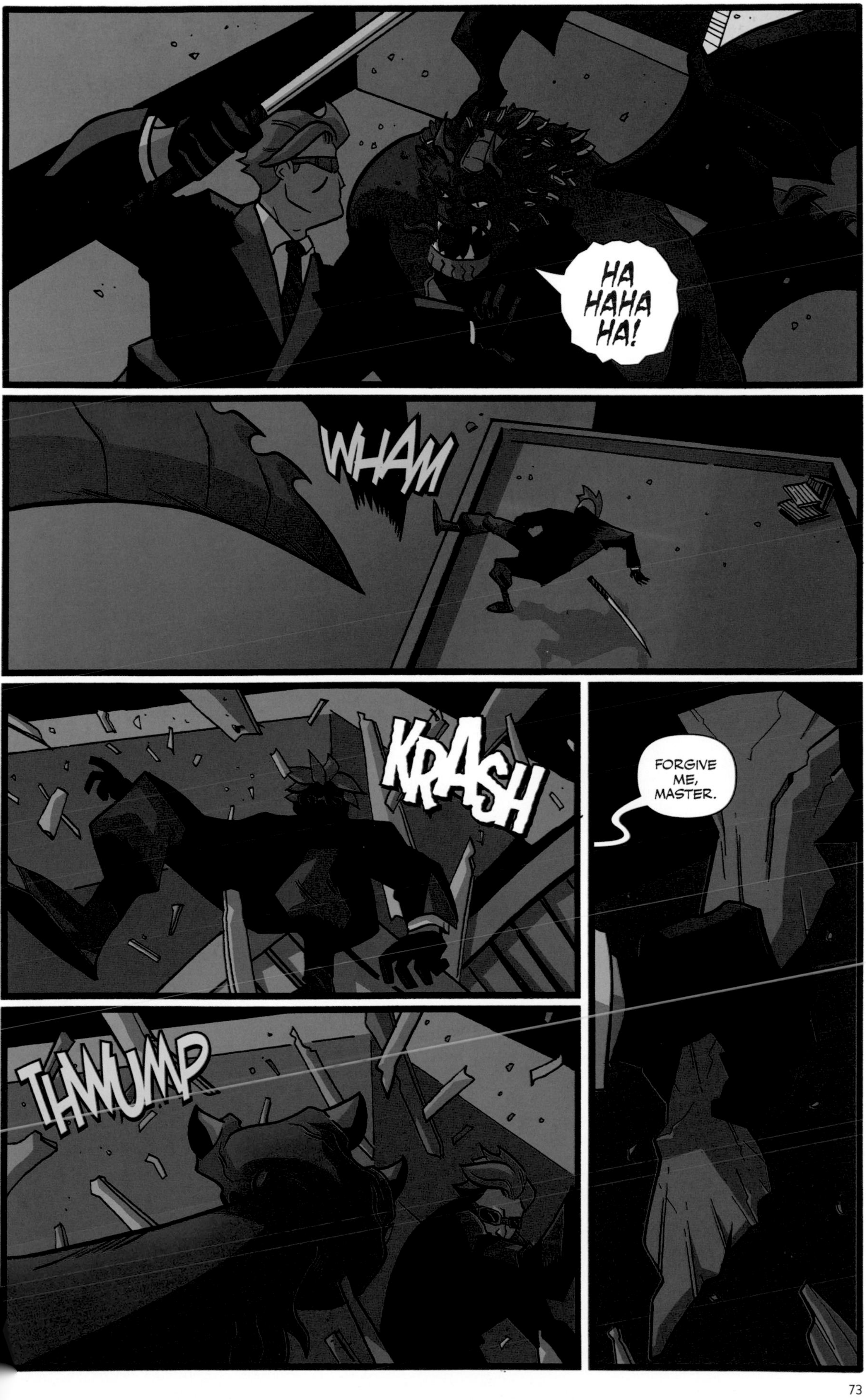
HA HAHAHA HA!
WHAM
KRASH
FORGIVE ME, MASTER.
THWUMP

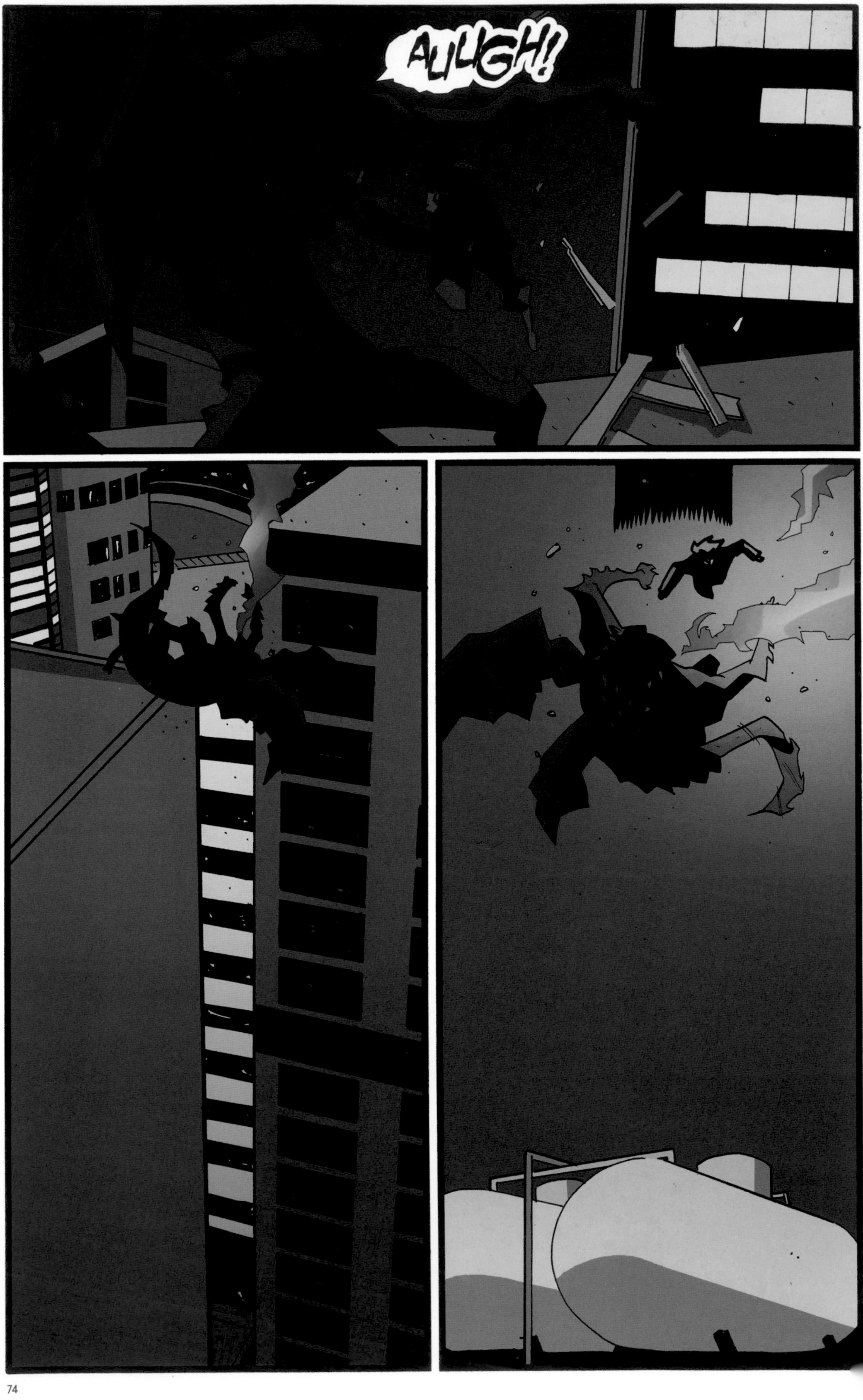
AULUGH!

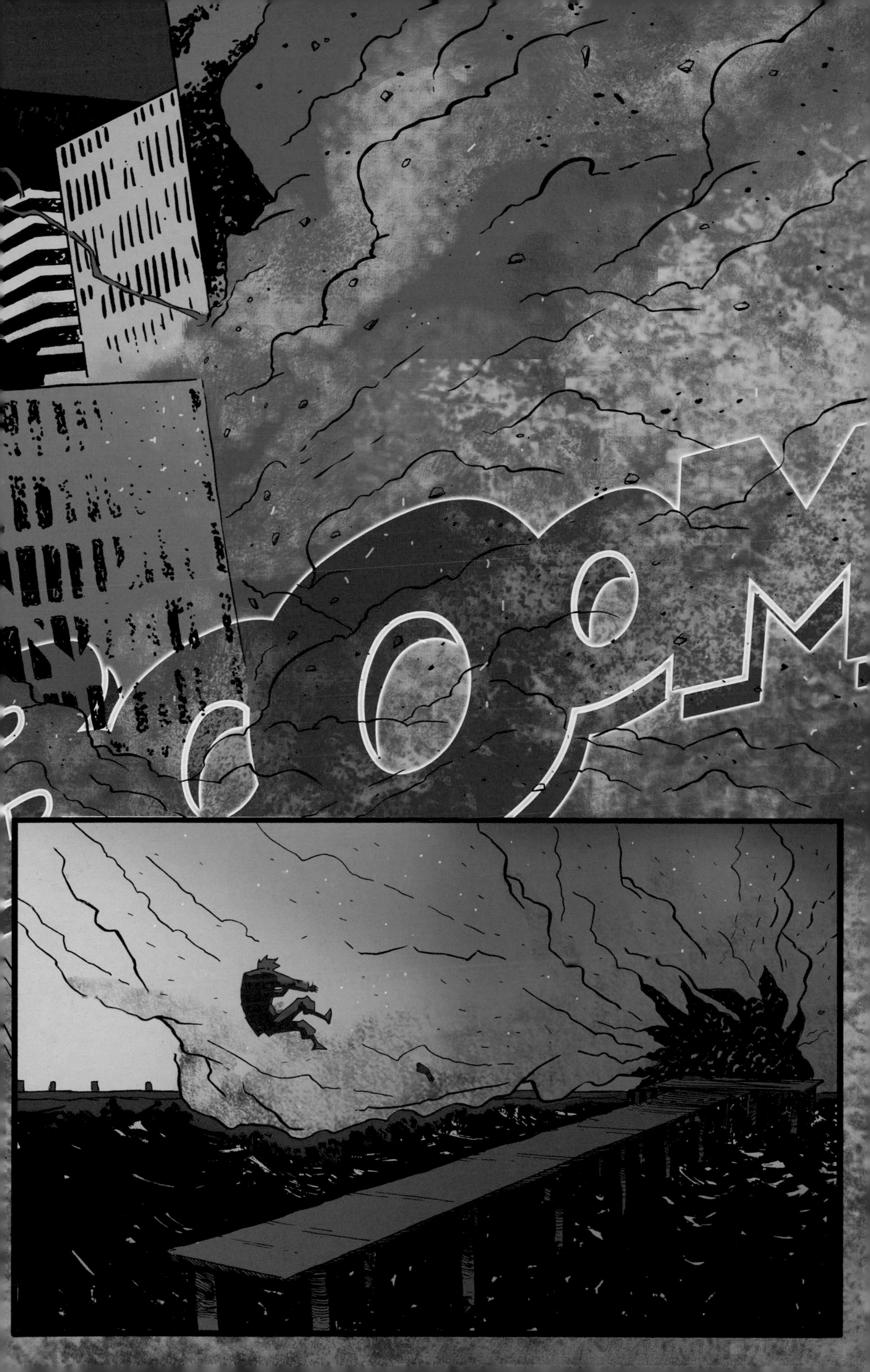
BOOOM

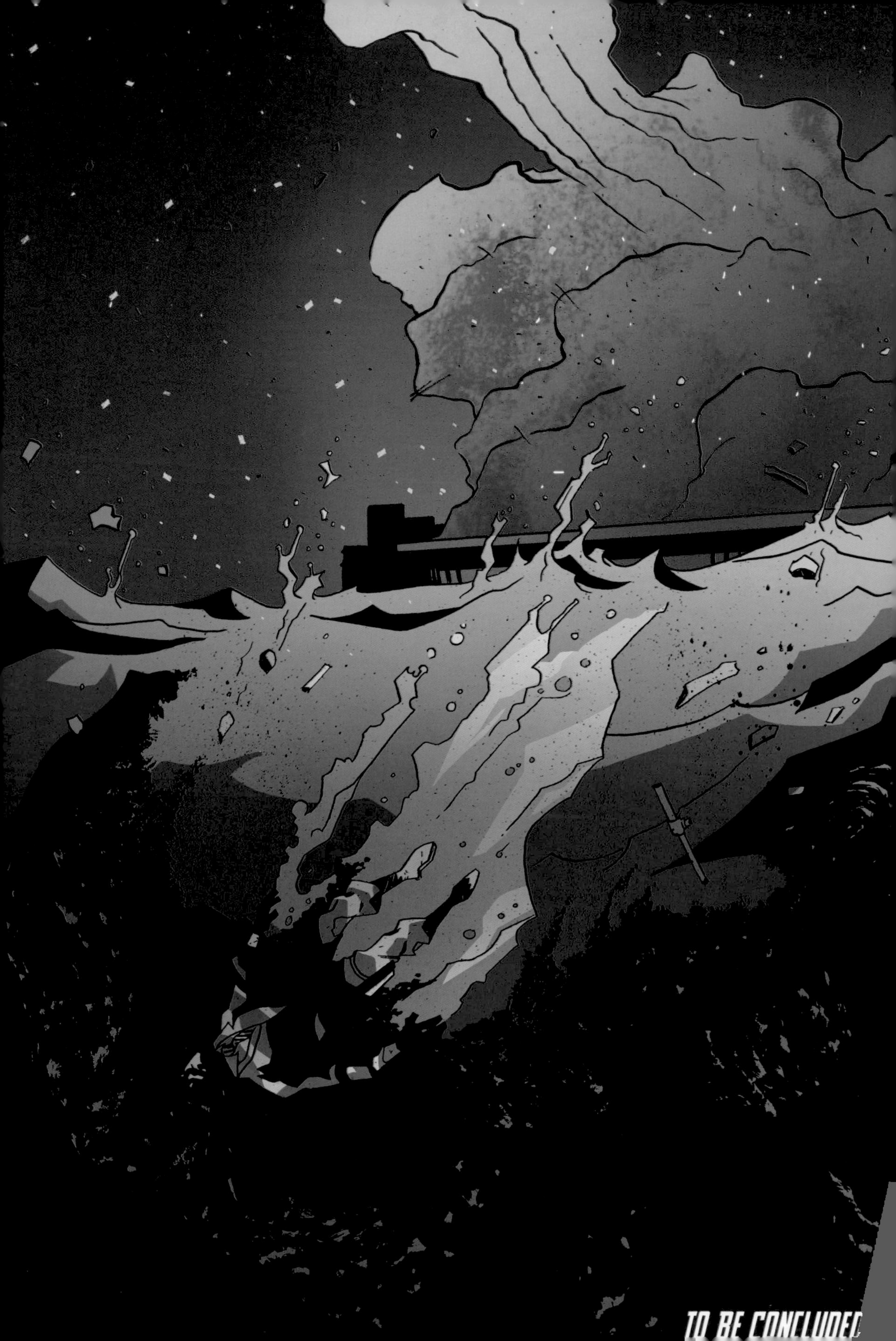
TO BE CONCLUDED

THE CURSE
OF ATLANTIS

SCRIPT BY **FABIAN RANGEL JR.**

ART BY **RYAN CODY**

LETTERS BY **ED BRISSON**

BEFORE.

"HOW DO I REPAY YOU?"

"THERE'S A LETTER IN MY DESK."

"IT'S SIGNED TO MY WIFE."

"SEE THAT SHE GETS IT AND WE'LL CALL IT EVEN."

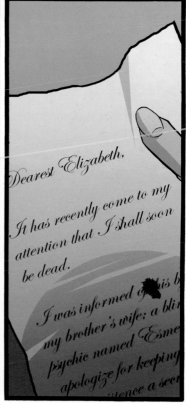

Dearest Elizabeth,

It has recently come to my attention that I shall soon be dead.

I was informed of this by my brother's wife: a blind psychic named Esme... apologize for keeping ...tence a secr...

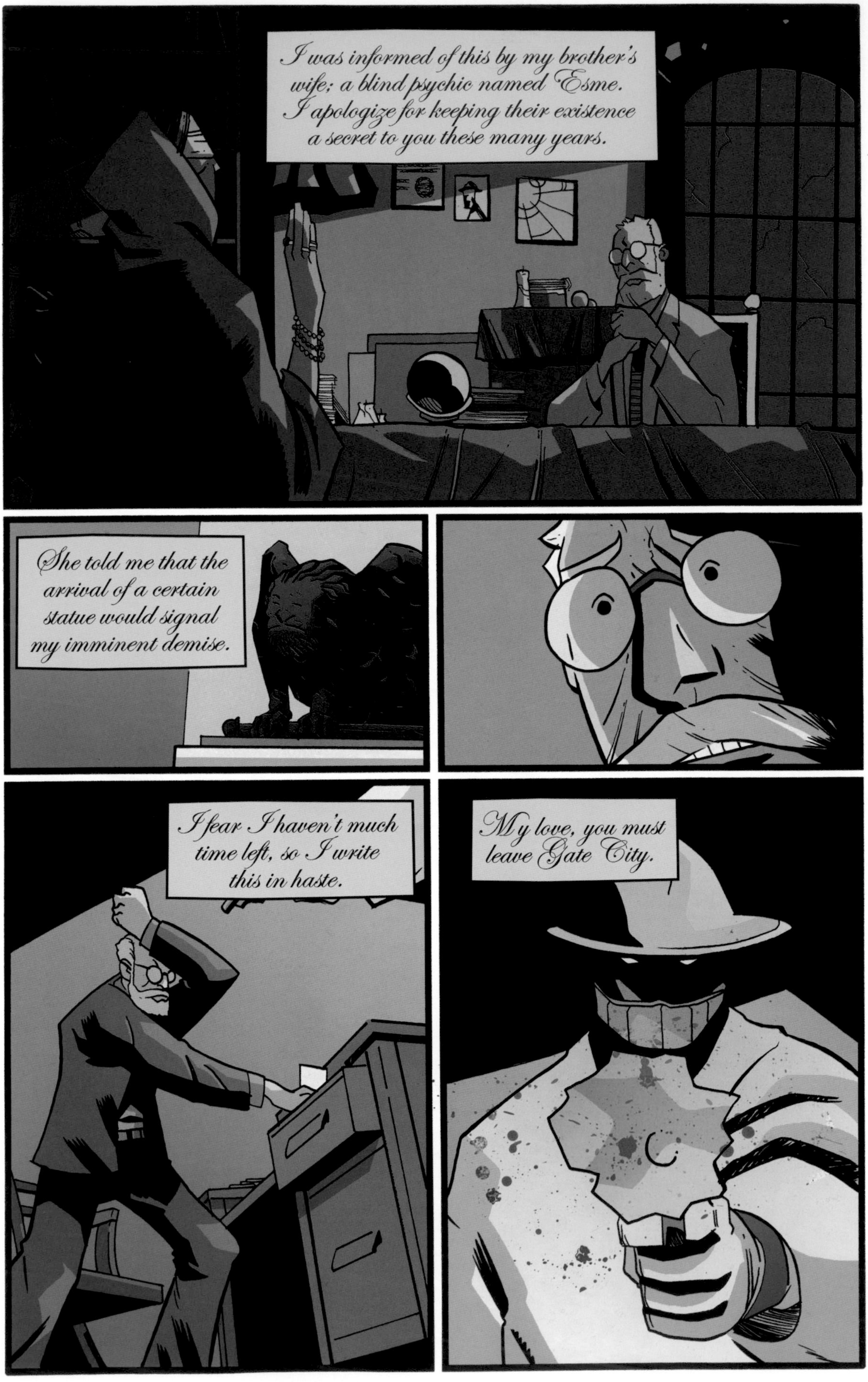
I was informed of this by my brother's wife; a blind psychic named Esme. I apologize for keeping their existence a secret to you these many years.
She told me that the arrival of a certain statue would signal my imminent demise.
I fear I haven't much time left, so I write this in haste.
My love, you must leave Gate City.

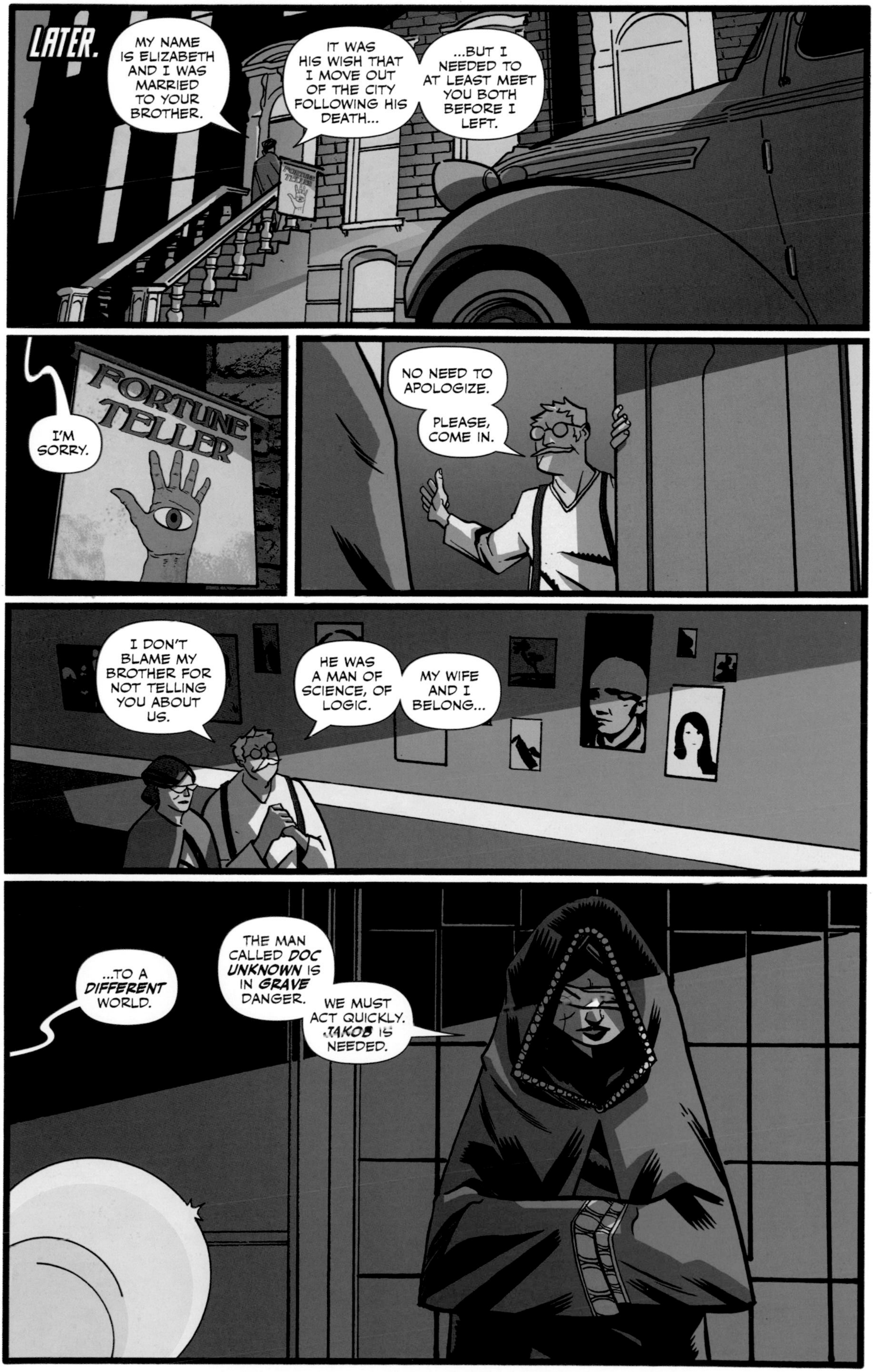
LATER.
MY NAME IS ELIZABETH AND I WAS MARRIED TO YOUR BROTHER.
IT WAS HIS WISH THAT I MOVE OUT OF THE CITY FOLLOWING HIS DEATH...
...BUT I NEEDED TO AT LEAST MEET YOU BOTH BEFORE I LEFT.
FORTUNE TELLER
FORTUNE TELLER
I'M SORRY.
NO NEED TO APOLOGIZE.
PLEASE, COME IN.
I DON'T BLAME MY BROTHER FOR NOT TELLING YOU ABOUT US.
HE WAS A MAN OF SCIENCE, OF LOGIC.
MY WIFE AND I BELONG...
...TO A *DIFFERENT* WORLD.
THE MAN CALLED *DOC UNKNOWN* IS IN *GRAVE* DANGER.
WE MUST ACT QUICKLY. *JAKOB* IS NEEDED.

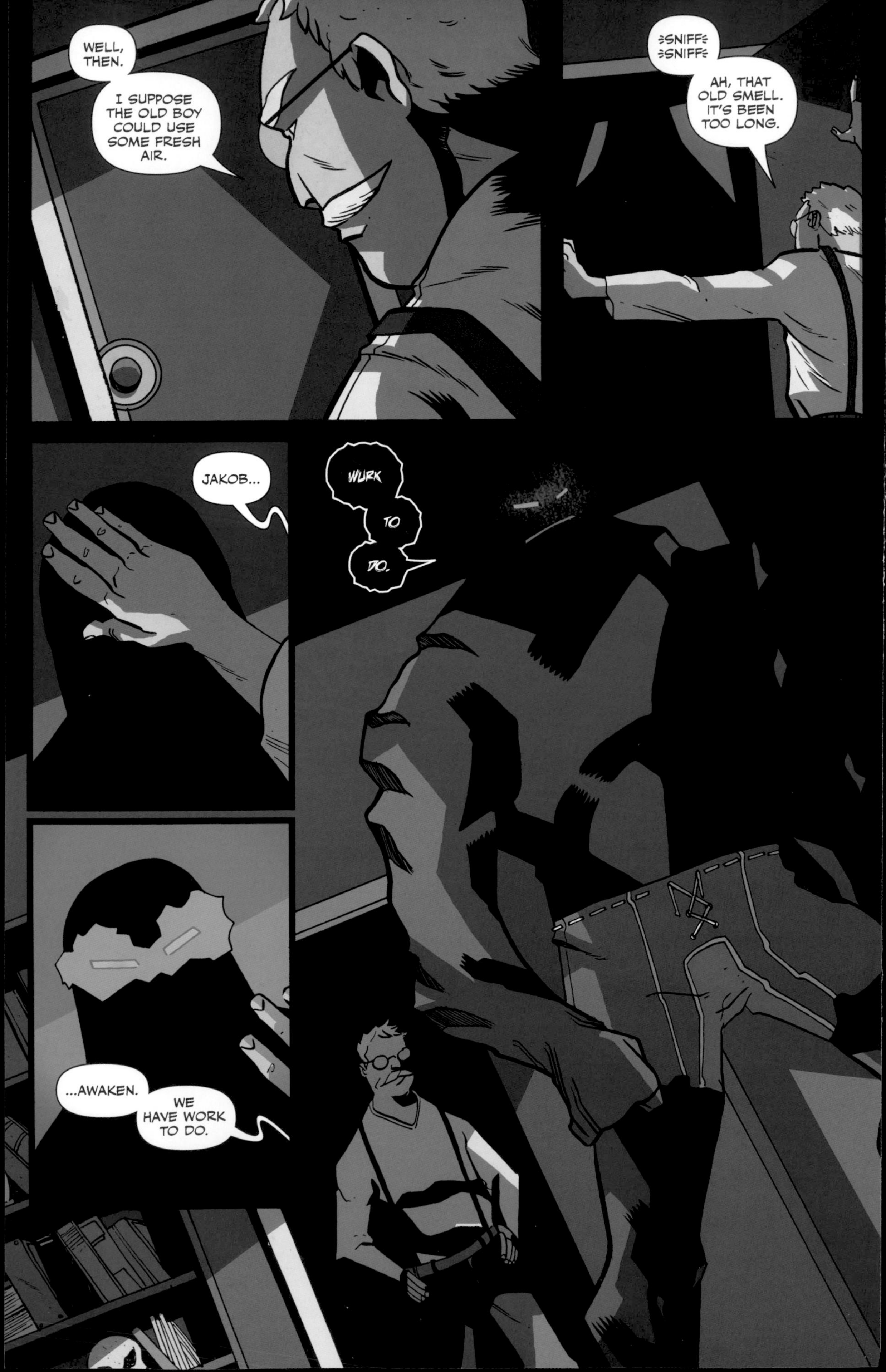
WELL, THEN.
I SUPPOSE THE OLD BOY COULD USE SOME FRESH AIR.
SNIFF SNIFF
AH, THAT OLD SMELL. IT'S BEEN TOO LONG.
JAKOB...
...AWAKEN.
WE HAVE WORK TO DO.
WURK TO DO.

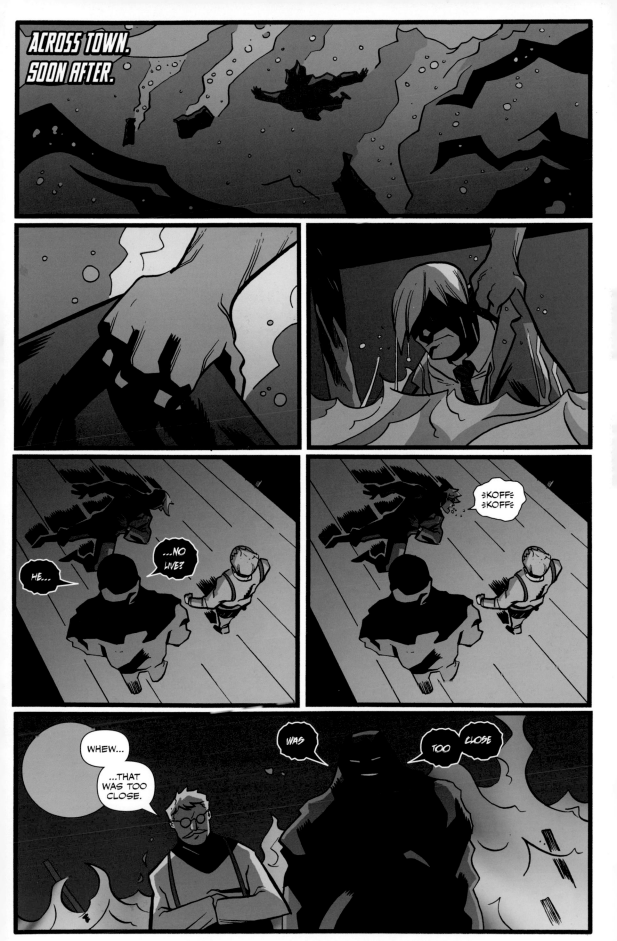

ACROSS TOWN.
SOON AFTER.

HE...

...NO LIVE?

≷KOFF≷
≷KOFF≷

WHEW...

...THAT WAS TOO CLOSE.

WAS

TOO CLOSE

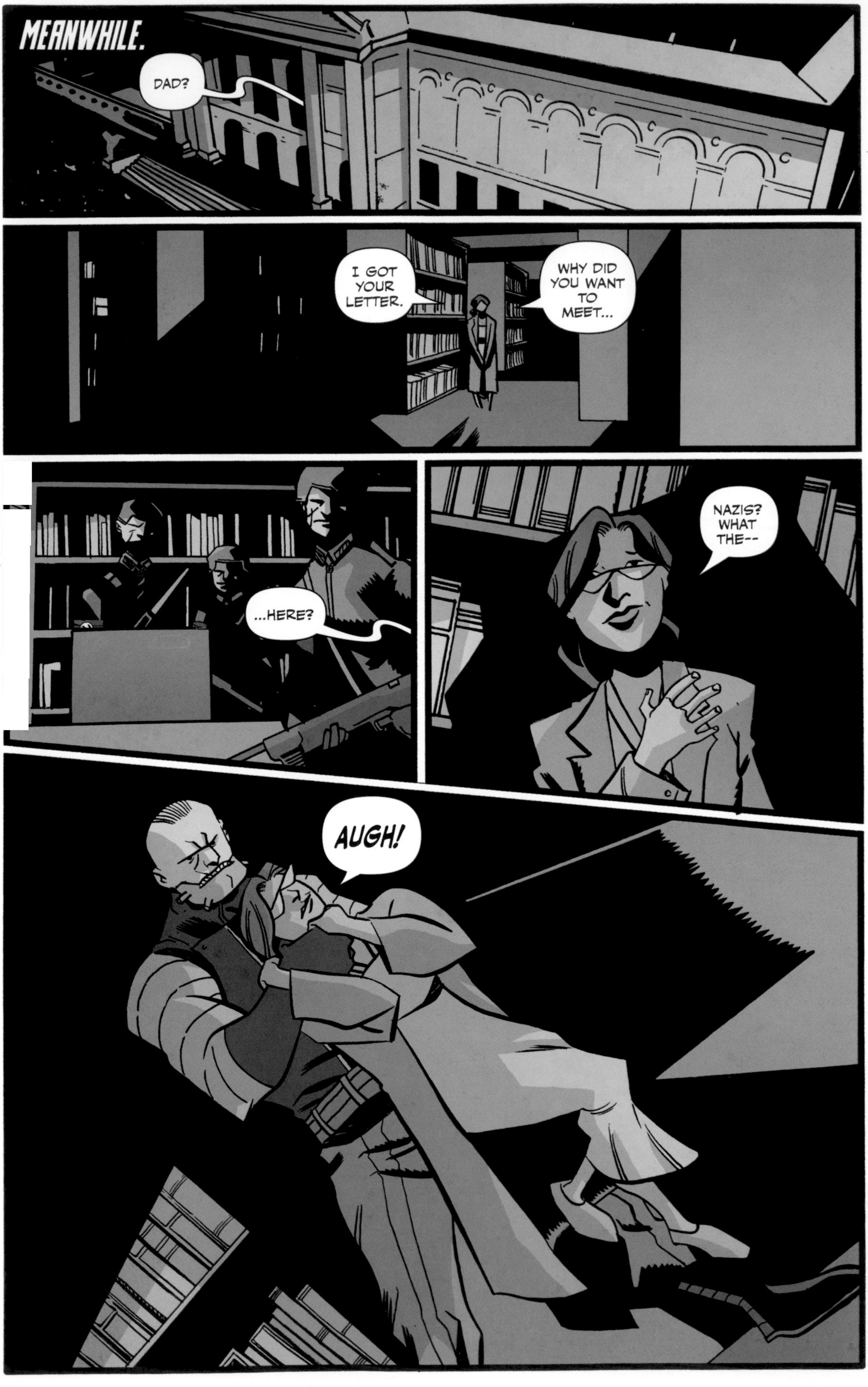
MEANWHILE.
DAD?
I GOT YOUR LETTER.
WHY DID YOU WANT TO MEET...
...HERE?
NAZIS? WHAT THE--
AUGH!

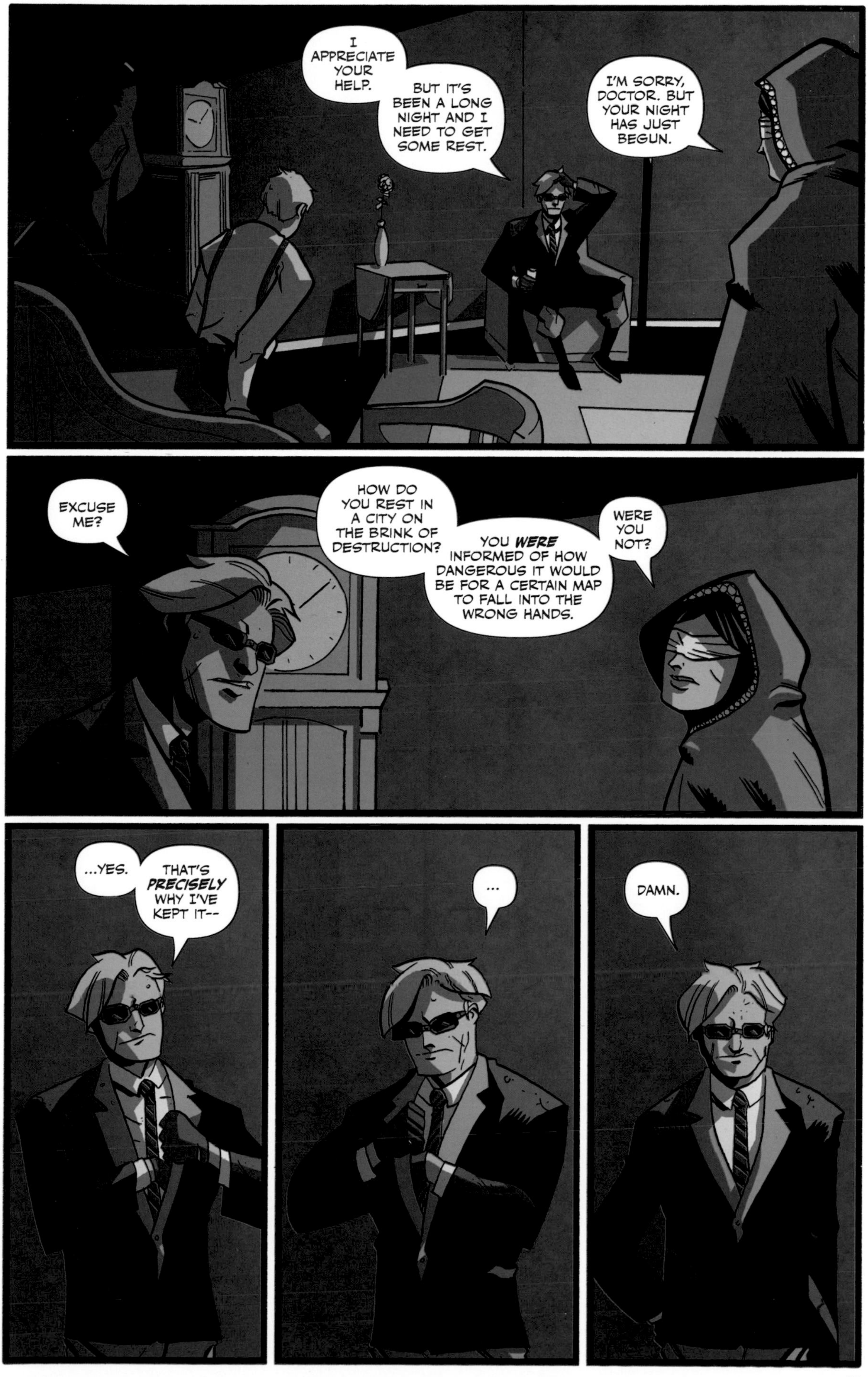
I APPRECIATE YOUR HELP.
BUT IT'S BEEN A LONG NIGHT AND I NEED TO GET SOME REST.
I'M SORRY, DOCTOR. BUT YOUR NIGHT HAS JUST BEGUN.
EXCUSE ME?
HOW DO YOU REST IN A CITY ON THE BRINK OF DESTRUCTION?
YOU *WERE* INFORMED OF HOW DANGEROUS IT WOULD BE FOR A CERTAIN MAP TO FALL INTO THE WRONG HANDS.
WERE YOU NOT?
...YES.
THAT'S *PRECISELY* WHY I'VE KEPT IT--
...
DAMN.

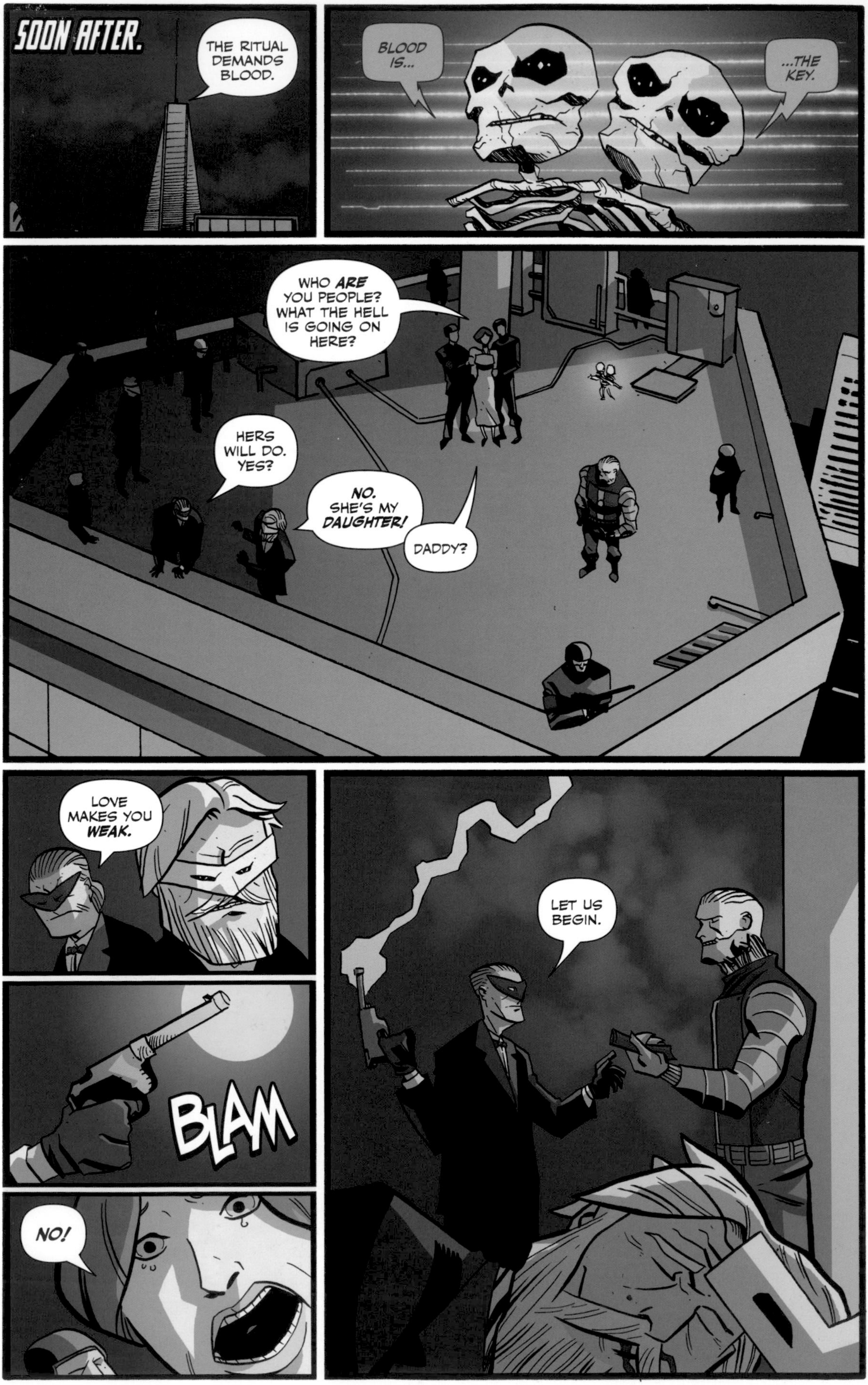
SOON AFTER.
THE RITUAL DEMANDS BLOOD.
BLOOD IS...
...THE KEY.
WHO ARE YOU PEOPLE? WHAT THE HELL IS GOING ON HERE?
HERS WILL DO. YES?
NO. SHE'S MY DAUGHTER!
DADDY?
LOVE MAKES YOU WEAK.
BLAM
NO!
LET US BEGIN.

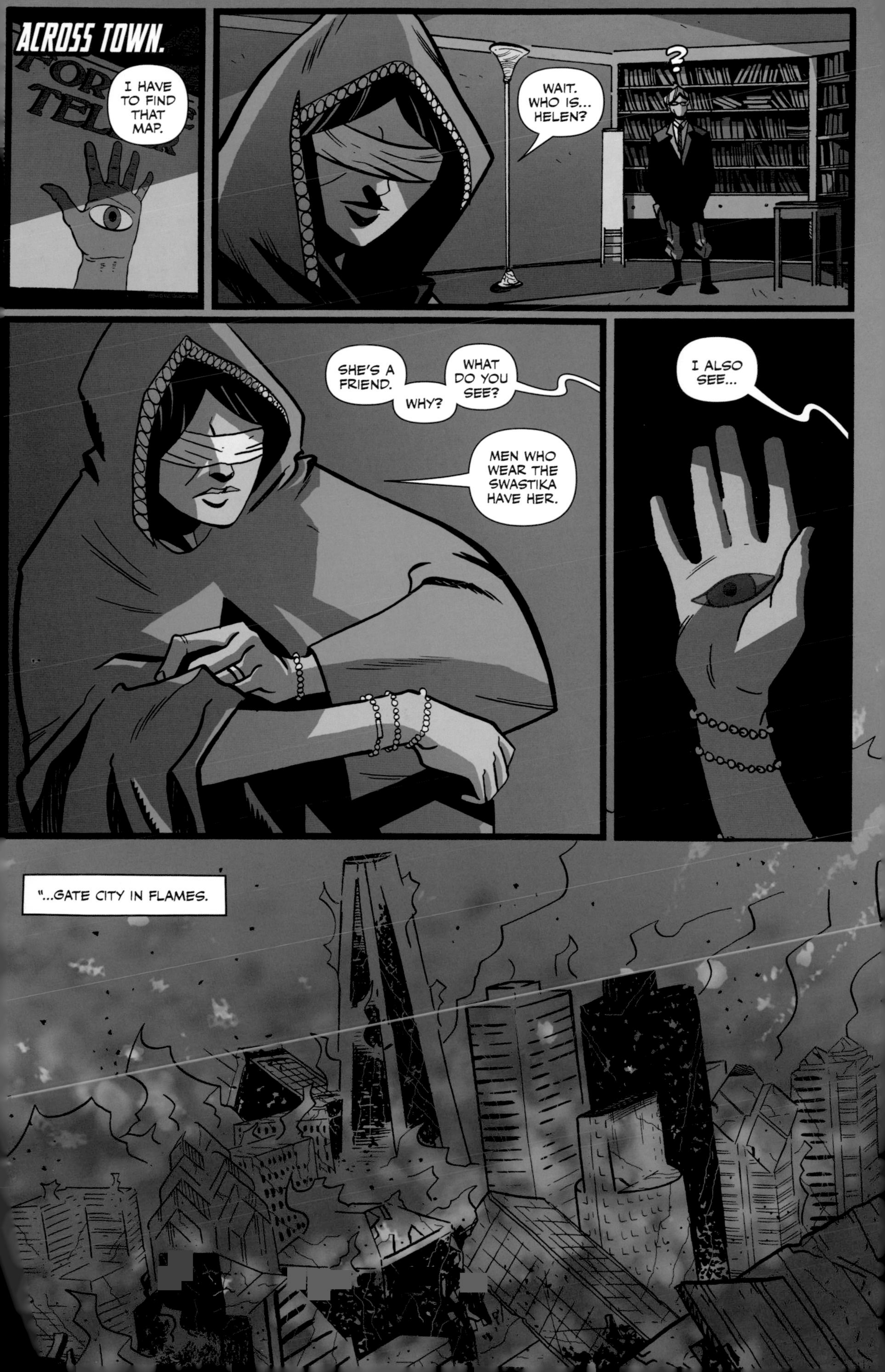
ACROSS TOWN.
I HAVE TO FIND THAT MAP.
WAIT. WHO IS... HELEN?
SHE'S A FRIEND.
WHY?
WHAT DO YOU SEE?
MEN WHO WEAR THE SWASTIKA HAVE HER.
I ALSO SEE...
"...GATE CITY IN FLAMES.

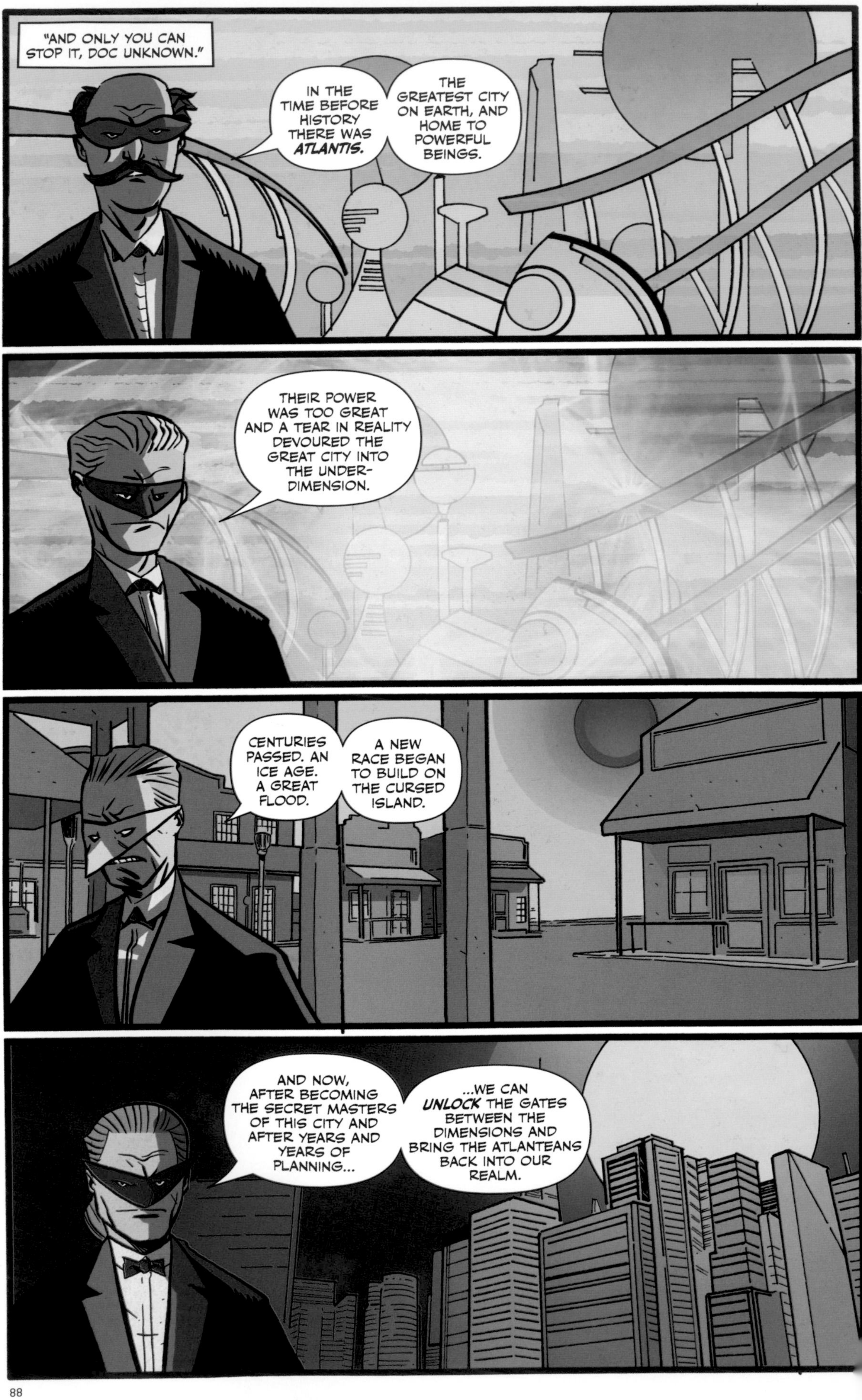
"AND ONLY YOU CAN STOP IT, DOC UNKNOWN."
IN THE TIME BEFORE HISTORY THERE WAS *ATLANTIS.*
THE GREATEST CITY ON EARTH, AND HOME TO POWERFUL BEINGS.
THEIR POWER WAS TOO GREAT AND A TEAR IN REALITY DEVOURED THE GREAT CITY INTO THE UNDER-DIMENSION.
CENTURIES PASSED. AN ICE AGE. A GREAT FLOOD.
A NEW RACE BEGAN TO BUILD ON THE CURSED ISLAND.
AND NOW, AFTER BECOMING THE SECRET MASTERS OF THIS CITY AND AFTER YEARS AND YEARS OF PLANNING...
...WE CAN *UNLOCK* THE GATES BETWEEN THE DIMENSIONS AND BRING THE ATLANTEANS BACK INTO OUR REALM.

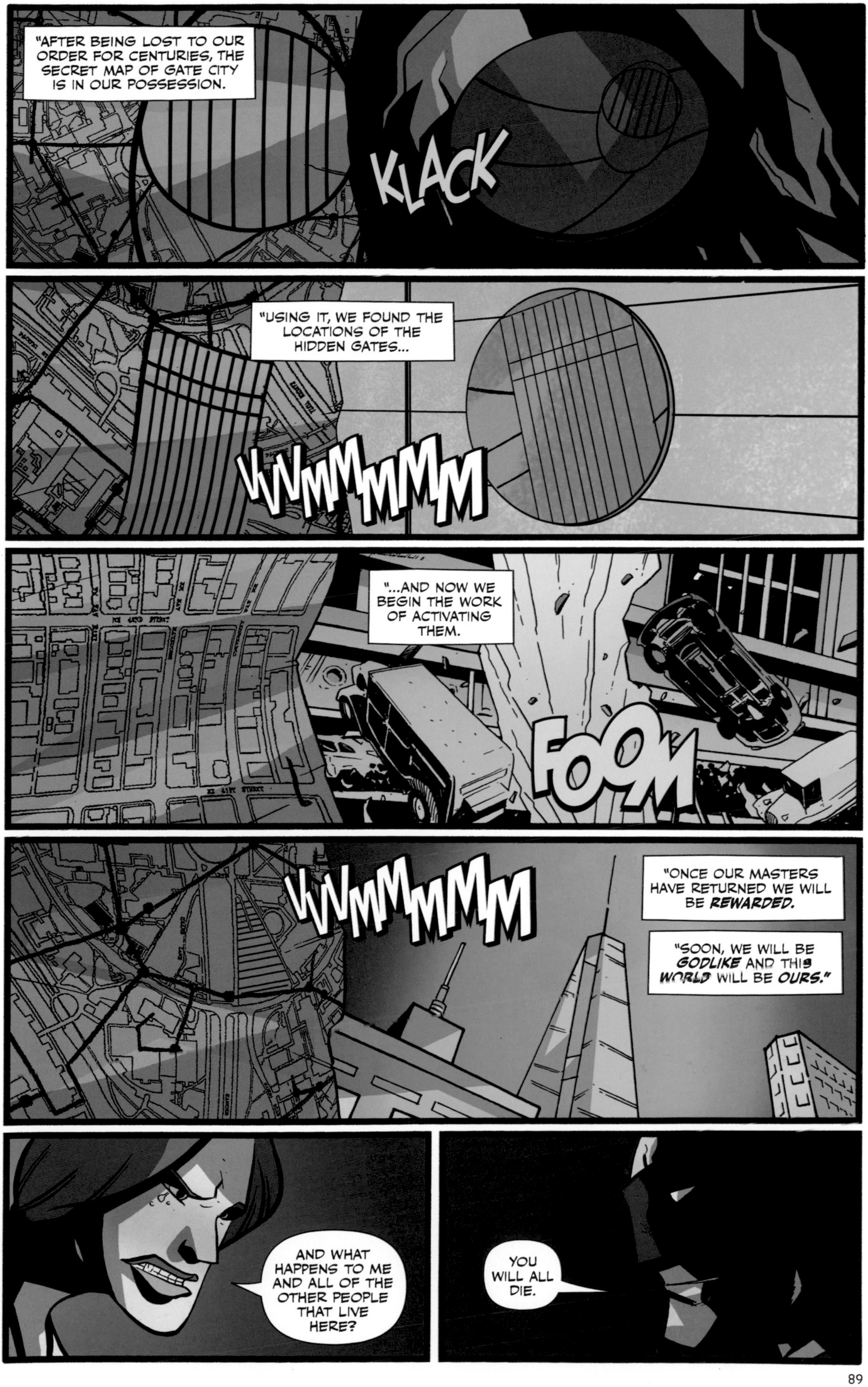
"AFTER BEING LOST TO OUR ORDER FOR CENTURIES, THE SECRET MAP OF GATE CITY IS IN OUR POSSESSION.
KLACK
"USING IT, WE FOUND THE LOCATIONS OF THE HIDDEN GATES...
VVVMMMMMM
"...AND NOW WE BEGIN THE WORK OF ACTIVATING THEM.
FOOM
VVVMMMMMM
"ONCE OUR MASTERS HAVE RETURNED WE WILL BE *REWARDED.*
"SOON, WE WILL BE *GODLIKE* AND THIS *WORLD* WILL BE *OURS."*
AND WHAT HAPPENS TO ME AND ALL OF THE OTHER PEOPLE THAT LIVE HERE?
YOU WILL ALL DIE.

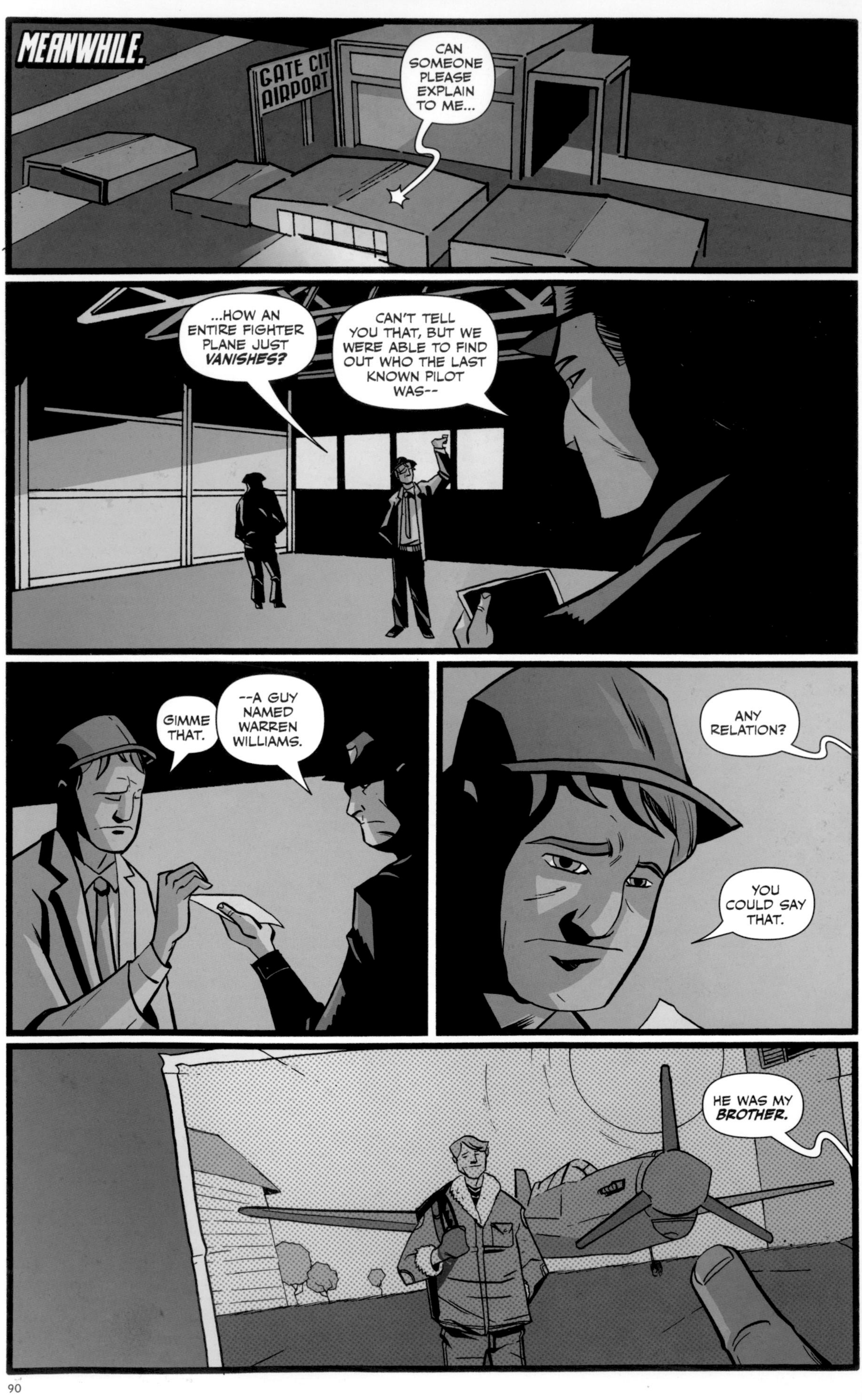
MEANWHILE.
GATE CIT
AIRPORT
CAN SOMEONE PLEASE EXPLAIN TO ME...
...HOW AN ENTIRE FIGHTER PLANE JUST *VANISHES?*
CAN'T TELL YOU THAT, BUT WE WERE ABLE TO FIND OUT WHO THE LAST KNOWN PILOT WAS--
--A GUY NAMED WARREN WILLIAMS.
GIMME THAT.
ANY RELATION?
YOU COULD SAY THAT.
HE WAS MY *BROTHER.*

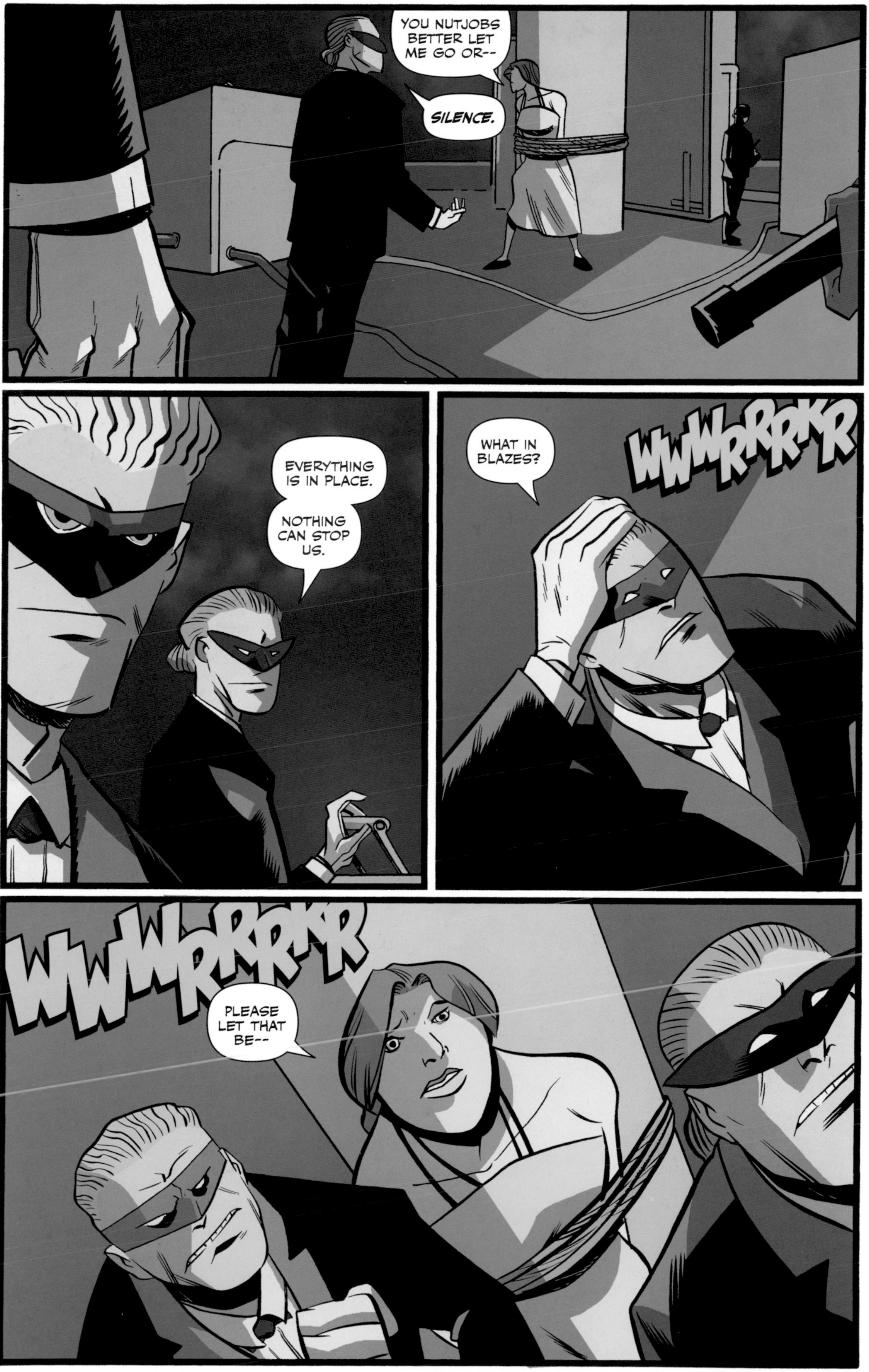
YOU NUTJOBS BETTER LET ME GO OR--
SILENCE.
EVERYTHING IS IN PLACE.
NOTHING CAN STOP US.
WHAT IN BLAZES?
WWWRRRKR
WWWRRRKR
PLEASE LET THAT BE--

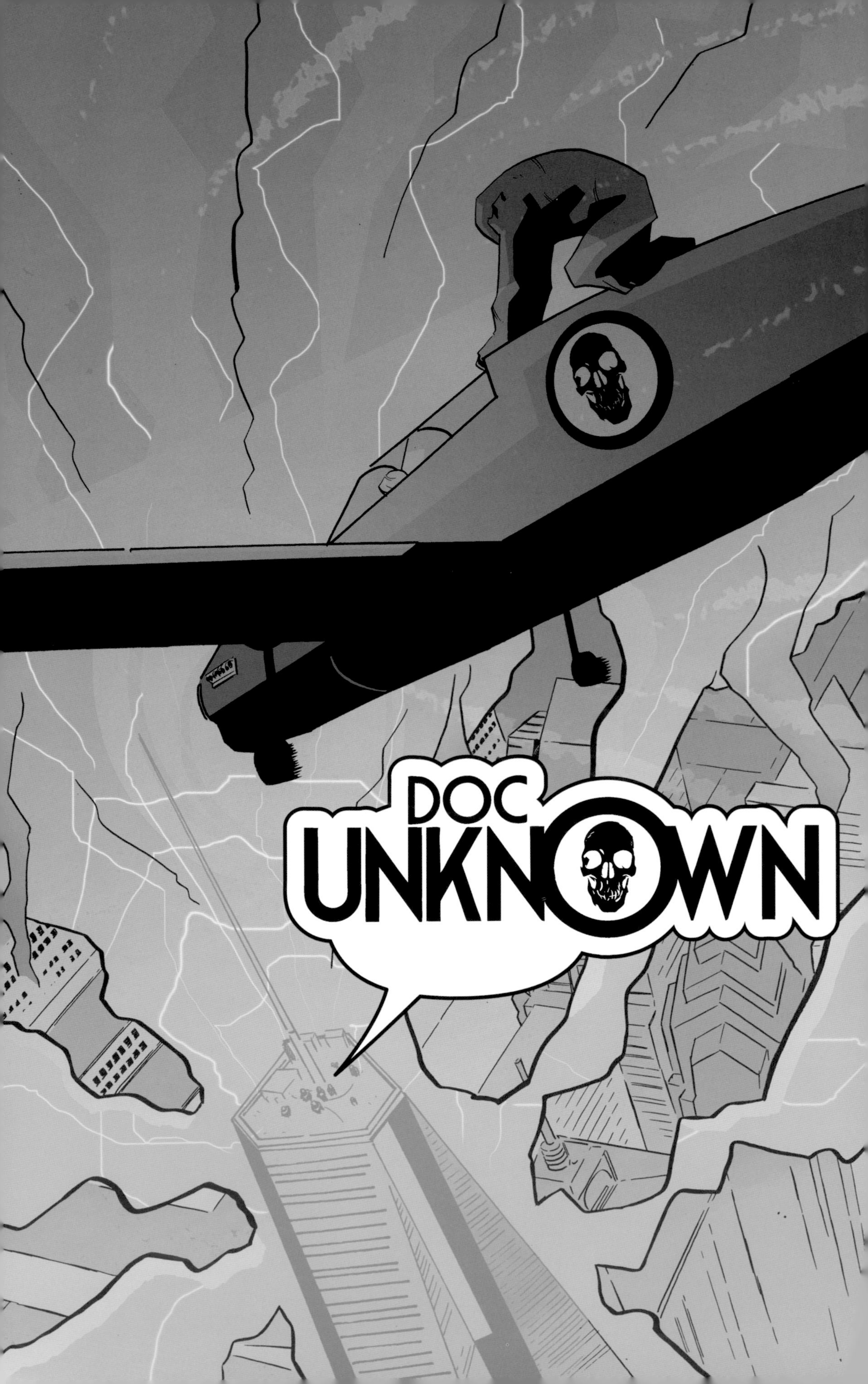
DOC UNKNOWN

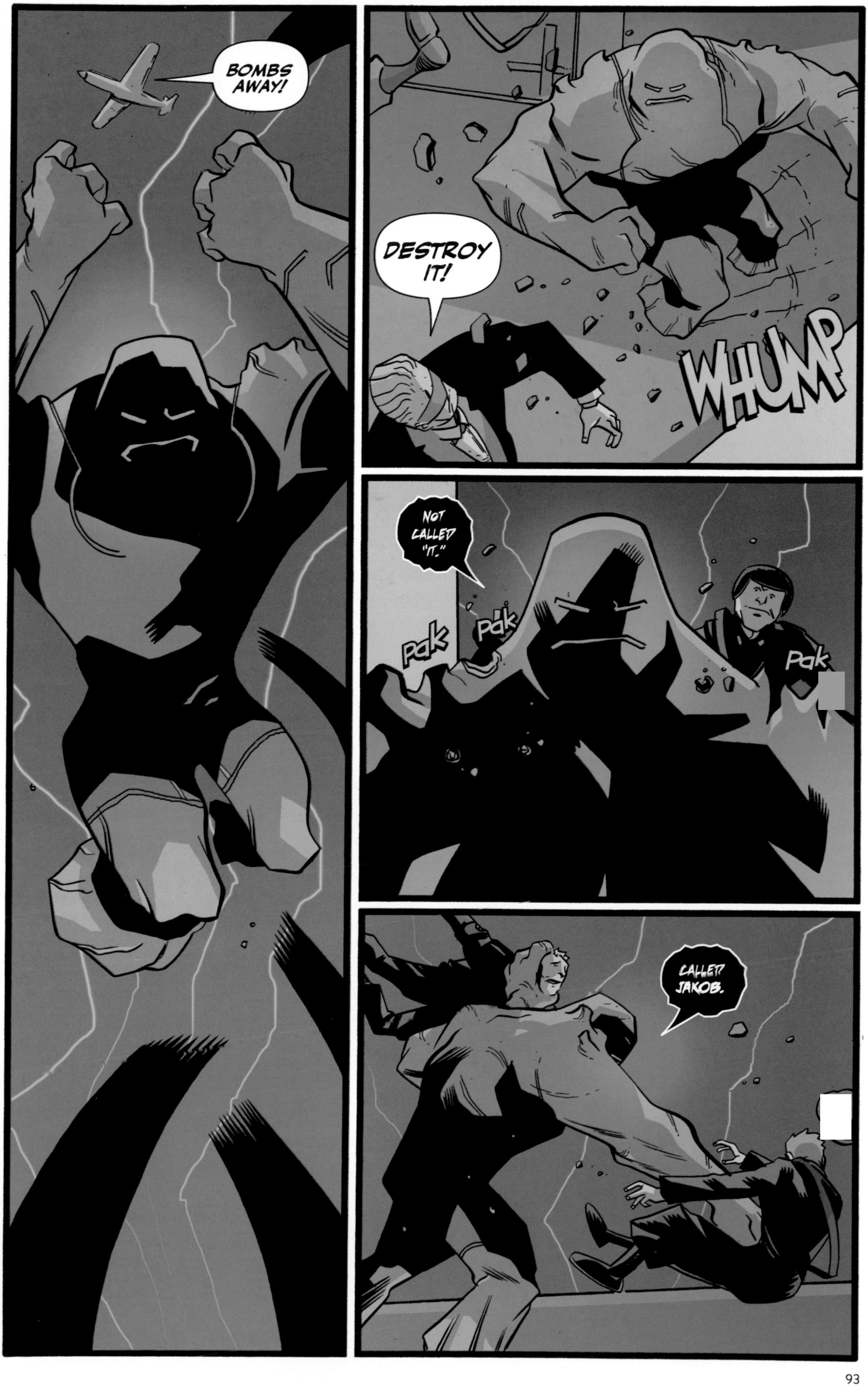
BOMBS AWAY!
DESTROY IT!
WHUMP
NOT CALLED "IT."
Pak
Pak
Pak
CALLED JAKOB.

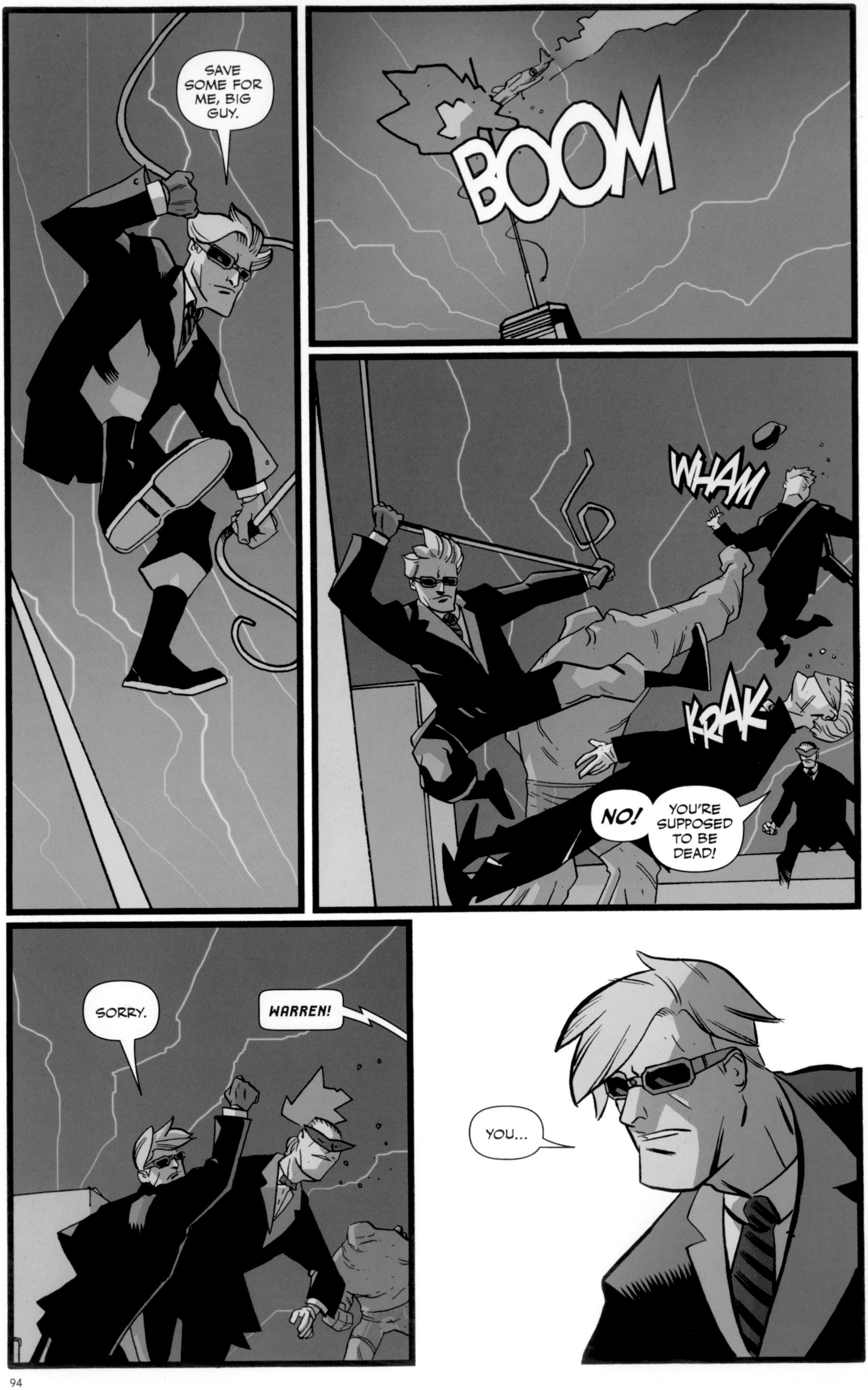
SAVE SOME FOR ME, BIG GUY.
BOOM
WHAM
KRAK
NO!
YOU'RE SUPPOSED TO BE DEAD!
SORRY.
WARREN!
YOU...

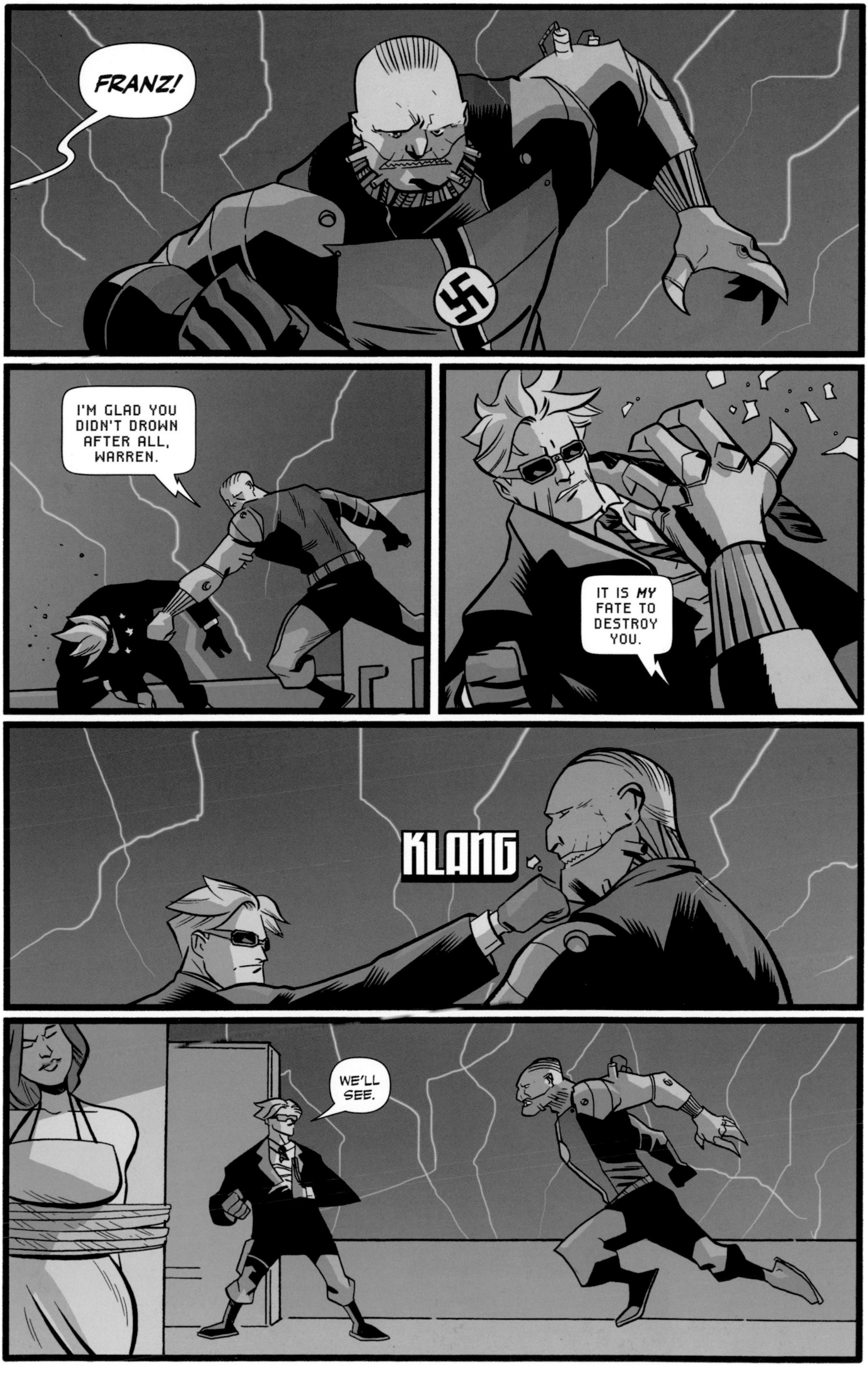
FRANZ!
I'M GLAD YOU DIDN'T DROWN AFTER ALL, WARREN.
IT IS *MY* FATE TO DESTROY YOU.
KLANG
WE'LL SEE.

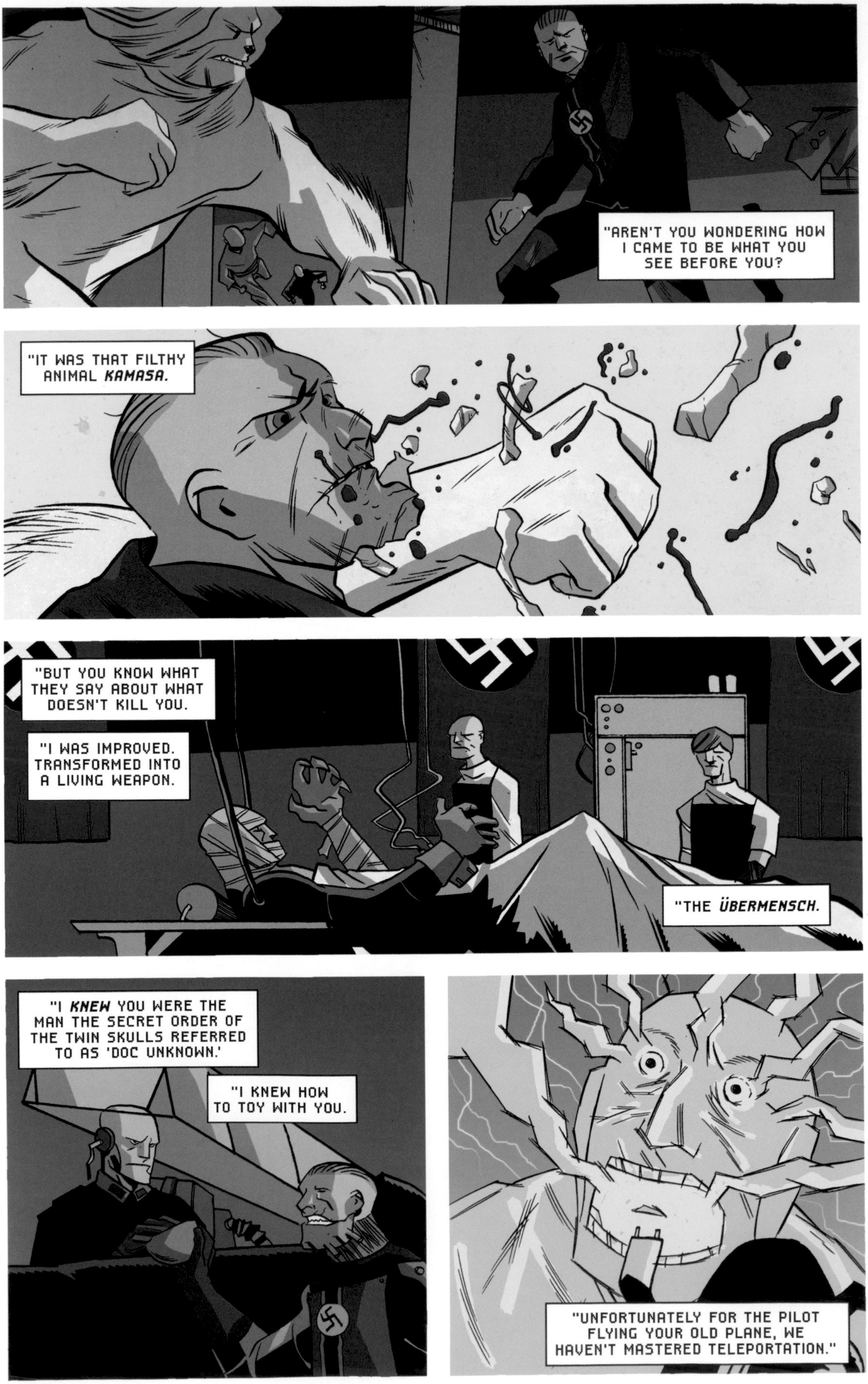
"AREN'T YOU WONDERING HOW I CAME TO BE WHAT YOU SEE BEFORE YOU?
"IT WAS THAT FILTHY ANIMAL *KAMASA.*
"BUT YOU KNOW WHAT THEY SAY ABOUT WHAT DOESN'T KILL YOU.
"I WAS IMPROVED. TRANSFORMED INTO A LIVING WEAPON.
"THE *ÜBERMENSCH.*
"I *KNEW* YOU WERE THE MAN THE SECRET ORDER OF THE TWIN SKULLS REFERRED TO AS 'DOC UNKNOWN.'
"I KNEW HOW TO TOY WITH YOU.
"UNFORTUNATELY FOR THE PILOT FLYING YOUR OLD PLANE, WE HAVEN'T MASTERED TELEPORTATION."

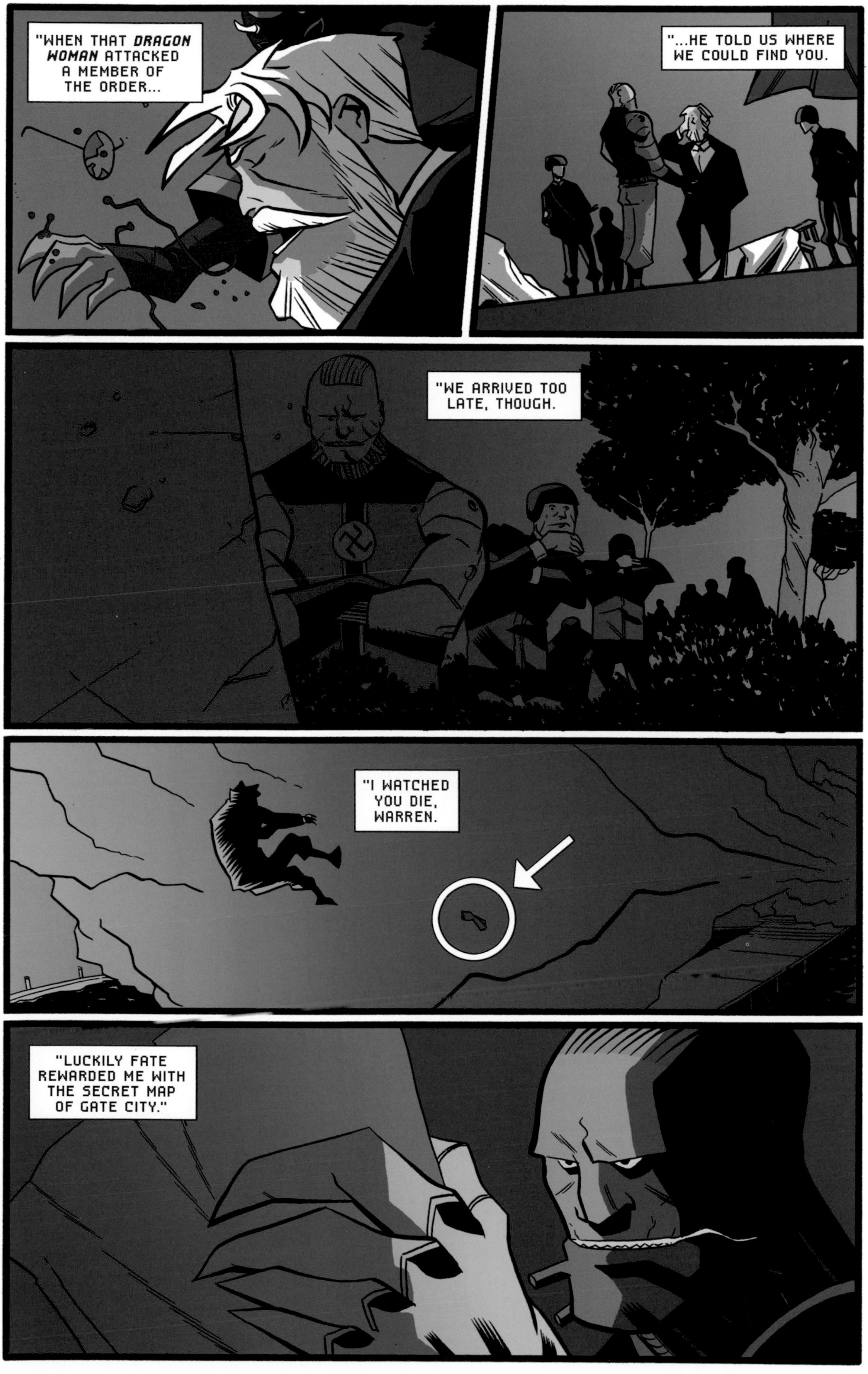
"WHEN THAT DRAGON WOMAN ATTACKED A MEMBER OF THE ORDER...
"...HE TOLD US WHERE WE COULD FIND YOU.
"WE ARRIVED TOO LATE, THOUGH.
"I WATCHED YOU DIE, WARREN.
"LUCKILY FATE REWARDED ME WITH THE SECRET MAP OF GATE CITY."

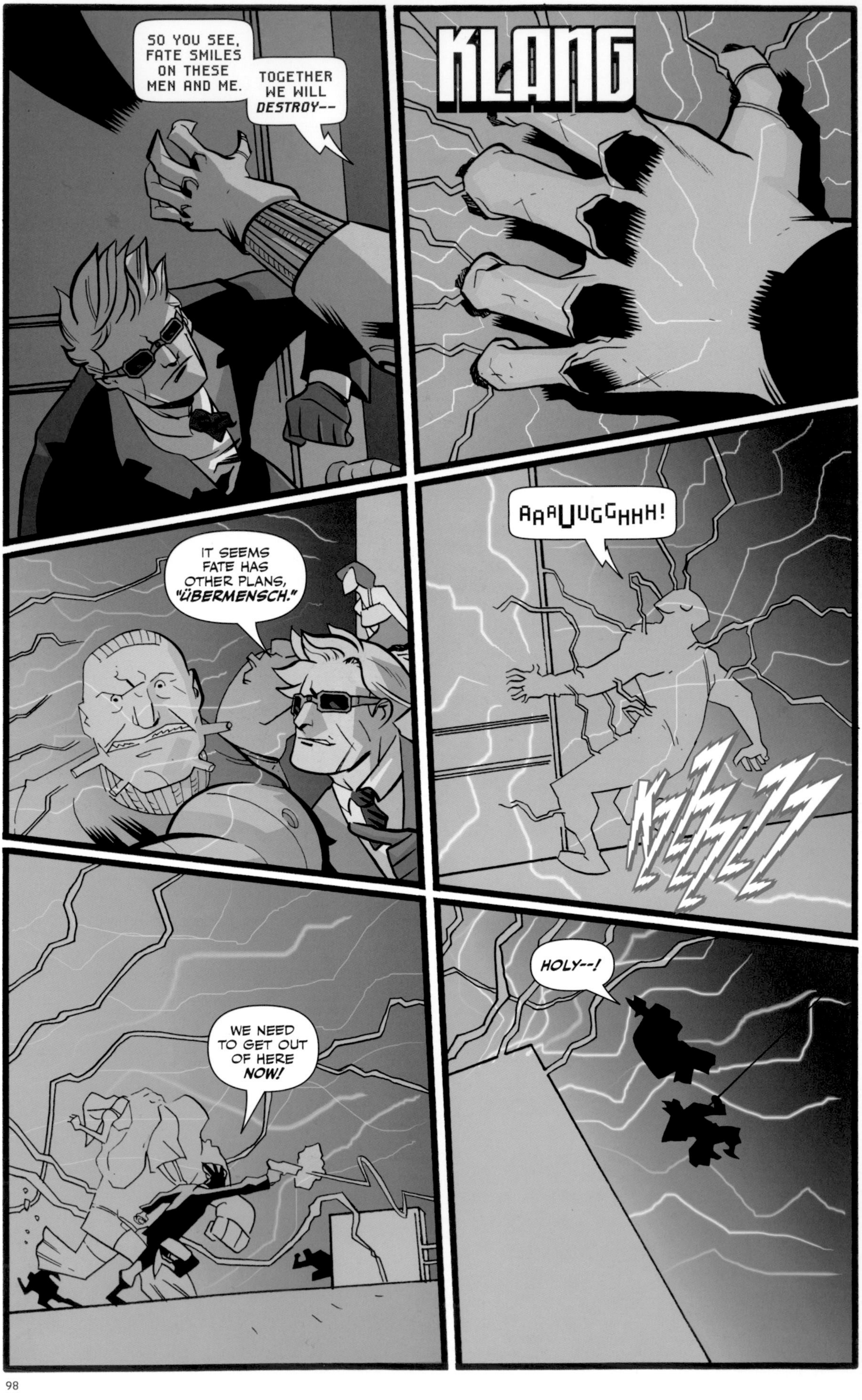
SO YOU SEE, FATE SMILES ON THESE MEN AND ME.
TOGETHER WE WILL *DESTROY--*
KLANG
IT SEEMS FATE HAS OTHER PLANS, *"ÜBERMENSCH."*
AAAUUGGHHH!
WE NEED TO GET OUT OF HERE *NOW!*
HOLY--!

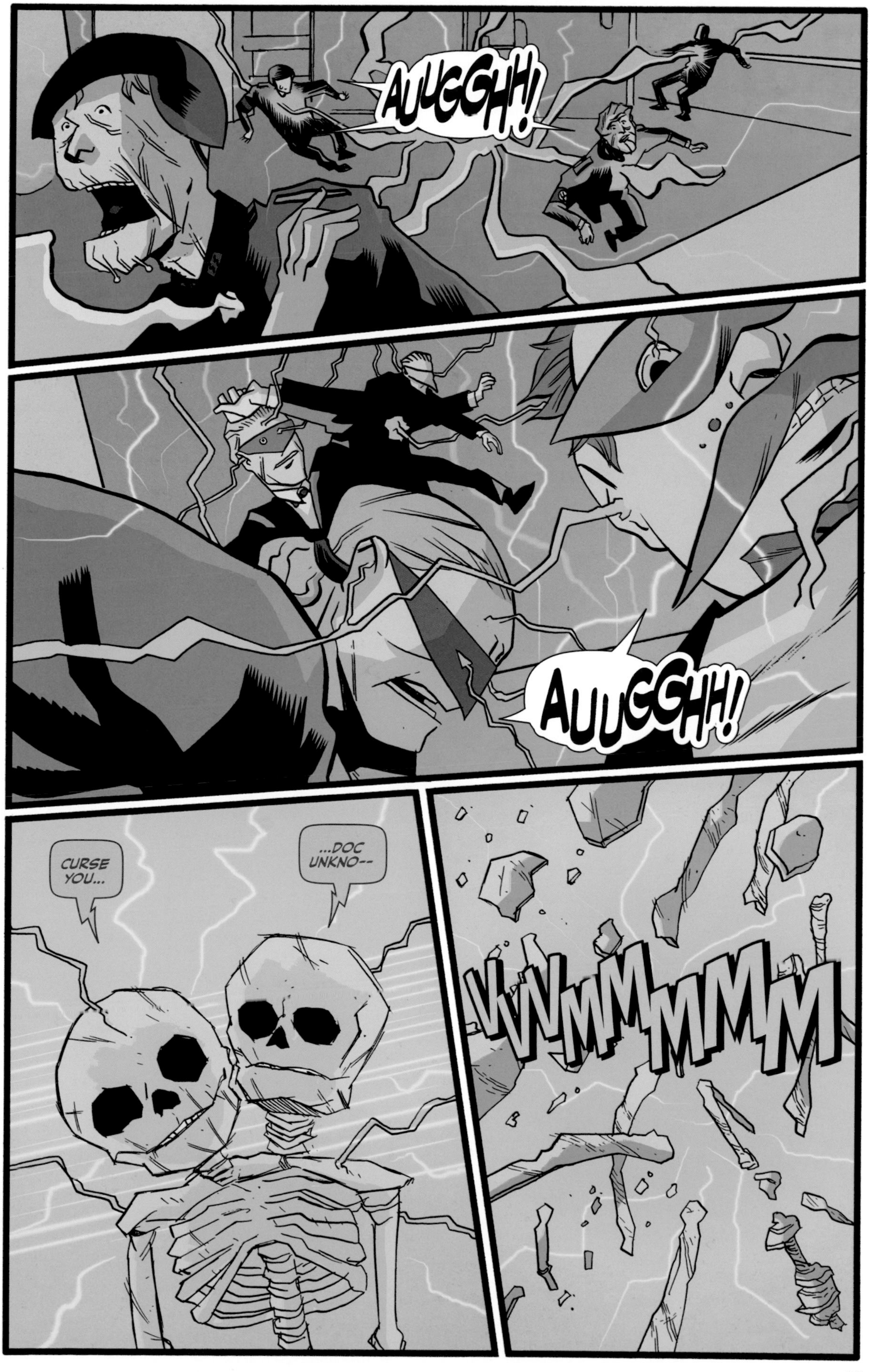

AUUGGHH!
AUUGGHH!
CURSE YOU...
...DOC UNKNO--
VVVMMMMMMM

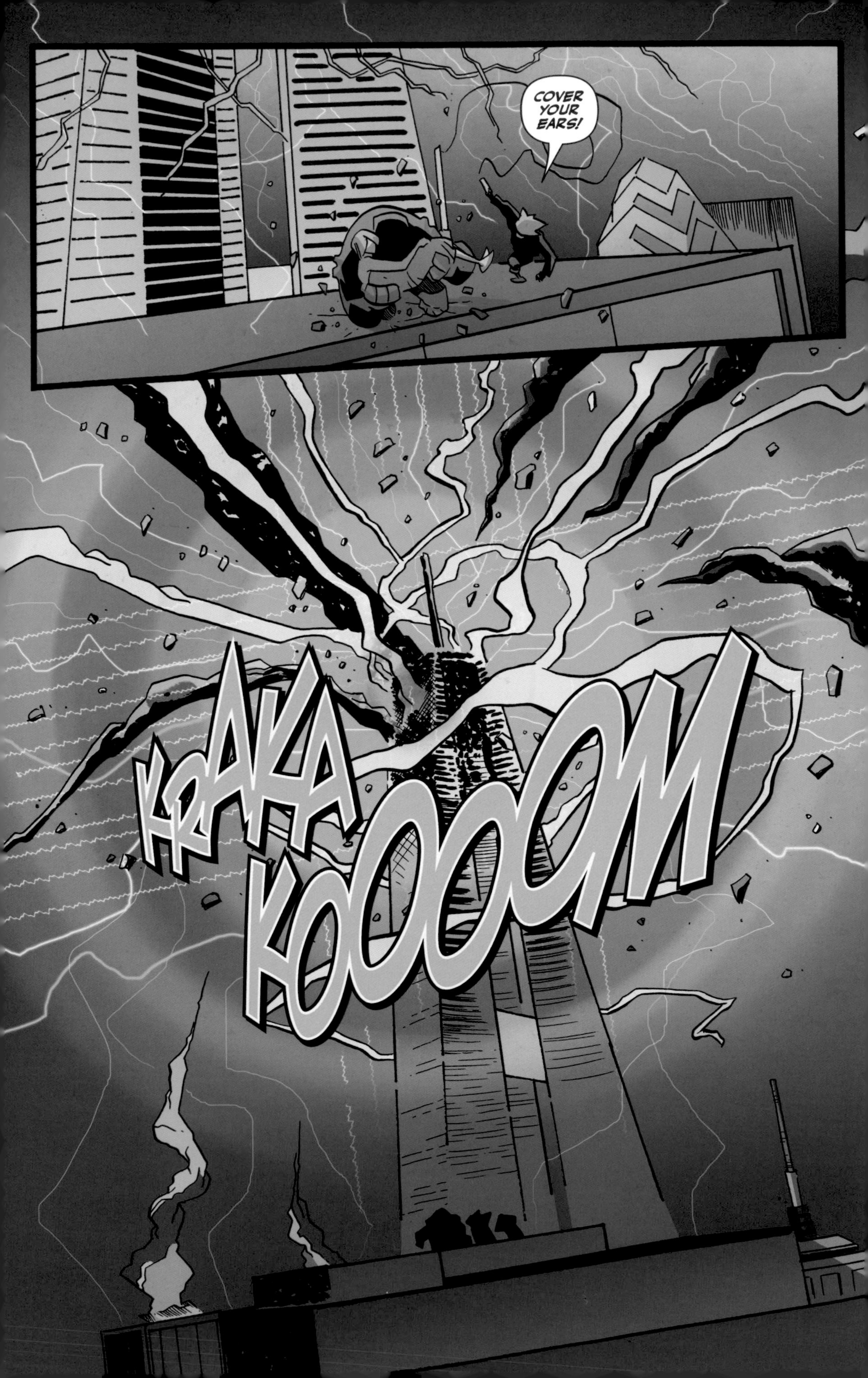
COVER YOUR EARS!
KRAKA KOOOOM

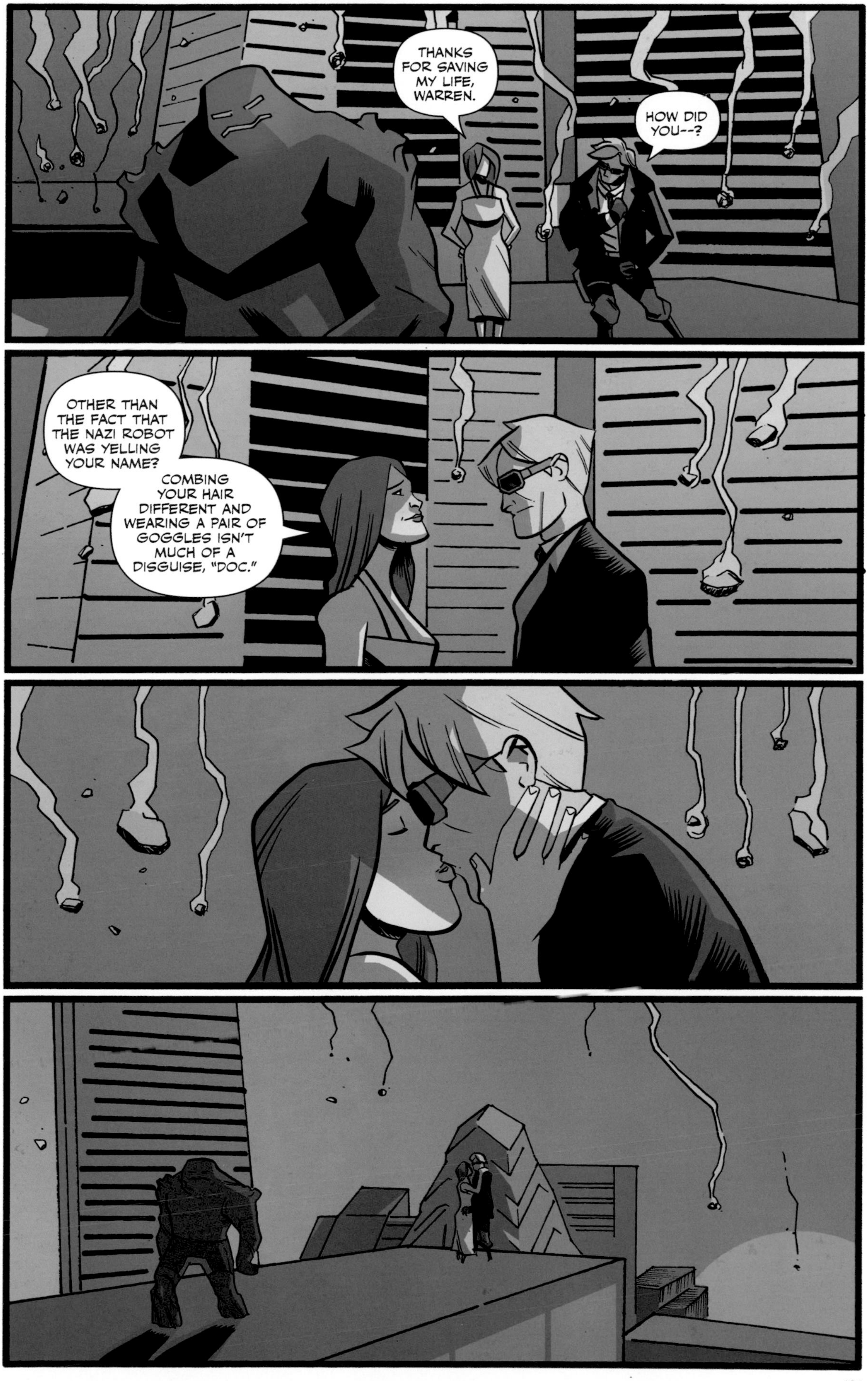
THANKS FOR SAVING MY LIFE, WARREN.
HOW DID YOU--?
OTHER THAN THE FACT THAT THE NAZI ROBOT WAS YELLING YOUR NAME?
COMBING YOUR HAIR DIFFERENT AND WEARING A PAIR OF GOGGLES ISN'T MUCH OF A DISGUISE, "DOC."

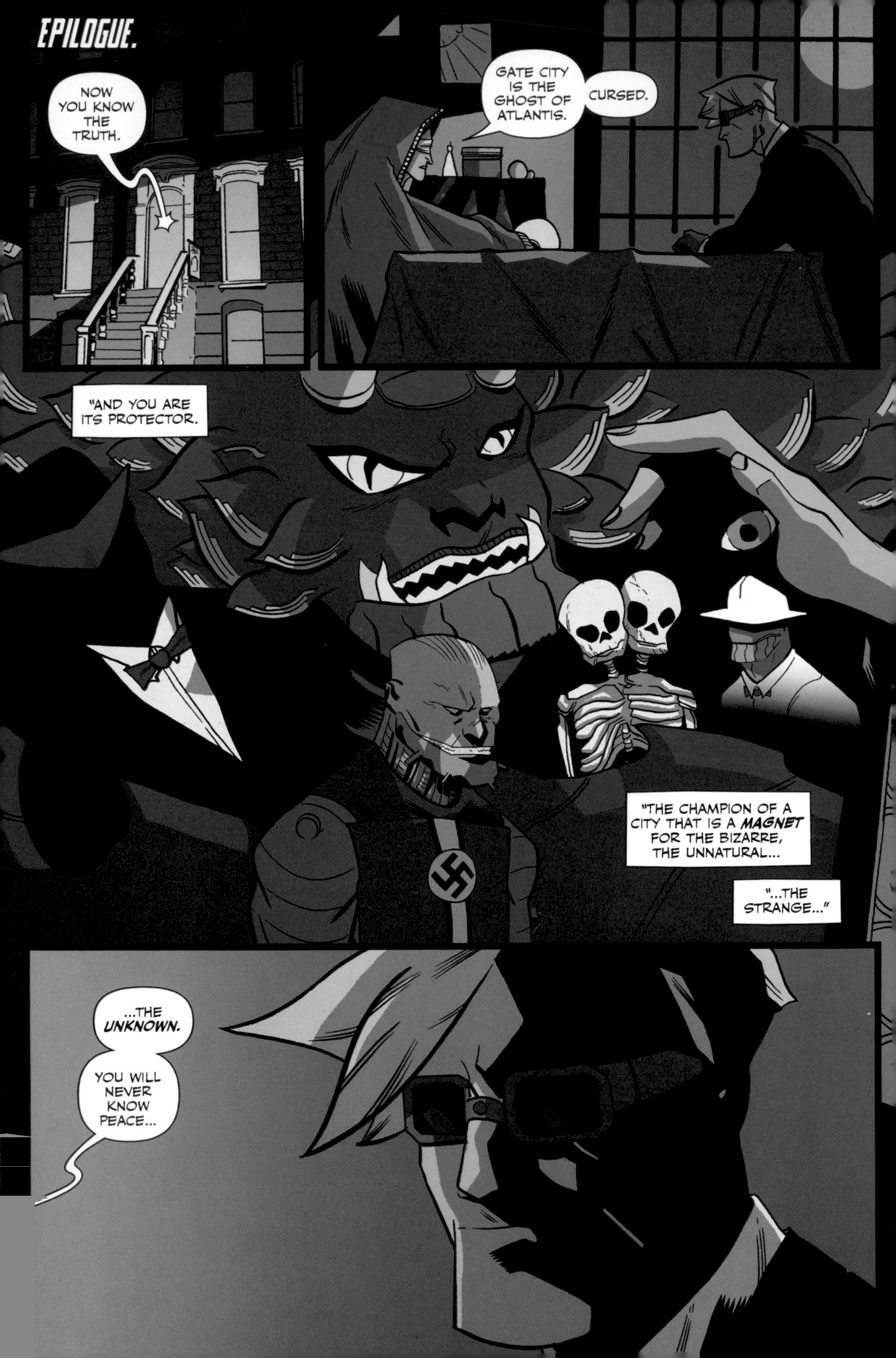
EPILOGUE.
NOW YOU KNOW THE TRUTH.
GATE CITY IS THE GHOST OF ATLANTIS.
CURSED.
"AND YOU ARE ITS PROTECTOR.
"THE CHAMPION OF A CITY THAT IS A MAGNET FOR THE BIZARRE, THE UNNATURAL...
"...THE STRANGE..."
...THE UNKNOWN.
YOU WILL NEVER KNOW PEACE...

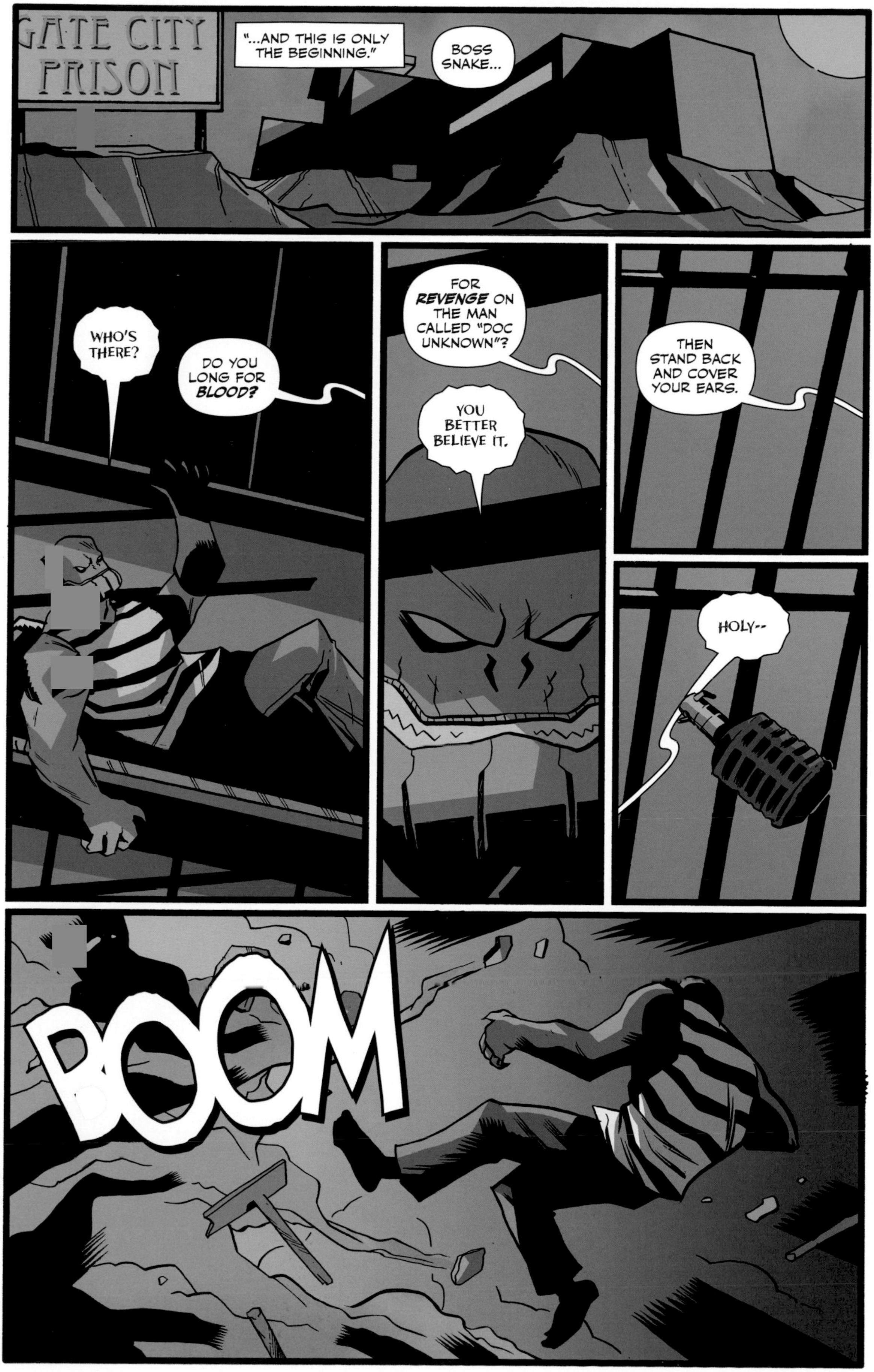
GATE CITY PRISON
"...AND THIS IS ONLY THE BEGINNING."
BOSS SNAKE...
WHO'S THERE?
DO YOU LONG FOR BLOOD?
FOR REVENGE ON THE MAN CALLED "DOC UNKNOWN"?
YOU BETTER BELIEVE IT.
THEN STAND BACK AND COVER YOUR EARS.
HOLY--
BOOM

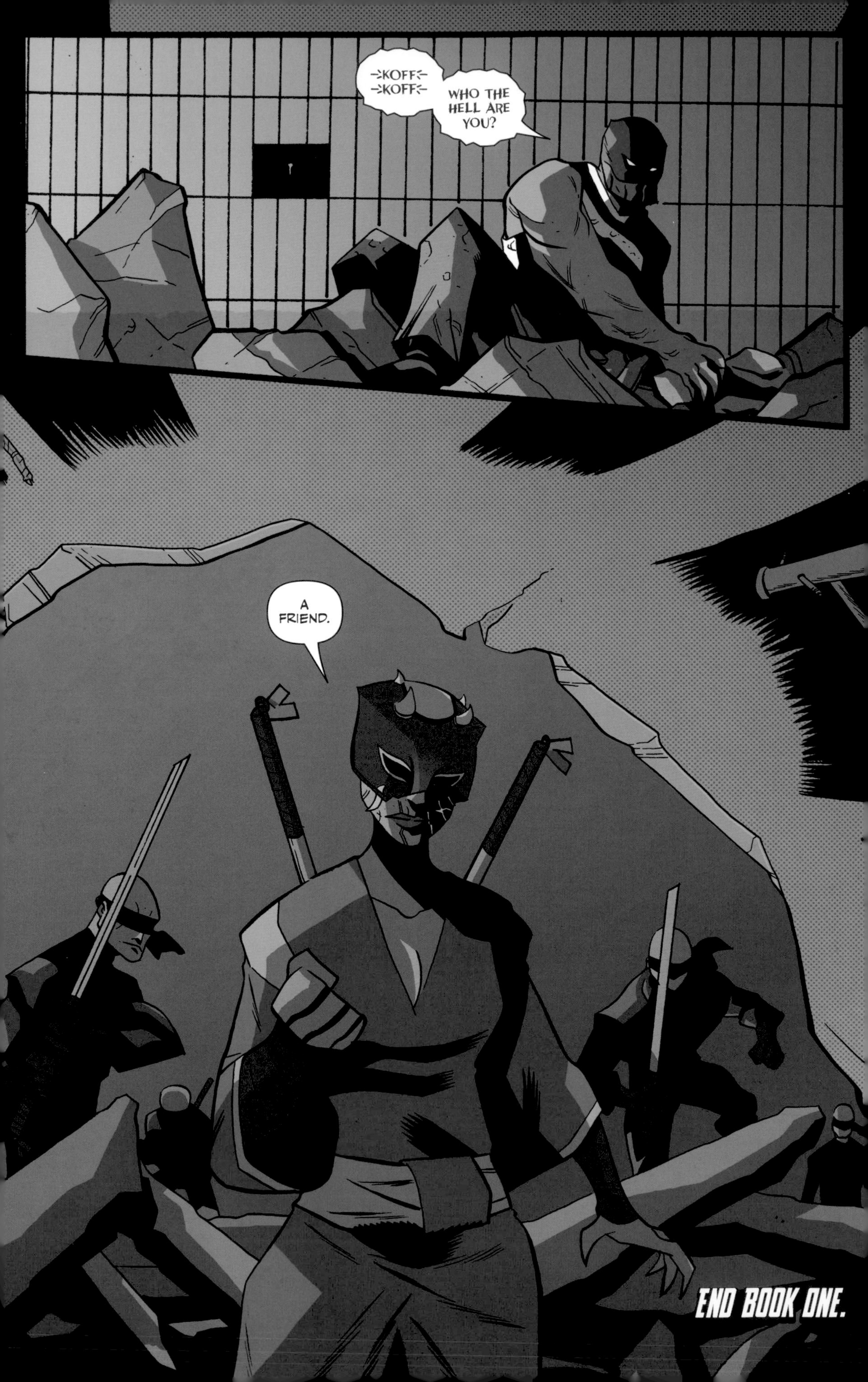
-KOFF- -KOFF-
WHO THE HELL ARE YOU?
A FRIEND.
END BOOK ONE.

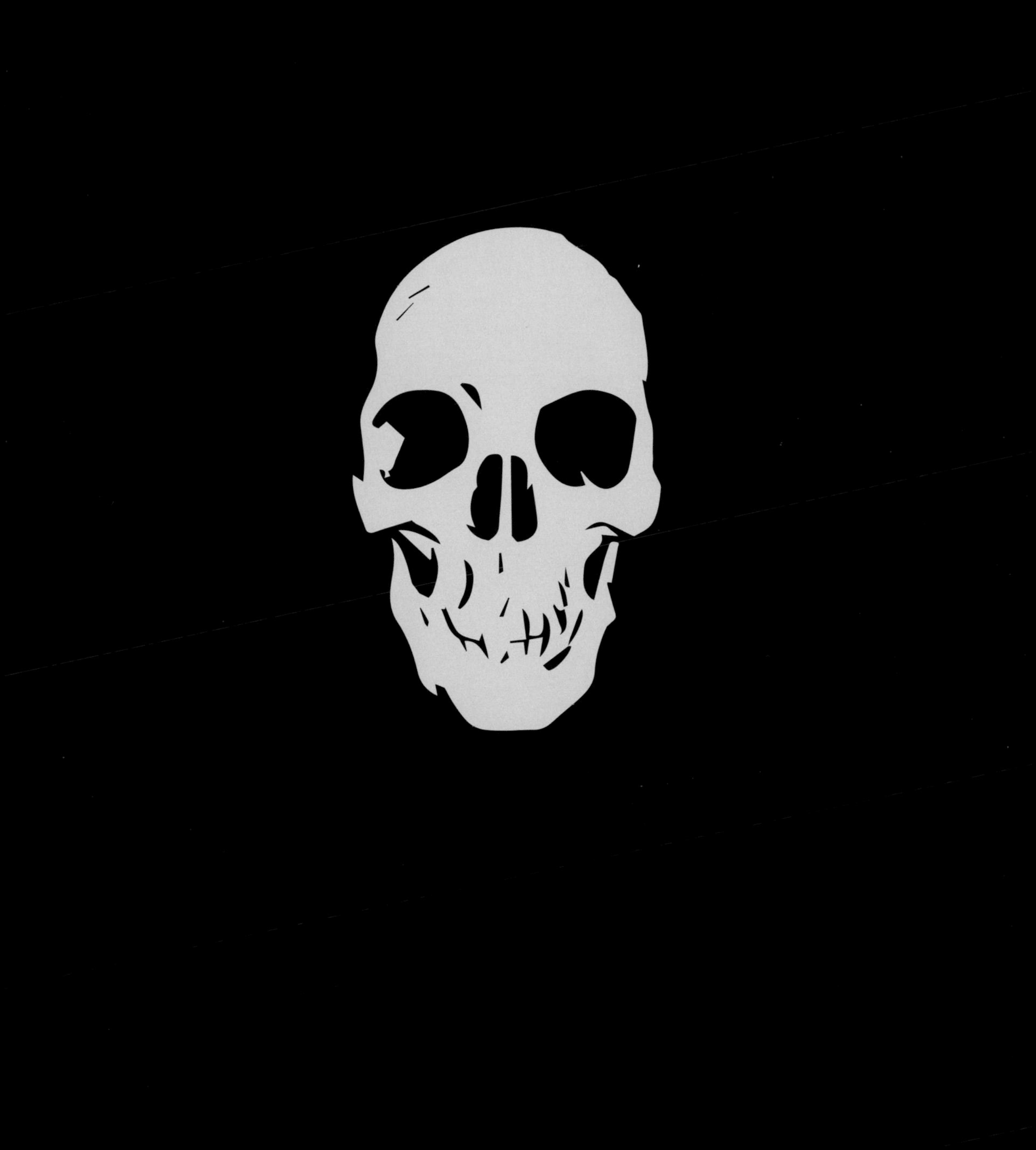

BOSS SNAKE

COLD BLOOD, COLD STREETS: A GATE CITY TALE

SCRIPT BY **FABIAN RANGEL JR.**

ART BY **RYAN CODY**

LETTERS BY **NIC SHAW**

EDITED BY **RYAN K LINDSAY**

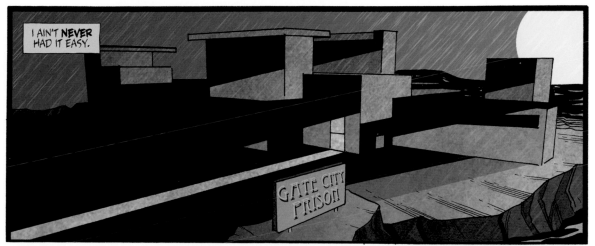

I AIN'T **NEVER** HAD IT EASY.

GATE CITY PRISON

ALL MY STINKIN' LIFE I'VE BEEN FIGHTIN' AND CLAWIN' FOR WHAT EVERYONE ELSE TAKES FOR GRANTED.

BUT WITH A MUG LIKE THIS--

--I GUESS I DIDN'T HAVE MUCH OF A CHOICE.

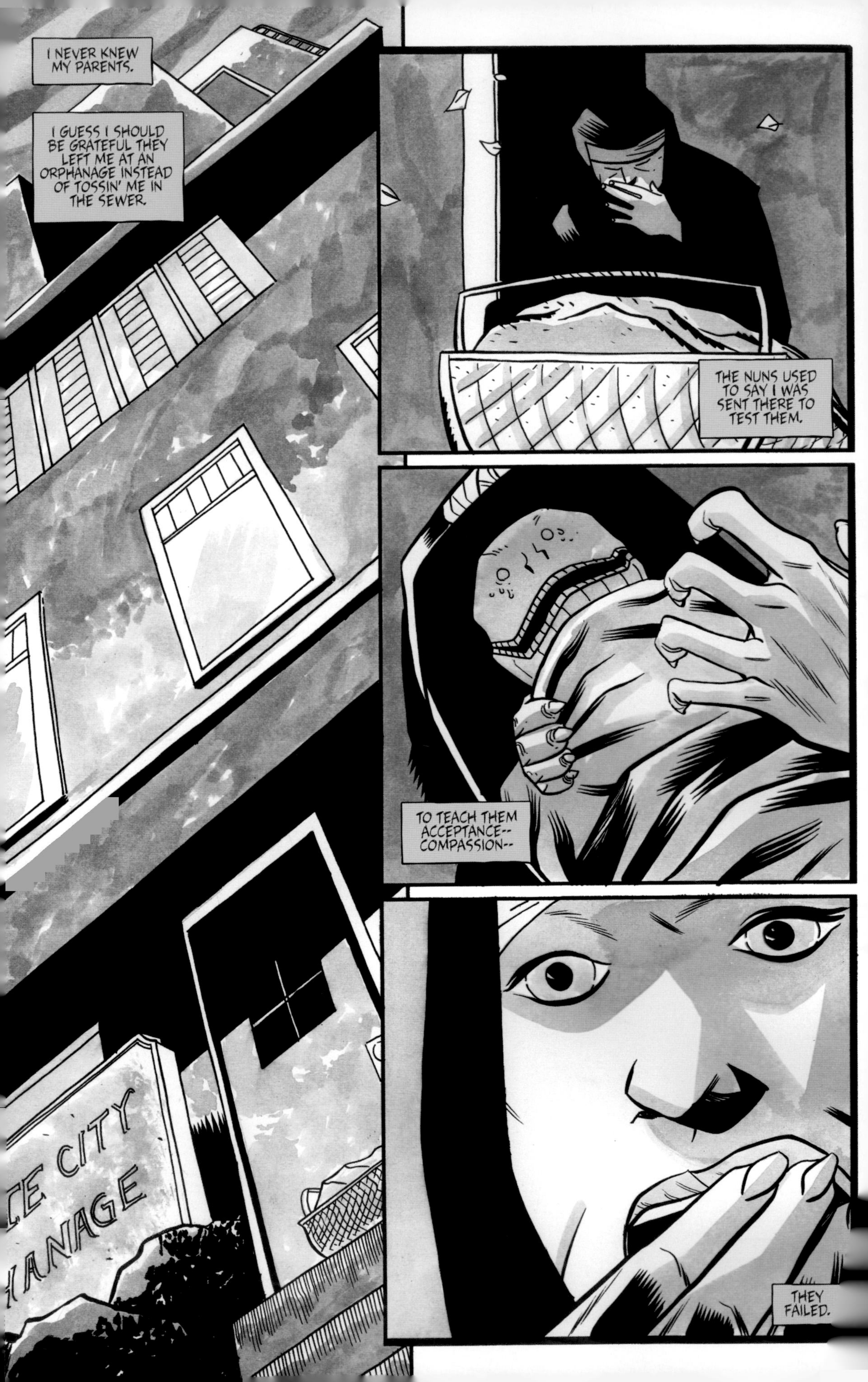
I NEVER KNEW MY PARENTS.
I GUESS I SHOULD BE GRATEFUL THEY LEFT ME AT AN ORPHANAGE INSTEAD OF TOSSIN' ME IN THE SEWER.
CE CITY
HANAGE
THE NUNS USED TO SAY I WAS SENT THERE TO TEST THEM.
TO TEACH THEM ACCEPTANCE-- COMPASSION--
THEY FAILED.

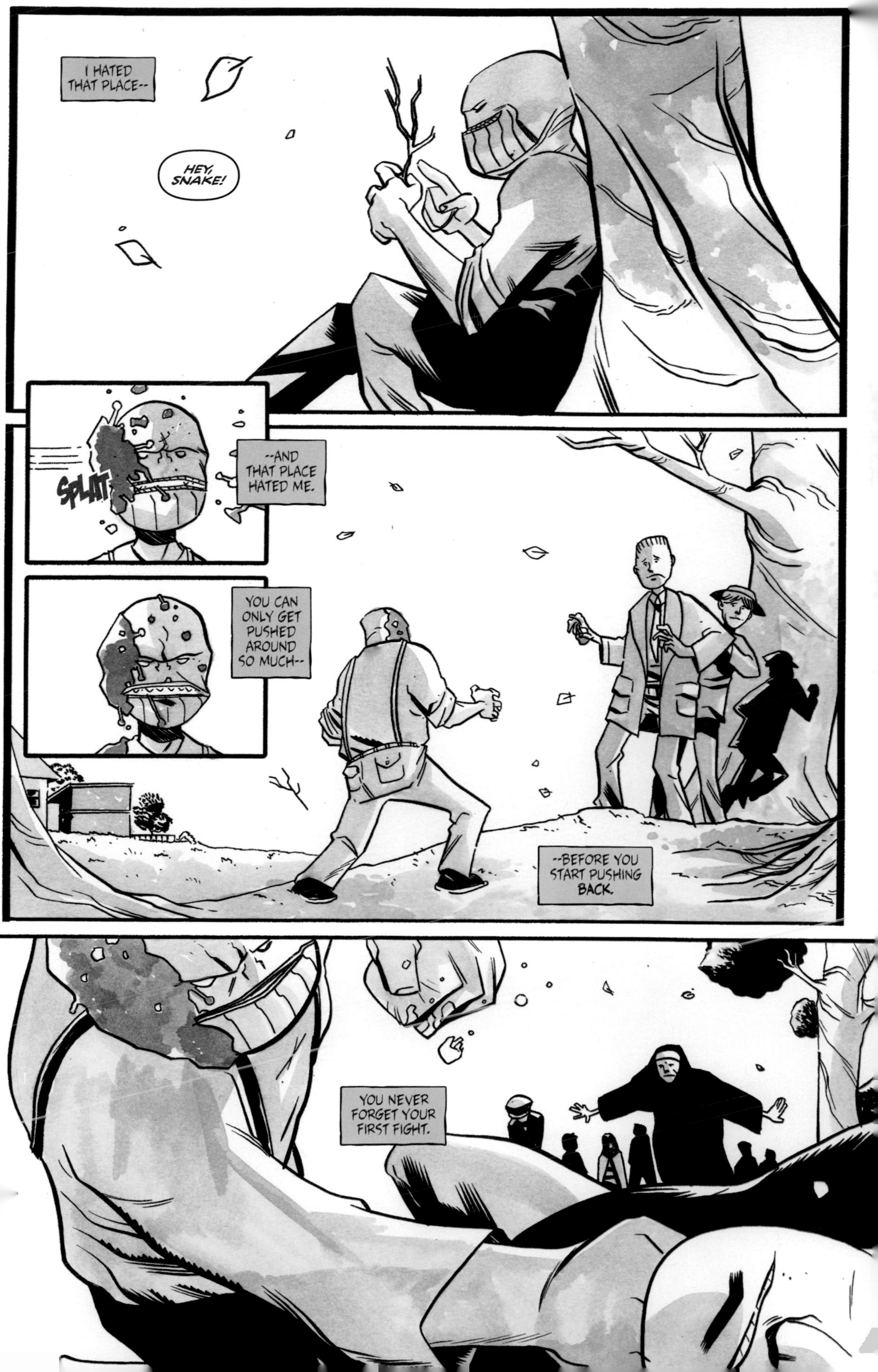
I HATED THAT PLACE--
HEY, SNAKE!
SPLAT
--AND THAT PLACE HATED ME.
YOU CAN ONLY GET PUSHED AROUND SO MUCH--
--BEFORE YOU START PUSHING BACK.
YOU NEVER FORGET YOUR FIRST FIGHT.

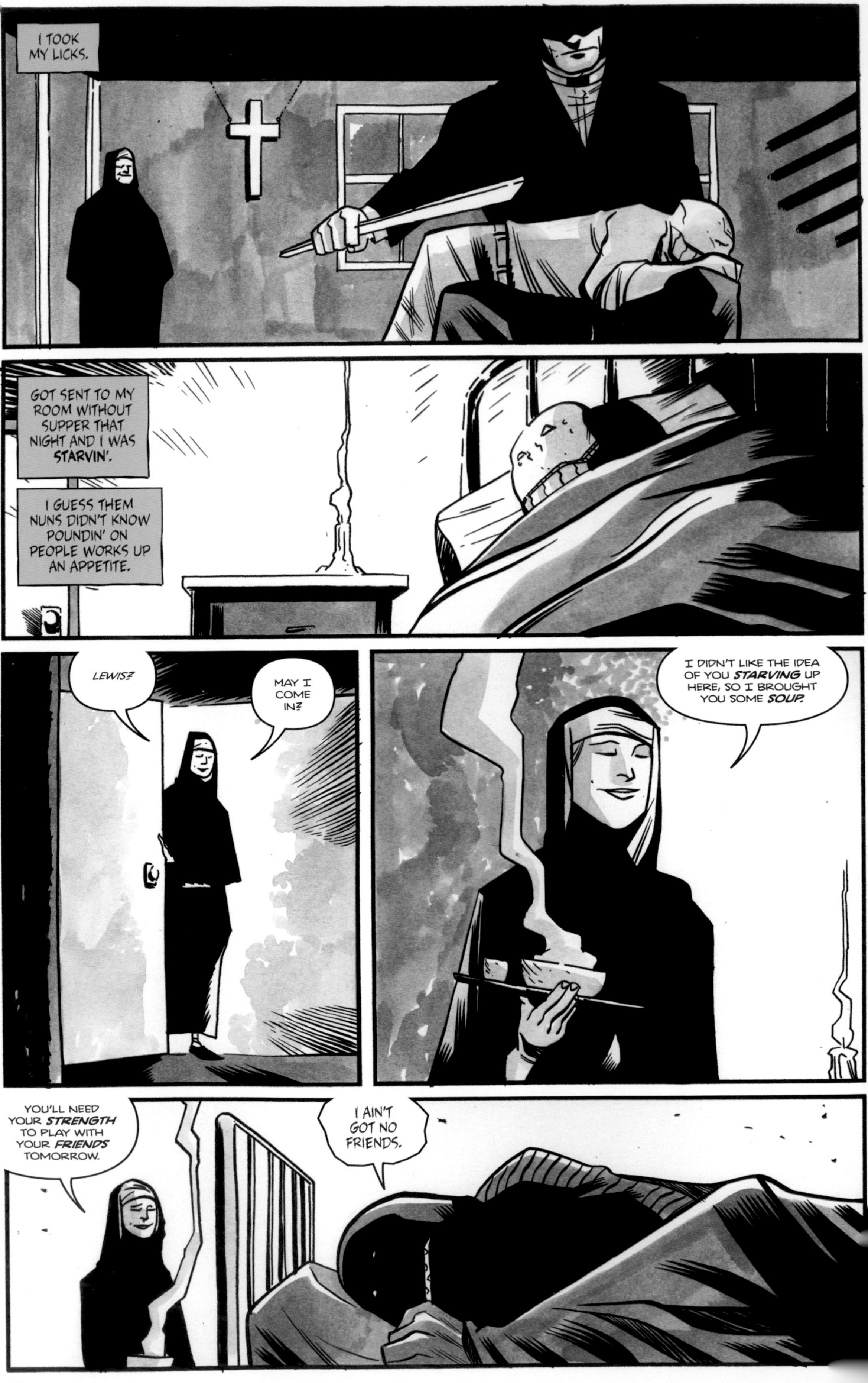
I TOOK MY LICKS.
GOT SENT TO MY ROOM WITHOUT SUPPER THAT NIGHT AND I WAS STARVIN'.
I GUESS THEM NUNS DIDN'T KNOW POUNDIN' ON PEOPLE WORKS UP AN APPETITE.
LEWIS?
MAY I COME IN?
I DIDN'T LIKE THE IDEA OF YOU STARVING UP HERE, SO I BROUGHT YOU SOME SOUP.
YOU'LL NEED YOUR STRENGTH TO PLAY WITH YOUR FRIENDS TOMORROW.
I AIN'T GOT NO FRIENDS.

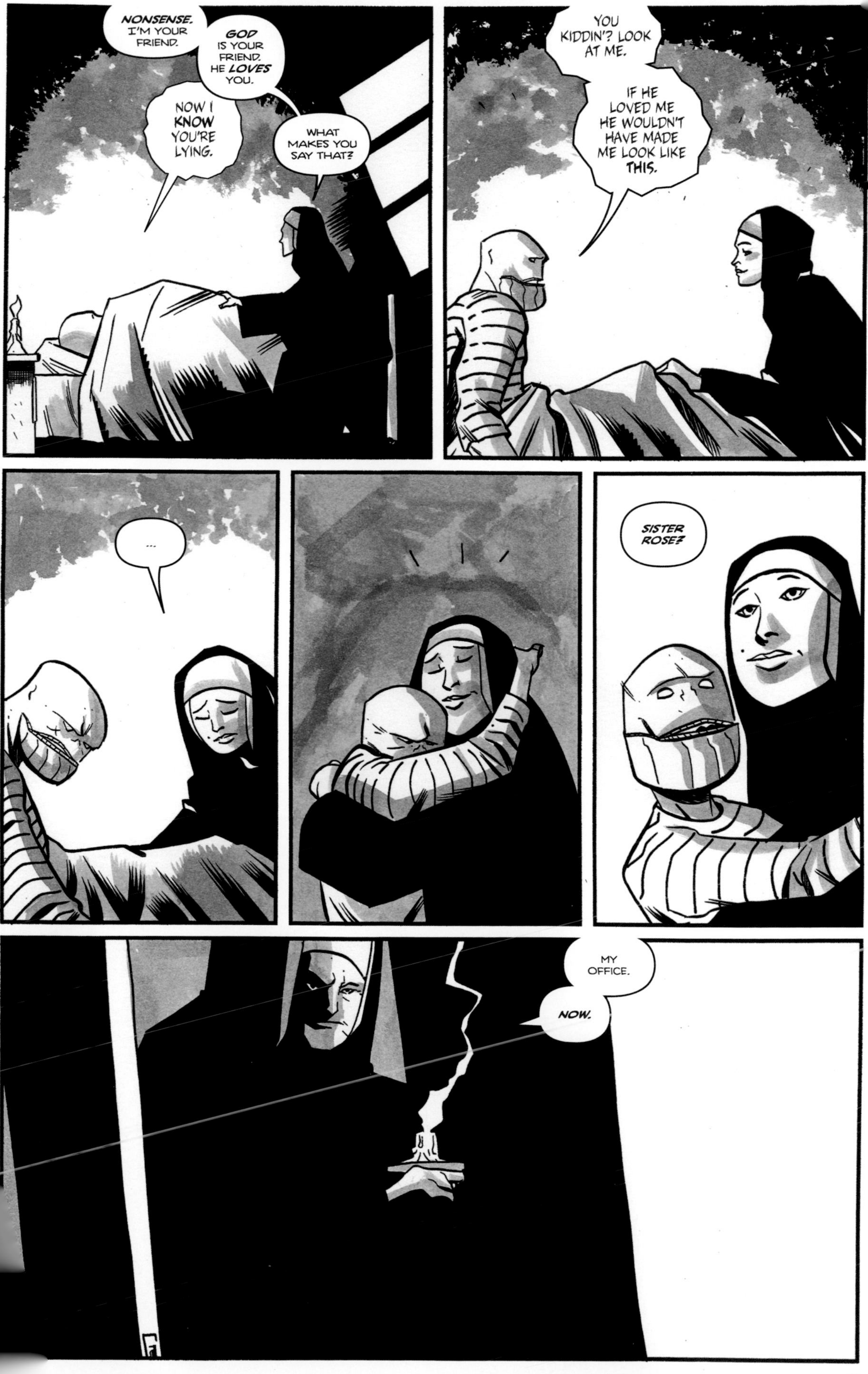
NONSENSE. I'M YOUR FRIEND.
GOD IS YOUR FRIEND. HE LOVES YOU.
NOW I KNOW YOU'RE LYING.
WHAT MAKES YOU SAY THAT?
YOU KIDDIN'? LOOK AT ME.
IF HE LOVED ME HE WOULDN'T HAVE MADE ME LOOK LIKE THIS.
...
SISTER ROSE?
MY OFFICE.
NOW.

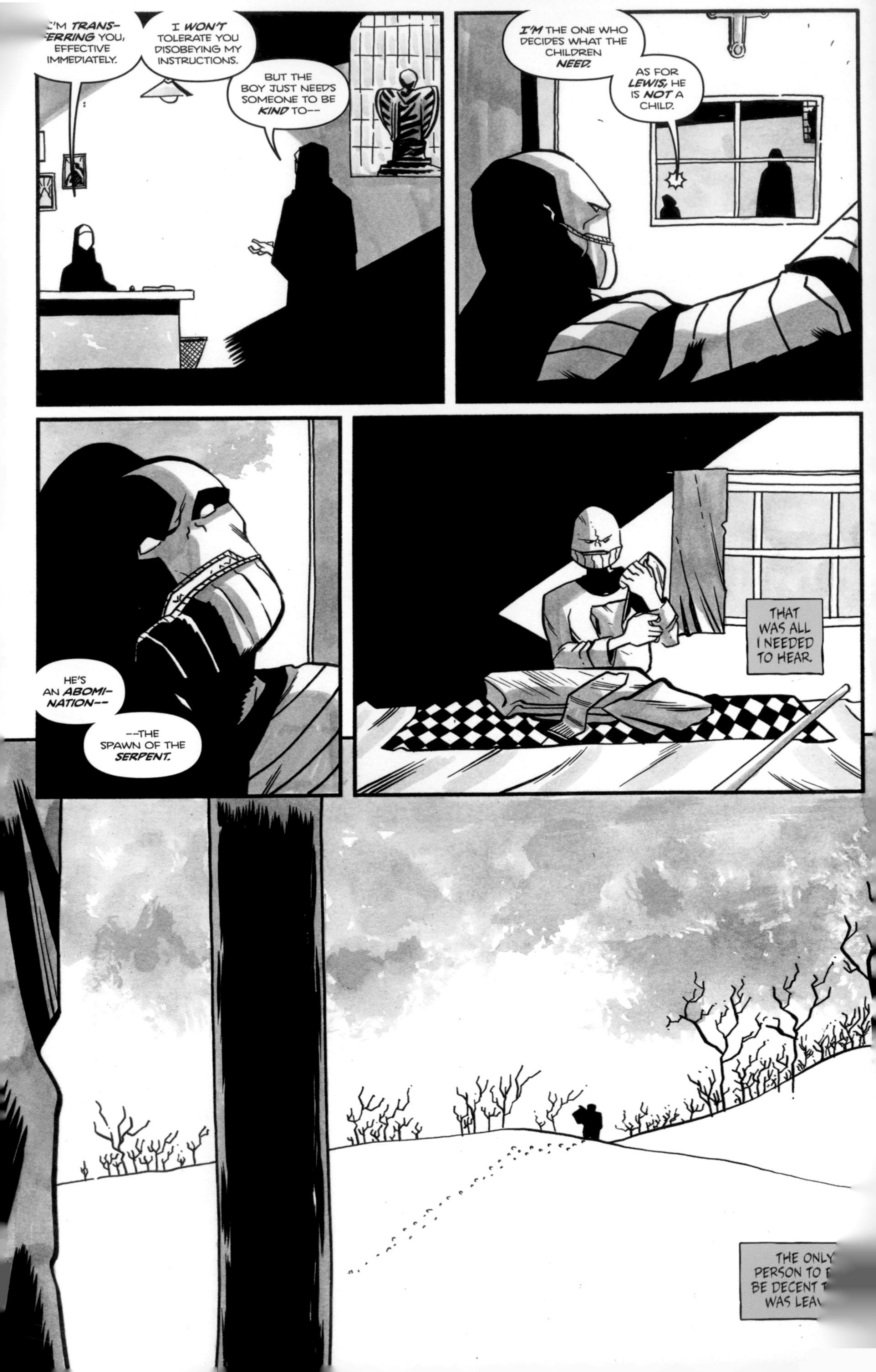
I'M TRANSFERRING YOU, EFFECTIVE IMMEDIATELY.
I WON'T TOLERATE YOU DISOBEYING MY INSTRUCTIONS.
BUT THE BOY JUST NEEDS SOMEONE TO BE KIND TO--
I'M THE ONE WHO DECIDES WHAT THE CHILDREN NEED.
AS FOR LEWIS, HE IS NOT A CHILD.
HE'S AN ABOMINATION--
--THE SPAWN OF THE SERPENT.
THAT WAS ALL I NEEDED TO HEAR.
THE ONLY PERSON TO
BE DECENT
WAS LEA

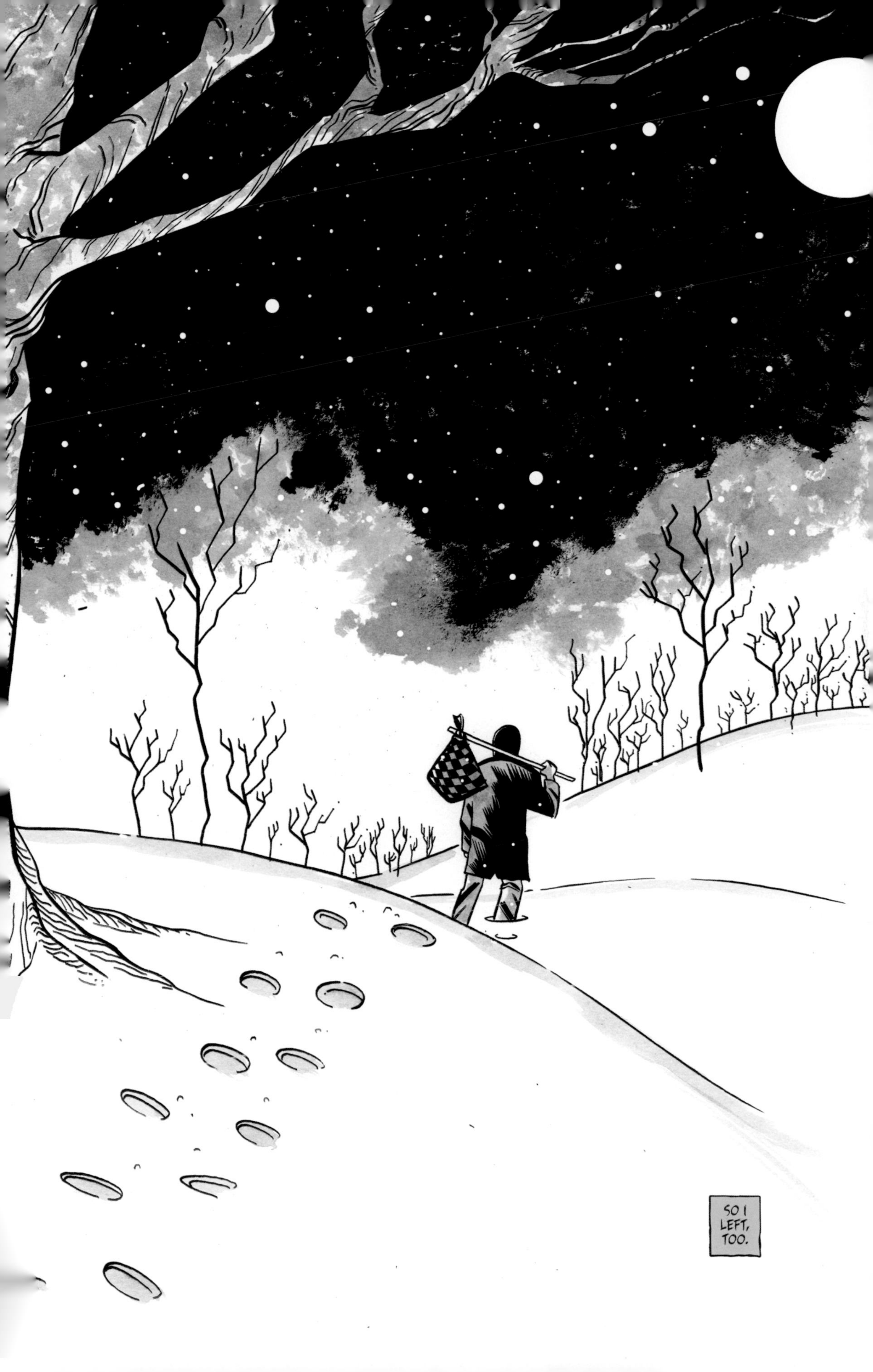
SO I LEFT, TOO.

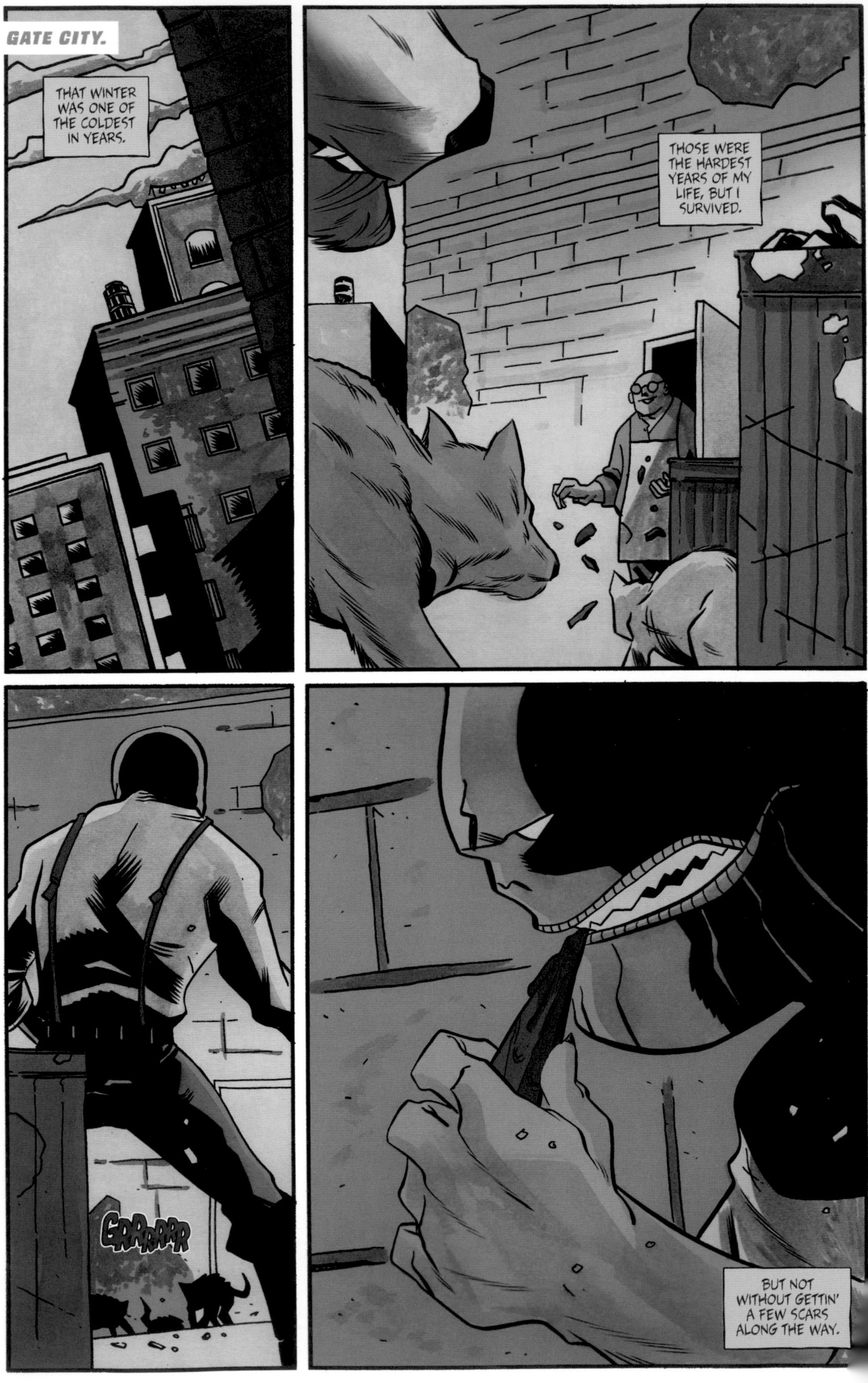
GATE CITY.
THAT WINTER WAS ONE OF THE COLDEST IN YEARS.
THOSE WERE THE HARDEST YEARS OF MY LIFE, BUT I SURVIVED.
GRRRRRR
BUT NOT WITHOUT GETTIN' A FEW SCARS ALONG THE WAY.

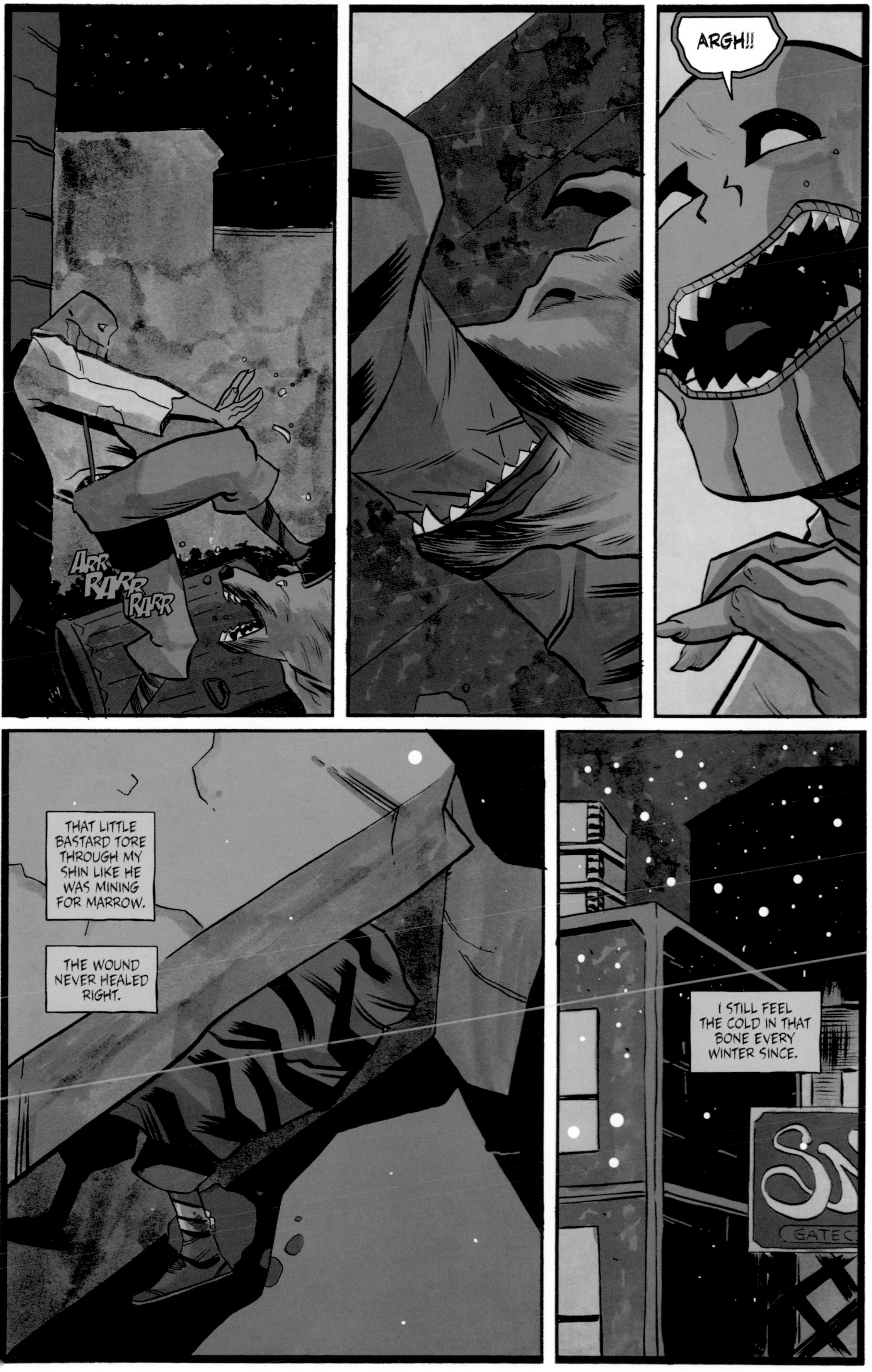
ARR
RARR
RARR
ARGH!!
THAT LITTLE BASTARD TORE THROUGH MY SHIN LIKE HE WAS MINING FOR MARROW.
THE WOUND NEVER HEALED RIGHT.
I STILL FEEL THE COLD IN THAT BONE EVERY WINTER SINCE.
GATEC

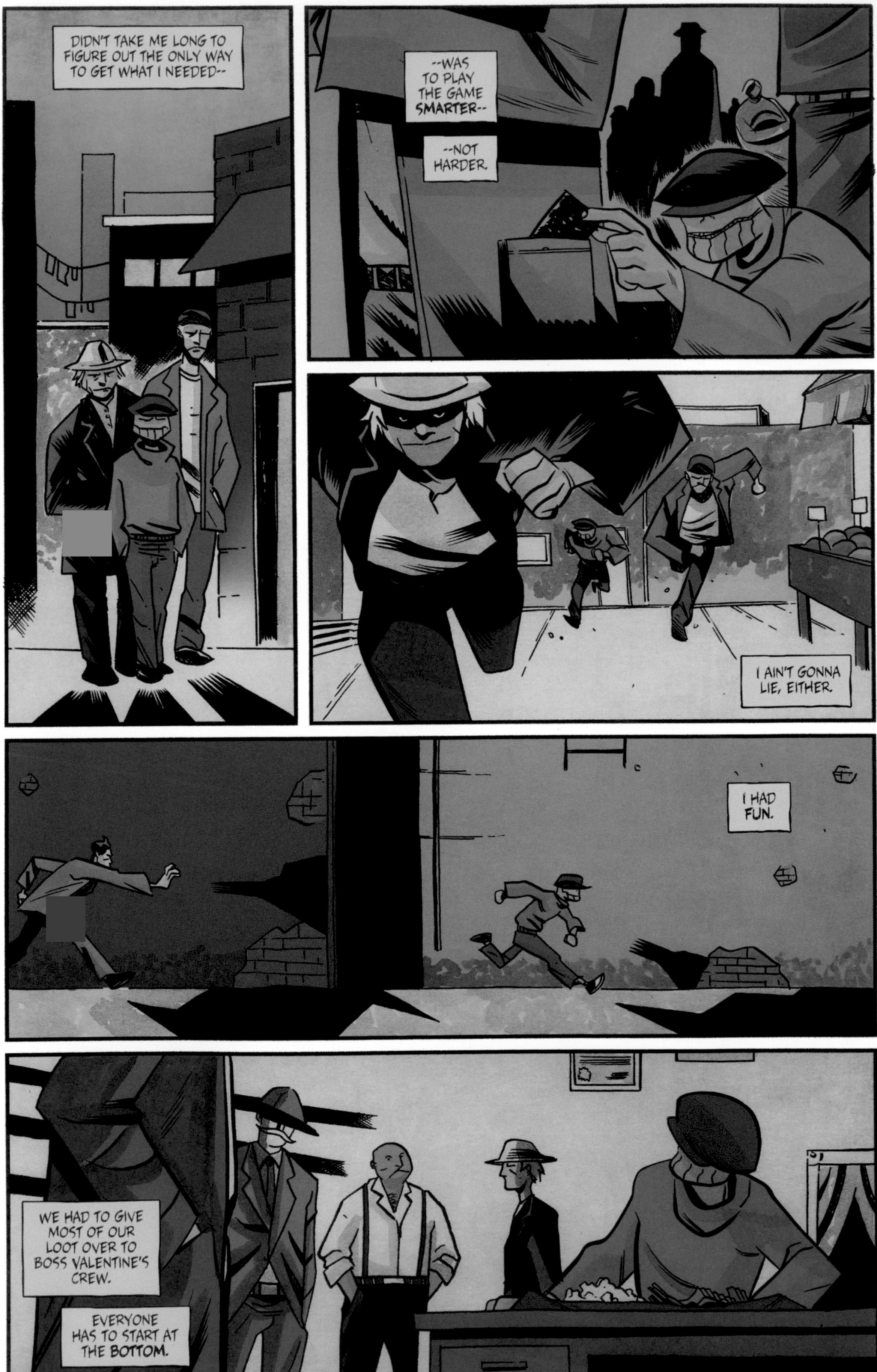
DIDN'T TAKE ME LONG TO FIGURE OUT THE ONLY WAY TO GET WHAT I NEEDED--
--WAS TO PLAY THE GAME SMARTER--
--NOT HARDER.
I AIN'T GONNA LIE, EITHER.
I HAD FUN.
WE HAD TO GIVE MOST OF OUR LOOT OVER TO BOSS VALENTINE'S CREW.
EVERYONE HAS TO START AT THE BOTTOM.

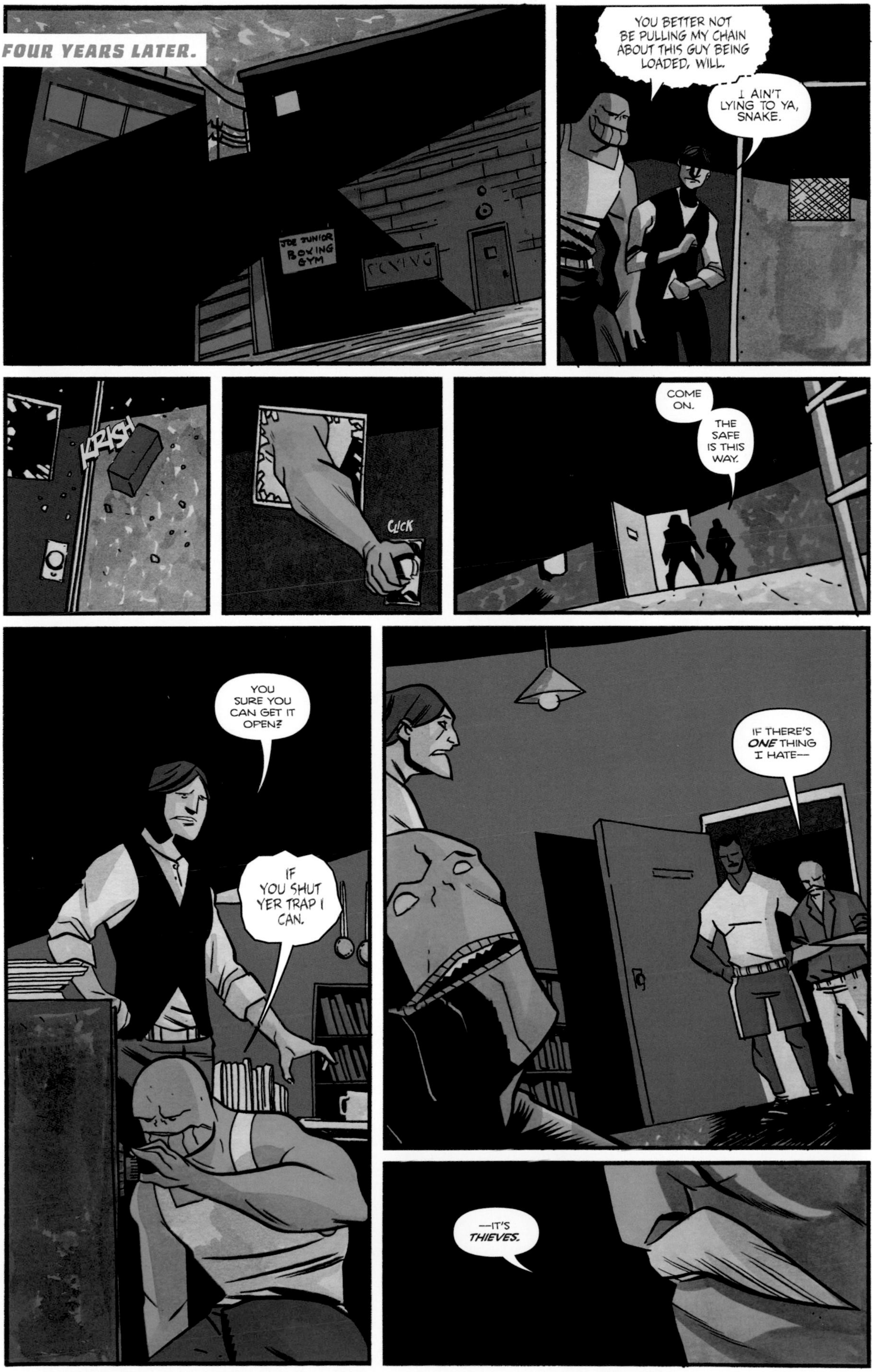
FOUR YEARS LATER.
JOE JUNIOR BOXING GYM
YOU BETTER NOT BE PULLING MY CHAIN ABOUT THIS GUY BEING LOADED, WILL.
I AIN'T LYING TO YA, SNAKE.
KRISH
CLICK
COME ON.
THE SAFE IS THIS WAY.
YOU SURE YOU CAN GET IT OPEN?
IF YOU SHUT YER TRAP I CAN.
IF THERE'S ONE THING I HATE--
--IT'S THIEVES.

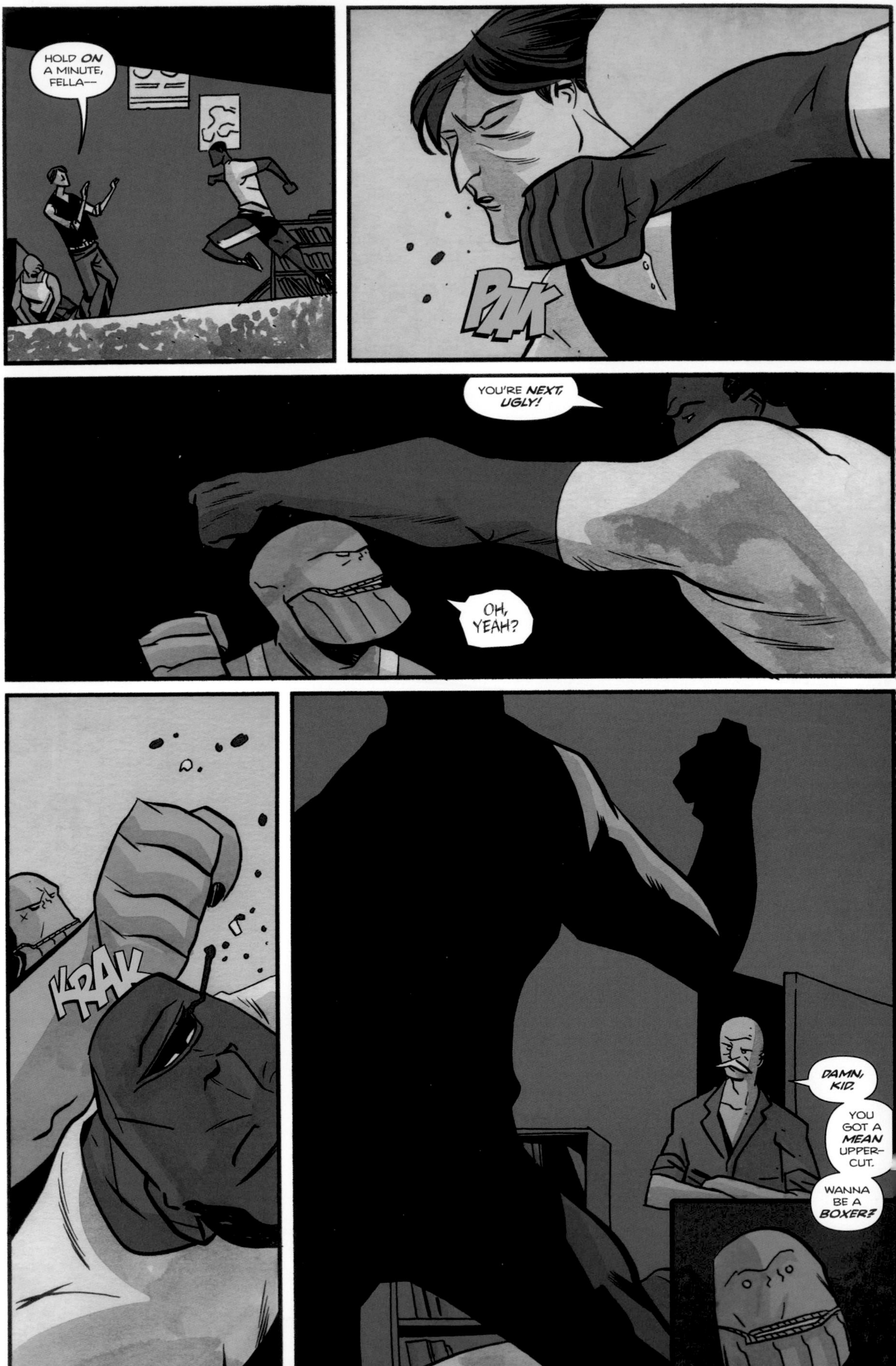
HOLD ON A MINUTE, FELLA--
PAK
YOU'RE NEXT, UGLY!
OH, YEAH?
KRAK
DAMN, KID.
YOU GOT A MEAN UPPER-CUT.
WANNA BE A BOXER?

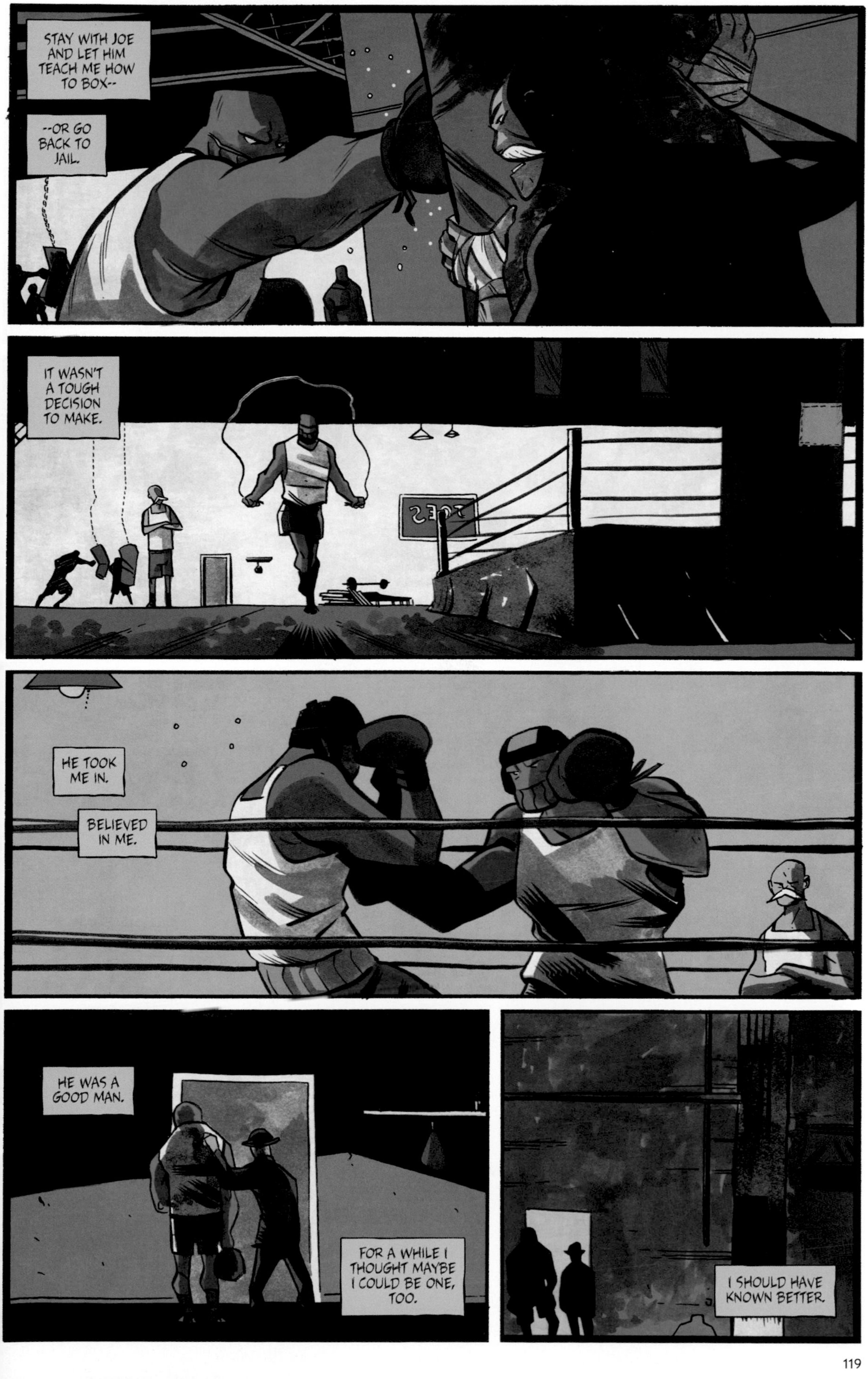
STAY WITH JOE AND LET HIM TEACH ME HOW TO BOX--
--OR GO BACK TO JAIL.
IT WASN'T A TOUGH DECISION TO MAKE.
HE TOOK ME IN.
BELIEVED IN ME.
HE WAS A GOOD MAN.
FOR A WHILE I THOUGHT MAYBE I COULD BE ONE, TOO.
I SHOULD HAVE KNOWN BETTER.

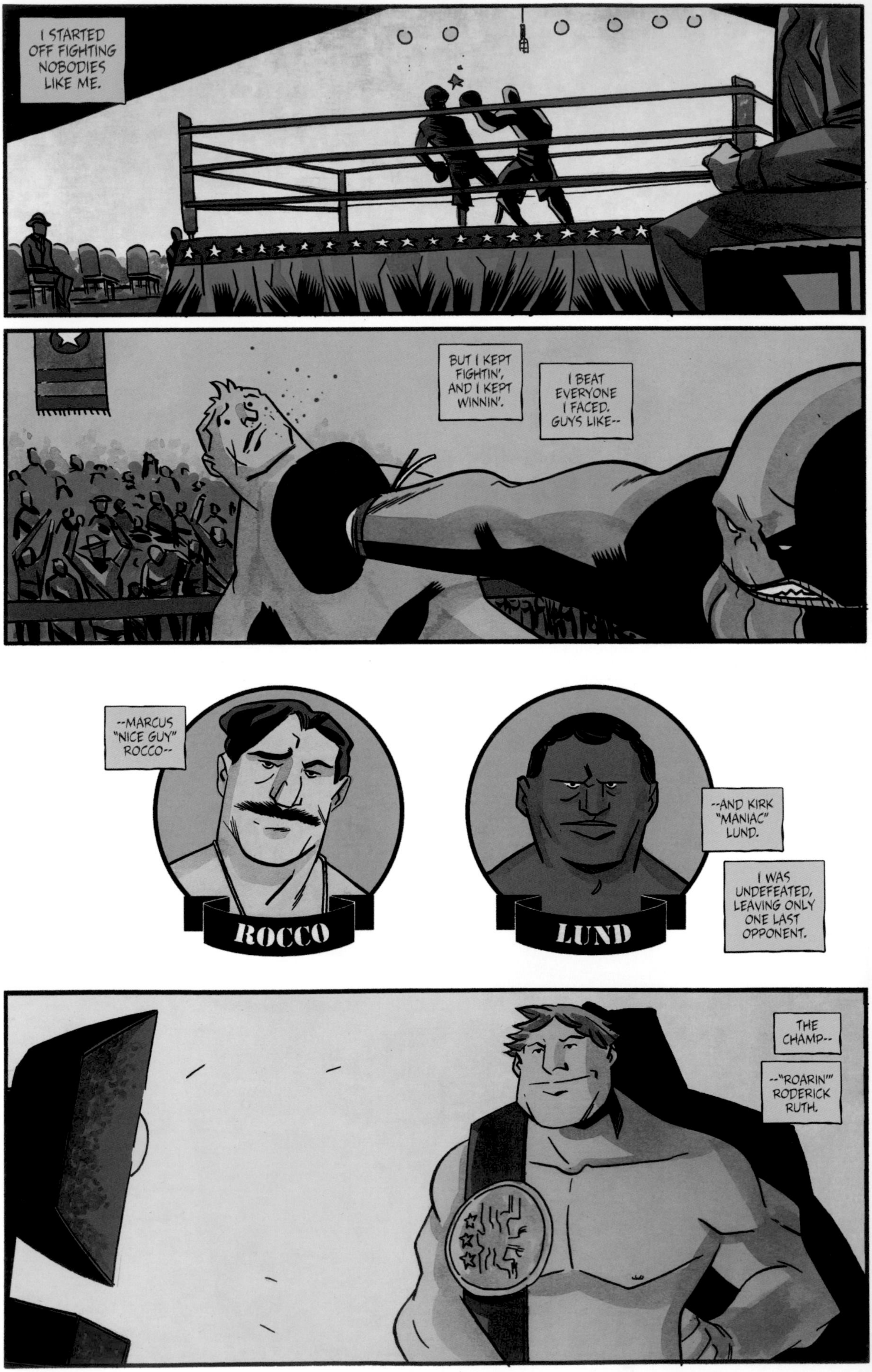

I STARTED OFF FIGHTING NOBODIES LIKE ME.
BUT I KEPT FIGHTIN', AND I KEPT WINNIN'.
I BEAT EVERYONE I FACED. GUYS LIKE--
--MARCUS "NICE GUY" ROCCO--
ROCCO
LUND
--AND KIRK "MANIAC" LUND.
I WAS UNDEFEATED, LEAVING ONLY ONE LAST OPPONENT.
THE CHAMP--
--"ROARIN'" RODERICK RUTH.

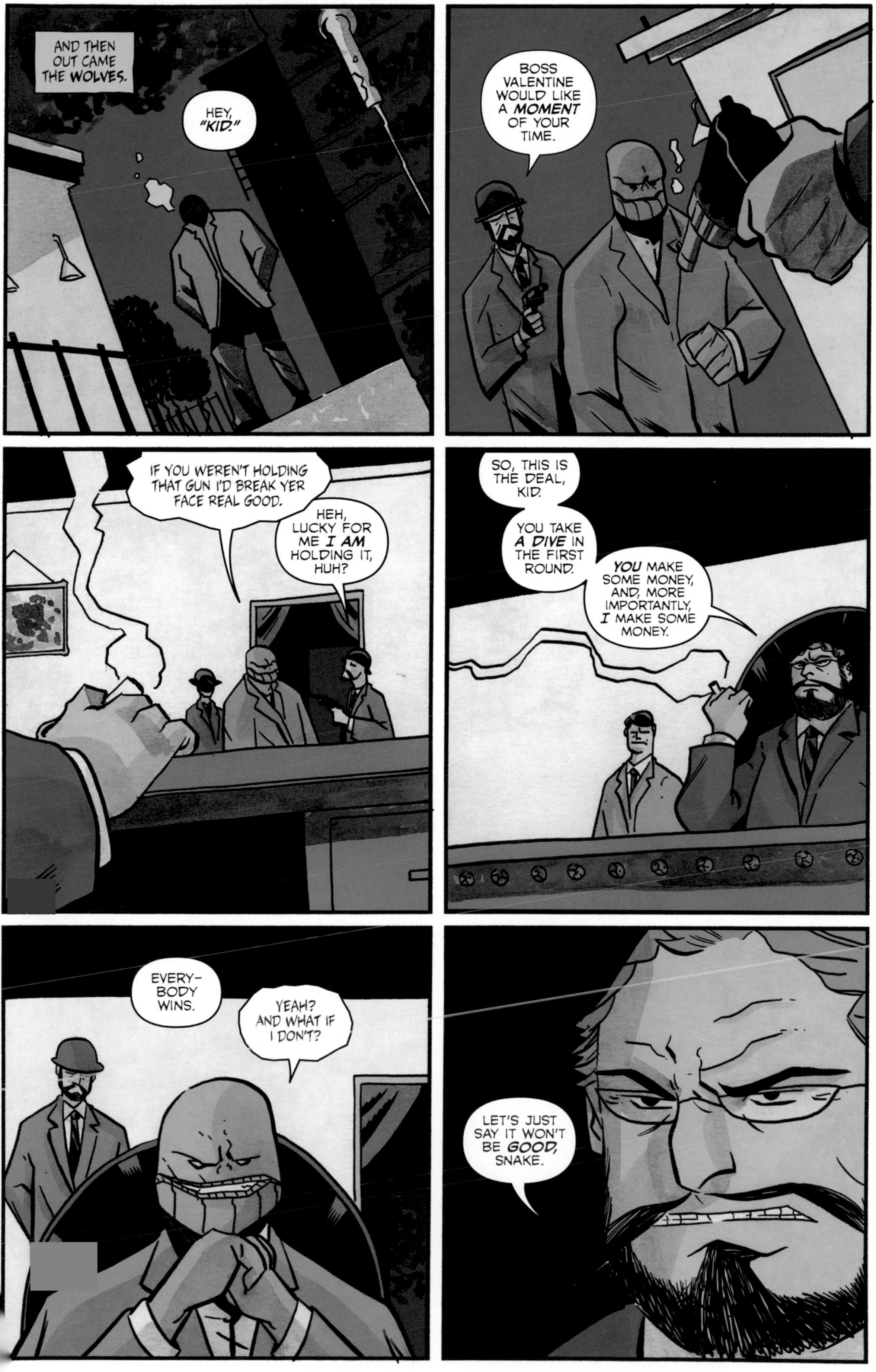
AND THEN OUT CAME THE WOLVES.
HEY, "KID."
BOSS VALENTINE WOULD LIKE A MOMENT OF YOUR TIME.
IF YOU WEREN'T HOLDING THAT GUN I'D BREAK YER FACE REAL GOOD.
HEH, LUCKY FOR ME I AM HOLDING IT, HUH?
SO, THIS IS THE DEAL, KID.
YOU TAKE A DIVE IN THE FIRST ROUND.
YOU MAKE SOME MONEY, AND, MORE IMPORTANTLY, I MAKE SOME MONEY.
EVERY-BODY WINS.
YEAH? AND WHAT IF I DON'T?
LET'S JUST SAY IT WON'T BE GOOD, SNAKE.

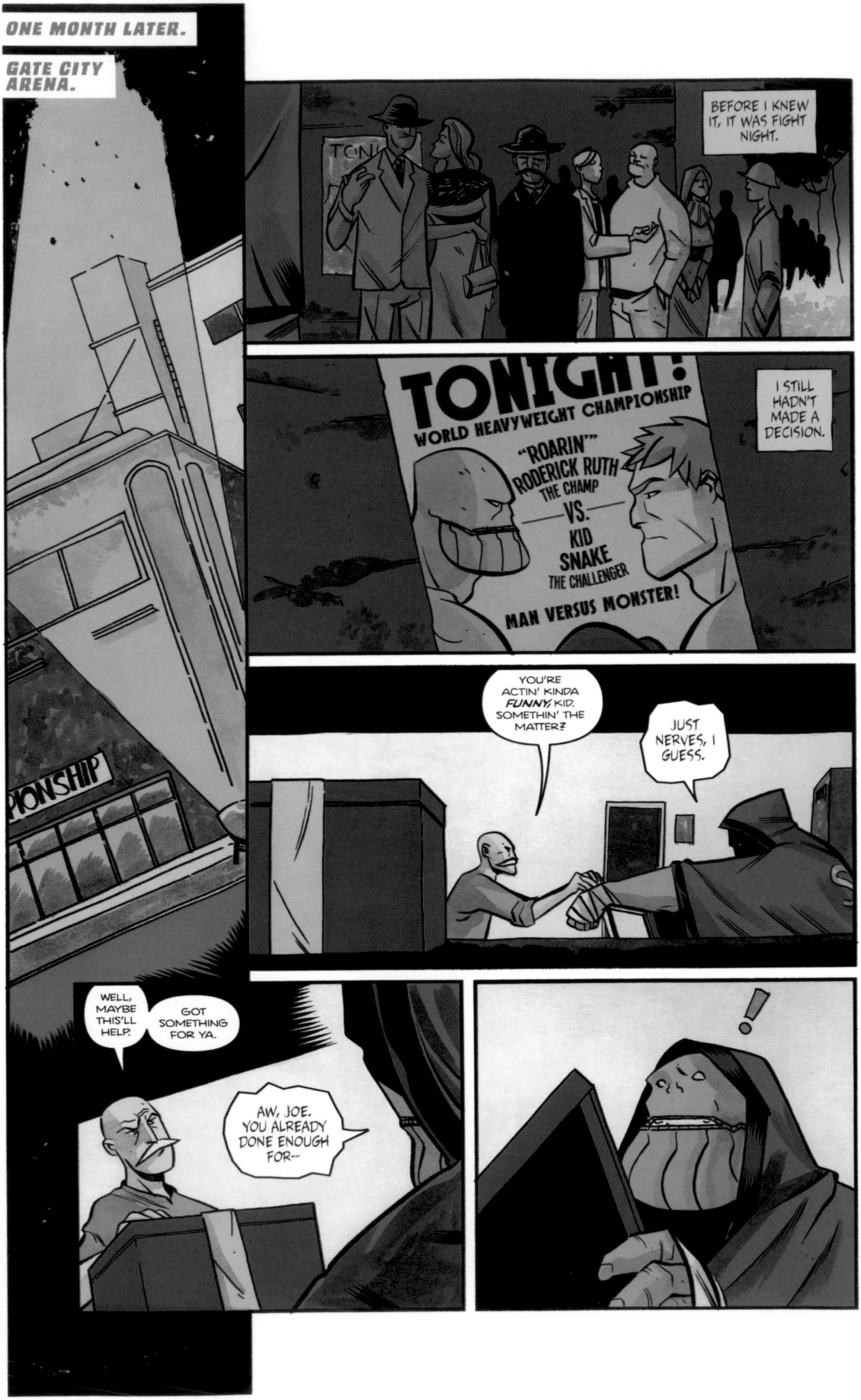
ONE MONTH LATER.
GATE CITY ARENA.
BEFORE I KNEW IT, IT WAS FIGHT NIGHT.
TONIGHT! WORLD HEAVYWEIGHT CHAMPIONSHIP "ROARIN'" RODERICK RUTH THE CHAMP —VS.— KID SNAKE THE CHALLENGER MAN VERSUS MONSTER!
I STILL HADN'T MADE A DECISION.
PIONSHIP
YOU'RE ACTIN' KINDA FUNNY, KID. SOMETHIN' THE MATTER?
JUST NERVES, I GUESS.
WELL, MAYBE THIS'LL HELP.
GOT SOMETHING FOR YA.
AW, JOE. YOU ALREADY DONE ENOUGH FOR--
!

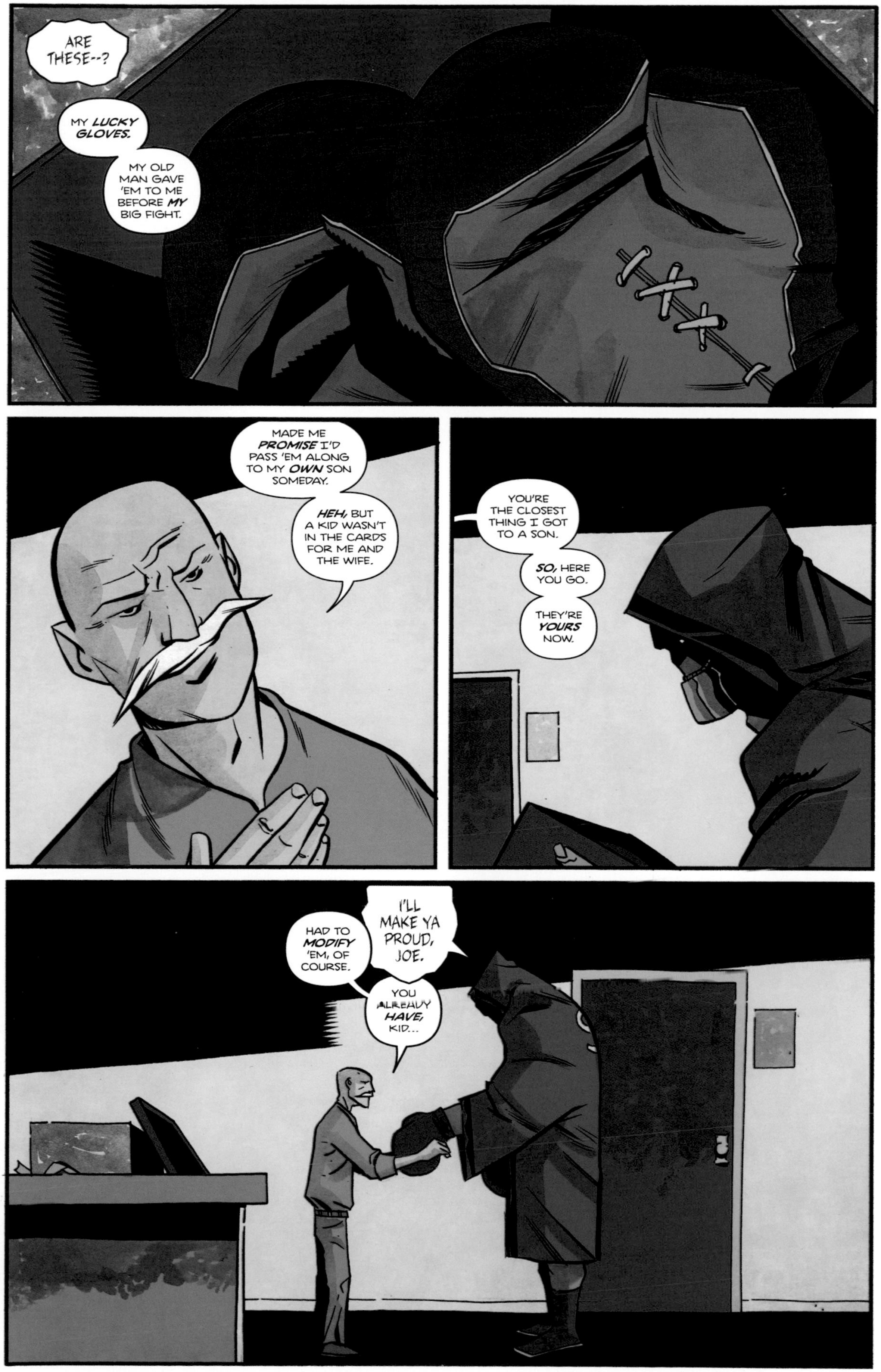
ARE THESE--?
MY LUCKY GLOVES.
MY OLD MAN GAVE 'EM TO ME BEFORE MY BIG FIGHT.
MADE ME PROMISE I'D PASS 'EM ALONG TO MY OWN SON SOMEDAY.
HEH, BUT A KID WASN'T IN THE CARDS FOR ME AND THE WIFE.
YOU'RE THE CLOSEST THING I GOT TO A SON.
SO, HERE YOU GO.
THEY'RE YOURS NOW.
HAD TO MODIFY 'EM, OF COURSE.
I'LL MAKE YA PROUD, JOE.
YOU ALREADY HAVE, KID...

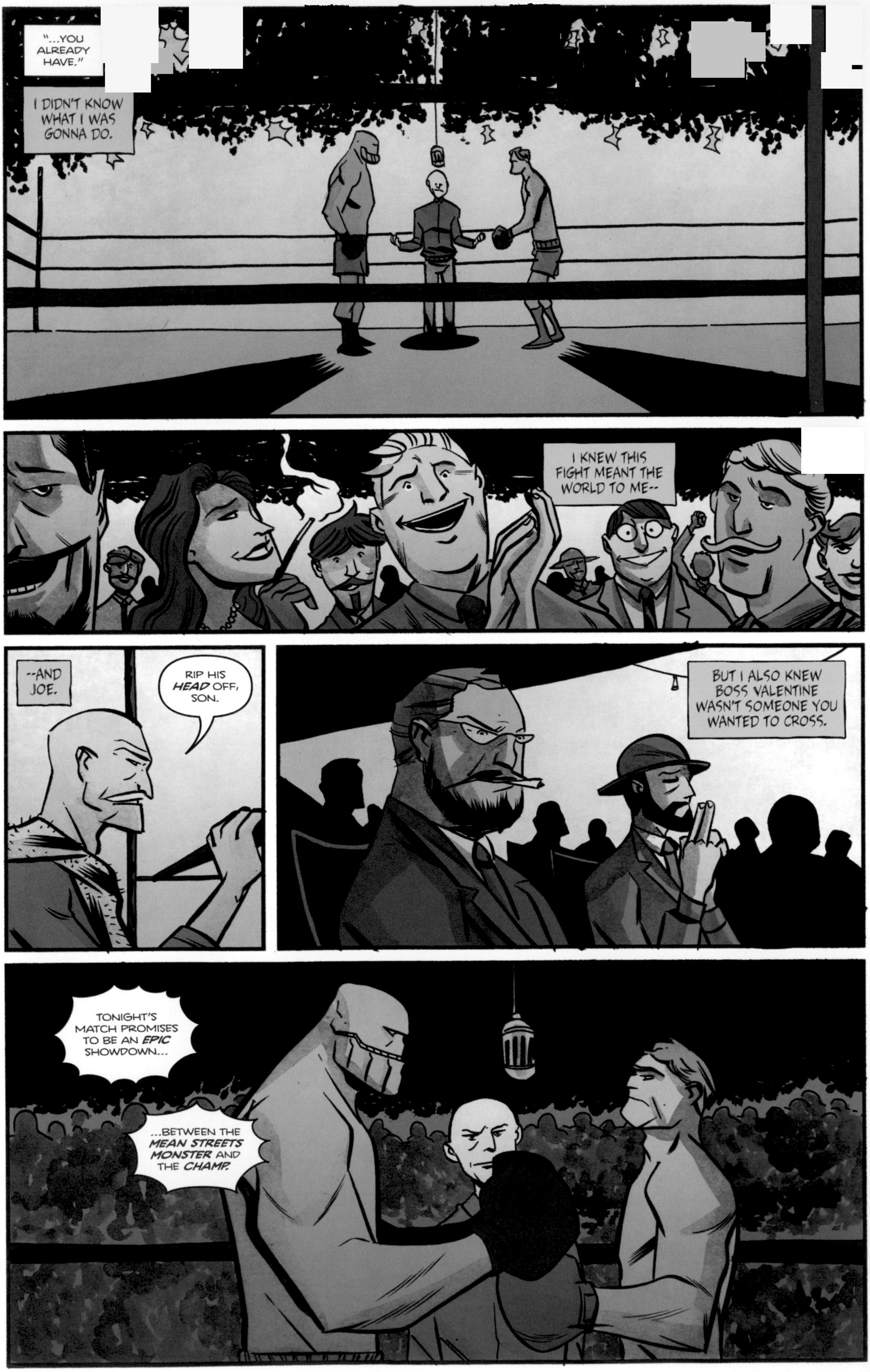
"...YOU ALREADY HAVE."
I DIDN'T KNOW WHAT I WAS GONNA DO.
I KNEW THIS FIGHT MEANT THE WORLD TO ME--
--AND JOE.
RIP HIS HEAD OFF, SON.
BUT I ALSO KNEW BOSS VALENTINE WASN'T SOMEONE YOU WANTED TO CROSS.
TONIGHT'S MATCH PROMISES TO BE AN EPIC SHOWDOWN...
...BETWEEN THE MEAN STREETS MONSTER AND THE CHAMP.

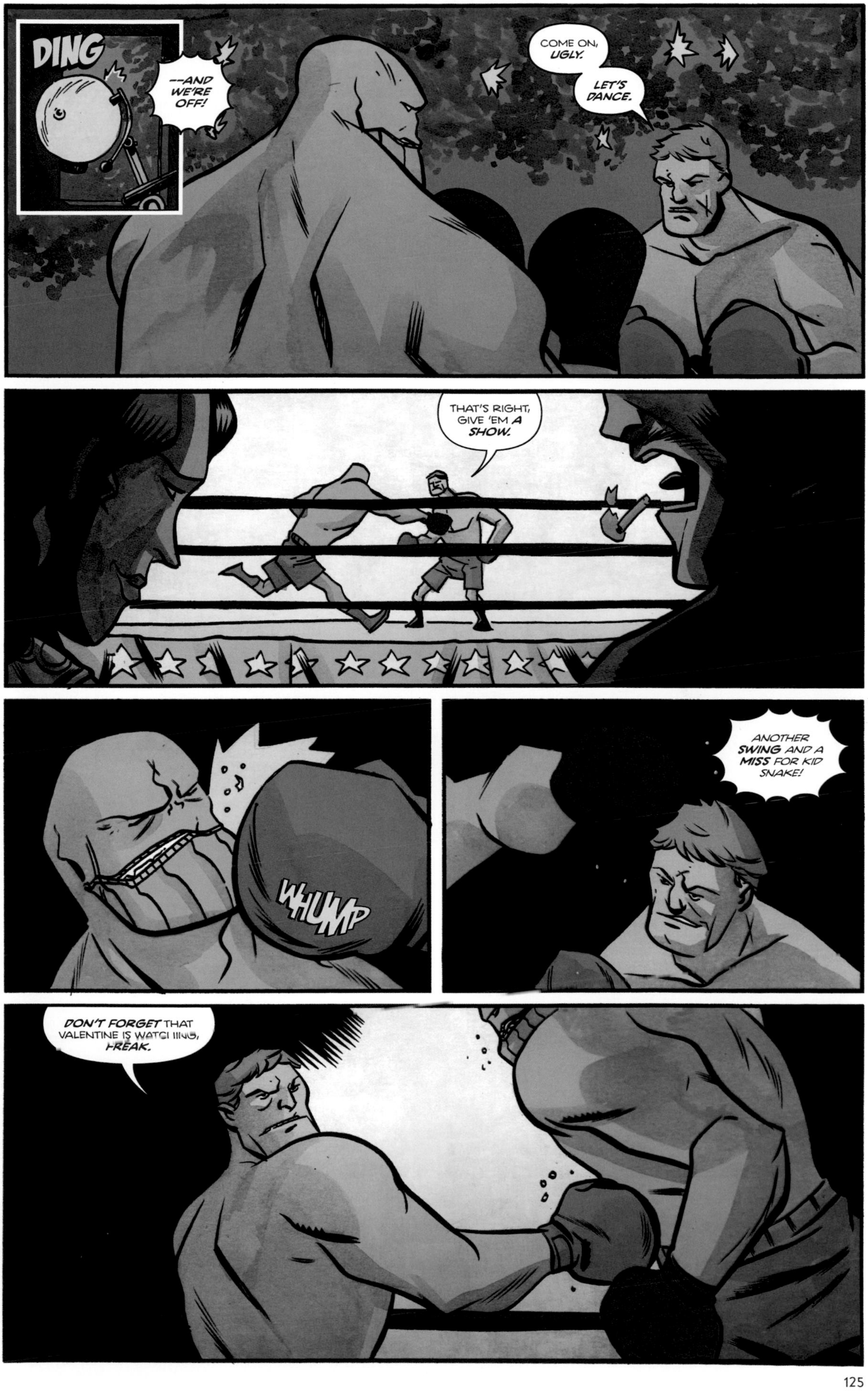
DING
--AND WE'RE OFF!
COME ON, UGLY.
LET'S DANCE.
THAT'S RIGHT, GIVE 'EM A SHOW.
WHUMP
ANOTHER SWING AND A MISS FOR KID SNAKE!
DON'T FORGET THAT VALENTINE IS WATCHING, FREAK.

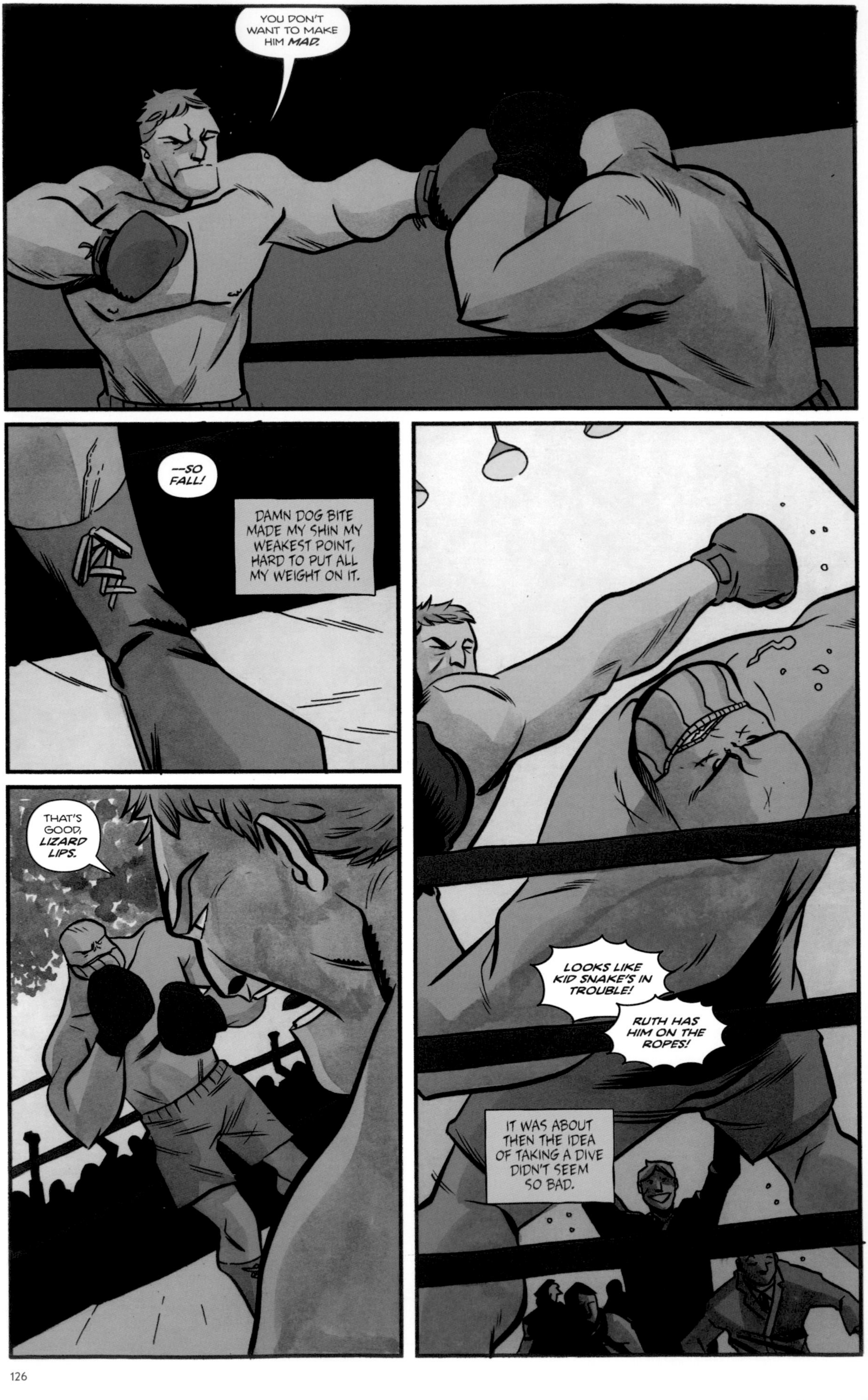
YOU DON'T WANT TO MAKE HIM MAD.
--SO FALL!
DAMN DOG BITE MADE MY SHIN MY WEAKEST POINT, HARD TO PUT ALL MY WEIGHT ON IT.
THAT'S GOOD, LIZARD LIPS.
LOOKS LIKE KID SNAKE'S IN TROUBLE!
RUTH HAS HIM ON THE ROPES!
IT WAS ABOUT THEN THE IDEA OF TAKING A DIVE DIDN'T SEEM SO BAD.

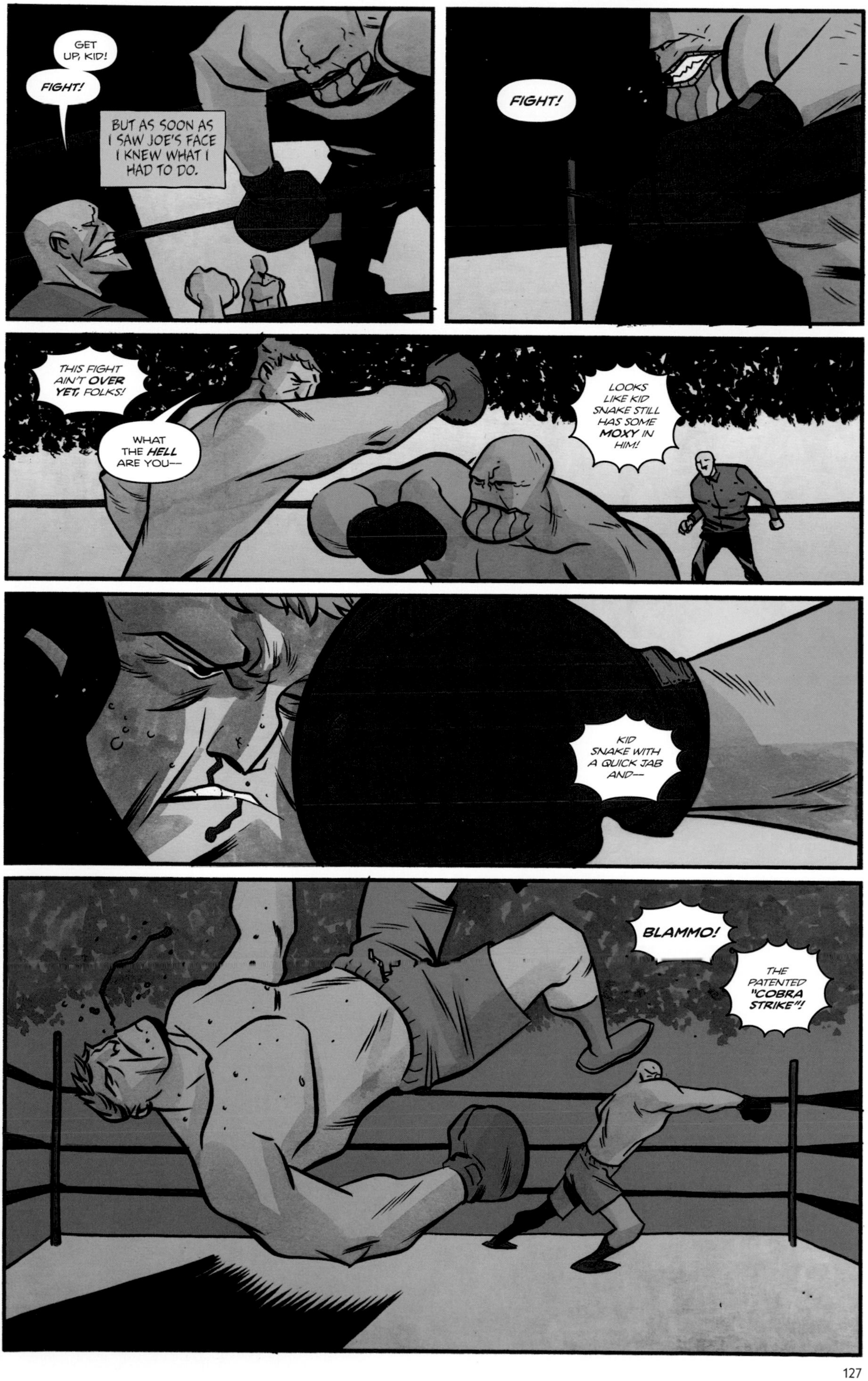
GET UP, KID!
FIGHT!
BUT AS SOON AS I SAW JOE'S FACE I KNEW WHAT I HAD TO DO.
FIGHT!
THIS FIGHT AIN'T OVER YET, FOLKS!
WHAT THE HELL ARE YOU--
LOOKS LIKE KID SNAKE STILL HAS SOME MOXY IN HIM!
KID SNAKE WITH A QUICK JAB AND--
BLAMMO!
THE PATENTED "COBRA STRIKE"!

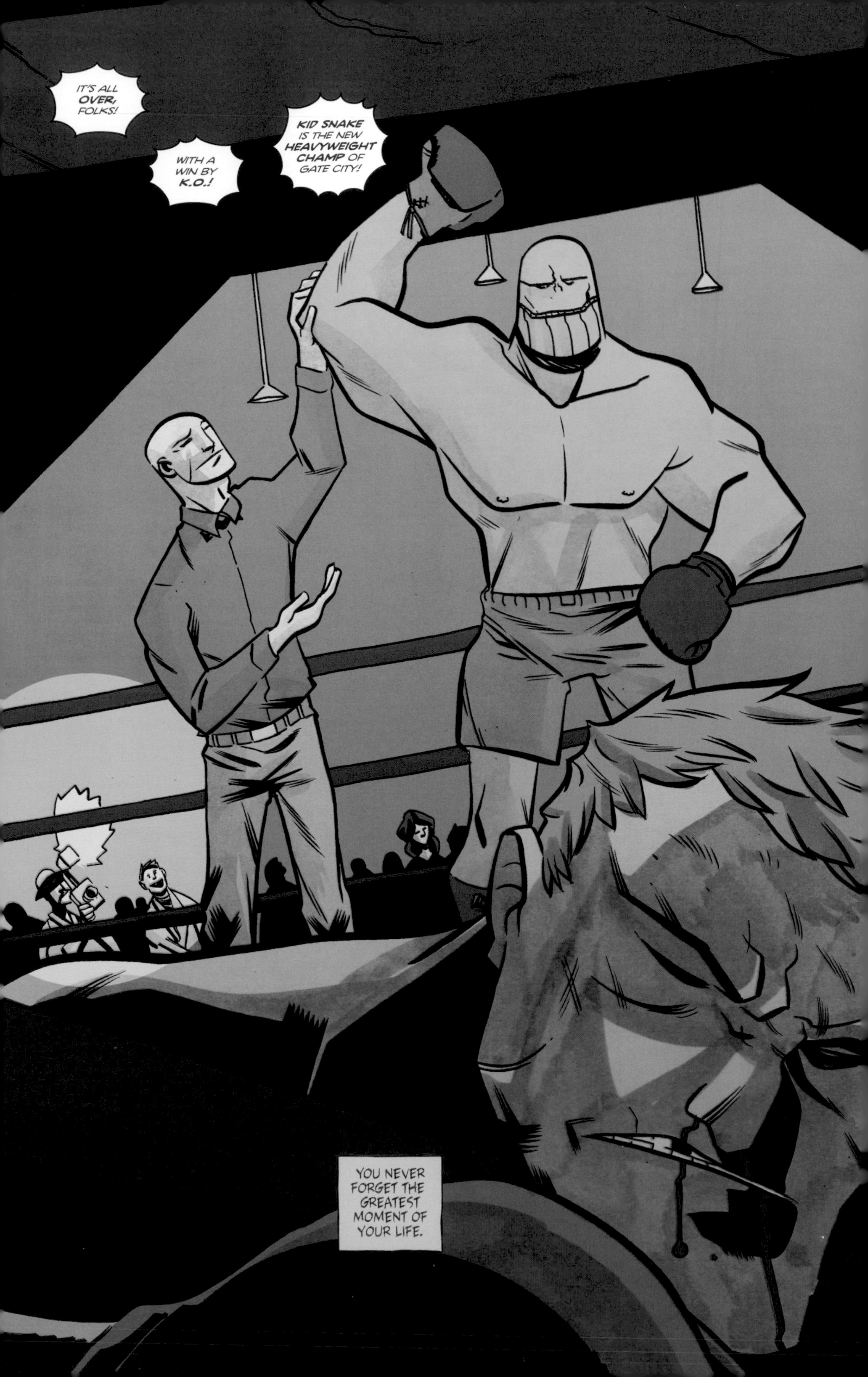
IT'S ALL OVER, FOLKS!
WITH A WIN BY K.O.!
KID SNAKE IS THE NEW HEAVYWEIGHT CHAMP OF GATE CITY!
YOU NEVER FORGET THE GREATEST MOMENT OF YOUR LIFE.

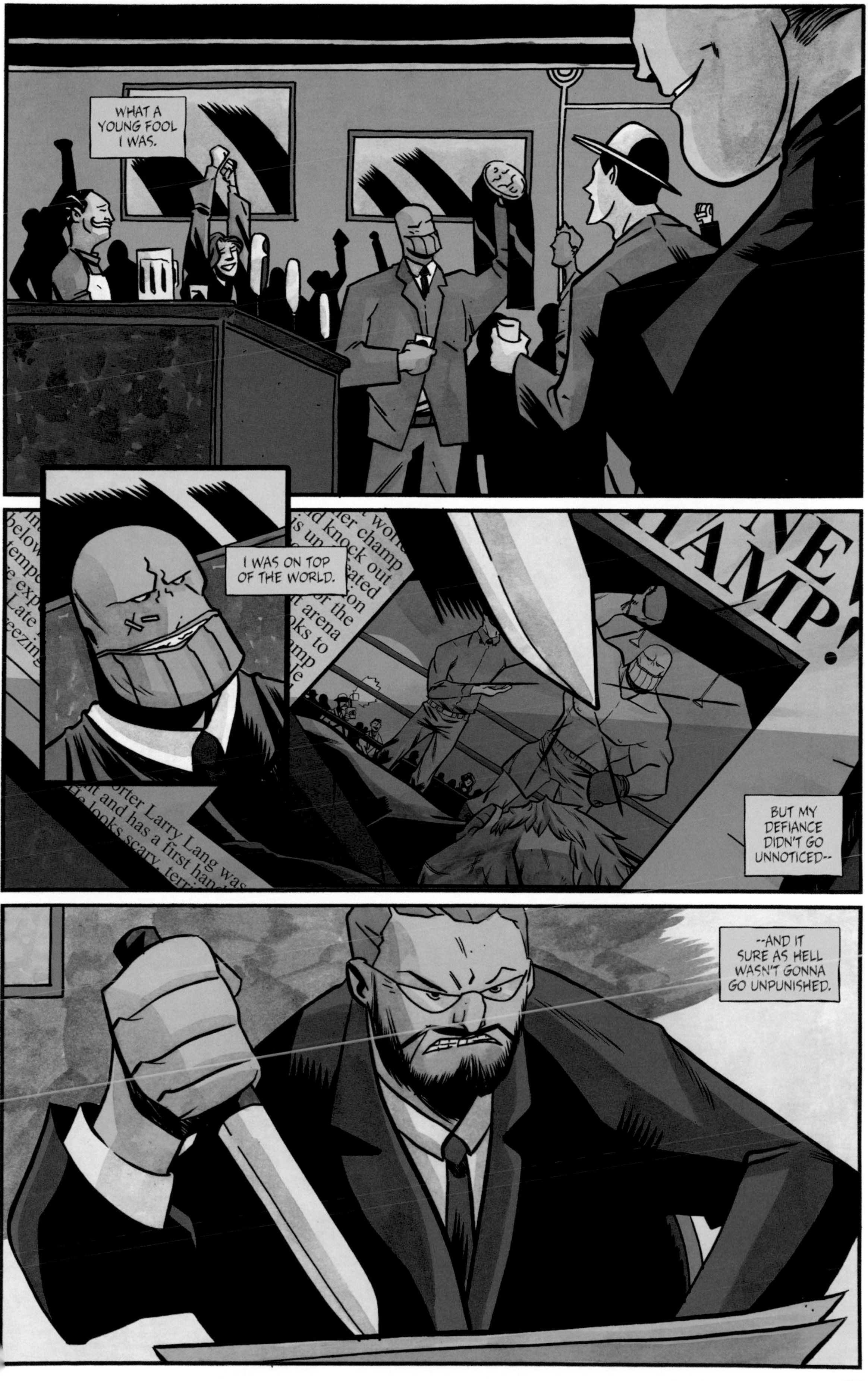
WHAT A YOUNG FOOL I WAS.
I WAS ON TOP OF THE WORLD.
BUT MY DEFIANCE DIDN'T GO UNNOTICED--
--AND IT SURE AS HELL WASN'T GONNA GO UNPUNISHED.

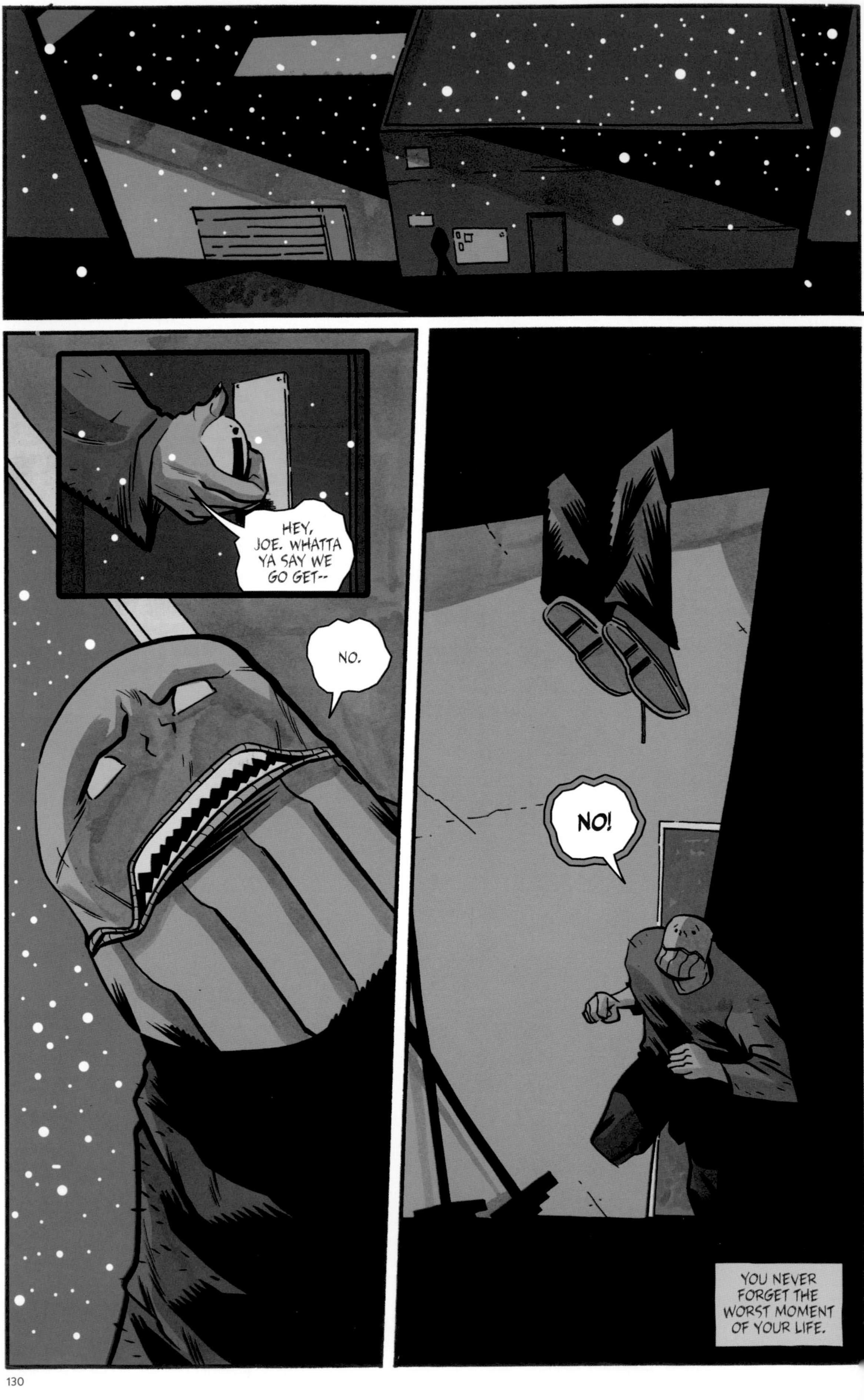
HEY, JOE. WHATTA YA SAY WE GO GET--
NO.
NO!
YOU NEVER FORGET THE WORST MOMENT OF YOUR LIFE.

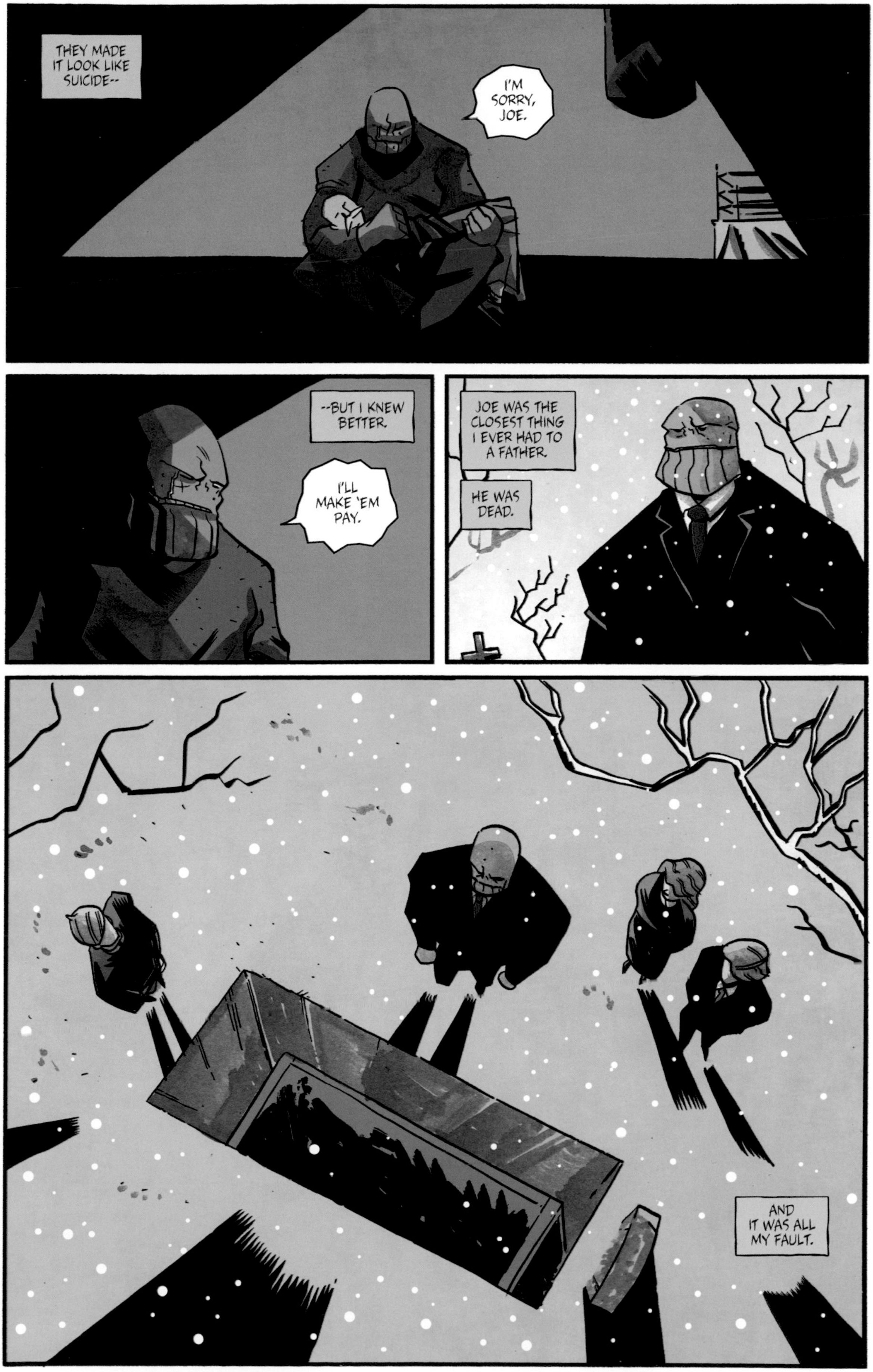
THEY MADE IT LOOK LIKE SUICIDE--
I'M SORRY, JOE.
--BUT I KNEW BETTER.
I'LL MAKE 'EM PAY.
JOE WAS THE CLOSEST THING I EVER HAD TO A FATHER.
HE WAS DEAD.
AND IT WAS ALL MY FAULT.

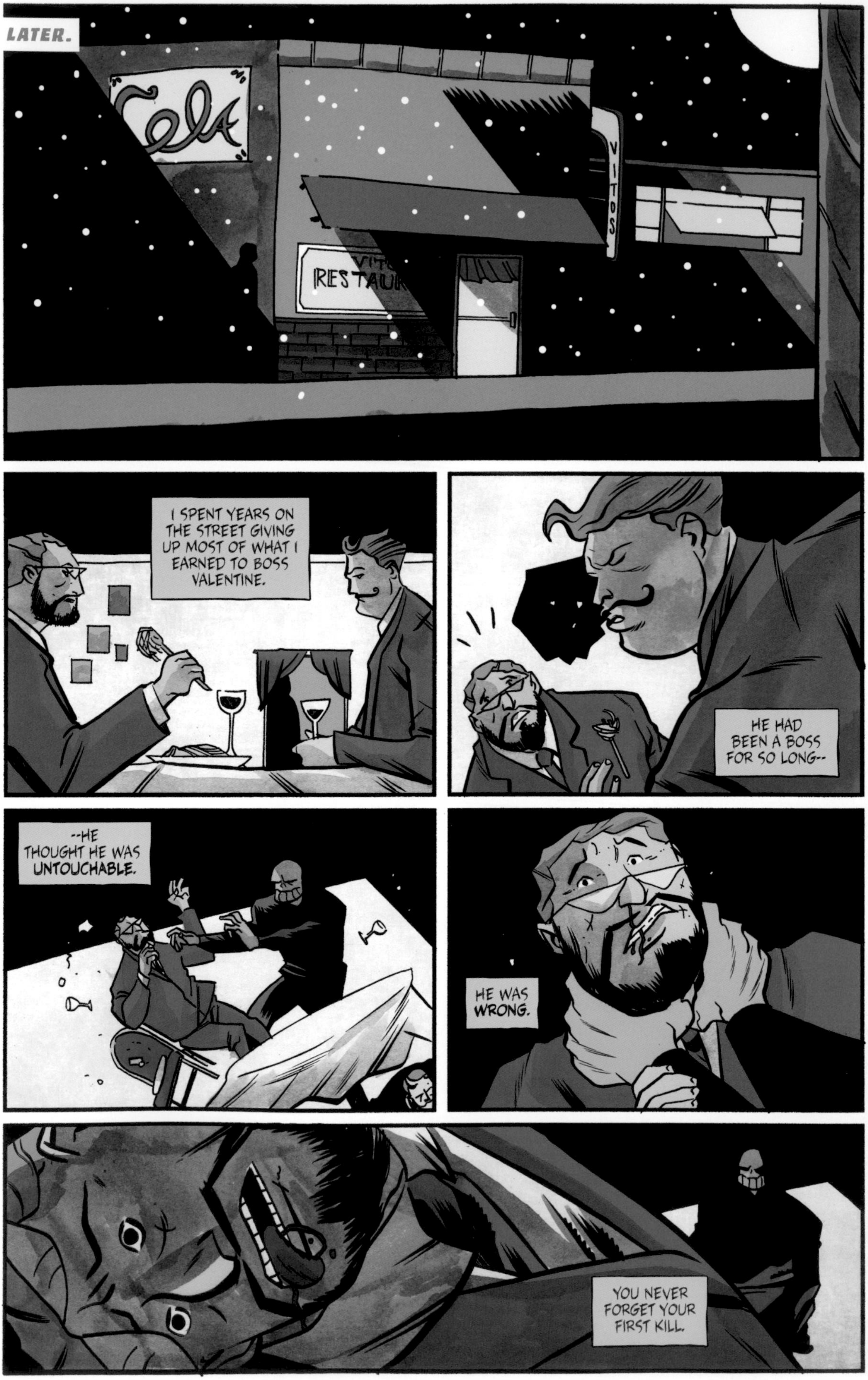
LATER.
VITOS
RESTAU
I SPENT YEARS ON THE STREET GIVING UP MOST OF WHAT I EARNED TO BOSS VALENTINE.
HE HAD BEEN A BOSS FOR SO LONG--
--HE THOUGHT HE WAS UNTOUCHABLE.
HE WAS WRONG.
YOU NEVER FORGET YOUR FIRST KILL.

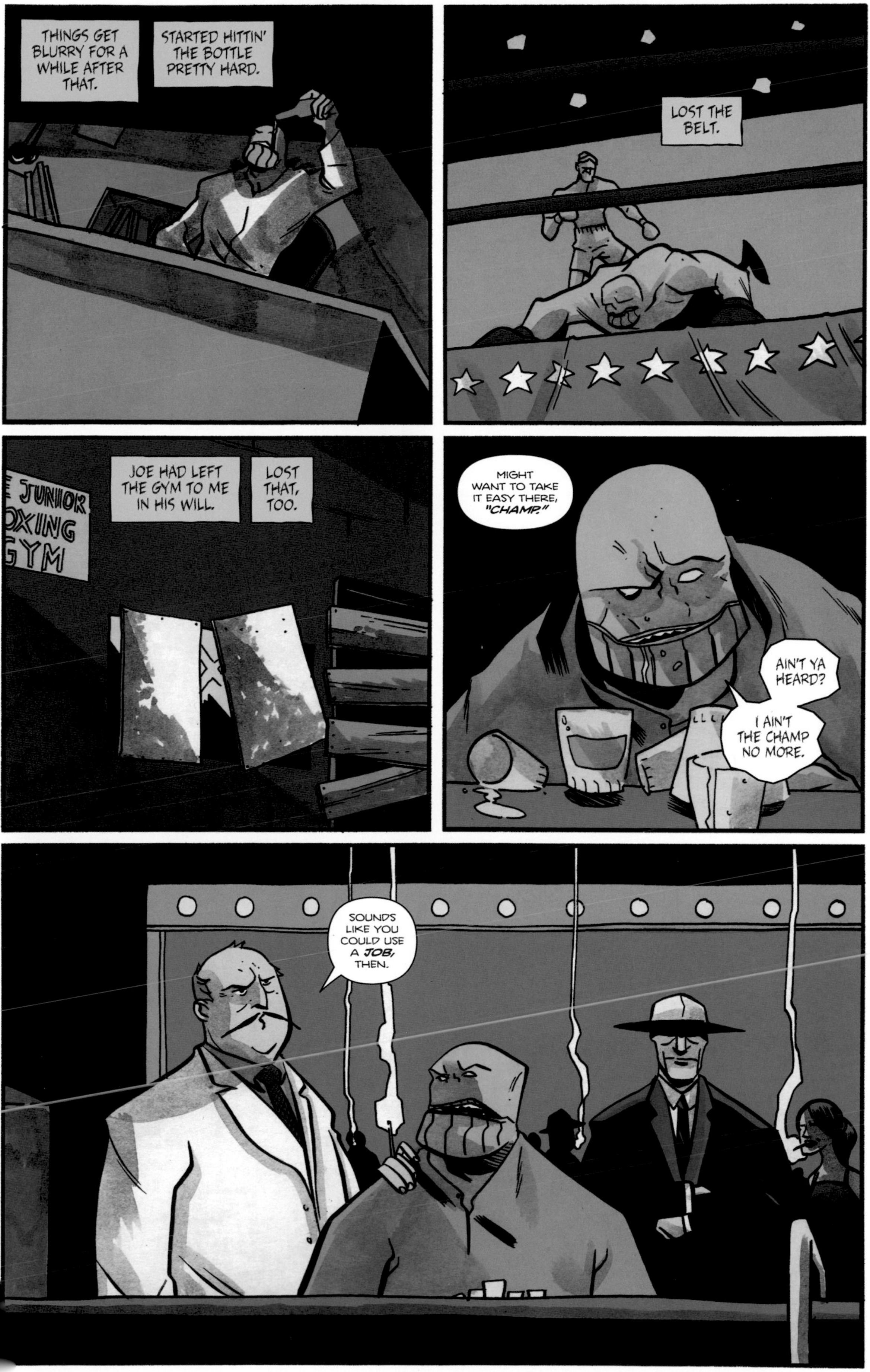
THINGS GET BLURRY FOR A WHILE AFTER THAT.
STARTED HITTIN' THE BOTTLE PRETTY HARD.
LOST THE BELT.
JOE HAD LEFT THE GYM TO ME IN HIS WILL.
LOST THAT, TOO.
JUNIOR
OXING
GYM
MIGHT WANT TO TAKE IT EASY THERE, "CHAMP."
AIN'T YA HEARD?
I AIN'T THE CHAMP NO MORE.
SOUNDS LIKE YOU COULD USE A JOB, THEN.

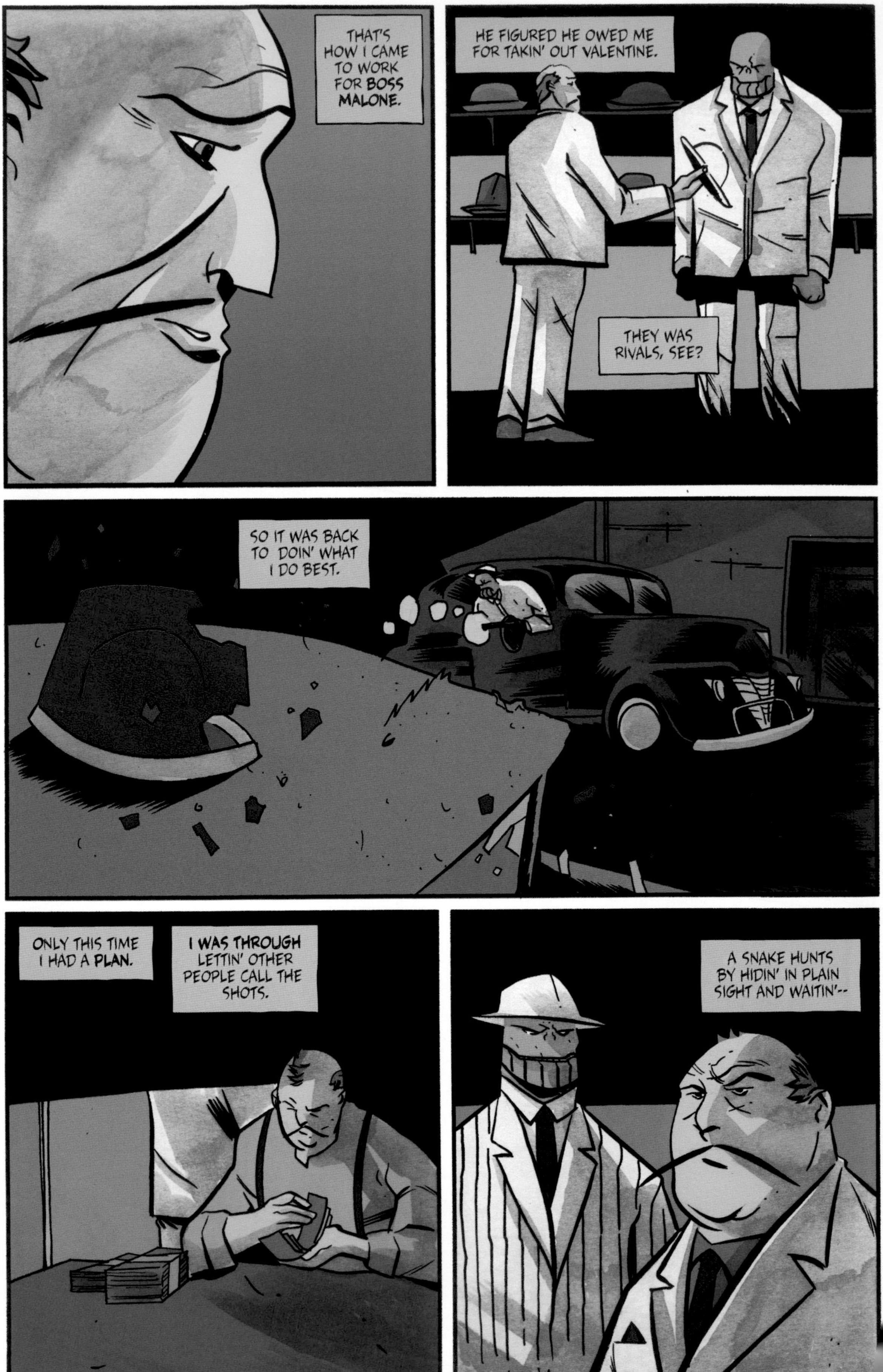
THAT'S HOW I CAME TO WORK FOR BOSS MALONE.
HE FIGURED HE OWED ME FOR TAKIN' OUT VALENTINE.
THEY WAS RIVALS, SEE?
SO IT WAS BACK TO DOIN' WHAT I DO BEST.
ONLY THIS TIME I HAD A PLAN.
I WAS THROUGH LETTIN' OTHER PEOPLE CALL THE SHOTS.
A SNAKE HUNTS BY HIDIN' IN PLAIN SIGHT AND WAITIN'--

--FOR THE RIGHT MOMENT TO STRIKE.

MY LIFE WASN'T MUCH OF A LIFE AT THAT POINT.

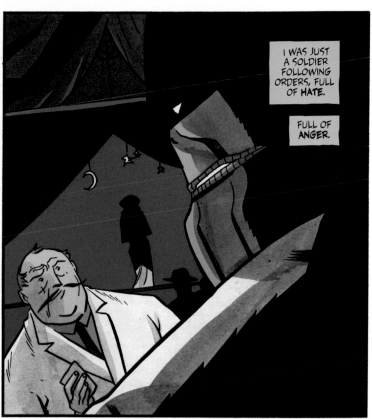

I WAS JUST A SOLDIER FOLLOWING ORDERS, FULL OF HATE.

FULL OF ANGER.

BUT THEN I SAW HER

I TELL YA IT WAS LOVE AT FIRST SIGHT.

SHE WAS THE MOST BEAUTIFUL THING I EVER LAID MY EYES ON.

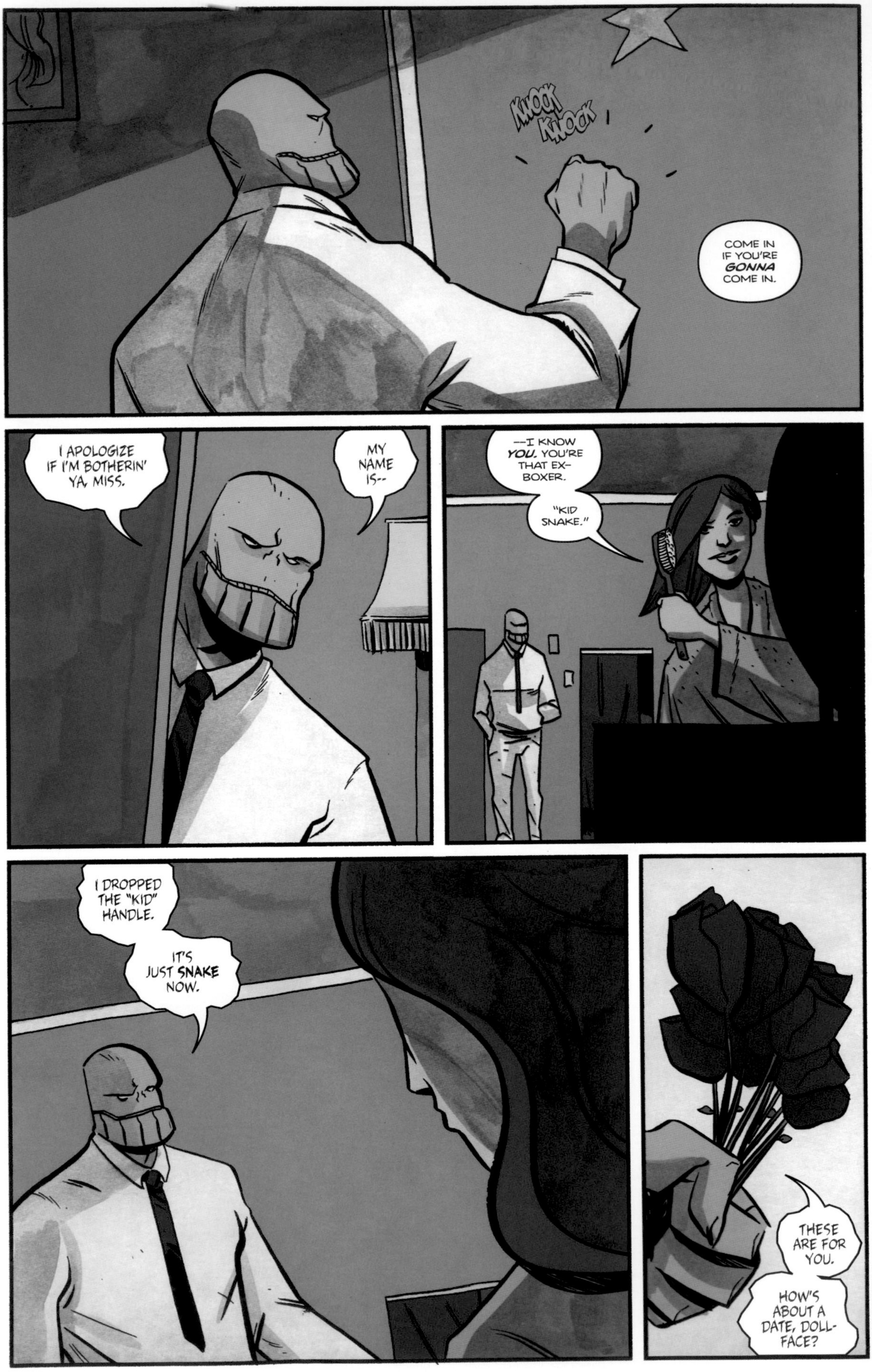
KNOCK KNOCK
COME IN IF YOU'RE GONNA COME IN.
I APOLOGIZE IF I'M BOTHERIN' YA, MISS.
MY NAME IS--
--I KNOW YOU. YOU'RE THAT EX-BOXER.
"KID SNAKE."
I DROPPED THE "KID" HANDLE.
IT'S JUST SNAKE NOW.
THESE ARE FOR YOU.
HOW'S ABOUT A DATE, DOLL-FACE?

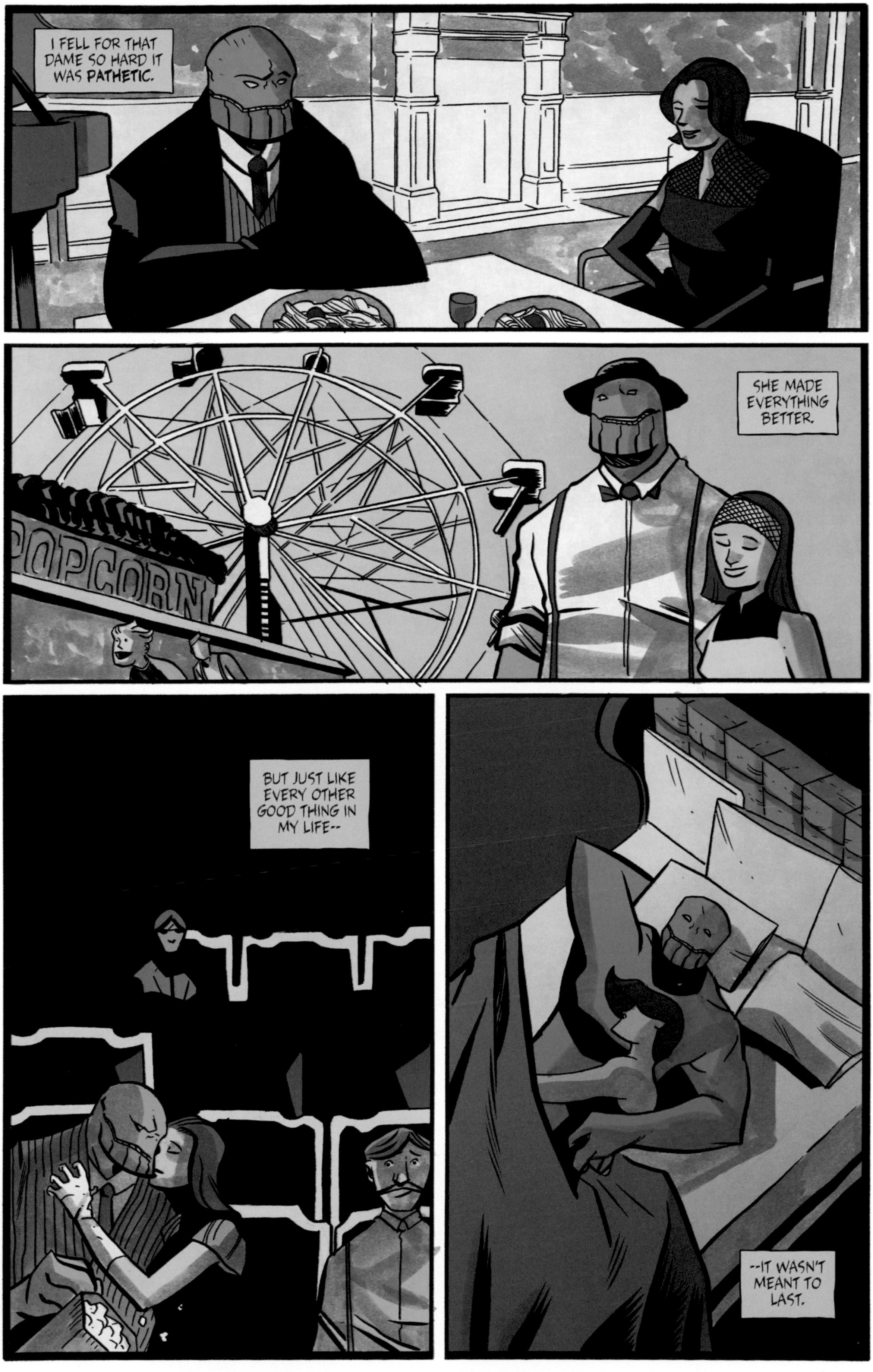
I FELL FOR THAT DAME SO HARD IT WAS **PATHETIC.**
SHE MADE EVERYTHING BETTER.
POPCORN
BUT JUST LIKE EVERY OTHER GOOD THING IN MY LIFE--
--IT WASN'T MEANT TO LAST.

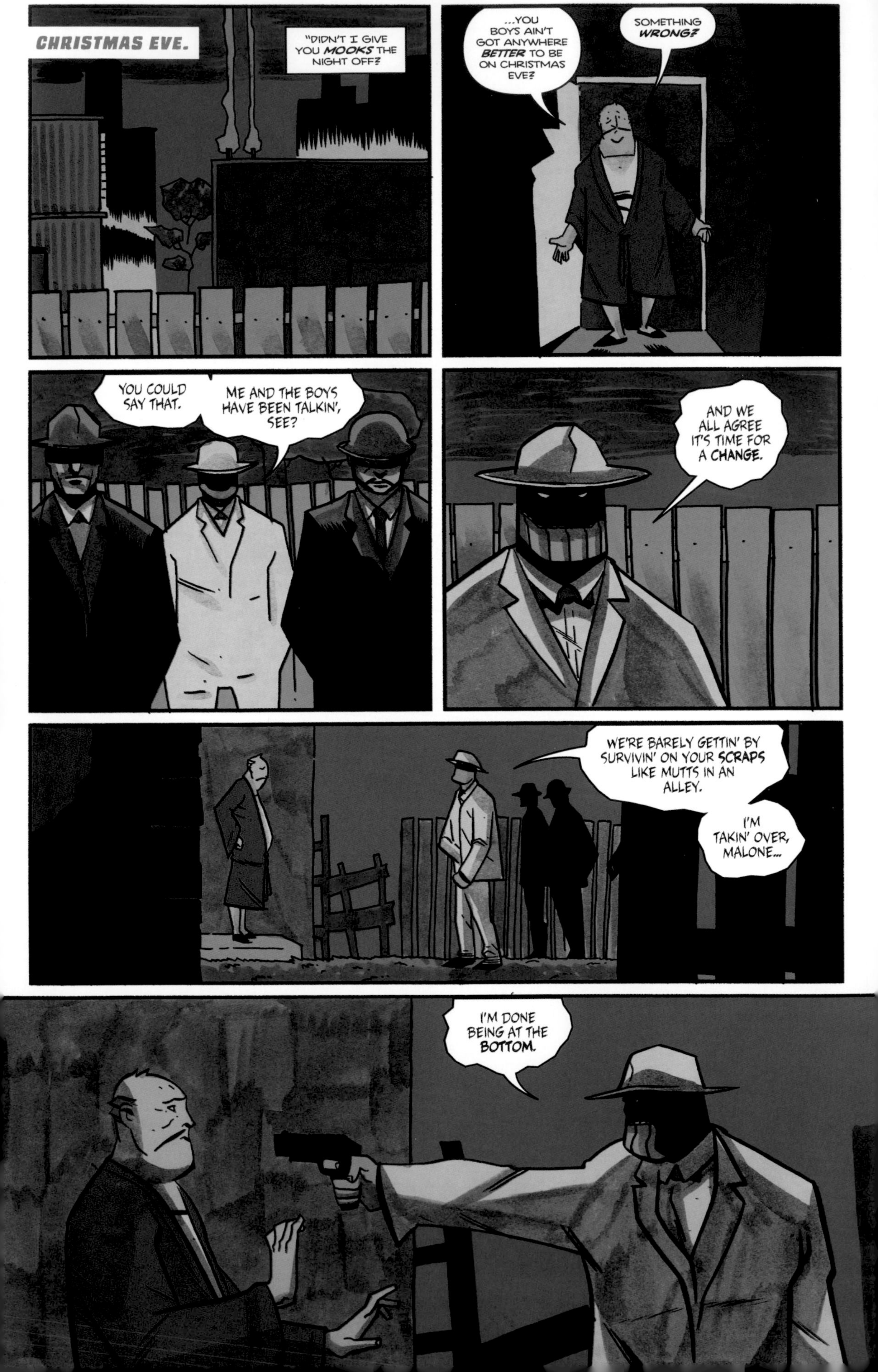
CHRISTMAS EVE.
"DIDN'T I GIVE YOU MOOKS THE NIGHT OFF?
...YOU BOYS AIN'T GOT ANYWHERE BETTER TO BE ON CHRISTMAS EVE?
SOMETHING WRONG?
YOU COULD SAY THAT.
ME AND THE BOYS HAVE BEEN TALKIN', SEE?
AND WE ALL AGREE IT'S TIME FOR A CHANGE.
WE'RE BARELY GETTIN' BY SURVIVIN' ON YOUR SCRAPS LIKE MUTTS IN AN ALLEY.
I'M TAKIN' OVER, MALONE...
I'M DONE BEING AT THE BOTTOM.

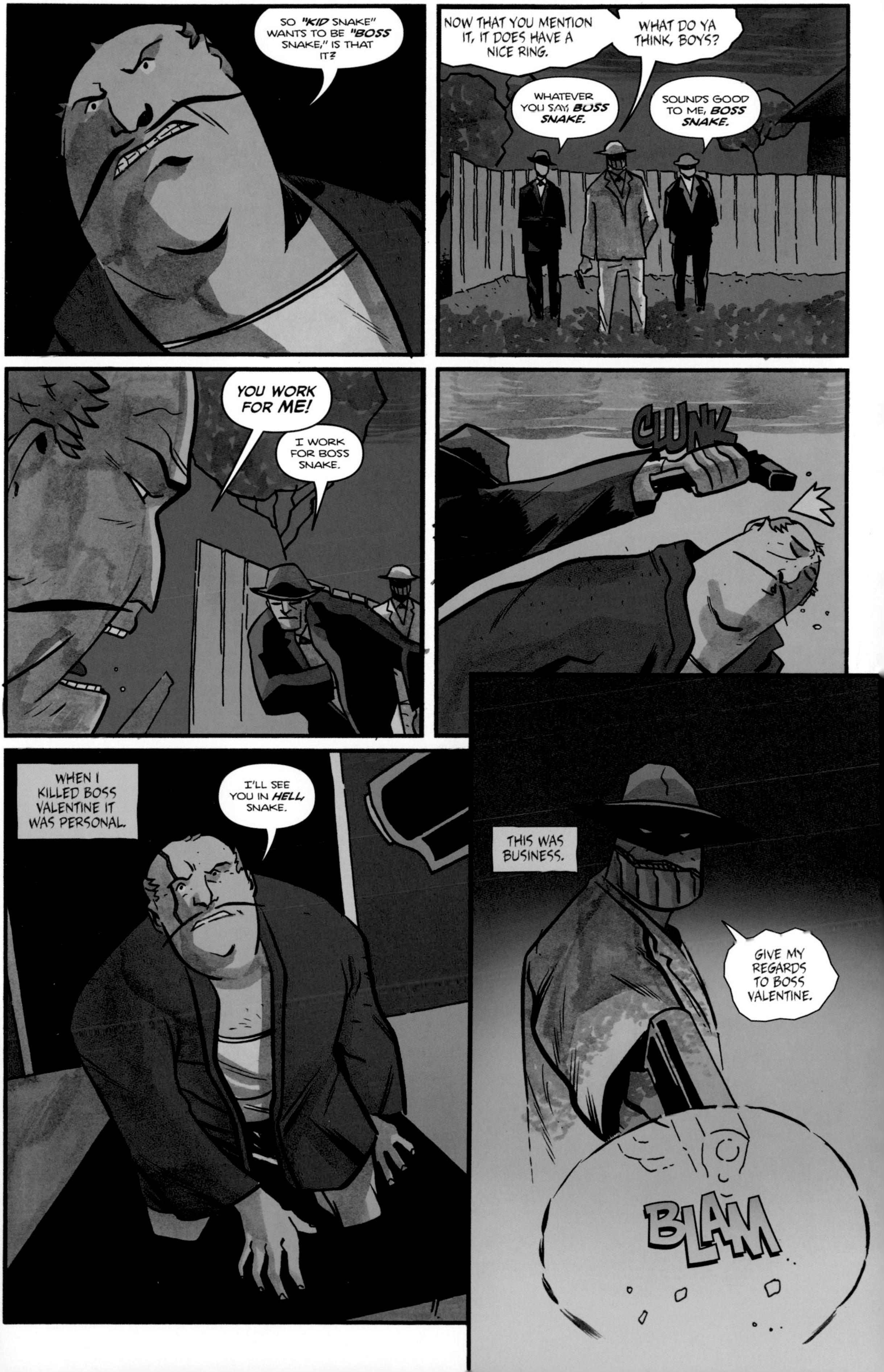
SO "KID SNAKE" WANTS TO BE "BOSS SNAKE," IS THAT IT?
NOW THAT YOU MENTION IT, IT DOES HAVE A NICE RING.
WHAT DO YA THINK, BOYS?
WHATEVER YOU SAY, BOSS SNAKE.
SOUNDS GOOD TO ME, BOSS SNAKE.
YOU WORK FOR ME!
I WORK FOR BOSS SNAKE.
CLUNK
WHEN I KILLED BOSS VALENTINE IT WAS PERSONAL.
I'LL SEE YOU IN HELL, SNAKE.
THIS WAS BUSINESS.
GIVE MY REGARDS TO BOSS VALENTINE.
BLAM

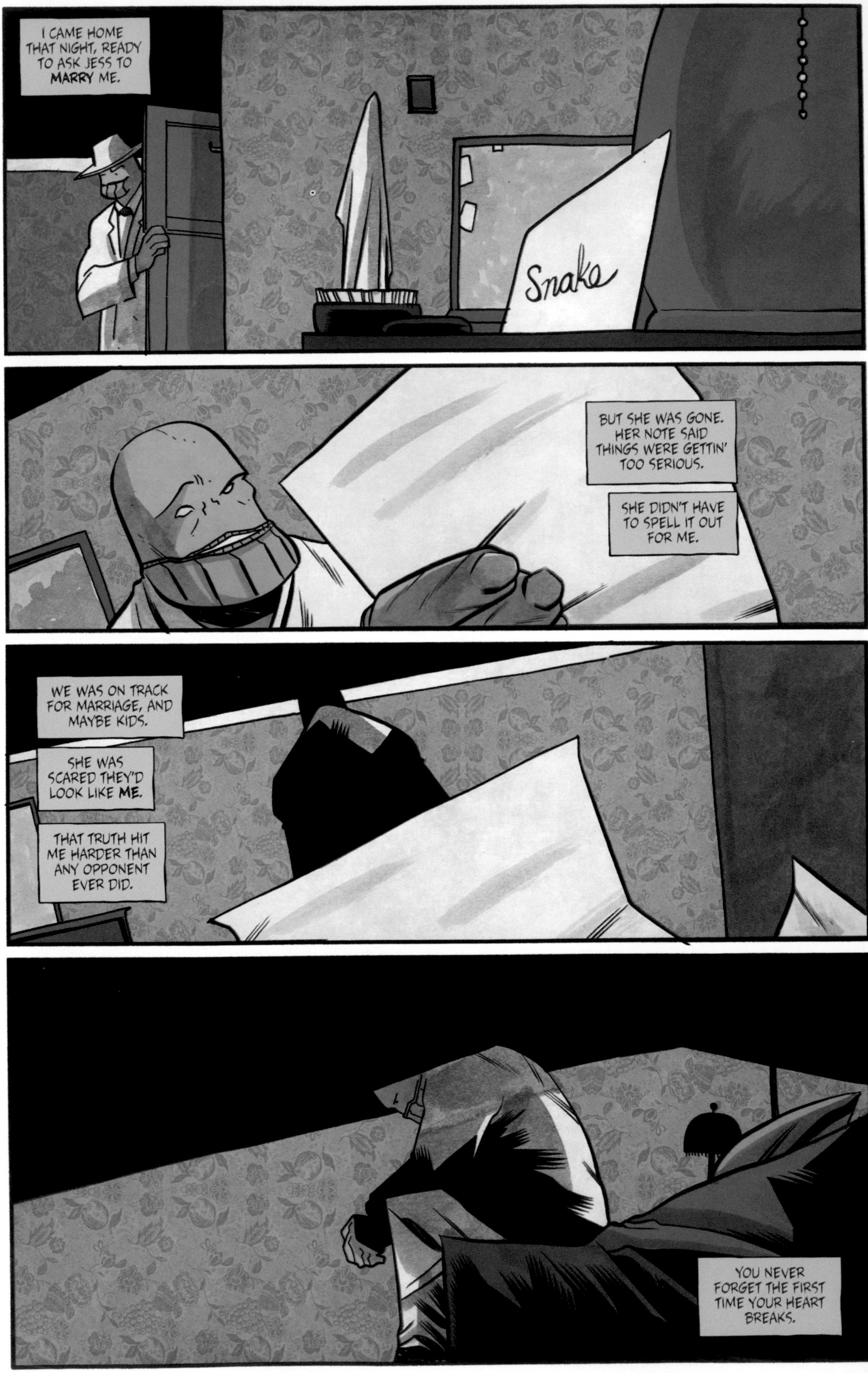
I CAME HOME THAT NIGHT, READY TO ASK JESS TO MARRY ME.
Snake
BUT SHE WAS GONE. HER NOTE SAID THINGS WERE GETTIN' TOO SERIOUS.
SHE DIDN'T HAVE TO SPELL IT OUT FOR ME.
WE WAS ON TRACK FOR MARRIAGE, AND MAYBE KIDS.
SHE WAS SCARED THEY'D LOOK LIKE ME.
THAT TRUTH HIT ME HARDER THAN ANY OPPONENT EVER DID.
YOU NEVER FORGET THE FIRST TIME YOUR HEART BREAKS.

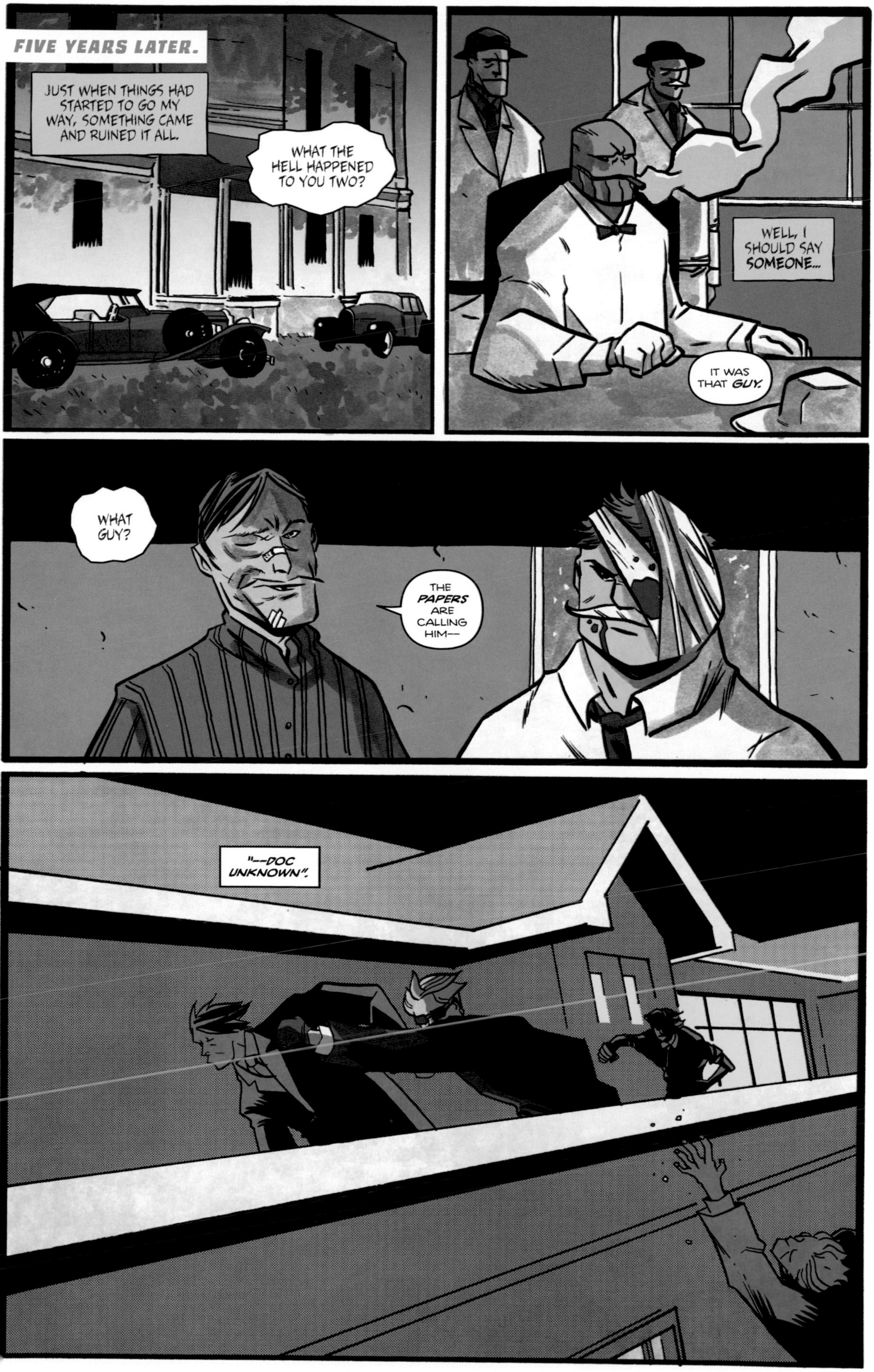
FIVE YEARS LATER.
JUST WHEN THINGS HAD STARTED TO GO MY WAY, SOMETHING CAME AND RUINED IT ALL.
WHAT THE HELL HAPPENED TO YOU TWO?
WELL, I SHOULD SAY SOMEONE...
IT WAS THAT GUY.
WHAT GUY?
THE PAPERS ARE CALLING HIM--
"--DOC UNKNOWN".

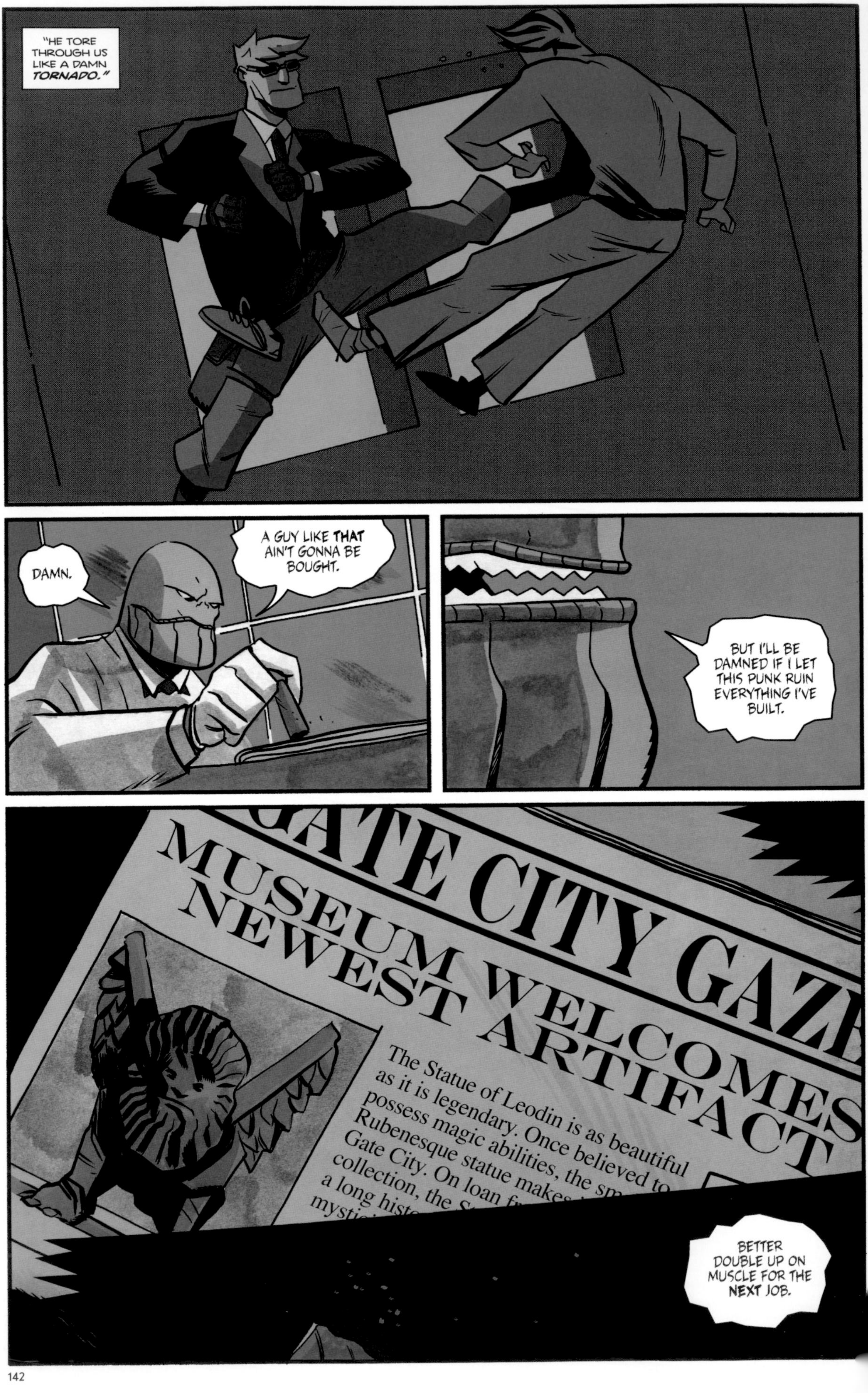
"HE TORE THROUGH US LIKE A DAMN *TORNADO.*"
DAMN.
A GUY LIKE **THAT** AIN'T GONNA BE BOUGHT.
BUT I'LL BE DAMNED IF I LET THIS PUNK RUIN EVERYTHING I'VE BUILT.
GATE CITY GAZE
MUSEUM WELCOMES NEWEST ARTIFACT
The Statue of Leodin is as beautiful as it is legendary. Once believed to possess magic abilities, the sm
Rubenesque statue makes
Gate City. On loan f
collection, the S
a long hist
mystic
BETTER DOUBLE UP ON MUSCLE FOR THE **NEXT** JOB.

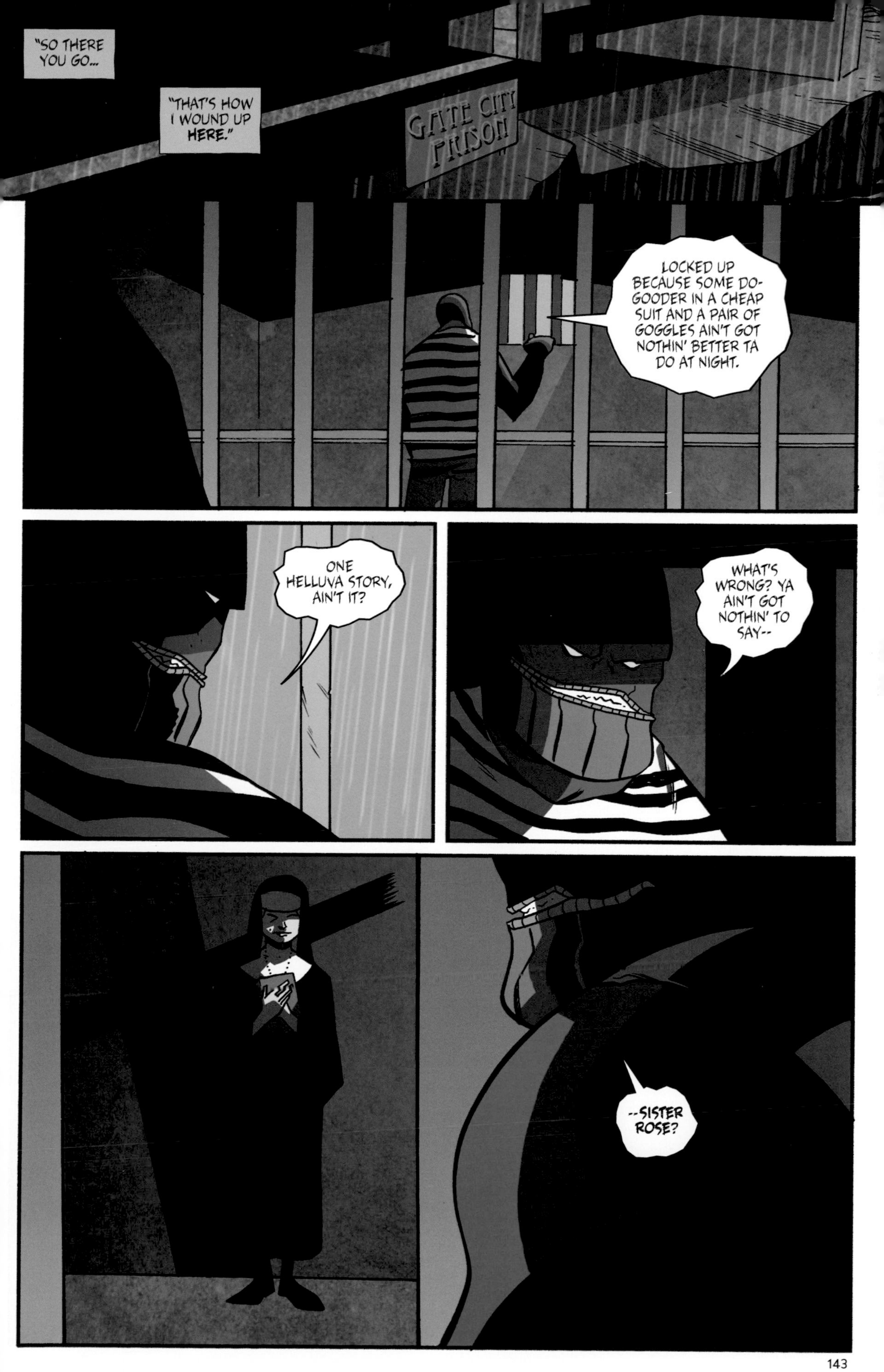
"SO THERE YOU GO...
"THAT'S HOW I WOUND UP HERE."
GATE CITY PRISON
LOCKED UP BECAUSE SOME DO-GOODER IN A CHEAP SUIT AND A PAIR OF GOGGLES AIN'T GOT NOTHIN' BETTER TA DO AT NIGHT.
ONE HELLUVA STORY, AIN'T IT?
WHAT'S WRONG? YA AIN'T GOT NOTHIN' TO SAY--
--SISTER ROSE?

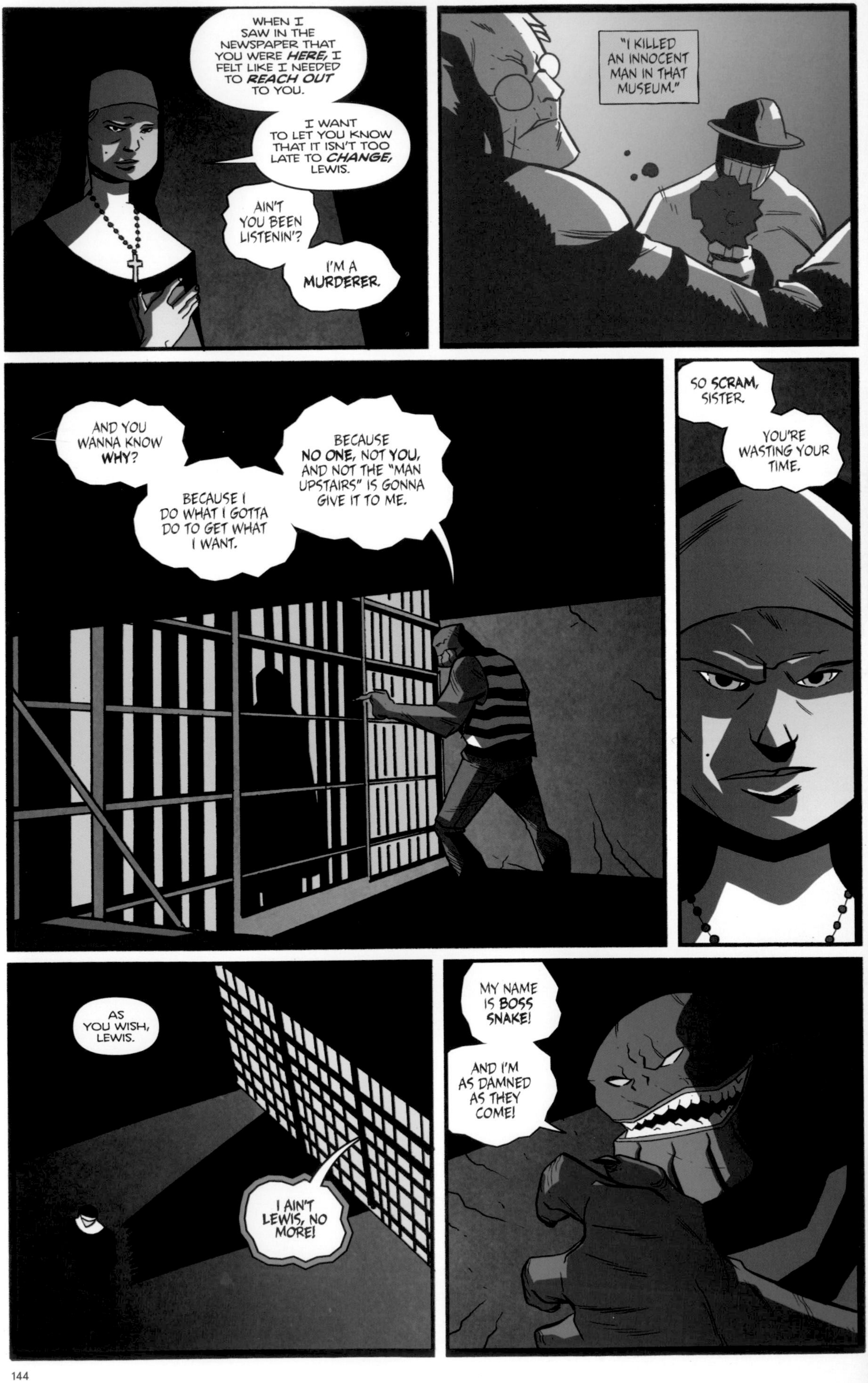
WHEN I SAW IN THE NEWSPAPER THAT YOU WERE *HERE,* I FELT LIKE I NEEDED TO *REACH OUT* TO YOU.
I WANT TO LET YOU KNOW THAT IT ISN'T TOO LATE TO *CHANGE,* LEWIS.
AIN'T YOU BEEN LISTENIN'?
I'M A **MURDERER.**
"I KILLED AN INNOCENT MAN IN THAT MUSEUM."
AND YOU WANNA KNOW **WHY**?
BECAUSE I DO WHAT I GOTTA DO TO GET WHAT I WANT.
BECAUSE **NO ONE**, NOT **YOU**, AND NOT THE "MAN UPSTAIRS" IS GONNA GIVE IT TO ME.
SO **SCRAM**, SISTER.
YOU'RE WASTING YOUR TIME.
AS YOU WISH, LEWIS.
I AIN'T LEWIS, NO MORE!
MY NAME IS **BOSS SNAKE!**
AND I'M AS DAMNED AS THEY COME!

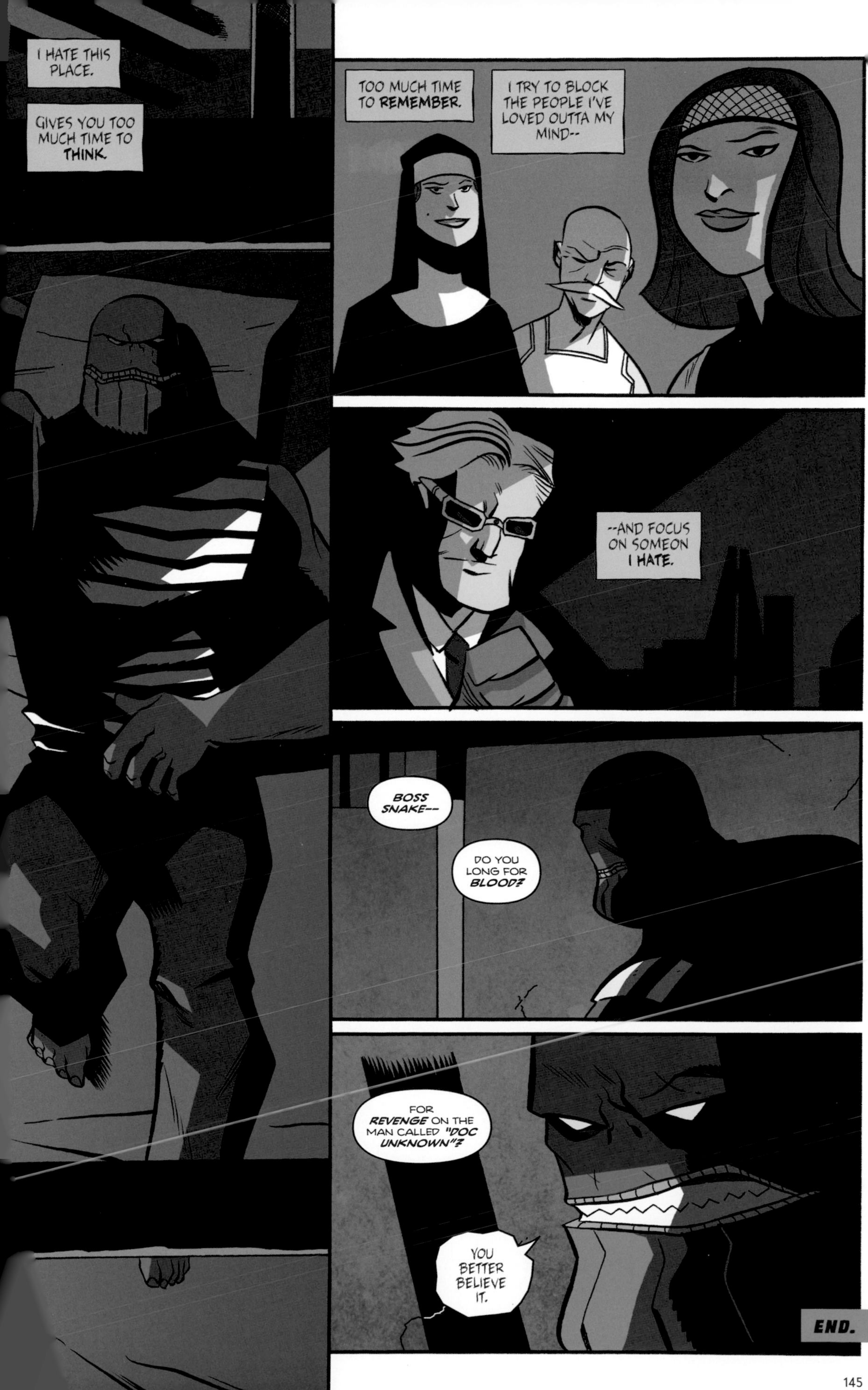
I HATE THIS PLACE.
GIVES YOU TOO MUCH TIME TO THINK.
TOO MUCH TIME TO REMEMBER.
I TRY TO BLOCK THE PEOPLE I'VE LOVED OUTTA MY MIND--
--AND FOCUS ON SOMEON I HATE.
BOSS SNAKE--
DO YOU LONG FOR BLOOD?
FOR REVENGE ON THE MAN CALLED "DOC UNKNOWN"?
YOU BETTER BELIEVE IT.
END.

WINTER OF THE DAMNED

SCRIPT BY **FABIAN RANGEL JR.**

ART BY **RYAN CODY**

LETTERS BY **FRANK BARBIERE**

EDITED BY **MIKE EXNER**

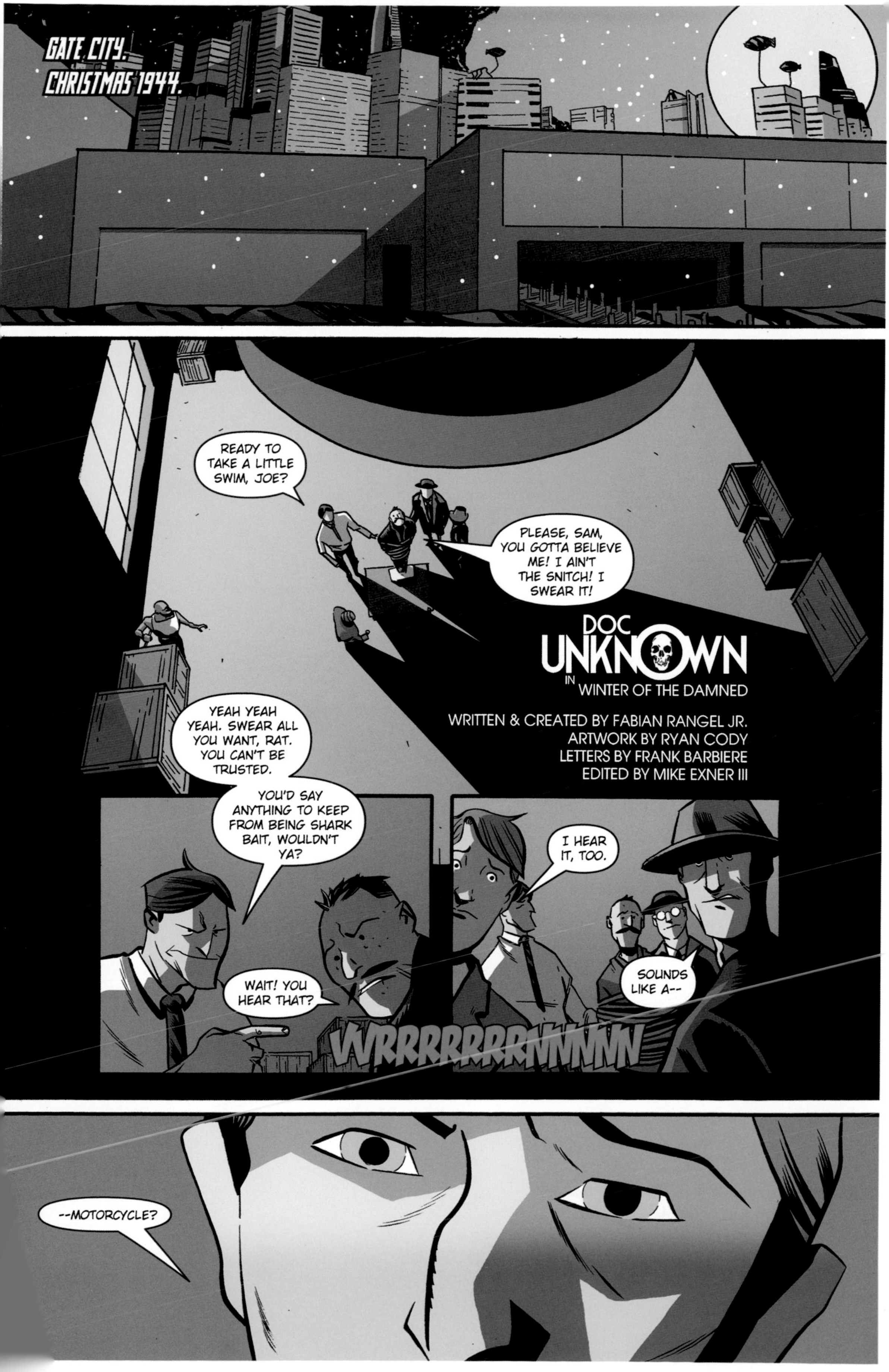
GATE CITY.
CHRISTMAS 1944.
READY TO TAKE A LITTLE SWIM, JOE?
PLEASE, SAM, YOU GOTTA BELIEVE ME! I AIN'T THE SNITCH! I SWEAR IT!
DOC UNKNOWN
IN WINTER OF THE DAMNED
WRITTEN & CREATED BY FABIAN RANGEL JR.
ARTWORK BY RYAN CODY
LETTERS BY FRANK BARBIERE
EDITED BY MIKE EXNER III
YEAH YEAH YEAH. SWEAR ALL YOU WANT, RAT. YOU CAN'T BE TRUSTED.
YOU'D SAY ANYTHING TO KEEP FROM BEING SHARK BAIT, WOULDN'T YA?
WAIT! YOU HEAR THAT?
I HEAR IT, TOO.
SOUNDS LIKE A--
VVRRRRRRRRNNNNNN
--MOTORCYCLE?

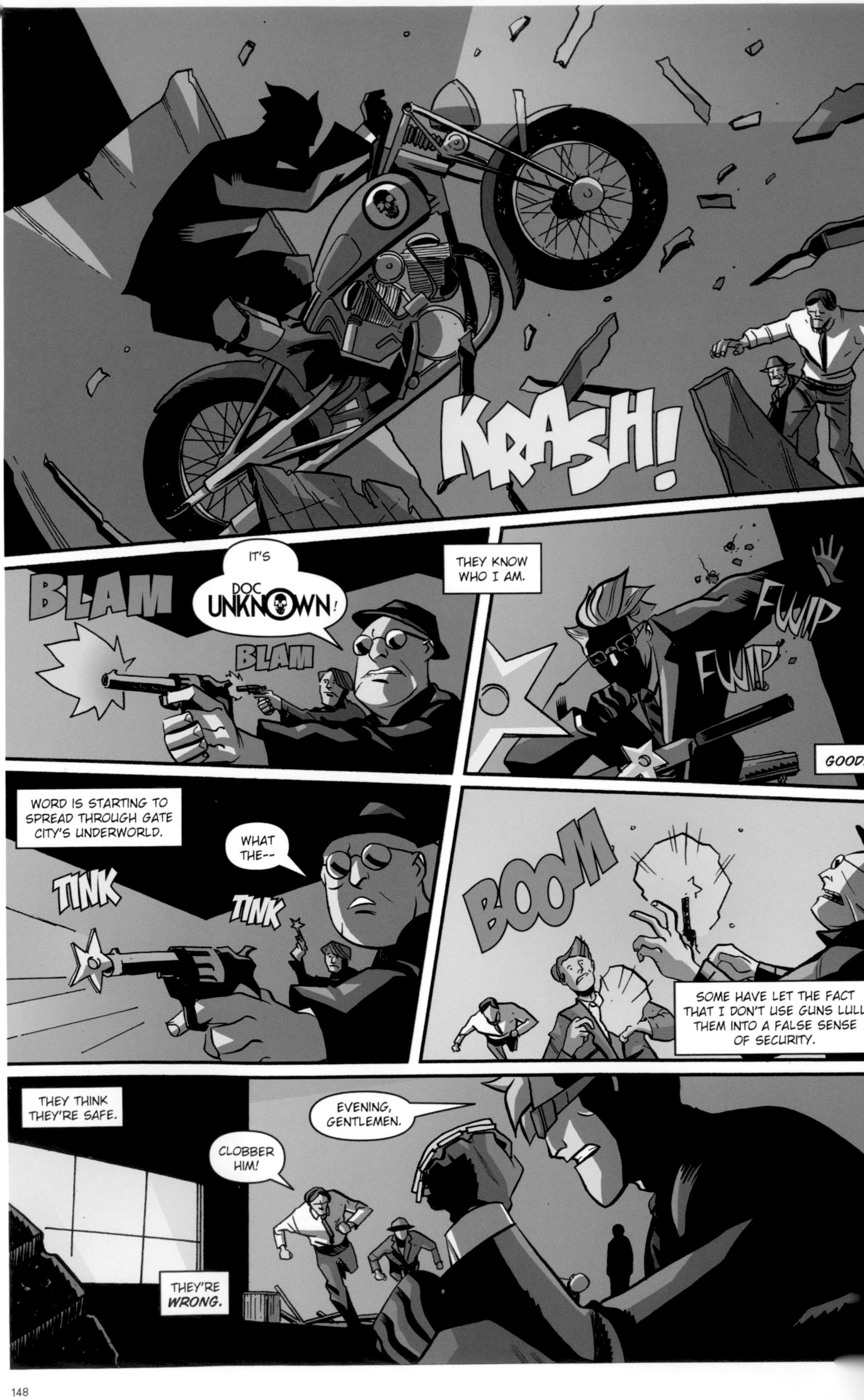
KRASH!
BLAM
IT'S DOC UNKNOWN!
BLAM
THEY KNOW WHO I AM.
FWIP
FWIP
GOOD.
WORD IS STARTING TO SPREAD THROUGH GATE CITY'S UNDERWORLD.
WHAT THE--
TINK
TINK
BOOM
SOME HAVE LET THE FACT THAT I DON'T USE GUNS LULL THEM INTO A FALSE SENSE OF SECURITY.
THEY THINK THEY'RE SAFE.
EVENING, GENTLEMEN.
CLOBBER HIM!
THEY'RE *WRONG.*

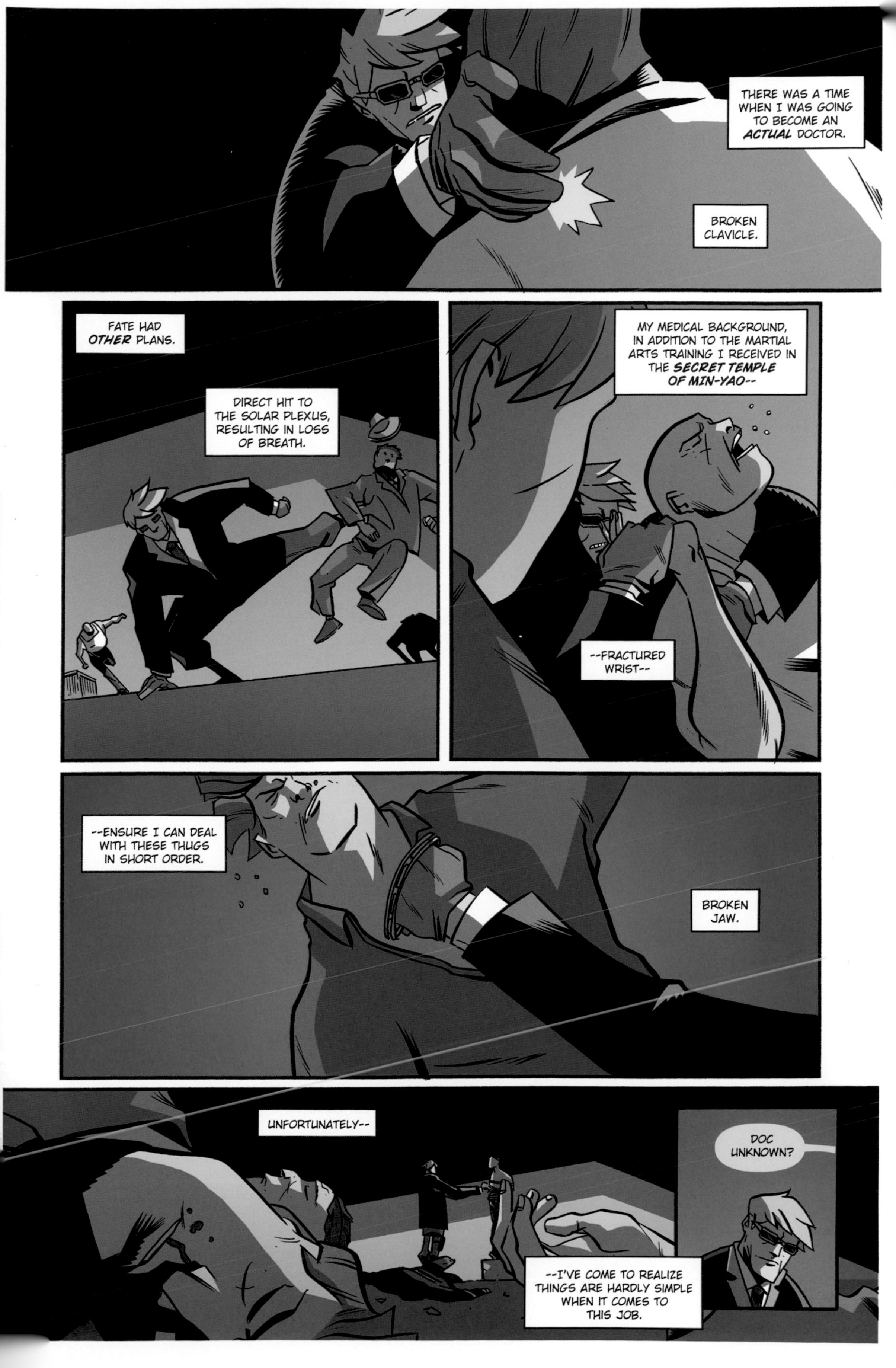
THERE WAS A TIME WHEN I WAS GOING TO BECOME AN ACTUAL DOCTOR.
BROKEN CLAVICLE.
FATE HAD OTHER PLANS.
DIRECT HIT TO THE SOLAR PLEXUS, RESULTING IN LOSS OF BREATH.
MY MEDICAL BACKGROUND, IN ADDITION TO THE MARTIAL ARTS TRAINING I RECEIVED IN THE SECRET TEMPLE OF MIN-YAO--
--FRACTURED WRIST--
--ENSURE I CAN DEAL WITH THESE THUGS IN SHORT ORDER.
BROKEN JAW.
UNFORTUNATELY--
DOC UNKNOWN?
--I'VE COME TO REALIZE THINGS ARE HARDLY SIMPLE WHEN IT COMES TO THIS JOB.

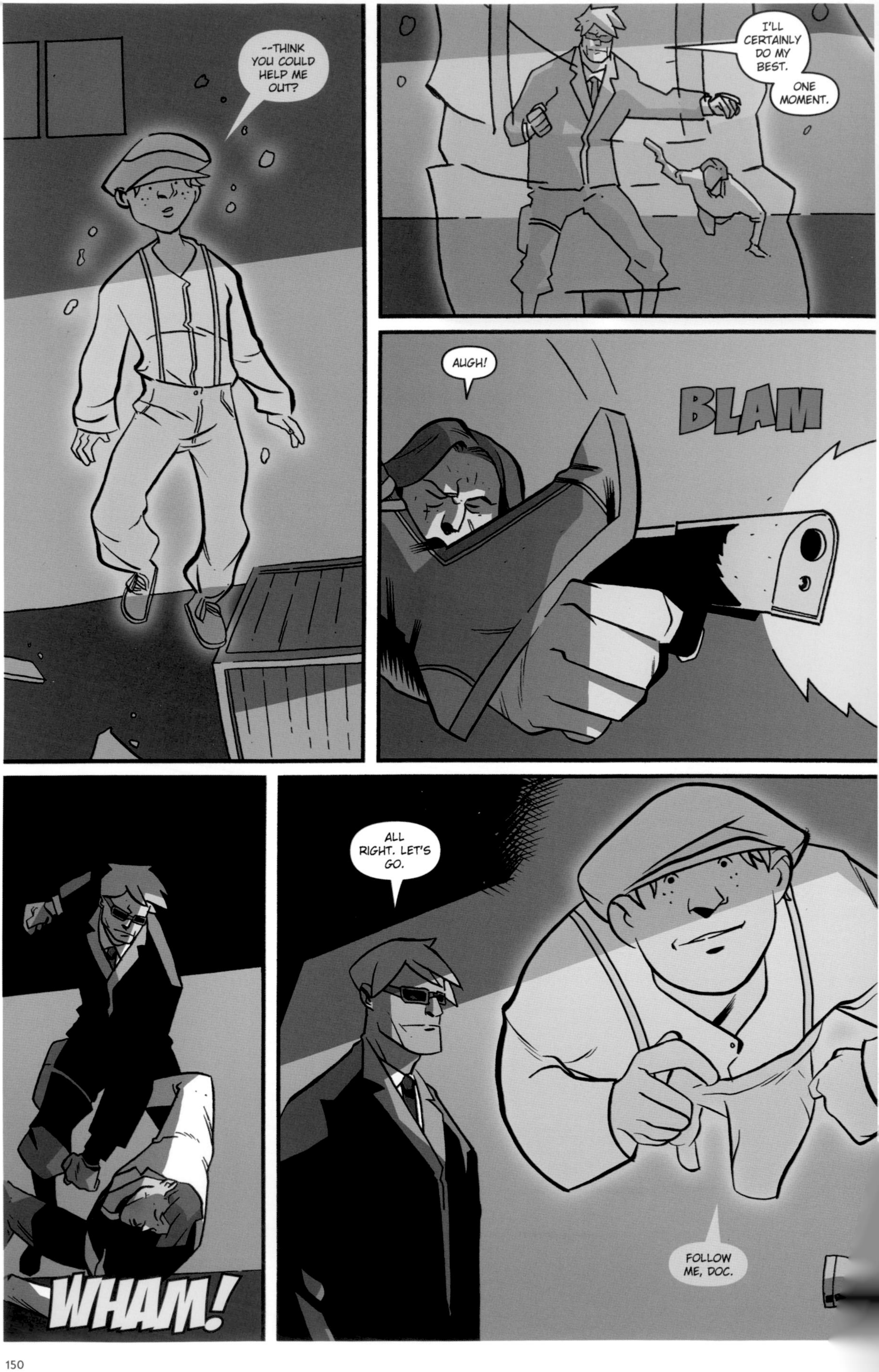
--THINK YOU COULD HELP ME OUT?
I'LL CERTAINLY DO MY BEST.
ONE MOMENT.
AUGH!
BLAM
WHAM!
ALL RIGHT. LET'S GO.
FOLLOW ME, DOC.

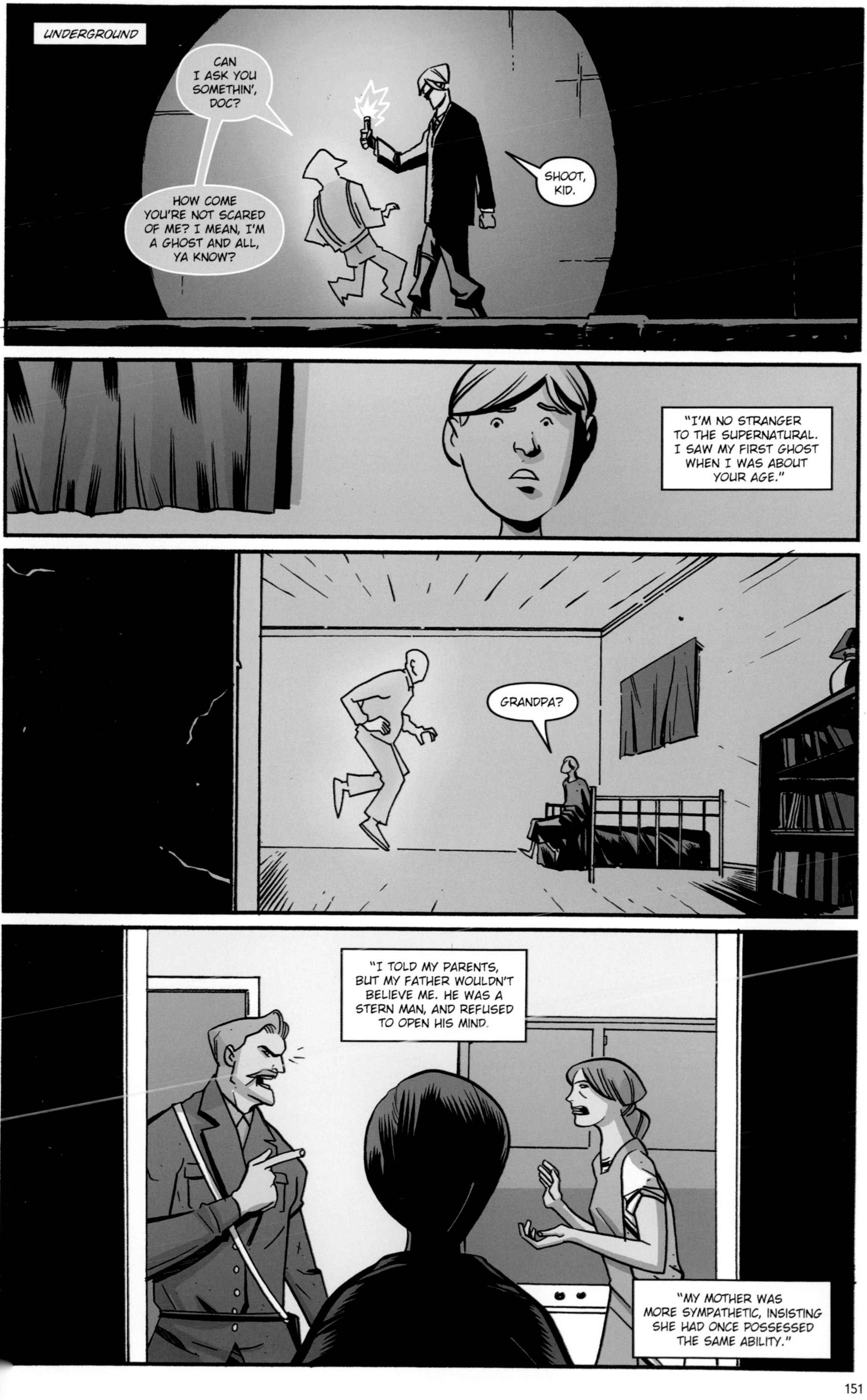
UNDERGROUND
CAN I ASK YOU SOMETHIN', DOC?
HOW COME YOU'RE NOT SCARED OF ME? I MEAN, I'M A GHOST AND ALL, YA KNOW?
SHOOT, KID.
"I'M NO STRANGER TO THE SUPERNATURAL. I SAW MY FIRST GHOST WHEN I WAS ABOUT YOUR AGE."
GRANDPA?
"I TOLD MY PARENTS, BUT MY FATHER WOULDN'T BELIEVE ME. HE WAS A STERN MAN, AND REFUSED TO OPEN HIS MIND.
"MY MOTHER WAS MORE SYMPATHETIC, INSISTING SHE HAD ONCE POSSESSED THE SAME ABILITY."

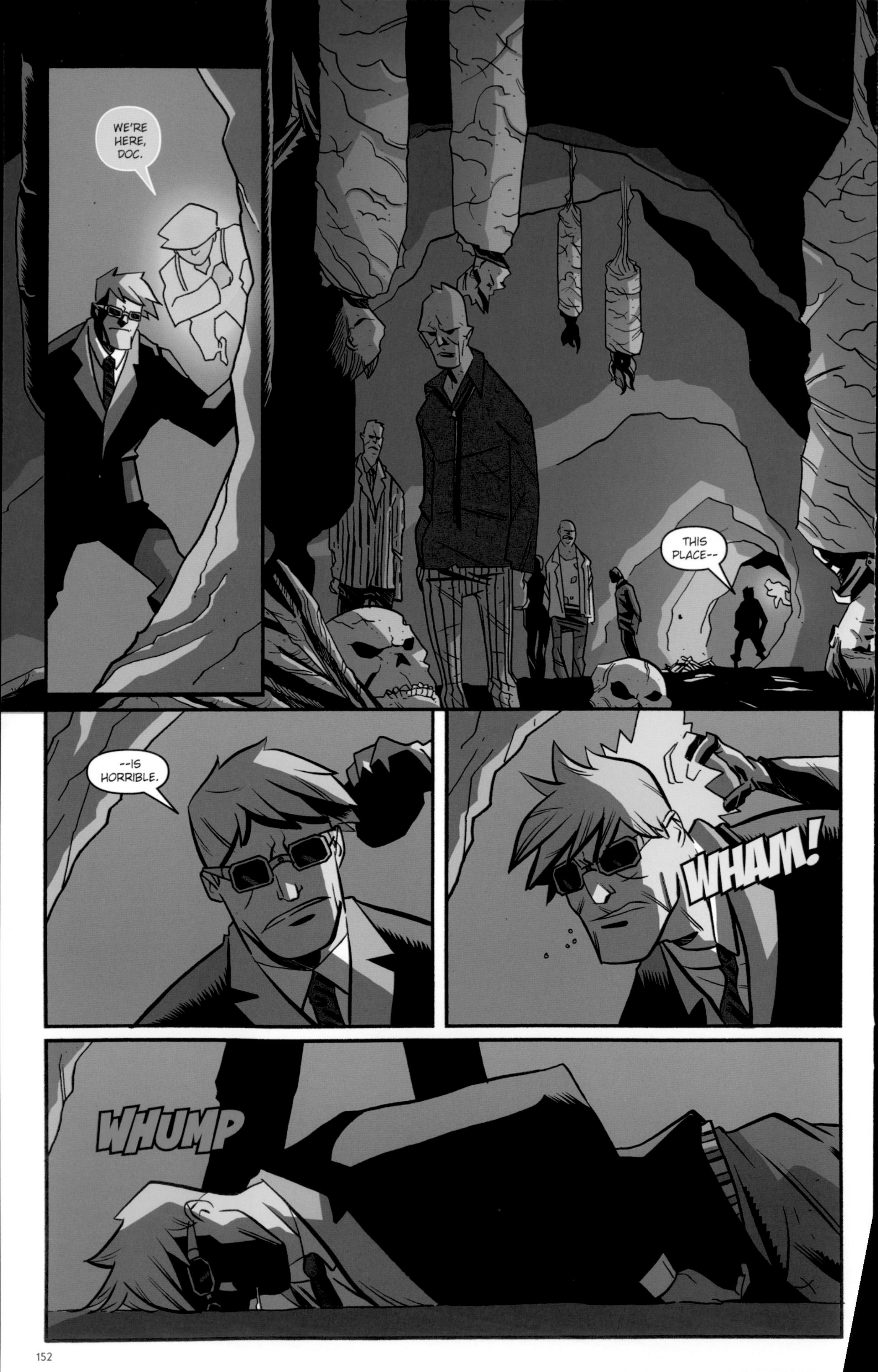
WE'RE HERE, DOC.
THIS PLACE--
--IS HORRIBLE.
WHAM!
WHUMP

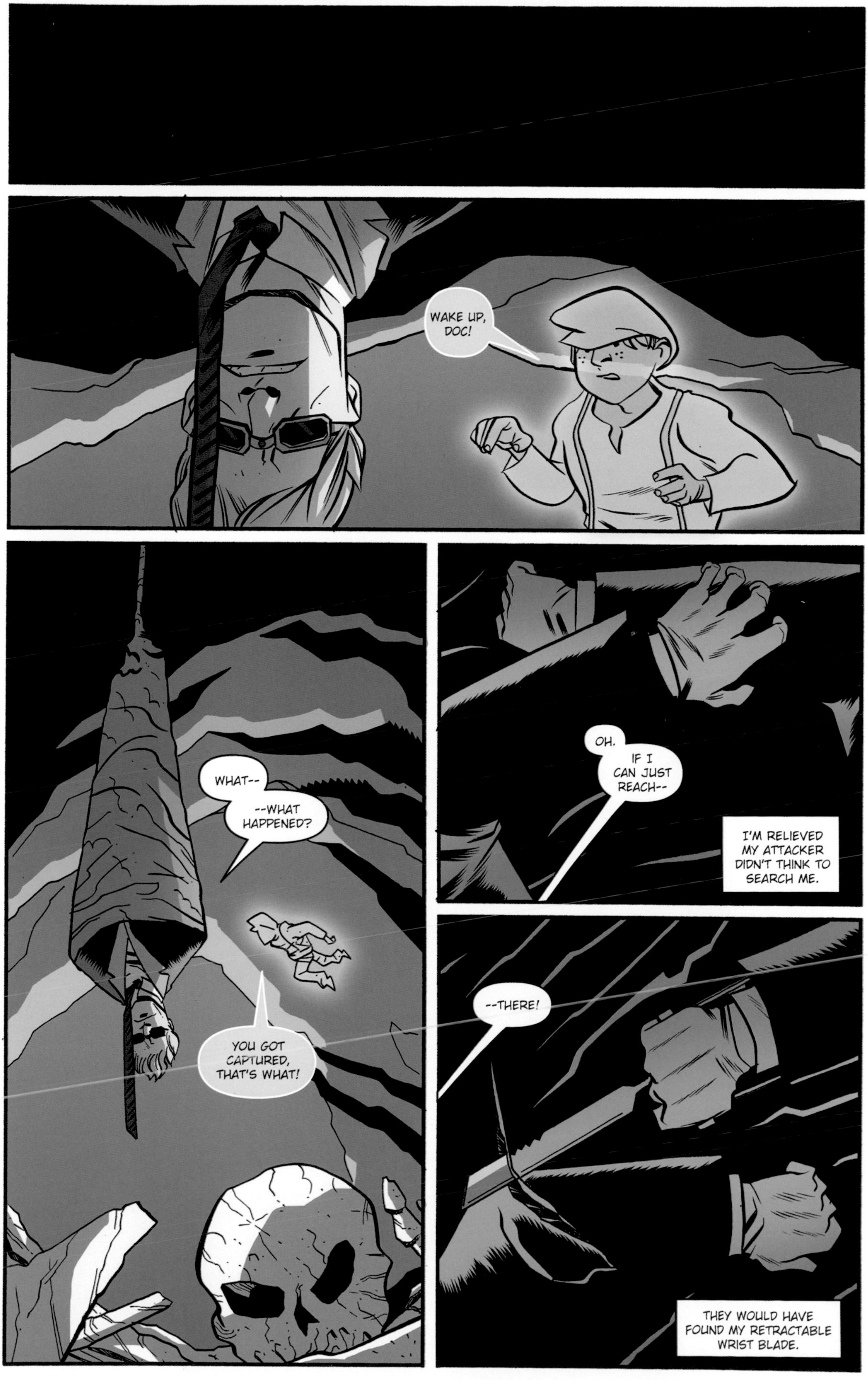
WAKE UP, DOC!
WHAT--
--WHAT HAPPENED?
YOU GOT CAPTURED, THAT'S WHAT!
OH.
IF I CAN JUST REACH--
I'M RELIEVED MY ATTACKER DIDN'T THINK TO SEARCH ME.
--THERE!
THEY WOULD HAVE FOUND MY RETRACTABLE WRIST BLADE.

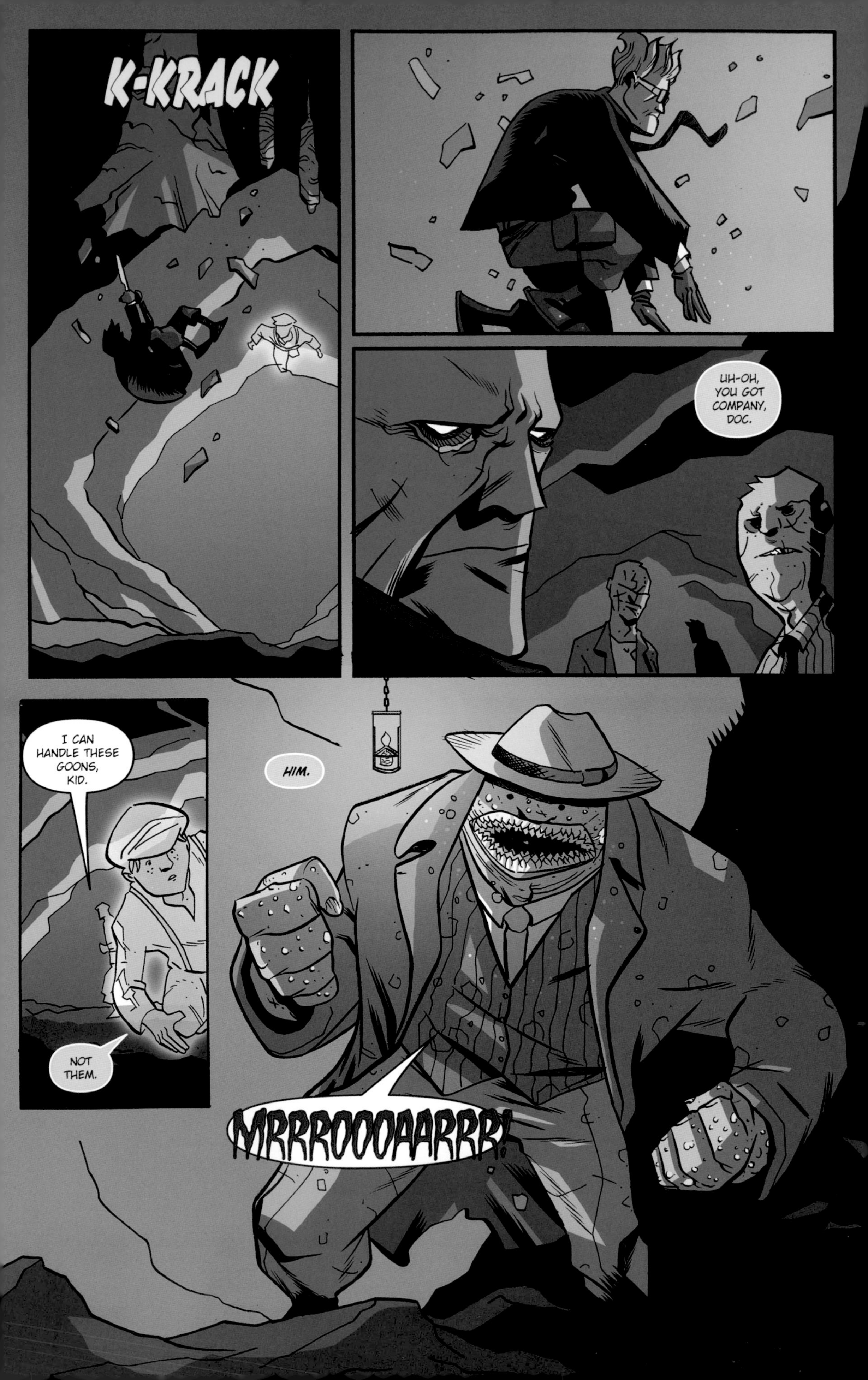

K-KRACK
UH-OH, YOU GOT COMPANY, DOC.
I CAN HANDLE THESE GOONS, KID.
NOT THEM.
HIM.
MRRROOOAARRR!

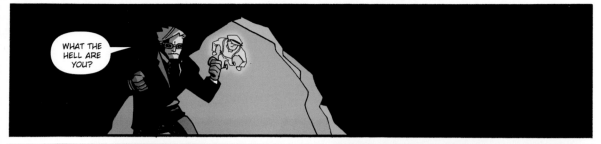

WHAT THE HELL ARE YOU?

MY NAME WAS *MAXWELL.* USED TO RUN BOOZE FOR BOSS MALONE TILL I GOT GREEDY.

"I WAS AS DOOMED AS THEY COME. I PRAYED THAT *SOMETHING* WOULD SAVE MY SORRY BUTT.

"SOMETHING HEARD ME.

"SOMETHING *STRANGE.*

"I GOT A SECOND CHANCE AT LIFE.

"WE *BOTH* DID."

SO WE'LL BE DAMNED IF SOME DO-GOODER IN A PAIR OF GOGGLES IS GONNA STOP US!

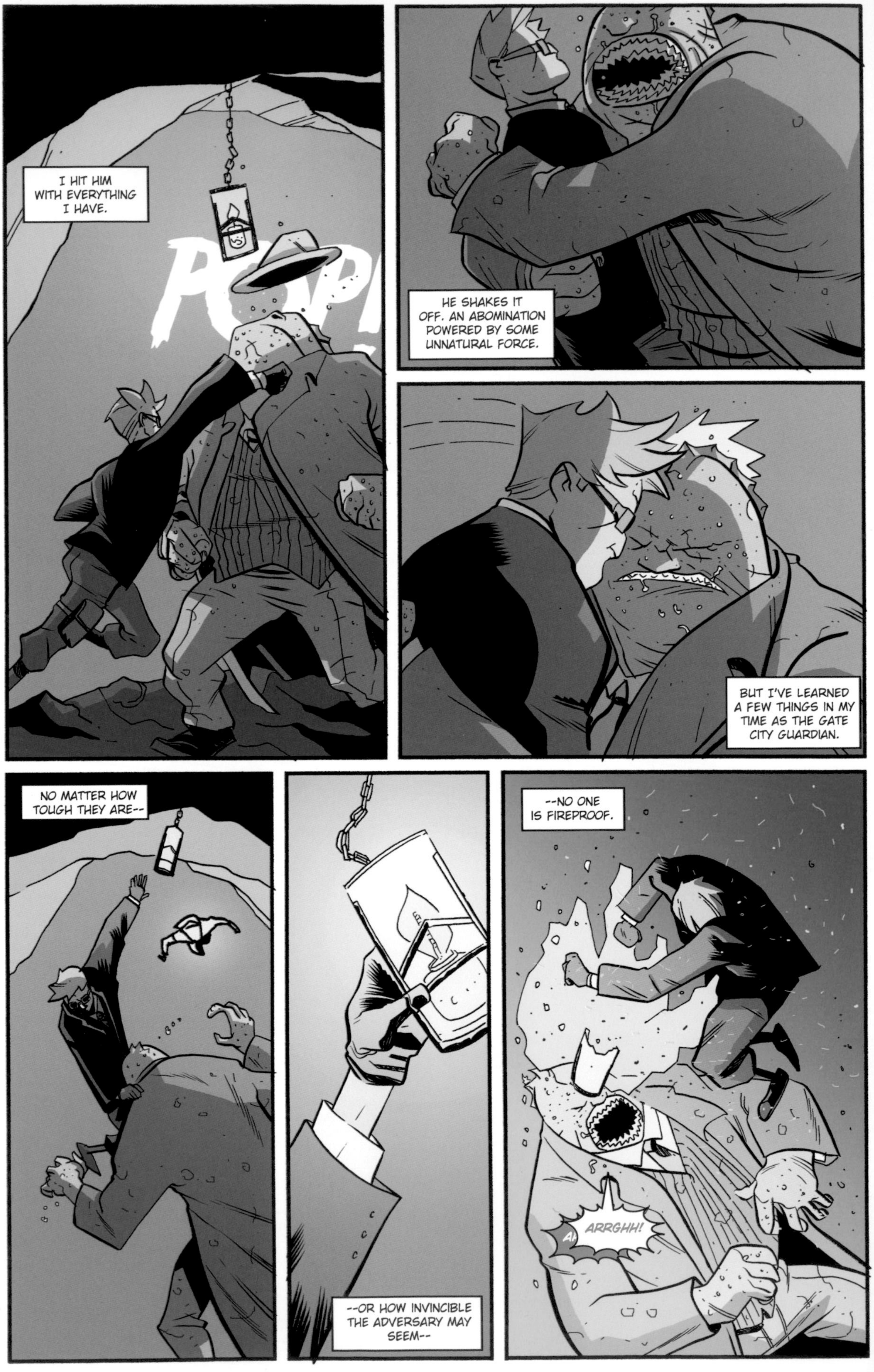
I HIT HIM WITH EVERYTHING I HAVE.
POP!
HE SHAKES IT OFF. AN ABOMINATION POWERED BY SOME UNNATURAL FORCE.
BUT I'VE LEARNED A FEW THINGS IN MY TIME AS THE GATE CITY GUARDIAN.
NO MATTER HOW TOUGH THEY ARE--
--OR HOW INVINCIBLE THE ADVERSARY MAY SEEM--
--NO ONE IS FIREPROOF.
ARRGHH!

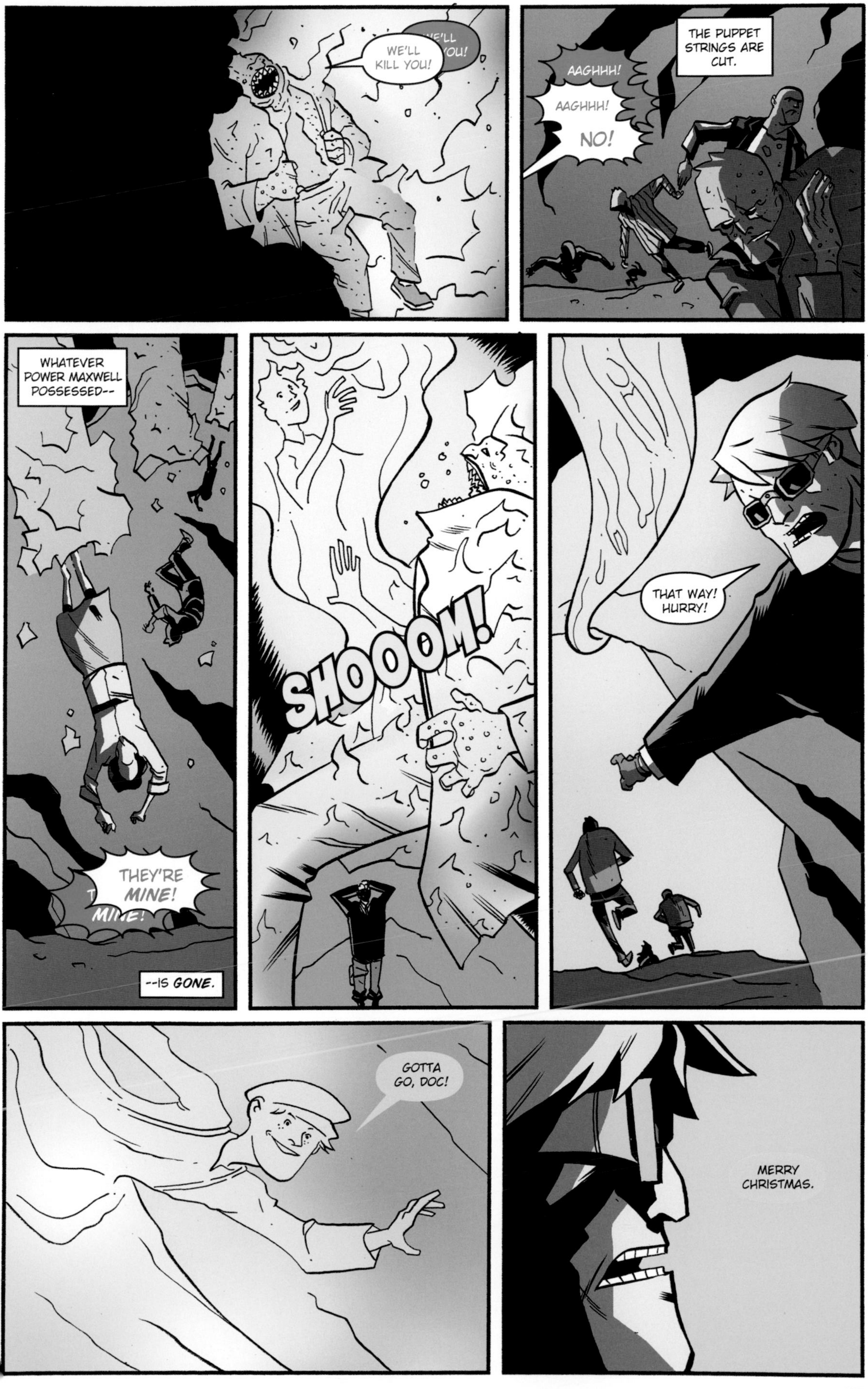
WE'LL KILL YOU!
THE PUPPET STRINGS ARE CUT.
AAGHHH!
AAGHHH!
NO!
WHATEVER POWER MAXWELL POSSESSED--
THEY'RE MINE!
--IS GONE.
SHOOOM!
THAT WAY! HURRY!
GOTTA GO, DOC!
MERRY CHRISTMAS.

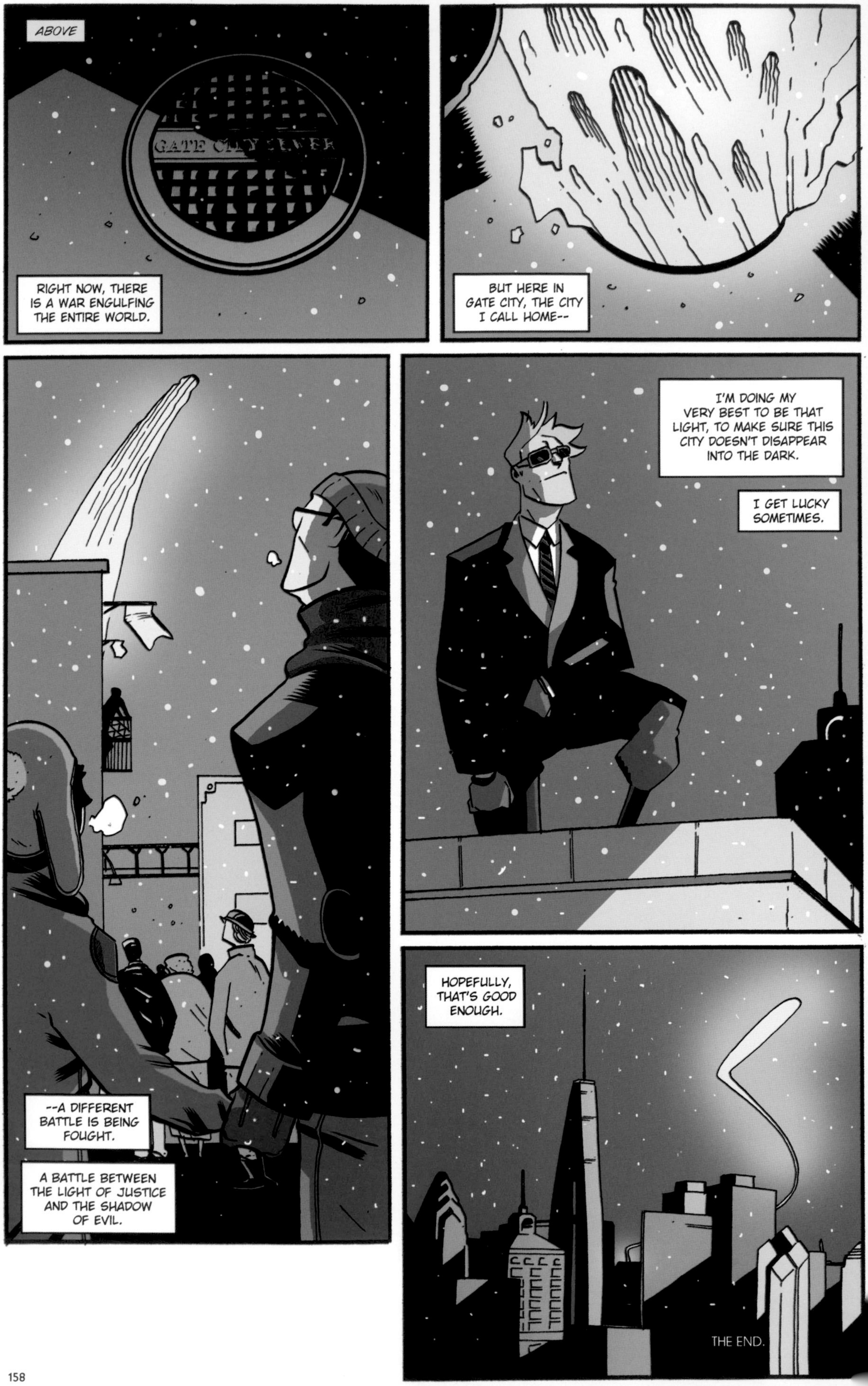
ABOVE
GATE CITY SEWER
RIGHT NOW, THERE IS A WAR ENGULFING THE ENTIRE WORLD.
BUT HERE IN GATE CITY, THE CITY I CALL HOME--
--A DIFFERENT BATTLE IS BEING FOUGHT.
A BATTLE BETWEEN THE LIGHT OF JUSTICE AND THE SHADOW OF EVIL.
I'M DOING MY VERY BEST TO BE THAT LIGHT, TO MAKE SURE THIS CITY DOESN'T DISAPPEAR INTO THE DARK.
I GET LUCKY SOMETIMES.
HOPEFULLY, THAT'S GOOD ENOUGH.
THE END.

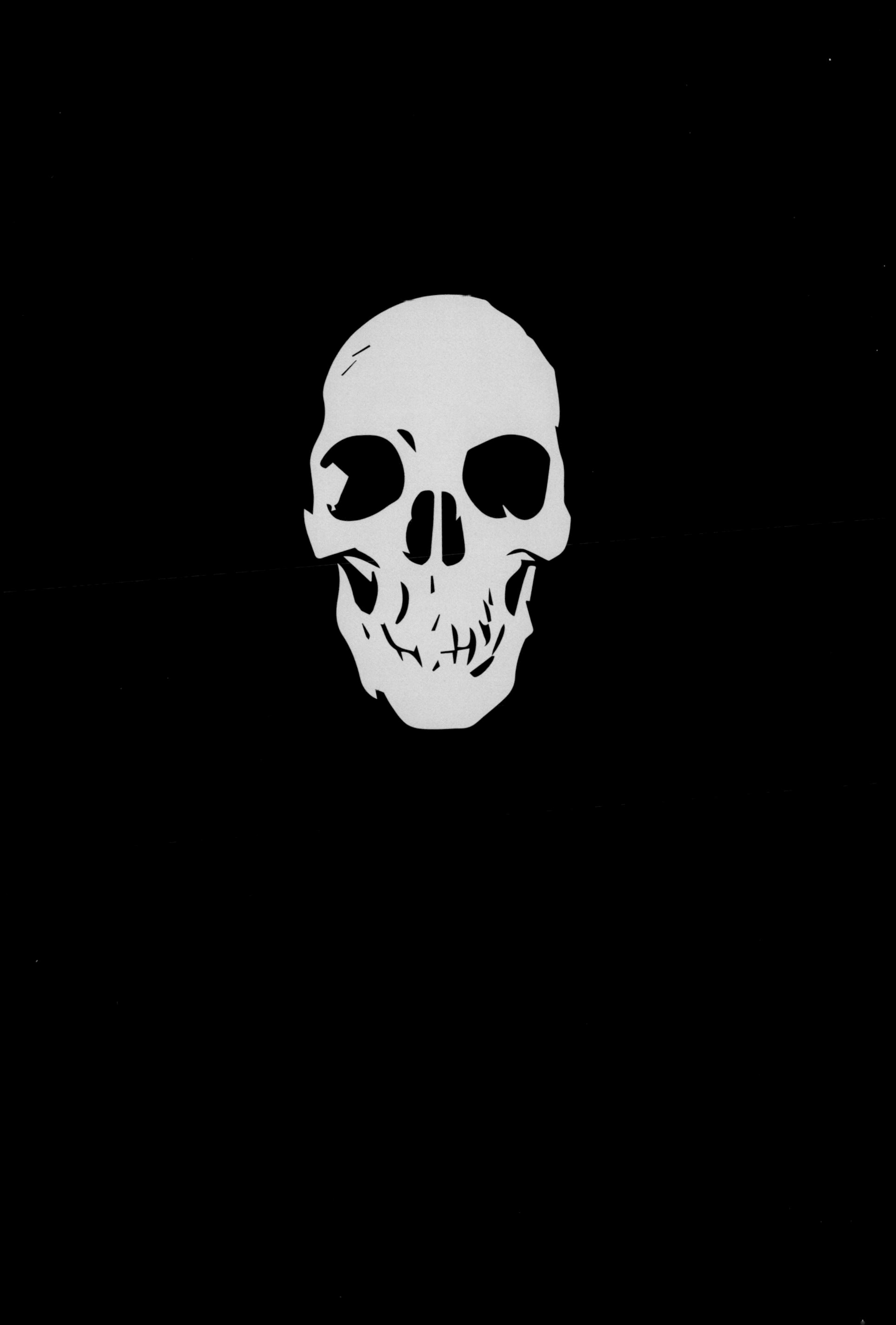

NOW I'M A SHADOW

SCRIPT BY **FABIAN RANGEL JR.**

ART BY **PHIL SLOAN**

LETTERS BY **RACHEL DEERING**

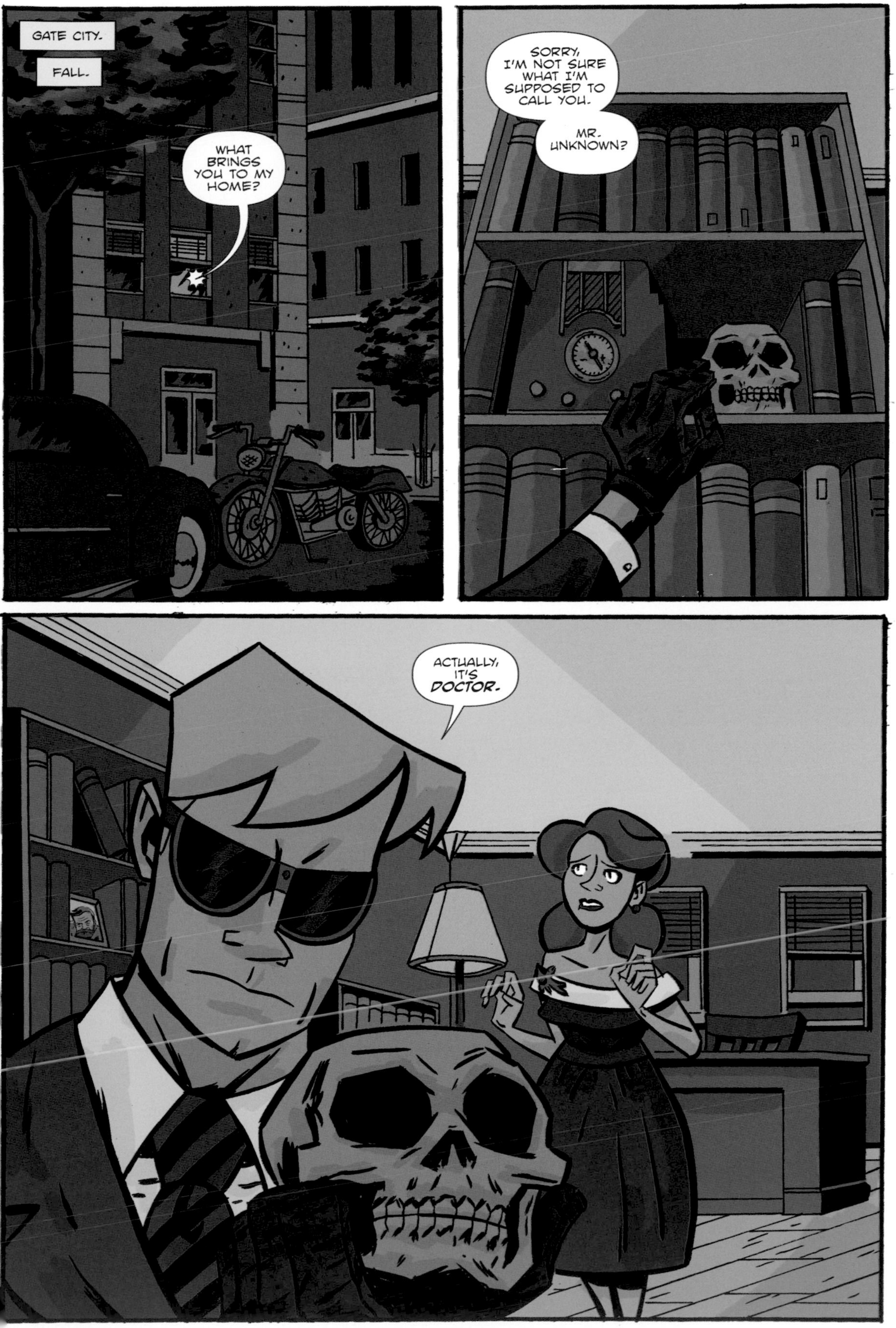
GATE CITY.
FALL.
WHAT BRINGS YOU TO MY HOME?
SORRY, I'M NOT SURE WHAT I'M SUPPOSED TO CALL YOU.
MR. UNKNOWN?
ACTUALLY, IT'S DOCTOR.

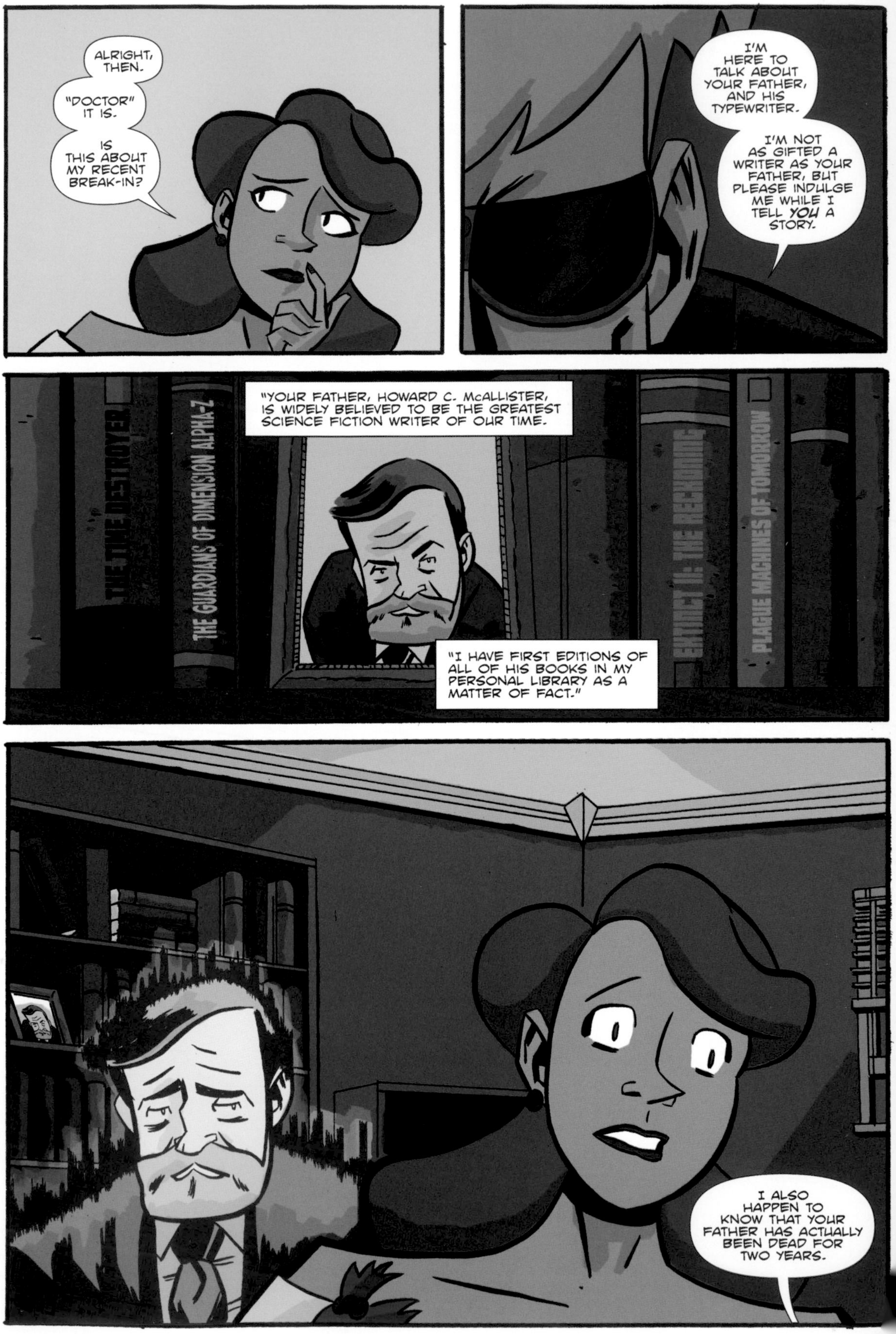

ALRIGHT, THEN.
"DOCTOR" IT IS.
IS THIS ABOUT MY RECENT BREAK-IN?
I'M HERE TO TALK ABOUT YOUR FATHER, AND HIS TYPEWRITER.
I'M NOT AS GIFTED A WRITER AS YOUR FATHER, BUT PLEASE INDULGE ME WHILE I TELL YOU A STORY.
"YOUR FATHER, HOWARD C. McALLISTER, IS WIDELY BELIEVED TO BE THE GREATEST SCIENCE FICTION WRITER OF OUR TIME.
THE TIME DESTROYER
THE GUARDIANS OF DIMENSION ALPHA-Z
EXTINCT II: THE RECKONING
PLAGUE MACHINES OF TOMORROW
"I HAVE FIRST EDITIONS OF ALL OF HIS BOOKS IN MY PERSONAL LIBRARY AS A MATTER OF FACT."
I ALSO HAPPEN TO KNOW THAT YOUR FATHER HAS ACTUALLY BEEN DEAD FOR TWO YEARS.

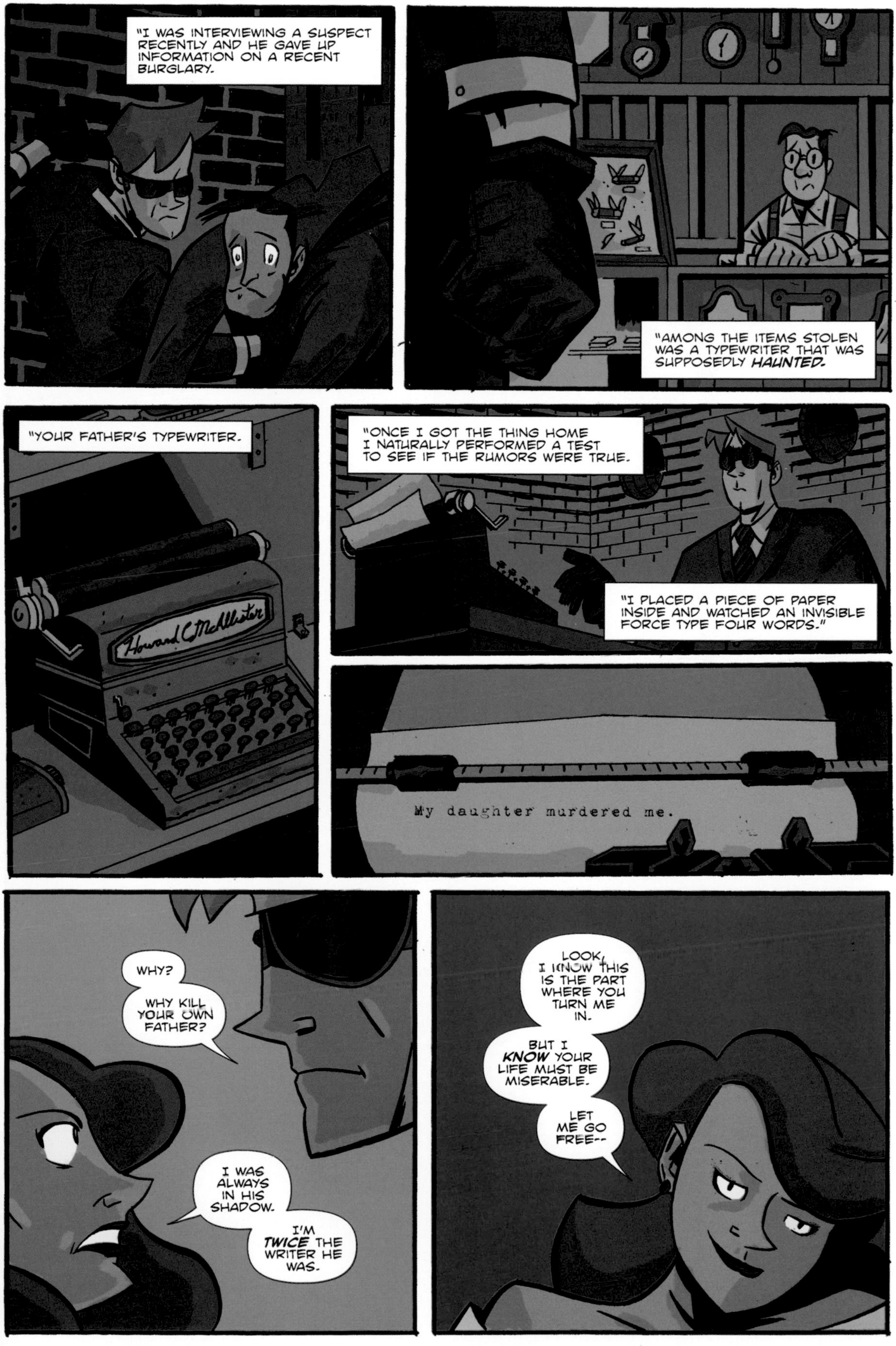
"I WAS INTERVIEWING A SUSPECT RECENTLY AND HE GAVE UP INFORMATION ON A RECENT BURGLARY.
"AMONG THE ITEMS STOLEN WAS A TYPEWRITER THAT WAS SUPPOSEDLY **HAUNTED**.
"YOUR FATHER'S TYPEWRITER.
Howard C. McAllister
"ONCE I GOT THE THING HOME I NATURALLY PERFORMED A TEST TO SEE IF THE RUMORS WERE TRUE.
"I PLACED A PIECE OF PAPER INSIDE AND WATCHED AN INVISIBLE FORCE TYPE FOUR WORDS."
My daughter murdered me.
WHY?
WHY KILL YOUR OWN FATHER?
I WAS ALWAYS IN HIS SHADOW.
I'M **TWICE** THE WRITER HE WAS.
LOOK, I KNOW THIS IS THE PART WHERE YOU TURN ME IN.
BUT I **KNOW** YOUR LIFE MUST BE MISERABLE.
LET ME GO FREE--

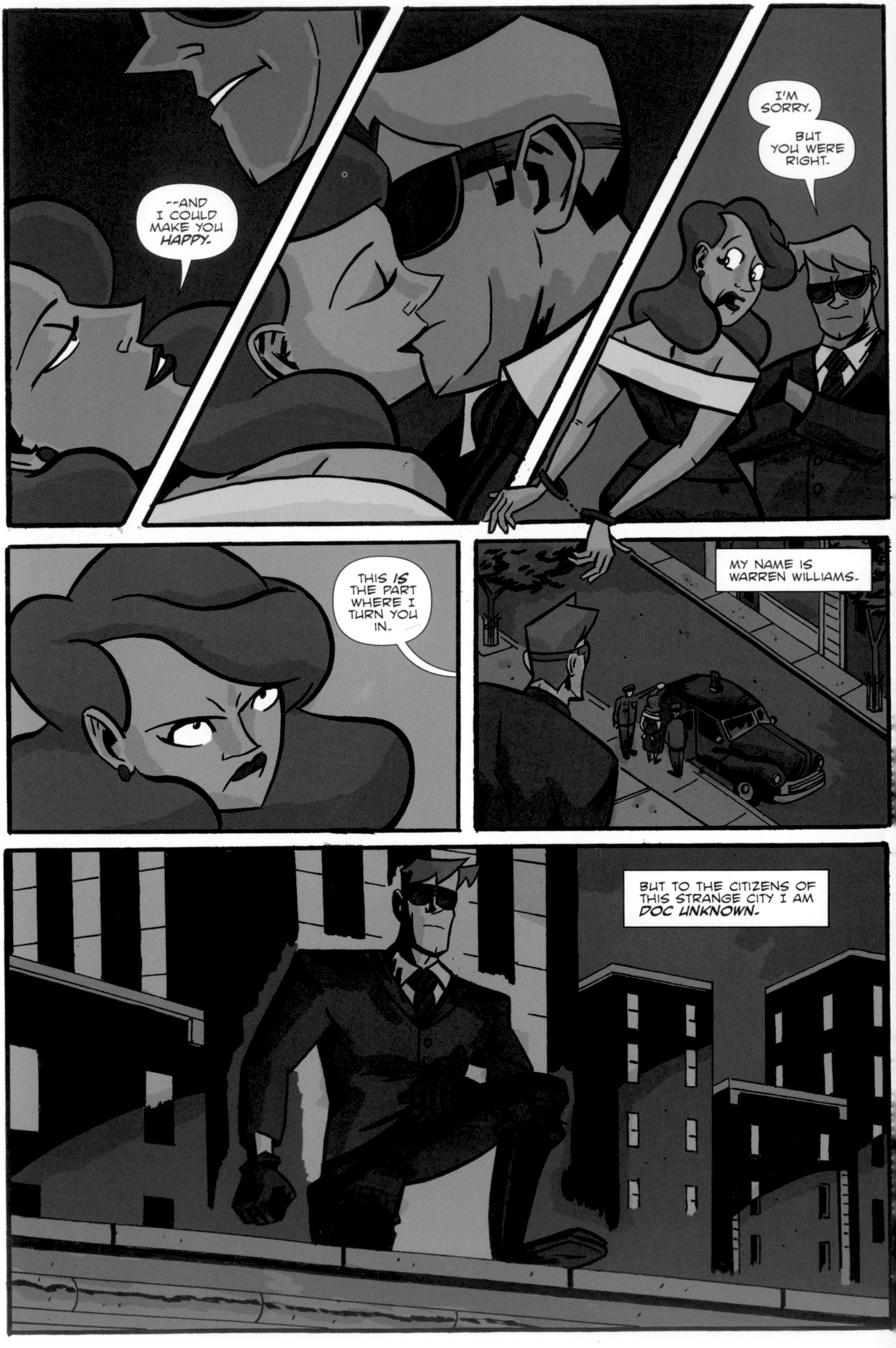
--AND I COULD MAKE YOU HAPPY.
I'M SORRY.
BUT YOU WERE RIGHT.
THIS IS THE PART WHERE I TURN YOU IN.
MY NAME IS WARREN WILLIAMS.
BUT TO THE CITIZENS OF THIS STRANGE CITY I AM DOC UNKNOWN.

I HAVE SEEN EXTRAORDINARY THINGS IN MY LIFETIME.

I HAVE SEEN THINGS TO DRIVE ALL COURAGE FROM MY BONES.

BUT AT THE END OF THE DAY--

--IT IS MY DUTY, MY *DESTINY*--

--TO BE A LIGHT IN THE DARK--

--TO MAKE SURE JUSTICE IS SERVED.

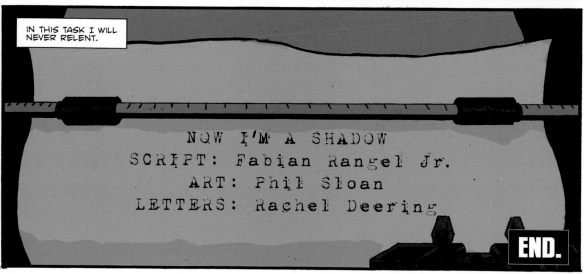

IN THIS TASK I WILL NEVER RELENT.

NOW I'M A SHADOW
SCRIPT: Fabian Rangel Jr.
ART: Phil Sloan
LETTERS: Rachel Deering

END.

CONSTELLATIONS

SCRIPT BY **FABIAN RANGEL JR.**

ART BY **JIM McMUNN**

LETTERS BY **EVELYN RANGEL**

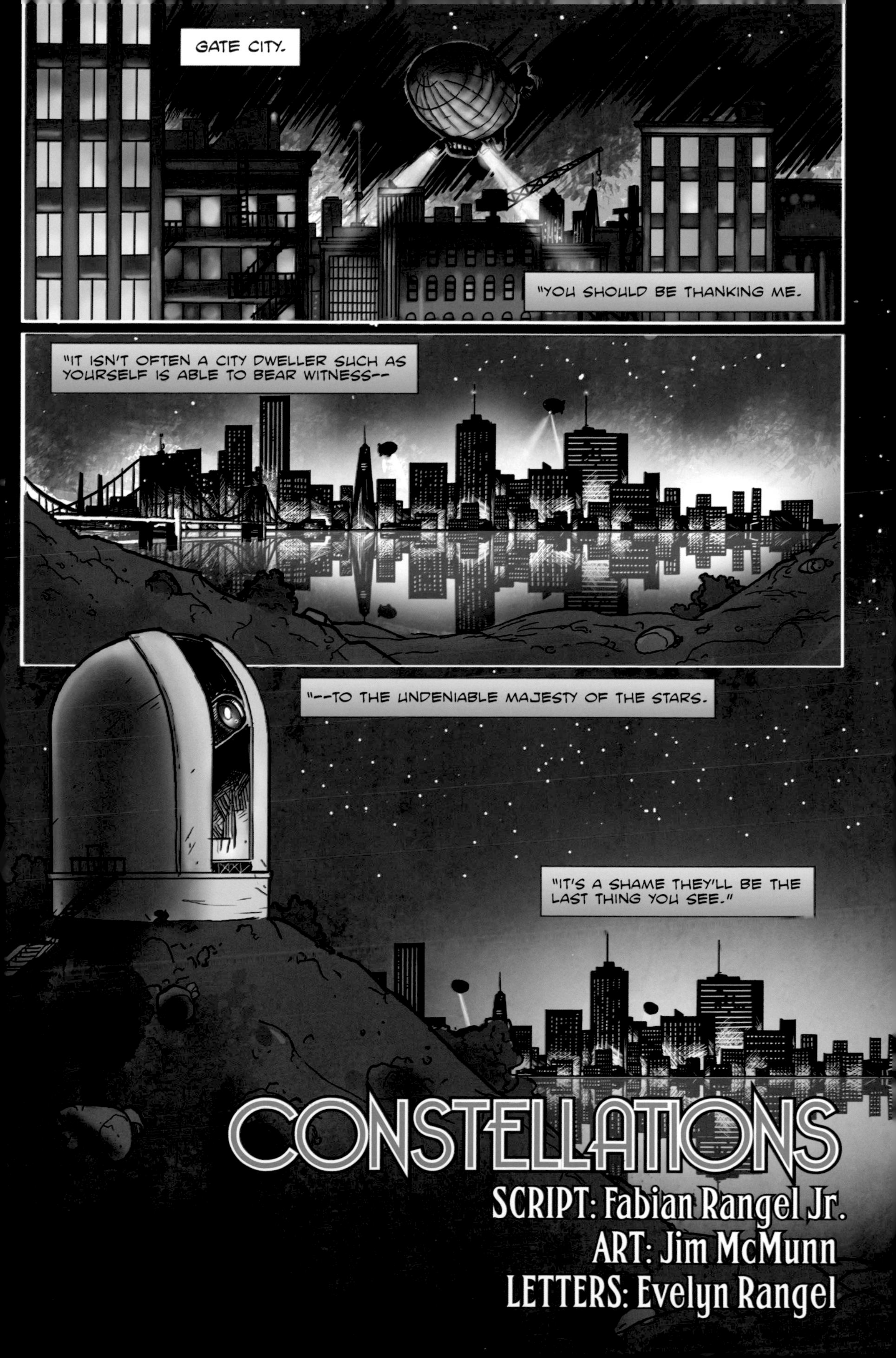
GATE CITY.
"YOU SHOULD BE THANKING ME.
"IT ISN'T OFTEN A CITY DWELLER SUCH AS YOURSELF IS ABLE TO BEAR WITNESS--
"--TO THE UNDENIABLE MAJESTY OF THE STARS.
"IT'S A SHAME THEY'LL BE THE LAST THING YOU SEE."
CONSTELLATIONS
SCRIPT: Fabian Rangel Jr.
ART: Jim McMunn
LETTERS: Evelyn Rangel

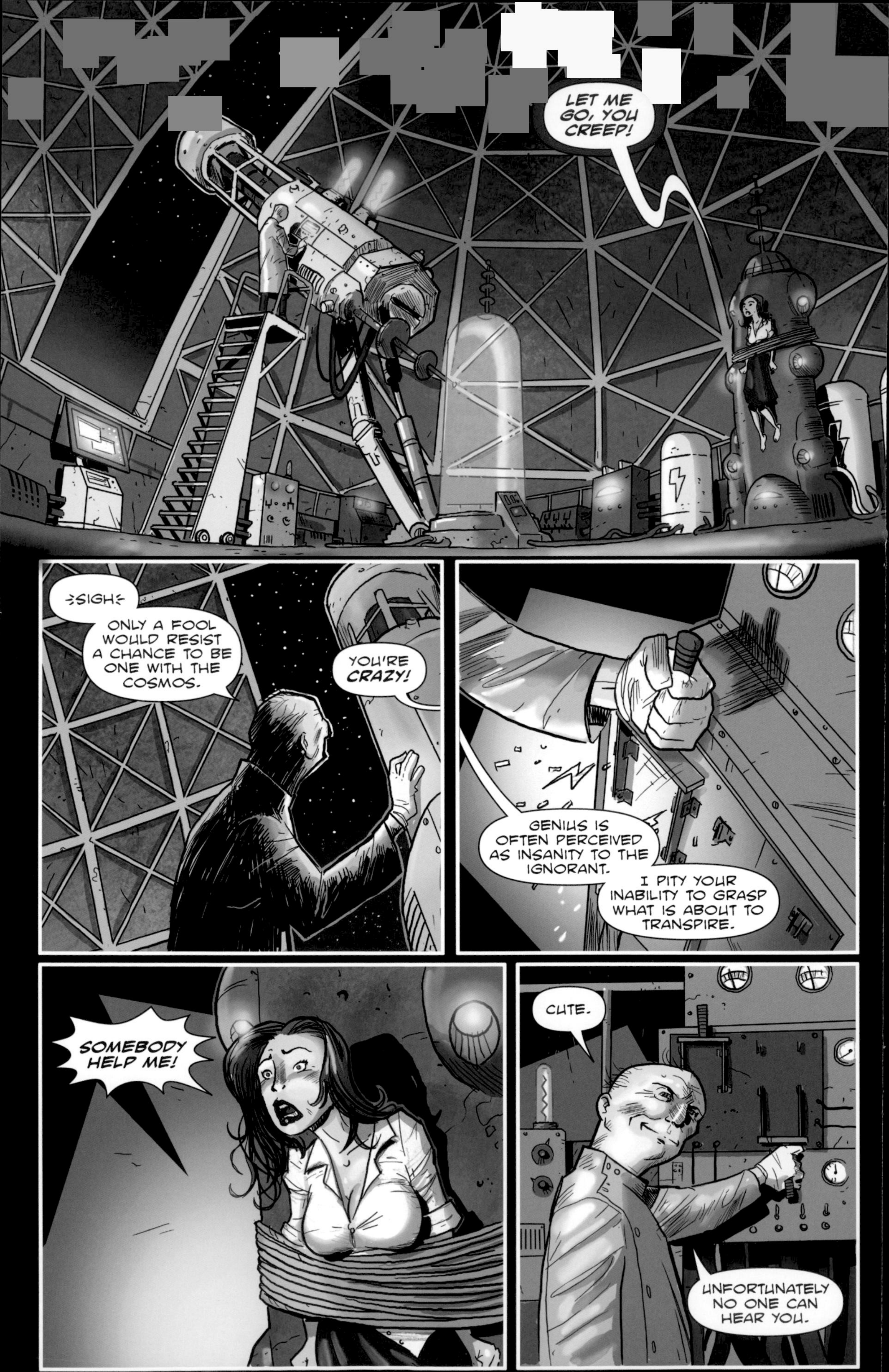
LET ME GO, YOU CREEP!
-SIGH-
ONLY A FOOL WOULD RESIST A CHANCE TO BE ONE WITH THE COSMOS.
YOU'RE CRAZY!
GENIUS IS OFTEN PERCEIVED AS INSANITY TO THE IGNORANT.
I PITY YOUR INABILITY TO GRASP WHAT IS ABOUT TO TRANSPIRE.
SOMEBODY HELP ME!
CUTE.
UNFORTUNATELY NO ONE CAN HEAR YOU.

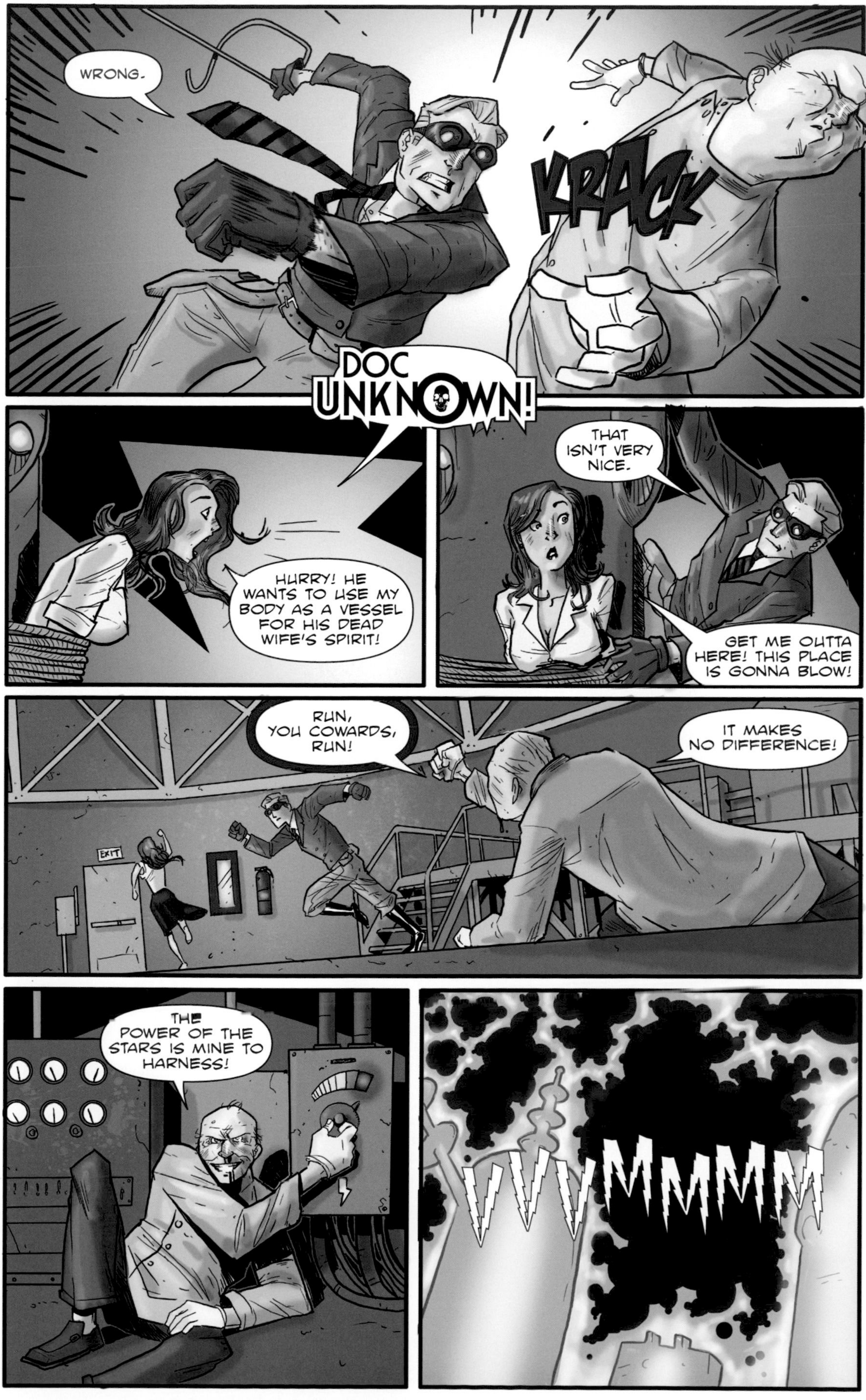

WRONG.
KRACK
DOC UNKNOWN!
HURRY! HE WANTS TO USE MY BODY AS A VESSEL FOR HIS DEAD WIFE'S SPIRIT!
THAT ISN'T VERY NICE.
GET ME OUTTA HERE! THIS PLACE IS GONNA BLOW!
RUN, YOU COWARDS, RUN!
IT MAKES NO DIFFERENCE!
EXIT
THE POWER OF THE STARS IS MINE TO HARNESS!
VVVMMMM

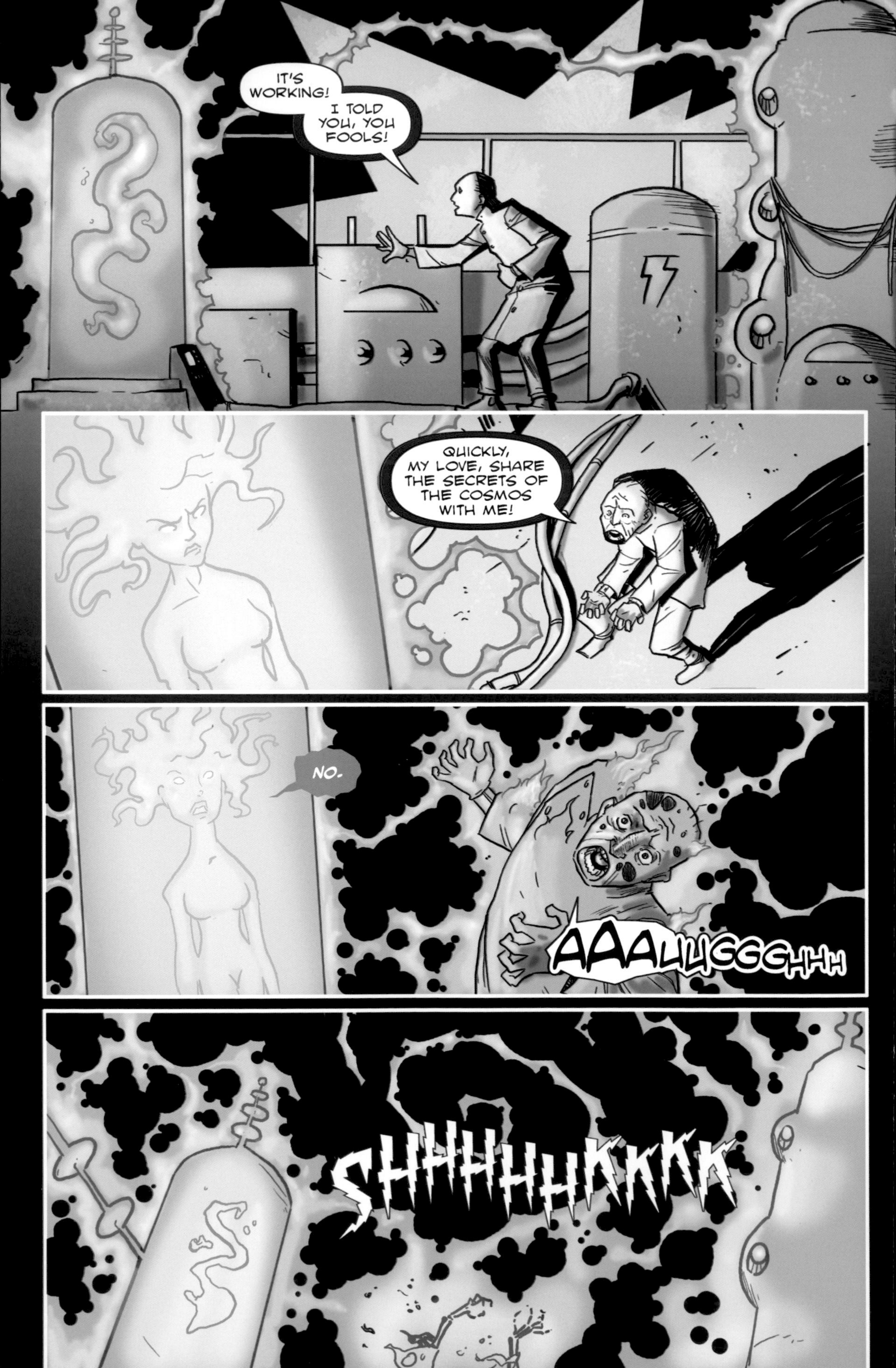
IT'S WORKING!
I TOLD YOU, YOU FOOLS!
QUICKLY, MY LOVE, SHARE THE SECRETS OF THE COSMOS WITH ME!
NO.
AAAIIUGGGHHH
SHHHHHKKKK

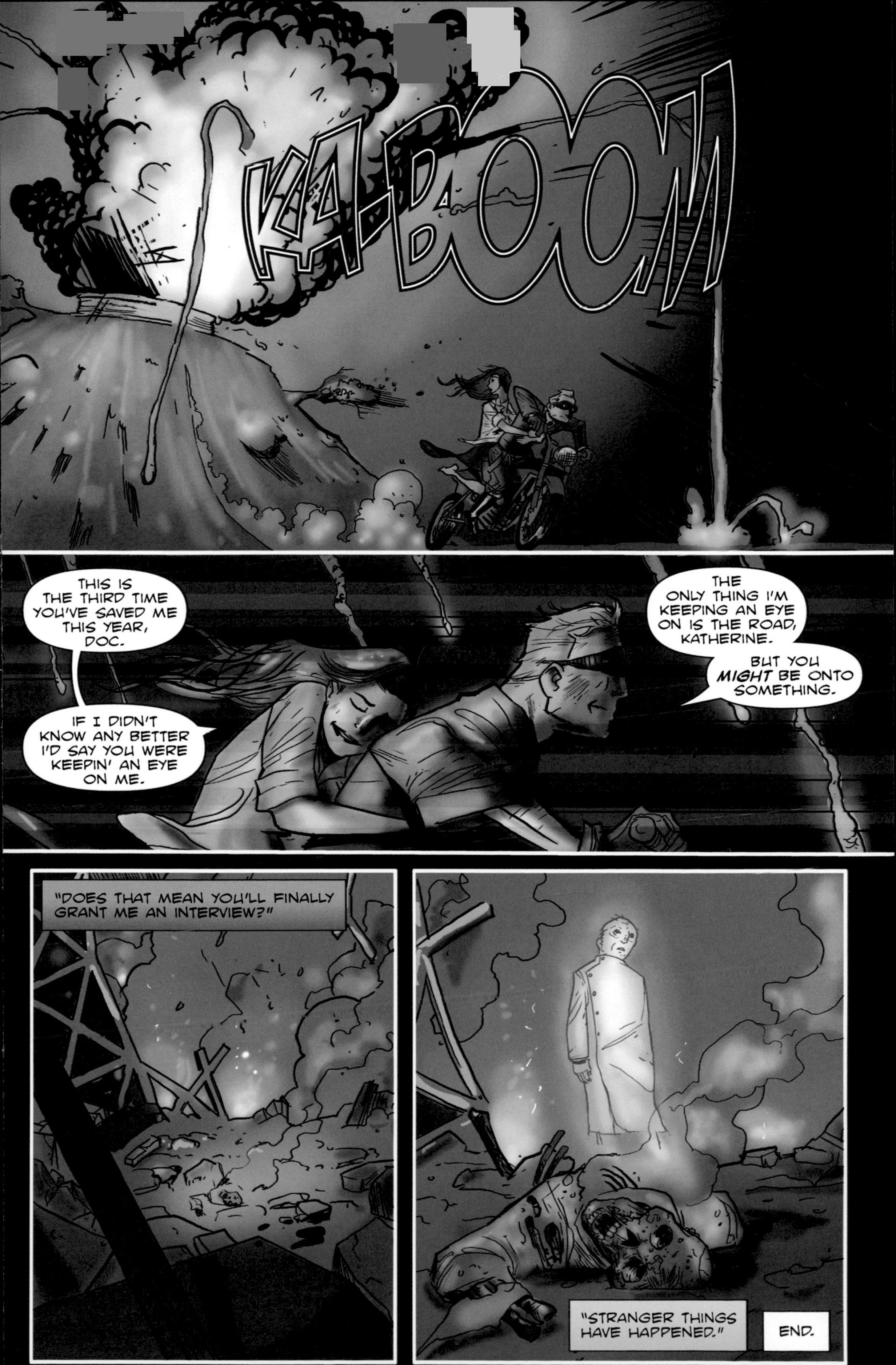
KA-BOOM
THIS IS THE THIRD TIME YOU'VE SAVED ME THIS YEAR, DOC.
IF I DIDN'T KNOW ANY BETTER I'D SAY YOU WERE KEEPIN' AN EYE ON ME.
THE ONLY THING I'M KEEPING AN EYE ON IS THE ROAD, KATHERINE.
BUT YOU *MIGHT* BE ONTO SOMETHING.
"DOES THAT MEAN YOU'LL FINALLY GRANT ME AN INTERVIEW?"
"STRANGER THINGS HAVE HAPPENED."
END.

THE ECHO FROM BEYOND TIME

SCRIPT BY **FABIAN RANGEL JR.**

LINE ART BY **JOHN BROGLIA**

COLORS BY **RYAN CODY**

LETTERS BY **EVELYN RANGEL**

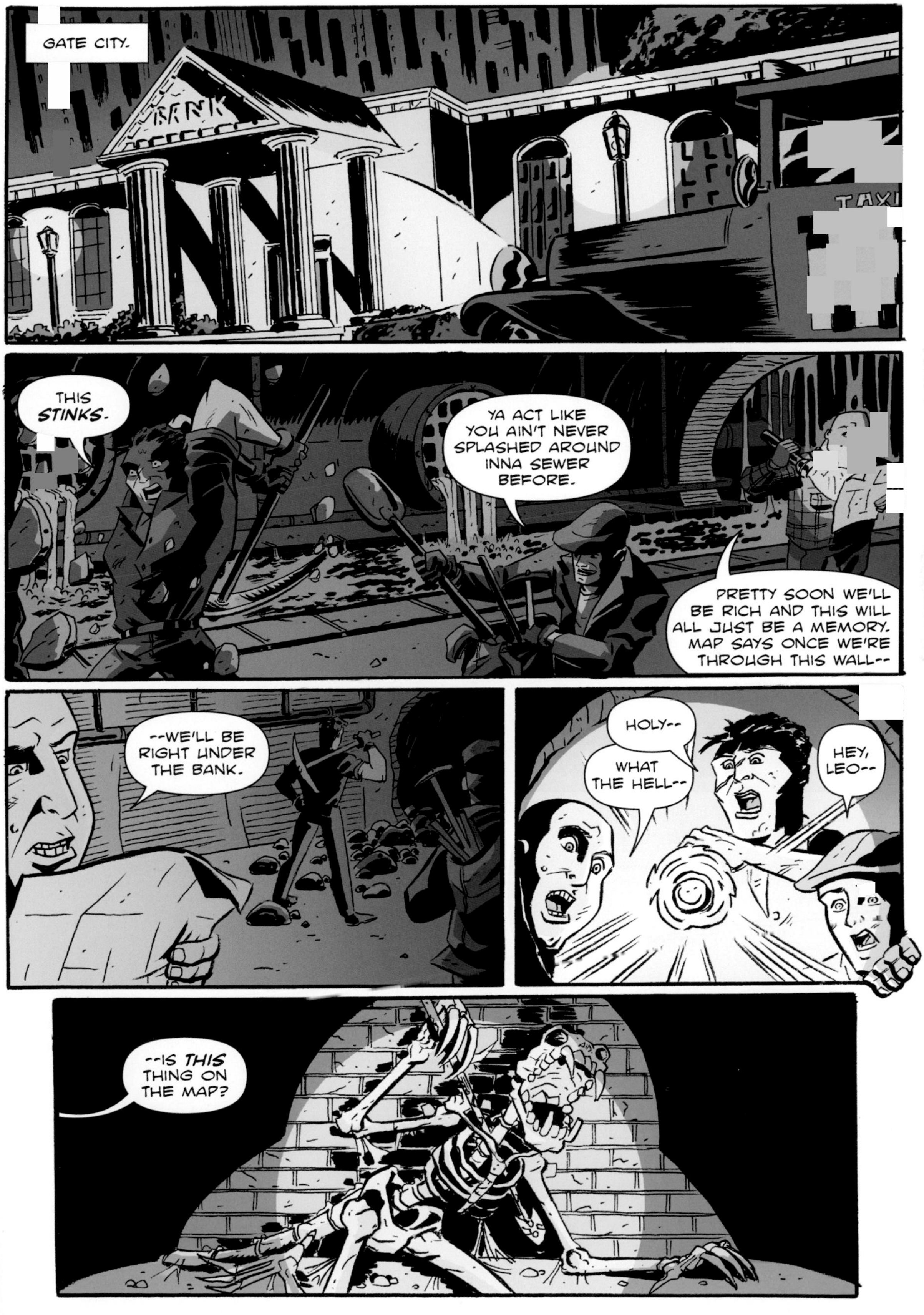
GATE CITY.
THIS STINKS.
YA ACT LIKE YOU AIN'T NEVER SPLASHED AROUND INNA SEWER BEFORE.
PRETTY SOON WE'LL BE RICH AND THIS WILL ALL JUST BE A MEMORY. MAP SAYS ONCE WE'RE THROUGH THIS WALL--
--WE'LL BE RIGHT UNDER THE BANK.
HOLY--
WHAT THE HELL--
HEY, LEO--
--IS THIS THING ON THE MAP?

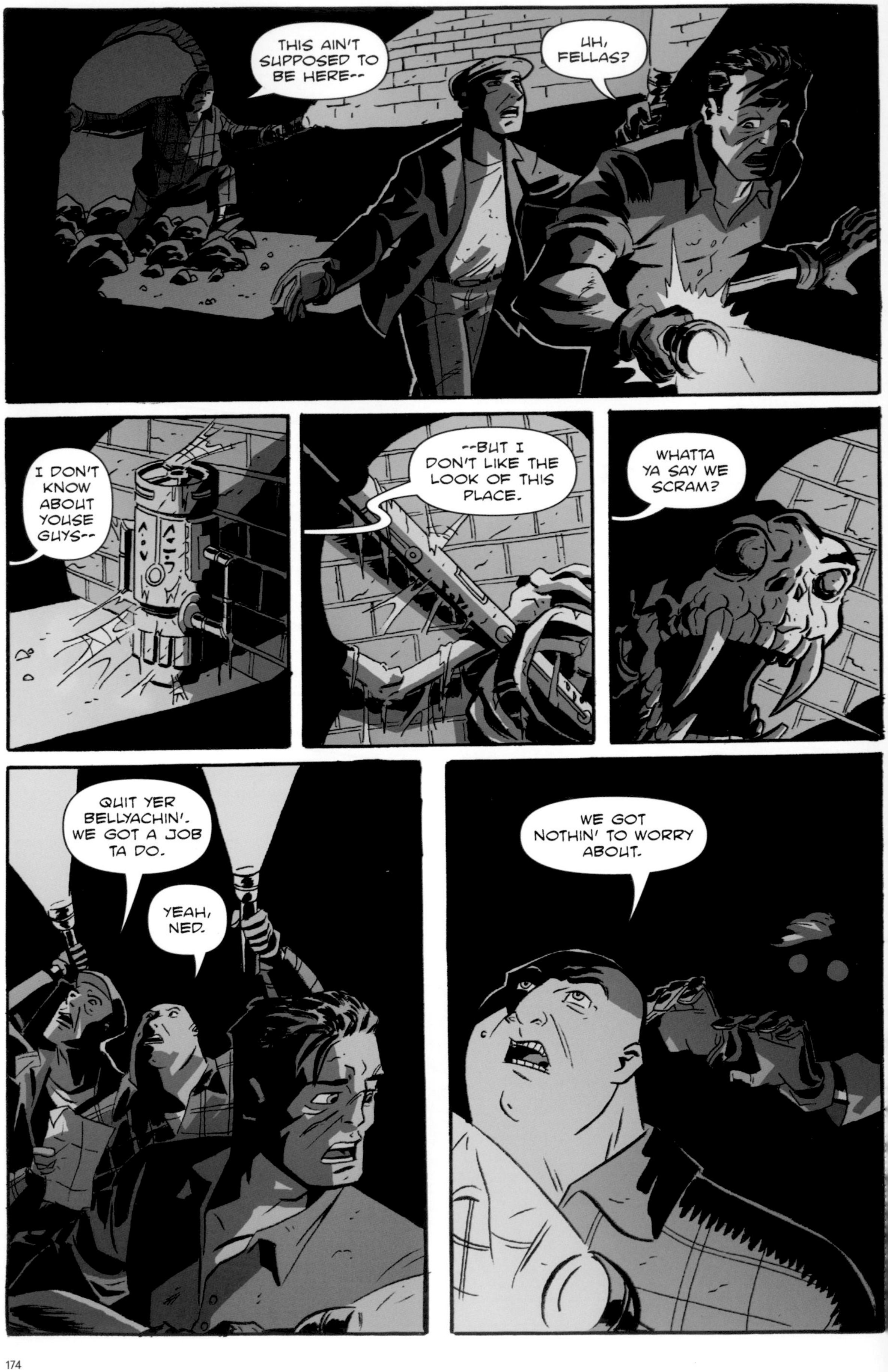
THIS AIN'T SUPPOSED TO BE HERE--
UH, FELLAS?
I DON'T KNOW ABOUT YOUSE GUYS--
--BUT I DON'T LIKE THE LOOK OF THIS PLACE.
WHATTA YA SAY WE SCRAM?
QUIT YER BELLYACHIN'. WE GOT A JOB TA DO.
YEAH, NED.
WE GOT NOTHIN' TO WORRY ABOUT.

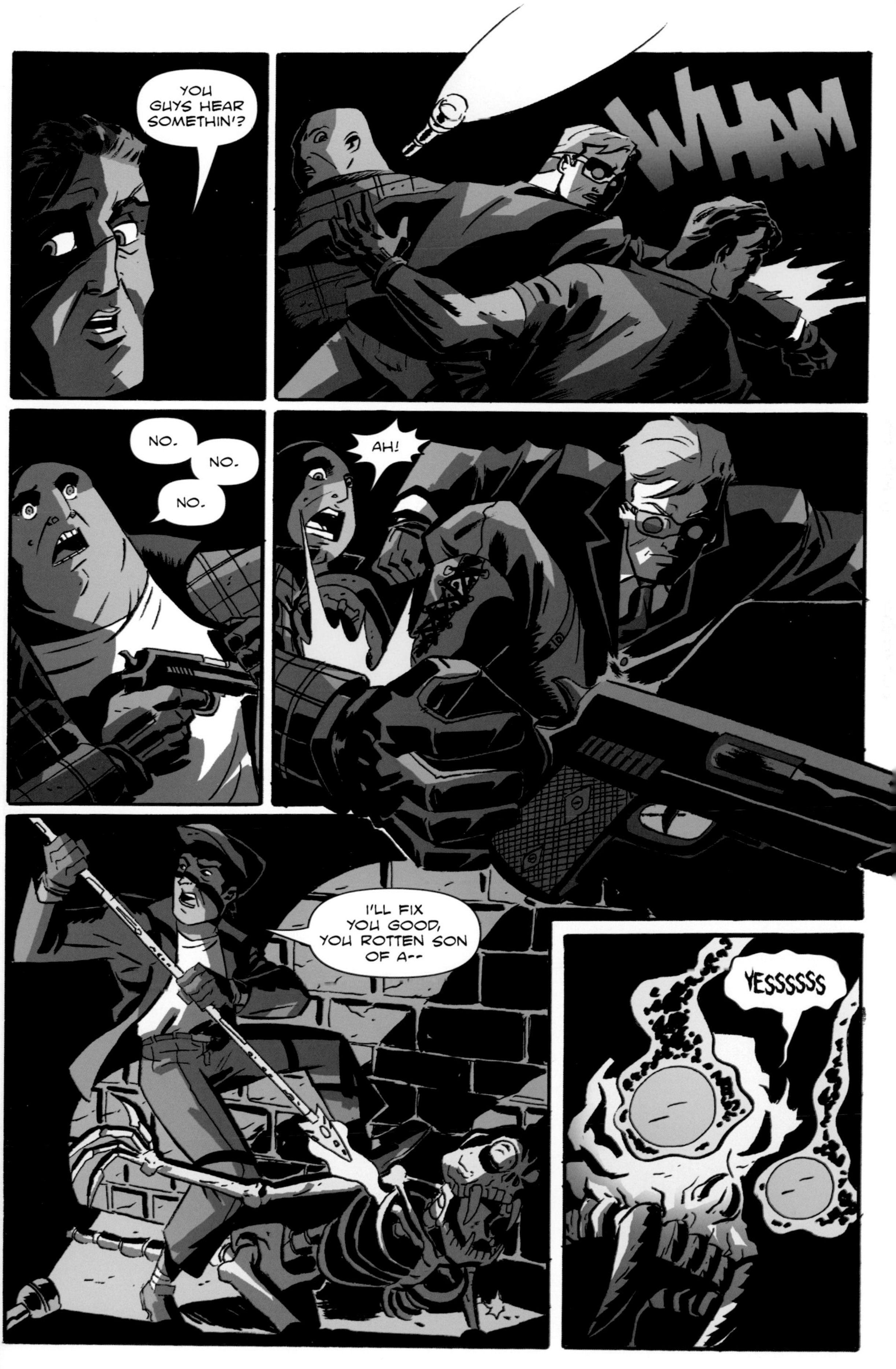
YOU GUYS HEAR SOMETHIN'?
WHAM
NO.
NO.
NO.
AH!
I'LL FIX YOU GOOD, YOU ROTTEN SON OF A--
YESSSSSS

HOLY--

AU GGH TH

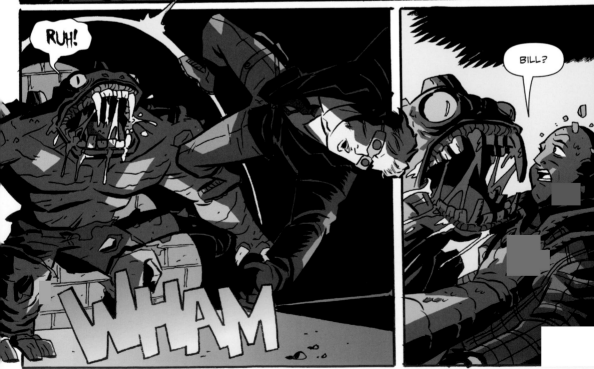

RUH!

BILL?

WHAM

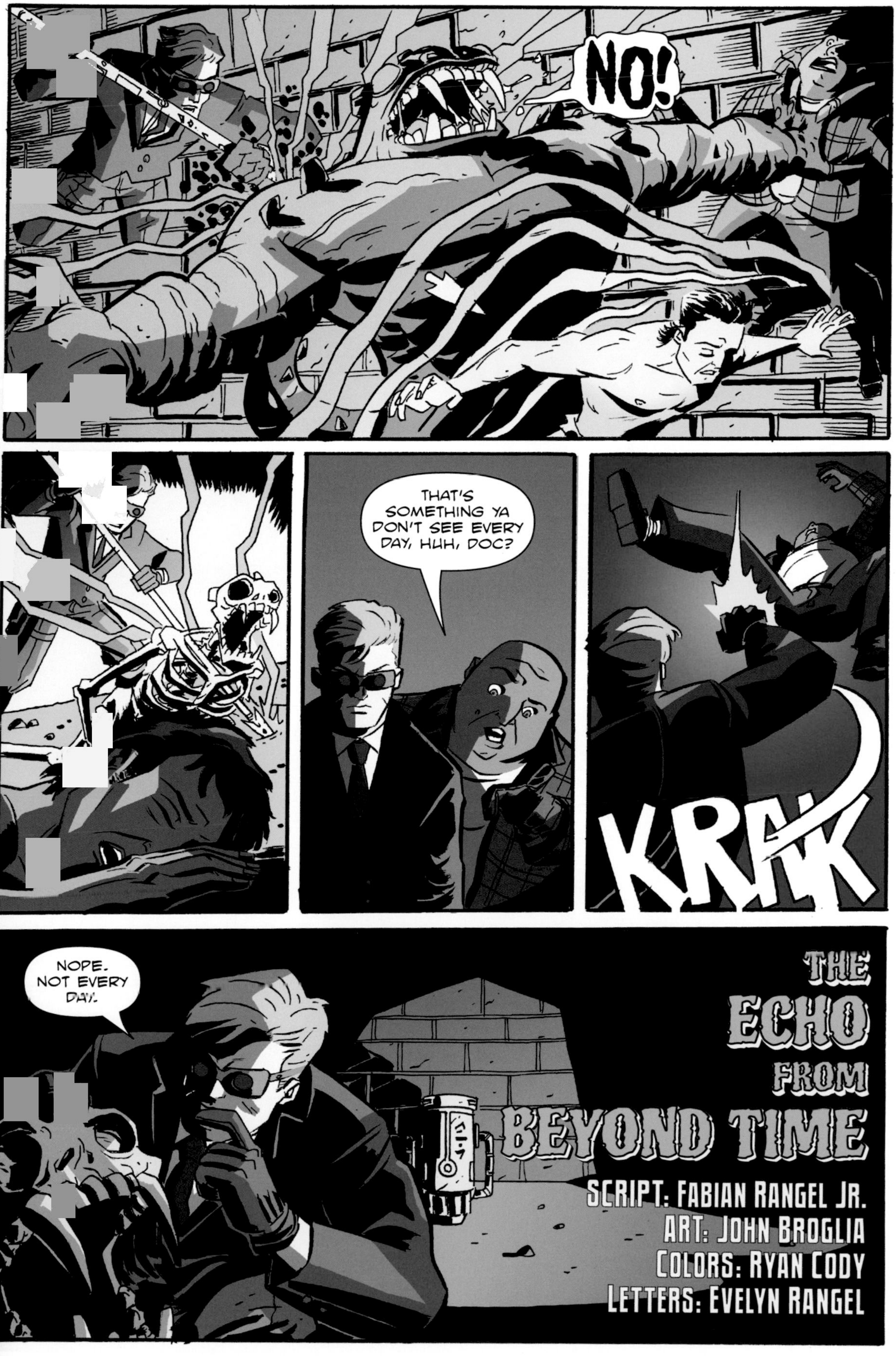
NO!
THAT'S SOMETHING YA DON'T SEE EVERY DAY, HUH, DOC?
KRAK
NOPE. NOT EVERY DAY.
THE ECHO FROM BEYOND TIME
SCRIPT: FABIAN RANGEL JR.
ART: JOHN BROGLIA
COLORS: RYAN CODY
LETTERS: EVELYN RANGEL

THE GHOST AND THE TIME MACHINE

SCRIPT BY **FABIAN RANGEL JR.**

ART AND LETTERS BY **RYAN CODY**

The Ghost and the Time Machine
by Fabian Rangel Jr. and Ryan Cody

THE PAST.

How much loot ya think we got?

Enough to retire and move to a nice little island somewhere.

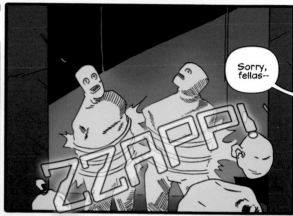

Sorry, fellas--

ZZAPP!

--but the only island you're headed to is Alcatraz.

Come on, be a pal and let us go.

You're no pal of mine, buster.

Ray...

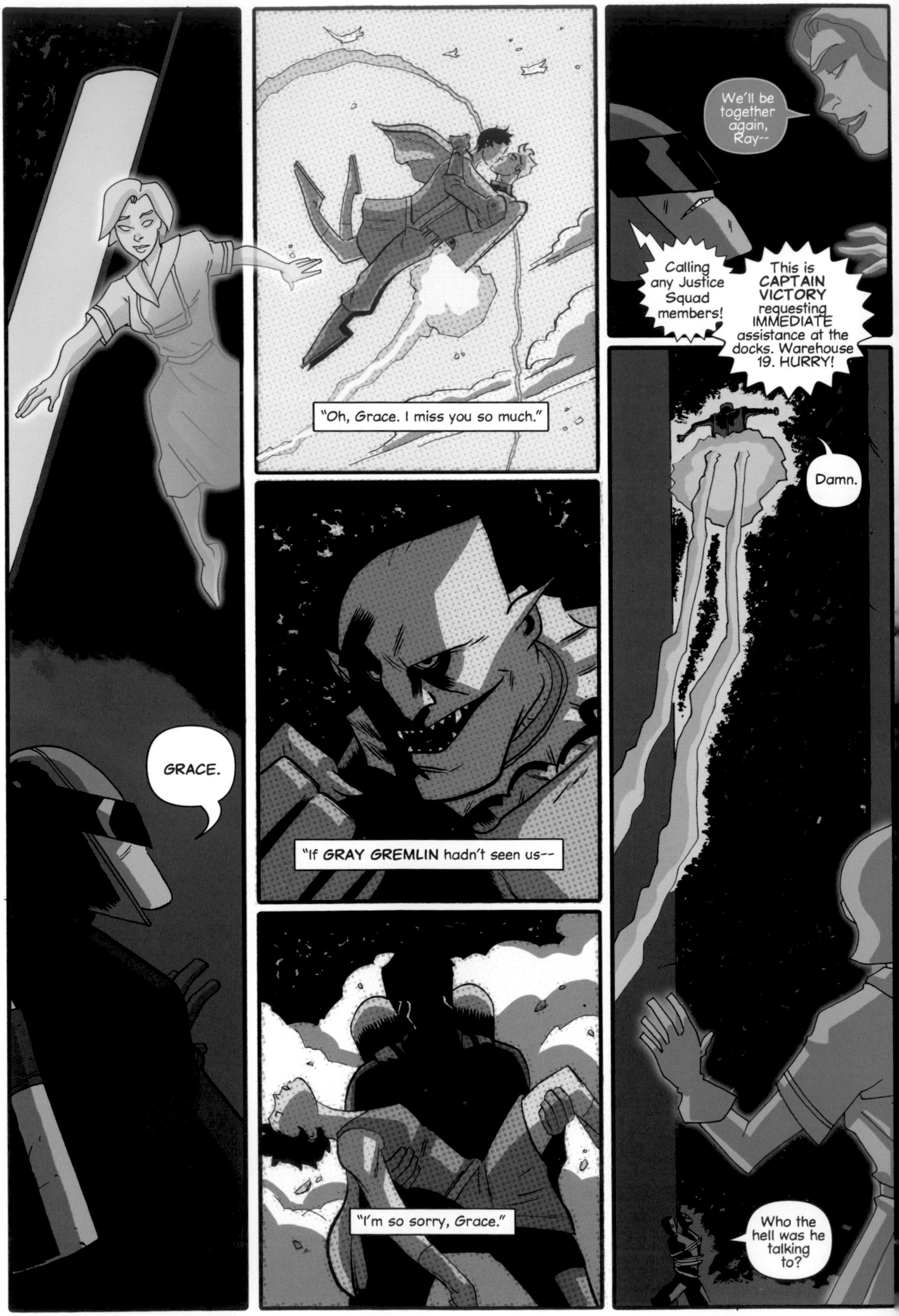

"Oh, Grace. I miss you so much."
We'll be together again, Ray--
GRACE.
"If GRAY GREMLIN hadn't seen us--
Calling any Justice Squad members!
This is CAPTAIN VICTORY requesting IMMEDIATE assistance at the docks. Warehouse 19. HURRY!
Damn.
"I'm so sorry, Grace."
Who the hell was he talking to?

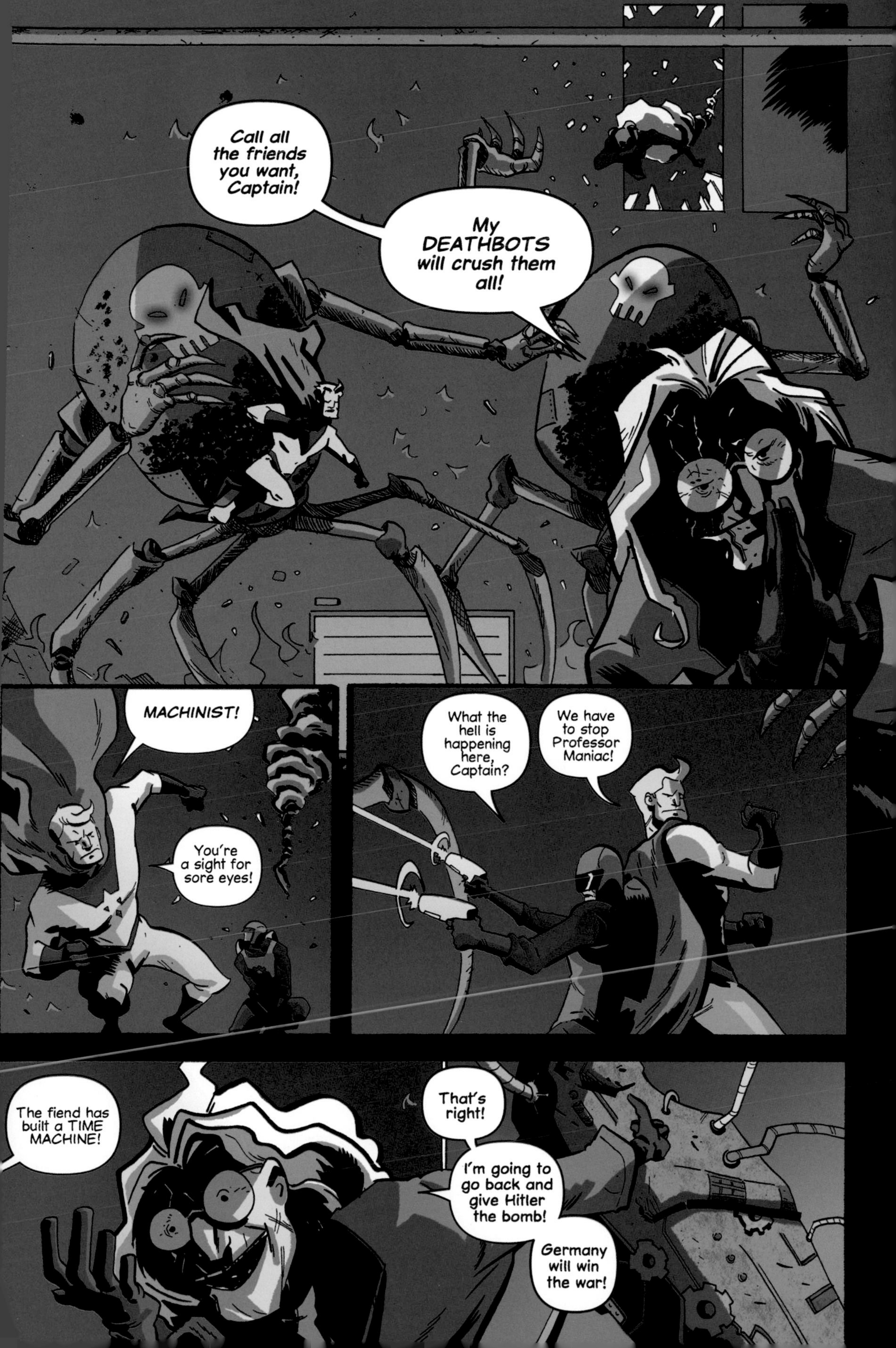
Call all the friends you want, Captain!
My DEATHBOTS will crush them all!
MACHINIST!
You're a sight for sore eyes!
What the hell is happening here, Captain?
We have to stop Professor Maniac!
The fiend has built a TIME MACHINE!
That's right!
I'm going to go back and give Hitler the bomb!
Germany will win the war!

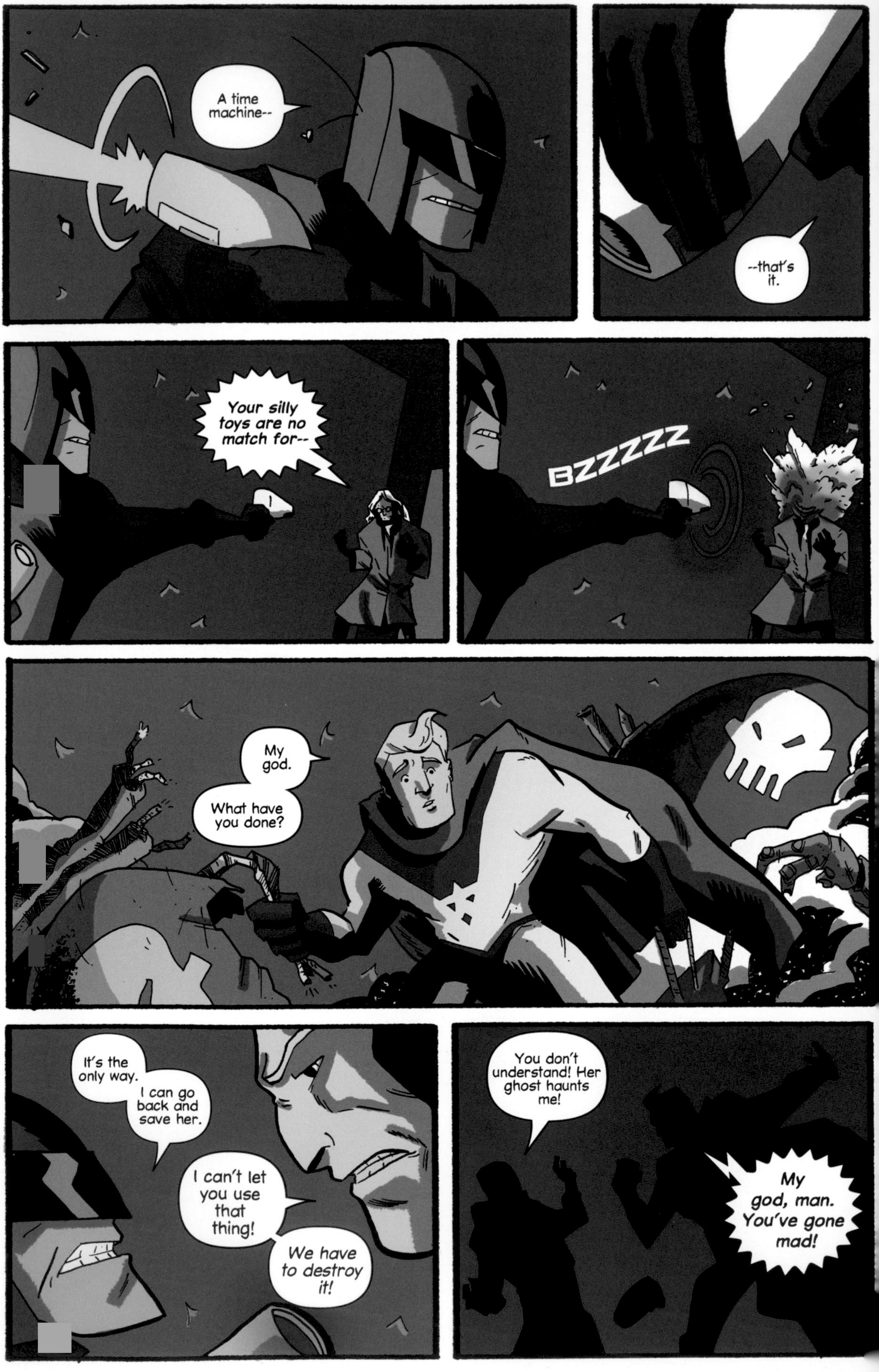
A time machine--
--that's it.
Your silly toys are no match for--
BZZZZZ
My god.
What have you done?
It's the only way.
I can go back and save her.
I can't let you use that thing!
We have to destroy it!
You don't understand! Her ghost haunts me!
My god, man. You've gone mad!

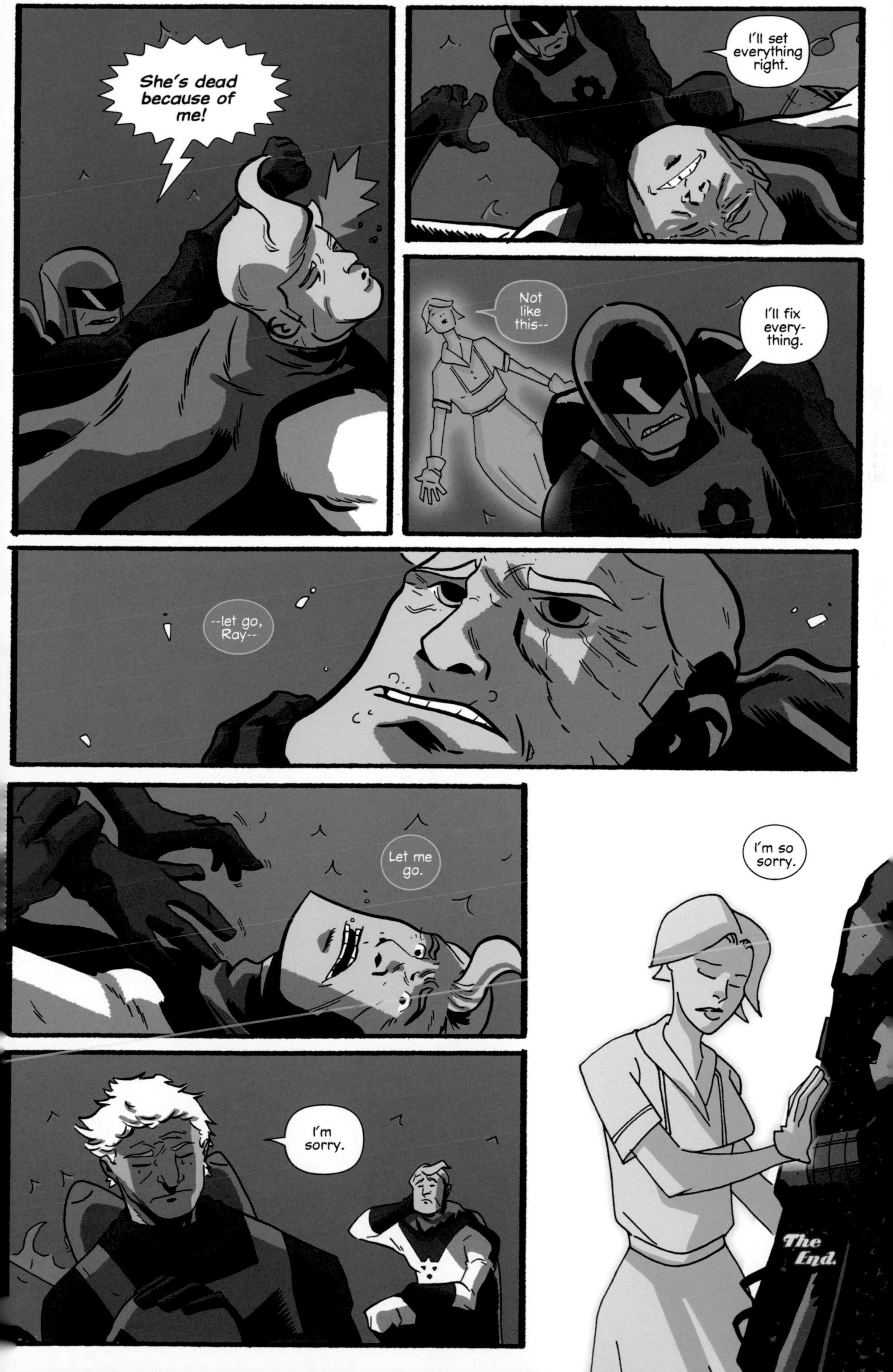
She's dead because of me!
I'll set everything right.
Not like this--
I'll fix every-thing.
--let go, Ray--
Let me go.
I'm sorry.
I'm so sorry.
The End.

CENTURIES

SCRIPT, ART, AND LETTERS BY **RYAN CODY**

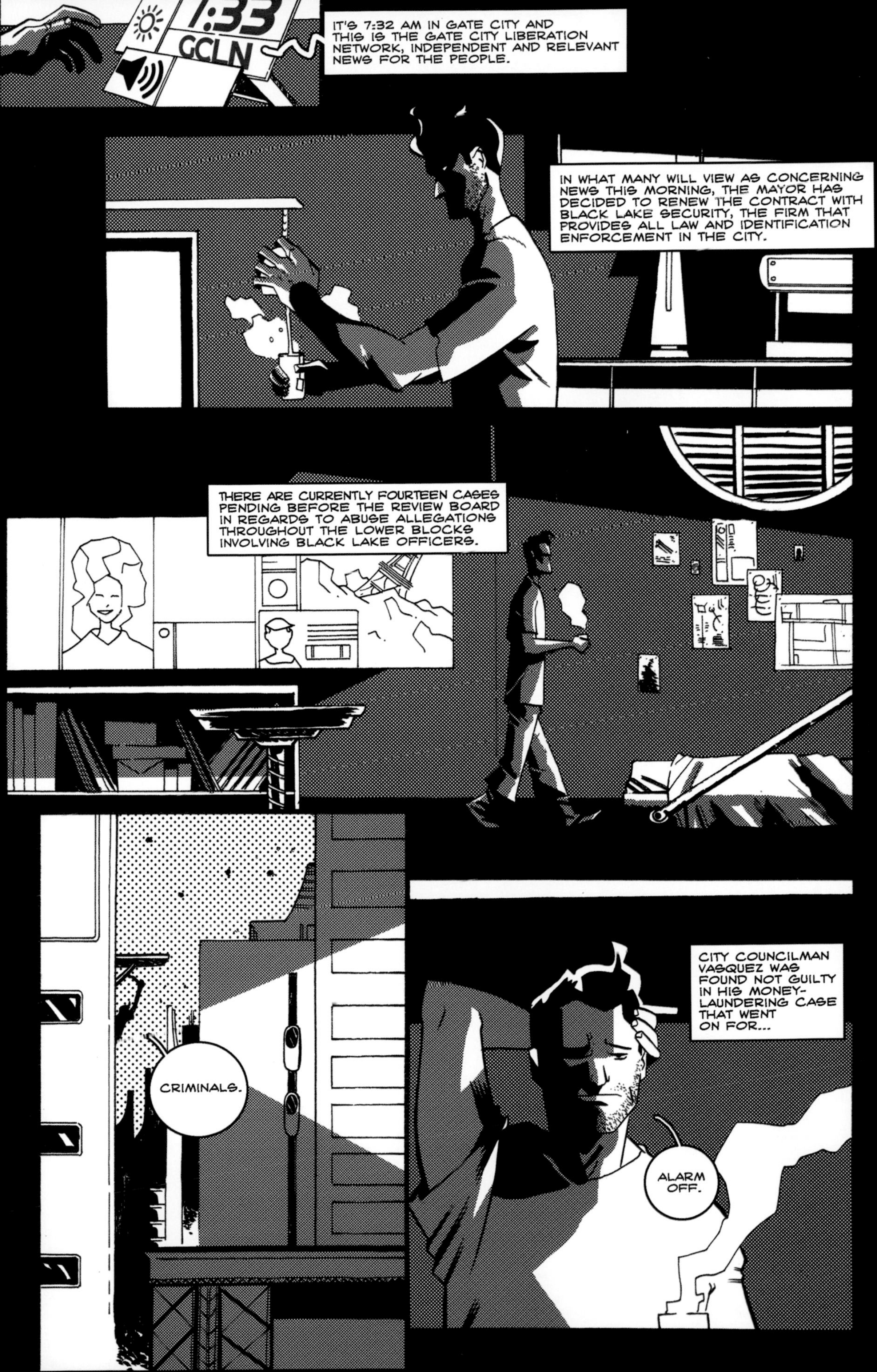
7:33
GCLN
IT'S 7:32 AM IN GATE CITY AND THIS IS THE GATE CITY LIBERATION NETWORK, INDEPENDENT AND RELEVANT NEWS FOR THE PEOPLE.
IN WHAT MANY WILL VIEW AS CONCERNING NEWS THIS MORNING, THE MAYOR HAS DECIDED TO RENEW THE CONTRACT WITH BLACK LAKE SECURITY, THE FIRM THAT PROVIDES ALL LAW AND IDENTIFICATION ENFORCEMENT IN THE CITY.
THERE ARE CURRENTLY FOURTEEN CASES PENDING BEFORE THE REVIEW BOARD IN REGARDS TO ABUSE ALLEGATIONS THROUGHOUT THE LOWER BLOCKS INVOLVING BLACK LAKE OFFICERS.
CRIMINALS.
CITY COUNCILMAN VASQUEZ WAS FOUND NOT GUILTY IN HIS MONEY-LAUNDERING CASE THAT WENT ON FOR...
ALARM OFF.

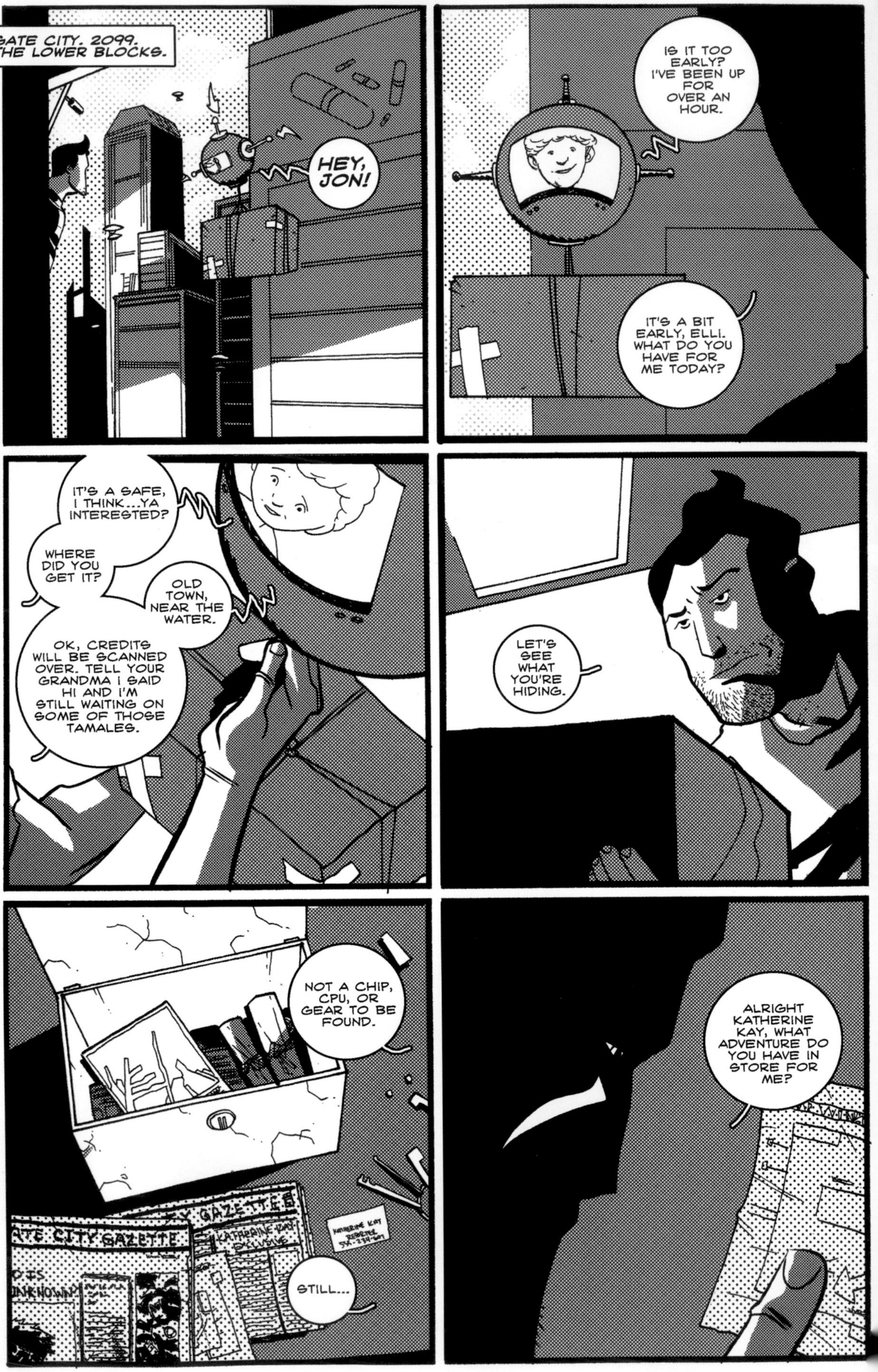
GATE CITY. 2099. THE LOWER BLOCKS.
HEY, JON!
IS IT TOO EARLY? I'VE BEEN UP FOR OVER AN HOUR.
IT'S A BIT EARLY, ELLI. WHAT DO YOU HAVE FOR ME TODAY?
IT'S A SAFE, I THINK...YA INTERESTED?
WHERE DID YOU GET IT?
OLD TOWN, NEAR THE WATER.
OK, CREDITS WILL BE SCANNED OVER. TELL YOUR GRANDMA I SAID HI AND I'M STILL WAITING ON SOME OF THOSE TAMALES.
LET'S SEE WHAT YOU'RE HIDING.
NOT A CHIP, CPU, OR GEAR TO BE FOUND.
STILL...
ALRIGHT KATHERINE KAY, WHAT ADVENTURE DO YOU HAVE IN STORE FOR ME?

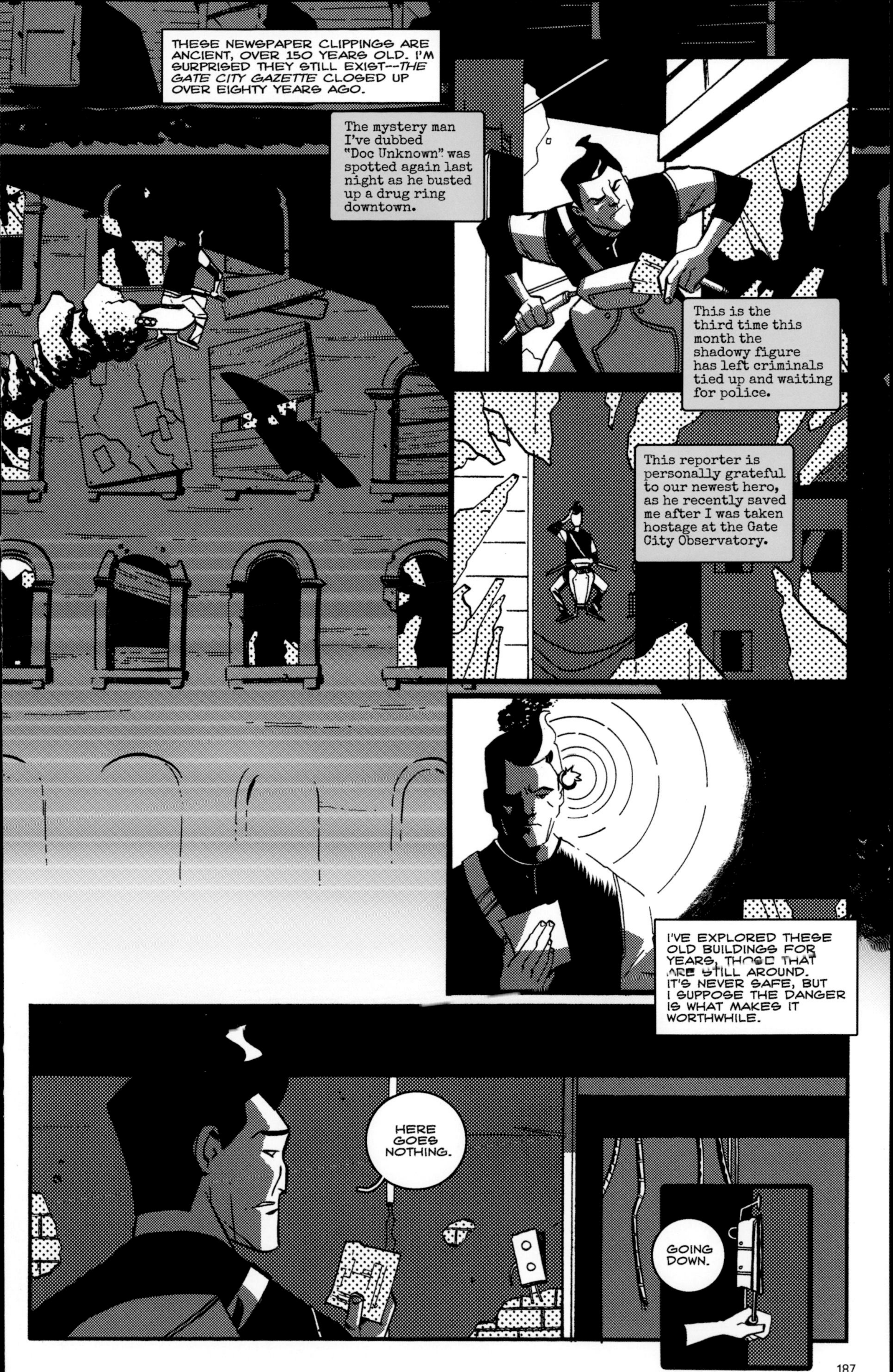

THESE NEWSPAPER CLIPPINGS ARE ANCIENT, OVER 150 YEARS OLD. I'M SURPRISED THEY STILL EXIST--THE GATE CITY GAZETTE CLOSED UP OVER EIGHTY YEARS AGO.
The mystery man I've dubbed "Doc Unknown" was spotted again last night as he busted up a drug ring downtown.
This is the third time this month the shadowy figure has left criminals tied up and waiting for police.
This reporter is personally grateful to our newest hero, as he recently saved me after I was taken hostage at the Gate City Observatory.
I'VE EXPLORED THESE OLD BUILDINGS FOR YEARS, THOSE THAT ARE STILL AROUND. IT'S NEVER SAFE, BUT I SUPPOSE THE DANGER IS WHAT MAKES IT WORTHWHILE.
HERE GOES NOTHING.
GOING DOWN.

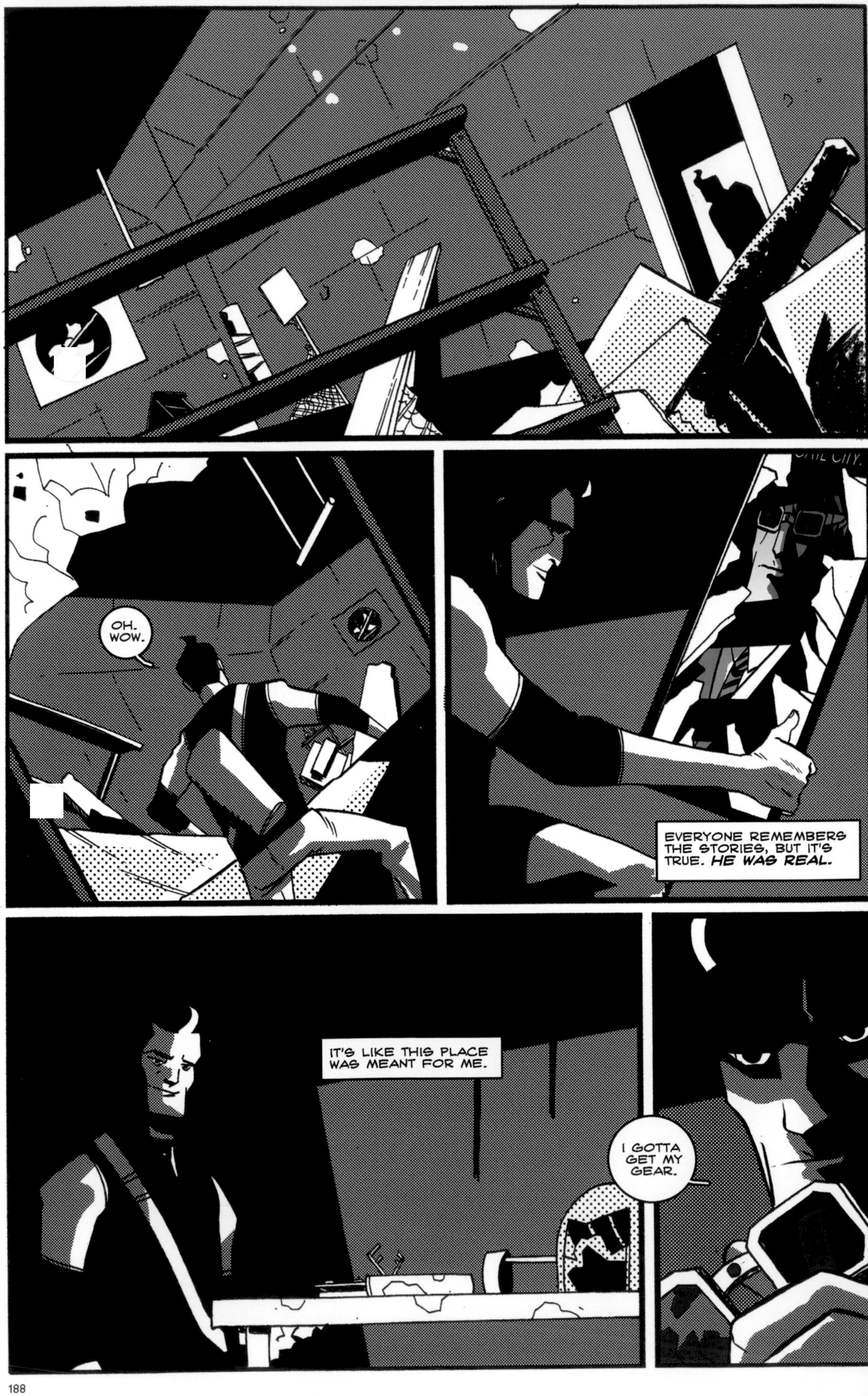
OH. WOW.
EVERYONE REMEMBERS THE STORIES, BUT IT'S TRUE. *HE WAS REAL.*
IT'S LIKE THIS PLACE WAS MEANT FOR ME.
I GOTTA GET MY GEAR.

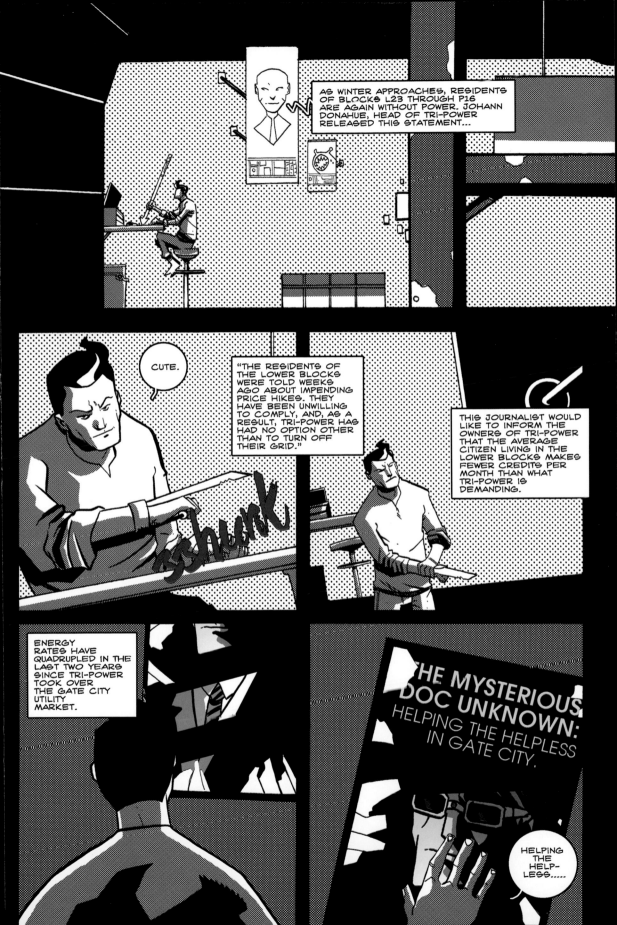

AS WINTER APPROACHES, RESIDENTS OF BLOCKS L23 THROUGH P16 ARE AGAIN WITHOUT POWER. JOHANN DONAHUE, HEAD OF TRI-POWER RELEASED THIS STATEMENT...

CUTE.

"THE RESIDENTS OF THE LOWER BLOCKS WERE TOLD WEEKS AGO ABOUT IMPENDING PRICE HIKES. THEY HAVE BEEN UNWILLING TO COMPLY, AND, AS A RESULT, TRI-POWER HAS HAD NO OPTION OTHER THAN TO TURN OFF THEIR GRID."

THIS JOURNALIST WOULD LIKE TO INFORM THE OWNERS OF TRI-POWER THAT THE AVERAGE CITIZEN LIVING IN THE LOWER BLOCKS MAKES FEWER CREDITS PER MONTH THAN WHAT TRI-POWER IS DEMANDING.

ENERGY RATES HAVE QUADRUPLED IN THE LAST TWO YEARS SINCE TRI-POWER TOOK OVER THE GATE CITY UTILITY MARKET.

THE MYSTERIOUS DOC UNKNOWN: HELPING THE HELPLESS IN GATE CITY.

HELPING THE HELPLESS......

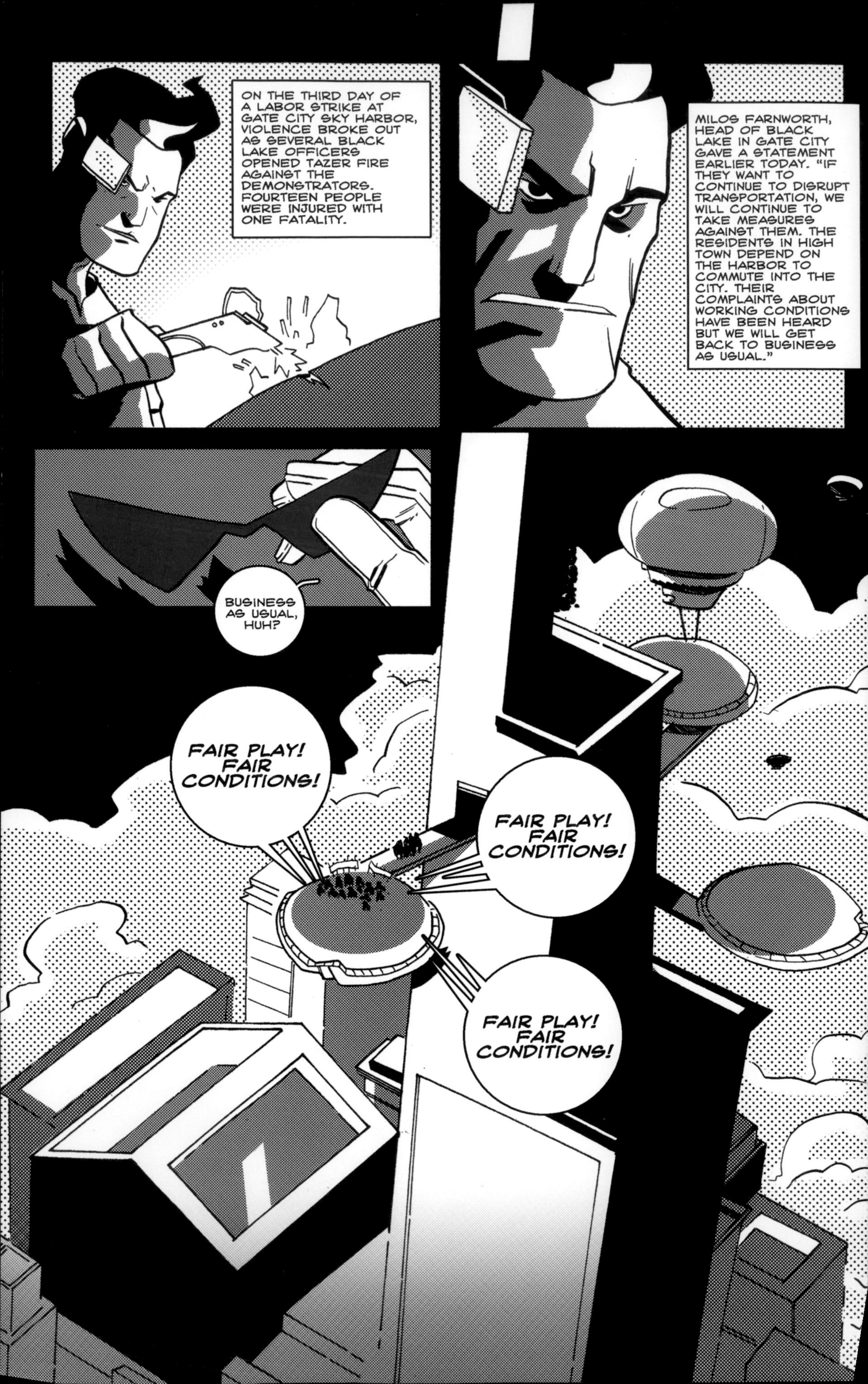
ON THE THIRD DAY OF A LABOR STRIKE AT GATE CITY SKY HARBOR, VIOLENCE BROKE OUT AS SEVERAL BLACK LAKE OFFICERS OPENED TAZER FIRE AGAINST THE DEMONSTRATORS. FOURTEEN PEOPLE WERE INJURED WITH ONE FATALITY.
MILOS FARNWORTH, HEAD OF BLACK LAKE IN GATE CITY GAVE A STATEMENT EARLIER TODAY. "IF THEY WANT TO CONTINUE TO DISRUPT TRANSPORTATION, WE WILL CONTINUE TO TAKE MEASURES AGAINST THEM. THE RESIDENTS IN HIGH TOWN DEPEND ON THE HARBOR TO COMMUTE INTO THE CITY. THEIR COMPLAINTS ABOUT WORKING CONDITIONS HAVE BEEN HEARD BUT WE WILL GET BACK TO BUSINESS AS USUAL."
BUSINESS AS USUAL, HUH?
FAIR PLAY! FAIR CONDITIONS!
FAIR PLAY! FAIR CONDITIONS!
FAIR PLAY! FAIR CONDITIONS!

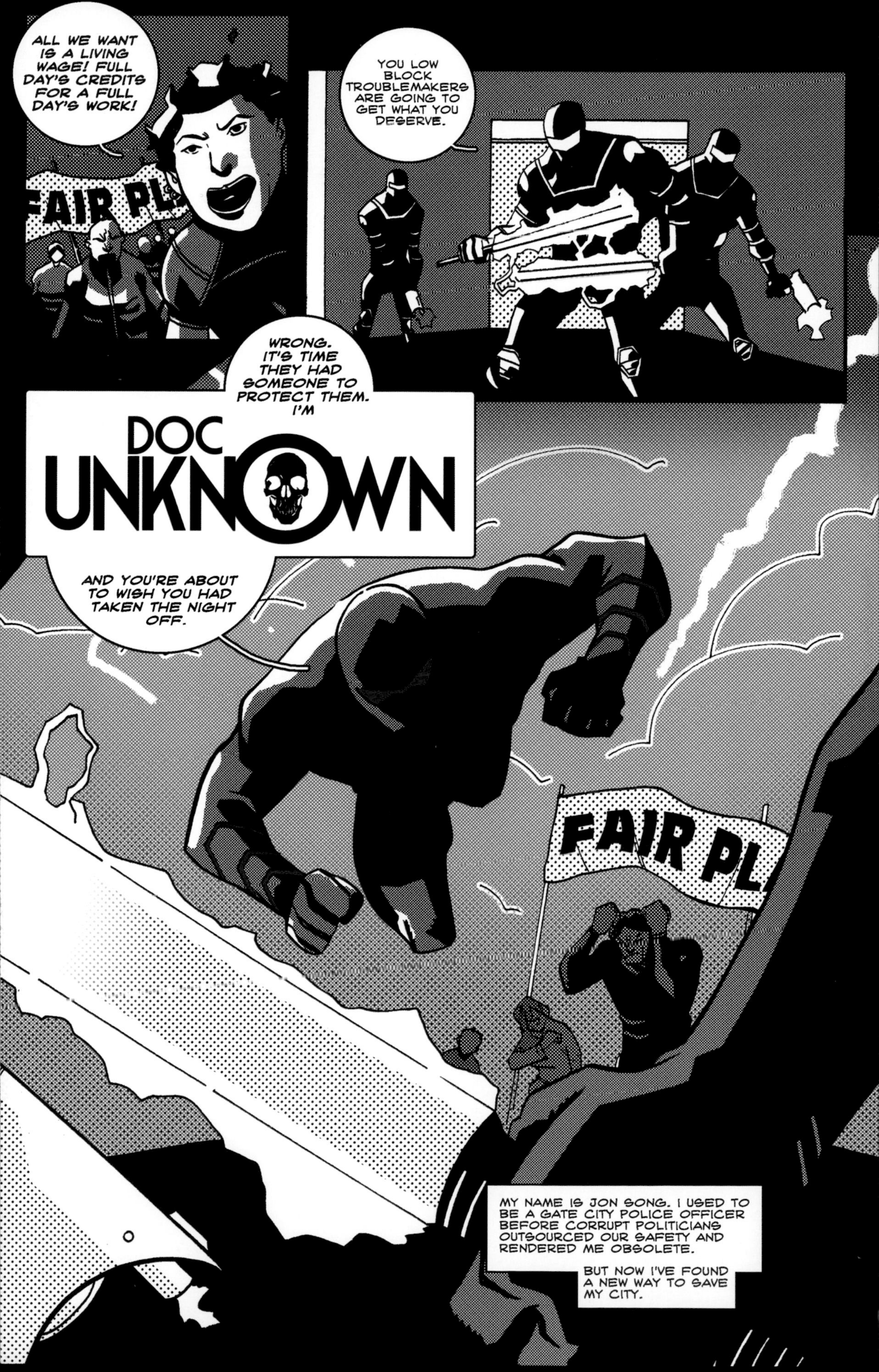

ALL WE WANT IS A LIVING WAGE! FULL DAY'S CREDITS FOR A FULL DAY'S WORK!
FAIR PL
YOU LOW BLOCK TROUBLEMAKERS ARE GOING TO GET WHAT YOU DESERVE.
WRONG. IT'S TIME THEY HAD SOMEONE TO PROTECT THEM. I'M
DOC UNKNOWN
AND YOU'RE ABOUT TO WISH YOU HAD TAKEN THE NIGHT OFF.
FAIR PL
MY NAME IS JON SONG. I USED TO BE A GATE CITY POLICE OFFICER BEFORE CORRUPT POLITICIANS OUTSOURCED OUR SAFETY AND RENDERED ME OBSOLETE.
BUT NOW I'VE FOUND A NEW WAY TO SAVE MY CITY.

THE SONGS OF THE FORGOTTEN

SCRIPT BY **FABIAN RANGEL JR.**

ART BY **RYAN CODY**

LETTERS BY **NIC SHAW**

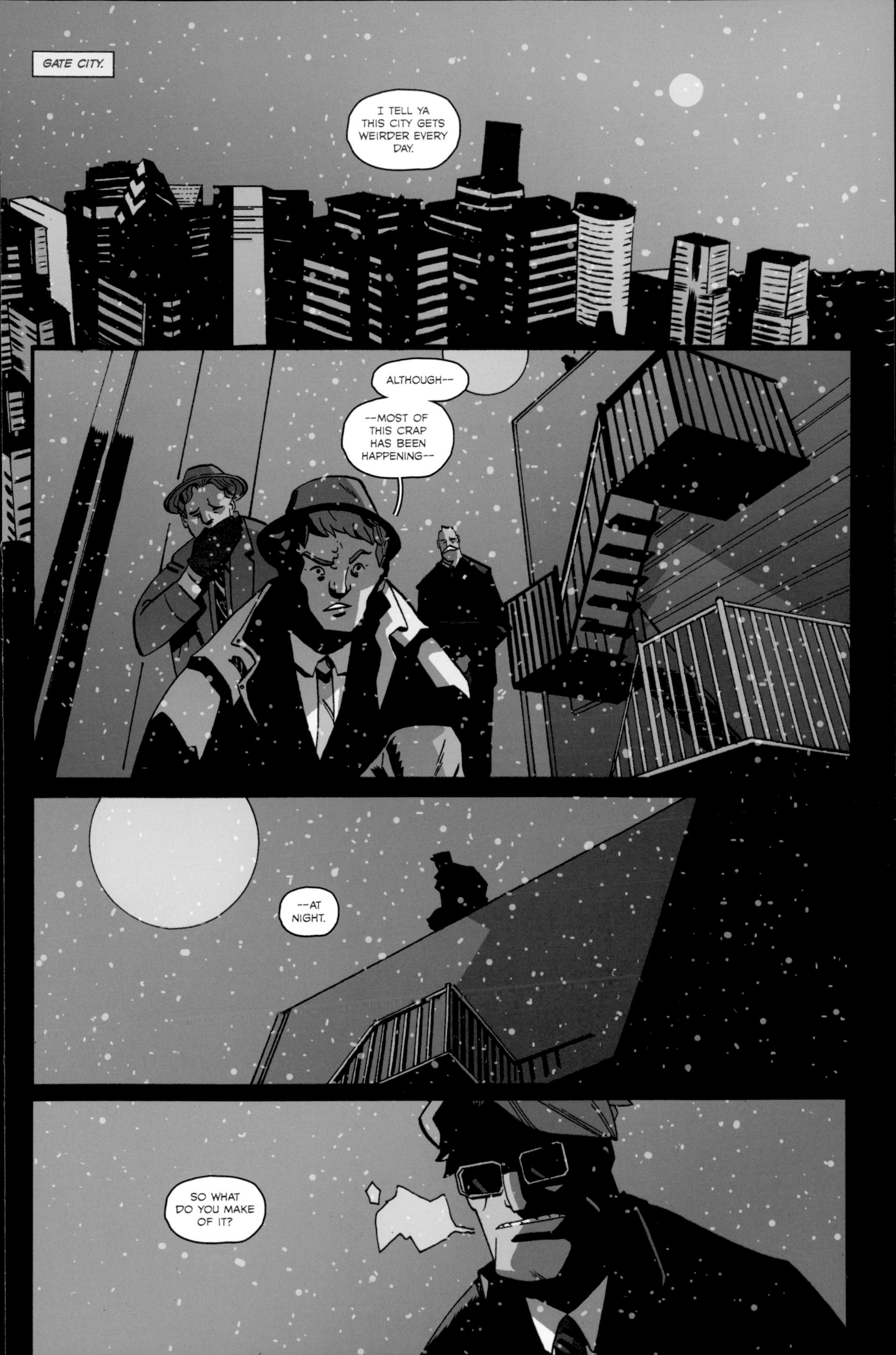

GATE CITY.
I TELL YA THIS CITY GETS WEIRDER EVERY DAY.
ALTHOUGH--
--MOST OF THIS CRAP HAS BEEN HAPPENING--
--AT NIGHT.
SO WHAT DO YOU MAKE OF IT?

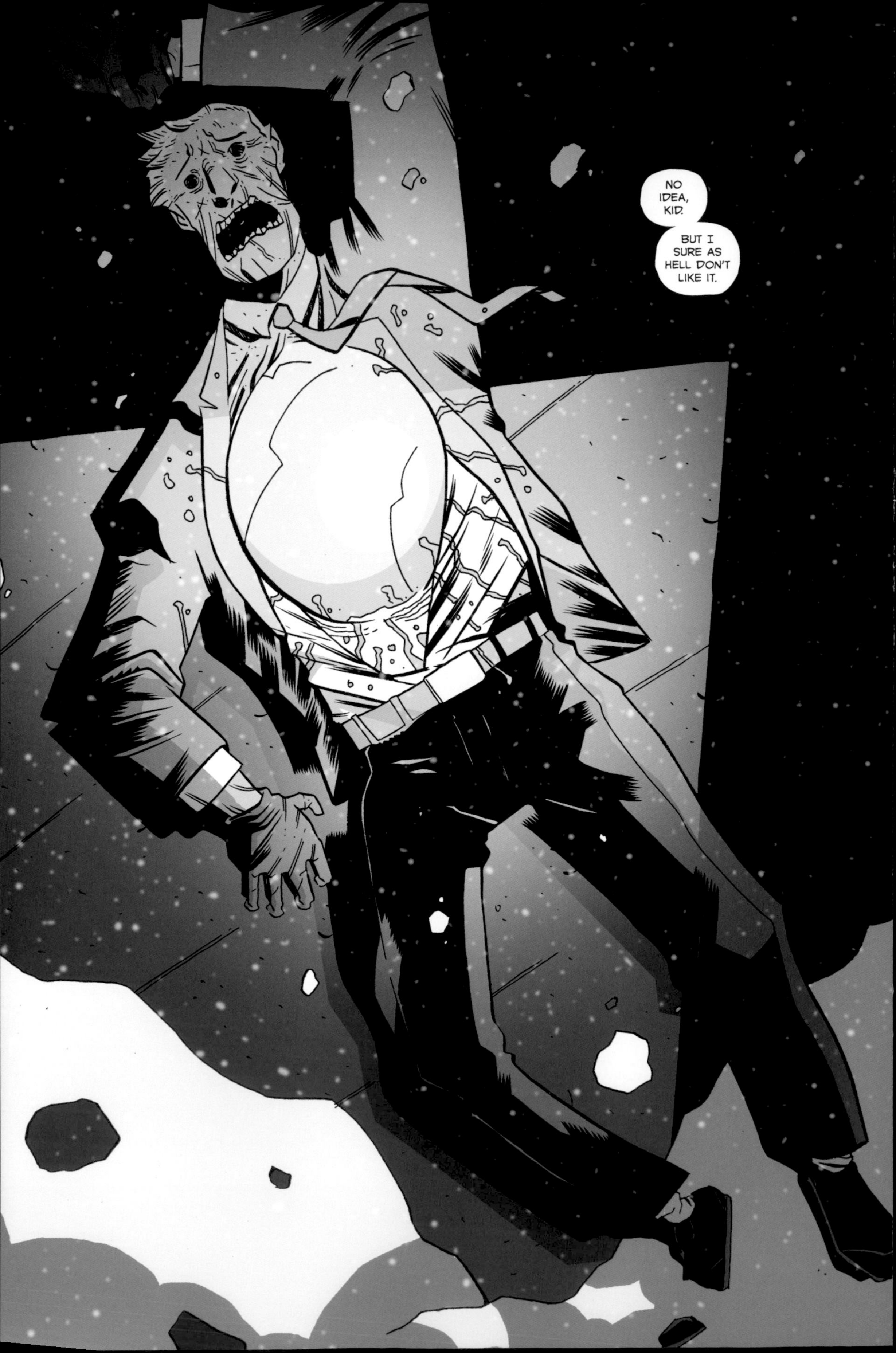
NO IDEA, KID.
BUT I SURE AS HELL DON'T LIKE IT.

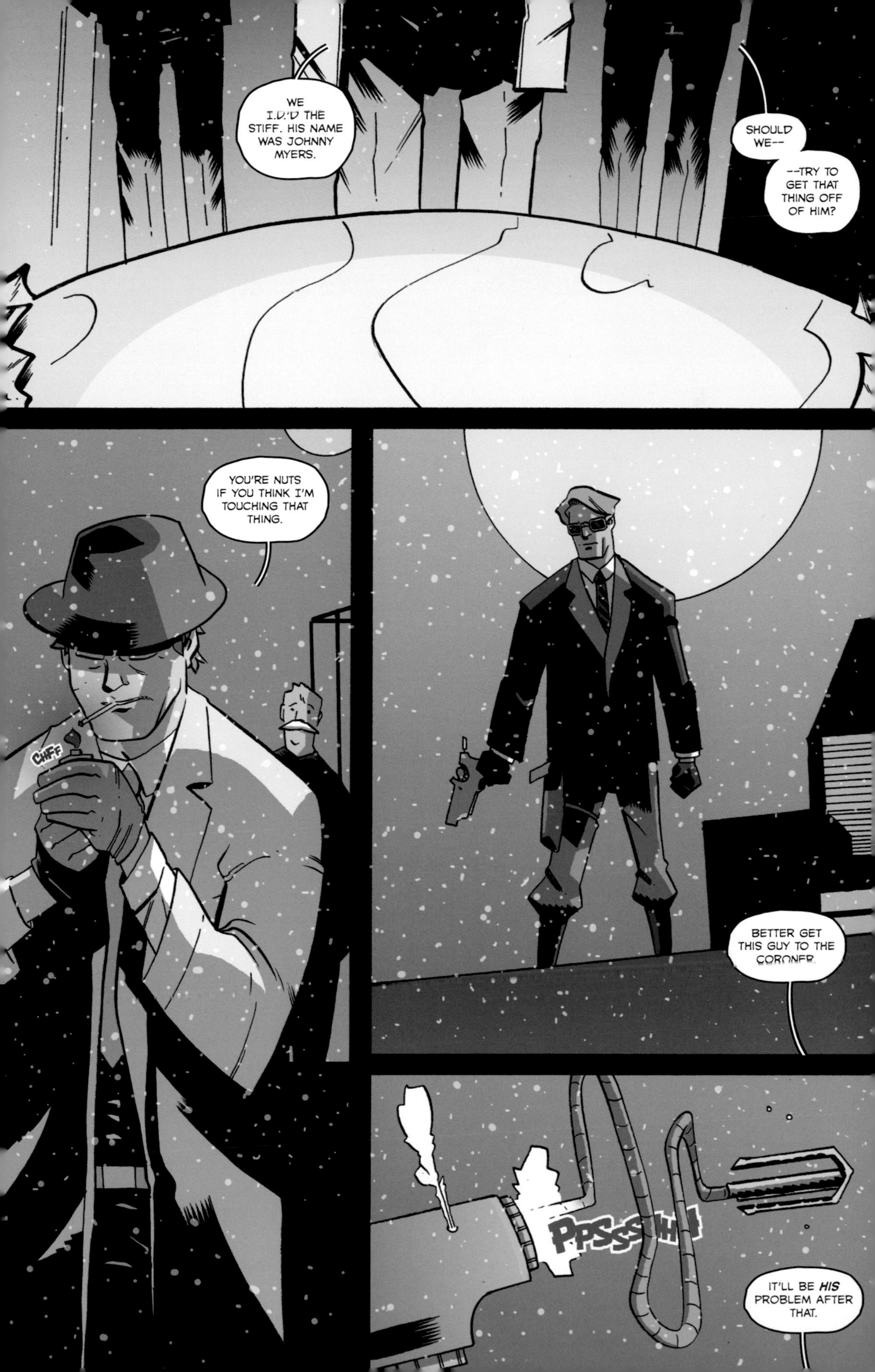
WE I.D.'D THE STIFF. HIS NAME WAS JOHNNY MYERS.
SHOULD WE--
--TRY TO GET THAT THING OFF OF HIM?
YOU'RE NUTS IF YOU THINK I'M TOUCHING THAT THING.
CHFF
BETTER GET THIS GUY TO THE CORONER.
PPSSSHH
IT'LL BE *HIS* PROBLEM AFTER THAT.

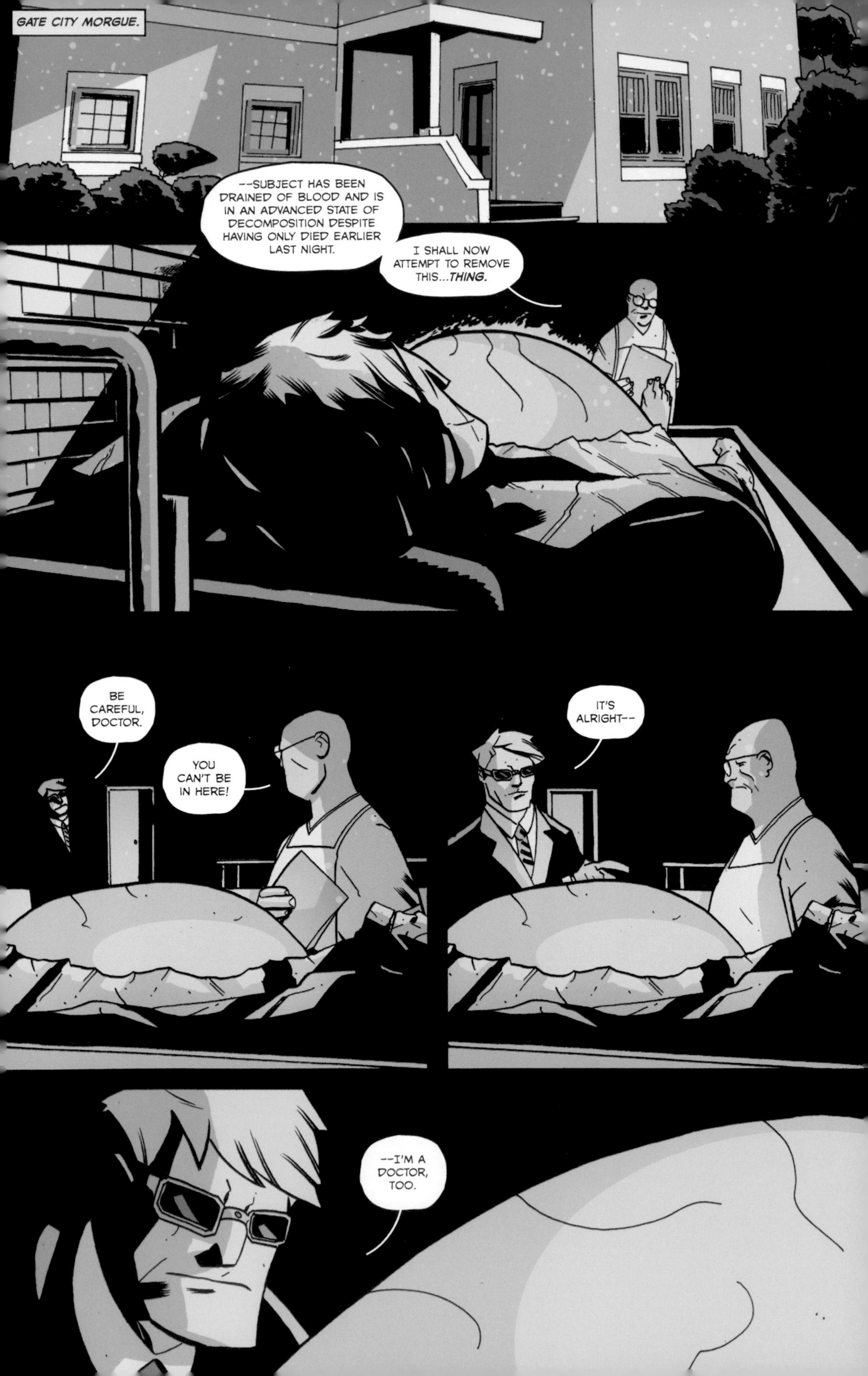
GATE CITY MORGUE.
--SUBJECT HAS BEEN DRAINED OF BLOOD AND IS IN AN ADVANCED STATE OF DECOMPOSITION DESPITE HAVING ONLY DIED EARLIER LAST NIGHT.
I SHALL NOW ATTEMPT TO REMOVE THIS...*THING.*
BE CAREFUL, DOCTOR.
YOU CAN'T BE IN HERE!
IT'S ALRIGHT--
--I'M A DOCTOR, TOO.

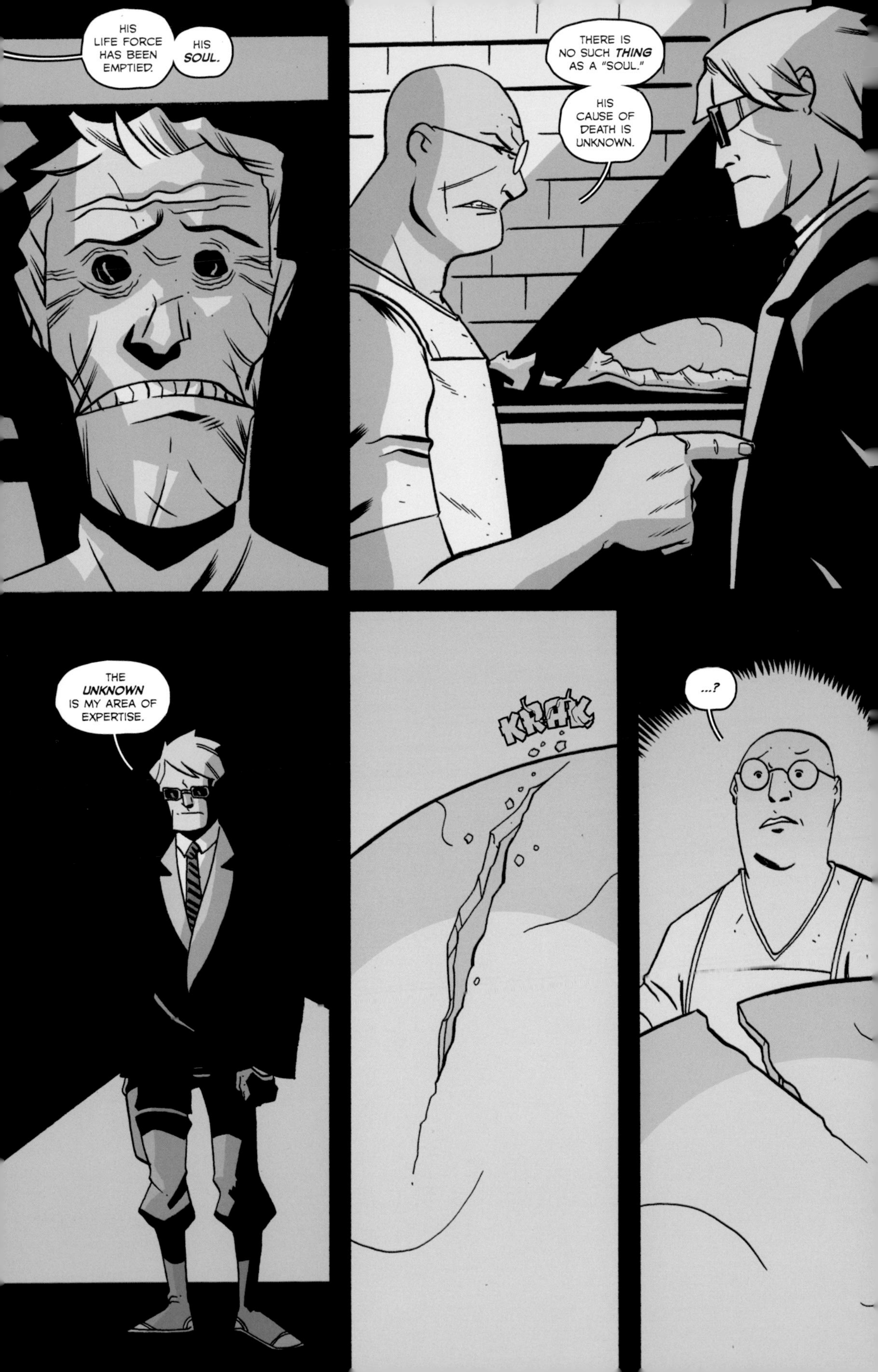

HIS LIFE FORCE HAS BEEN EMPTIED.
HIS SOUL.
THERE IS NO SUCH THING AS A "SOUL."
HIS CAUSE OF DEATH IS UNKNOWN.
THE UNKNOWN IS MY AREA OF EXPERTISE.
KRAK
...?

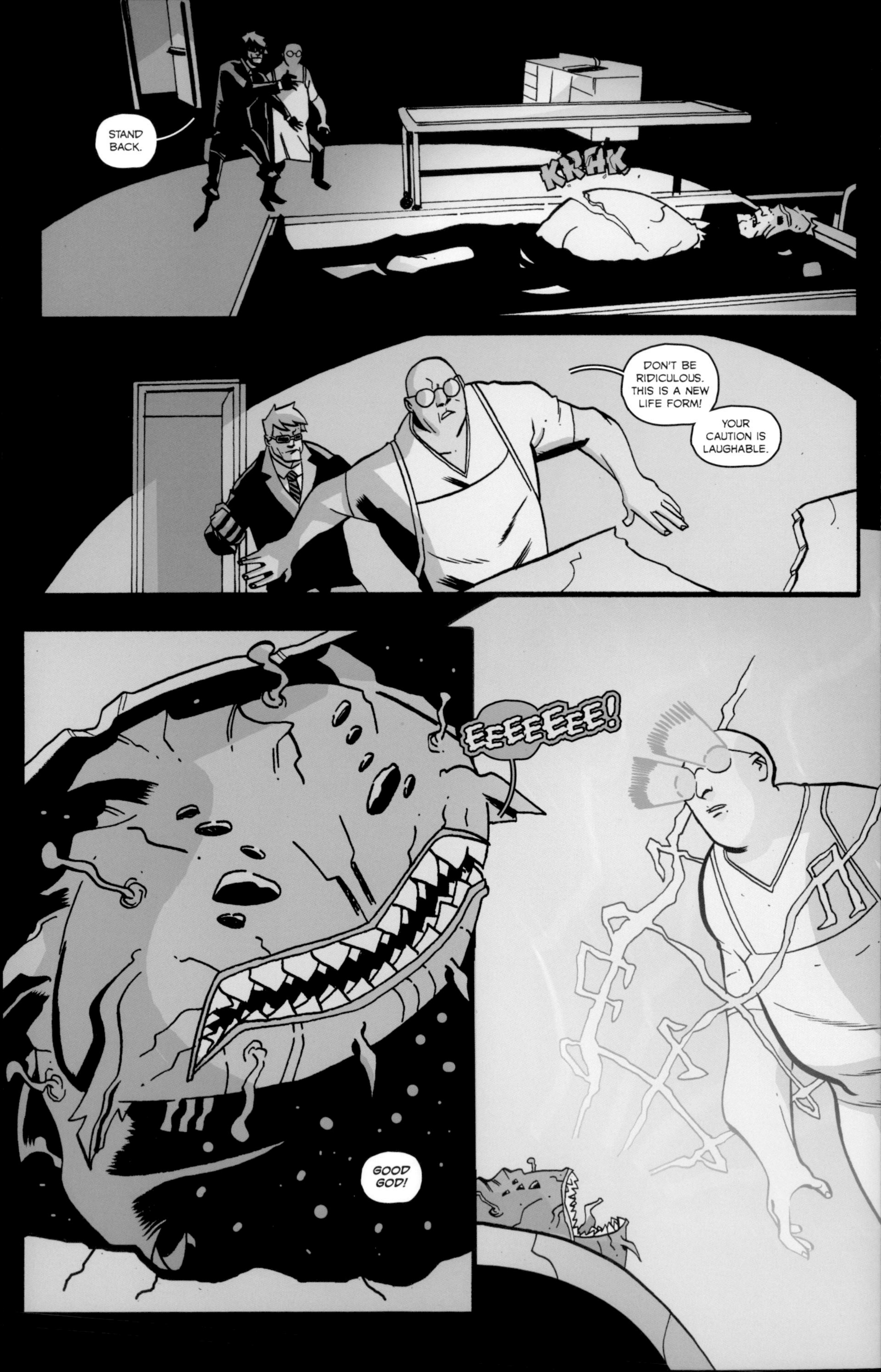
STAND BACK.
KRAK
DON'T BE RIDICULOUS. THIS IS A NEW LIFE FORM!
YOUR CAUTION IS LAUGHABLE.
EEEEEEE!
GOOD GOD!

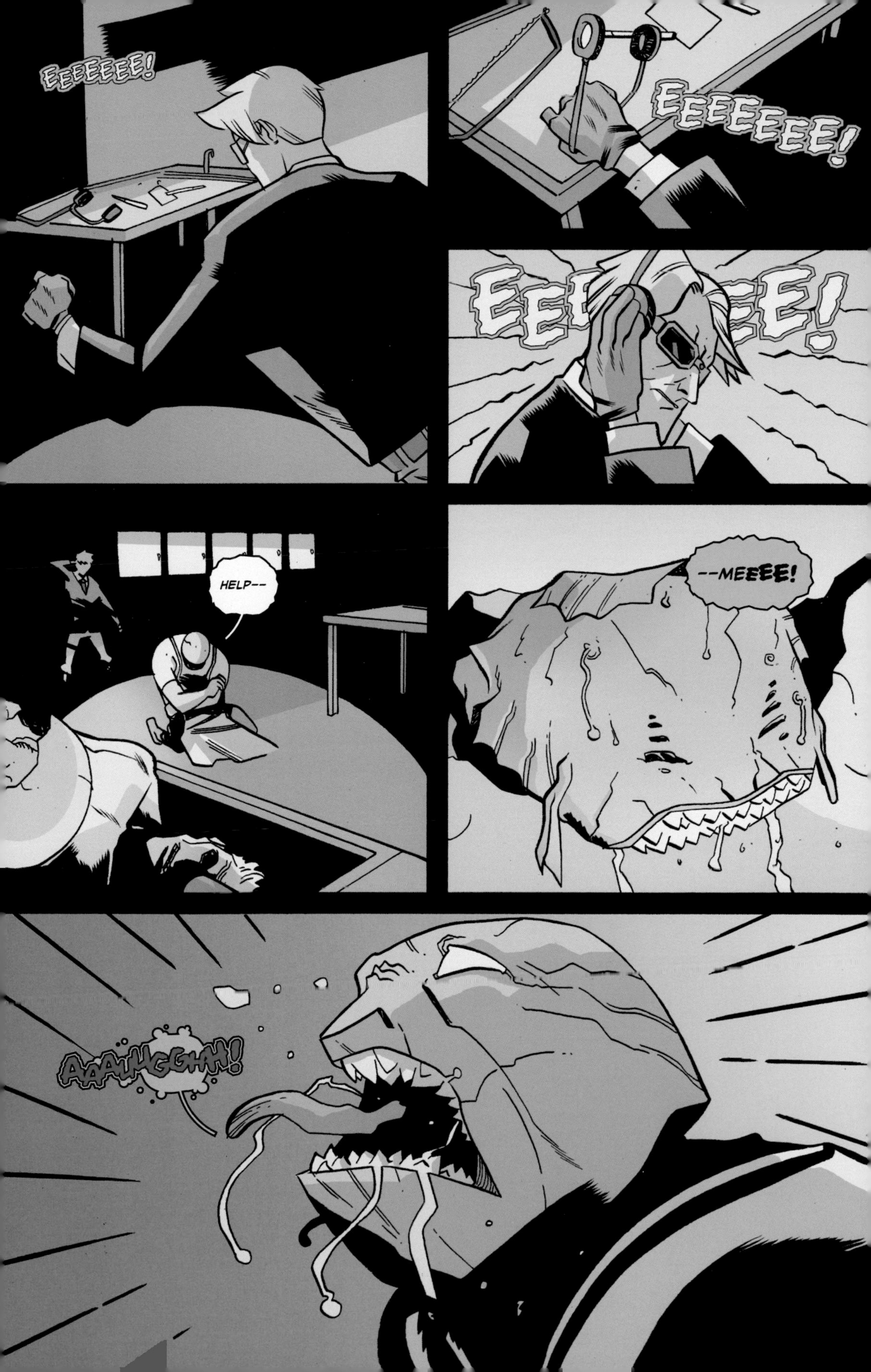

EEEEEEE!
EEEEEEEE!
EEEEEEEE!
HELP--
--MEEEE!
AAAUUGGHH!

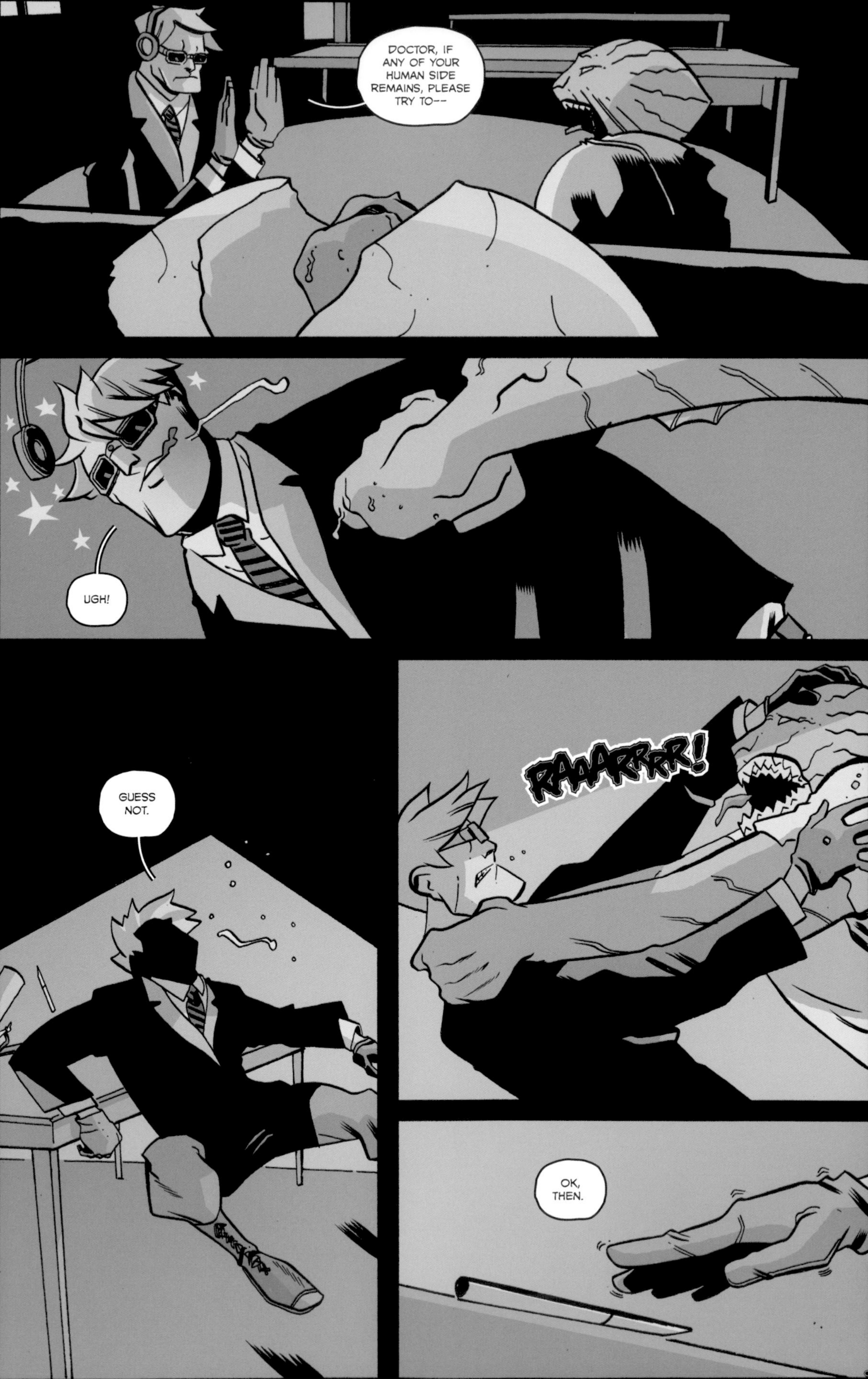

DOCTOR, IF ANY OF YOUR HUMAN SIDE REMAINS, PLEASE TRY TO--
UGH!
GUESS NOT.
RAAARRRR!
OK, THEN.

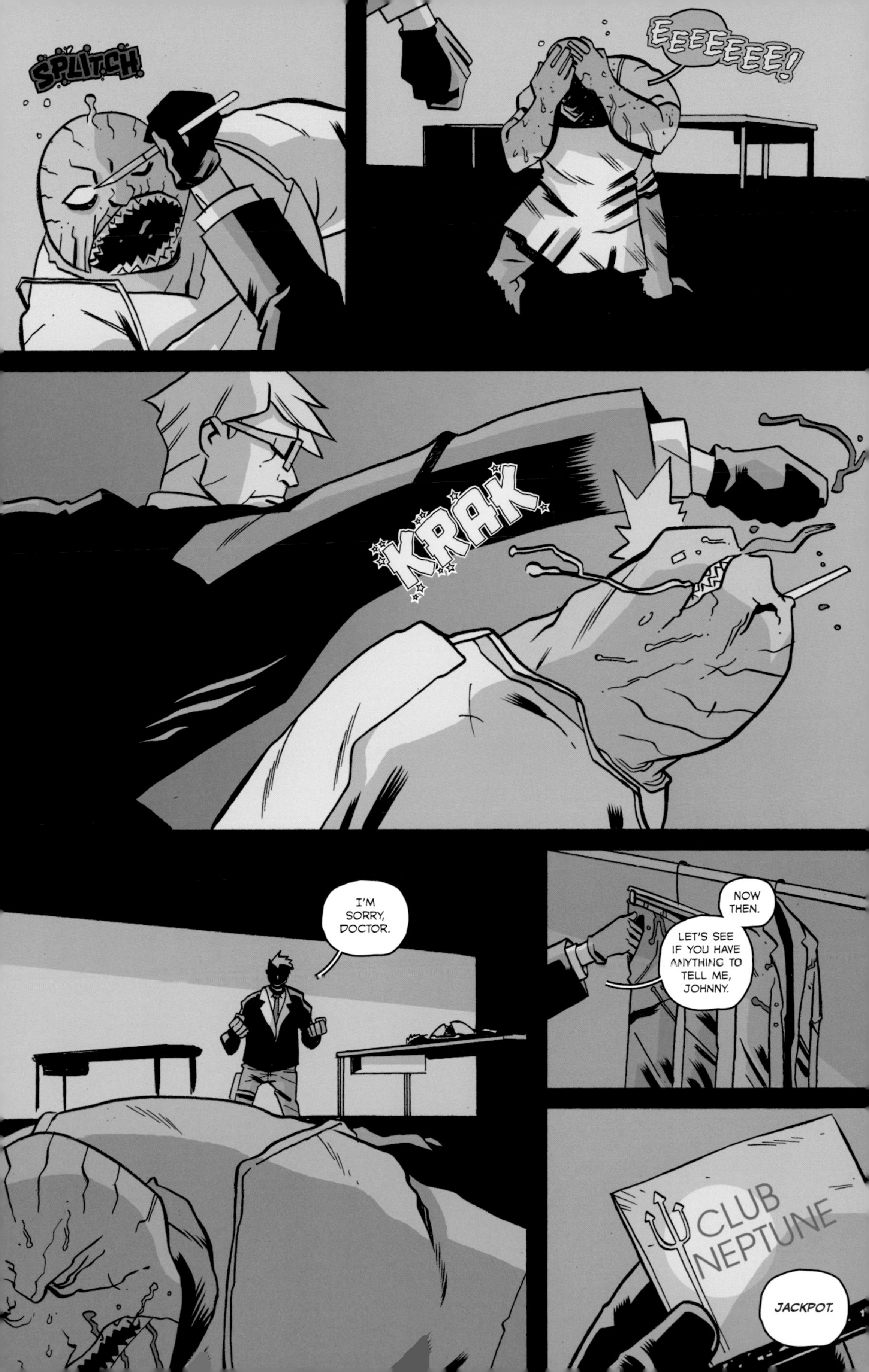

SPLITCH
EEEEEEEE!
KRAK
I'M SORRY, DOCTOR.
NOW THEN.
LET'S SEE IF YOU HAVE ANYTHING TO TELL ME, JOHNNY.
CLUB NEPTUNE
JACKPOT.

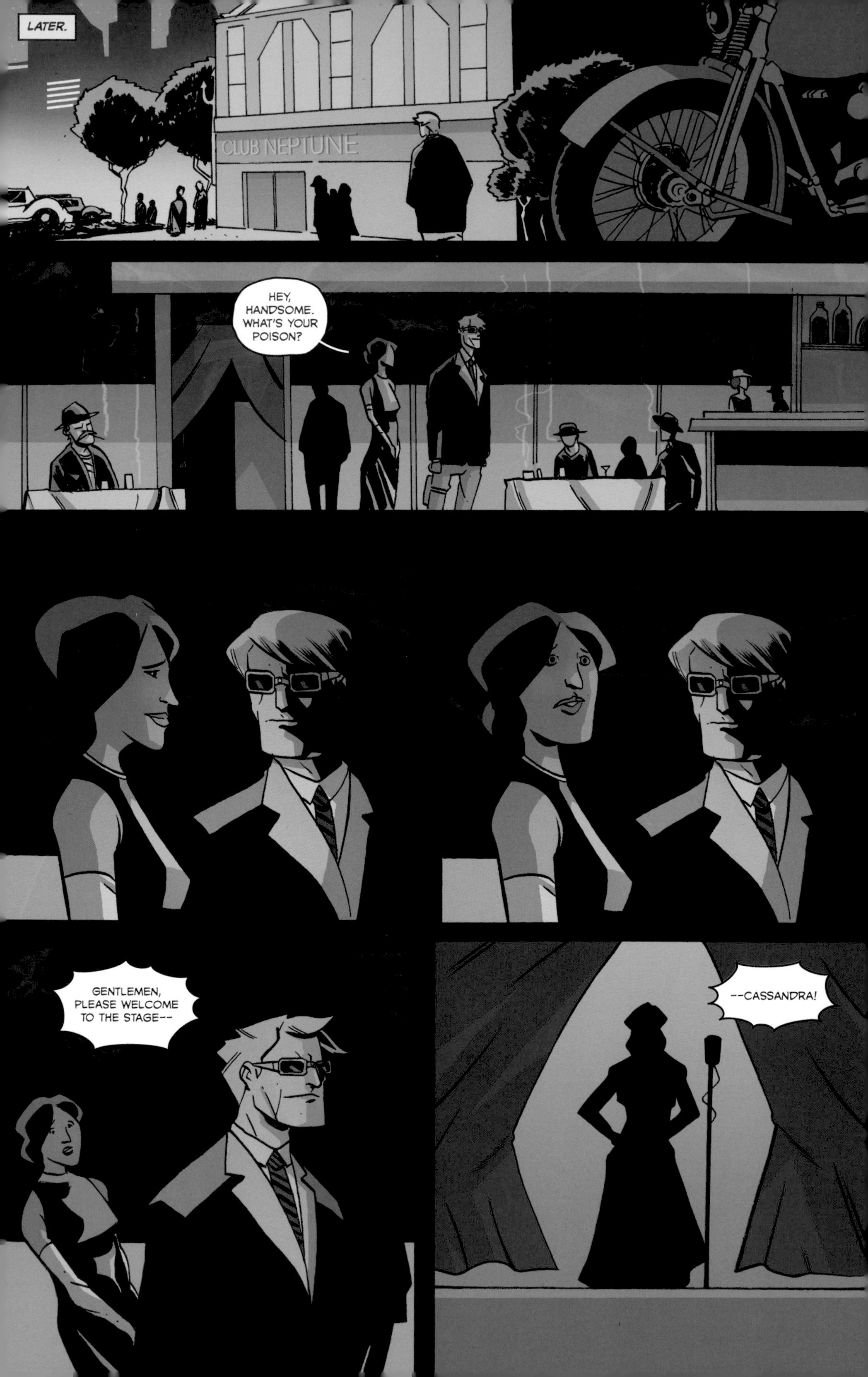
LATER.
CLUB NEPTUNE
HEY, HANDSOME. WHAT'S YOUR POISON?
GENTLEMEN, PLEASE WELCOME TO THE STAGE--
--CASSANDRA!

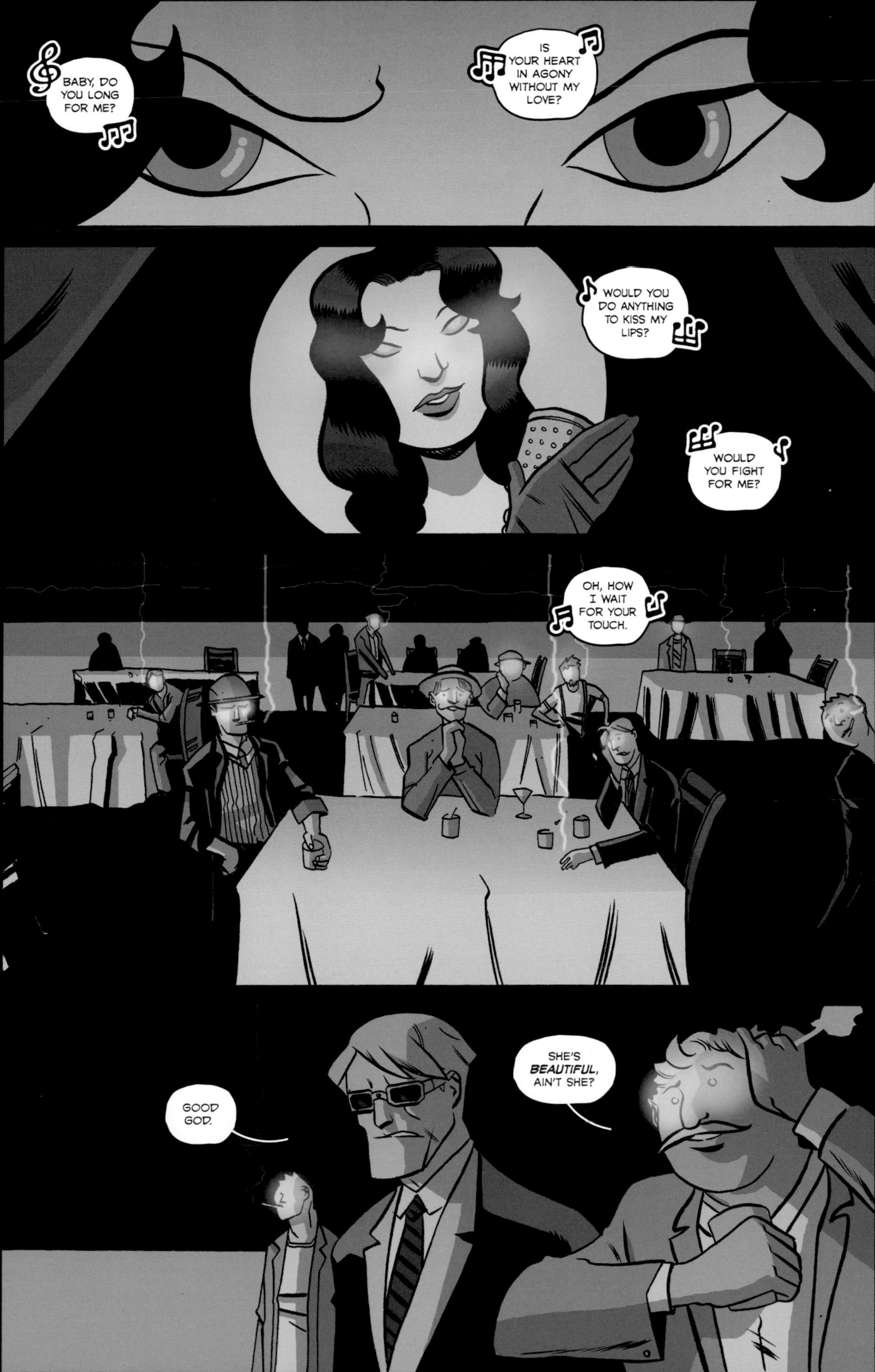

BABY, DO YOU LONG FOR ME?
IS YOUR HEART IN AGONY WITHOUT MY LOVE?
WOULD YOU DO ANYTHING TO KISS MY LIPS?
WOULD YOU FIGHT FOR ME?
OH, HOW I WAIT FOR YOUR TOUCH.
SHE'S *BEAUTIFUL*, AIN'T SHE?
GOOD GOD.

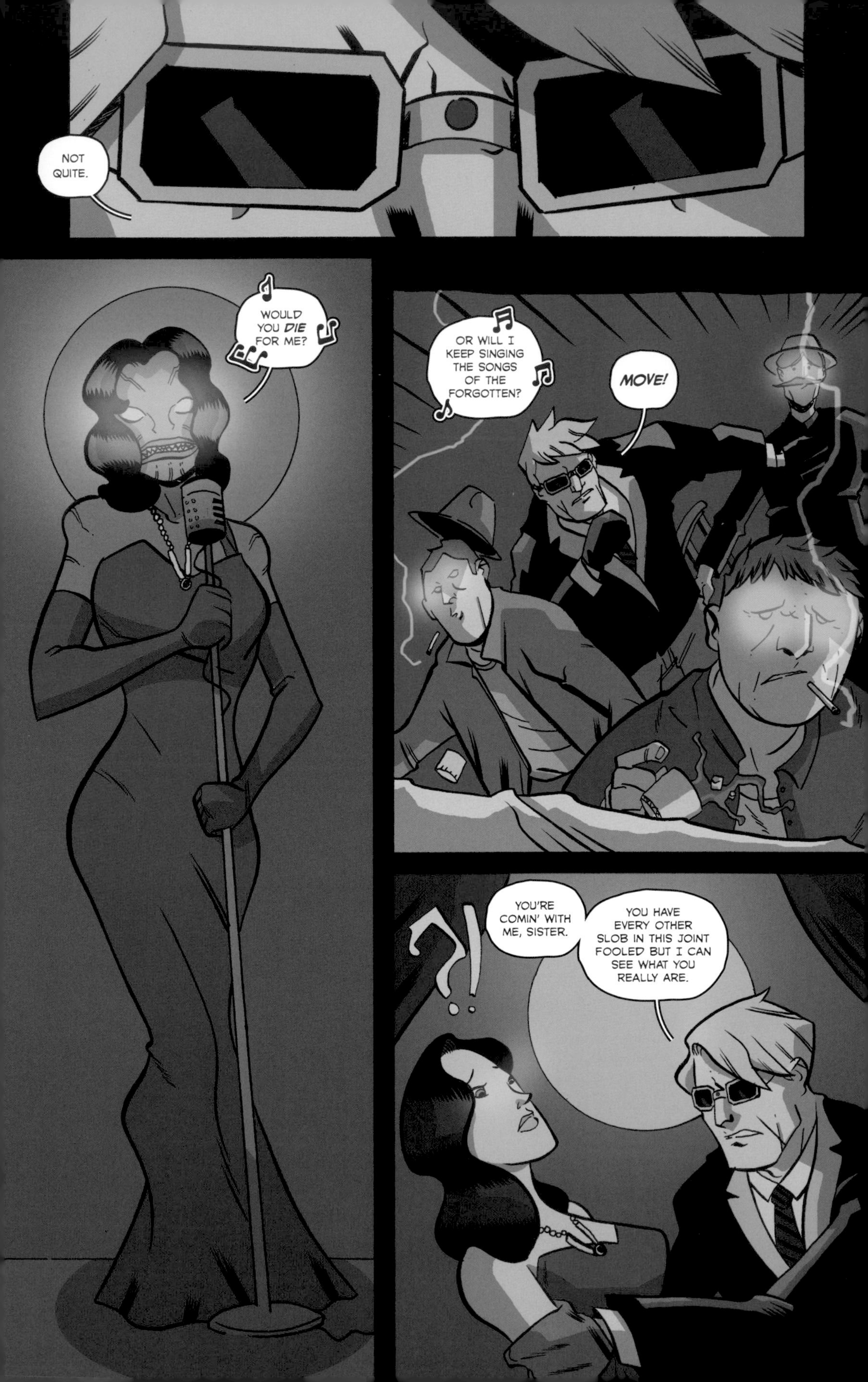
NOT QUITE.
WOULD YOU DIE FOR ME?
OR WILL I KEEP SINGING THE SONGS OF THE FORGOTTEN?
MOVE!
?!
YOU'RE COMIN' WITH ME, SISTER.
YOU HAVE EVERY OTHER SLOB IN THIS JOINT FOOLED BUT I CAN SEE WHAT YOU REALLY ARE.

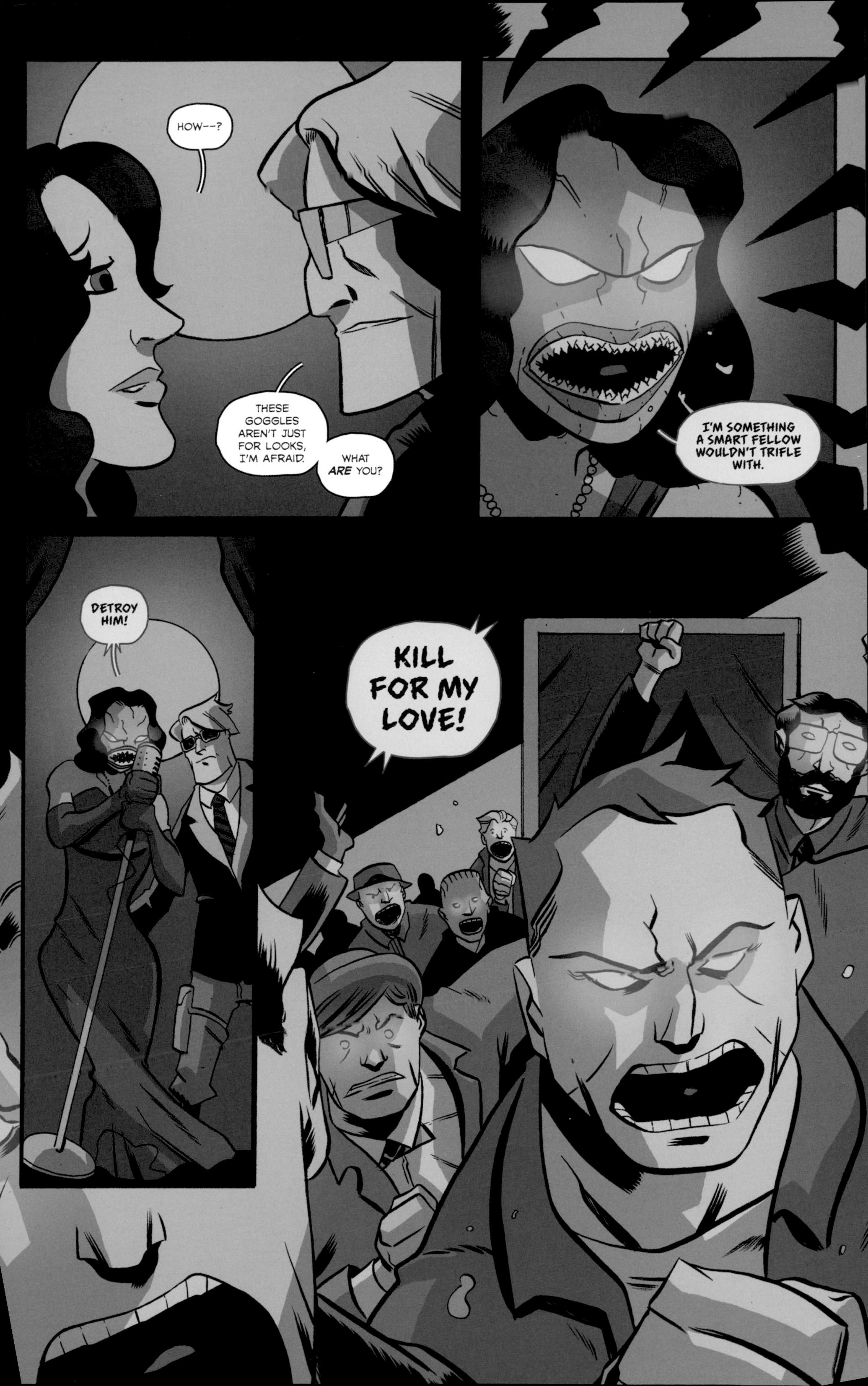
HOW--?
THESE GOGGLES AREN'T JUST FOR LOOKS, I'M AFRAID.
WHAT *ARE* YOU?
I'M SOMETHING A SMART FELLOW WOULDN'T TRIFLE WITH.
DETROY HIM!
KILL FOR MY LOVE!

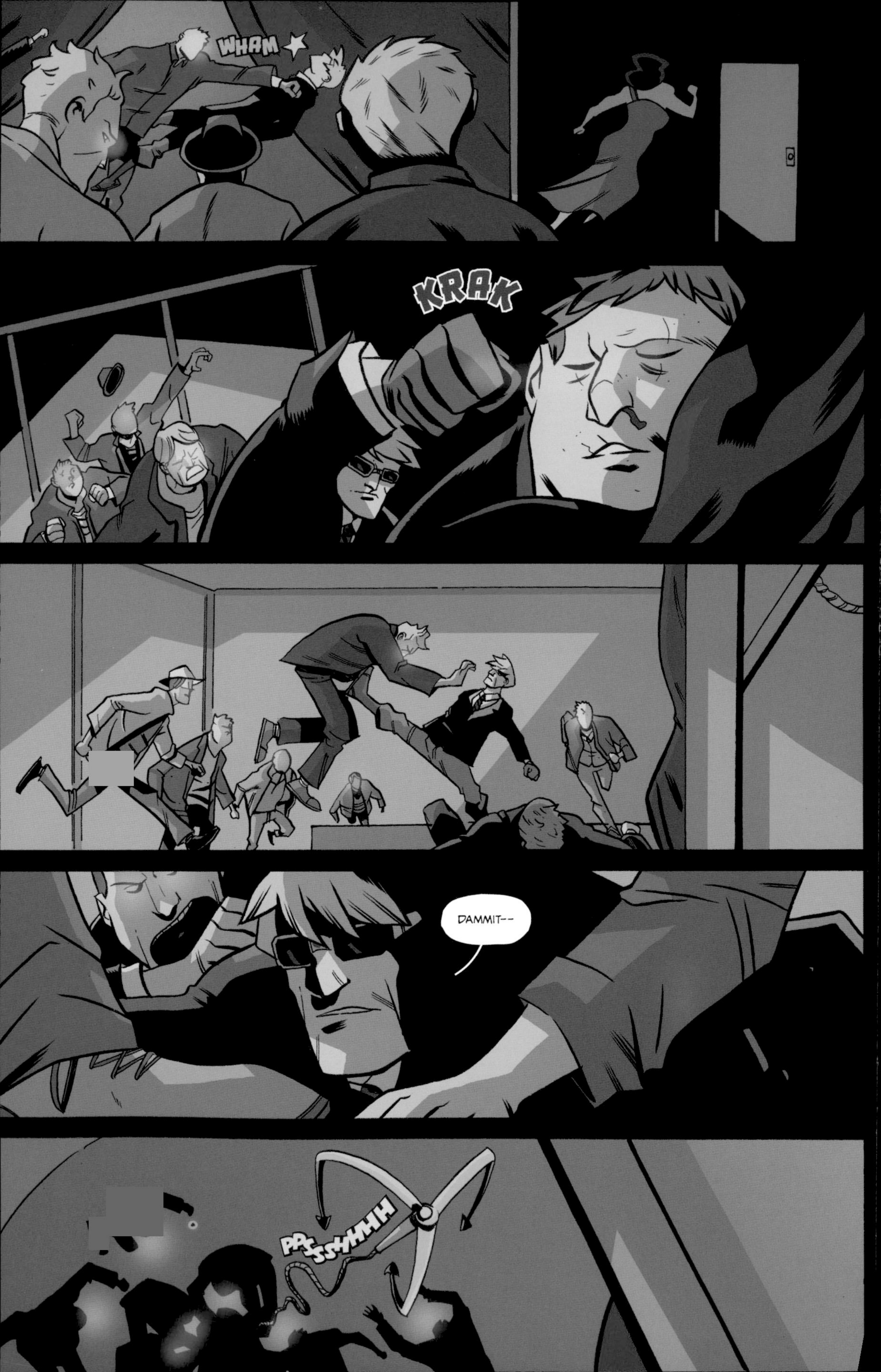
WHAM
KRAK
DAMMIT--
PPSSSHHHHH

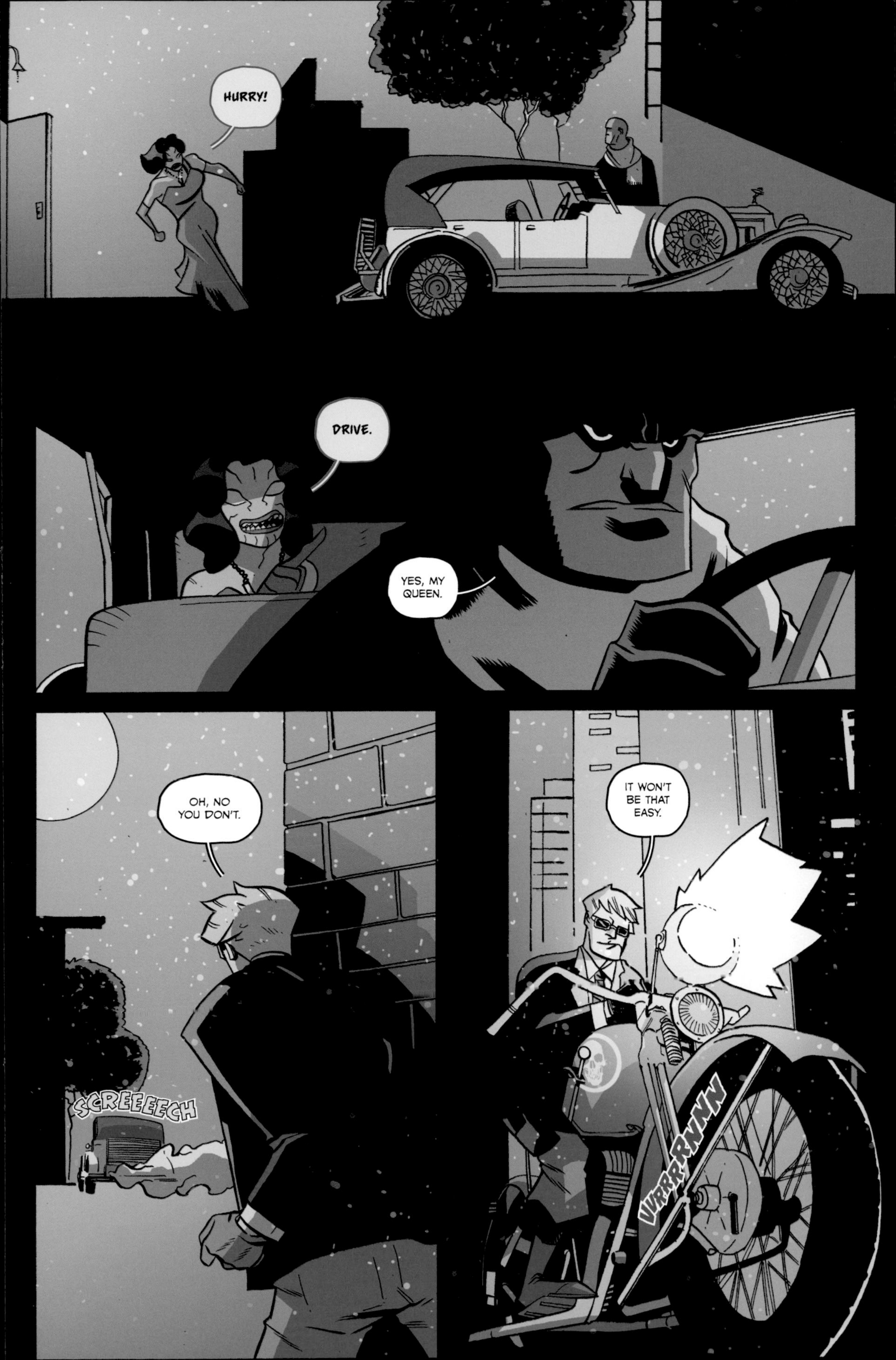
HURRY!
DRIVE.
YES, MY QUEEN.
OH, NO YOU DON'T.
SCREEEEECH
IT WON'T BE THAT EASY.
VVRRRRNNN

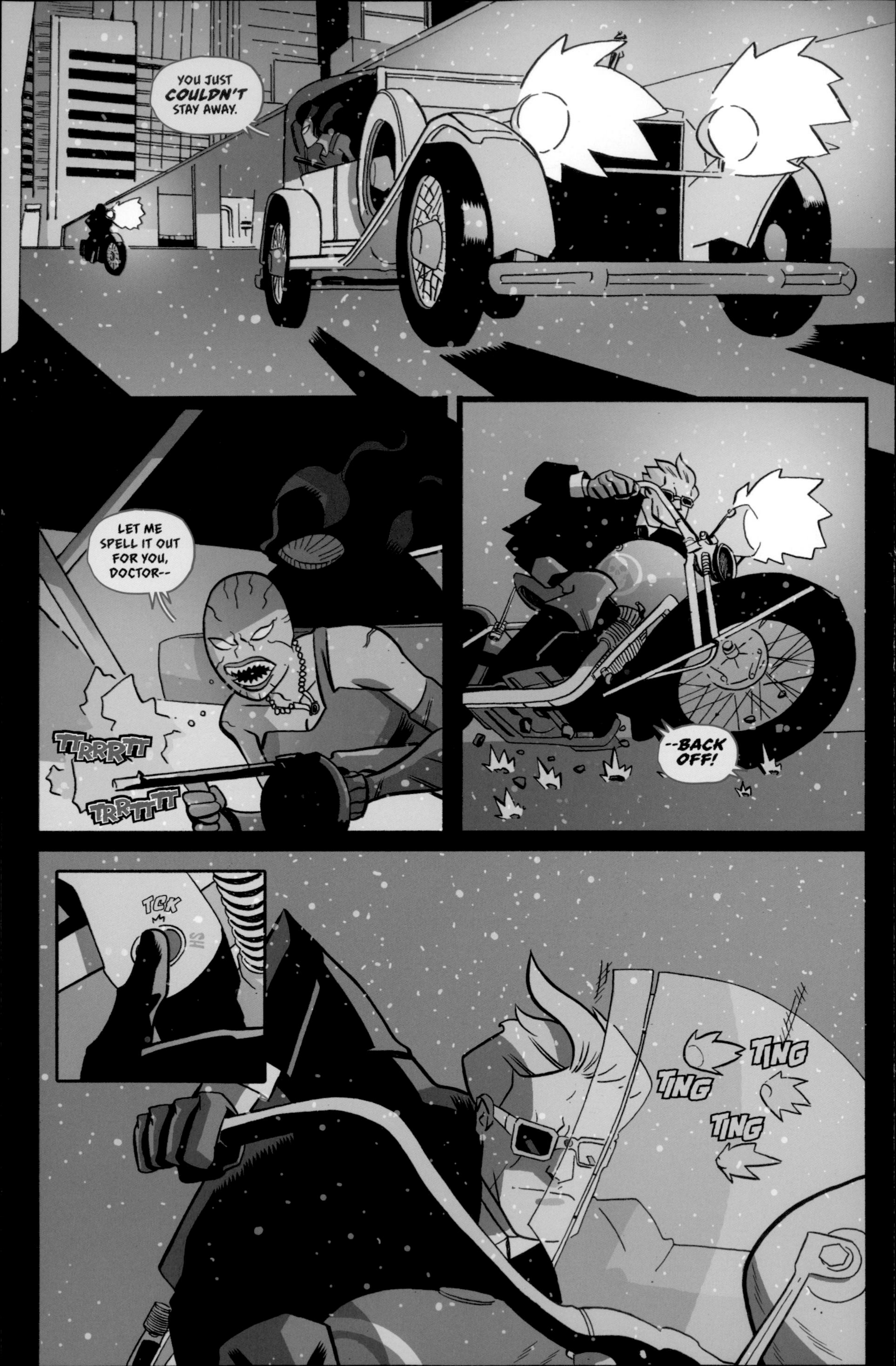
YOU JUST COULDN'T STAY AWAY.
LET ME SPELL IT OUT FOR YOU, DOCTOR--
TTRRRTT
TRRTTTT
--BACK OFF!
TCK
TING
TING
TING

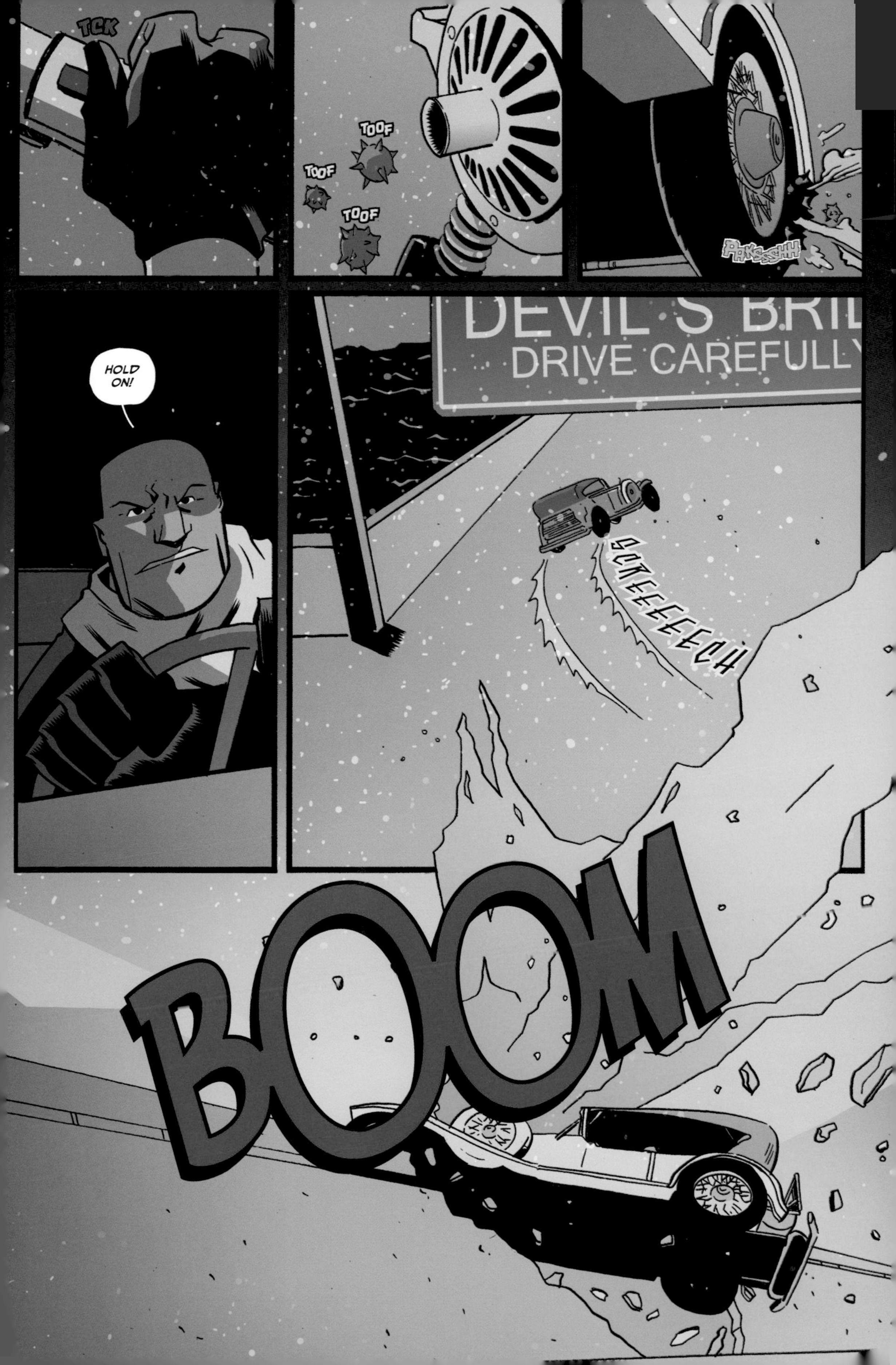
TCK
TOOF
TOOF
TOOF
PAKSSSHH
HOLD ON!
DEVIL'S BRI
DRIVE CAREFULLY
SCREEEEECH
BOOM

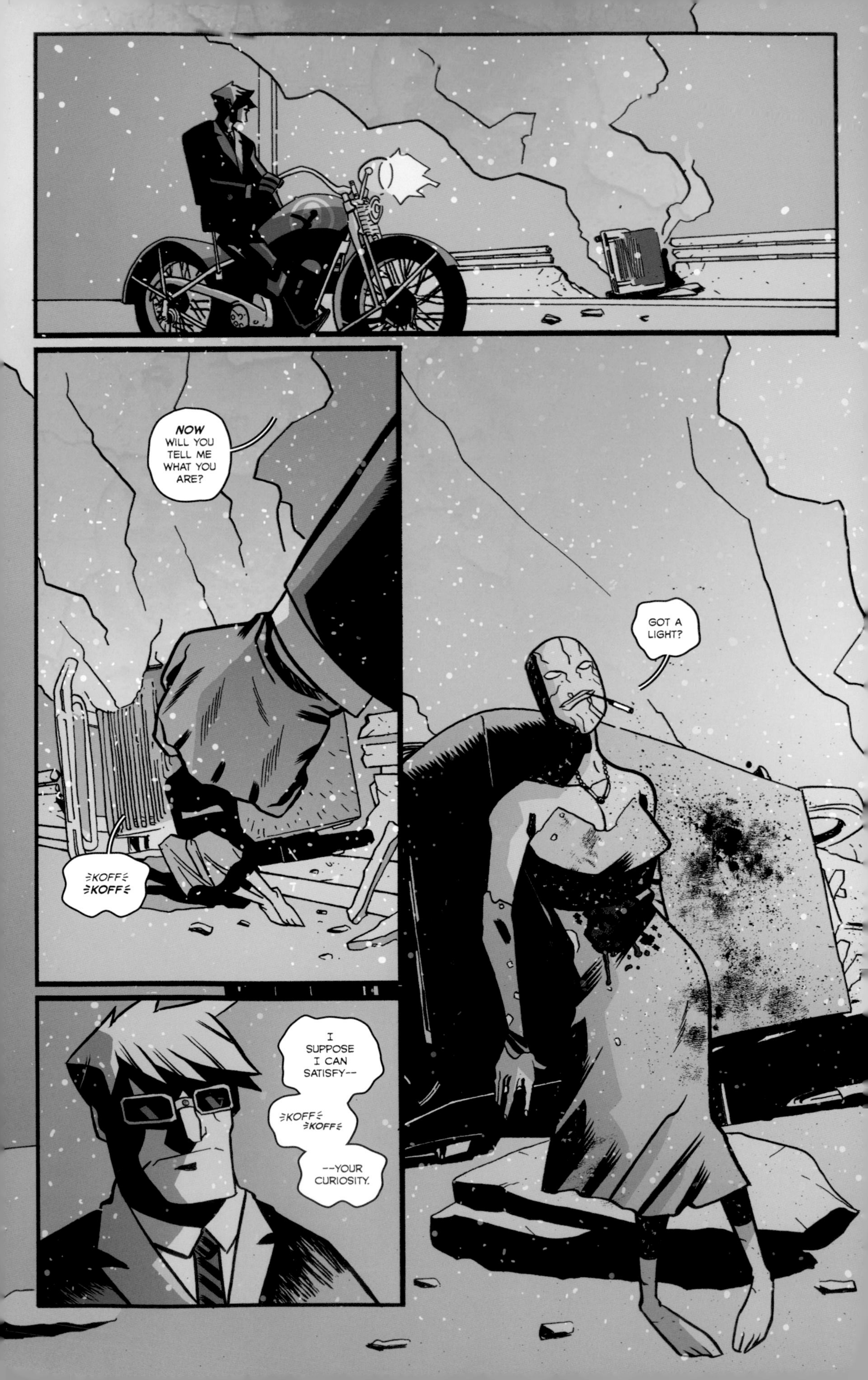
NOW WILL YOU TELL ME WHAT YOU ARE?
KOFF KOFF
GOT A LIGHT?
I SUPPOSE I CAN SATISFY--
KOFF KOFF
--YOUR CURIOSITY.

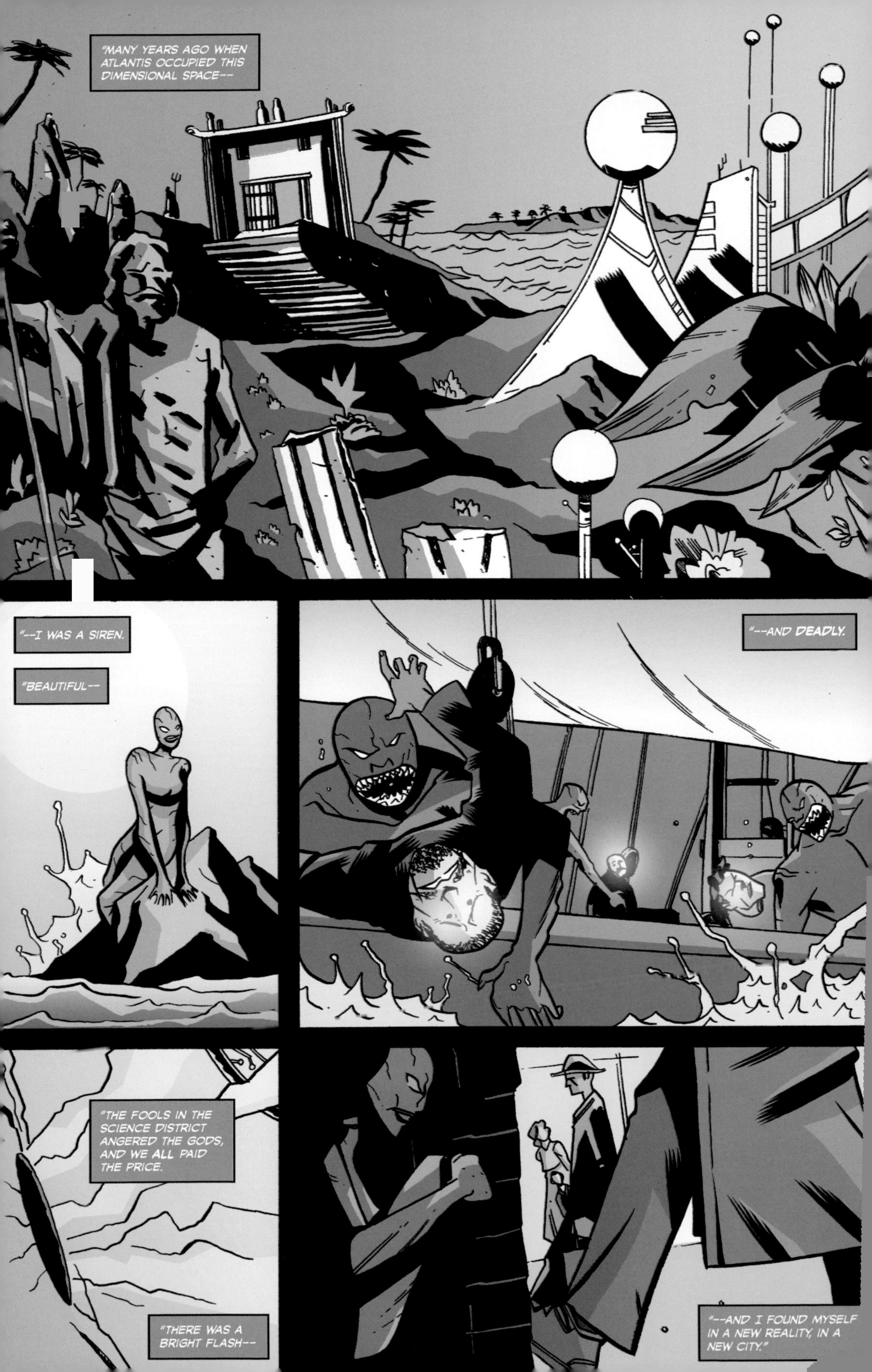
"MANY YEARS AGO WHEN ATLANTIS OCCUPIED THIS DIMENSIONAL SPACE--
"--I WAS A SIREN.
"BEAUTIFUL--
"--AND DEADLY.
"THE FOOLS IN THE SCIENCE DISTRICT ANGERED THE GODS, AND WE ALL PAID THE PRICE.
"THERE WAS A BRIGHT FLASH--
"--AND I FOUND MYSELF IN A NEW REALITY, IN A NEW CITY."

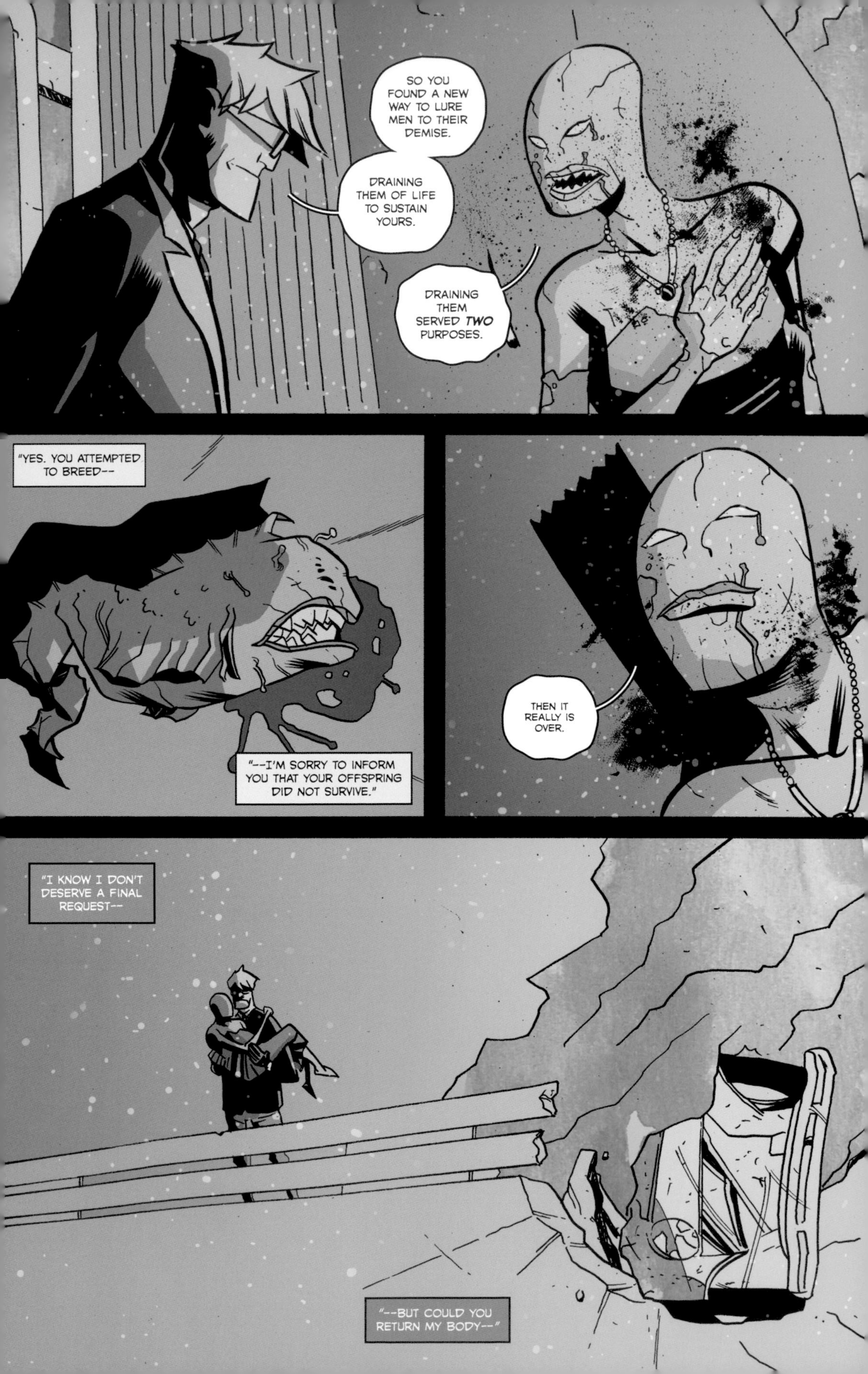
SO YOU FOUND A NEW WAY TO LURE MEN TO THEIR DEMISE.
DRAINING THEM OF LIFE TO SUSTAIN YOURS.
DRAINING THEM SERVED **TWO** PURPOSES.
"YES. YOU ATTEMPTED TO BREED--
"--I'M SORRY TO INFORM YOU THAT YOUR OFFSPRING DID NOT SURVIVE."
THEN IT REALLY IS OVER.
"I KNOW I DON'T DESERVE A FINAL REQUEST--
"--BUT COULD YOU RETURN MY BODY--"

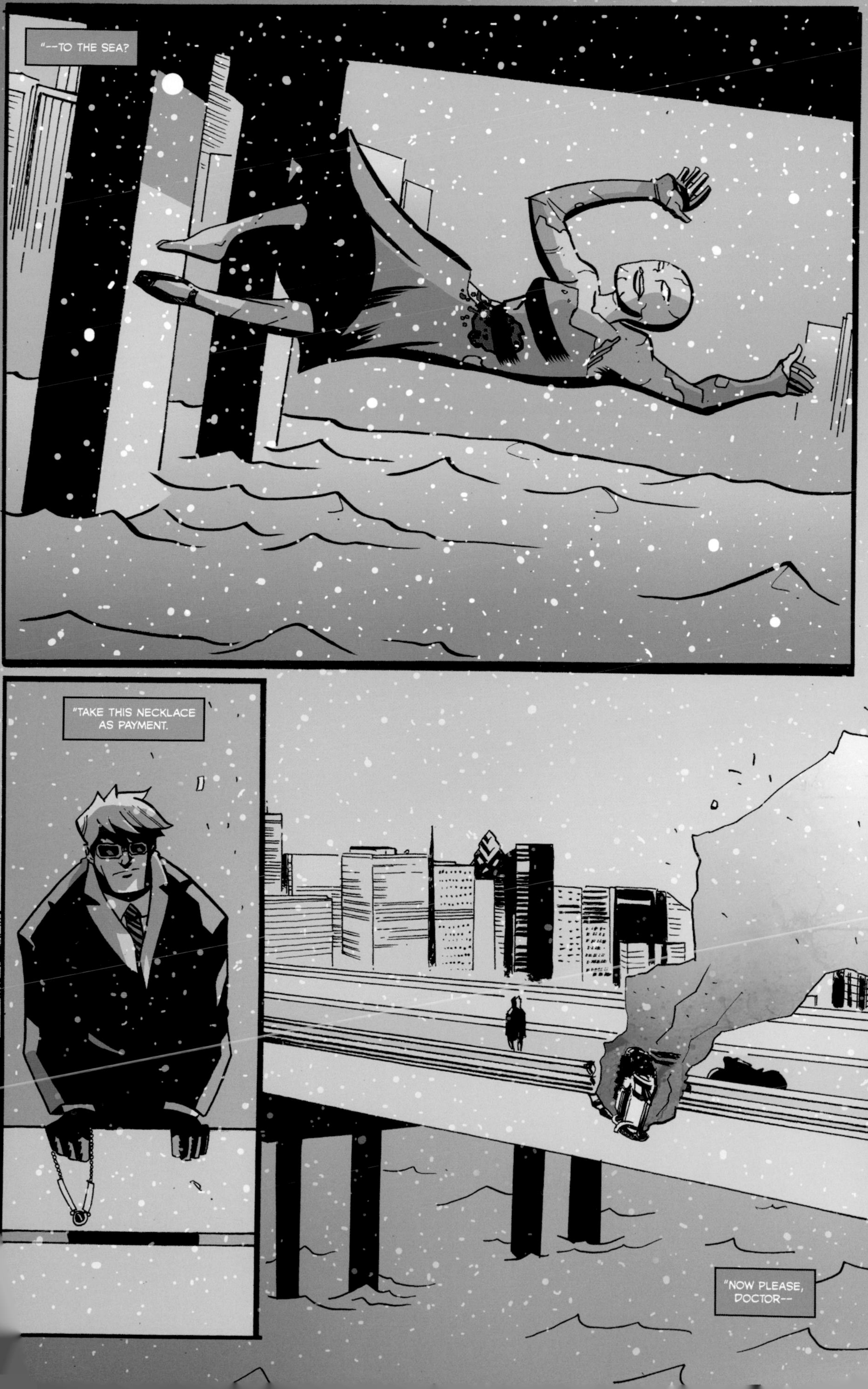
"--TO THE SEA?
"TAKE THIS NECKLACE AS PAYMENT.
"NOW PLEASE, DOCTOR--

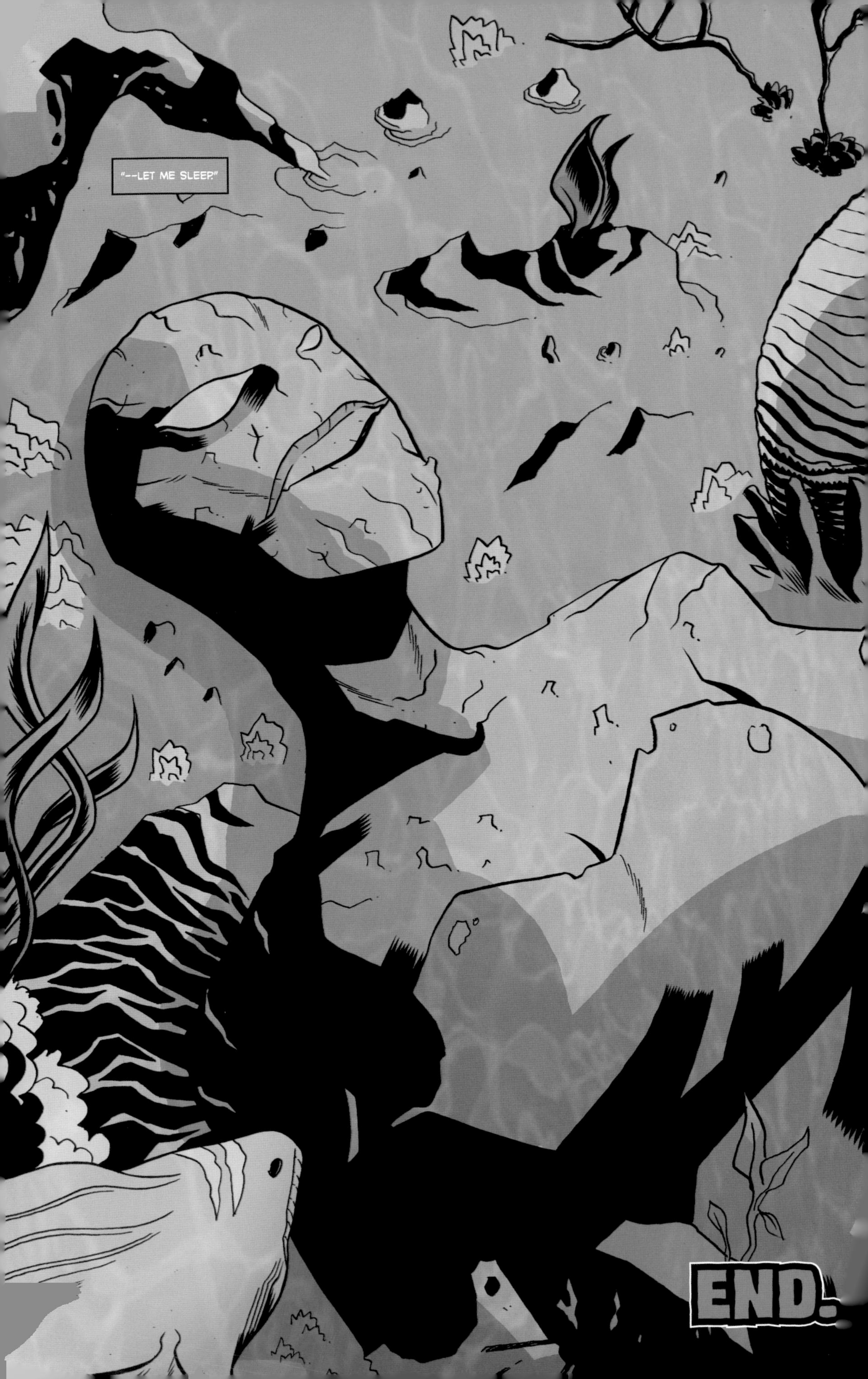
"--LET ME SLEEP."
END.

THE FREQUENCY OF FEAR

SCRIPT BY **FABIAN RANGEL JR.**

ART BY **RYAN CODY**

LETTERS BY **NIC SHAW**

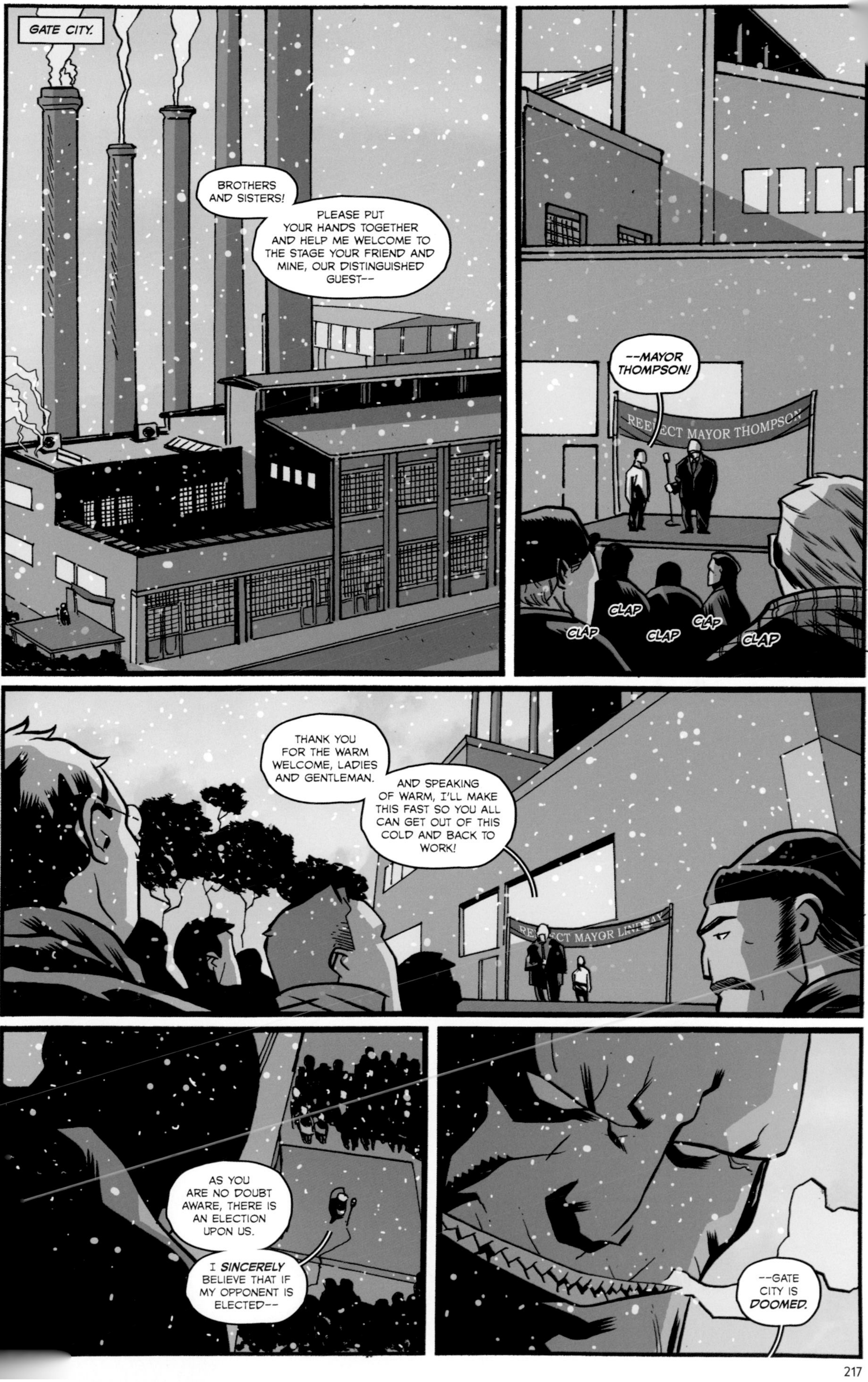
GATE CITY.
BROTHERS AND SISTERS!
PLEASE PUT YOUR HANDS TOGETHER AND HELP ME WELCOME TO THE STAGE YOUR FRIEND AND MINE, OUR DISTINGUISHED GUEST--
--MAYOR THOMPSON!
REELECT MAYOR THOMPSON
CLAP
CLAP
CLAP
CLAP
CLAP
THANK YOU FOR THE WARM WELCOME, LADIES AND GENTLEMAN.
AND SPEAKING OF WARM, I'LL MAKE THIS FAST SO YOU ALL CAN GET OUT OF THIS COLD AND BACK TO WORK!
AS YOU ARE NO DOUBT AWARE, THERE IS AN ELECTION UPON US.
I *SINCERELY* BELIEVE THAT IF MY OPPONENT IS ELECTED--
--GATE CITY IS *DOOMED.*

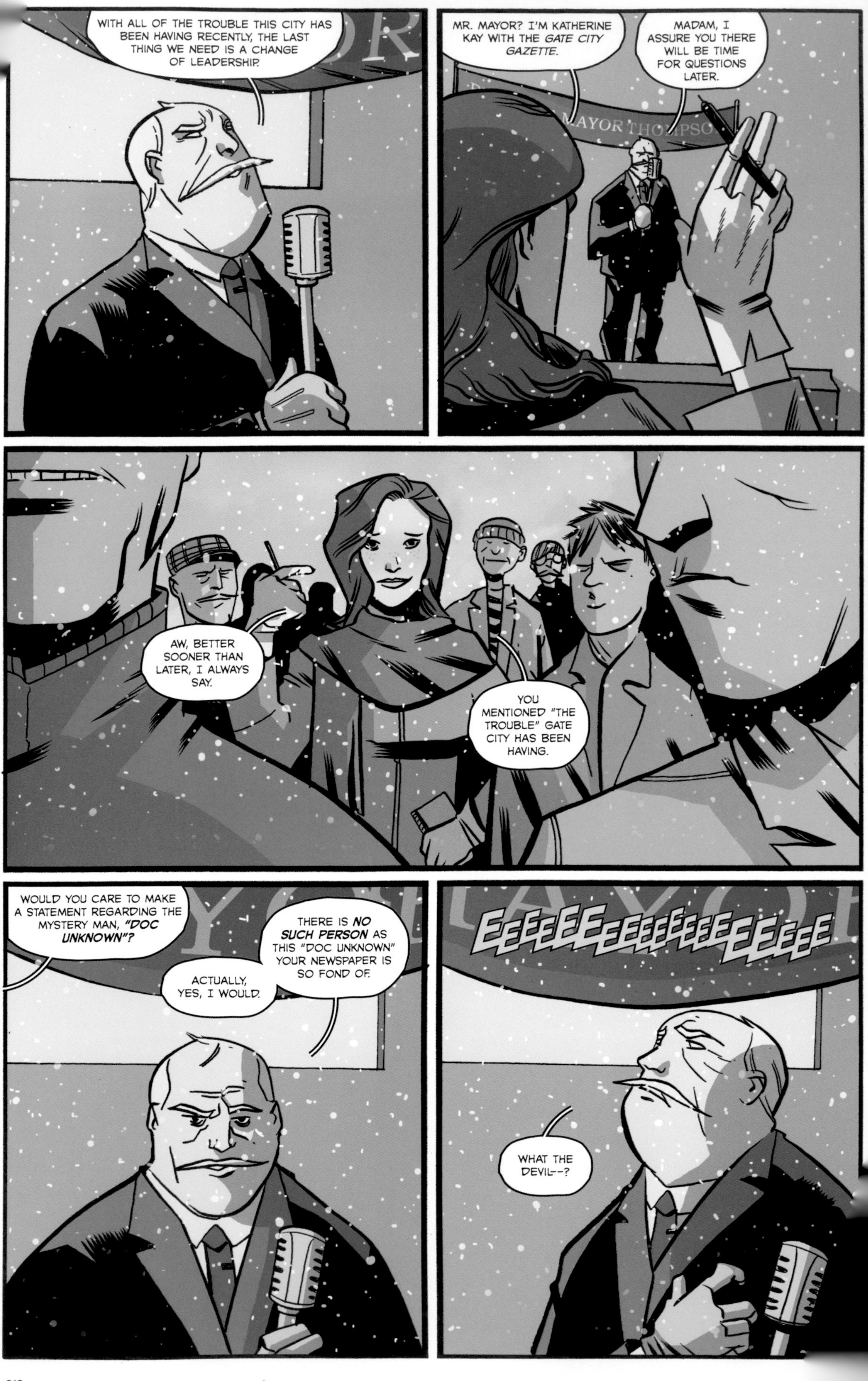

WITH ALL OF THE TROUBLE THIS CITY HAS BEEN HAVING RECENTLY, THE LAST THING WE NEED IS A CHANGE OF LEADERSHIP.
MR. MAYOR? I'M KATHERINE KAY WITH THE *GATE CITY GAZETTE.*
MADAM, I ASSURE YOU THERE WILL BE TIME FOR QUESTIONS LATER.
MAYOR THOMPSO
AW, BETTER SOONER THAN LATER, I ALWAYS SAY.
YOU MENTIONED "THE TROUBLE" GATE CITY HAS BEEN HAVING.
WOULD YOU CARE TO MAKE A STATEMENT REGARDING THE MYSTERY MAN, ***"DOC UNKNOWN"?***
ACTUALLY, YES, I WOULD.
THERE IS ***NO SUCH PERSON*** AS THIS "DOC UNKNOWN" YOUR NEWSPAPER IS SO FOND OF.
EEEEEEEEEEEEEEEEEEEEE
WHAT THE DEVIL--?

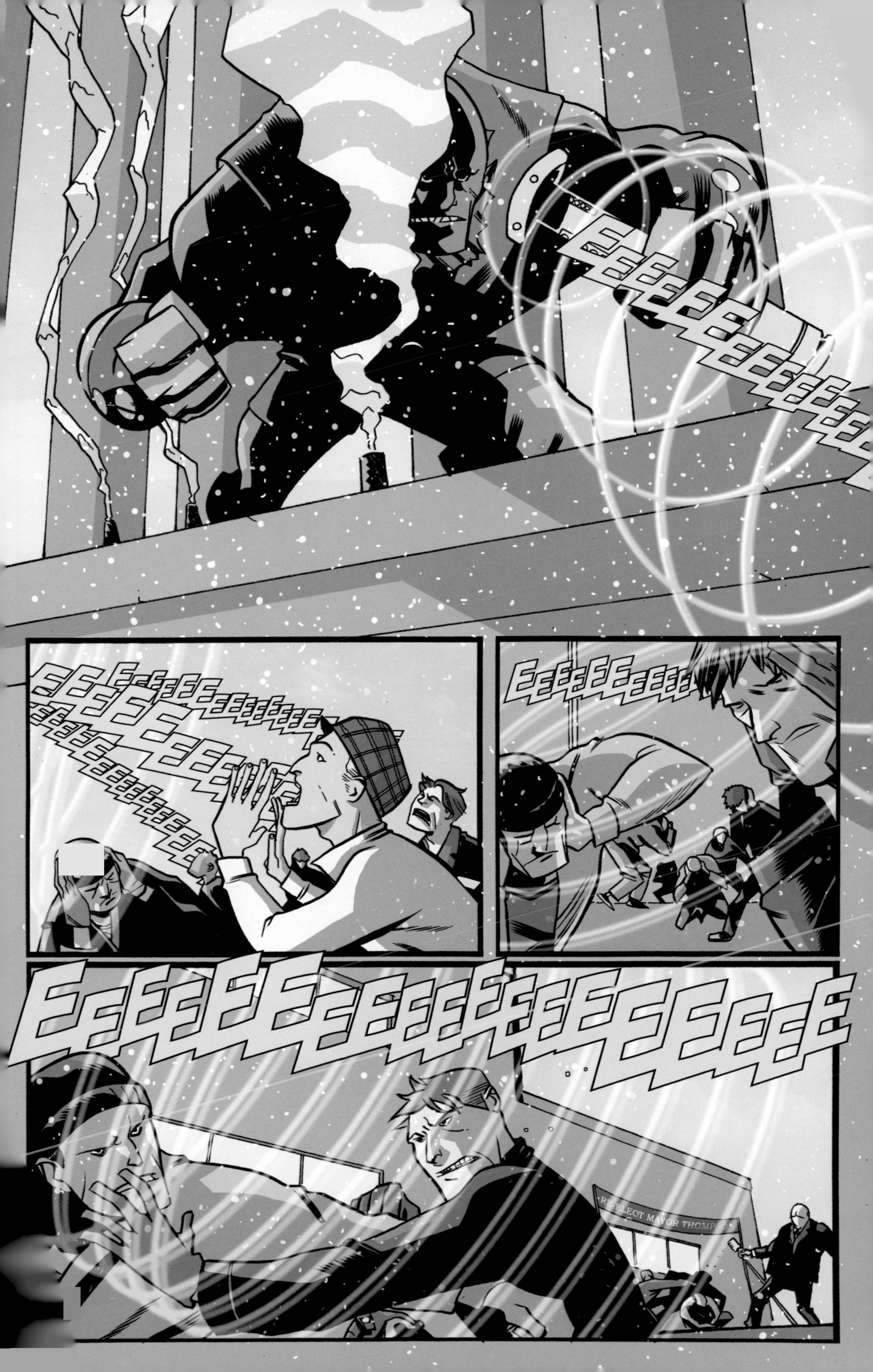
EEEEEEEEEEEEEEE
EEEEEEEEEEEEEEEEEEEE
EEEEEEEEEEEE
EEEEEEEEEEEEEEEEEEEEEEEEE
RE-ELECT MAYOR THOMPSON

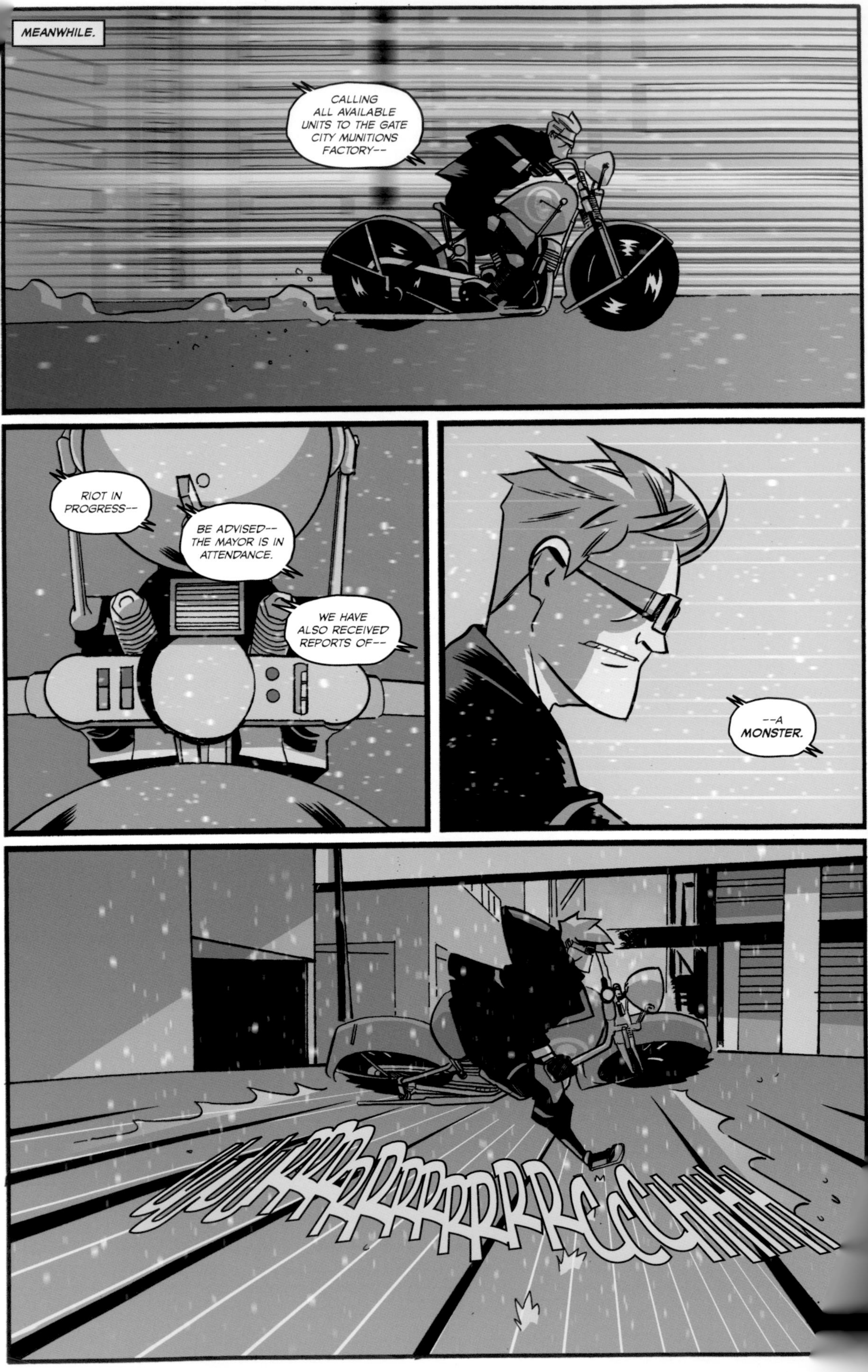
MEANWHILE.
CALLING ALL AVAILABLE UNITS TO THE GATE CITY MUNITIONS FACTORY--
RIOT IN PROGRESS--
BE ADVISED-- THE MAYOR IS IN ATTENDANCE.
WE HAVE ALSO RECEIVED REPORTS OF--
--A MONSTER.
WHHRRRRRRRRRRRRCCCHHH

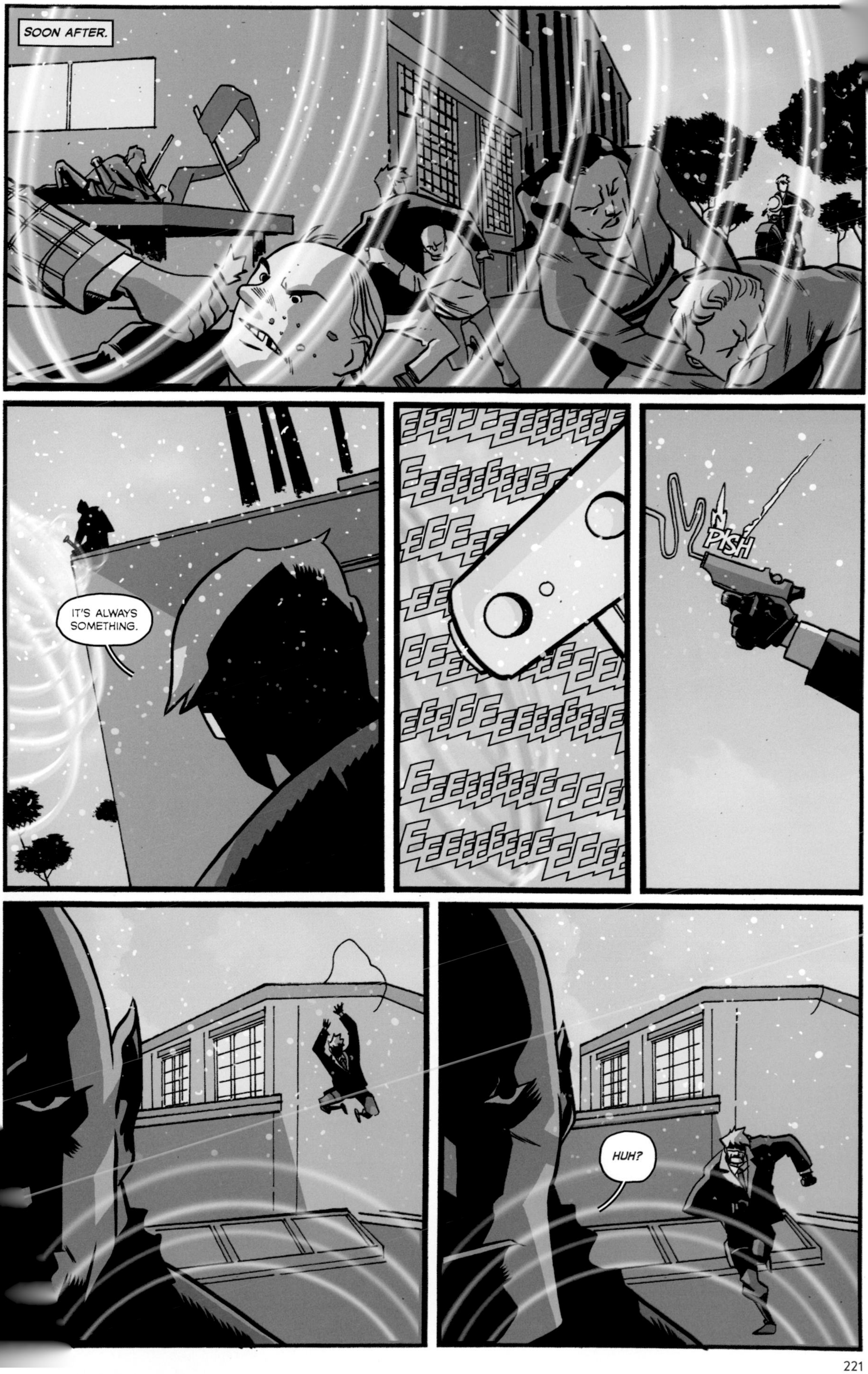
SOON AFTER.
IT'S ALWAYS SOMETHING.
EEEEEEEEEEEEEEEEEEEEEEEEEEEEEEEEEEE
PISH
HUH?

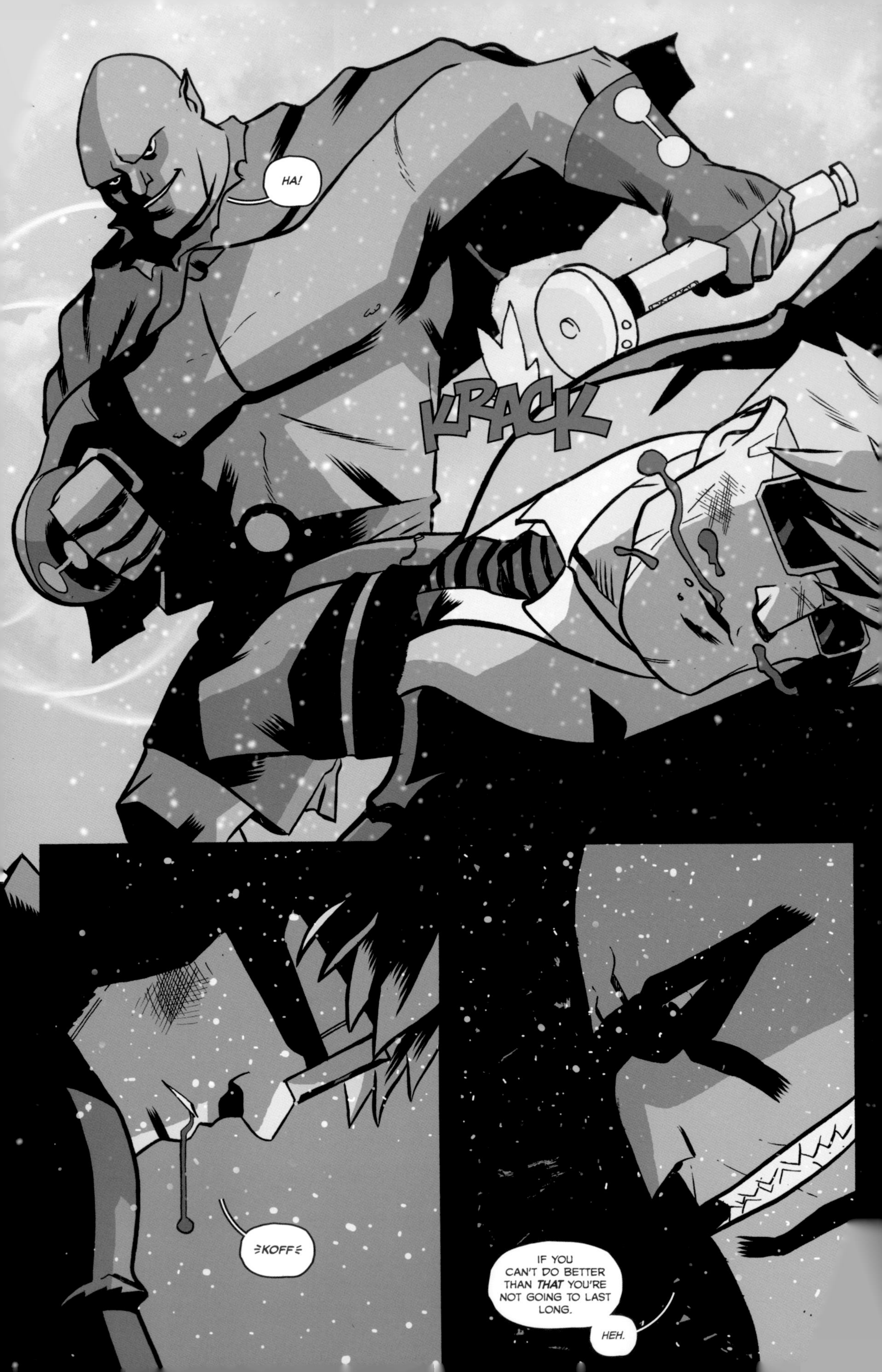
HA!
KRACK
KOFF
IF YOU CAN'T DO BETTER THAN THAT YOU'RE NOT GOING TO LAST LONG.
HEH.

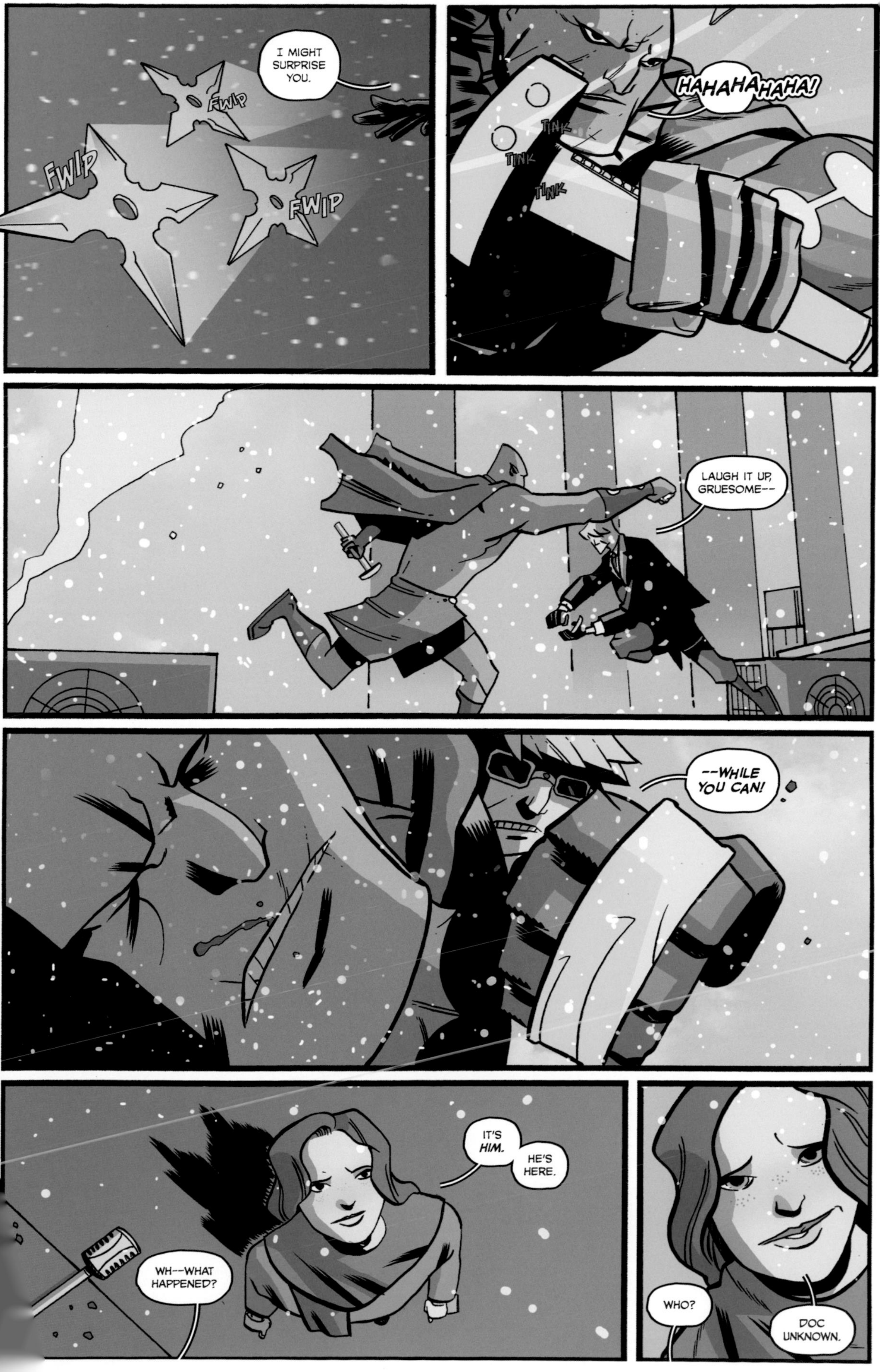
I MIGHT SURPRISE YOU.
FWIP
FWIP
FWIP
HAHAHAHAHAHA!
TINK
TINK
TINK
LAUGH IT UP, GRUESOME--
--WHILE YOU CAN!
IT'S *HIM.*
HE'S HERE.
WH--WHAT HAPPENED?
WHO?
DOC UNKNOWN.

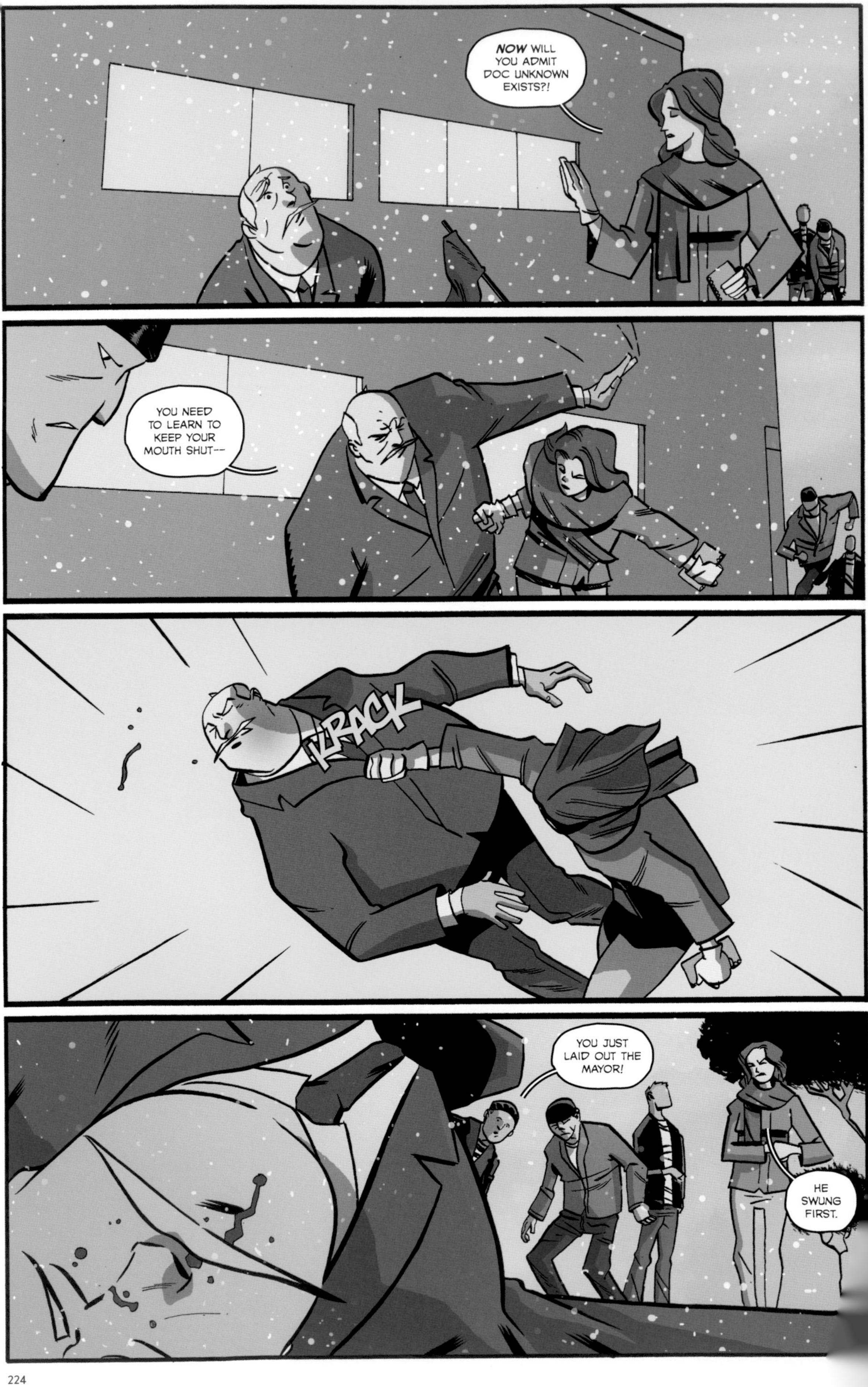
NOW WILL YOU ADMIT DOC UNKNOWN EXISTS?!
YOU NEED TO LEARN TO KEEP YOUR MOUTH SHUT--
KRACK
YOU JUST LAID OUT THE MAYOR!
HE SWUNG FIRST.

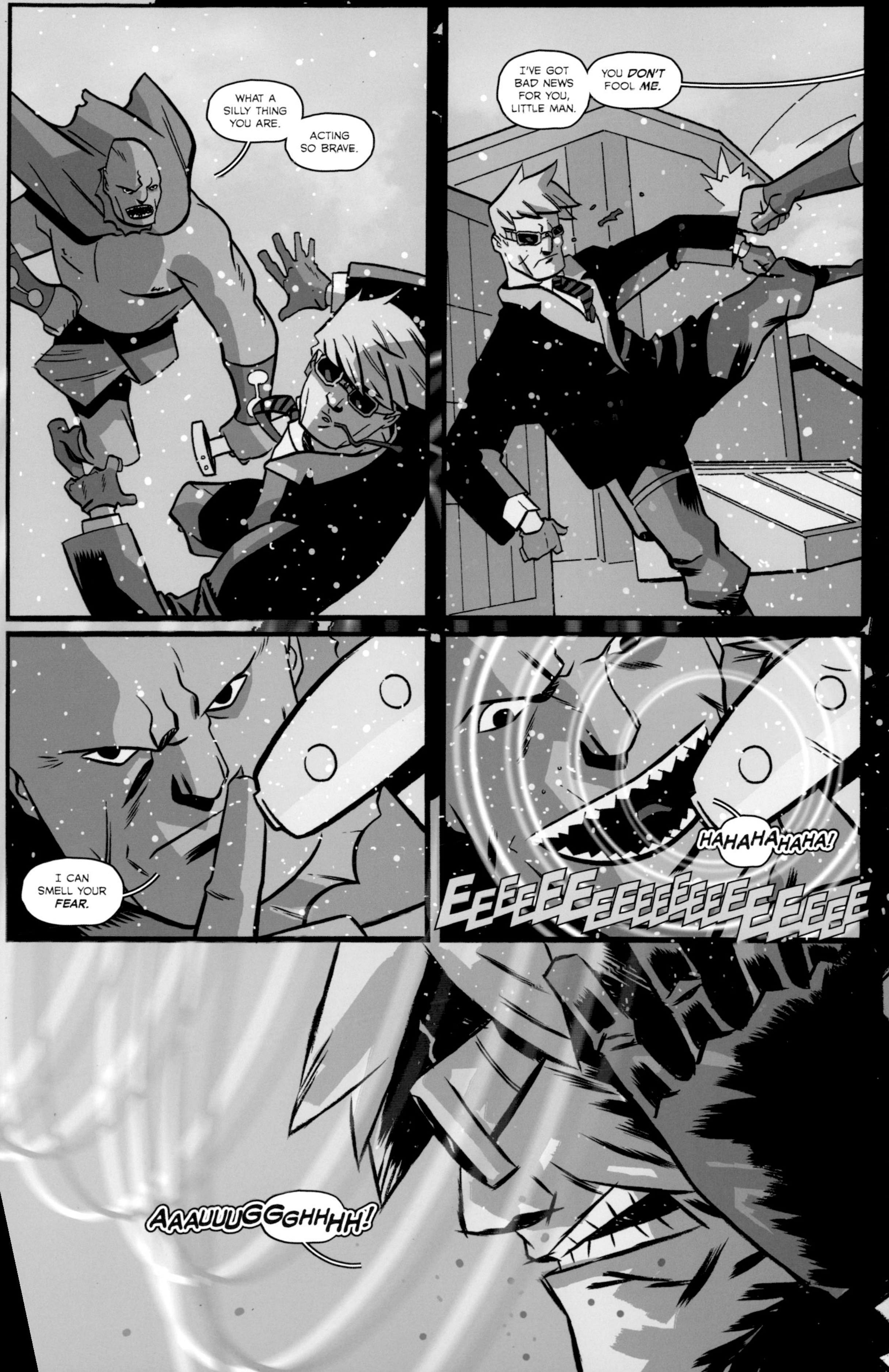
WHAT A SILLY THING YOU ARE.
ACTING SO BRAVE.
I'VE GOT BAD NEWS FOR YOU, LITTLE MAN.
YOU DON'T FOOL ME.
I CAN SMELL YOUR FEAR.
HAHAHAHAHA!
EEEEEEEEEEEEEEEEEEEEEE
AAAUUUGGGHHHHH!

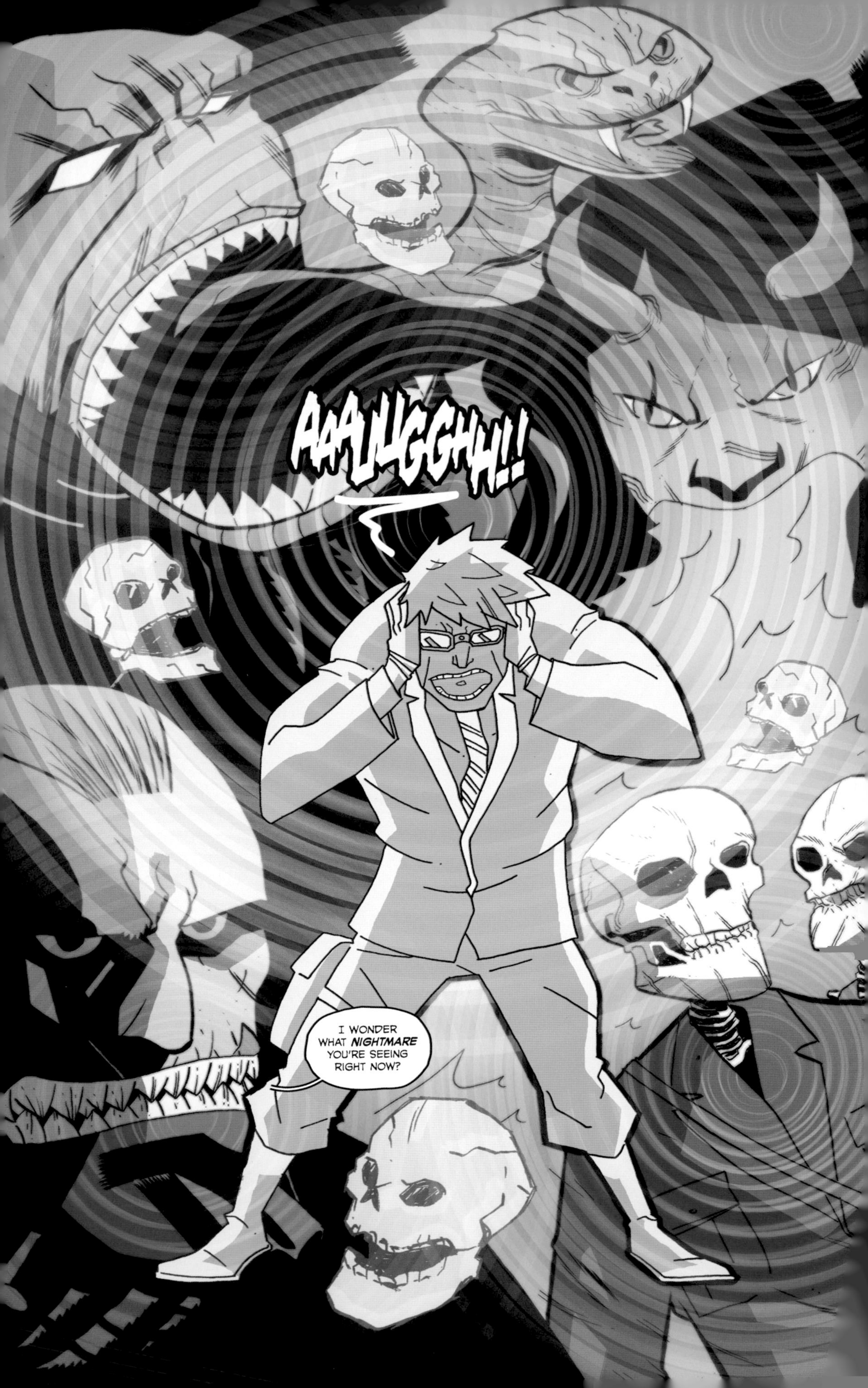
AAAUUGGHH!!
I WONDER WHAT NIGHTMARE YOU'RE SEEING RIGHT NOW?

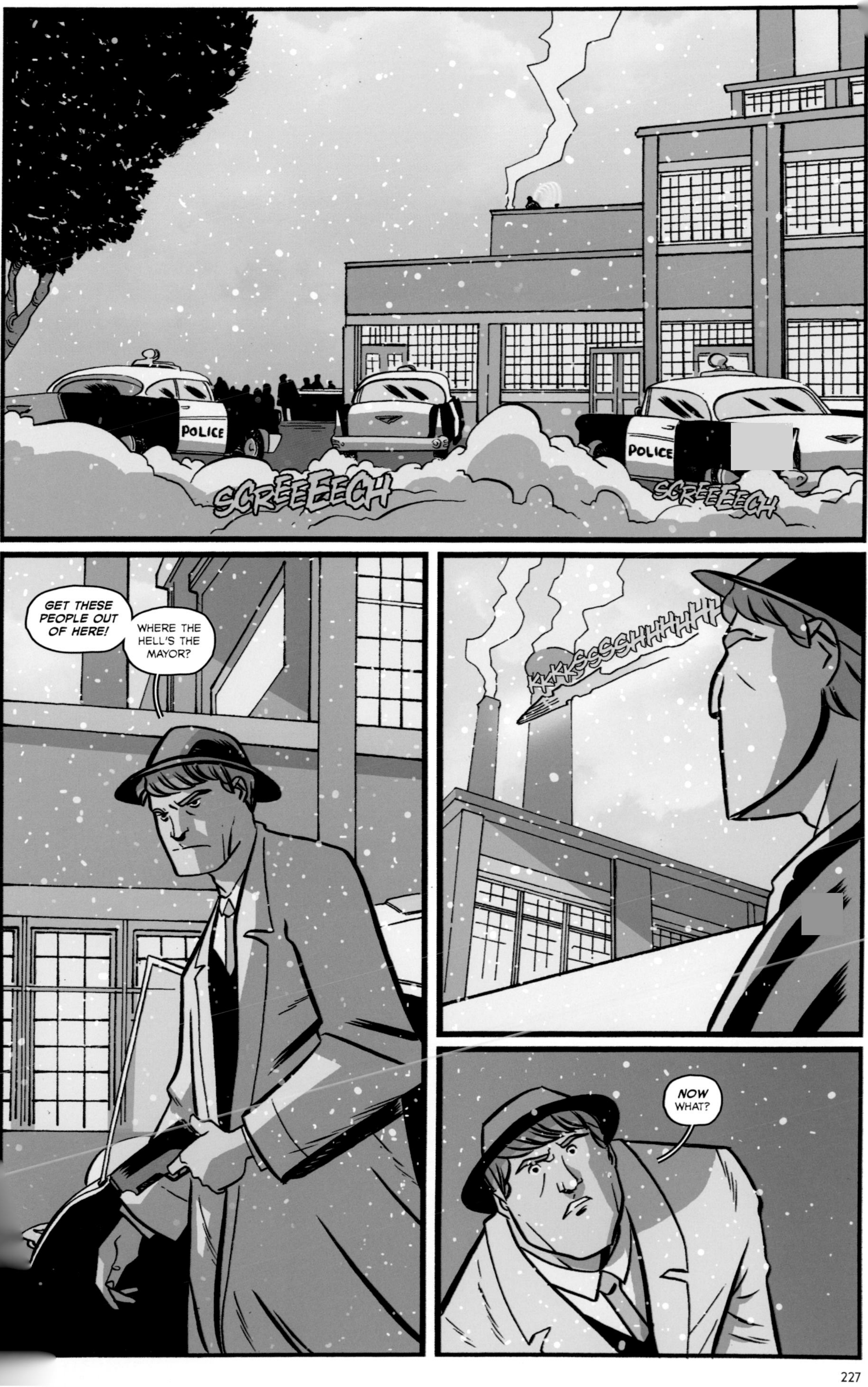

POLICE
POLICE
SCREEEEECH
SCREEEEECH
GET THESE PEOPLE OUT OF HERE!
WHERE THE HELL'S THE MAYOR?
KKKSSSSHHHHHHHH
NOW WHAT?

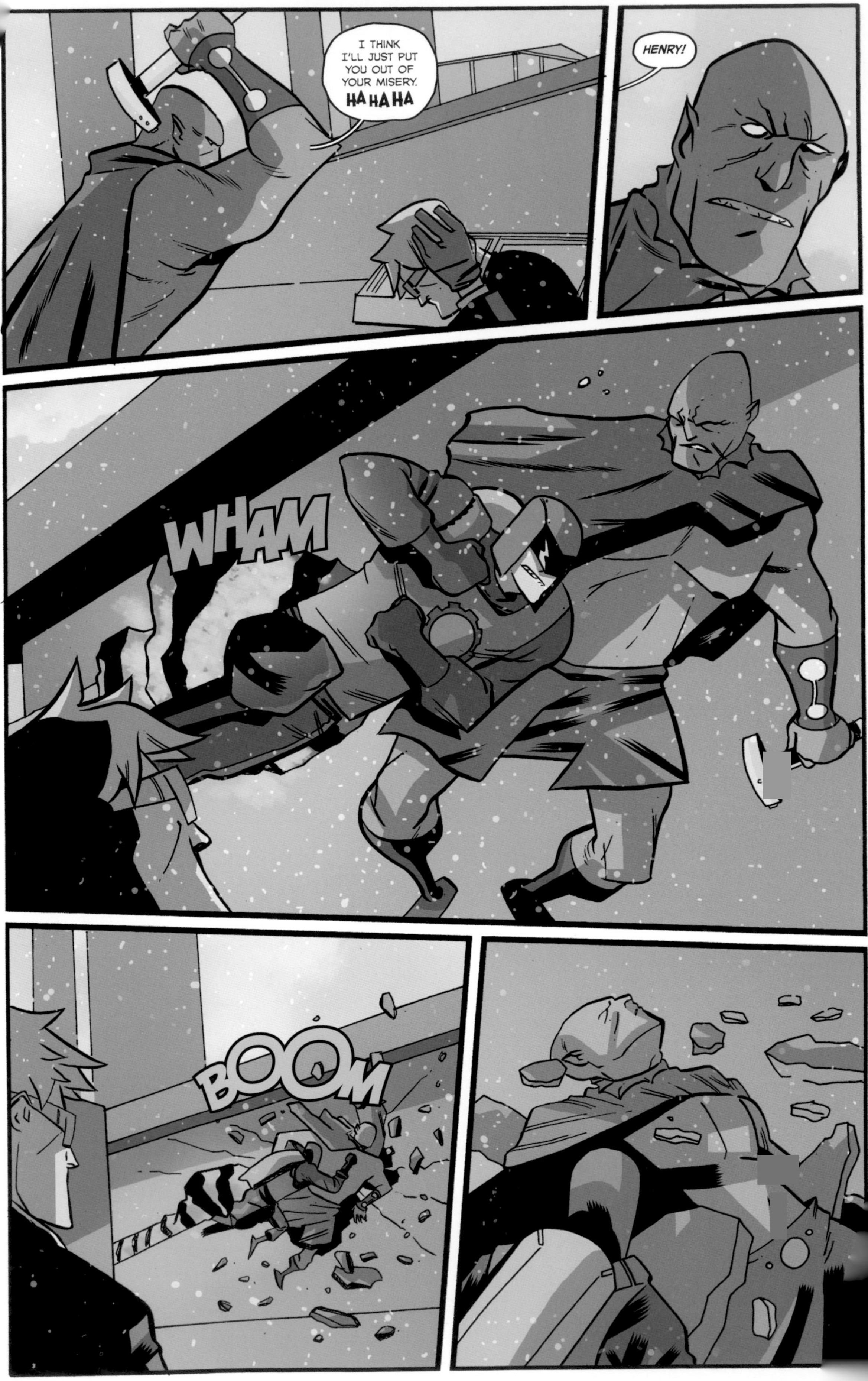
I THINK I'LL JUST PUT YOU OUT OF YOUR MISERY. HA HA HA
HENRY!
WHAM
BOOM

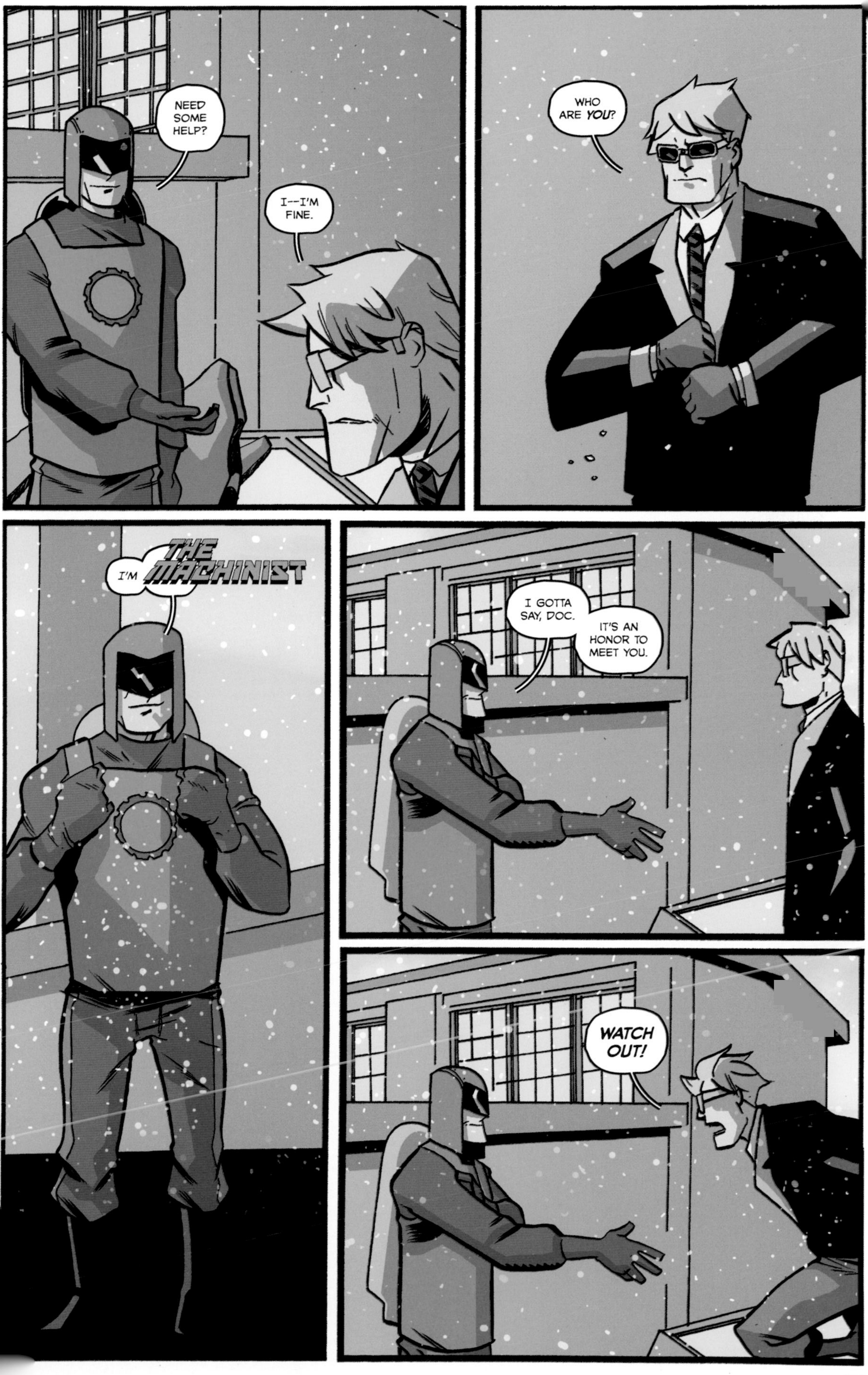
NEED SOME HELP?
I--I'M FINE.
WHO ARE YOU?
I'M THE MACHINIST
I GOTTA SAY, DOC.
IT'S AN HONOR TO MEET YOU.
WATCH OUT!

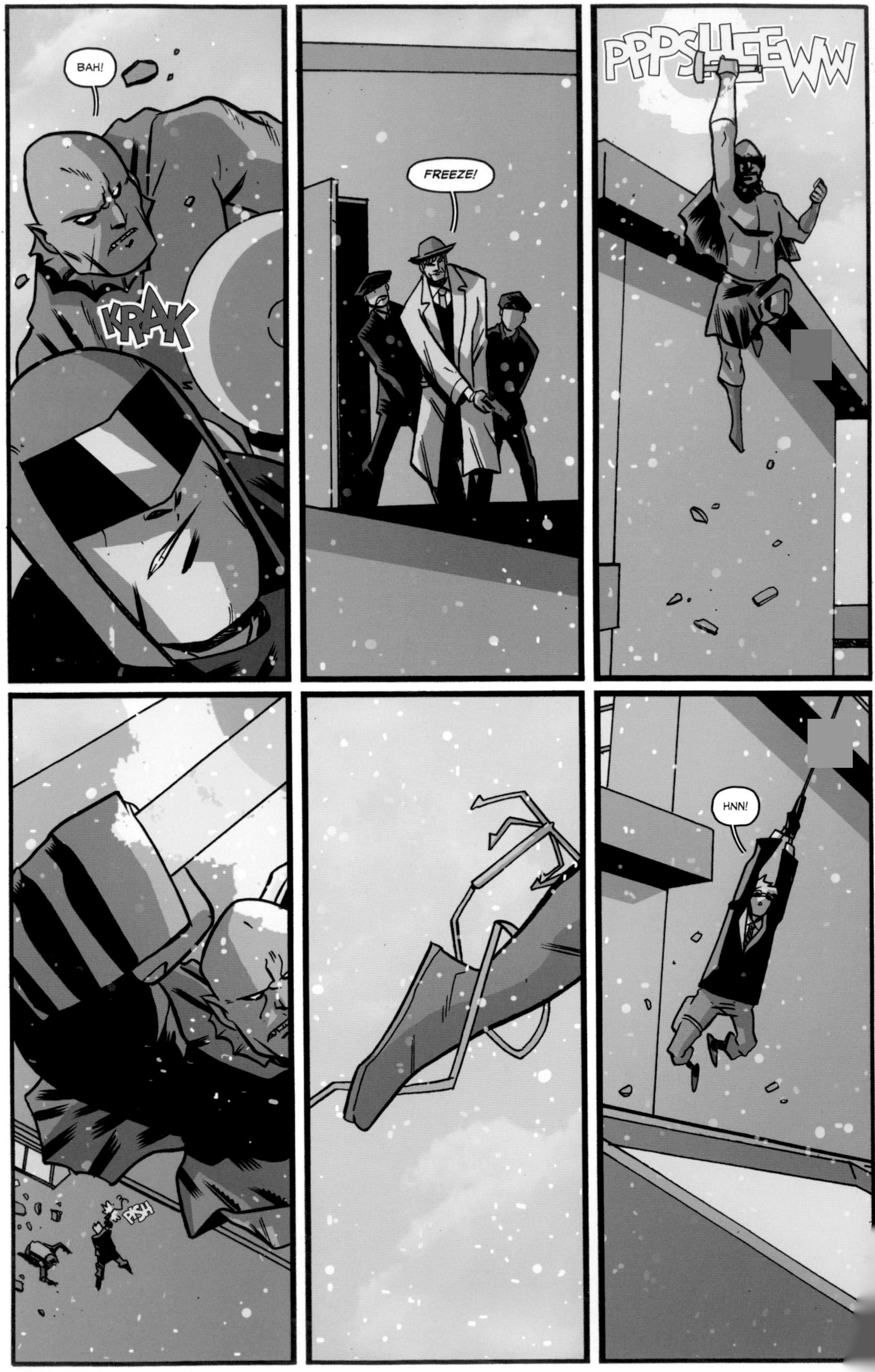
BAH!
KRAK
FREEZE!
PPPSHEEWW
PISH
HNN!

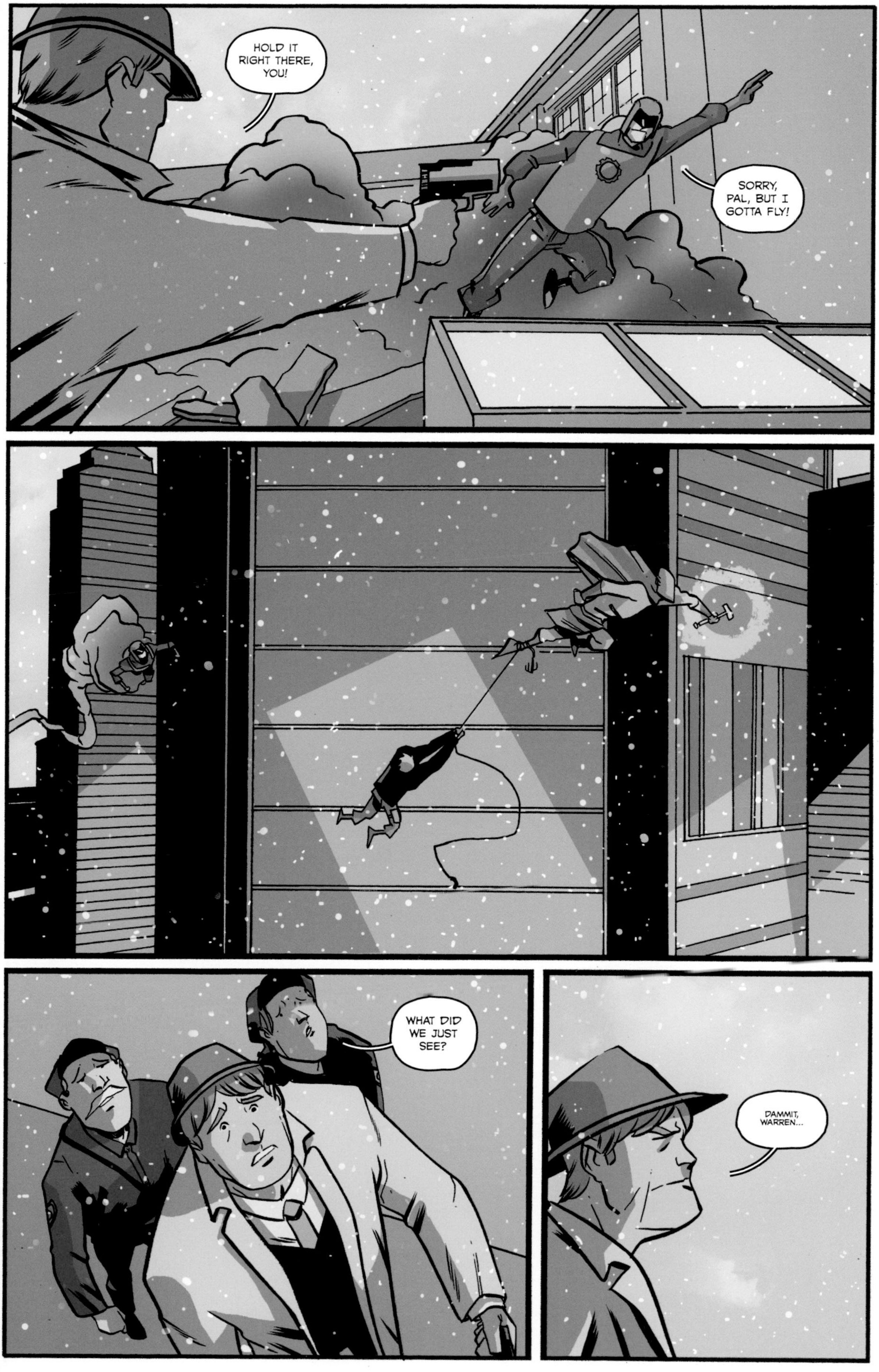
HOLD IT RIGHT THERE, YOU!
SORRY, PAL, BUT I GOTTA FLY!
WHAT DID WE JUST SEE?
DAMMIT, WARREN...

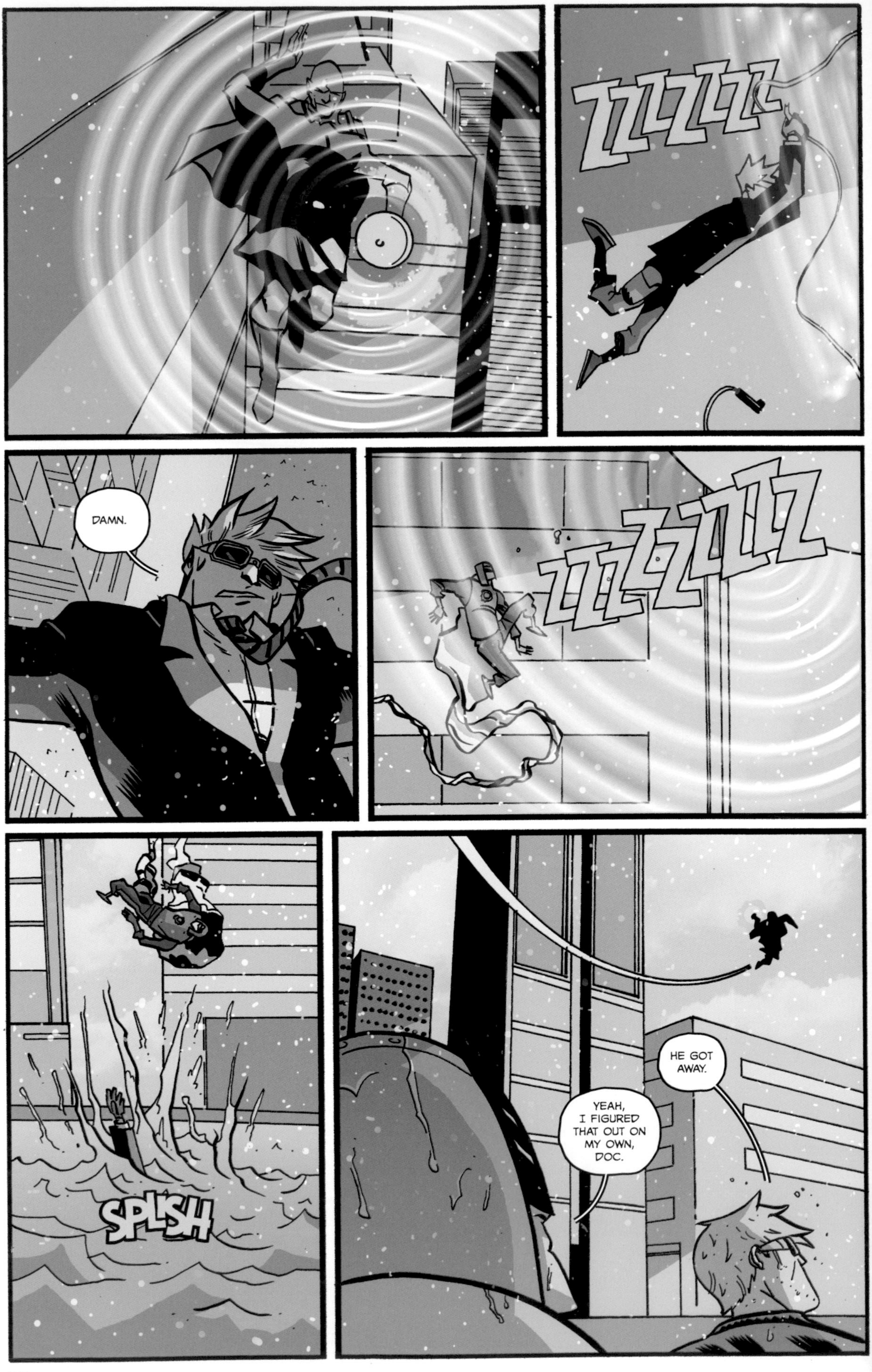
ZZZZZZZ
DAMN.
ZZZZZZZZZ
SPLISH
HE GOT AWAY.
YEAH, I FIGURED THAT OUT ON MY OWN, DOC.

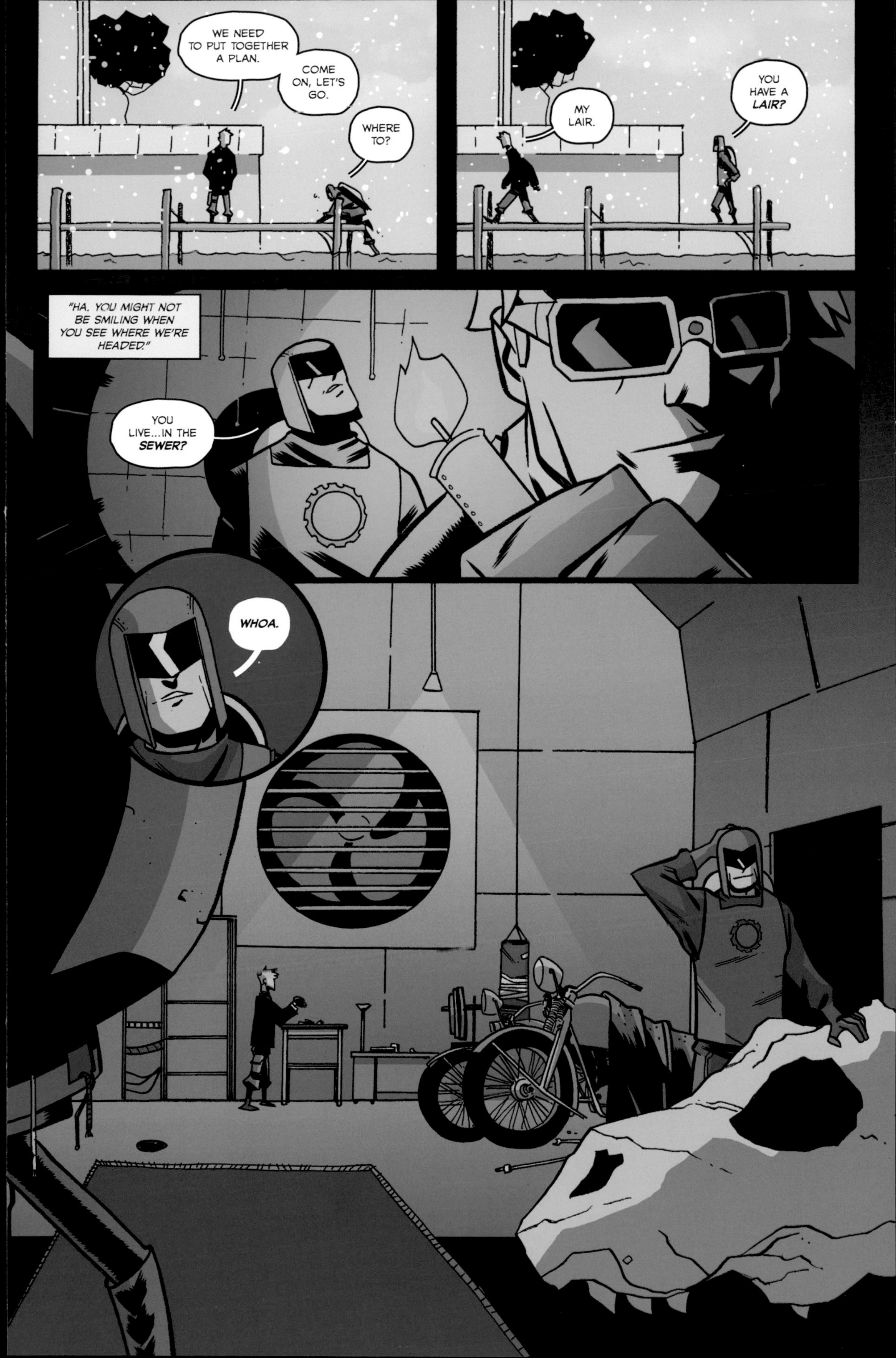
WE NEED TO PUT TOGETHER A PLAN.
COME ON, LET'S GO.
WHERE TO?
MY LAIR.
YOU HAVE A *LAIR?*
"HA. YOU MIGHT NOT BE SMILING WHEN YOU SEE WHERE WE'RE HEADED."
YOU LIVE...IN THE *SEWER?*
WHOA.

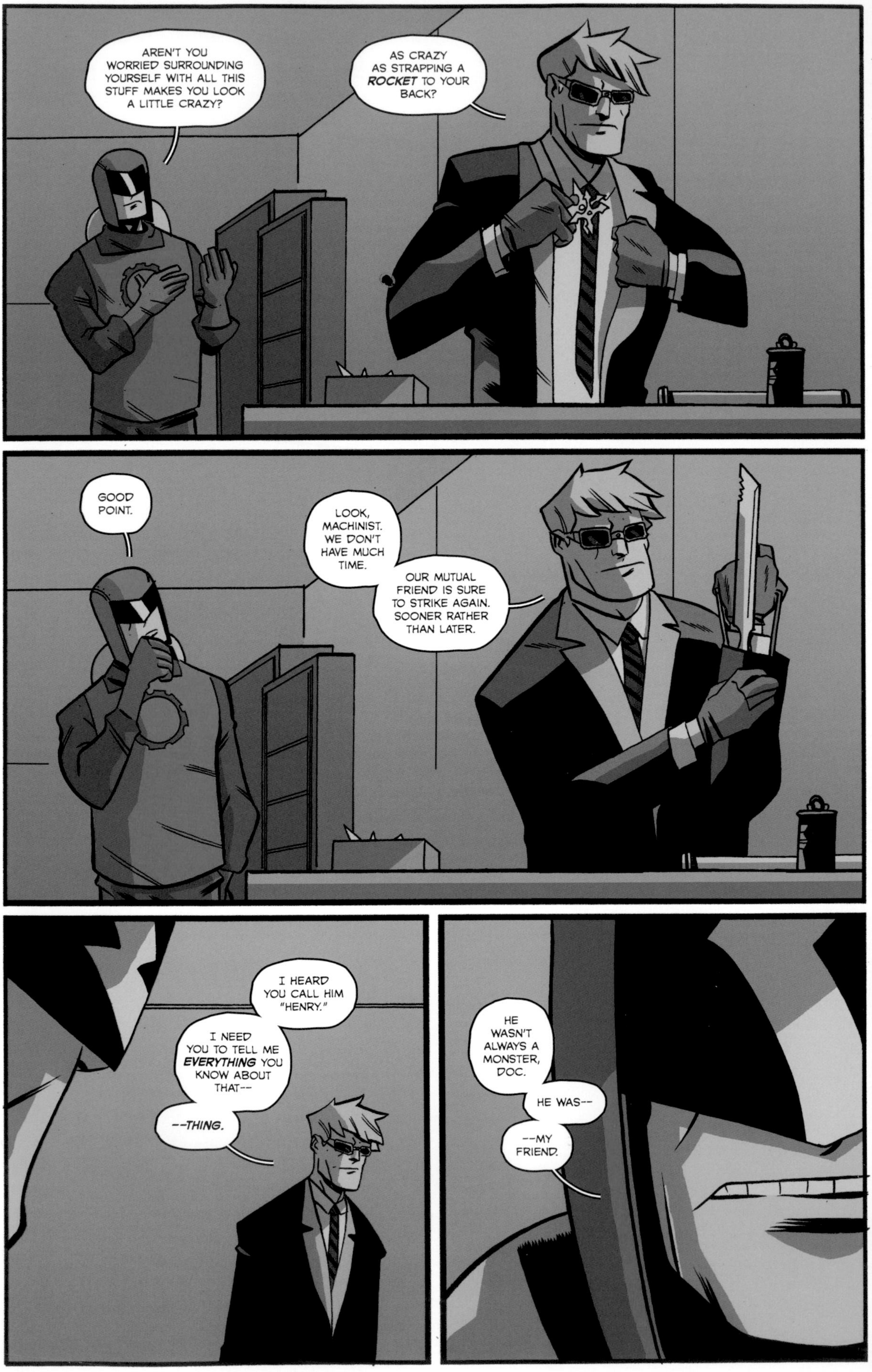
AREN'T YOU WORRIED SURROUNDING YOURSELF WITH ALL THIS STUFF MAKES YOU LOOK A LITTLE CRAZY?
AS CRAZY AS STRAPPING A *ROCKET* TO YOUR BACK?
GOOD POINT.
LOOK, MACHINIST. WE DON'T HAVE MUCH TIME.
OUR MUTUAL FRIEND IS SURE TO STRIKE AGAIN. SOONER RATHER THAN LATER.
I HEARD YOU CALL HIM "HENRY."
I NEED YOU TO TELL ME *EVERYTHING* YOU KNOW ABOUT THAT--
--THING.
HE WASN'T ALWAYS A MONSTER, DOC.
HE WAS--
--MY FRIEND.

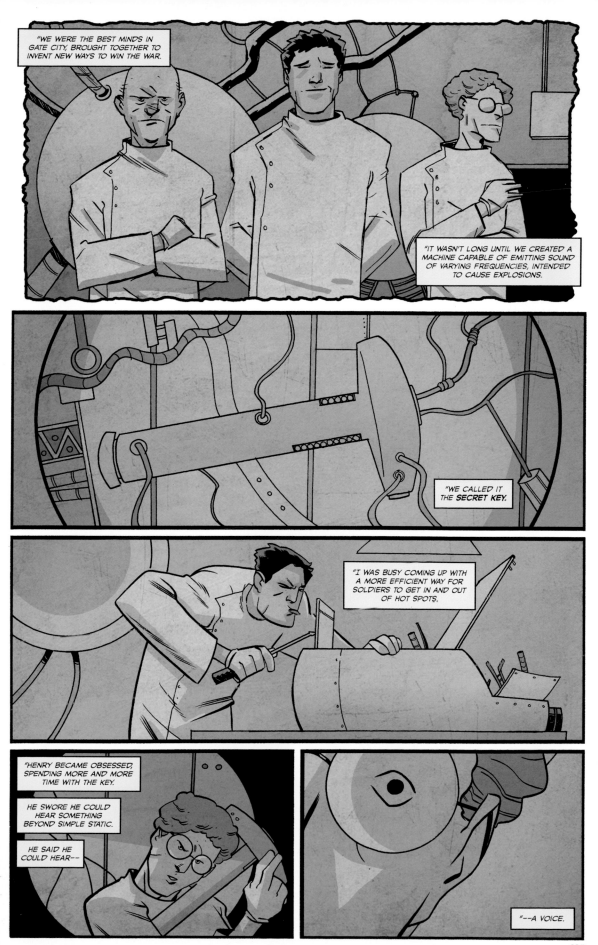

"WE WERE THE BEST MINDS IN GATE CITY, BROUGHT TOGETHER TO INVENT NEW WAYS TO WIN THE WAR.

"IT WASN'T LONG UNTIL WE CREATED A MACHINE CAPABLE OF EMITTING SOUND OF VARYING FREQUENCIES, INTENDED TO CAUSE EXPLOSIONS.

"WE CALLED IT THE *SECRET KEY.*

"I WAS BUSY COMING UP WITH A MORE EFFICIENT WAY FOR SOLDIERS TO GET IN AND OUT OF HOT SPOTS.

"HENRY BECAME OBSESSED, SPENDING MORE AND MORE TIME WITH THE KEY.

HE SWORE HE COULD HEAR SOMETHING BEYOND SIMPLE STATIC.

HE SAID HE COULD HEAR--

"--A VOICE.

235

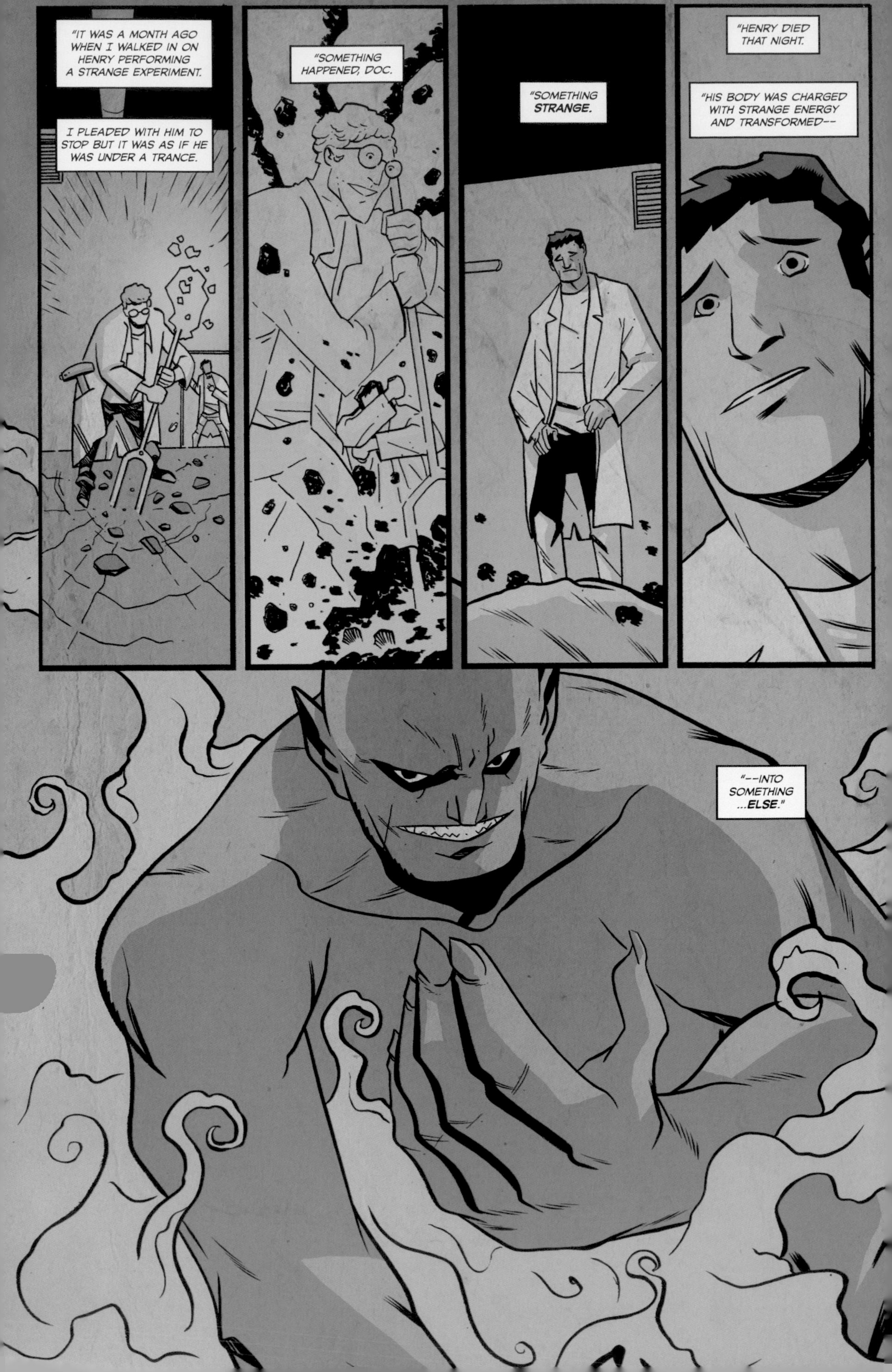
"IT WAS A MONTH AGO WHEN I WALKED IN ON HENRY PERFORMING A STRANGE EXPERIMENT.
I PLEADED WITH HIM TO STOP BUT IT WAS AS IF HE WAS UNDER A TRANCE.
"SOMETHING HAPPENED, DOC.
"SOMETHING **STRANGE.**
"HENRY DIED THAT NIGHT.
"HIS BODY WAS CHARGED WITH STRANGE ENERGY AND TRANSFORMED--
"--INTO SOMETHING ...**ELSE.**"

HENRY DESTROYED THE LAB, AND STOLE THE SECRET KEY.

"I KNEW HE'D BE TOO MUCH FOR THE COPS TO HANDLE--

"--SO I TOOK A PAGE FROM *YOUR* BOOK, DOC.

ALL AVAILABLE UNITS REPORT TO THE DOWNTOWN DISTRICT--

--*GRAY GREMLIN* IS ON SCENE CAUSING PROPERTY DAMAGE AND ASSAULTING POLICE OFFICERS--I REPEAT-- *THE GRAY GREMLIN*--

GRAY GREMLIN?

SOUNDS LIKE SOMETHING KATHERINE KAY CAME UP WITH.

SHE'S THE ONE WHO STARTED CALLING ME "DOC UNKNOWN."

LET'S GO.

NEED A LIFT?

NO THANKS.

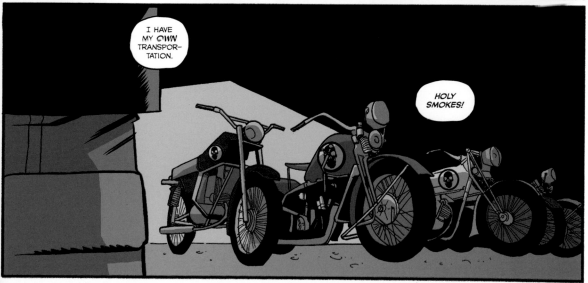

I HAVE MY *OWN* TRANSPOR-TATION.

HOLY SMOKES!

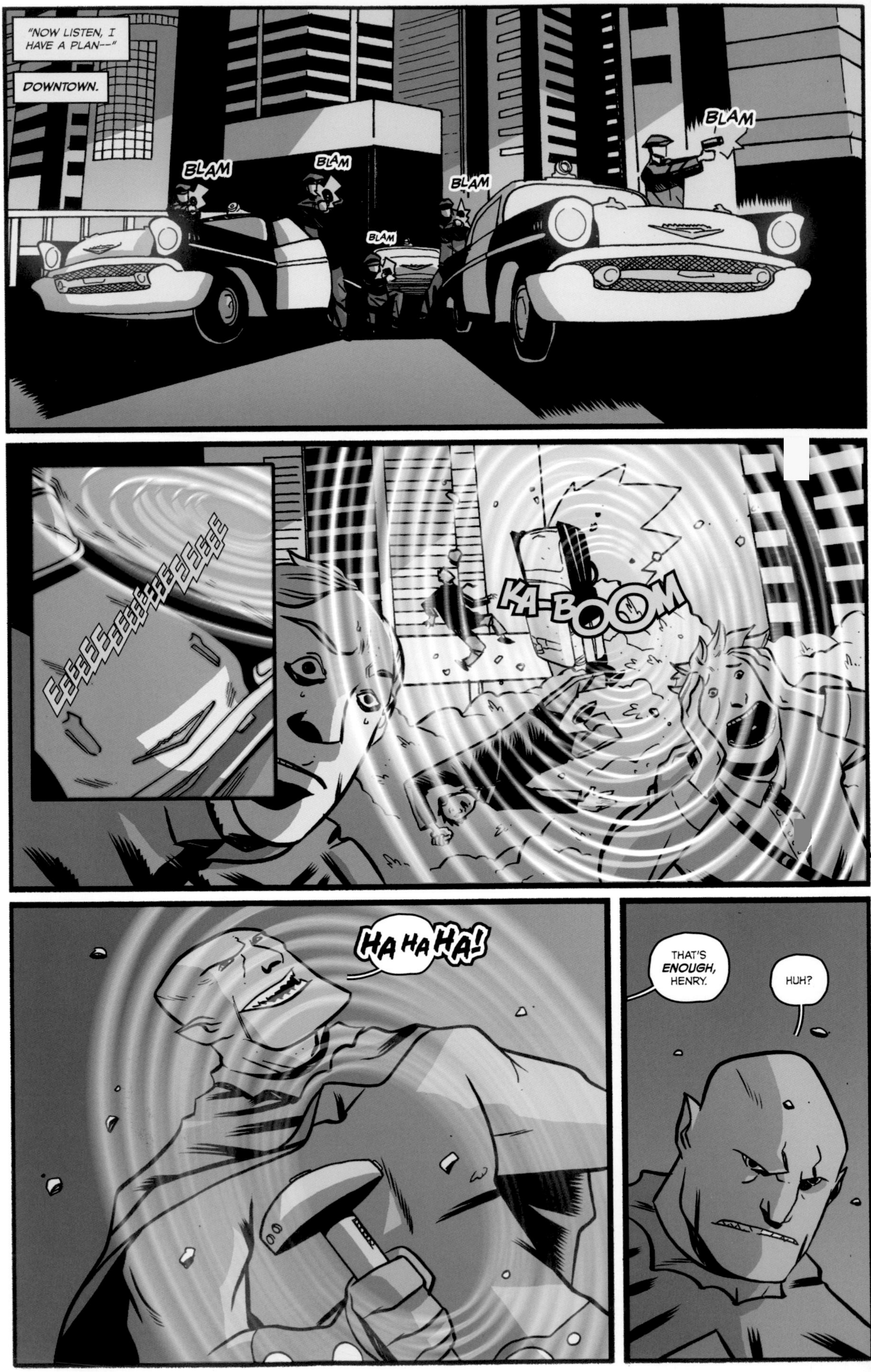
"NOW LISTEN, I HAVE A PLAN--"
DOWNTOWN.
BLAM
BLAM
BLAM
BLAM
BLAM
KA-BOOM
HA HA HA!
THAT'S ENOUGH, HENRY.
HUH?

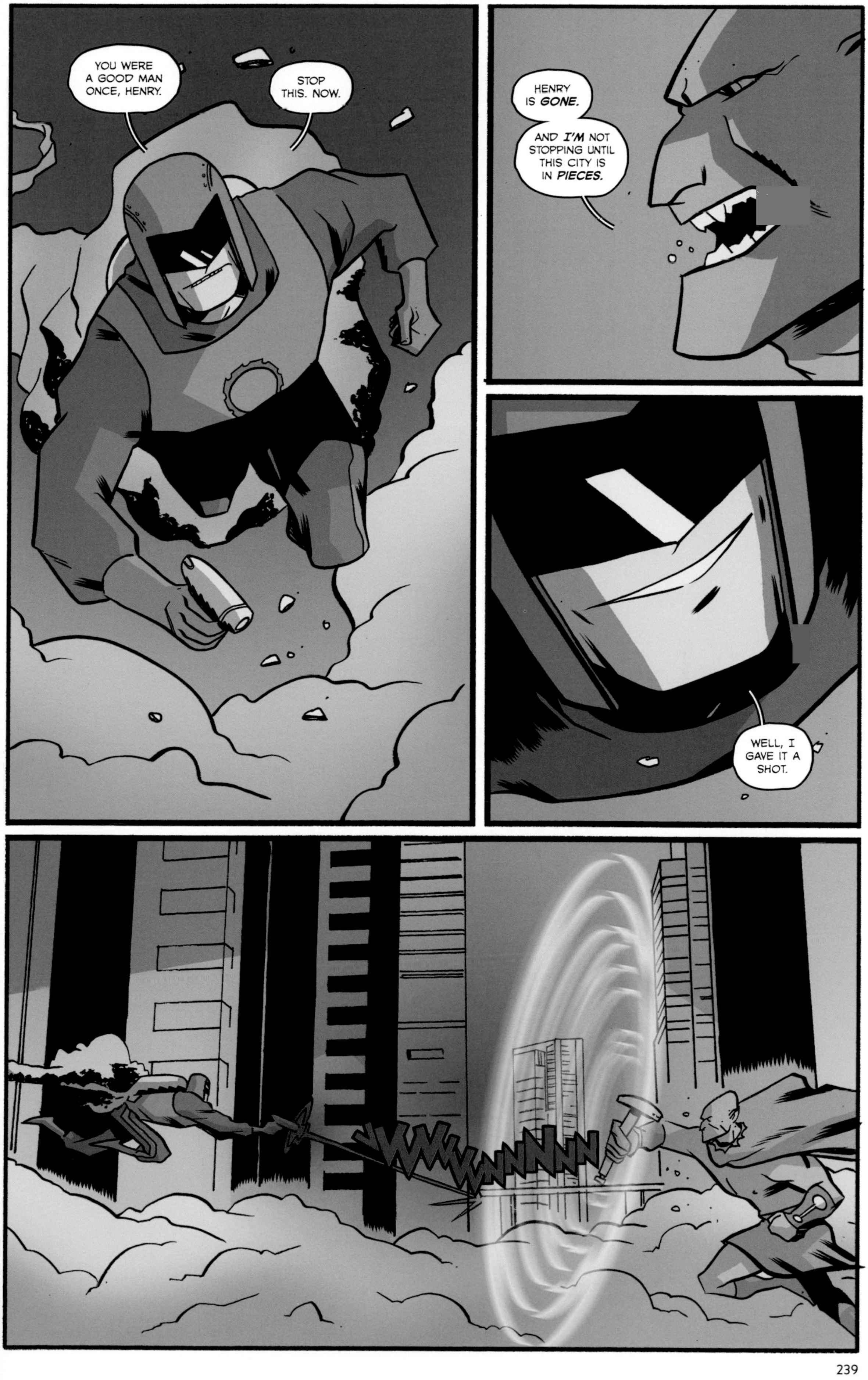
YOU WERE A GOOD MAN ONCE, HENRY.
STOP THIS. NOW.
HENRY IS *GONE.*
AND *I'M* NOT STOPPING UNTIL THIS CITY IS IN *PIECES.*
WELL, I GAVE IT A SHOT.

WHAM

KKSSSHHHH

NOW, DOC!

PPFSHHH

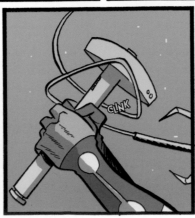

CLNK

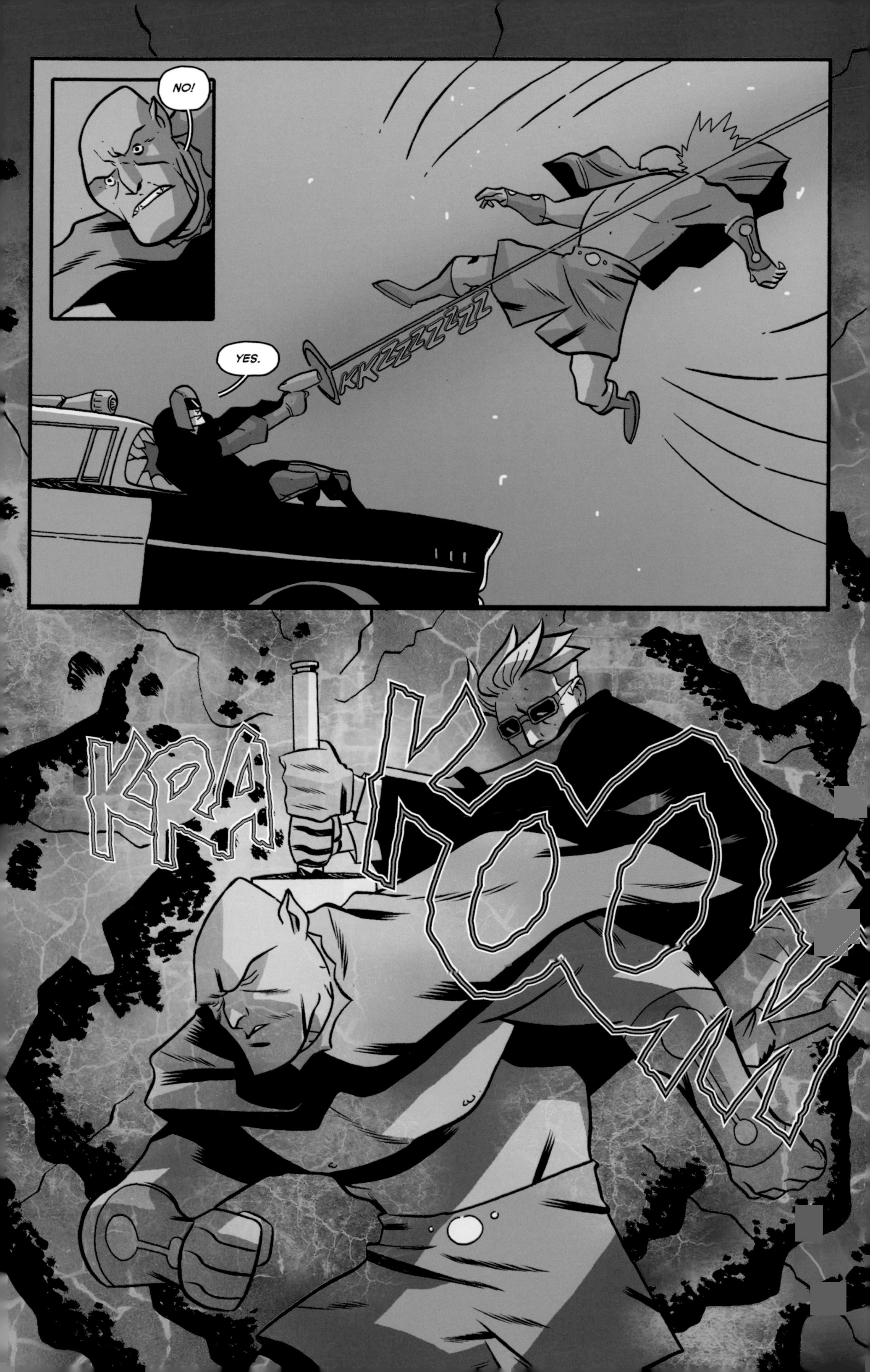
NO!
YES.
KKZZZZZZZZ
KRA
KOOM

KKSHOWWW

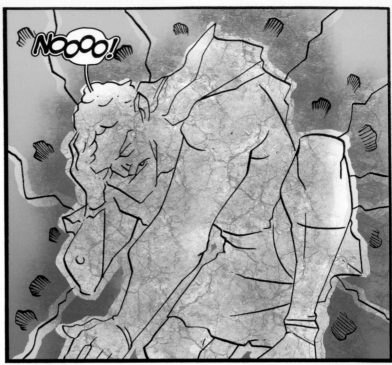

NOOOO!

NO.

I'LL KILL YOU!

KRAK

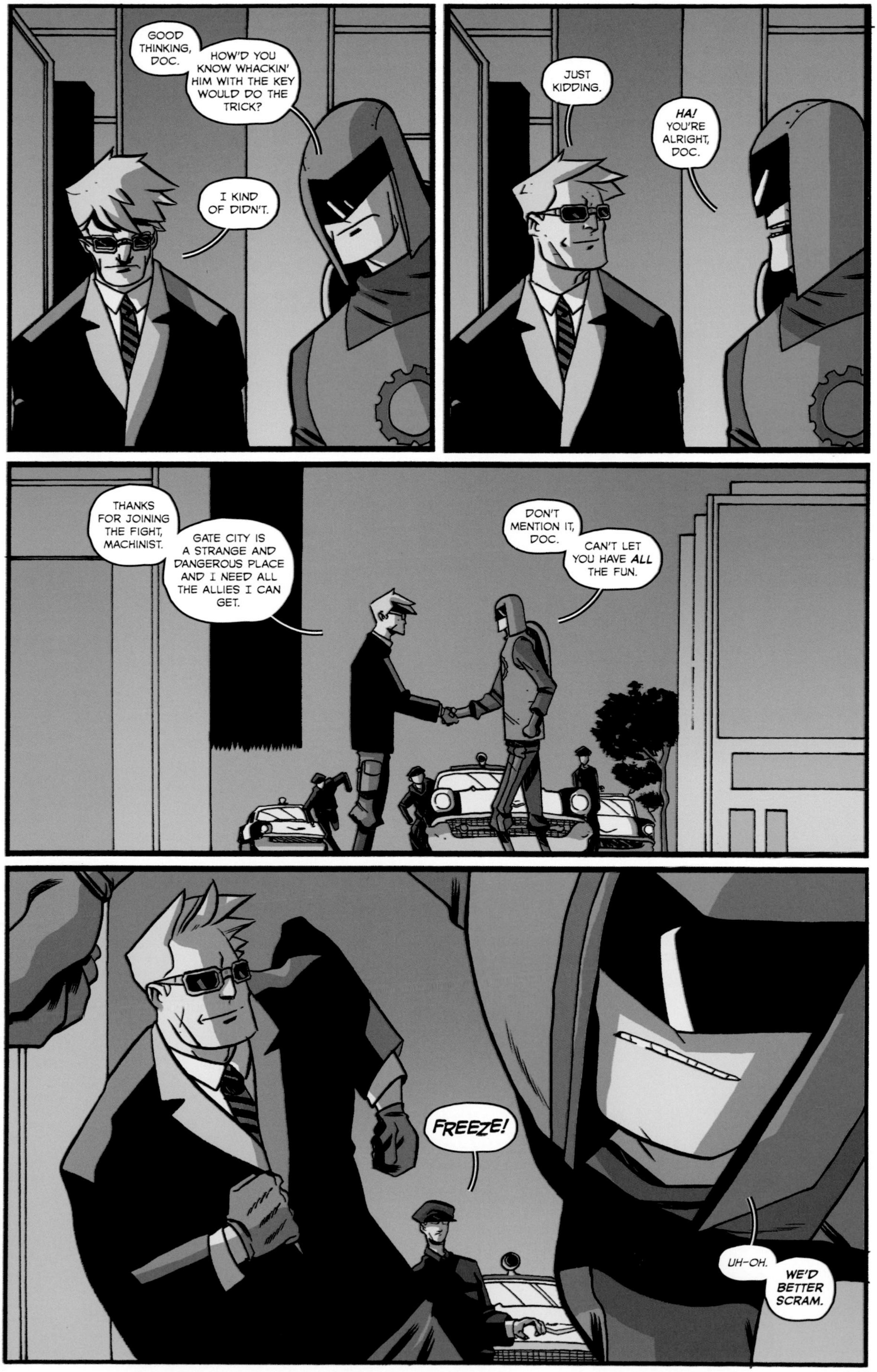
GOOD THINKING, DOC.
HOW'D YOU KNOW WHACKIN' HIM WITH THE KEY WOULD DO THE TRICK?
I KIND OF DIDN'T.
JUST KIDDING.
HA! YOU'RE ALRIGHT, DOC.
THANKS FOR JOINING THE FIGHT, MACHINIST.
GATE CITY IS A STRANGE AND DANGEROUS PLACE AND I NEED ALL THE ALLIES I CAN GET.
DON'T MENTION IT, DOC.
CAN'T LET YOU HAVE ALL THE FUN.
FREEZE!
UH-OH.
WE'D BETTER SCRAM.

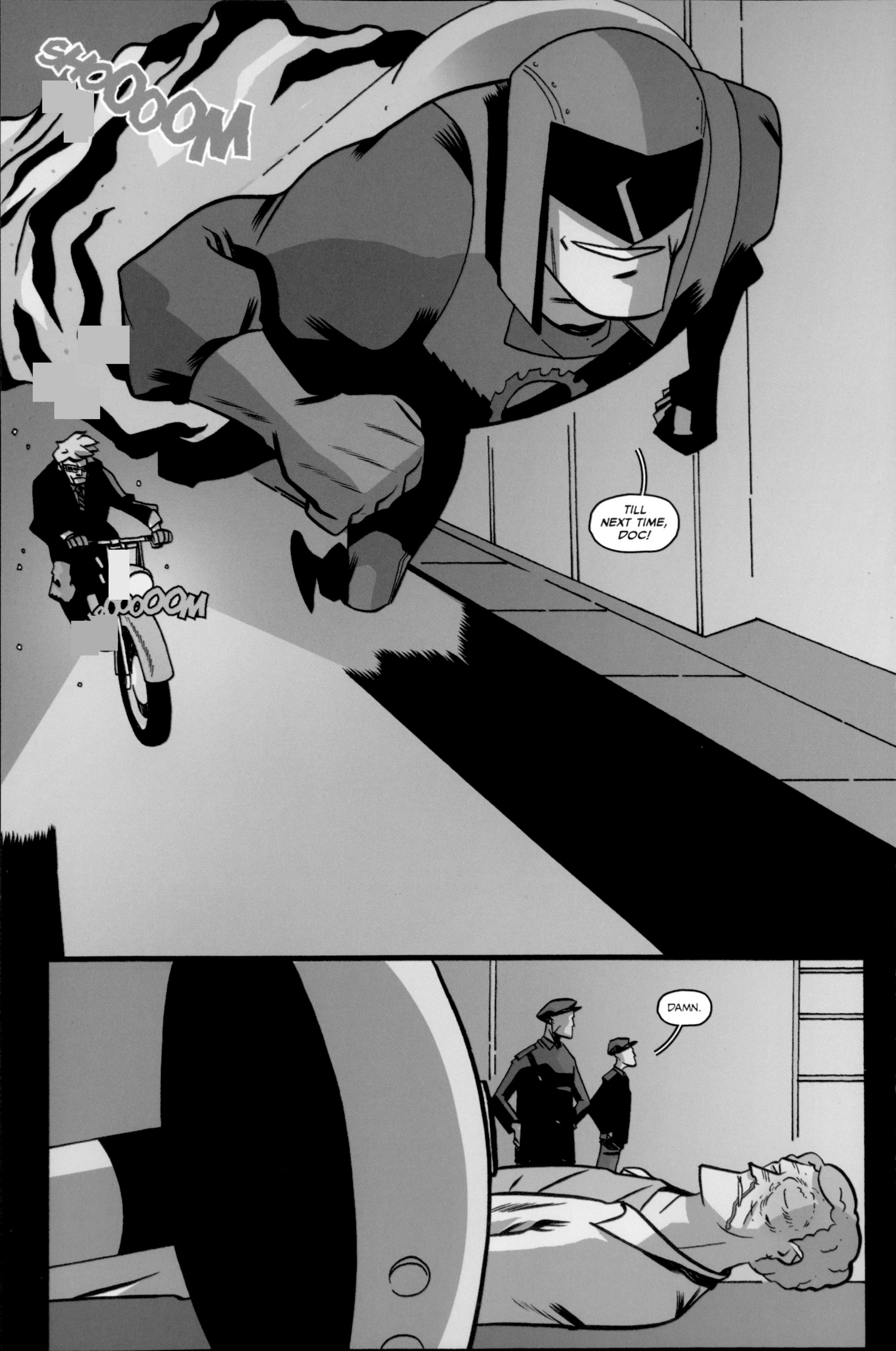
SHOOOOM
TILL NEXT TIME, DOC!
DAMN.

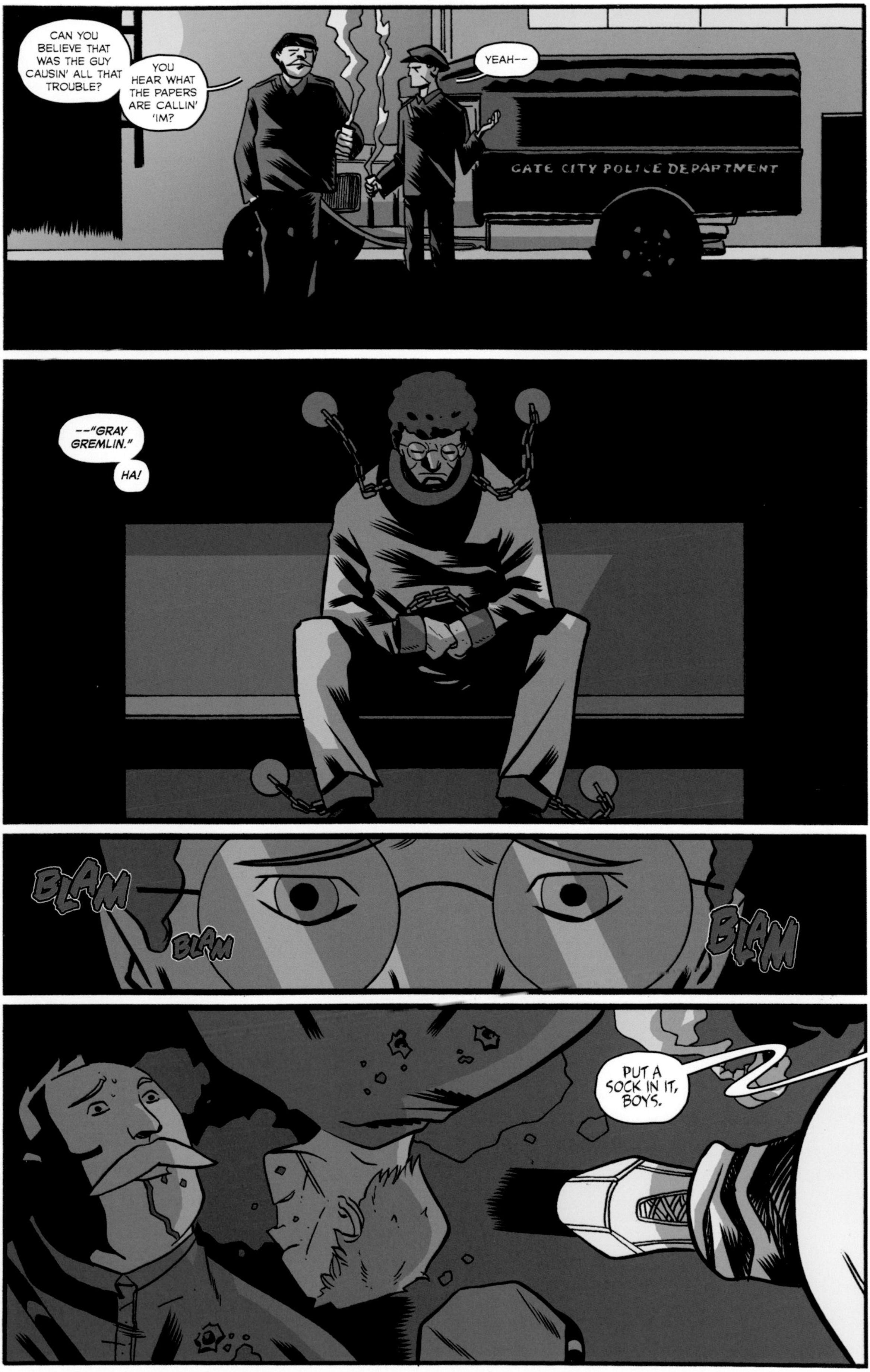
CAN YOU BELIEVE THAT WAS THE GUY CAUSIN' ALL THAT TROUBLE?
YOU HEAR WHAT THE PAPERS ARE CALLIN' 'IM?
YEAH--
GATE CITY POLICE DEPARTMENT
--"GRAY GREMLIN."
HA!
BLAM
BLAM
BLAM
PUT A SOCK IN IT, BOYS.

KKLAK

YOU SURE THIS IS THE GUY?

THAT'S HIM, SNAKE.

WHAT DO YOU WANT FROM ME?

HE DON'T LOOK LIKE MUCH.

NOT YET, HE DOESN'T.

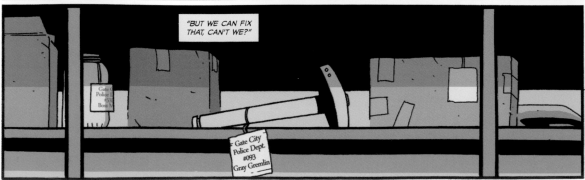

"BUT WE CAN FIX THAT, CAN'T WE?"

Gate City Police Dept. #093 Gray Gremlin

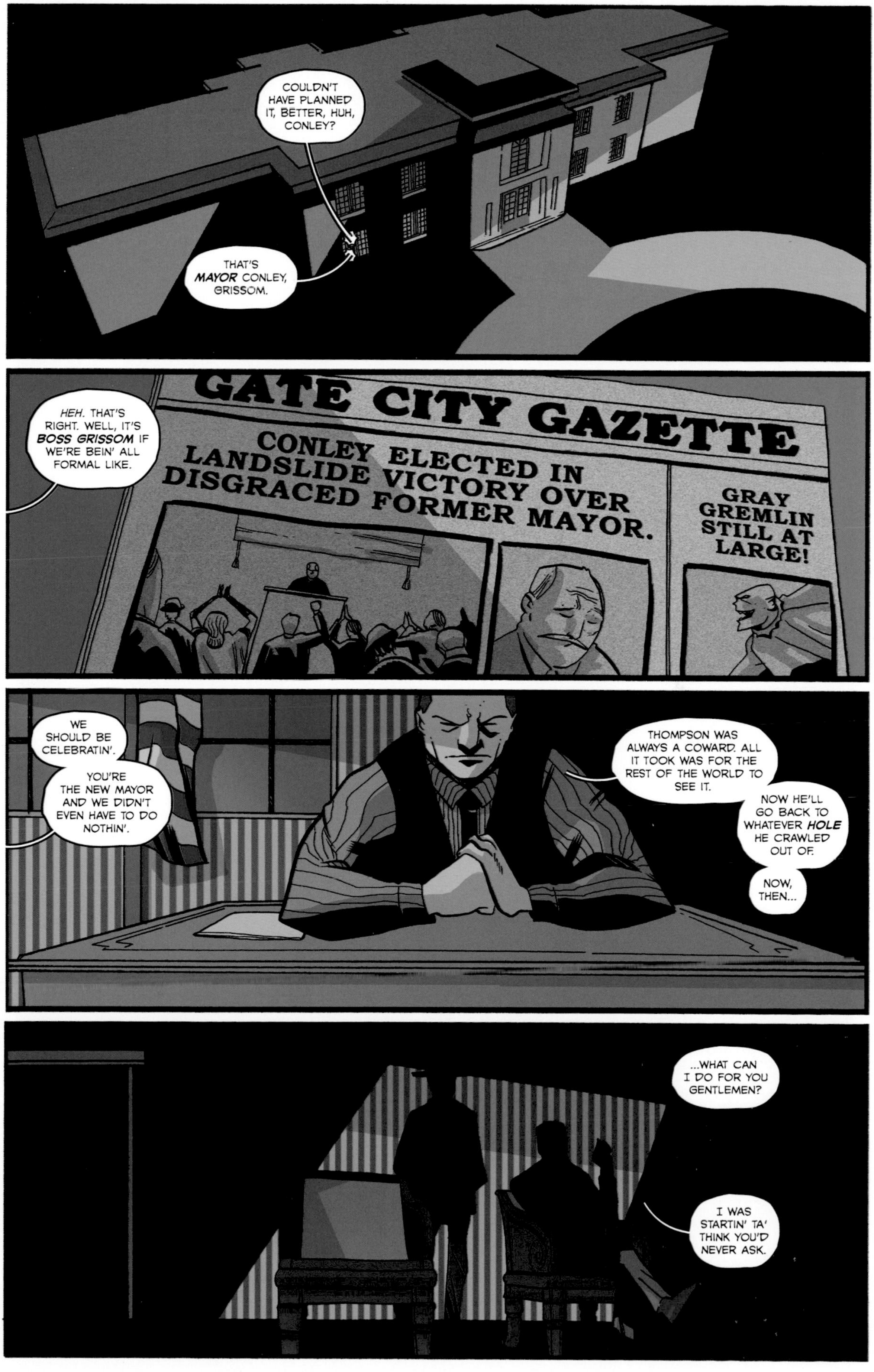
COULDN'T HAVE PLANNED IT, BETTER, HUH, CONLEY?
THAT'S MAYOR CONLEY, GRISSOM.
HEH. THAT'S RIGHT. WELL, IT'S BOSS GRISSOM IF WE'RE BEIN' ALL FORMAL LIKE.
GATE CITY GAZETTE
CONLEY ELECTED IN LANDSLIDE VICTORY OVER DISGRACED FORMER MAYOR.
GRAY GREMLIN STILL AT LARGE!
WE SHOULD BE CELEBRATIN'.
YOU'RE THE NEW MAYOR AND WE DIDN'T EVEN HAVE TO DO NOTHIN'.
THOMPSON WAS ALWAYS A COWARD. ALL IT TOOK WAS FOR THE REST OF THE WORLD TO SEE IT.
NOW HE'LL GO BACK TO WHATEVER HOLE HE CRAWLED OUT OF.
NOW, THEN...
...WHAT CAN I DO FOR YOU GENTLEMEN?
I WAS STARTIN' TA' THINK YOU'D NEVER ASK.

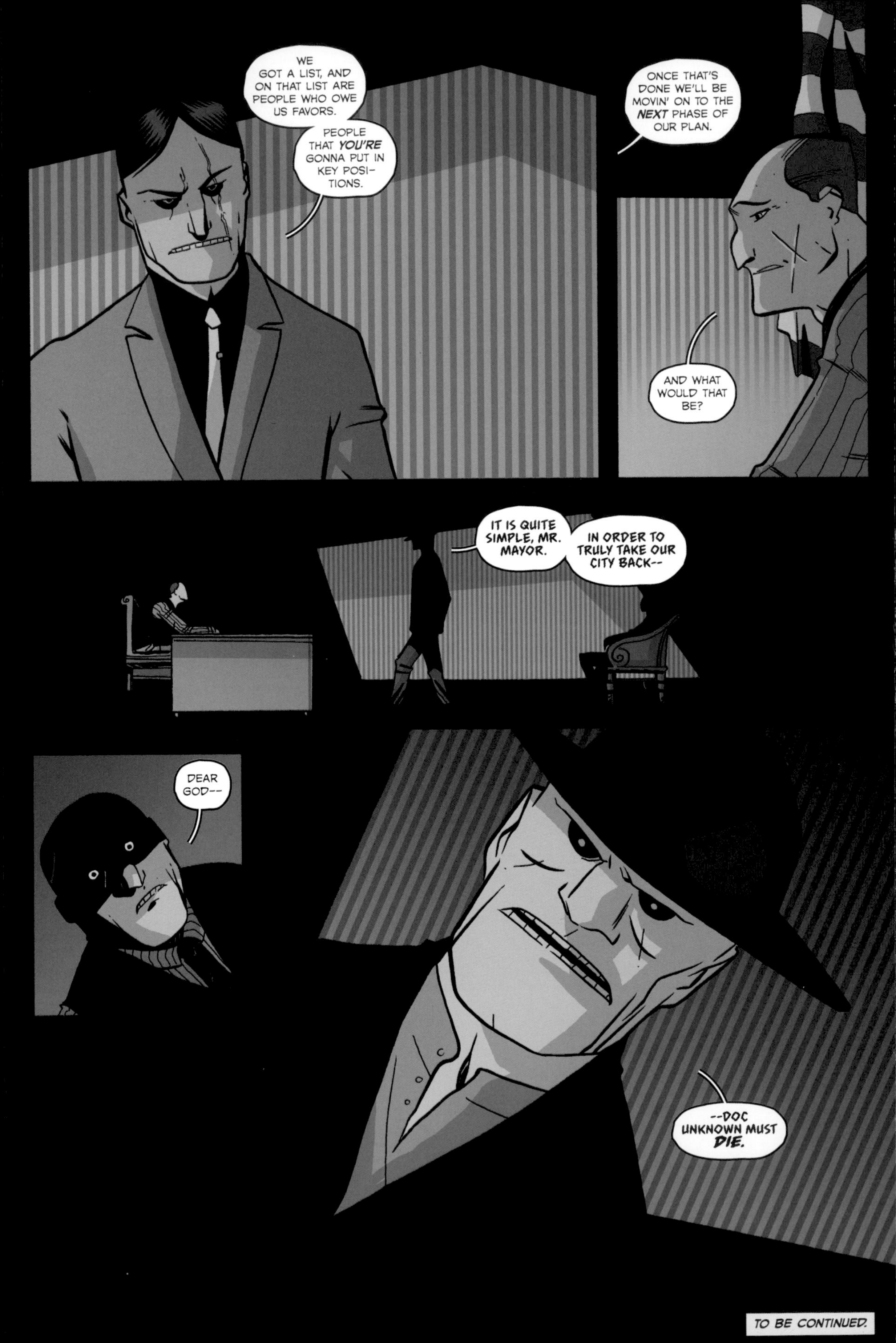
WE GOT A LIST, AND ON THAT LIST ARE PEOPLE WHO OWE US FAVORS.
PEOPLE THAT YOU'RE GONNA PUT IN KEY POSITIONS.
ONCE THAT'S DONE WE'LL BE MOVIN' ON TO THE NEXT PHASE OF OUR PLAN.
AND WHAT WOULD THAT BE?
IT IS QUITE SIMPLE, MR. MAYOR.
IN ORDER TO TRULY TAKE OUR CITY BACK--
DEAR GOD--
--DOC UNKNOWN MUST DIE.
TO BE CONTINUED.

THE CALL OF THE MIDNIGHT COUNCIL

SCRIPT BY **FABIAN RANGEL JR.**

ART BY **RYAN CODY**

LETTERS BY **EVELYN RANGEL**

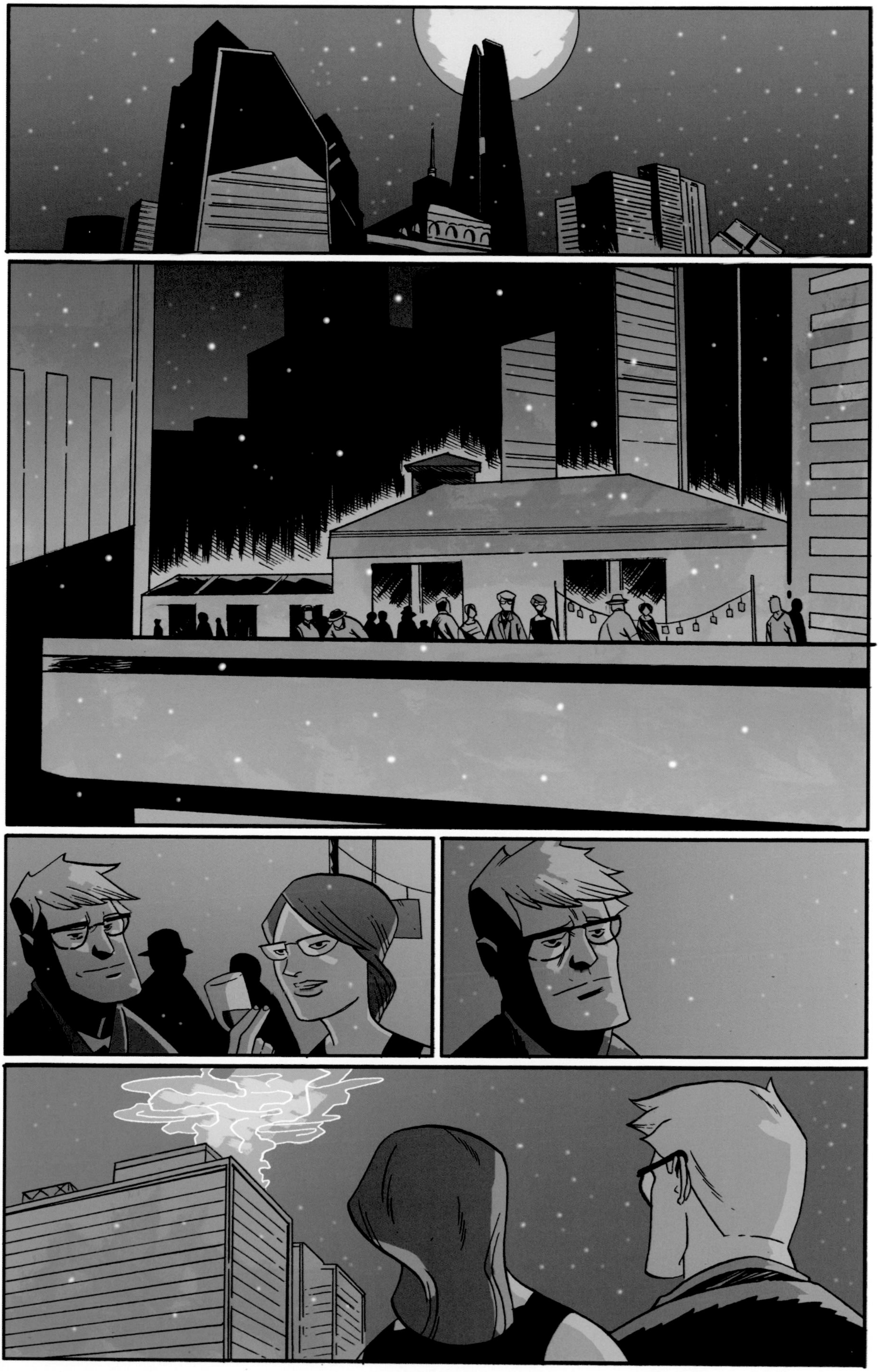

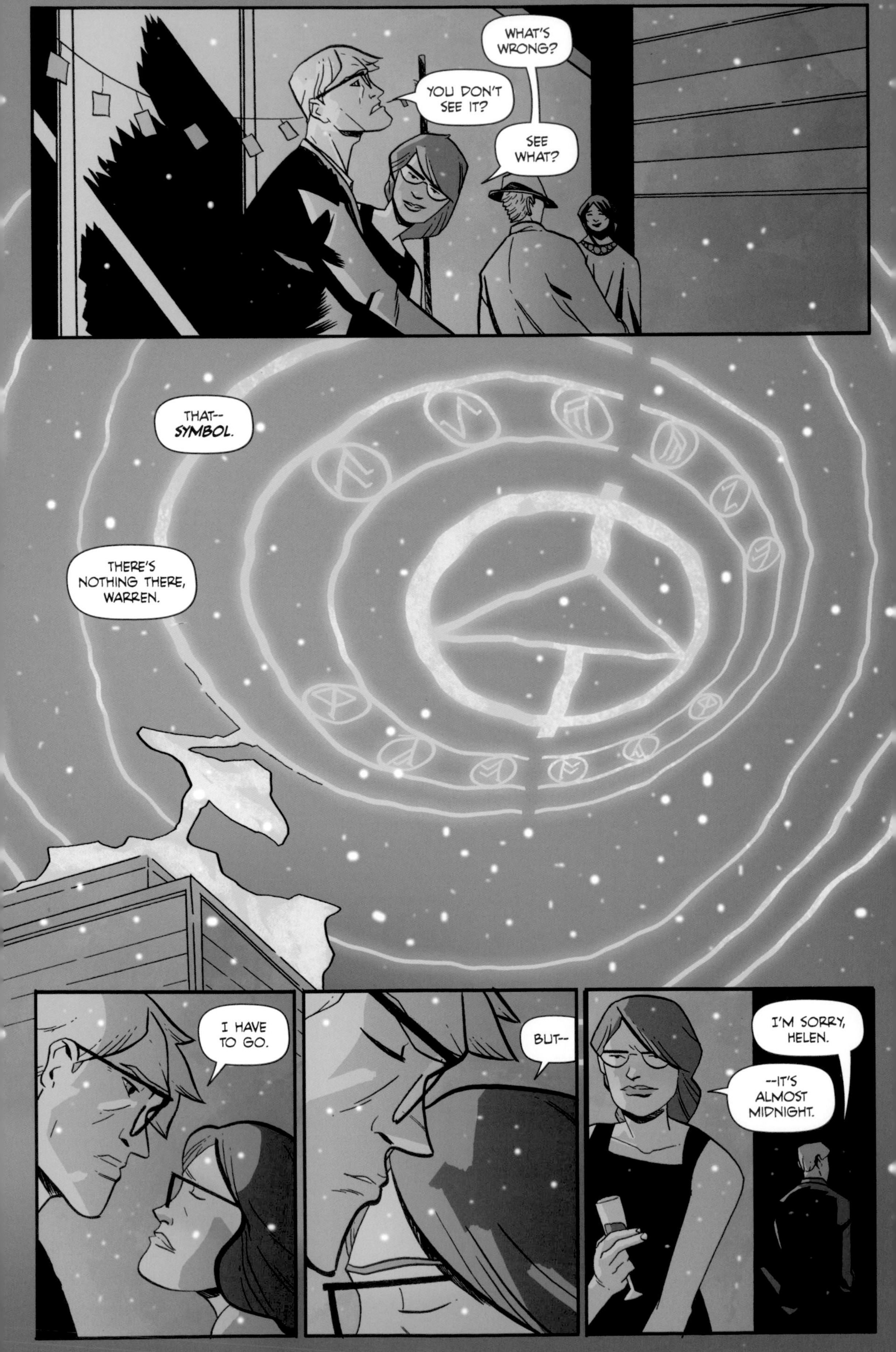
WHAT'S WRONG?
YOU DON'T SEE IT?
SEE WHAT?
THAT-- SYMBOL.
THERE'S NOTHING THERE, WARREN.
I HAVE TO GO.
BUT--
I'M SORRY, HELEN.
--IT'S ALMOST MIDNIGHT.

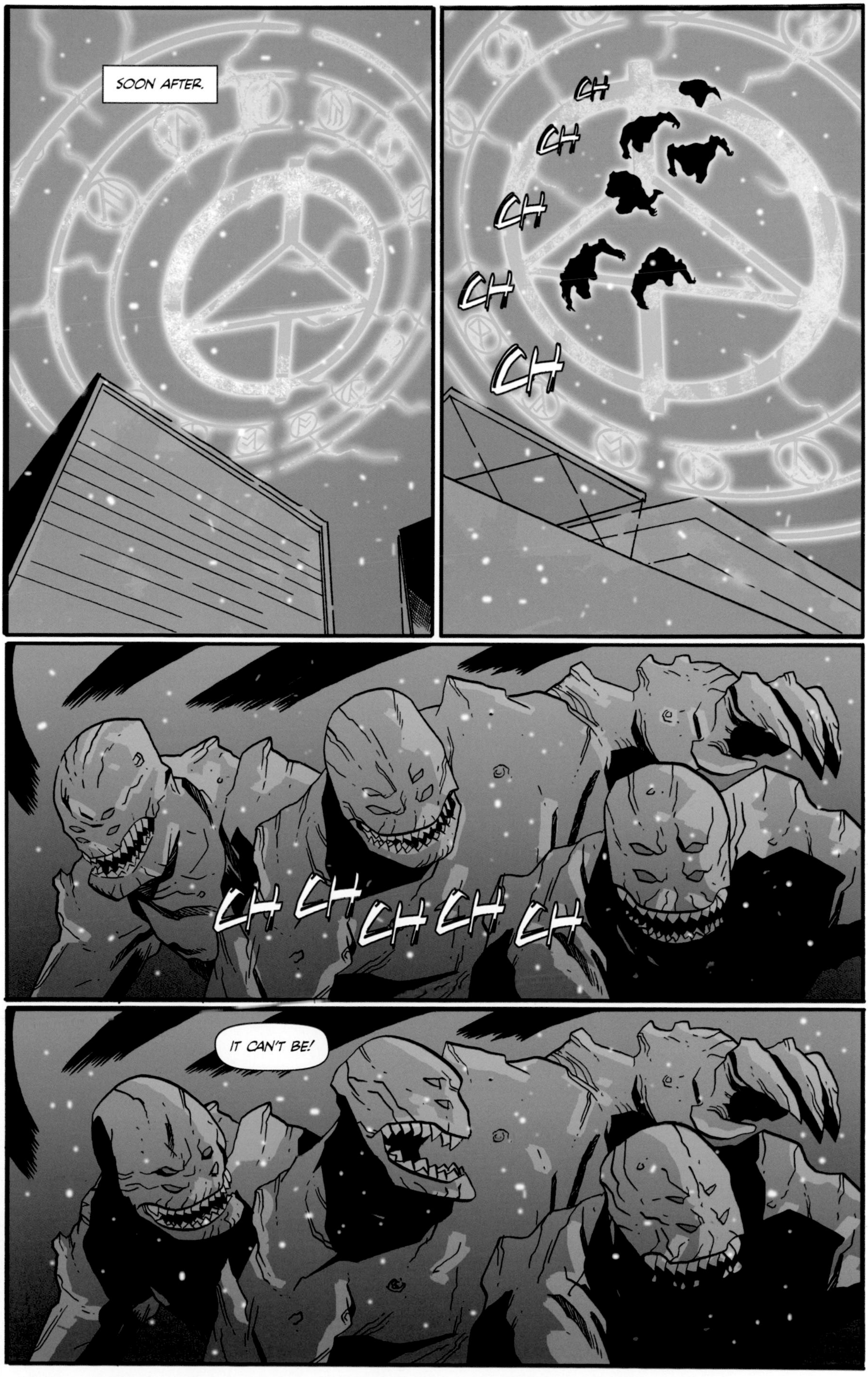
SOON AFTER.
CH
CH
CH
CH
CH
CH CH CH CH CH
IT CAN'T BE!

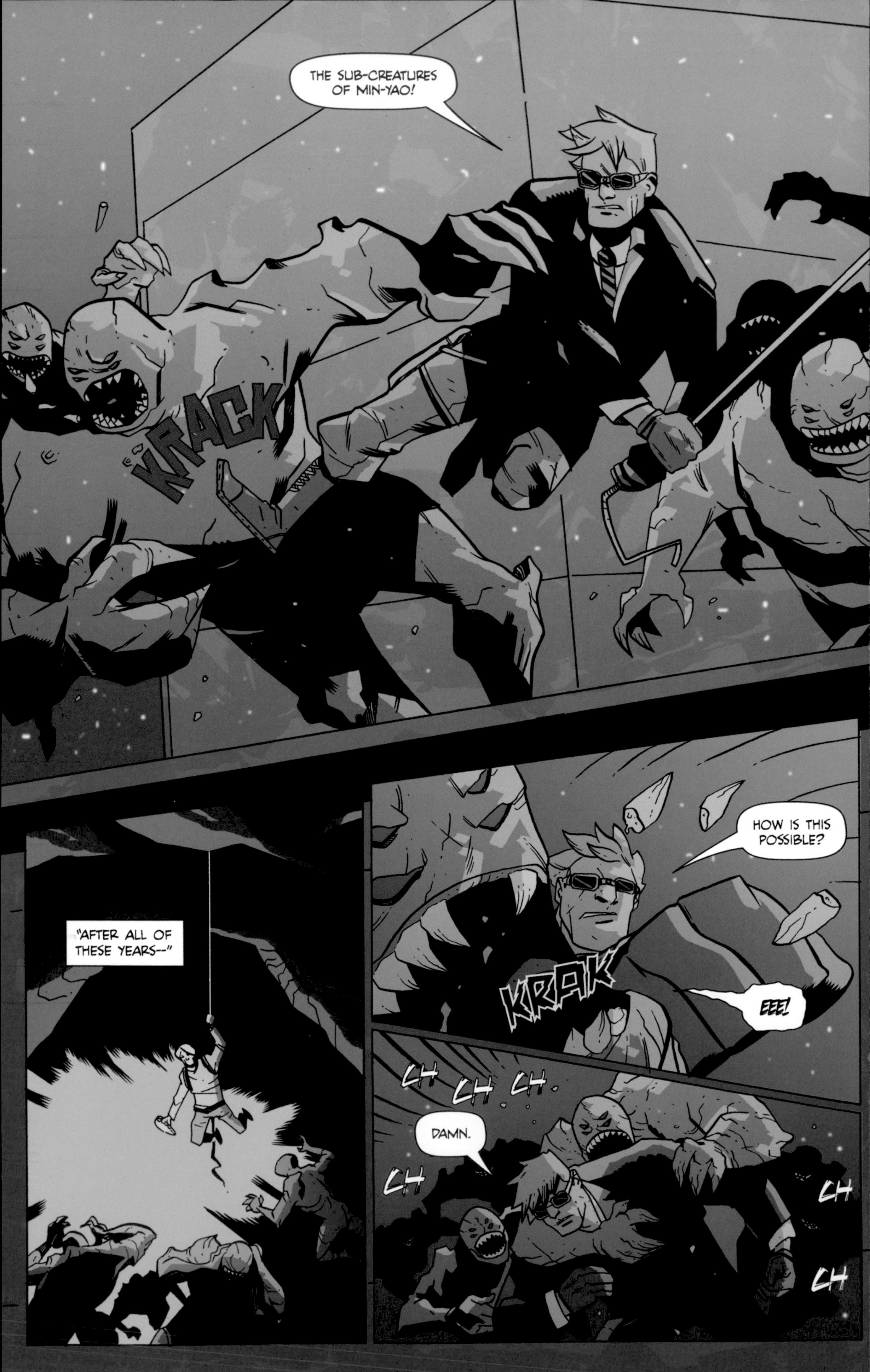

THE SUB-CREATURES OF MIN-YAO!
KRACK
"AFTER ALL OF THESE YEARS--"
HOW IS THIS POSSIBLE?
KRAK
EEE!
CH CH CH
DAMN.
CH
CH
CH

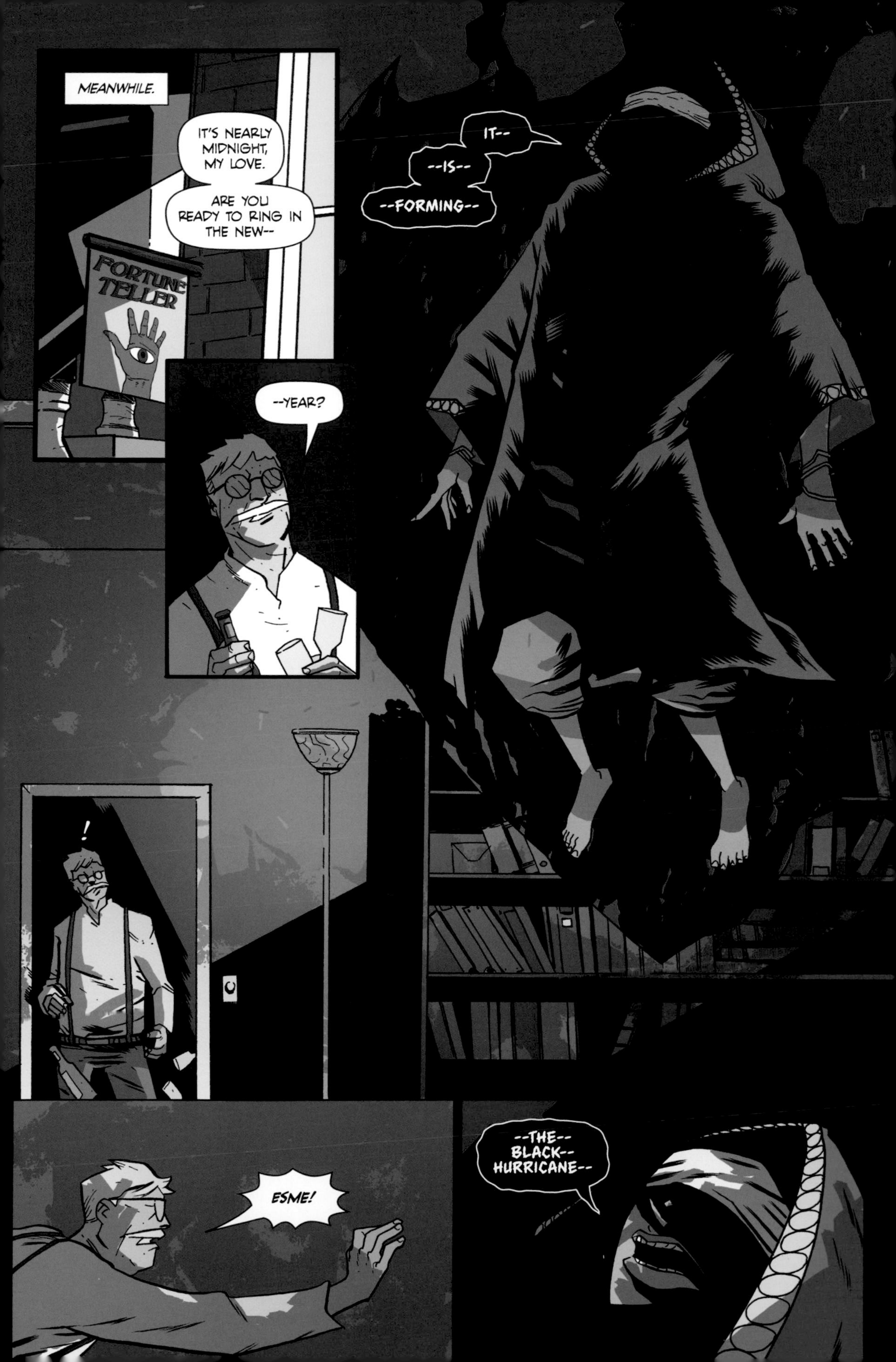
MEANWHILE.
IT'S NEARLY MIDNIGHT, MY LOVE.
ARE YOU READY TO RING IN THE NEW--
FORTUNE TELLER
--YEAR?
IT--
--IS--
--FORMING--
!
ESME!
--THE-- BLACK-- HURRICANE--

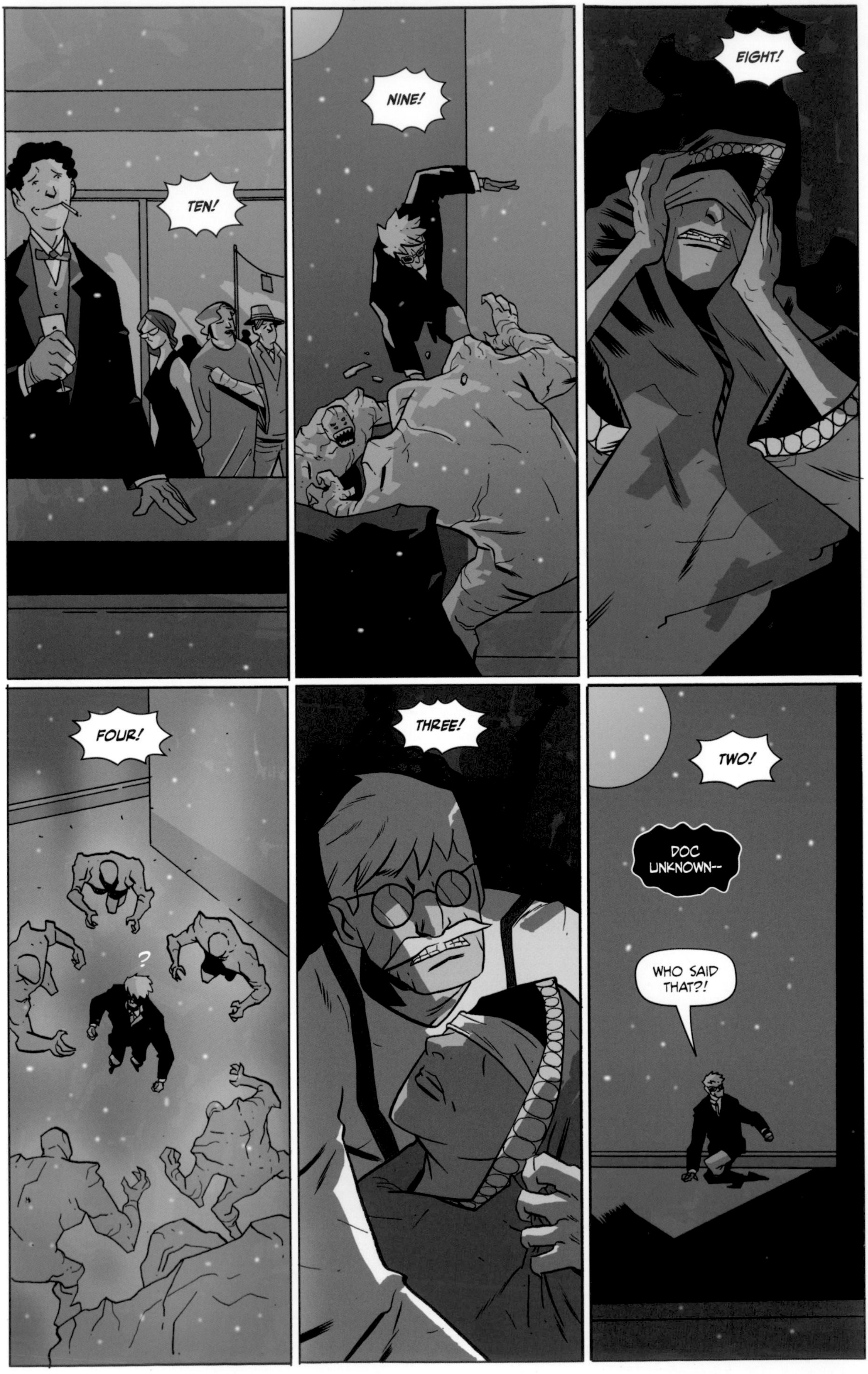
TEN!
NINE!
EIGHT!
FOUR!
?
THREE!
TWO!
DOC UNKNOWN--
WHO SAID THAT?!

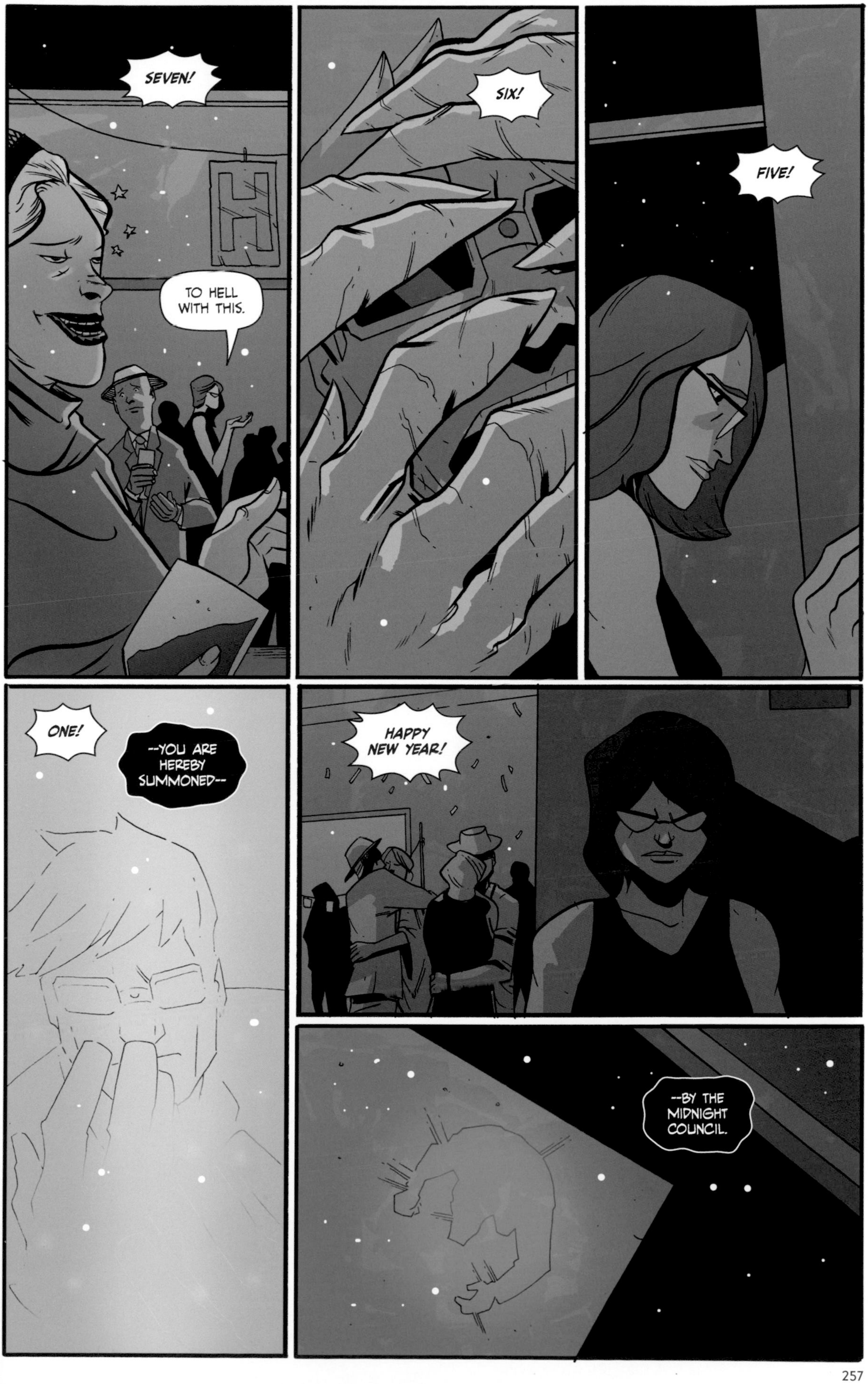
SEVEN!
TO HELL WITH THIS.
SIX!
FIVE!
ONE!
--YOU ARE HEREBY SUMMONED--
HAPPY NEW YEAR!
--BY THE MIDNIGHT COUNCIL.

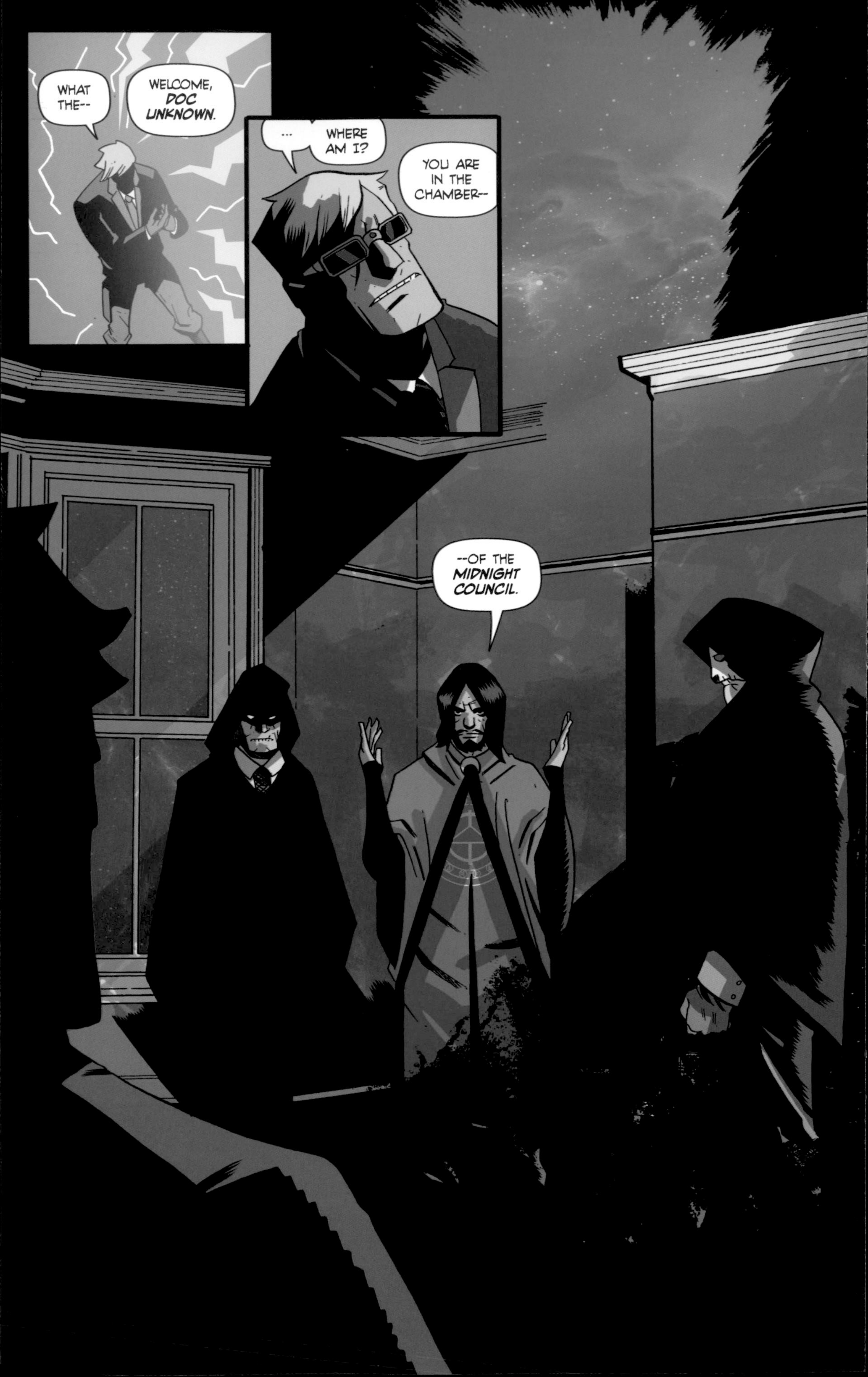
WHAT THE--
WELCOME, DOC UNKNOWN.
...
WHERE AM I?
YOU ARE IN THE CHAMBER--
--OF THE MIDNIGHT COUNCIL.

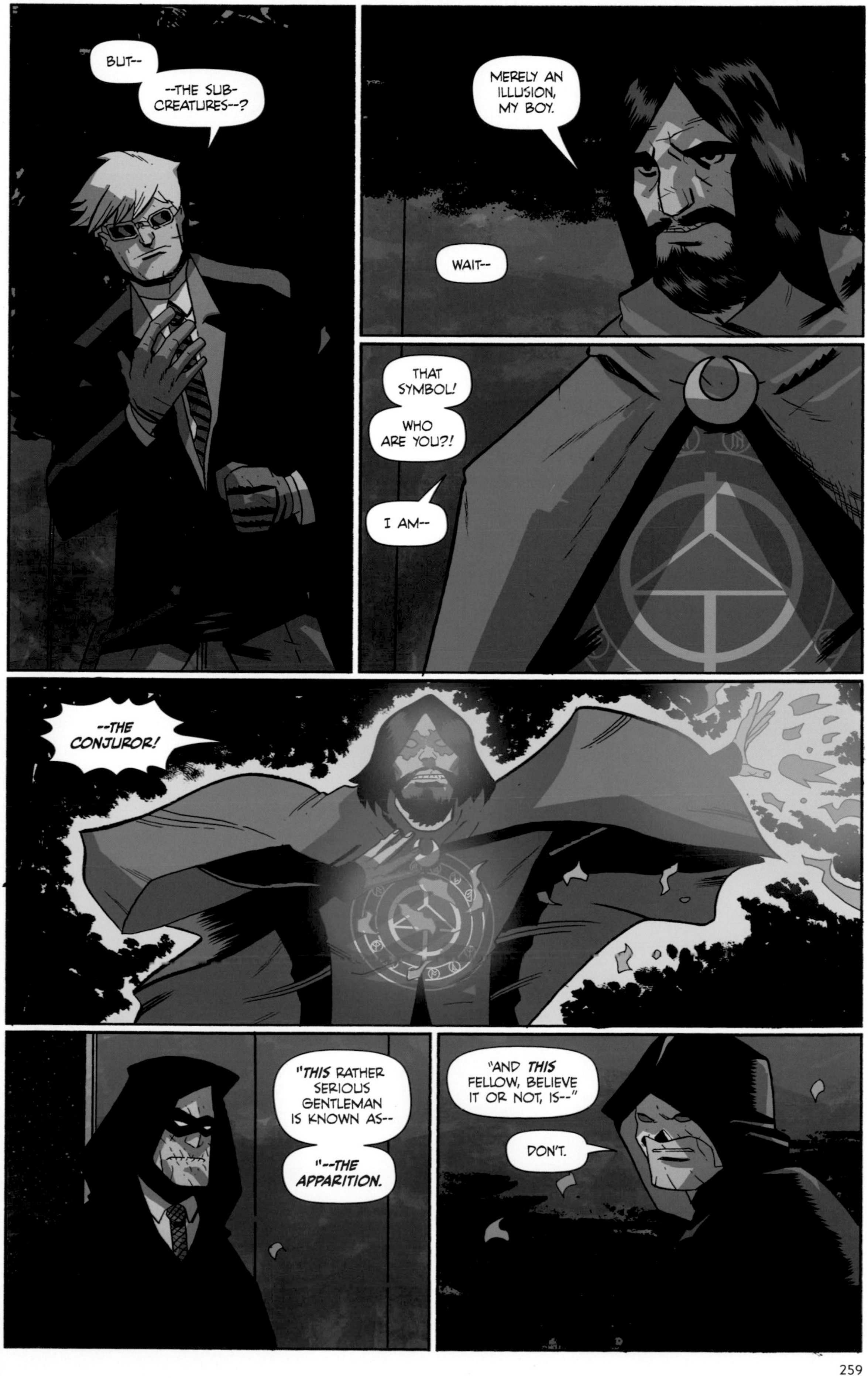
BUT--
--THE SUB-CREATURES--?
MERELY AN ILLUSION, MY BOY.
WAIT--
THAT SYMBOL!
WHO ARE YOU?!
I AM--
--THE CONJUROR!
"THIS RATHER SERIOUS GENTLEMAN IS KNOWN AS--
"--THE APPARITION.
"AND THIS FELLOW, BELIEVE IT OR NOT, IS--"
DON'T.

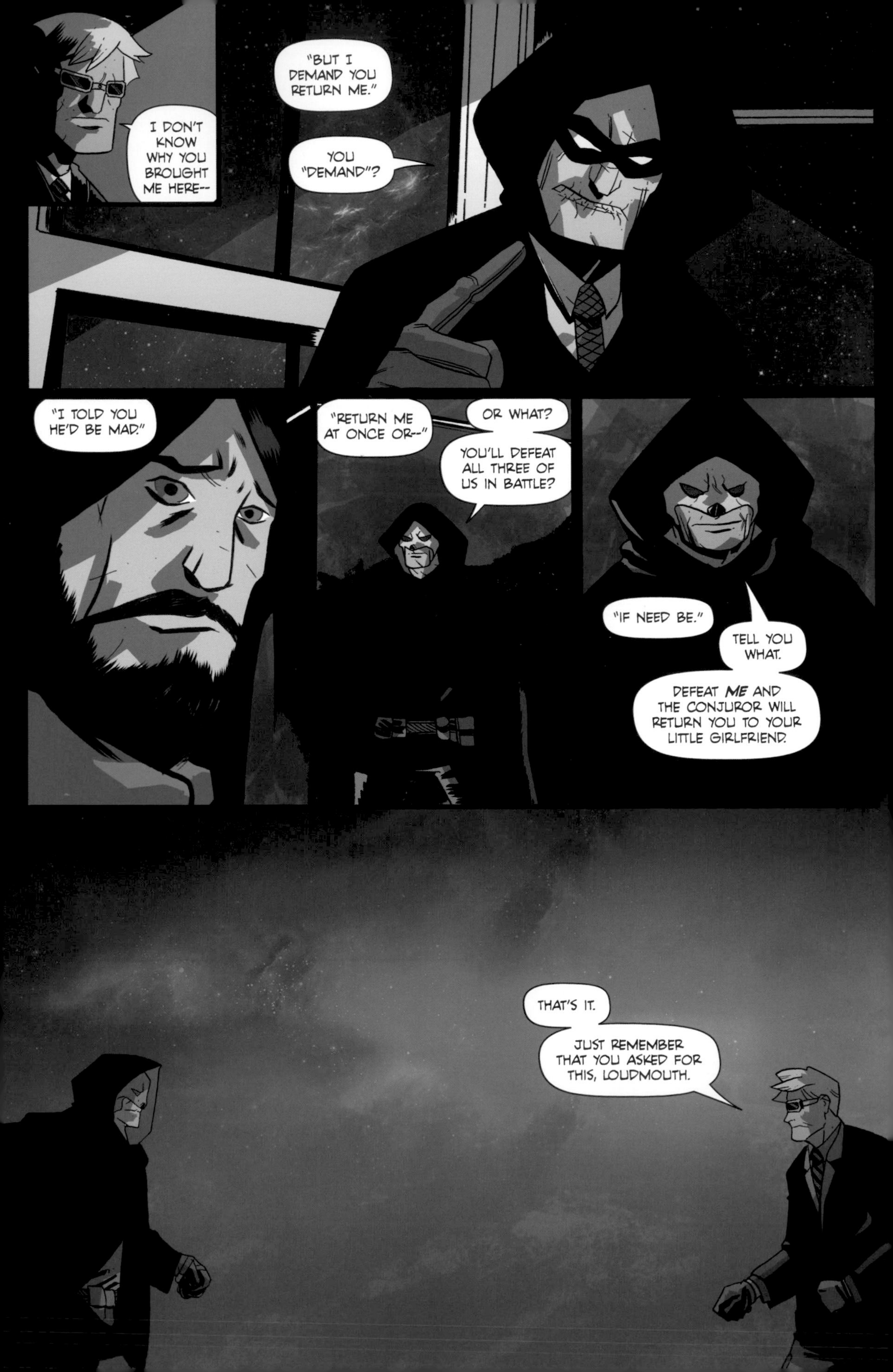
I DON'T KNOW WHY YOU BROUGHT ME HERE--
"BUT I DEMAND YOU RETURN ME."
YOU "DEMAND"?
"I TOLD YOU HE'D BE MAD."
"RETURN ME AT ONCE OR--"
OR WHAT?
YOU'LL DEFEAT ALL THREE OF US IN BATTLE?
"IF NEED BE."
TELL YOU WHAT.
DEFEAT ME AND THE CONJUROR WILL RETURN YOU TO YOUR LITTLE GIRLFRIEND.
THAT'S IT.
JUST REMEMBER THAT YOU ASKED FOR THIS, LOUDMOUTH.

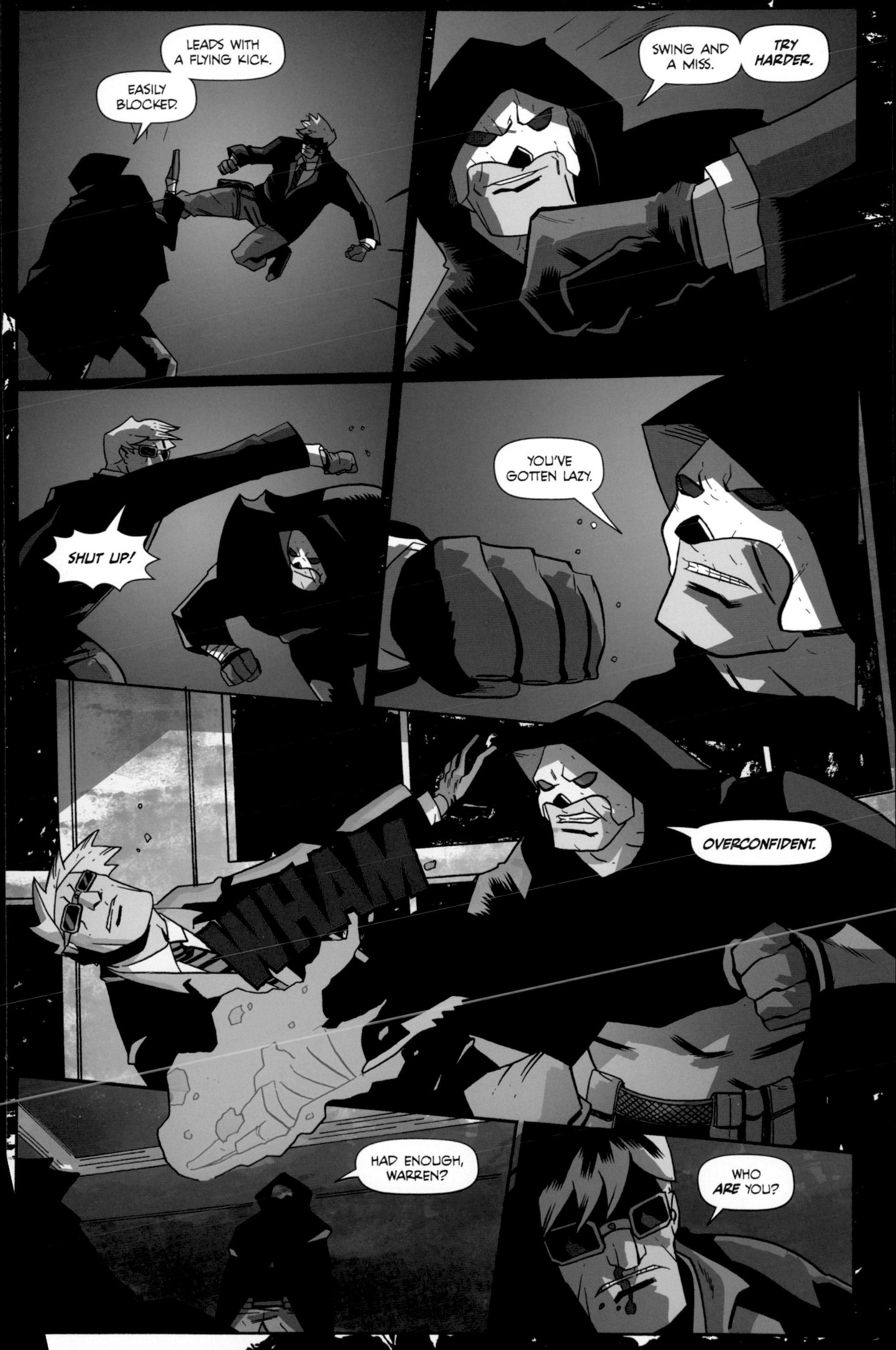

EASILY BLOCKED.
LEADS WITH A FLYING KICK.
SWING AND A MISS.
TRY HARDER.
SHUT UP!
YOU'VE GOTTEN LAZY.
OVERCONFIDENT.
WHAM
HAD ENOUGH, WARREN?
WHO ARE YOU?

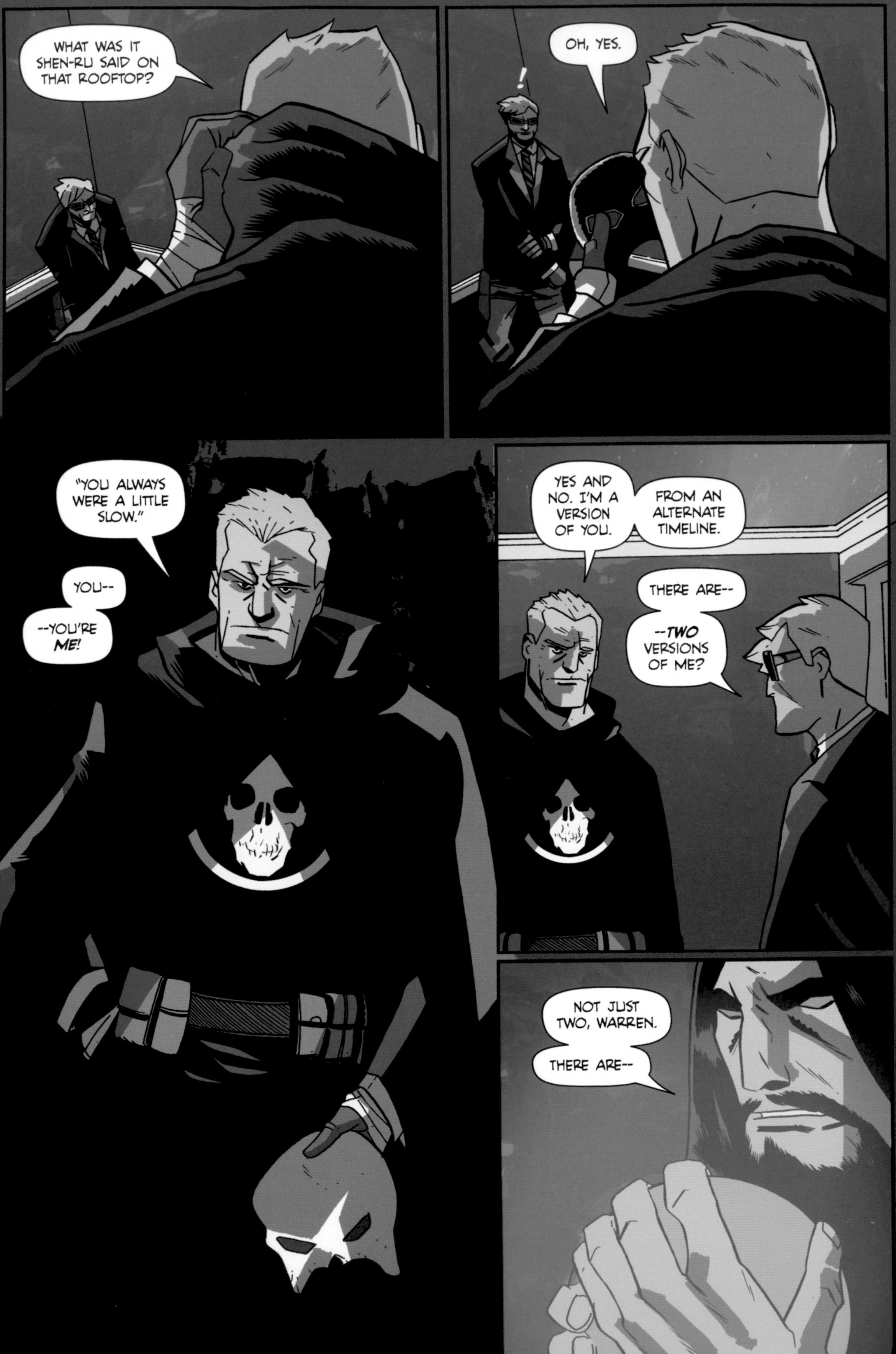
WHAT WAS IT SHEN-RU SAID ON THAT ROOFTOP?
OH, YES.
!
"YOU ALWAYS WERE A LITTLE SLOW."
YOU--
--YOU'RE ME!
YES AND NO. I'M A VERSION OF YOU.
FROM AN ALTERNATE TIMELINE.
THERE ARE--
--TWO VERSIONS OF ME?
NOT JUST TWO, WARREN.
THERE ARE--

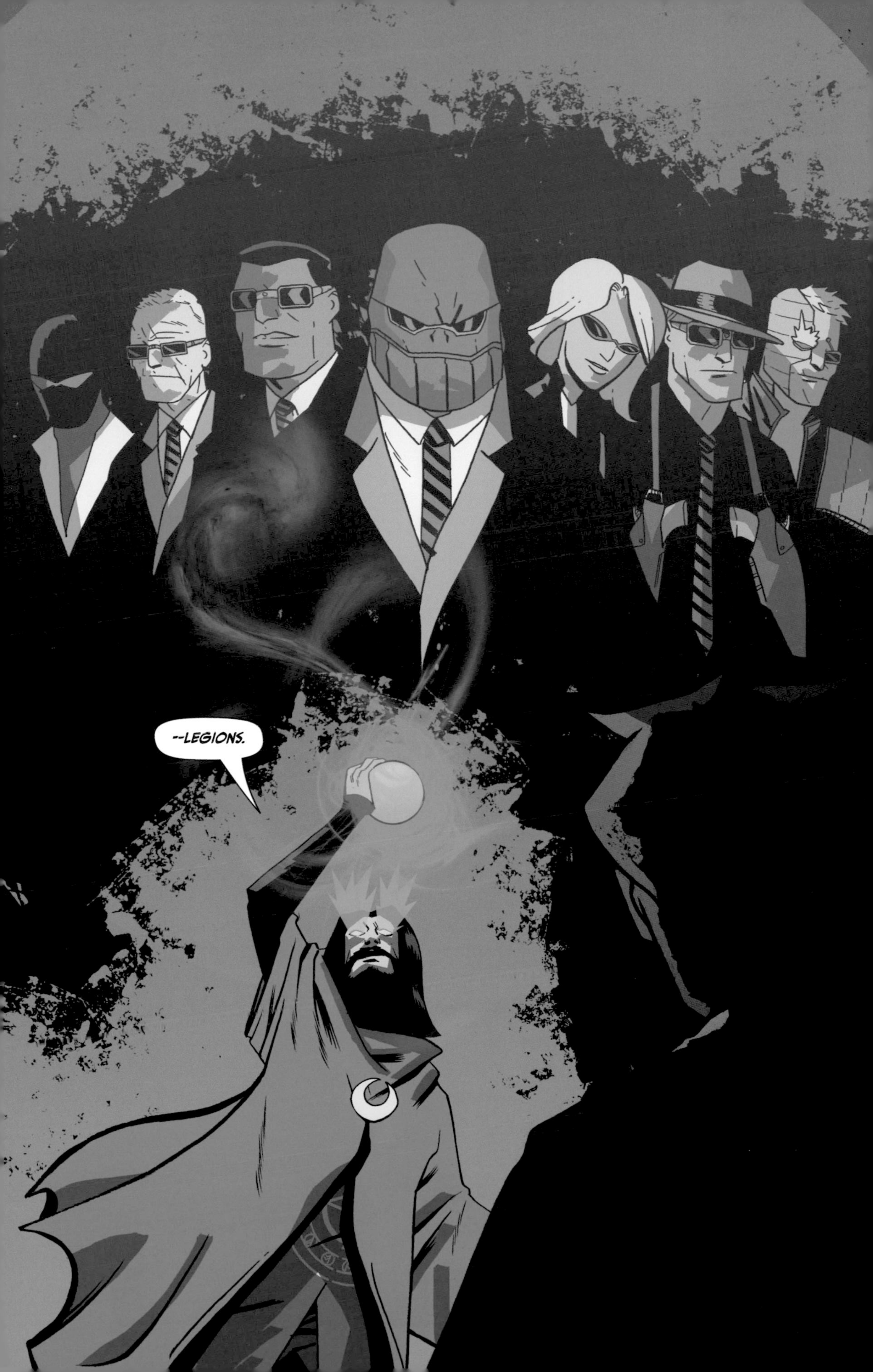
--LEGIONS.

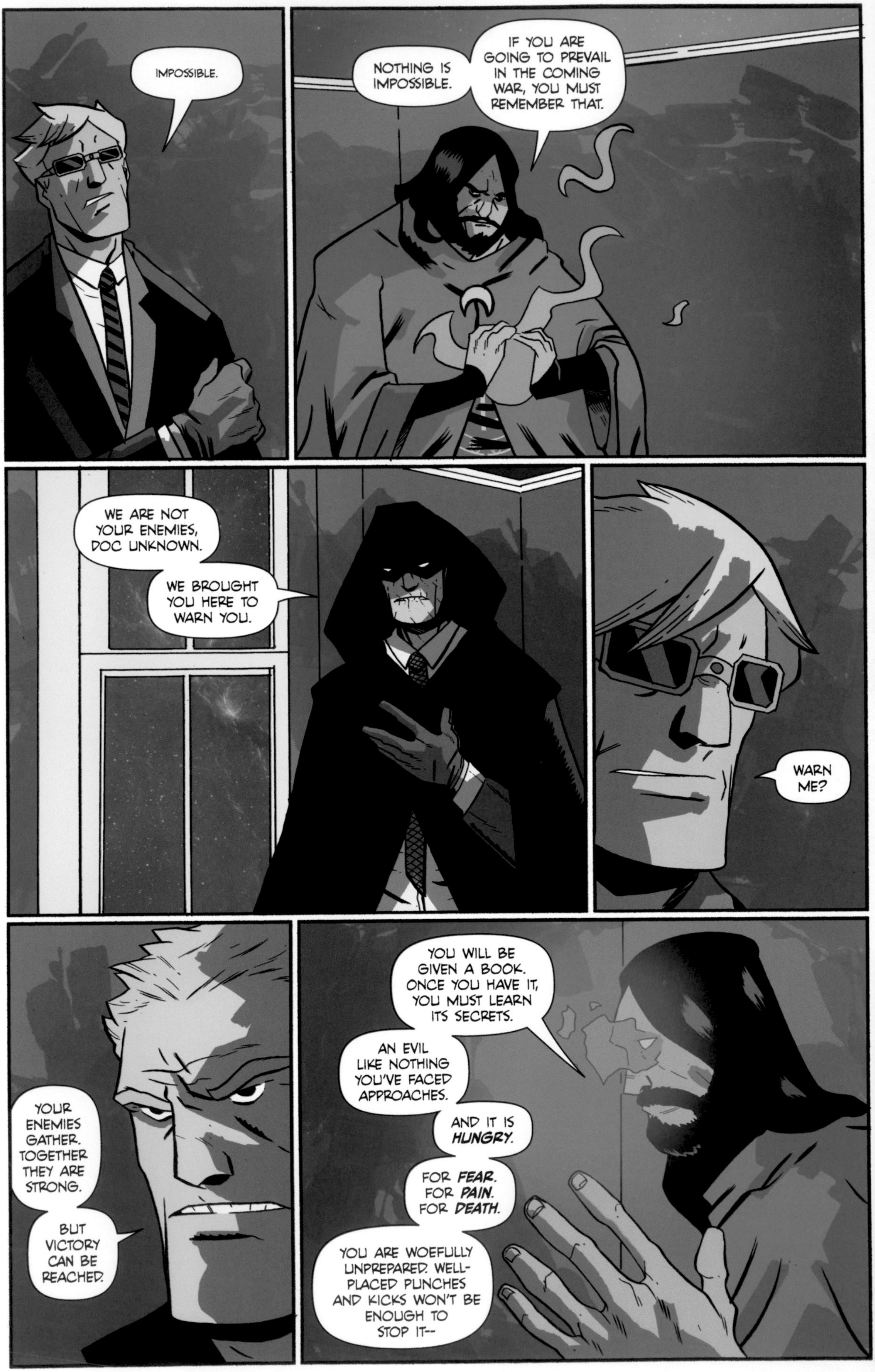
IMPOSSIBLE.
NOTHING IS IMPOSSIBLE.
IF YOU ARE GOING TO PREVAIL IN THE COMING WAR, YOU MUST REMEMBER THAT.
WE ARE NOT YOUR ENEMIES, DOC UNKNOWN.
WE BROUGHT YOU HERE TO WARN YOU.
WARN ME?
YOUR ENEMIES GATHER. TOGETHER THEY ARE STRONG.
BUT VICTORY CAN BE REACHED.
YOU WILL BE GIVEN A BOOK. ONCE YOU HAVE IT, YOU MUST LEARN ITS SECRETS.
AN EVIL LIKE NOTHING YOU'VE FACED APPROACHES.
AND IT IS *HUNGRY*.
FOR *FEAR*. FOR *PAIN*. FOR *DEATH*.
YOU ARE WOEFULLY UNPREPARED. WELL-PLACED PUNCHES AND KICKS WON'T BE ENOUGH TO STOP IT--

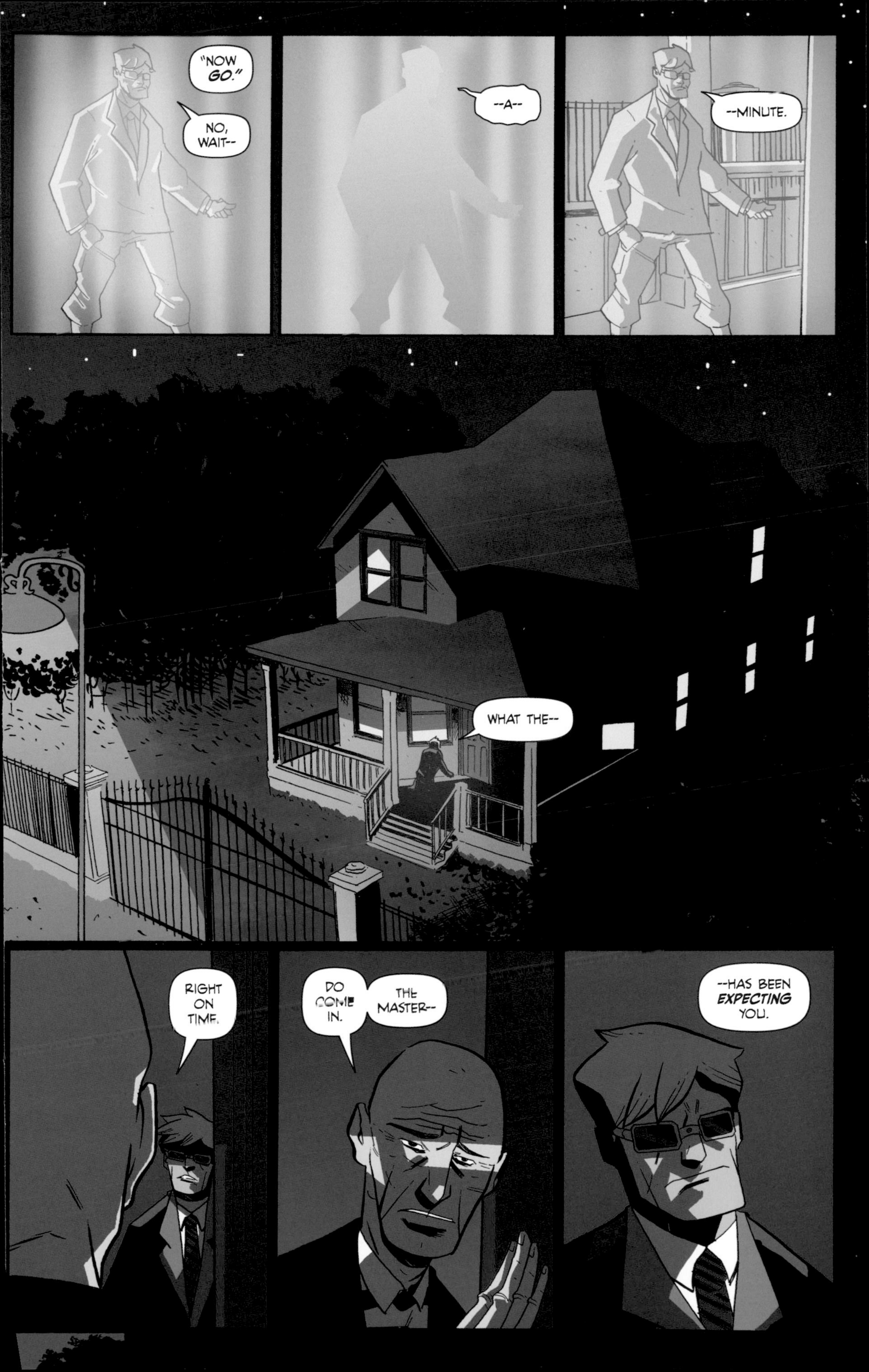
"NOW GO."
NO, WAIT--
--A--
--MINUTE.
WHAT THE--
RIGHT ON TIME.
DO COME IN.
THE MASTER--
--HAS BEEN EXPECTING YOU.

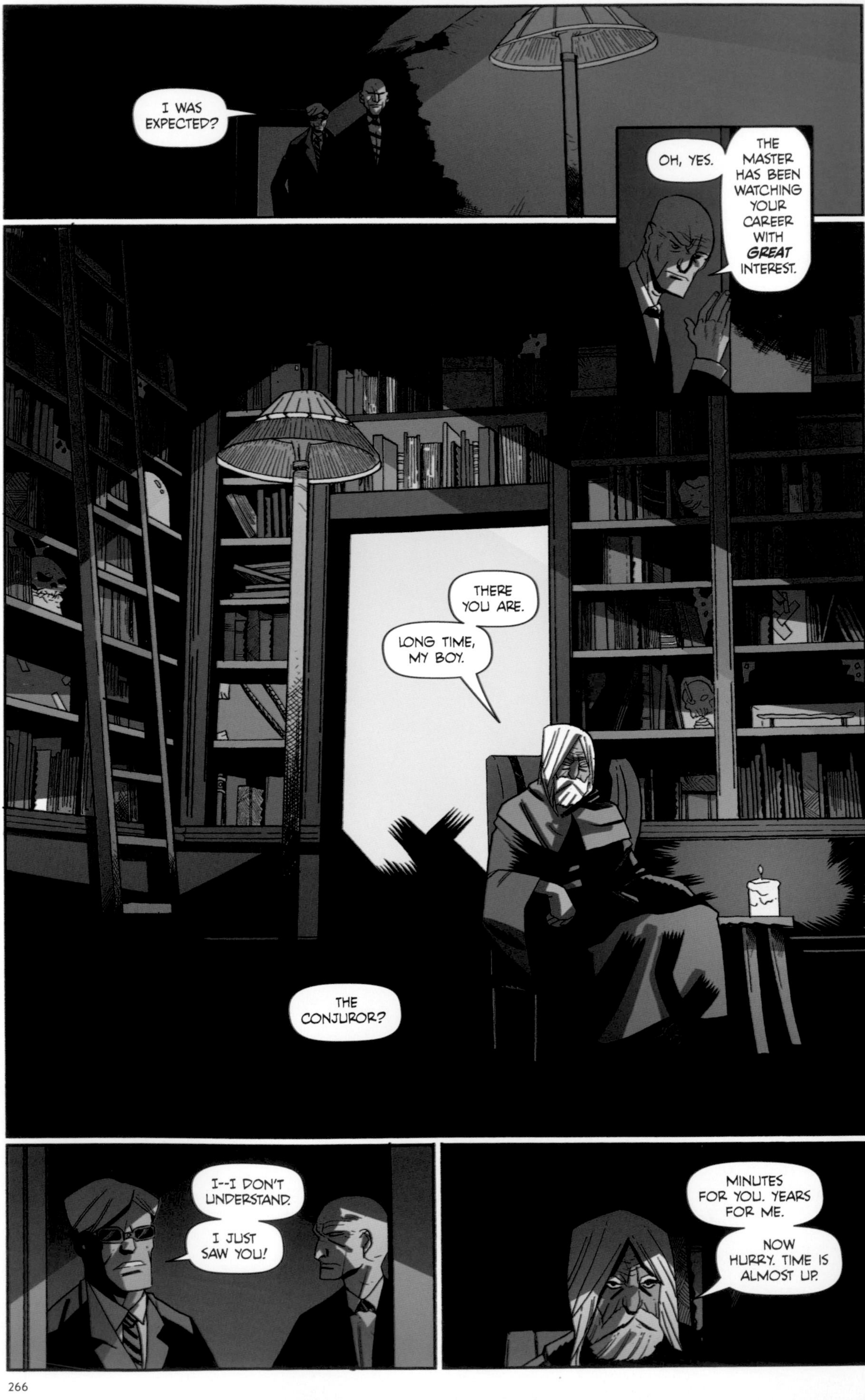
I WAS EXPECTED?
OH, YES.
THE MASTER HAS BEEN WATCHING YOUR CAREER WITH GREAT INTEREST.
THERE YOU ARE.
LONG TIME, MY BOY.
THE CONJUROR?
I--I DON'T UNDERSTAND.
I JUST SAW YOU!
MINUTES FOR YOU. YEARS FOR ME.
NOW HURRY. TIME IS ALMOST UP.

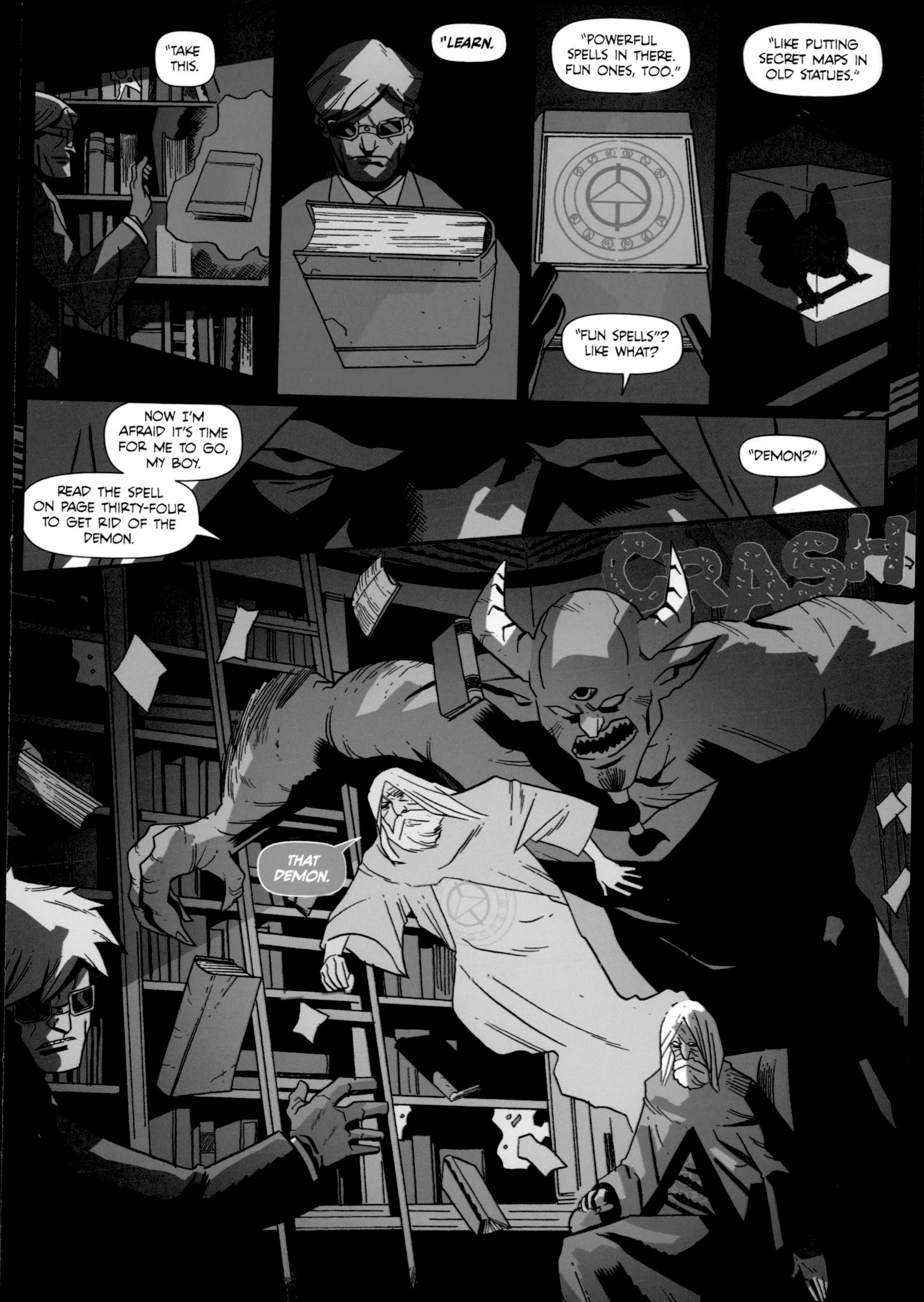
"TAKE THIS.
"LEARN.
"POWERFUL SPELLS IN THERE. FUN ONES, TOO."
"LIKE PUTTING SECRET MAPS IN OLD STATUES."
"FUN SPELLS"? LIKE WHAT?
NOW I'M AFRAID IT'S TIME FOR ME TO GO, MY BOY.
READ THE SPELL ON PAGE THIRTY-FOUR TO GET RID OF THE DEMON.
"DEMON?"
CRASH
THAT DEMON.

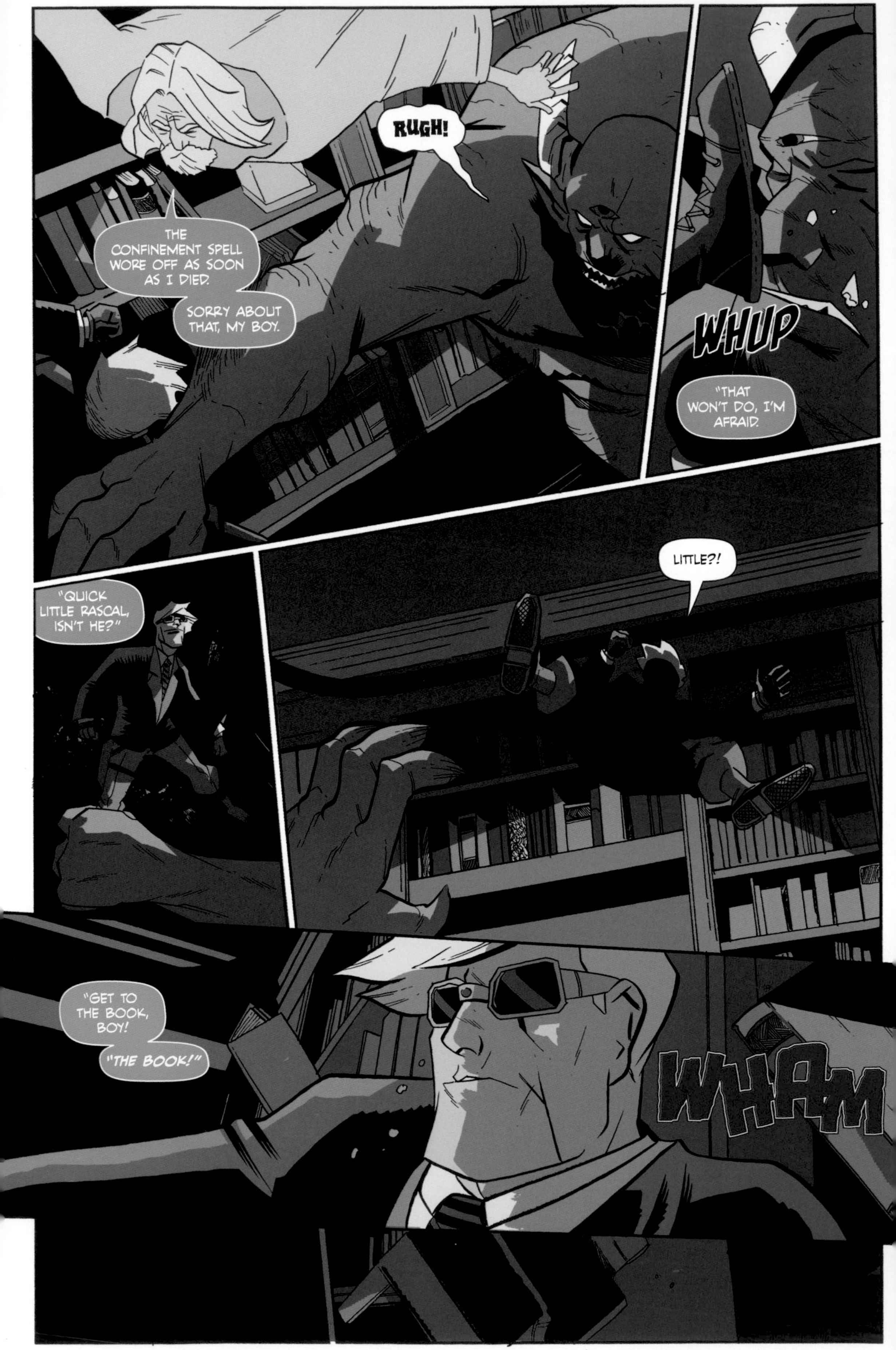
RUGH!
THE CONFINEMENT SPELL WORE OFF AS SOON AS I DIED.
SORRY ABOUT THAT, MY BOY.
WHUP
"THAT WON'T DO, I'M AFRAID.
"QUICK LITTLE RASCAL, ISN'T HE?"
LITTLE?!
"GET TO THE BOOK, BOY!
"THE BOOK!"
WHAM

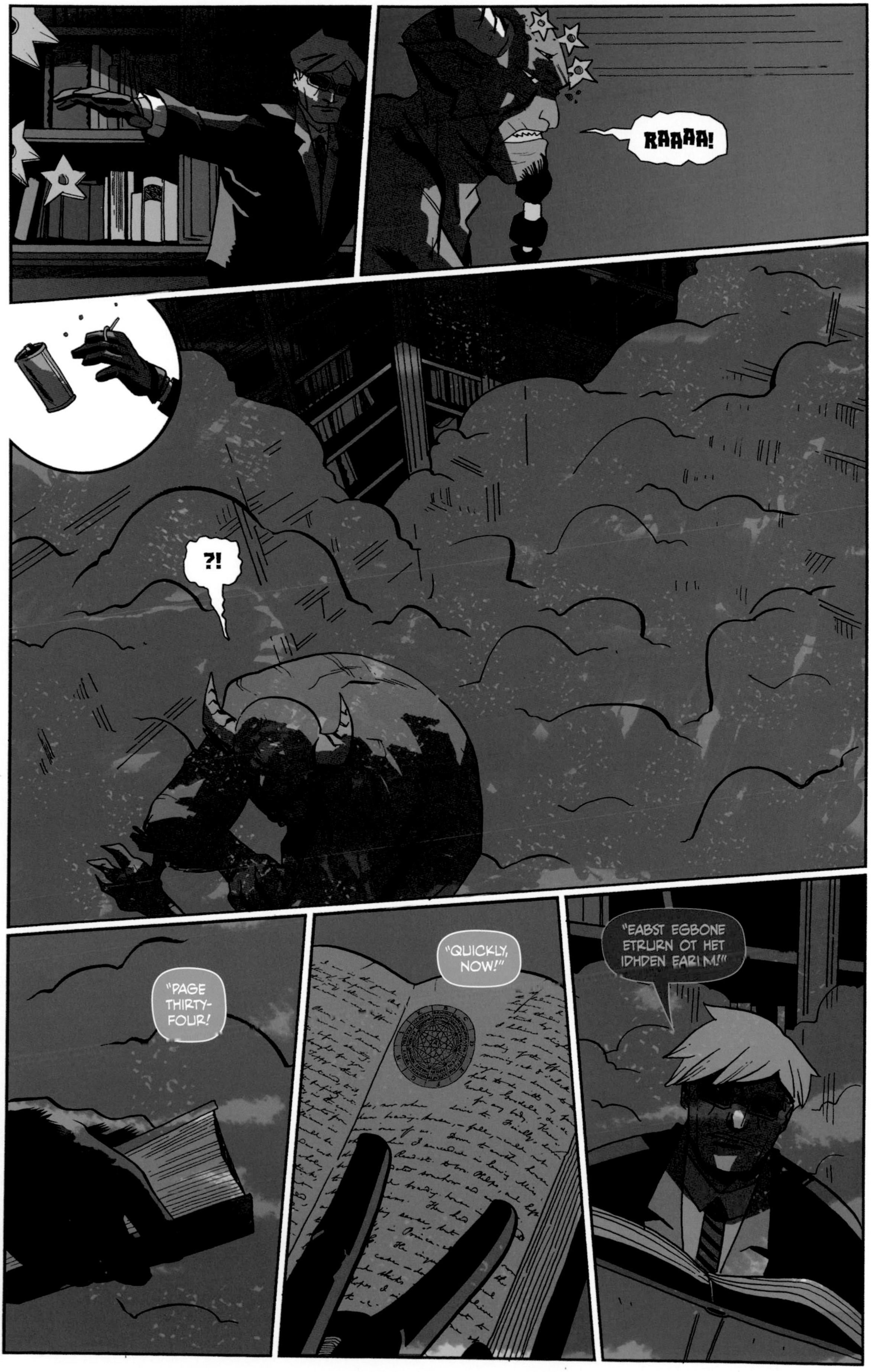
RAAAA!
?!
"PAGE THIRTY-FOUR!
"QUICKLY, NOW!"
"EABST EGBONE ETRURN OT HET IDHDEN EARLM!"

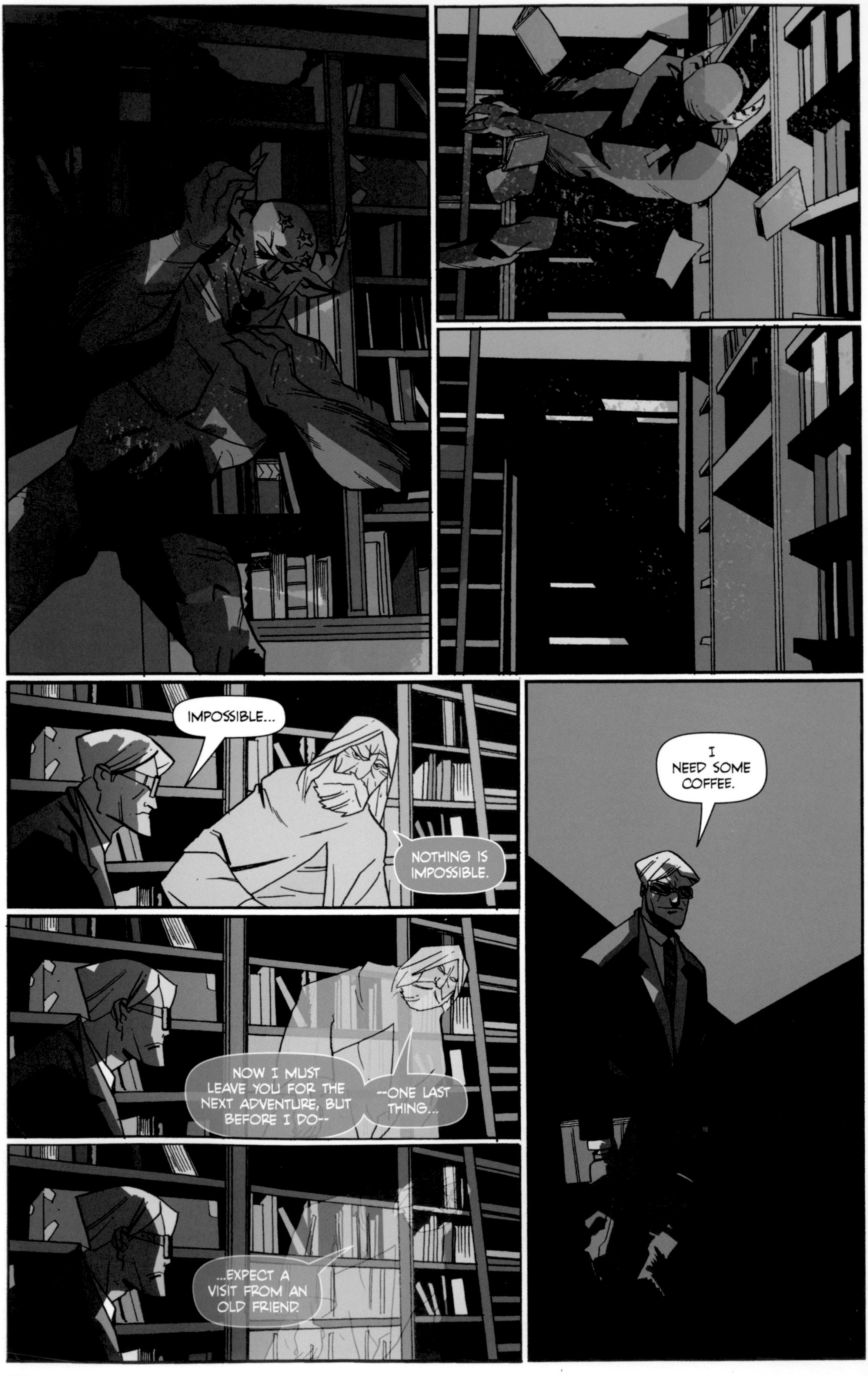
IMPOSSIBLE...
NOTHING IS IMPOSSIBLE.
NOW I MUST LEAVE YOU FOR THE NEXT ADVENTURE, BUT BEFORE I DO--
--ONE LAST THING...
...EXPECT A VISIT FROM AN OLD FRIEND.
I NEED SOME COFFEE.

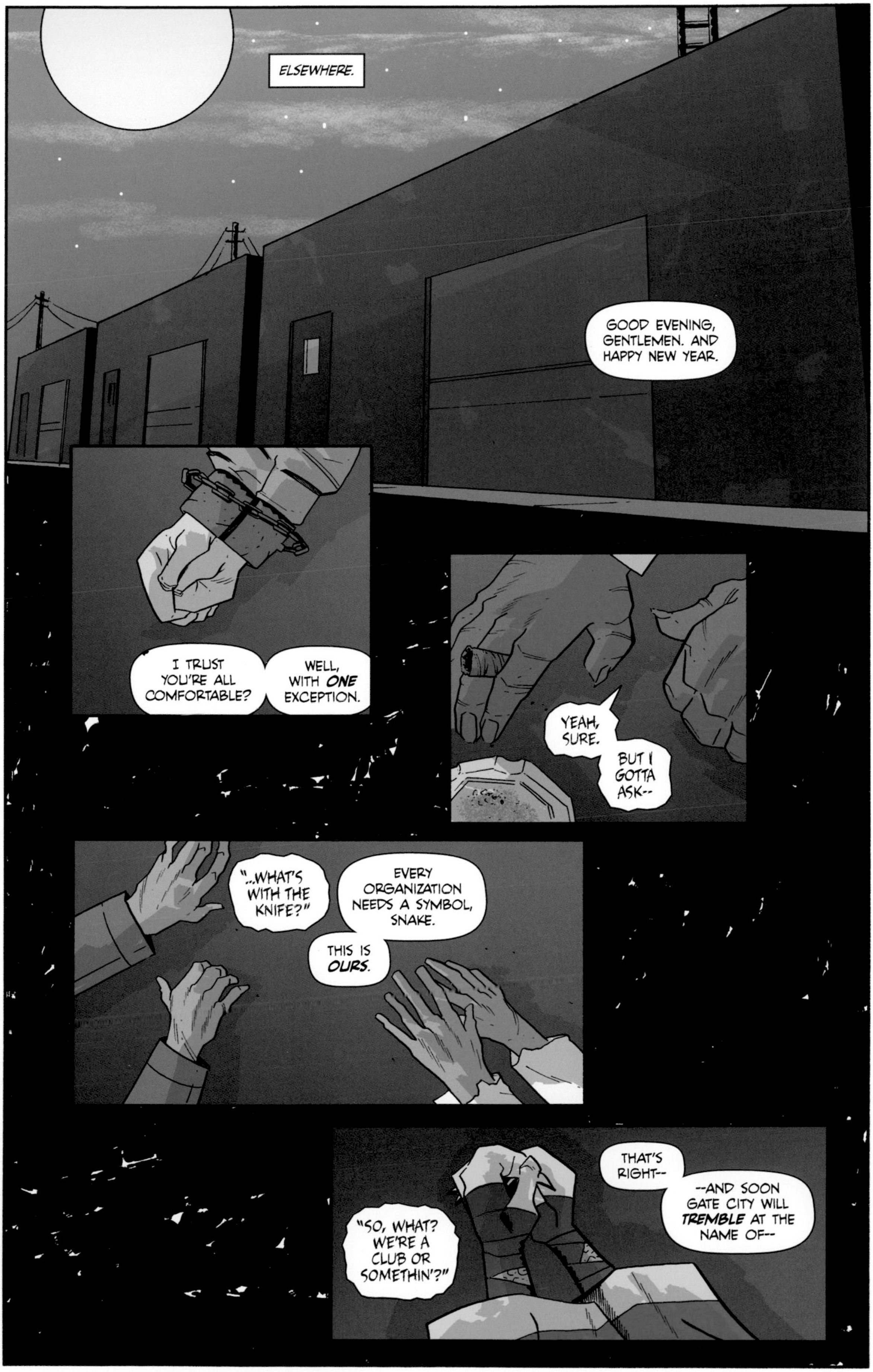
ELSEWHERE.
GOOD EVENING, GENTLEMEN. AND HAPPY NEW YEAR.
I TRUST YOU'RE ALL COMFORTABLE?
WELL, WITH ONE EXCEPTION.
YEAH, SURE.
BUT I GOTTA ASK--
"...WHAT'S WITH THE KNIFE?"
EVERY ORGANIZATION NEEDS A SYMBOL, SNAKE.
THIS IS OURS.
"SO, WHAT? WE'RE A CLUB OR SOMETHIN'?"
THAT'S RIGHT--
--AND SOON GATE CITY WILL TREMBLE AT THE NAME OF--

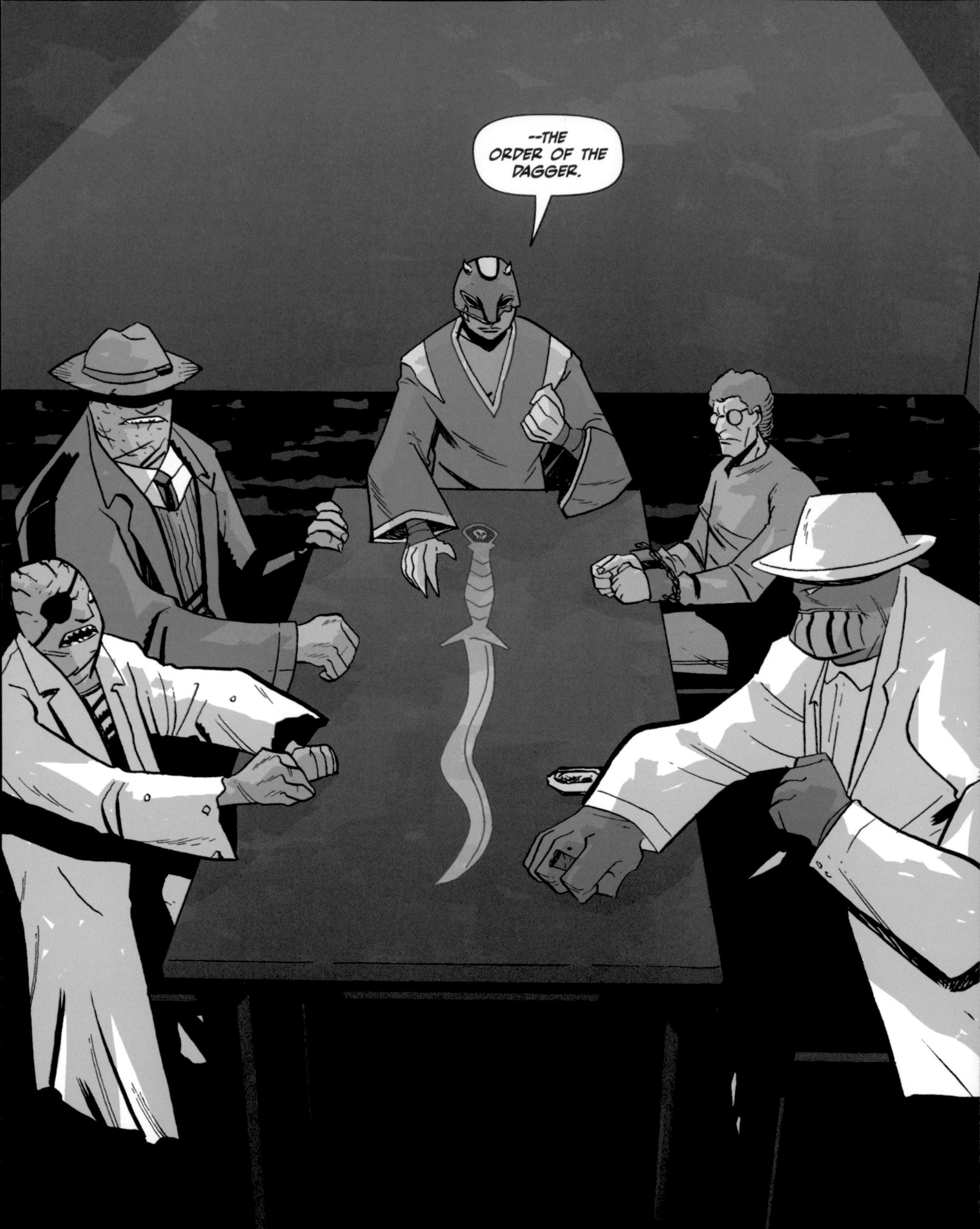
--THE ORDER OF THE DAGGER.

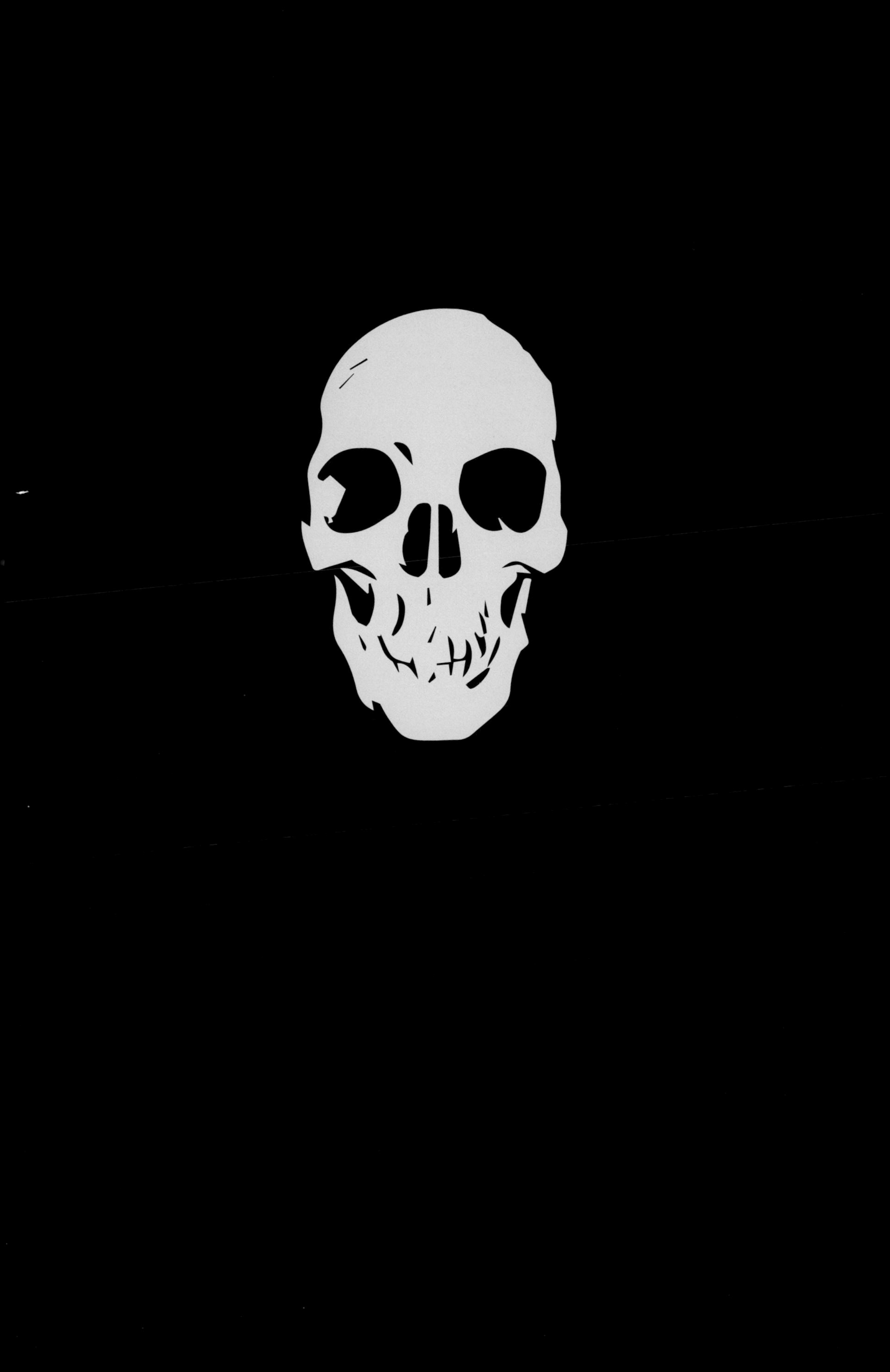

THE FIRE
OF TIME

SCRIPT BY **FABIAN RANGEL JR.**

ART BY **RYAN CODY**

LETTERS BY **EVELYN RANGEL**

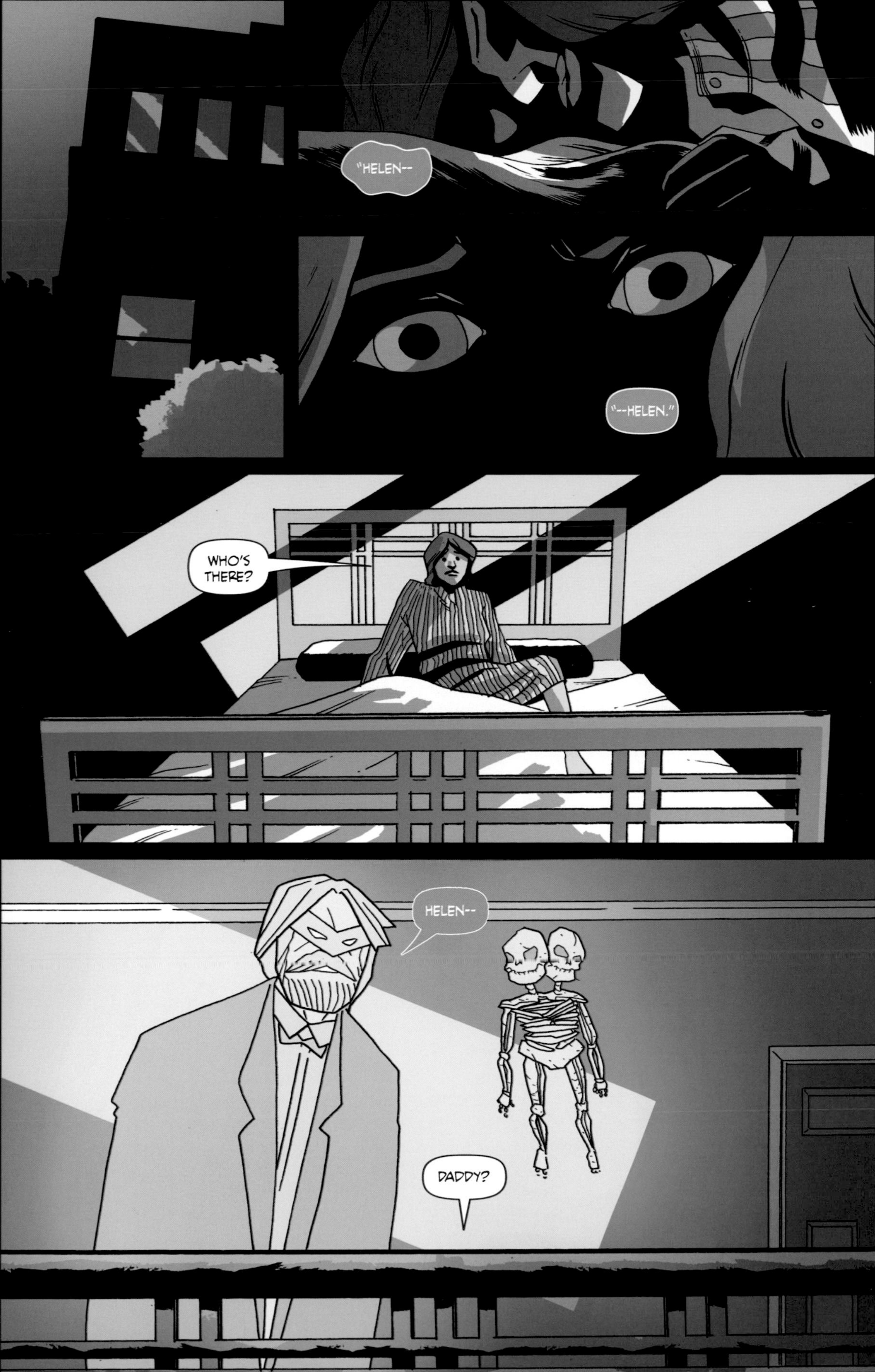
"HELEN--
"--HELEN."
WHO'S THERE?
HELEN--
DADDY?

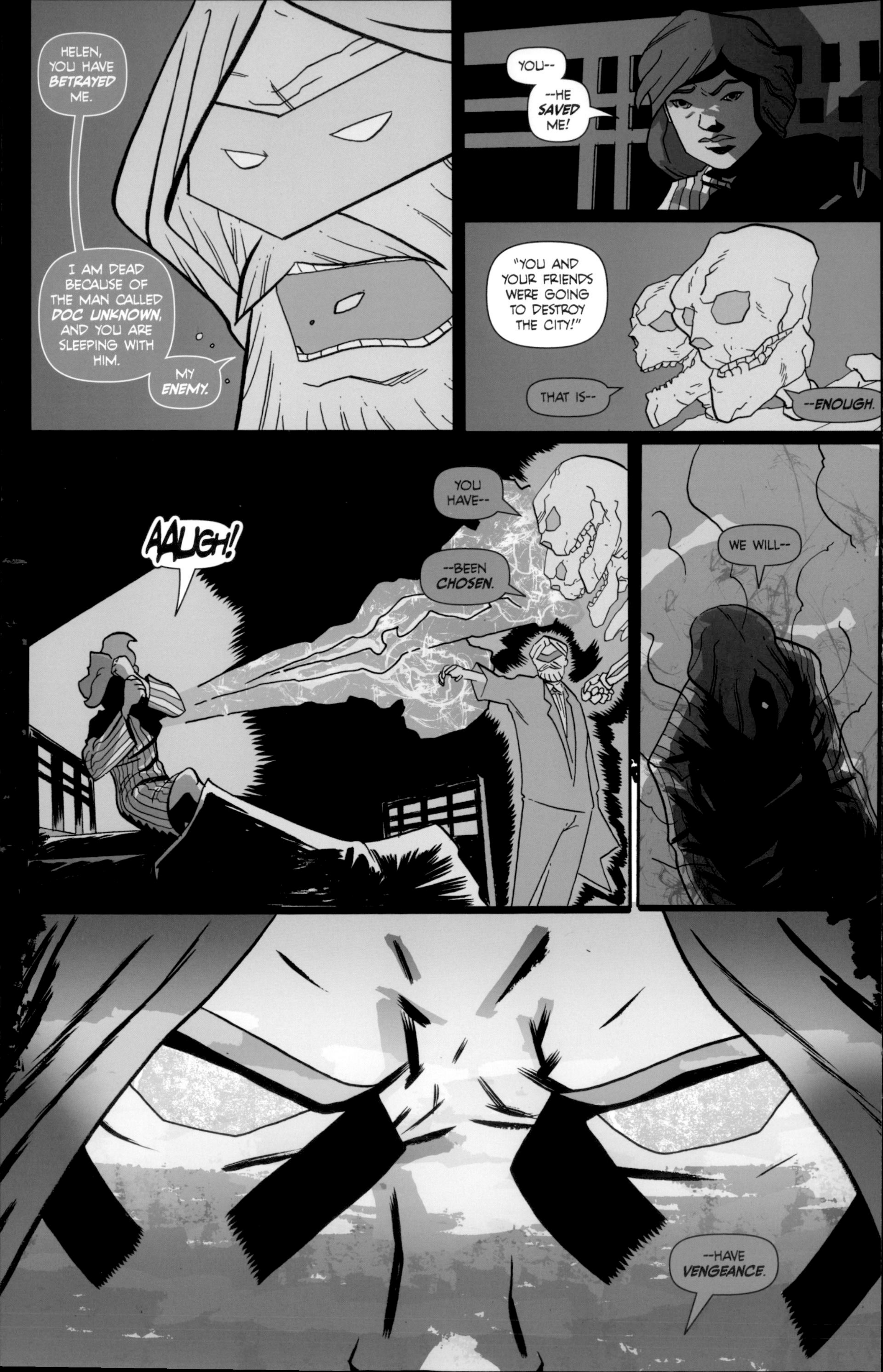

HELEN, YOU HAVE BETRAYED ME.
I AM DEAD BECAUSE OF THE MAN CALLED DOC UNKNOWN, AND YOU ARE SLEEPING WITH HIM.
MY ENEMY.
YOU--
--HE SAVED ME!
"YOU AND YOUR FRIENDS WERE GOING TO DESTROY THE CITY!"
THAT IS--
--ENOUGH.
AAUGH!
YOU HAVE--
--BEEN CHOSEN.
WE WILL--
--HAVE VENGEANCE.

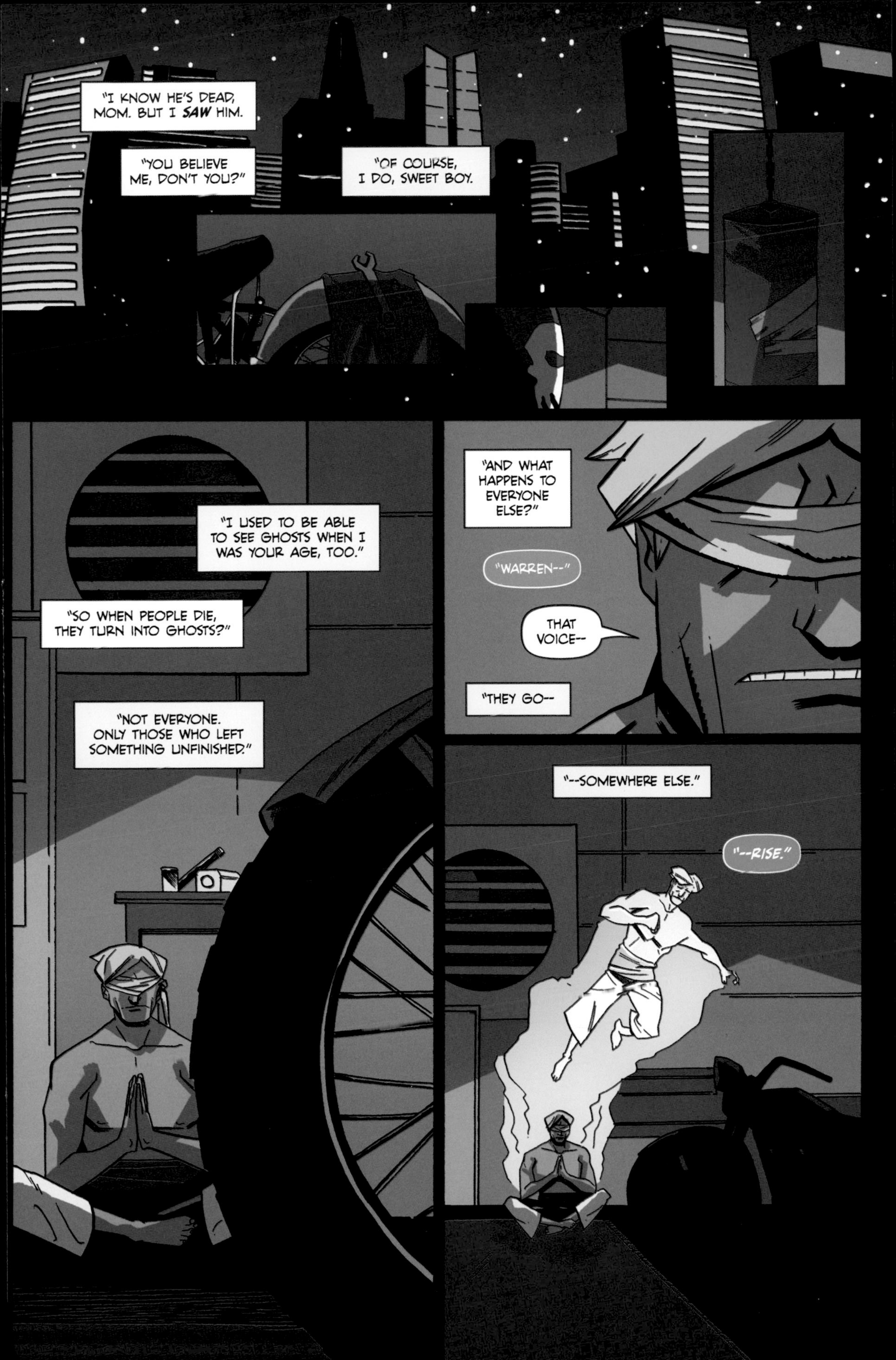
"I KNOW HE'S DEAD, MOM. BUT I SAW HIM.
"YOU BELIEVE ME, DON'T YOU?"
"OF COURSE, I DO, SWEET BOY.
"I USED TO BE ABLE TO SEE GHOSTS WHEN I WAS YOUR AGE, TOO."
"SO WHEN PEOPLE DIE, THEY TURN INTO GHOSTS?"
"NOT EVERYONE. ONLY THOSE WHO LEFT SOMETHING UNFINISHED."
"AND WHAT HAPPENS TO EVERYONE ELSE?"
"WARREN--"
THAT VOICE--
"THEY GO--
"--SOMEWHERE ELSE."
"--RISE."

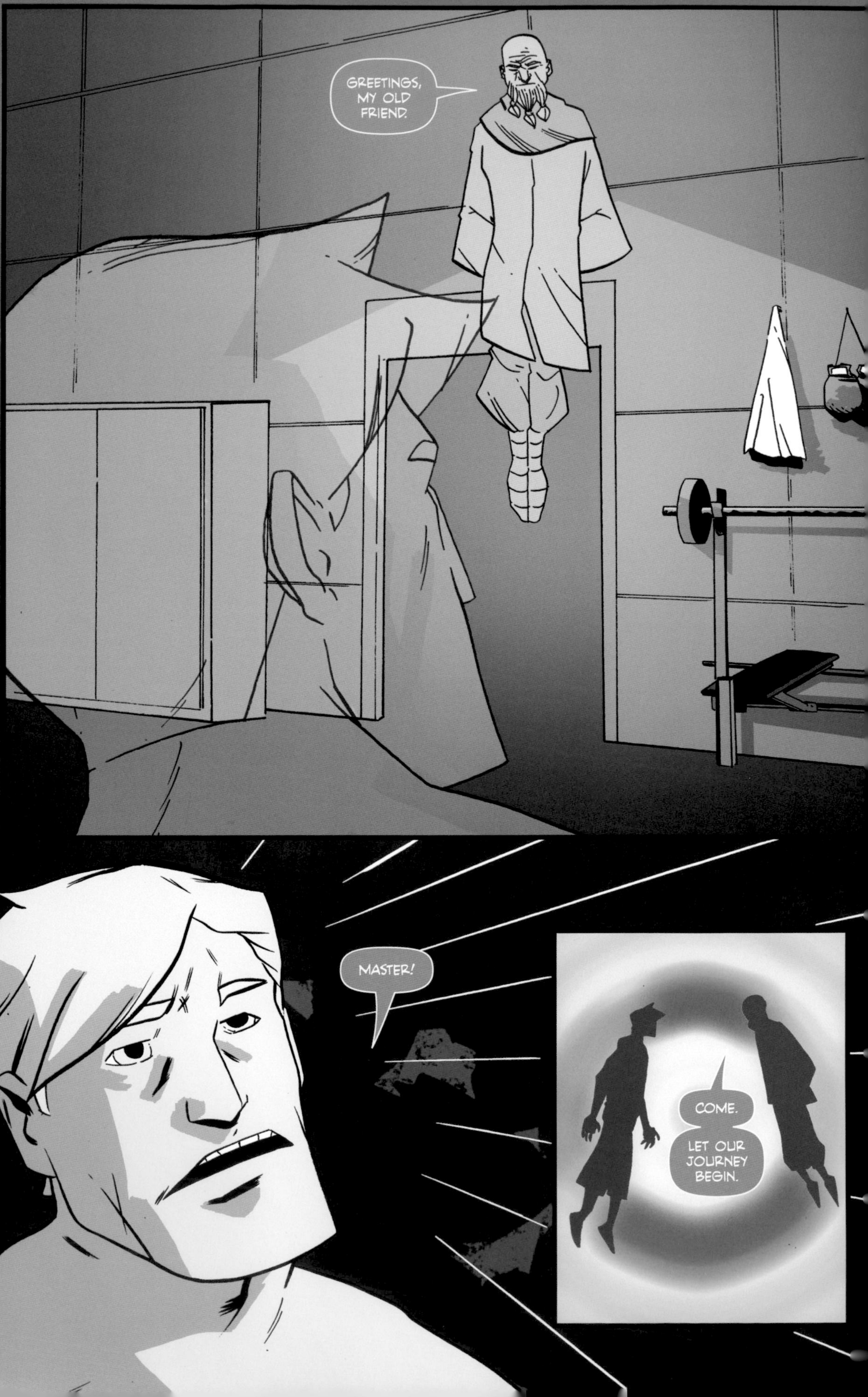
GREETINGS, MY OLD FRIEND.
MASTER!
COME.
LET OUR JOURNEY BEGIN.

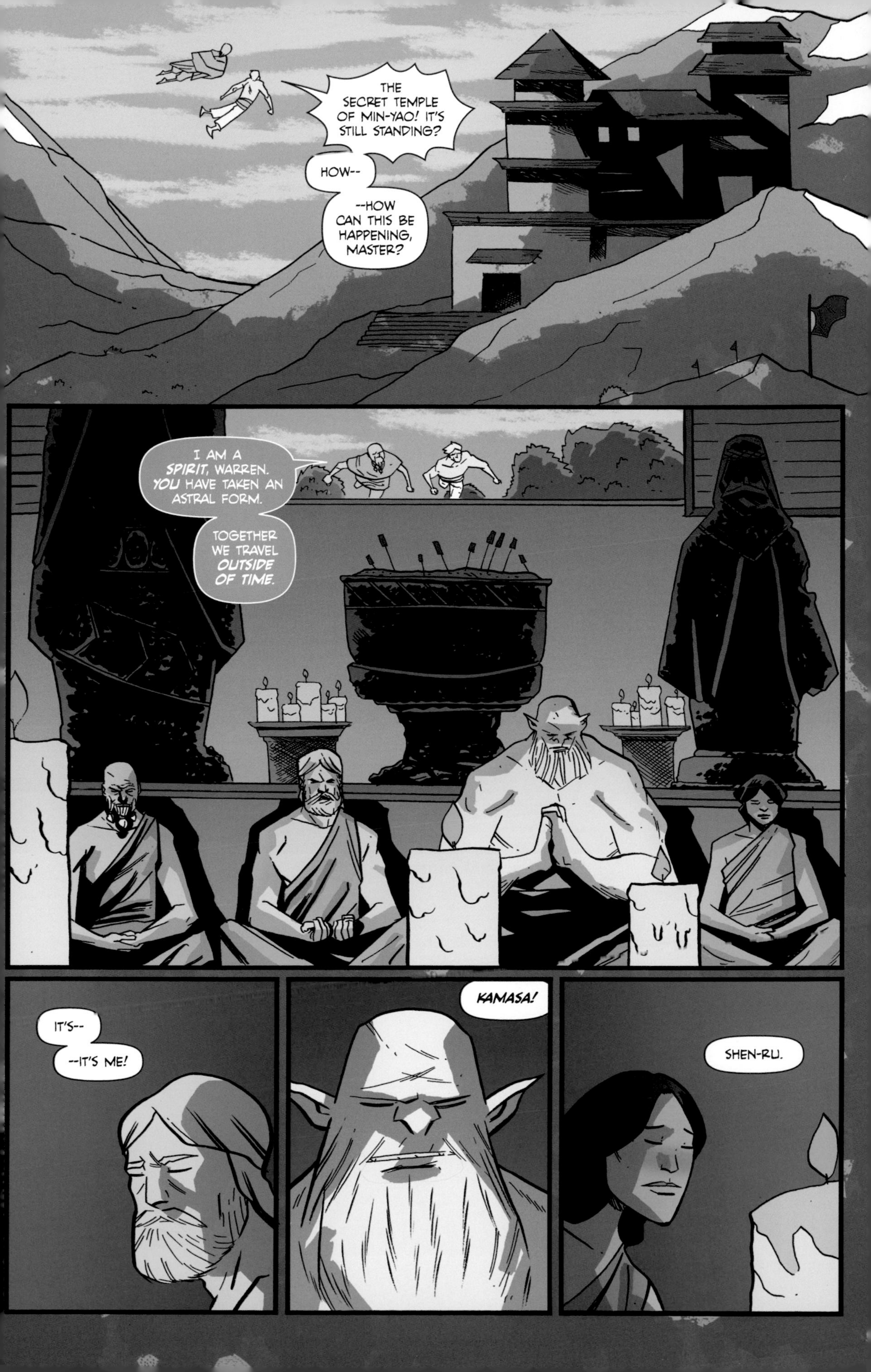
THE SECRET TEMPLE OF MIN-YAO! IT'S STILL STANDING?
HOW--
--HOW CAN THIS BE HAPPENING, MASTER?
I AM A SPIRIT, WARREN. YOU HAVE TAKEN AN ASTRAL FORM.
TOGETHER WE TRAVEL OUTSIDE OF TIME.
IT'S--
--IT'S ME!
KAMASA!
SHEN-RU.

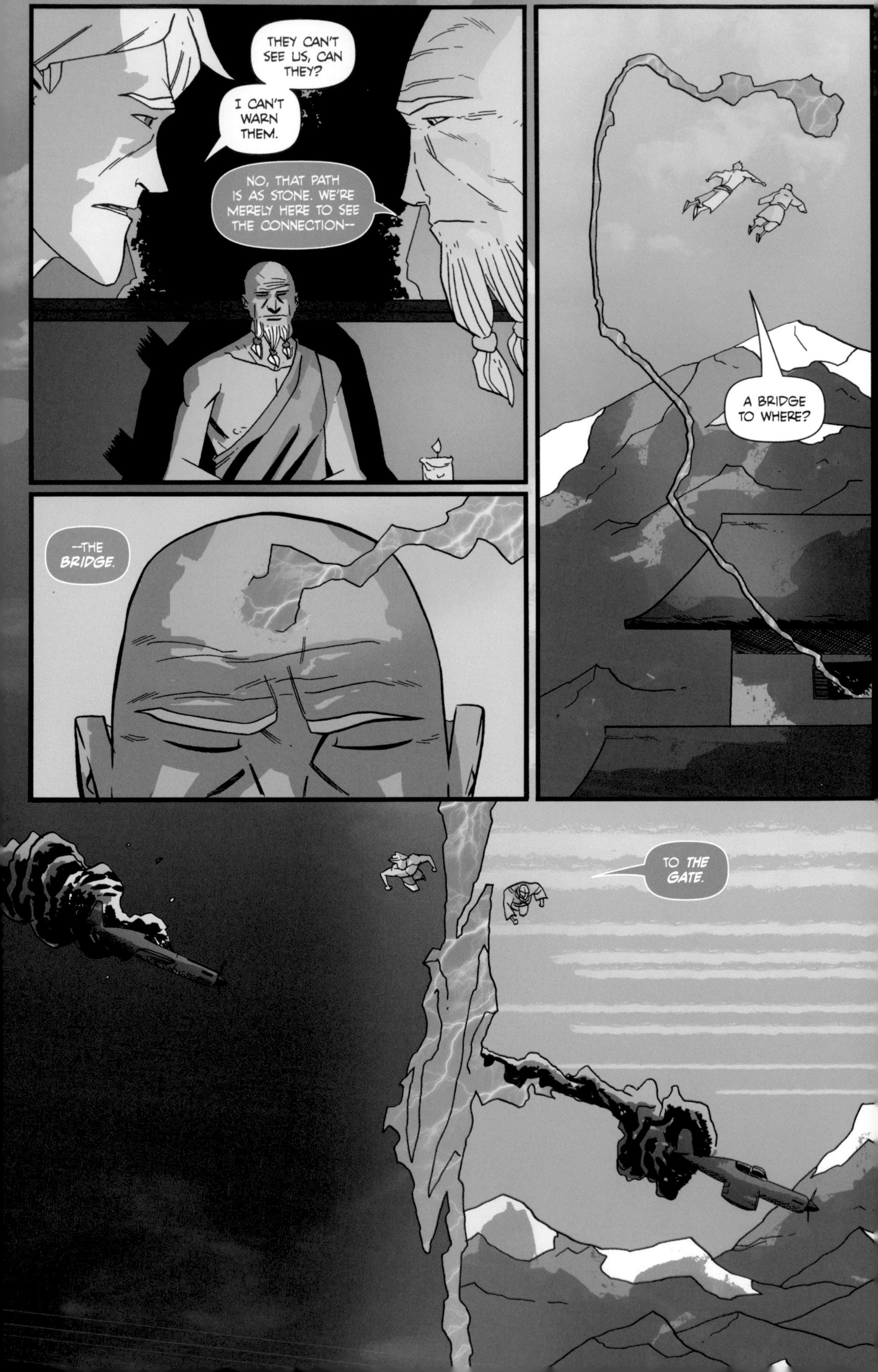
THEY CAN'T SEE US, CAN THEY?
I CAN'T WARN THEM.
NO, THAT PATH IS AS STONE. WE'RE MERELY HERE TO SEE THE CONNECTION--
--THE *BRIDGE.*
A BRIDGE TO WHERE?
TO *THE GATE.*

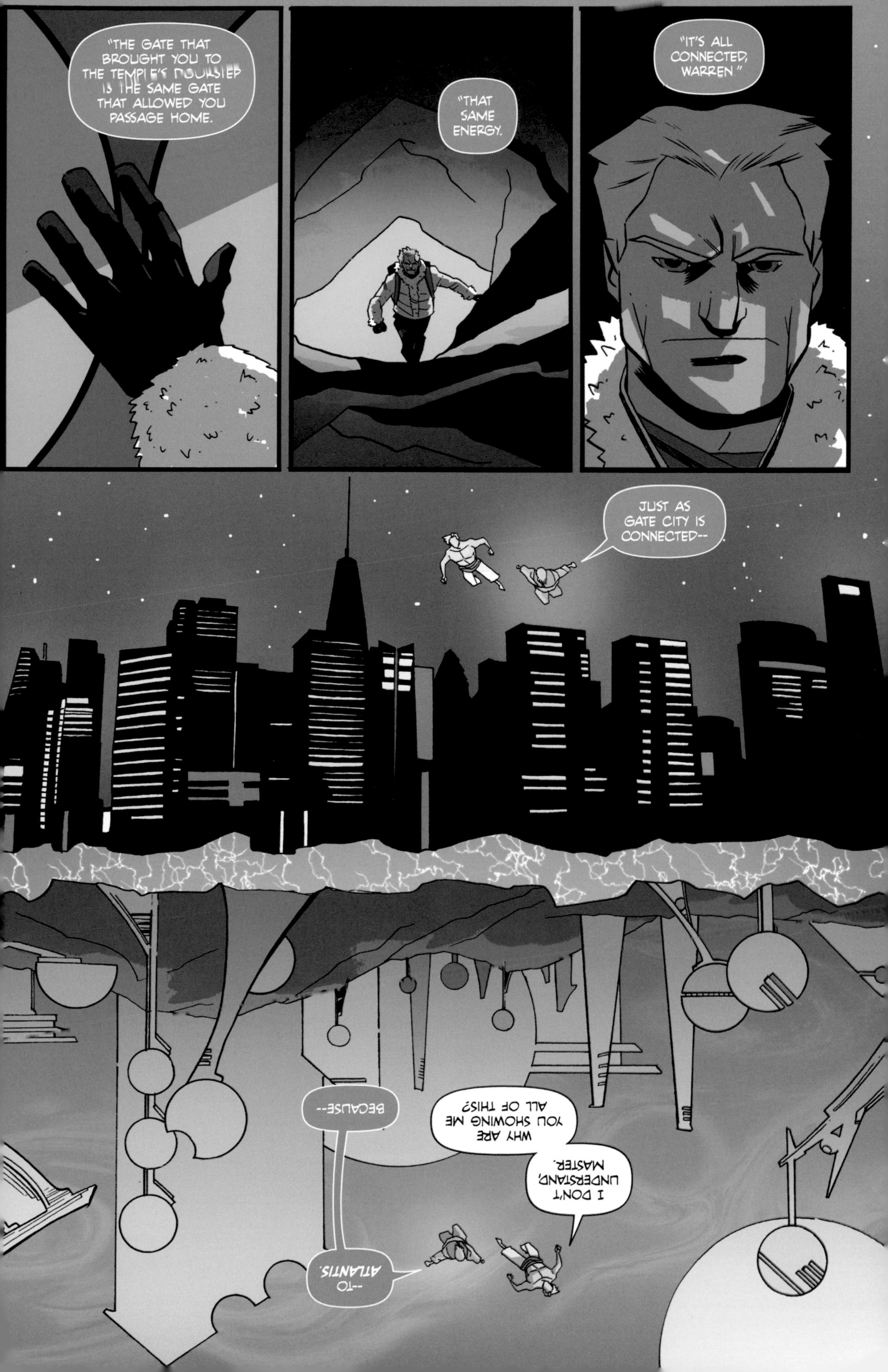
"THE GATE THAT BROUGHT YOU TO THE TEMPLE'S DOORSTEP IS THE SAME GATE THAT ALLOWED YOU PASSAGE HOME.
"THAT SAME ENERGY.
"IT'S ALL CONNECTED, WARREN."
JUST AS GATE CITY IS CONNECTED--
--TO ATLANTIS.
I DON'T UNDERSTAND, MASTER.
WHY ARE YOU SHOWING ME ALL OF THIS?
BECAUSE--

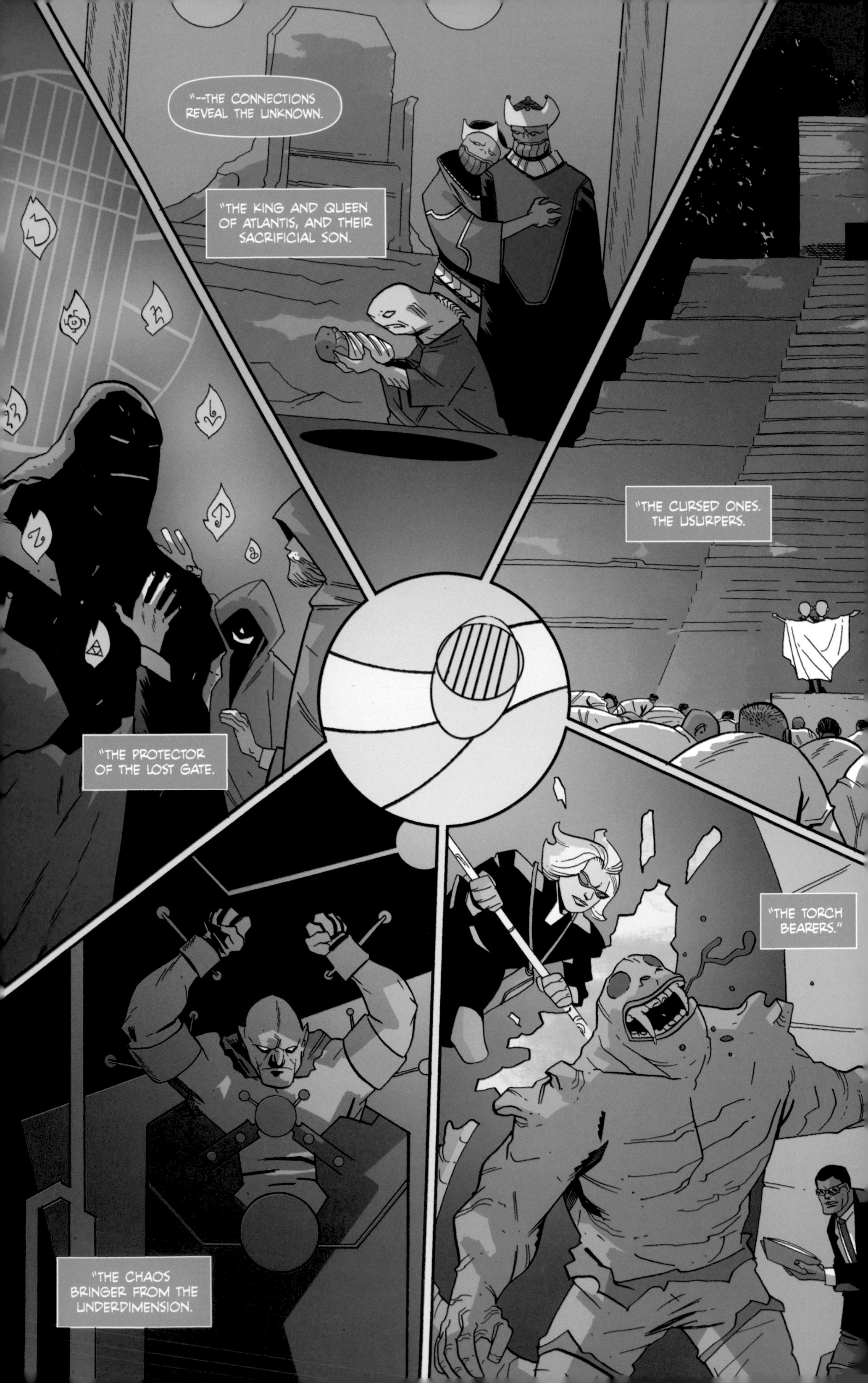
"--THE CONNECTIONS REVEAL THE UNKNOWN.
"THE KING AND QUEEN OF ATLANTIS, AND THEIR SACRIFICIAL SON.
"THE CURSED ONES. THE USURPERS.
"THE PROTECTOR OF THE LOST GATE.
"THE CHAOS BRINGER FROM THE UNDERDIMENSION.
"THE TORCH BEARERS."

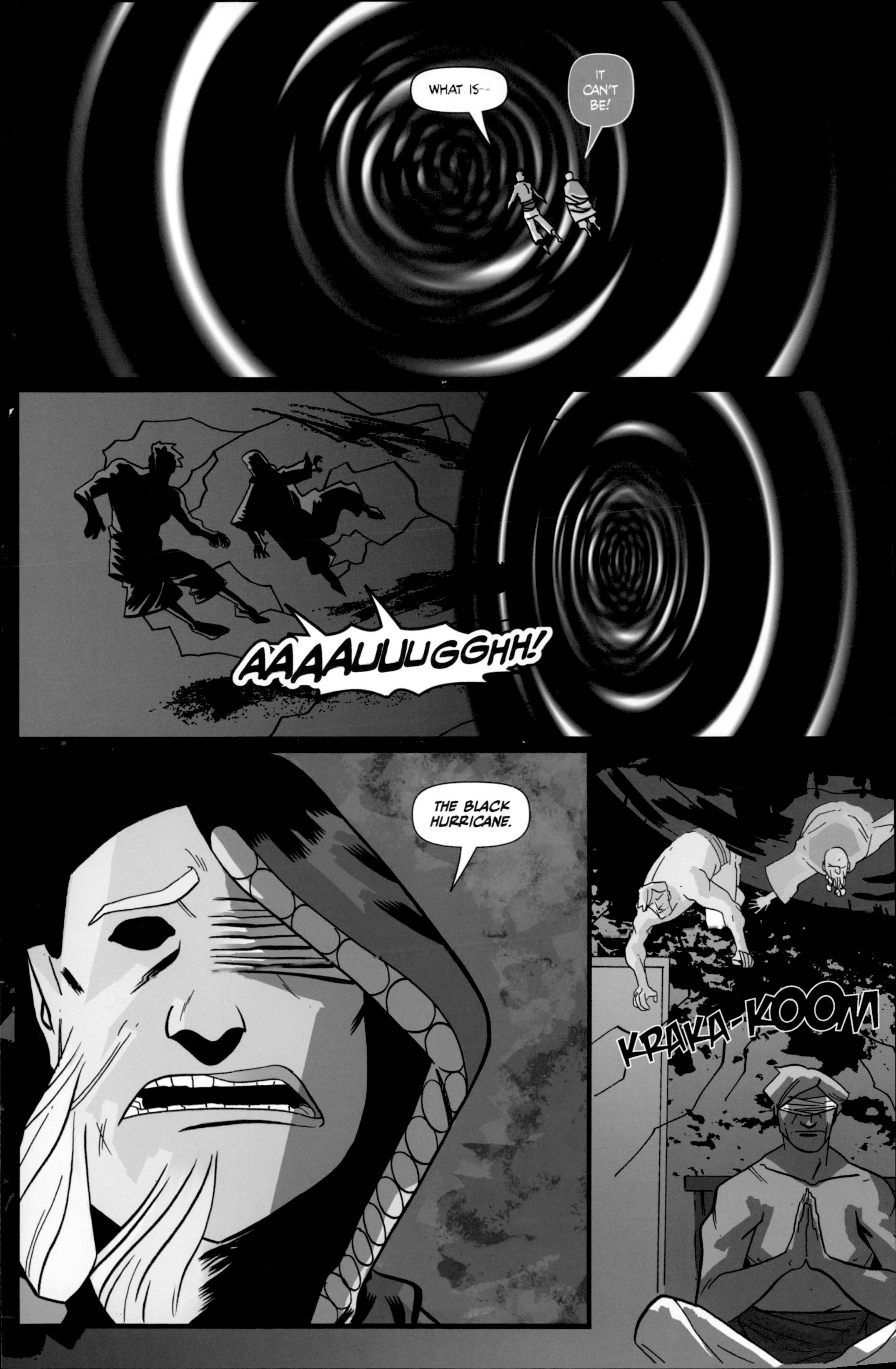
WHAT IS--
IT CAN'T BE!
AAAAUUUGGHH!
THE BLACK HURRICANE.
KRAKA-KOOM

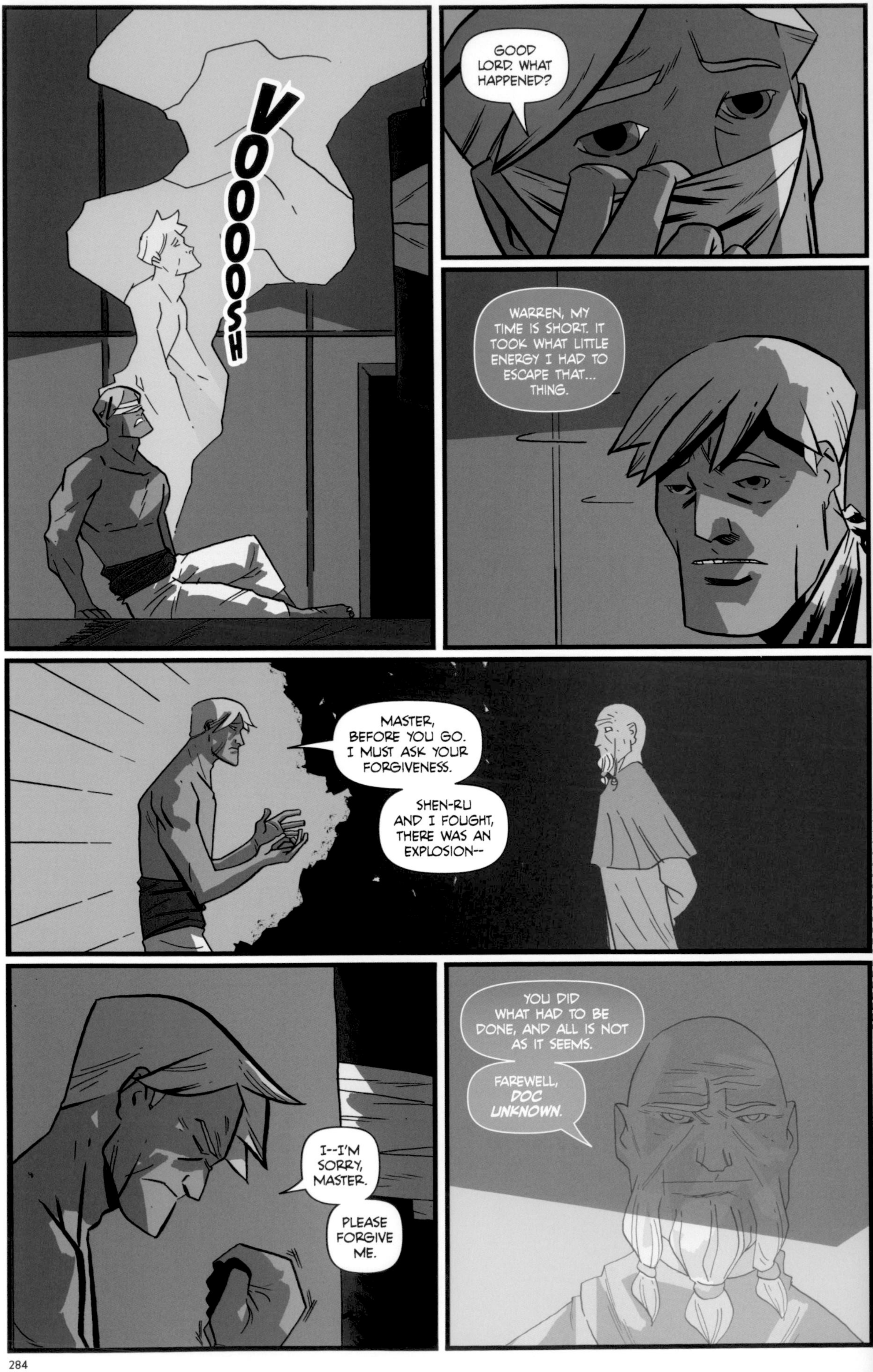
VOOOOOSH
GOOD LORD. WHAT HAPPENED?
WARREN, MY TIME IS SHORT. IT TOOK WHAT LITTLE ENERGY I HAD TO ESCAPE THAT... THING.
MASTER, BEFORE YOU GO. I MUST ASK YOUR FORGIVENESS.
SHEN-RU AND I FOUGHT, THERE WAS AN EXPLOSION--
I--I'M SORRY, MASTER.
PLEASE FORGIVE ME.
YOU DID WHAT HAD TO BE DONE, AND ALL IS NOT AS IT SEEMS.
FAREWELL, *DOC UNKNOWN*.

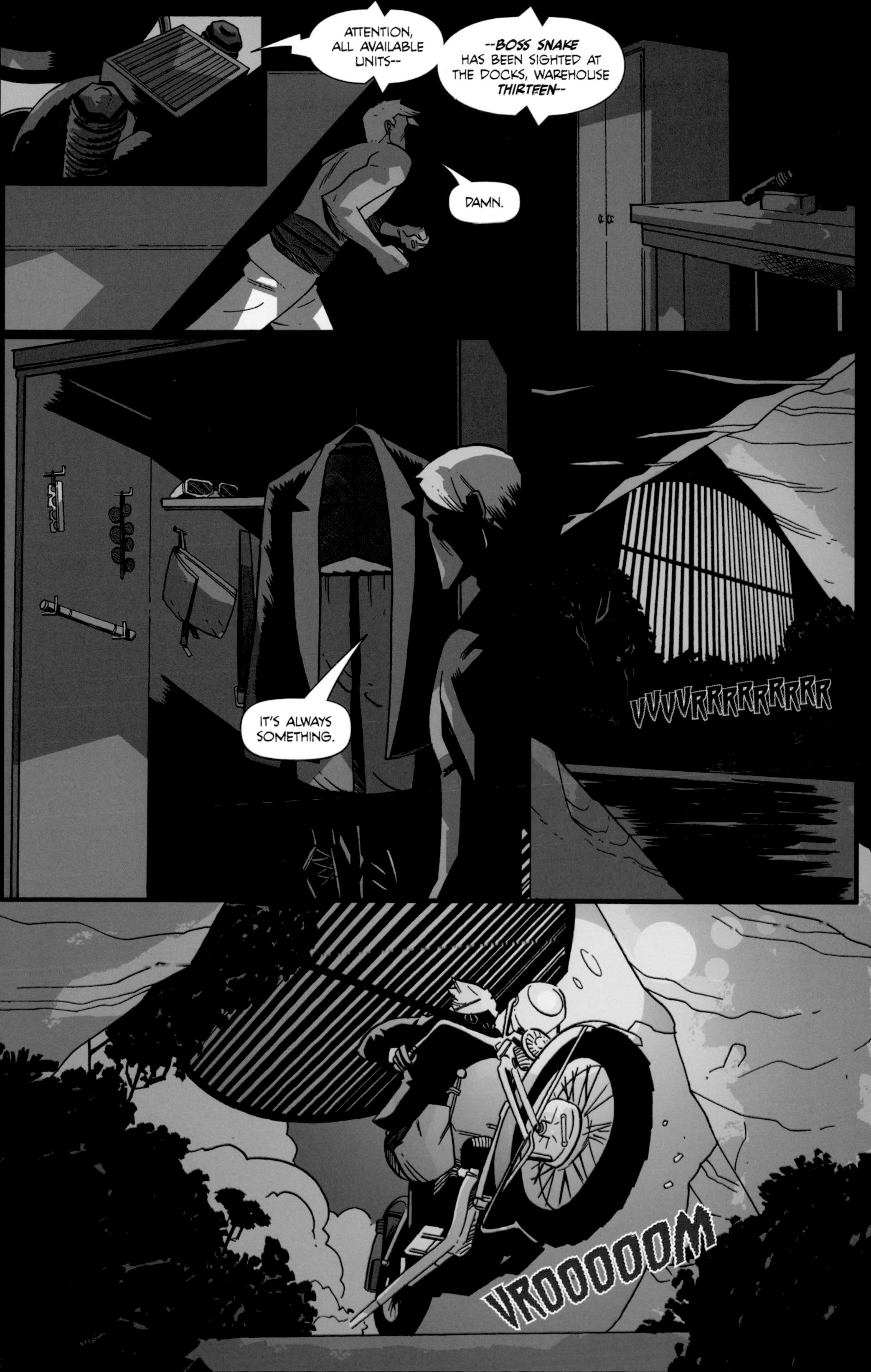
ATTENTION, ALL AVAILABLE UNITS--
--BOSS SNAKE HAS BEEN SIGHTED AT THE DOCKS, WAREHOUSE THIRTEEN--
DAMN.
IT'S ALWAYS SOMETHING.
VVVVRRRRRRRRR
VROOOOOOM

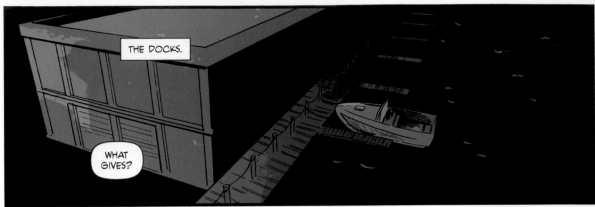

THE DOCKS.

WHAT GIVES?

I KNOW THIS DOESN'T HAVE ANYTHING TO DO WITH SNAKE.

WHAT'S THIS REALLY ABOUT?

AIN'T YA HEARD?

STRAIGHT FROM MAYOR CONLEY.

THIS IS AN AMBUSH.

AMBUSH?

FOR WHO?

FOR *DOC UNKNOWN.*

SHOOT TO KILL.

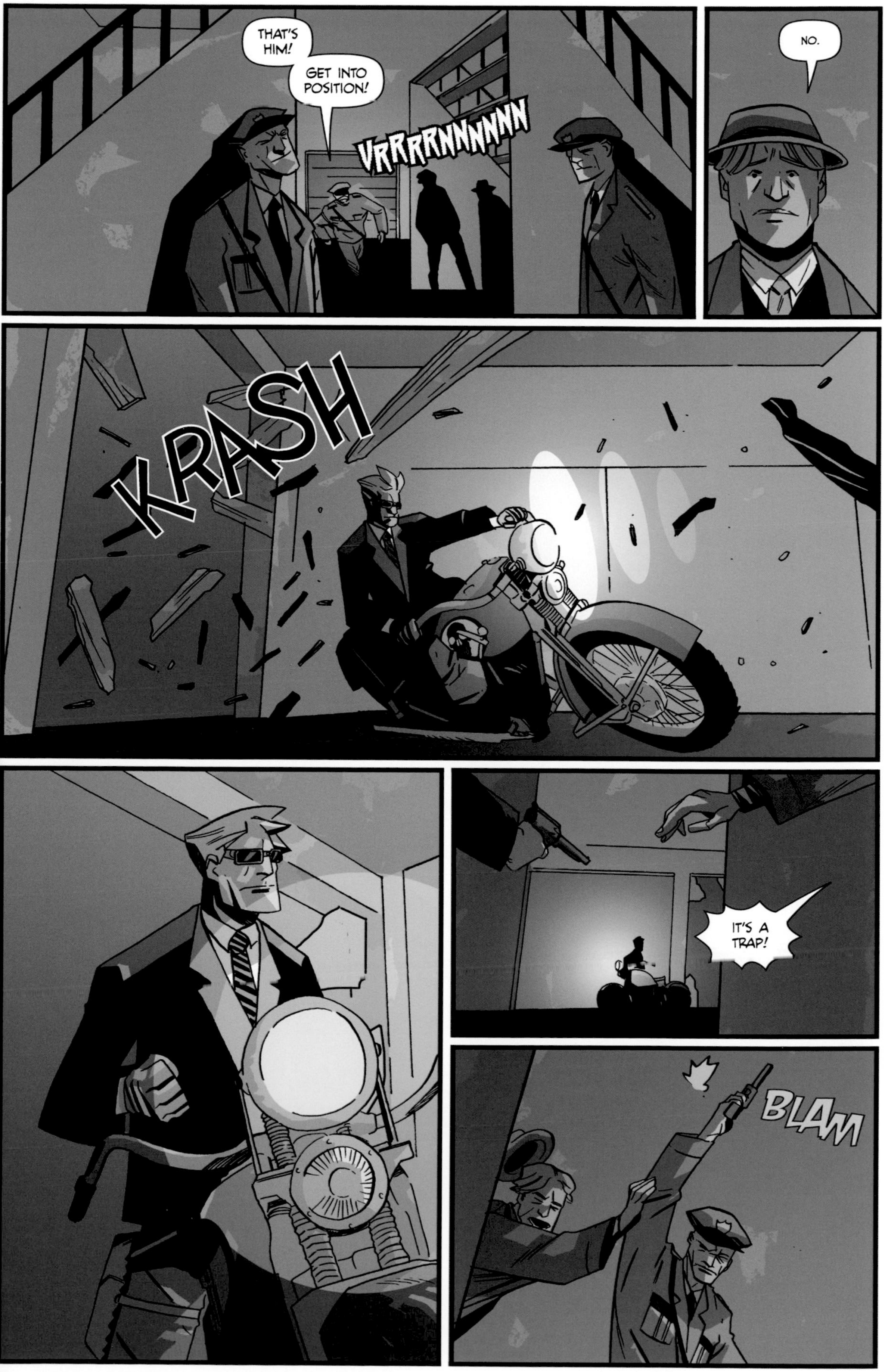
THAT'S HIM!
GET INTO POSITION!
VRRRRNNNNNN
NO.
KRASH
IT'S A TRAP!
BLAM

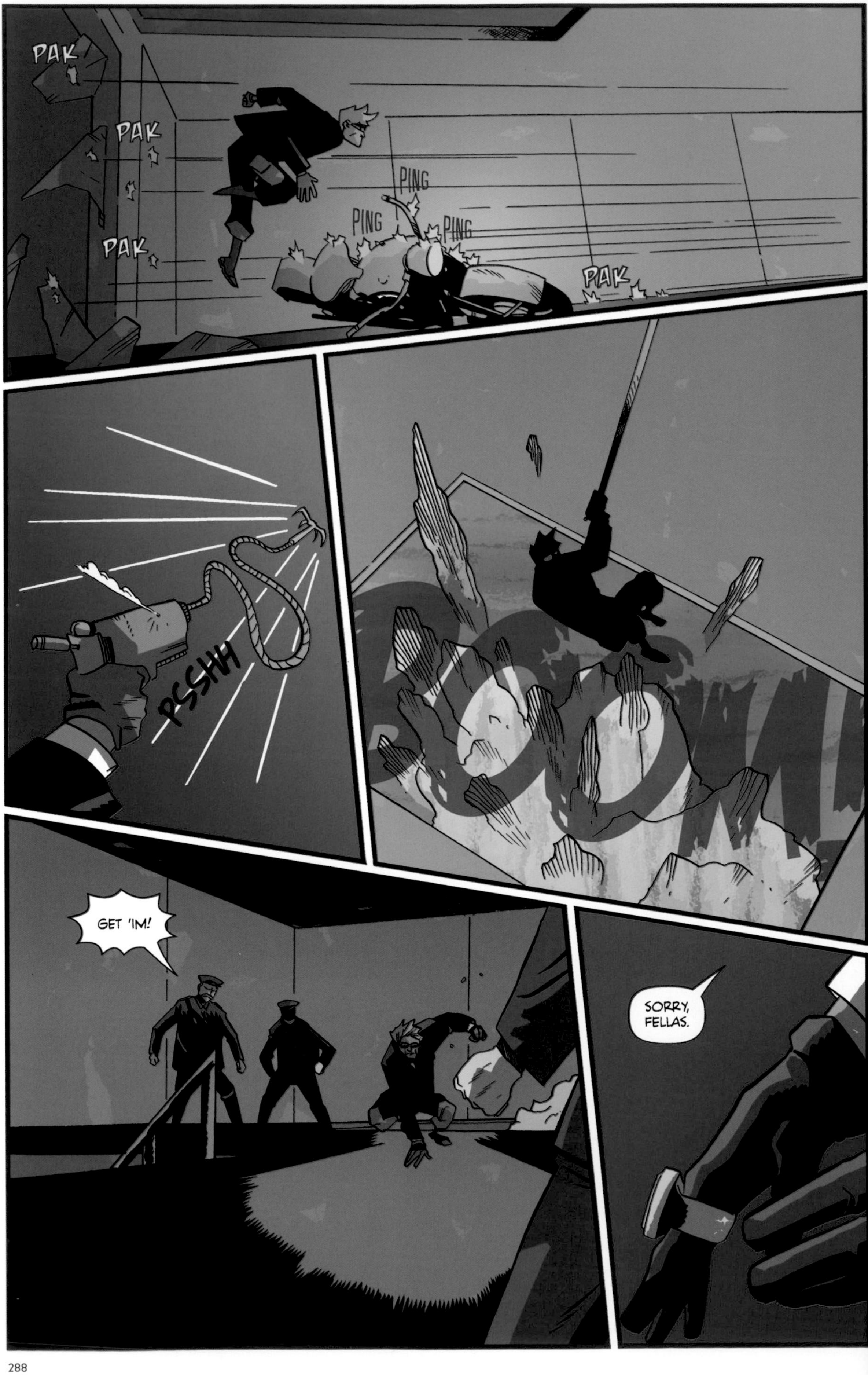
PAK
PAK
PAK
PING
PING
PING
PAK
PSSHH
GET 'IM!
SORRY, FELLAS.

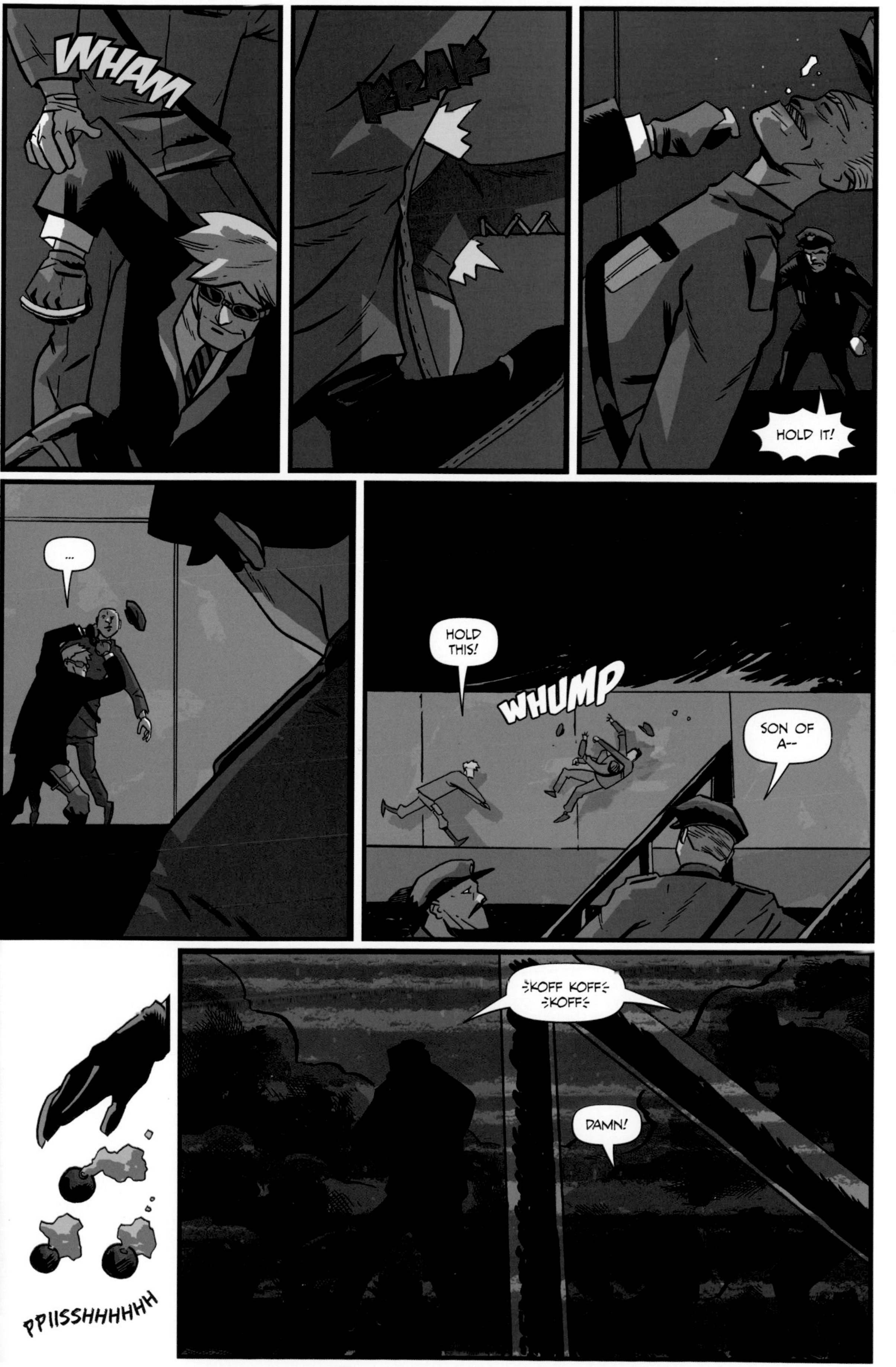
WHAM
KRAK
HOLD IT!
...
HOLD THIS!
WHUMP
SON OF A--
PPIISSHHHHHH
KOFF KOFF KOFF
DAMN!

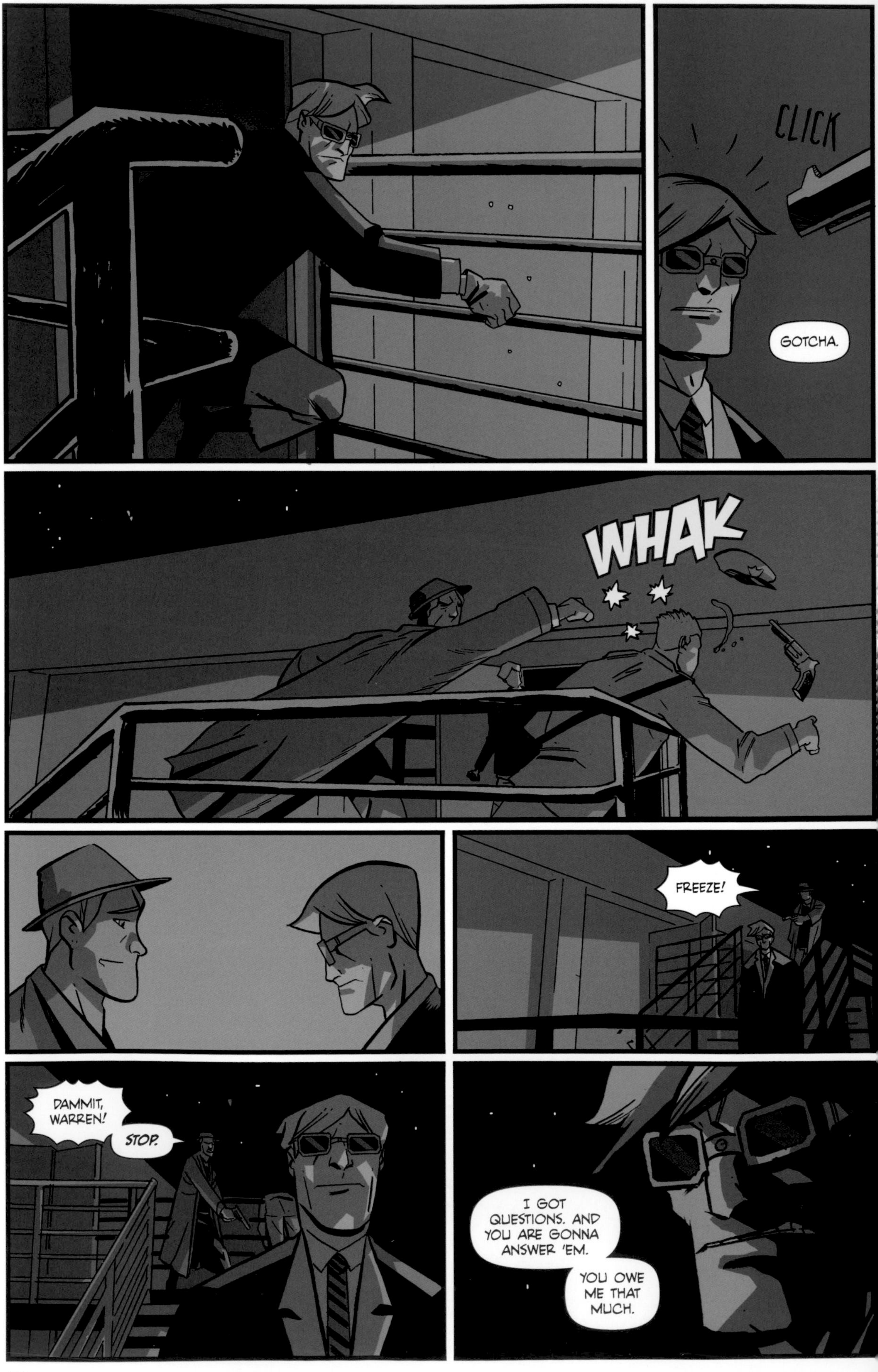
CLICK
GOTCHA.
WHAK
FREEZE!
DAMMIT, WARREN!
STOP.
I GOT QUESTIONS. AND YOU ARE GONNA ANSWER 'EM.
YOU OWE ME THAT MUCH.

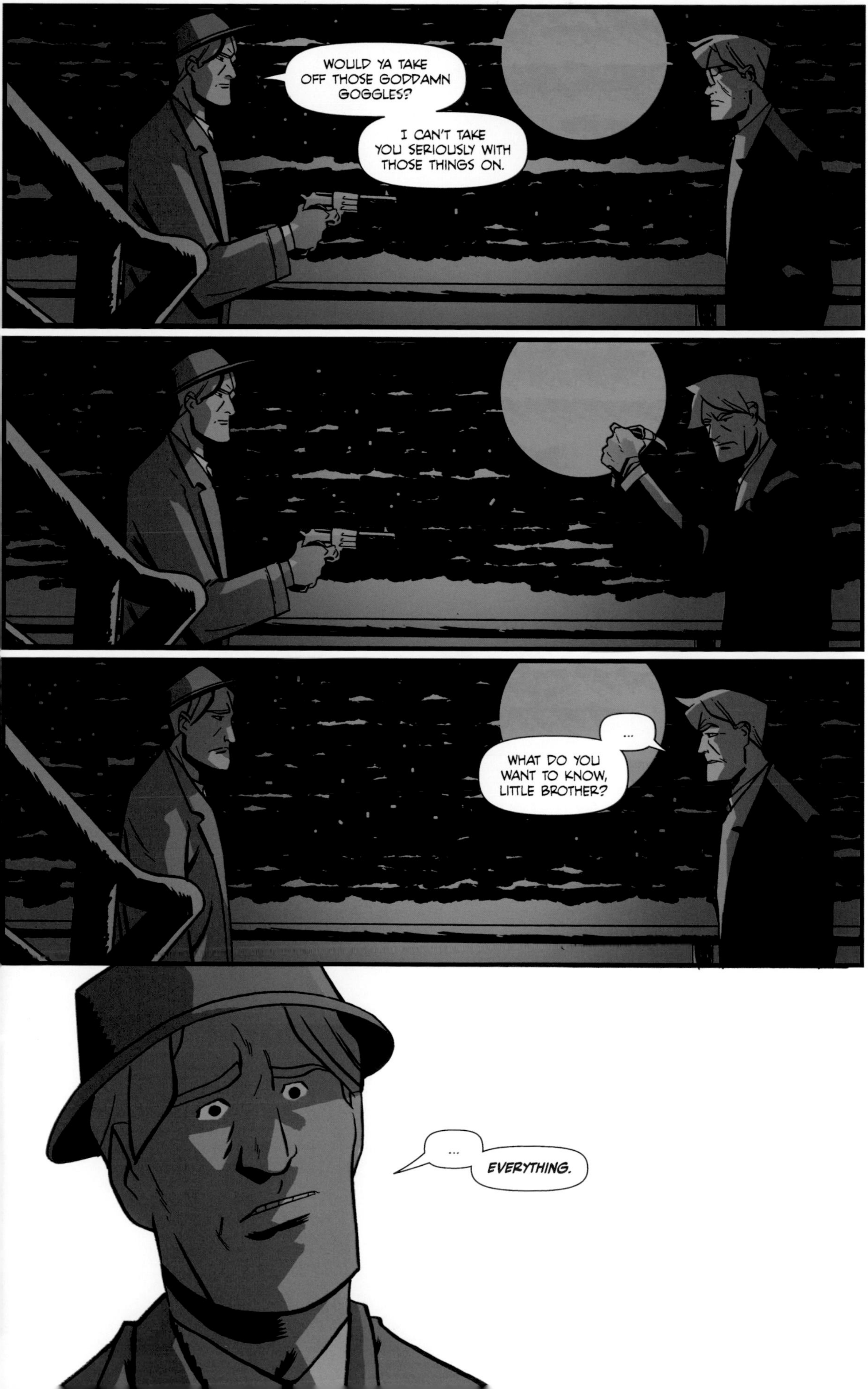
WOULD YA TAKE OFF THOSE GODDAMN GOGGLES?
I CAN'T TAKE YOU SERIOUSLY WITH THOSE THINGS ON.
...
WHAT DO YOU WANT TO KNOW, LITTLE BROTHER?
...
EVERYTHING.

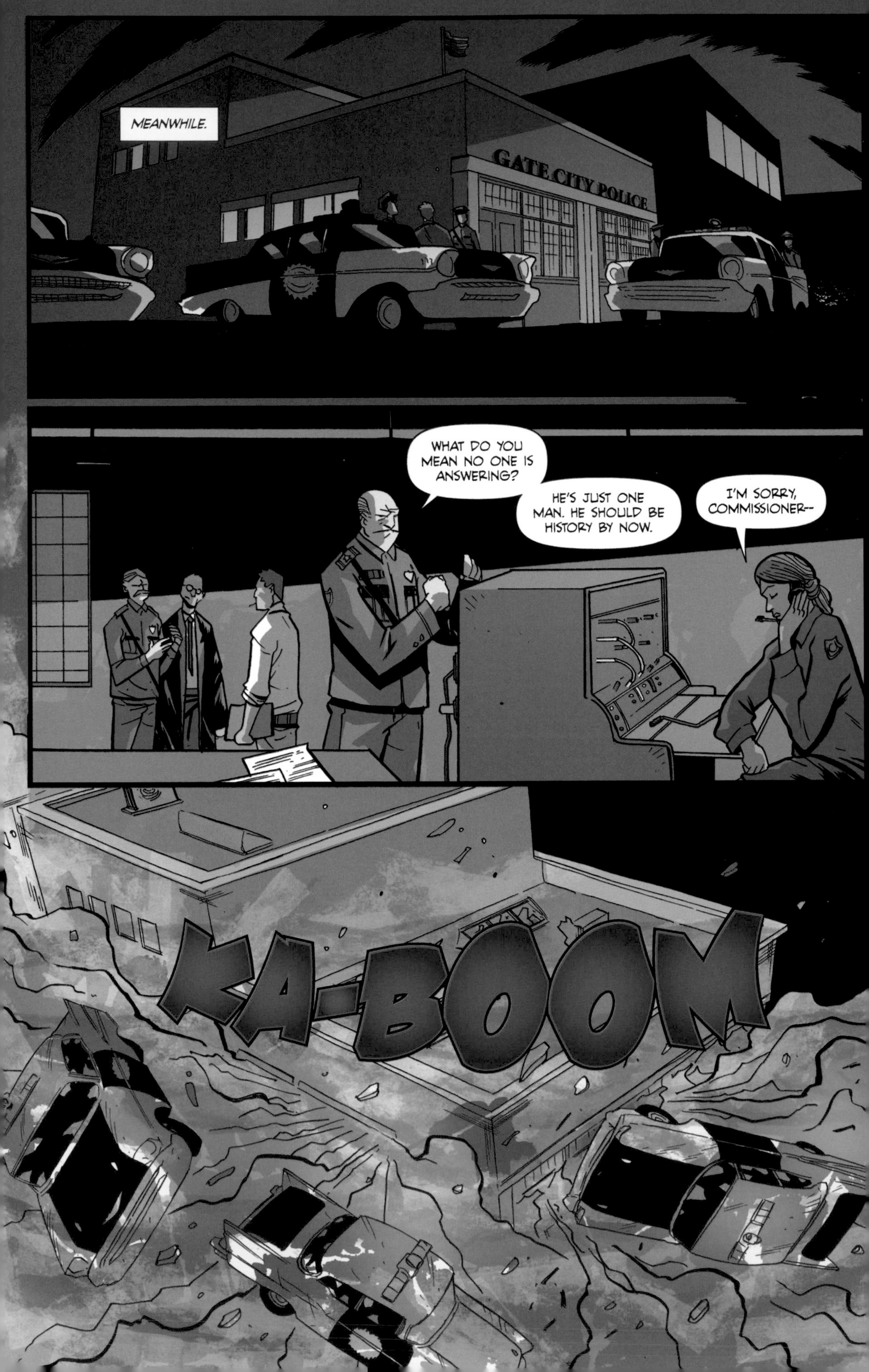

MEANWHILE.
GATE CITY POLICE
WHAT DO YOU MEAN NO ONE IS ANSWERING?
HE'S JUST ONE MAN. HE SHOULD BE HISTORY BY NOW.
I'M SORRY, COMMISSIONER--
KA-BOOM

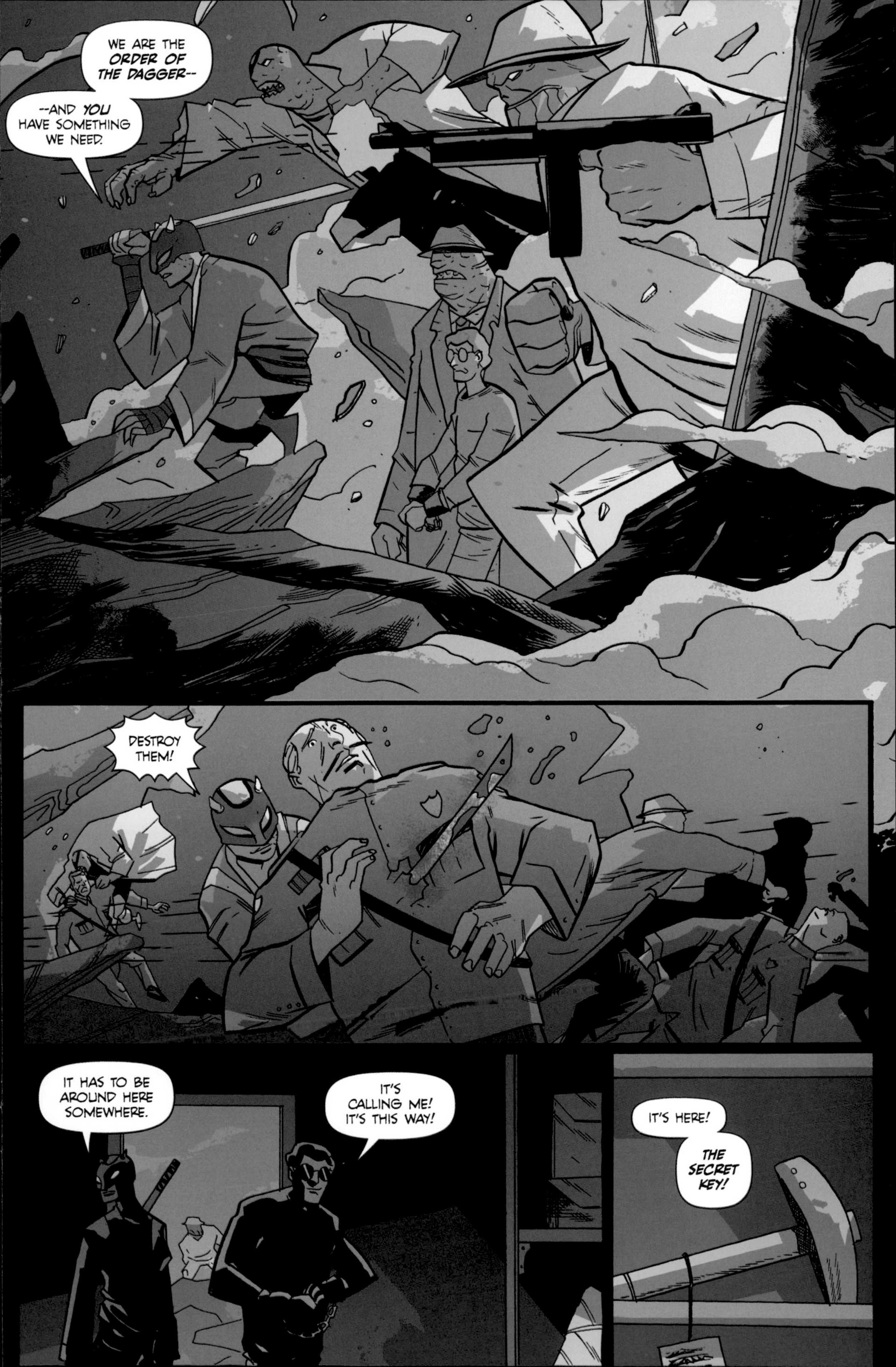
WE ARE THE ORDER OF THE DAGGER--
--AND YOU HAVE SOMETHING WE NEED.
DESTROY THEM!
IT HAS TO BE AROUND HERE SOMEWHERE.
IT'S CALLING ME! IT'S THIS WAY!
IT'S HERE!
THE SECRET KEY!

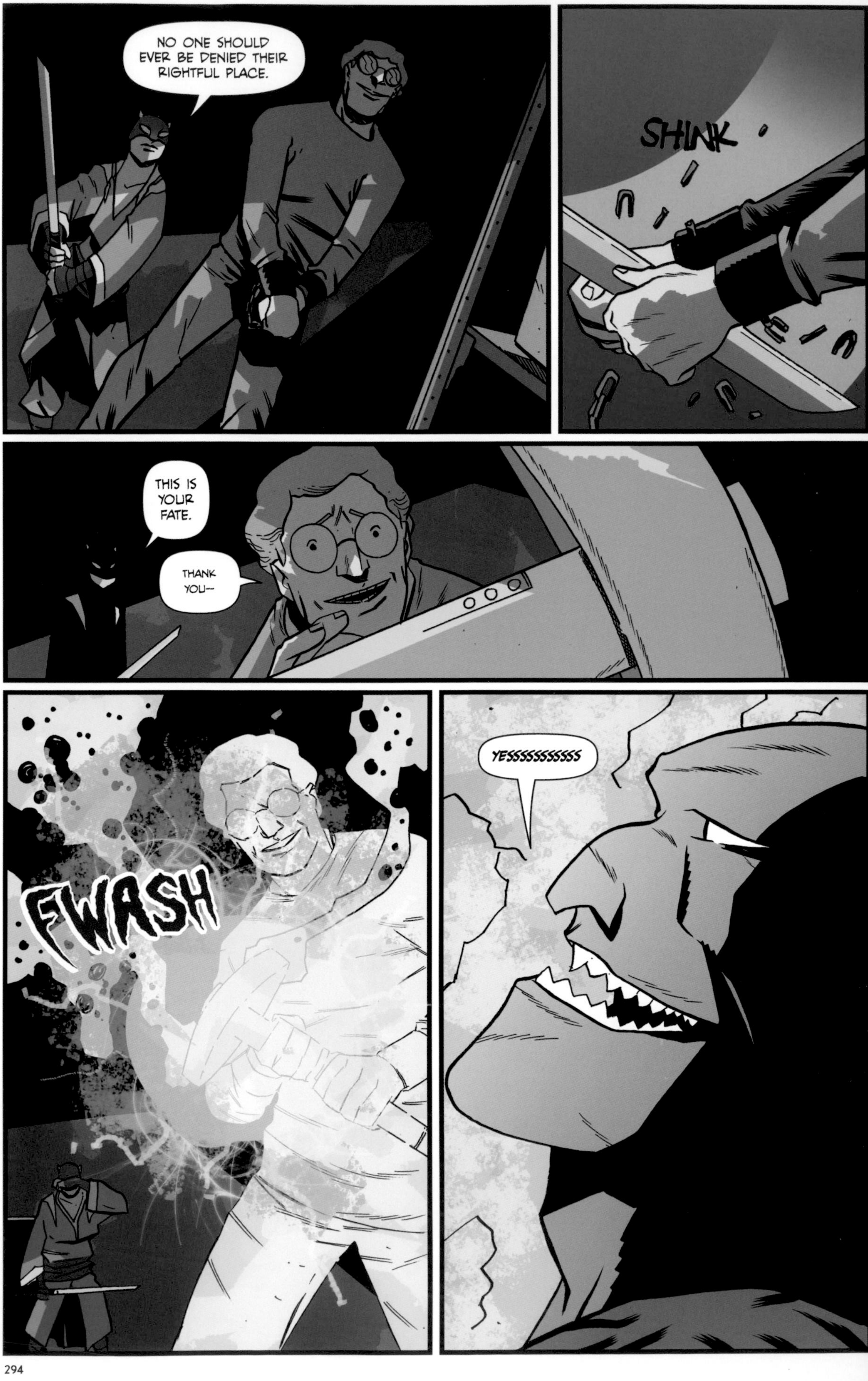
NO ONE SHOULD EVER BE DENIED THEIR RIGHTFUL PLACE.
SHINK
THIS IS YOUR FATE.
THANK YOU--
FWASH
YESSSSSSSSSSS

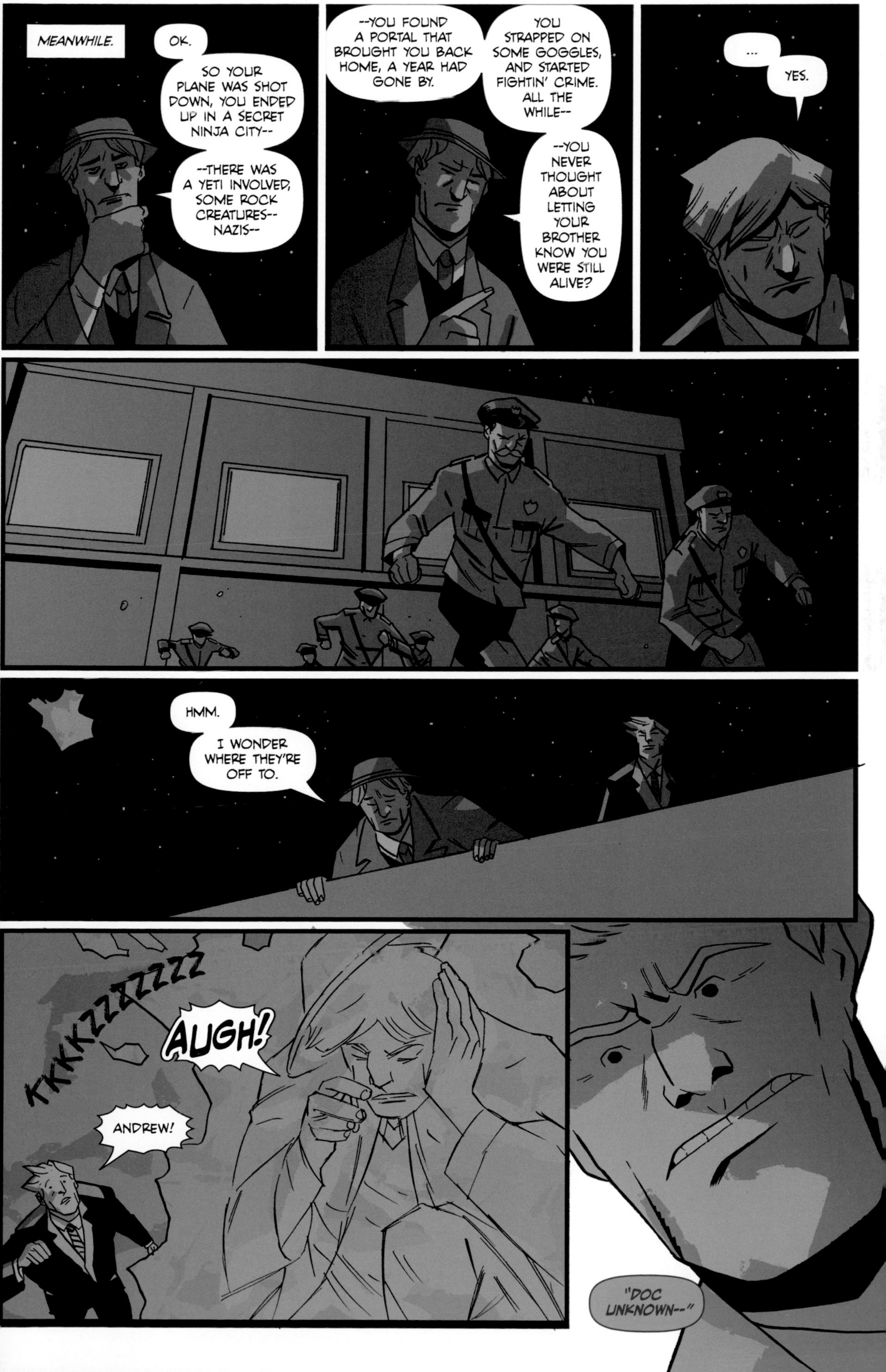
MEANWHILE.
OK.
SO YOUR PLANE WAS SHOT DOWN, YOU ENDED UP IN A SECRET NINJA CITY--
--THERE WAS A YETI INVOLVED, SOME ROCK CREATURES-- NAZIS--
--YOU FOUND A PORTAL THAT BROUGHT YOU BACK HOME, A YEAR HAD GONE BY.
YOU STRAPPED ON SOME GOGGLES, AND STARTED FIGHTIN' CRIME. ALL THE WHILE--
--YOU NEVER THOUGHT ABOUT LETTING YOUR BROTHER KNOW YOU WERE STILL ALIVE?
...
YES.
HMM.
I WONDER WHERE THEY'RE OFF TO.
KKKKZZZZZZZZ
AUGH!
ANDREW!
"DOC UNKNOWN--"

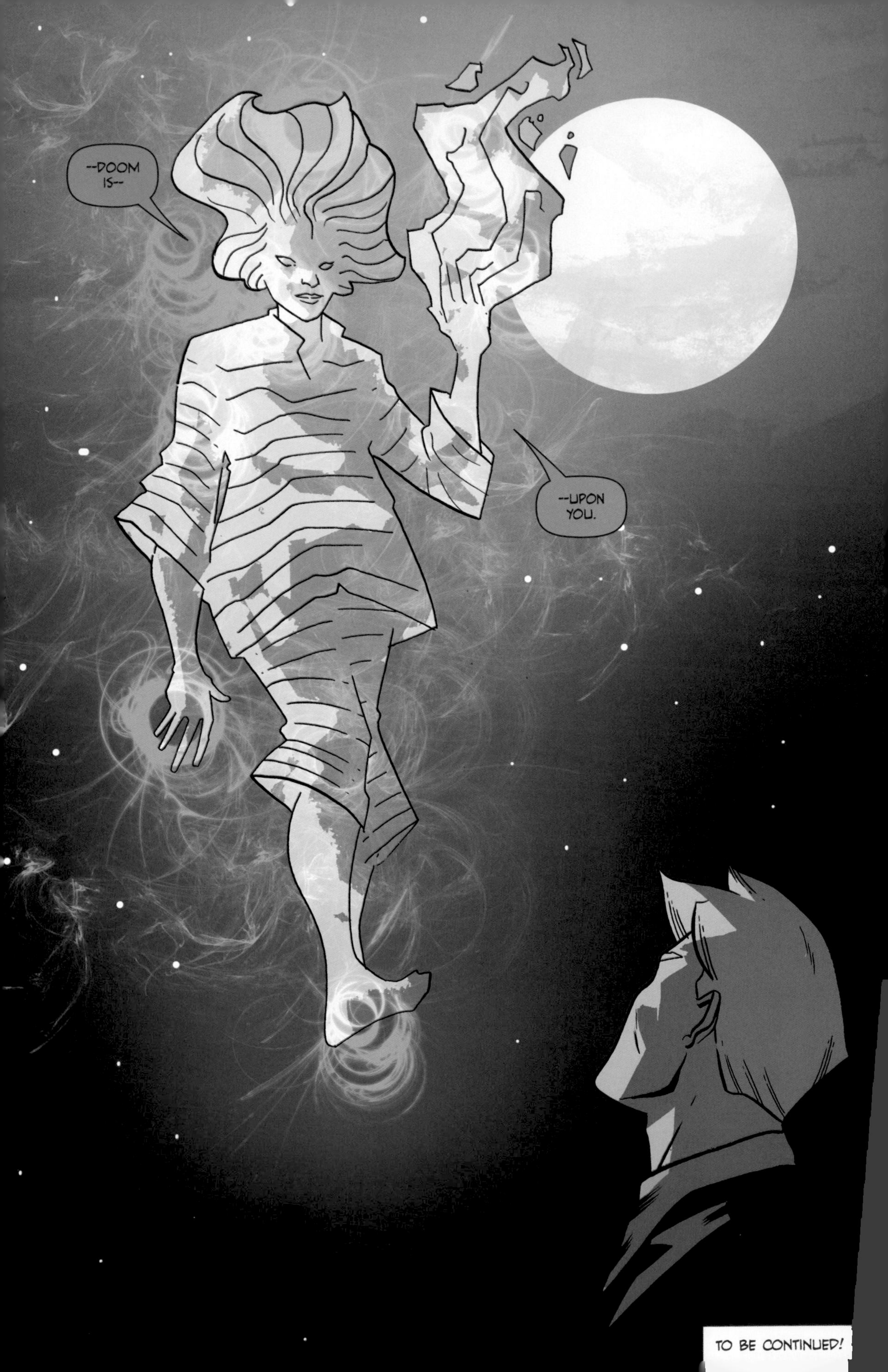
--DOOM IS--
--UPON YOU.
TO BE CONTINUED!

THE DOOM
OF GATE CITY

SCRIPT BY **FABIAN RANGEL JR.**

ART BY **RYAN CODY**

LETTERS BY **EVELYN RANGEL**

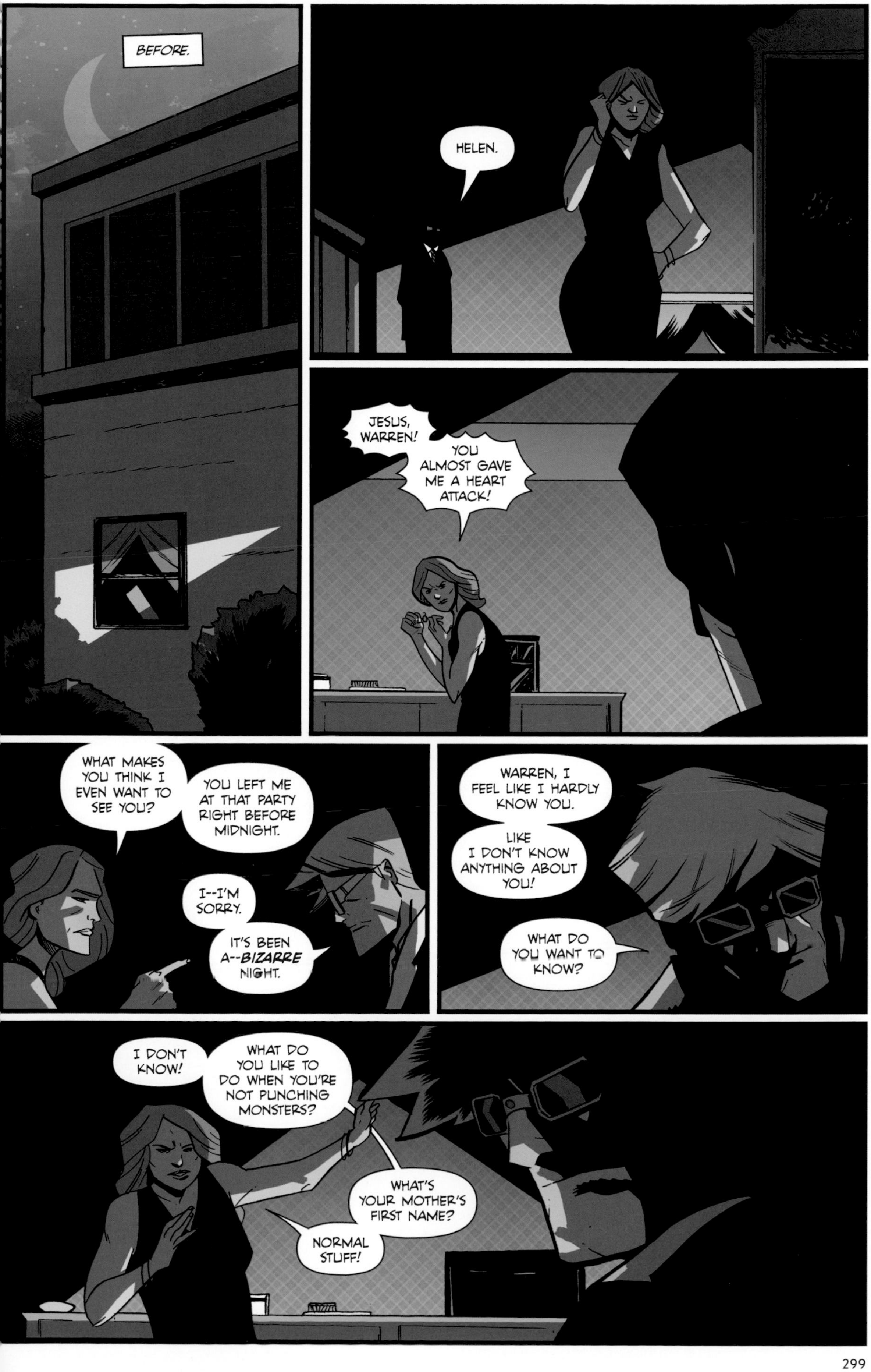
BEFORE.
HELEN.
JESUS, WARREN!
YOU ALMOST GAVE ME A HEART ATTACK!
WHAT MAKES YOU THINK I EVEN WANT TO SEE YOU?
YOU LEFT ME AT THAT PARTY RIGHT BEFORE MIDNIGHT.
I--I'M SORRY.
IT'S BEEN A--BIZARRE NIGHT.
WARREN, I FEEL LIKE I HARDLY KNOW YOU.
LIKE I DON'T KNOW ANYTHING ABOUT YOU!
WHAT DO YOU WANT TO KNOW?
I DON'T KNOW!
WHAT DO YOU LIKE TO DO WHEN YOU'RE NOT PUNCHING MONSTERS?
WHAT'S YOUR MOTHER'S FIRST NAME?
NORMAL STUFF!

I LIKE DRINKING COFFEE AND READING SCI-FI NOVELS.

MY MOTHER'S NAME WAS *SARAH*--

--AND I LOVE YOU.

I HAVE SINCE I MET YOU.

WARREN--

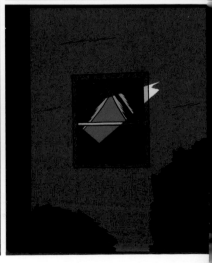

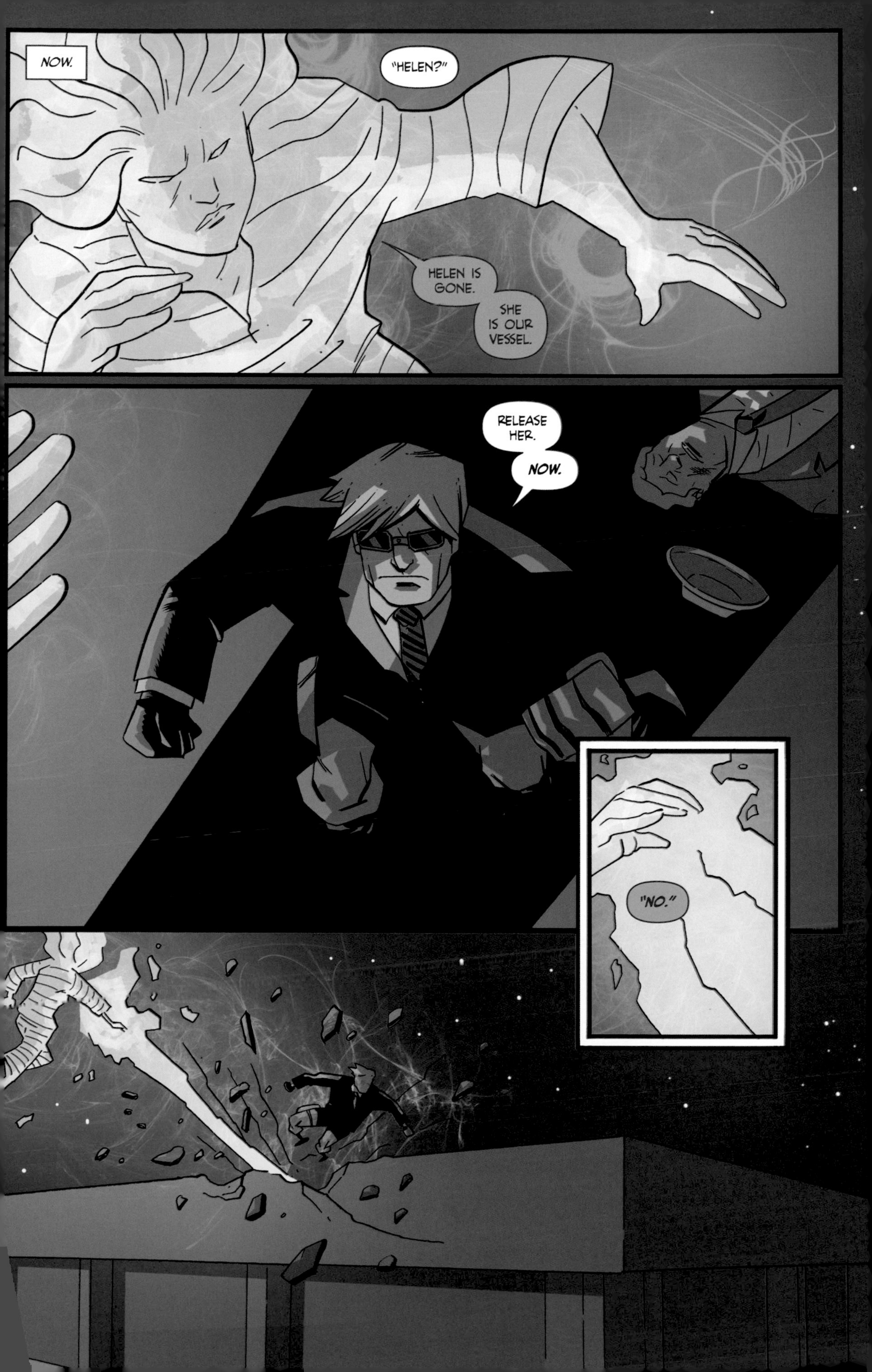
NOW.
"HELEN?"
HELEN IS GONE.
SHE IS OUR VESSEL.
RELEASE HER.
NOW.
"NO."

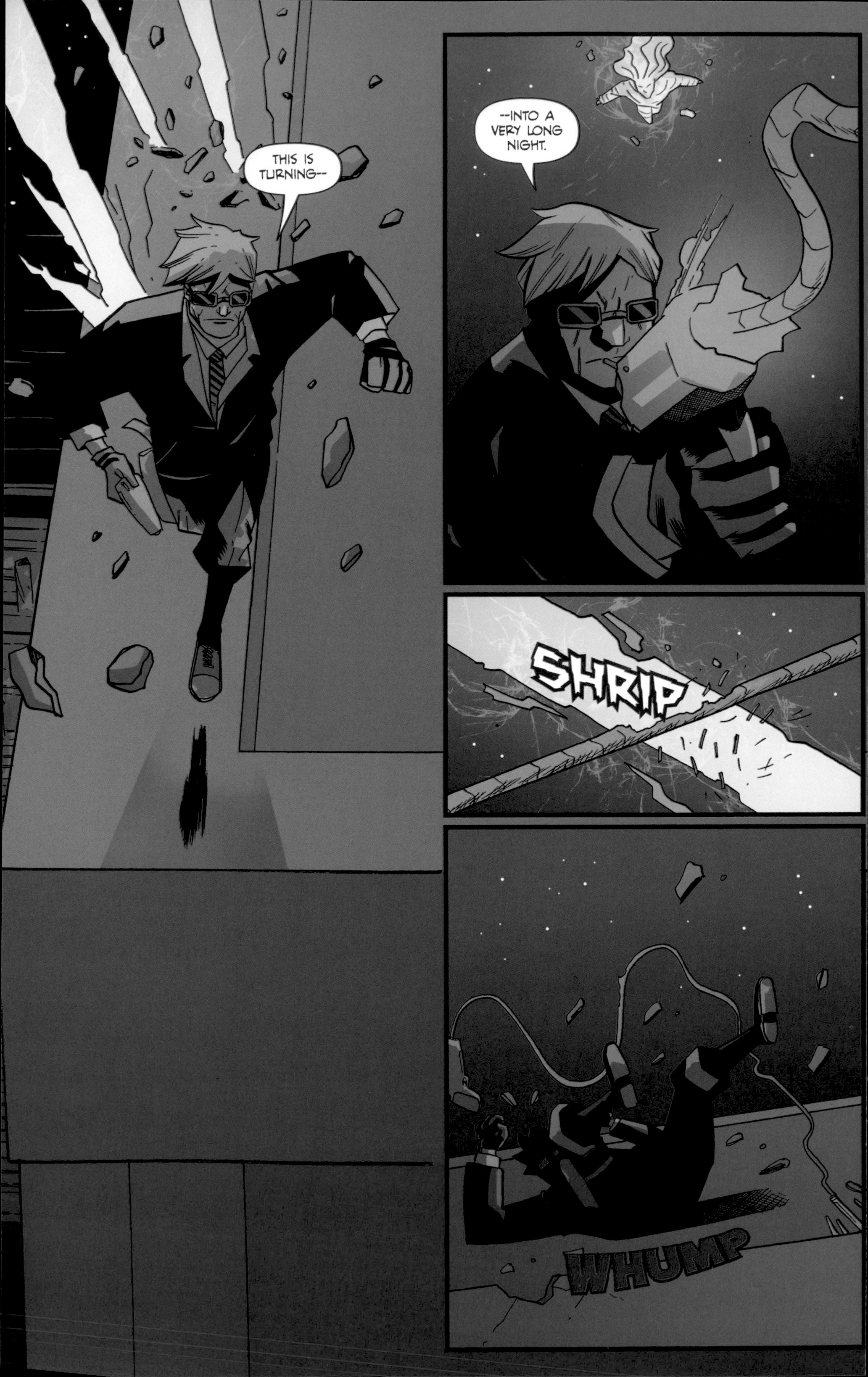
THIS IS TURNING--
--INTO A VERY LONG NIGHT.
SHRIP
WHUMP

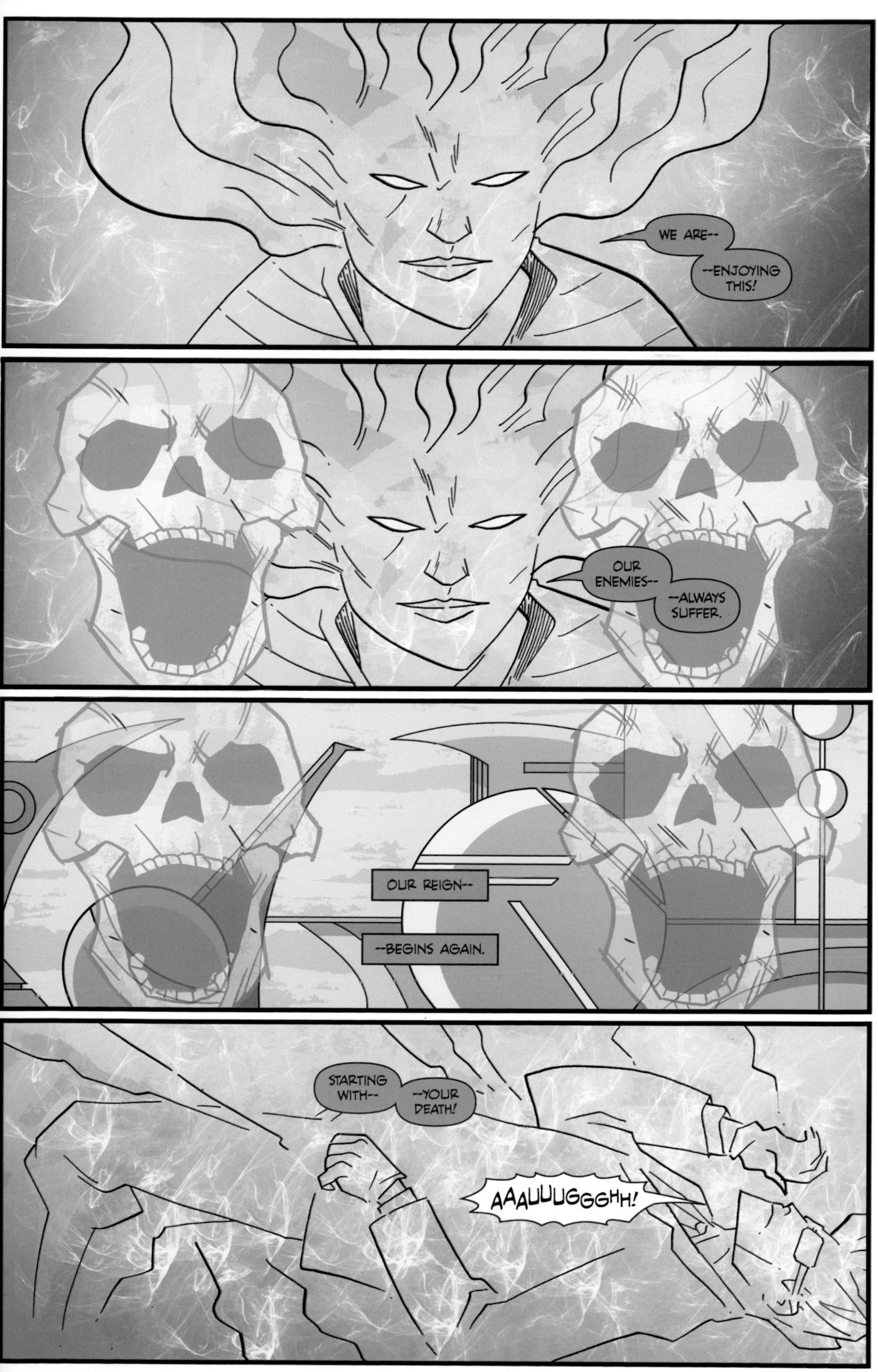
WE ARE--
--ENJOYING THIS!
OUR ENEMIES--
--ALWAYS SUFFER.
OUR REIGN--
--BEGINS AGAIN.
STARTING WITH--
--YOUR DEATH!
AAAUUUGGGHH!

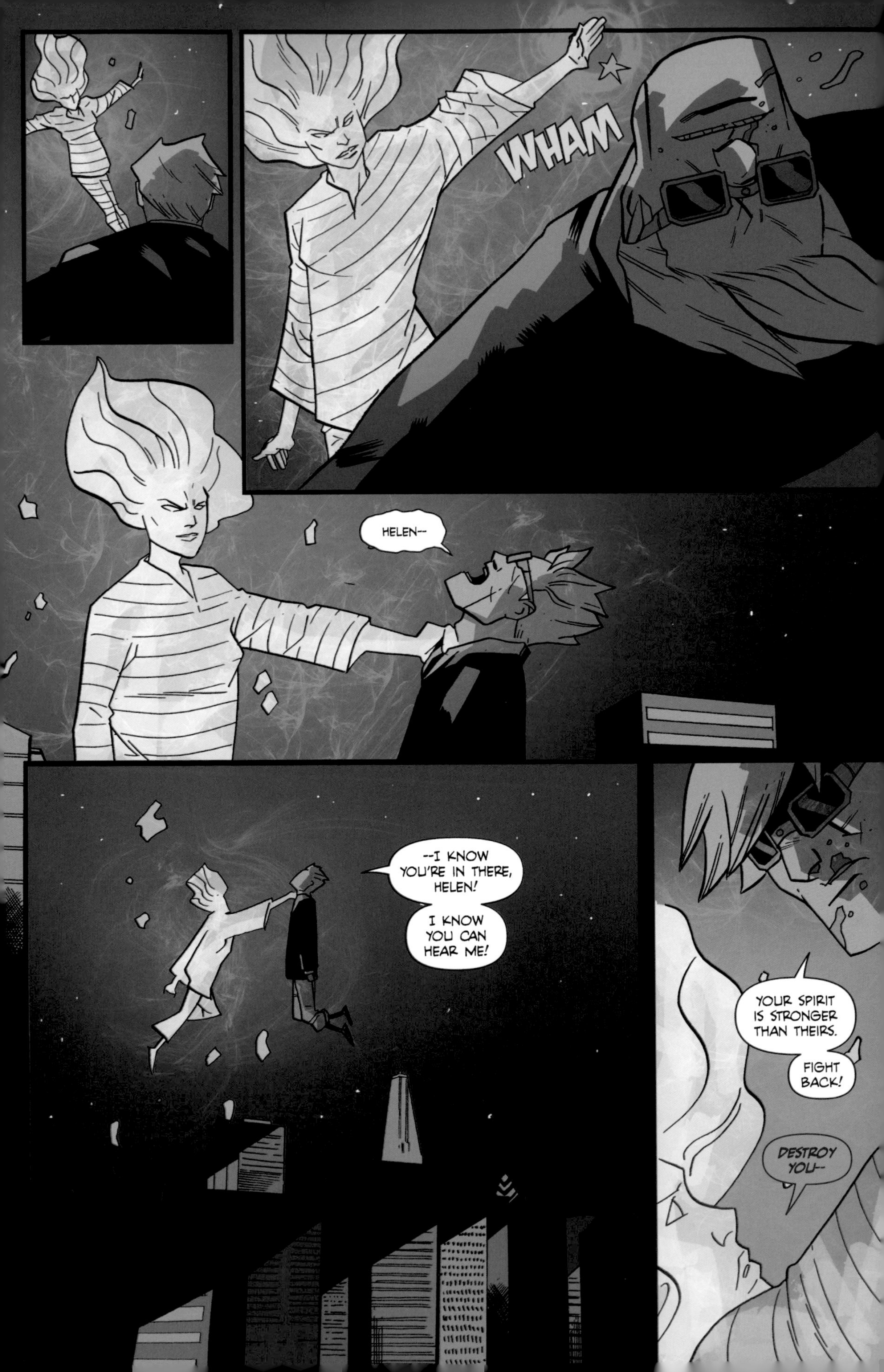
WHAM
HELEN--
--I KNOW YOU'RE IN THERE, HELEN!
I KNOW YOU CAN HEAR ME!
YOUR SPIRIT IS STRONGER THAN THEIRS.
FIGHT BACK!
DESTROY YOU--

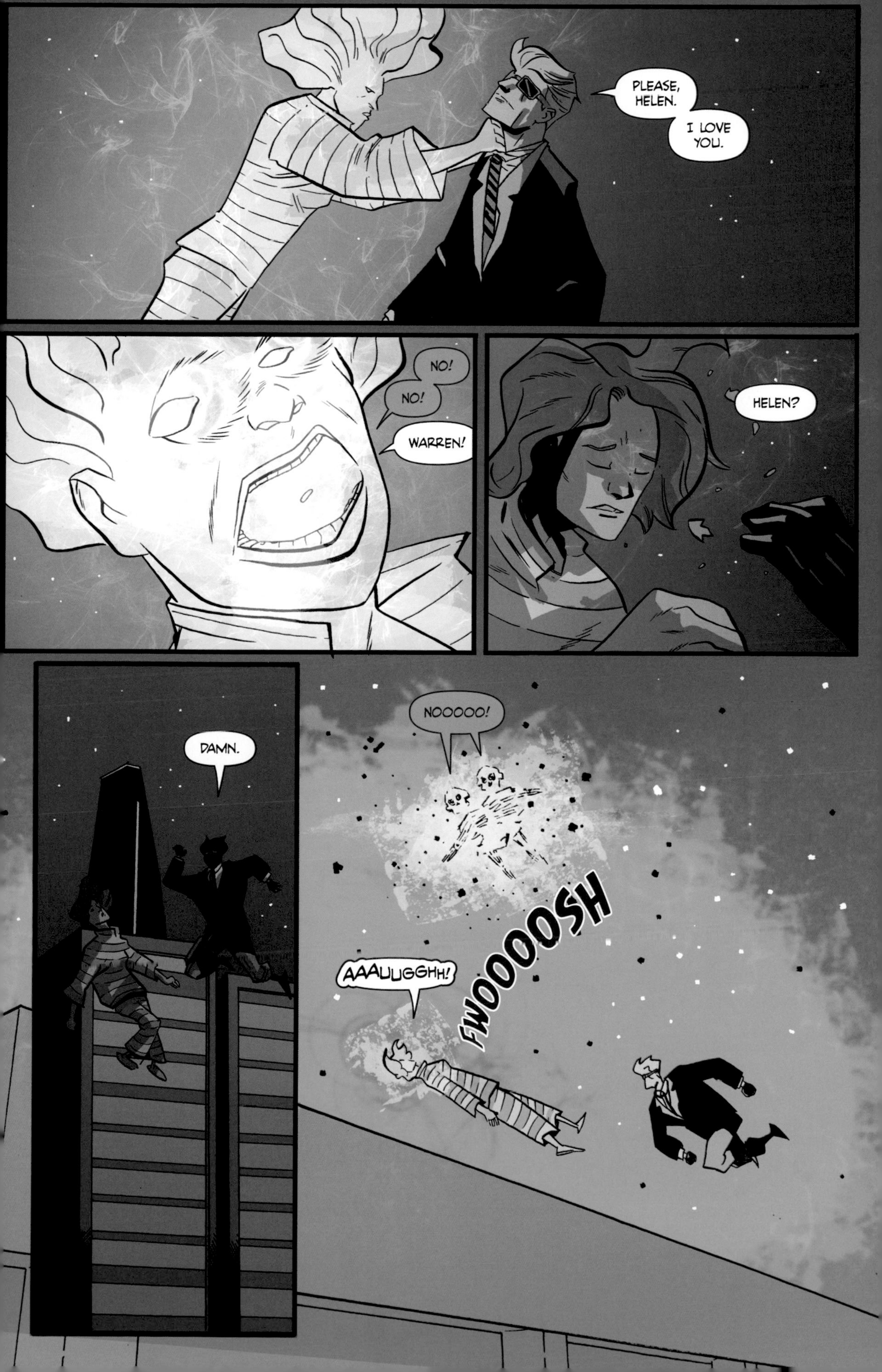
PLEASE, HELEN.
I LOVE YOU.
NO!
NO!
WARREN!
HELEN?
DAMN.
NOOOOO!
AAAUUGGHH!
FWOOOOOSH

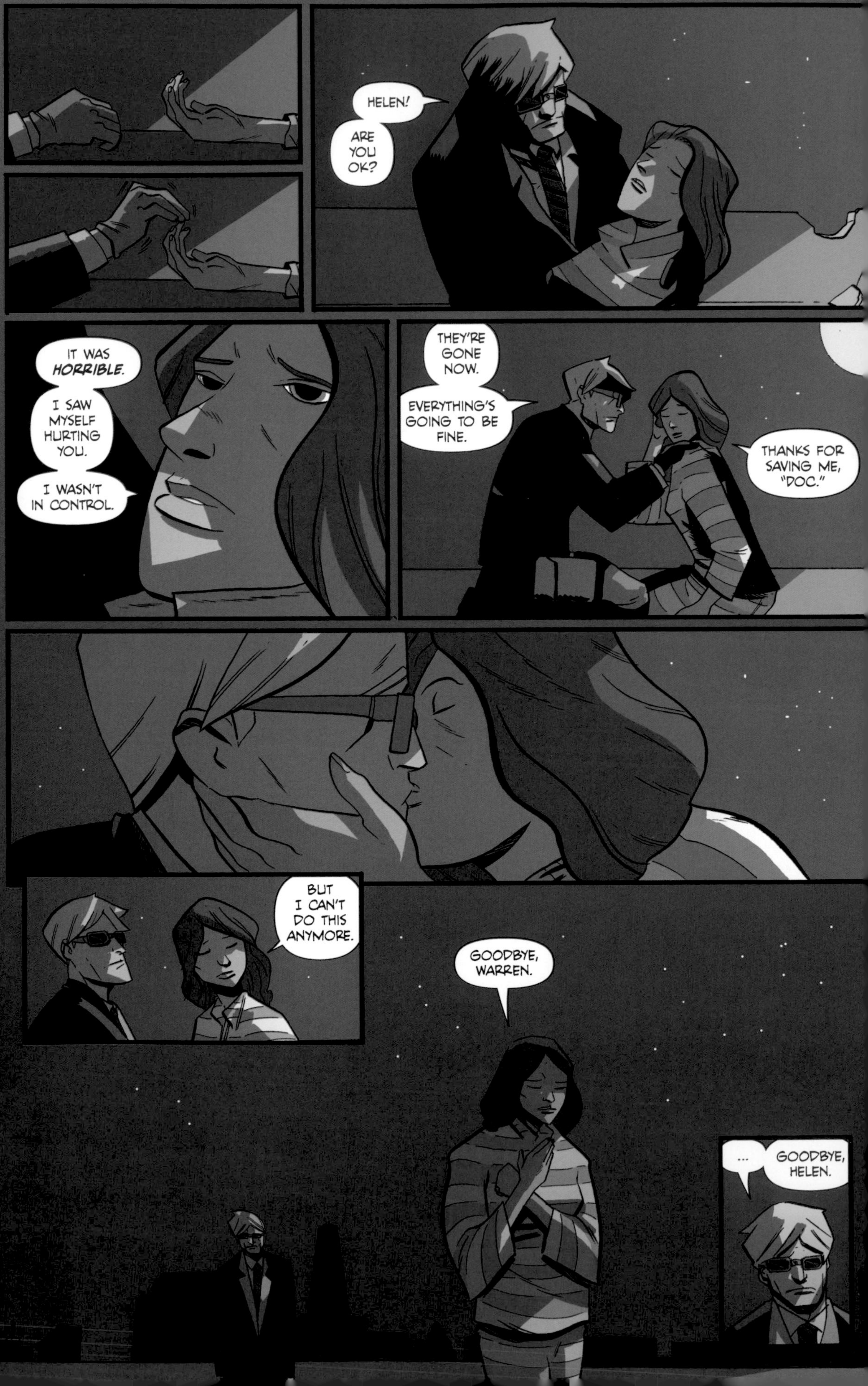
HELEN!
ARE YOU OK?
IT WAS *HORRIBLE.*
I SAW MYSELF HURTING YOU.
I WASN'T IN CONTROL.
THEY'RE GONE NOW.
EVERYTHING'S GOING TO BE FINE.
THANKS FOR SAVING ME, "DOC."
BUT I CAN'T DO THIS ANYMORE.
GOODBYE, WARREN.
...
GOODBYE, HELEN.

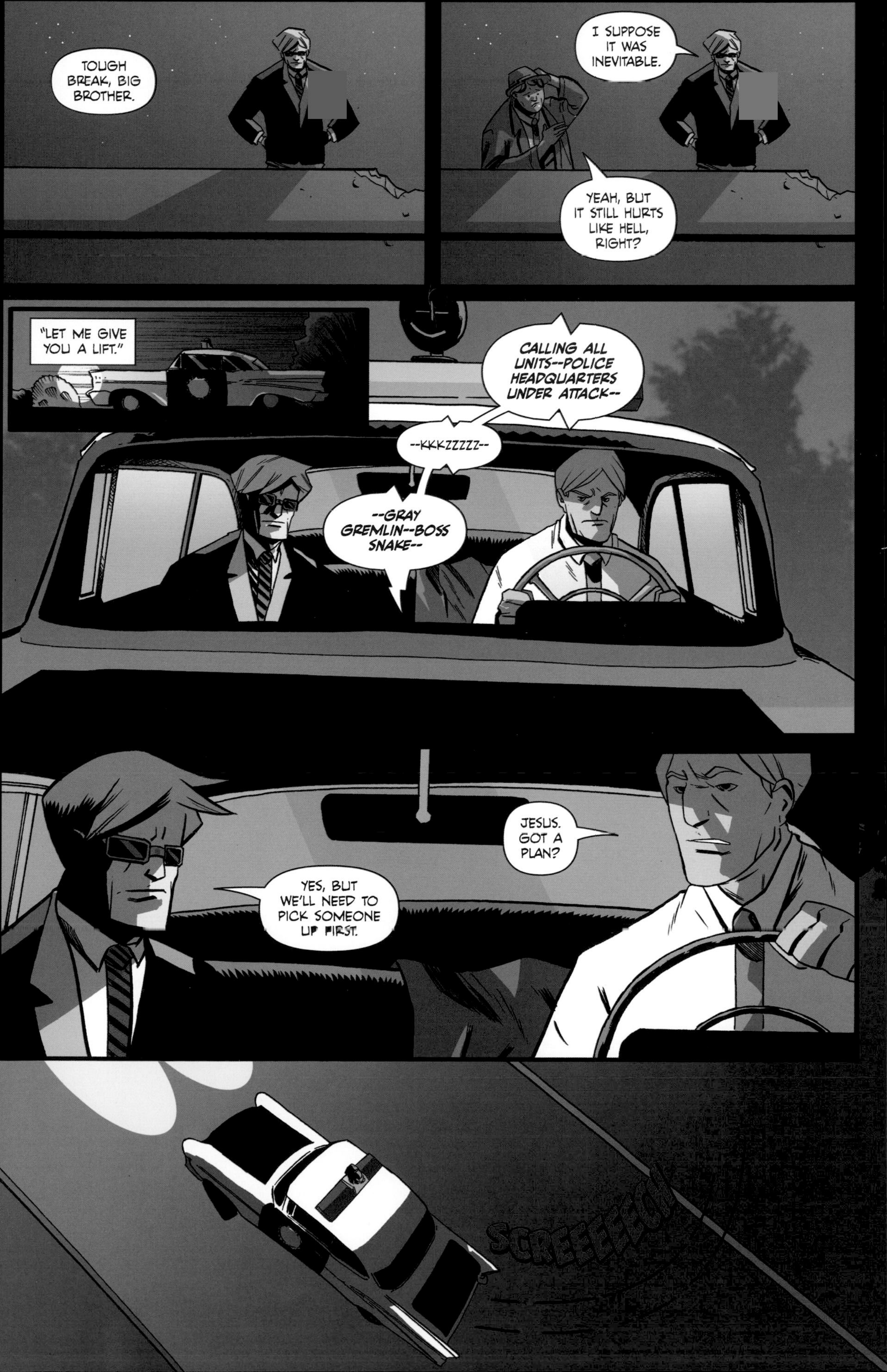
TOUGH BREAK, BIG BROTHER.
I SUPPOSE IT WAS INEVITABLE.
YEAH, BUT IT STILL HURTS LIKE HELL, RIGHT?
"LET ME GIVE YOU A LIFT."
CALLING ALL UNITS--POLICE HEADQUARTERS UNDER ATTACK--
--KKKZZZZZ--
--GRAY GREMLIN--BOSS SNAKE--
JESUS. GOT A PLAN?
YES, BUT WE'LL NEED TO PICK SOMEONE UP FIRST.
SCREEEECH!

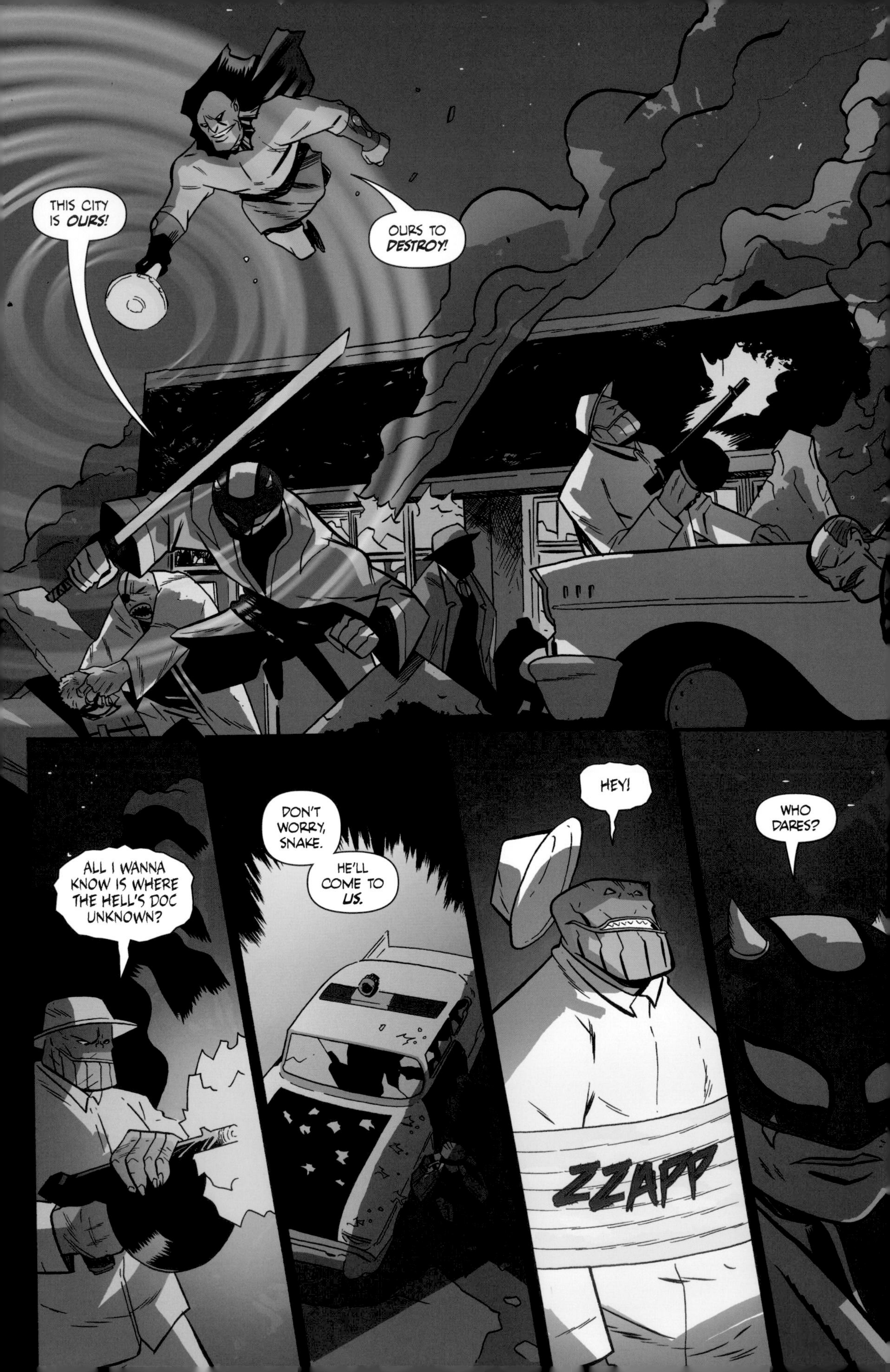
THIS CITY IS OURS!
OURS TO DESTROY!
ALL I WANNA KNOW IS WHERE THE HELL'S DOC UNKNOWN?
DON'T WORRY, SNAKE.
HE'LL COME TO US.
HEY!
ZZAPP
WHO DARES?

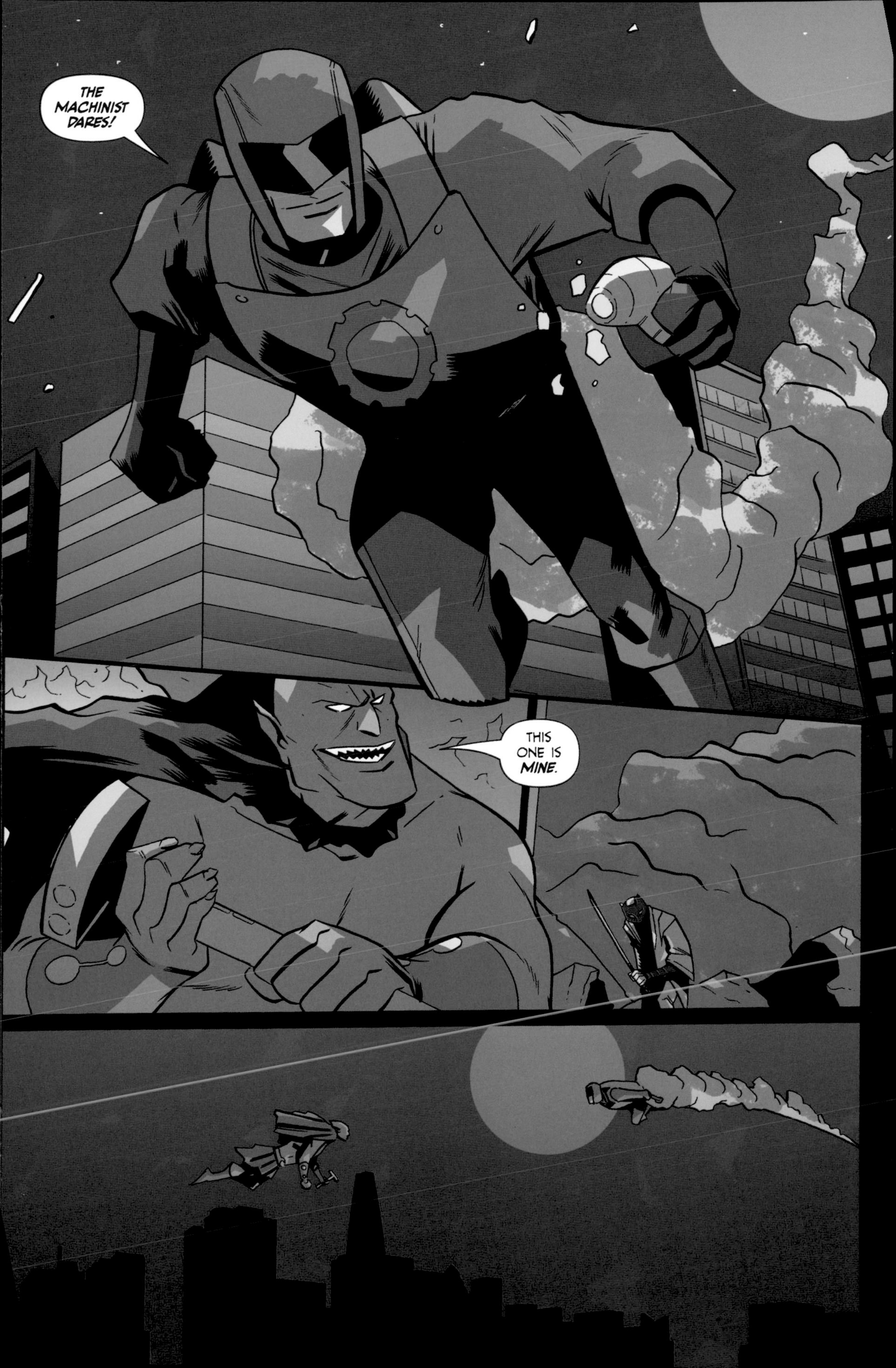
THE MACHINIST DARES!
THIS ONE IS MINE.

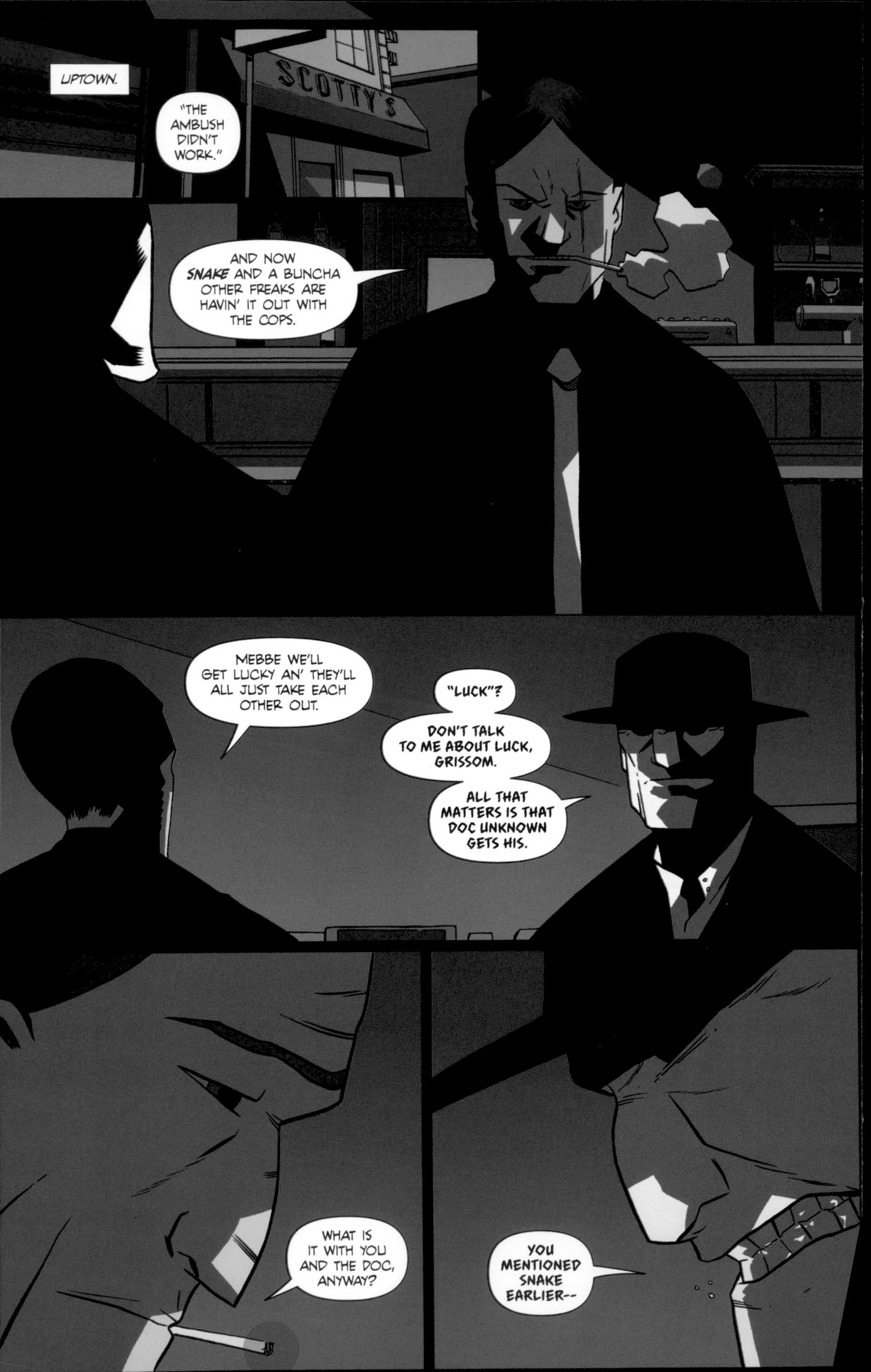

UPTOWN.
"THE AMBUSH DIDN'T WORK."
AND NOW SNAKE AND A BUNCHA OTHER FREAKS ARE HAVIN' IT OUT WITH THE COPS.
SCOTTY'S
MEBBE WE'LL GET LUCKY AN' THEY'LL ALL JUST TAKE EACH OTHER OUT.
"LUCK"?
DON'T TALK TO ME ABOUT LUCK, GRISSOM.
ALL THAT MATTERS IS THAT DOC UNKNOWN GETS HIS.
WHAT IS IT WITH YOU AND THE DOC, ANYWAY?
YOU MENTIONED SNAKE EARLIER--

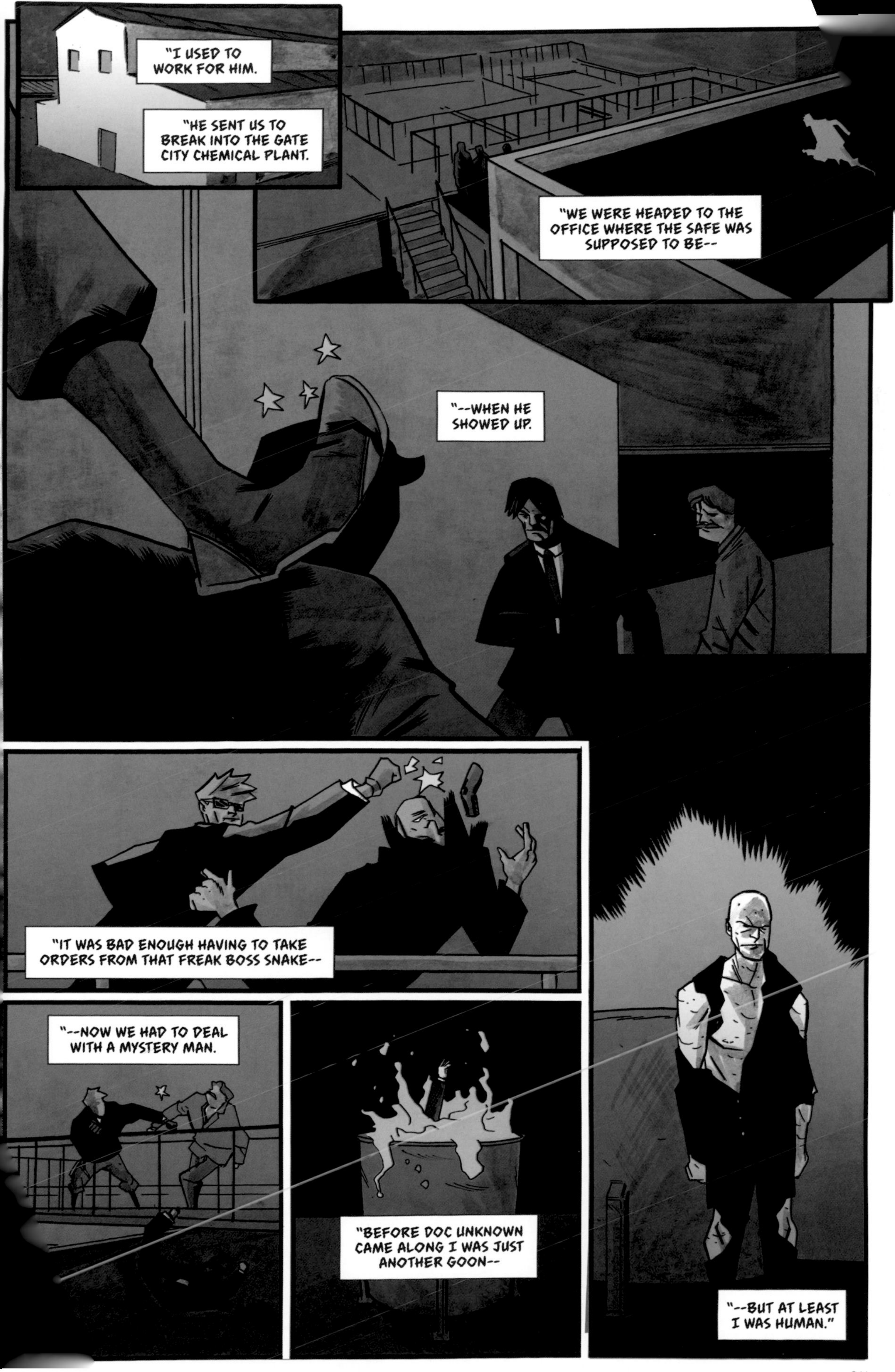
"I USED TO WORK FOR HIM.
"HE SENT US TO BREAK INTO THE GATE CITY CHEMICAL PLANT.
"WE WERE HEADED TO THE OFFICE WHERE THE SAFE WAS SUPPOSED TO BE--
"--WHEN HE SHOWED UP.
"IT WAS BAD ENOUGH HAVING TO TAKE ORDERS FROM THAT FREAK BOSS SNAKE--
"--NOW WE HAD TO DEAL WITH A MYSTERY MAN.
"BEFORE DOC UNKNOWN CAME ALONG I WAS JUST ANOTHER GOON--
"--BUT AT LEAST I WAS HUMAN."

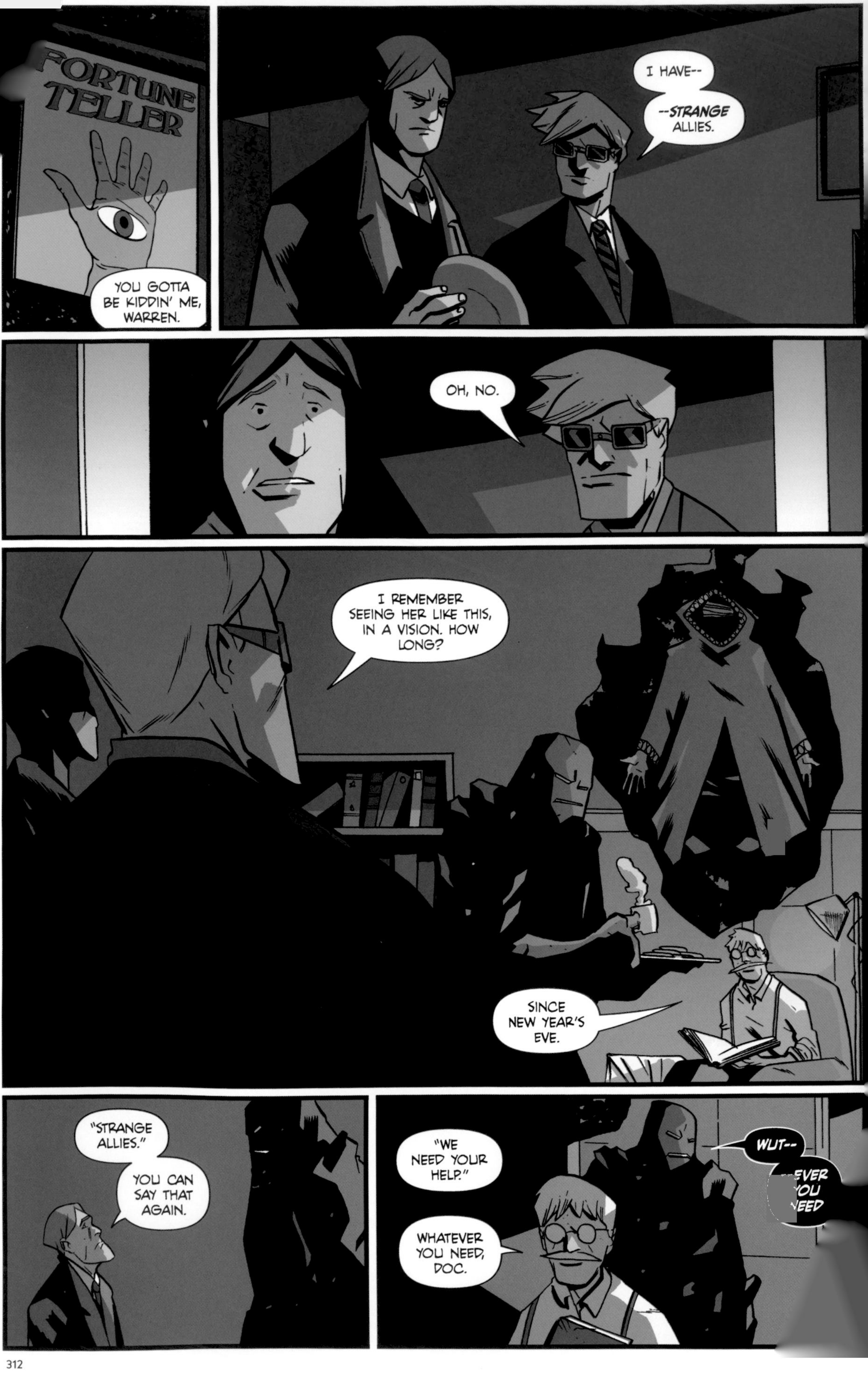
FORTUNE TELLER
YOU GOTTA BE KIDDIN' ME, WARREN.
I HAVE--
--STRANGE ALLIES.
OH, NO.
I REMEMBER SEEING HER LIKE THIS, IN A VISION. HOW LONG?
SINCE NEW YEAR'S EVE.
"STRANGE ALLIES."
YOU CAN SAY THAT AGAIN.
"WE NEED YOUR HELP."
WHATEVER YOU NEED, DOC.
WUT--

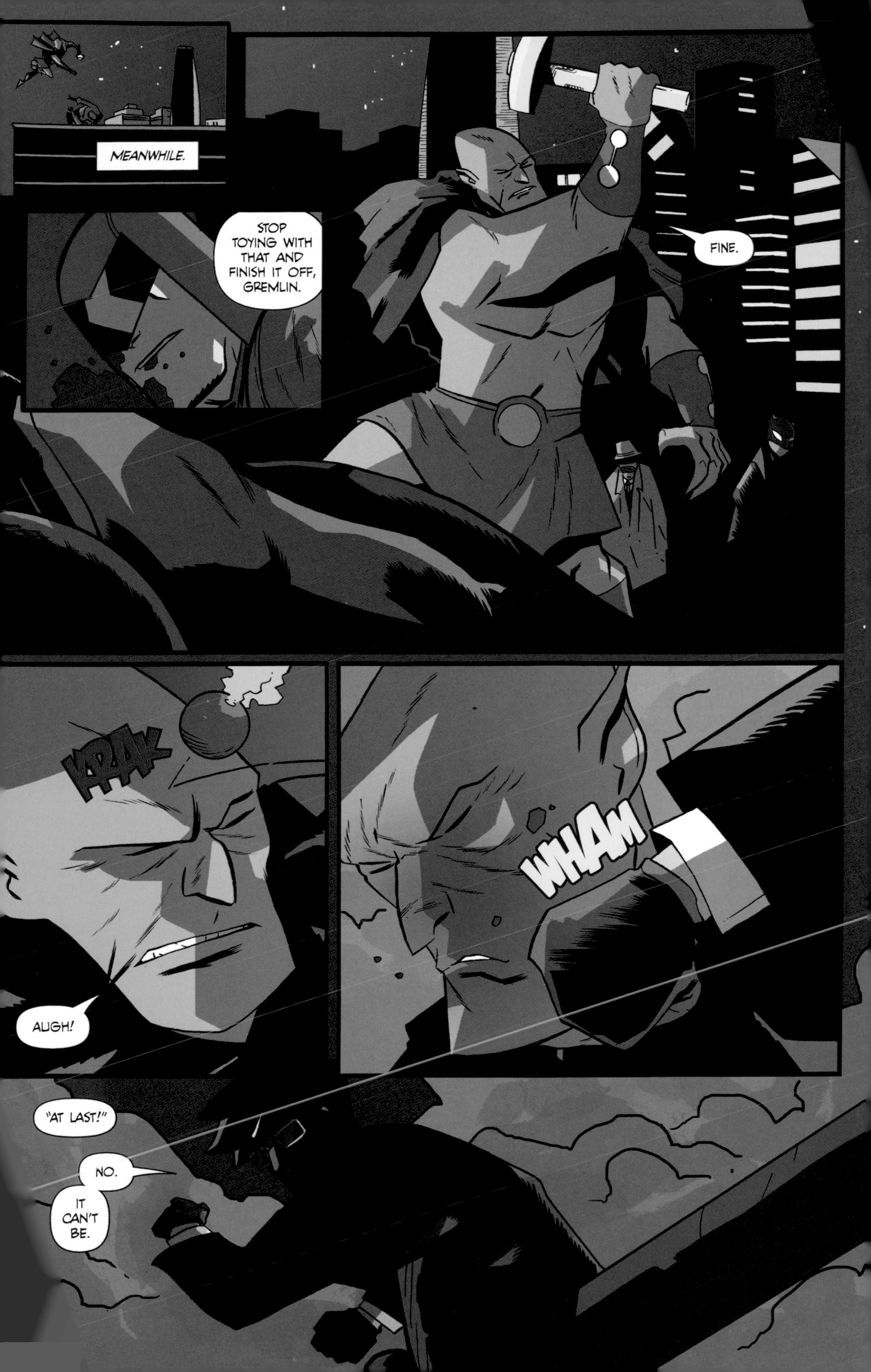
MEANWHILE.
STOP TOYING WITH THAT AND FINISH IT OFF, GREMLIN.
FINE.
KRAK
AUGH!
WHAM
"AT LAST!"
NO.
IT CAN'T BE.

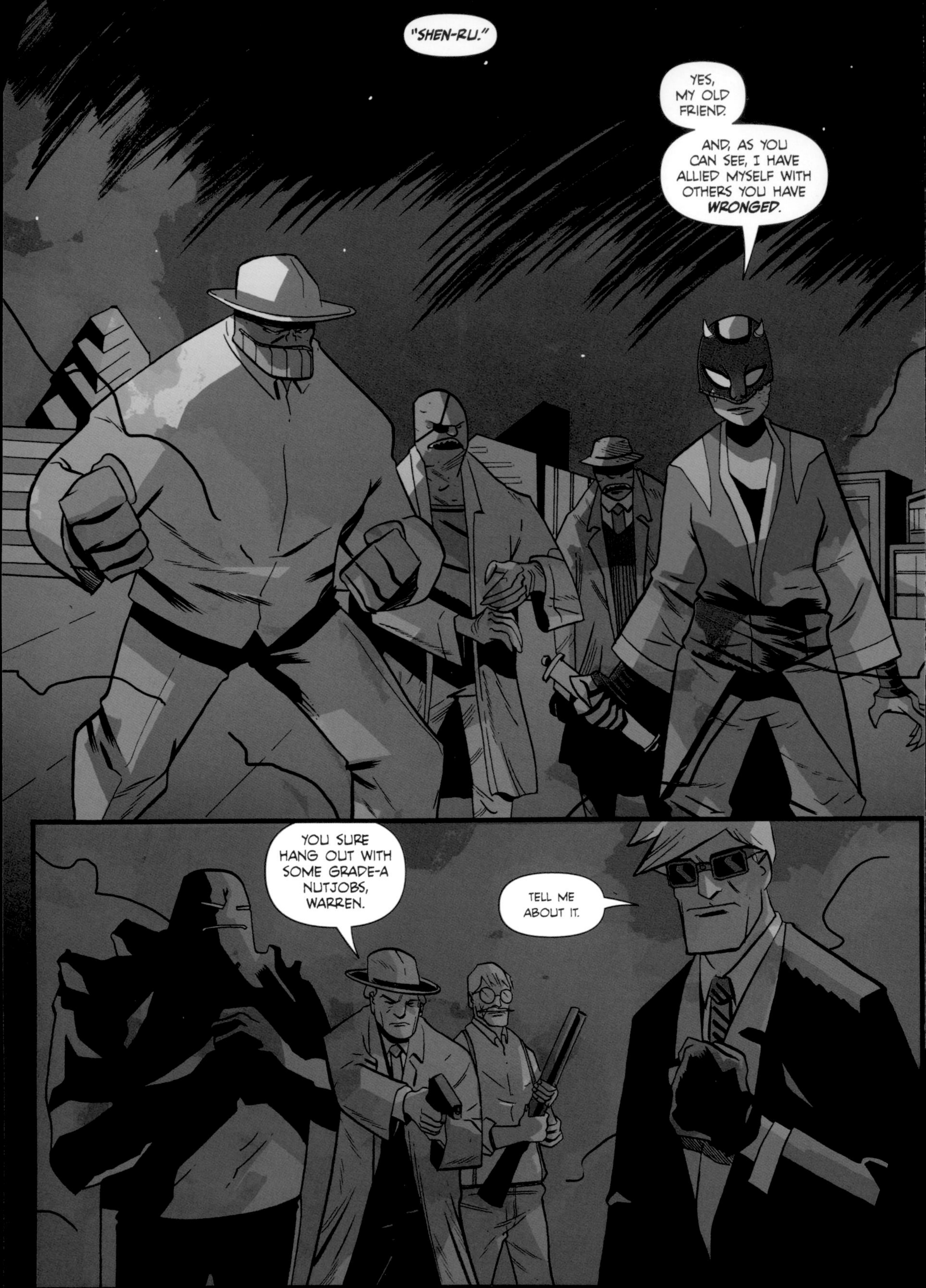
"SHEN-RU."
YES, MY OLD FRIEND.
AND, AS YOU CAN SEE, I HAVE ALLIED MYSELF WITH OTHERS YOU HAVE **WRONGED**.
YOU SURE HANG OUT WITH SOME GRADE-A NUTJOBS, WARREN.
TELL ME ABOUT IT.

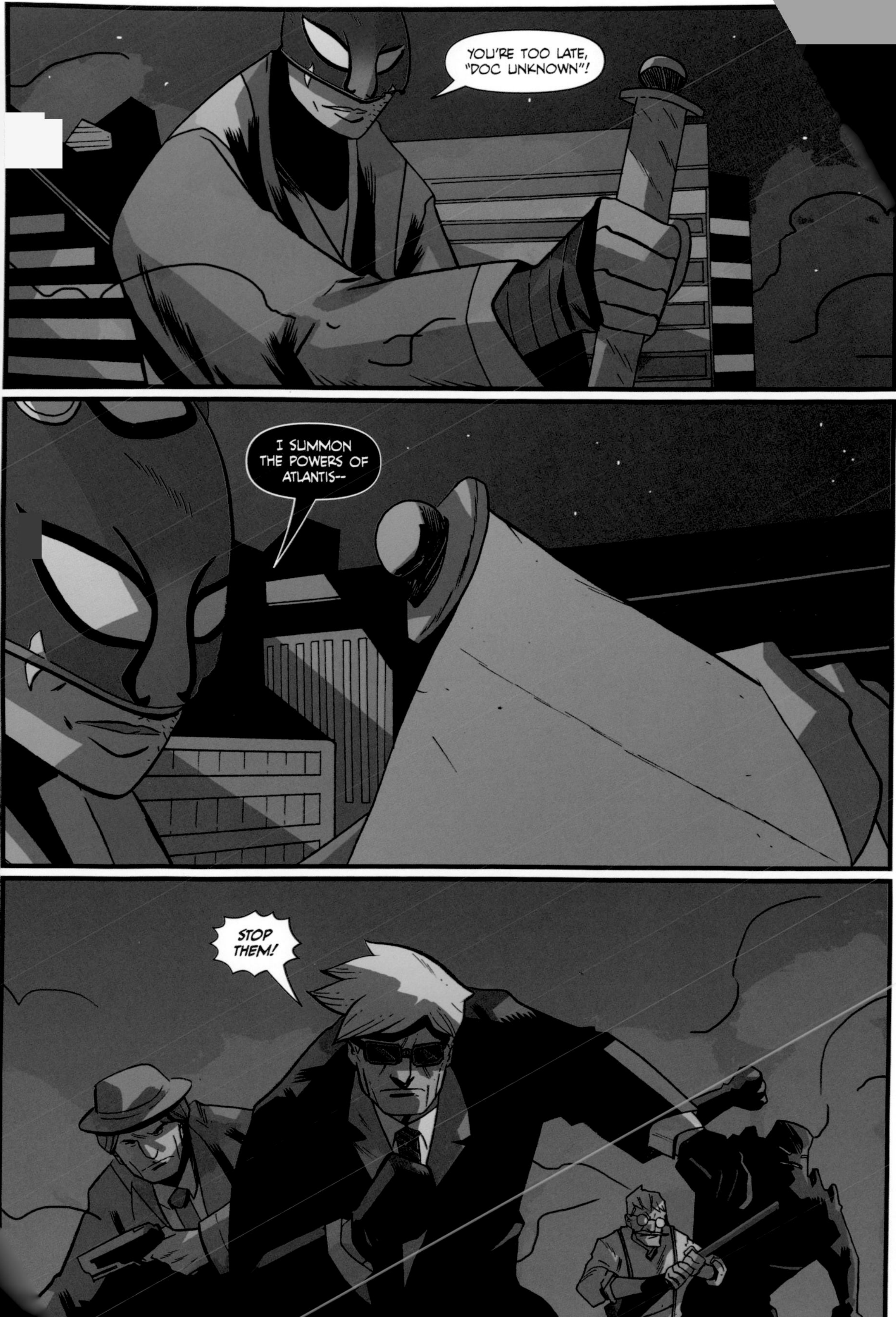
YOU'RE TOO LATE, "DOC UNKNOWN"!
I SUMMON THE POWERS OF ATLANTIS--
STOP THEM!

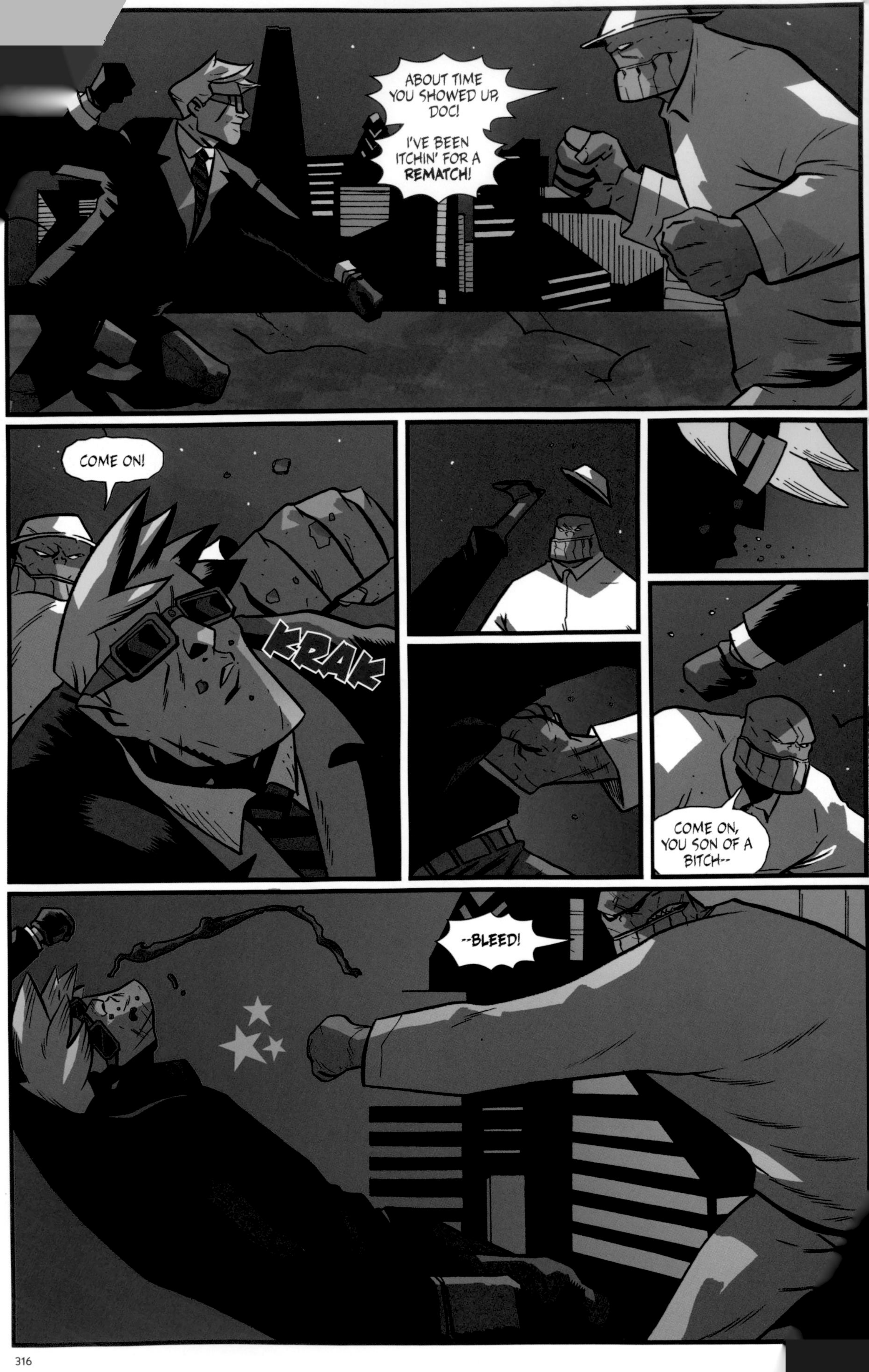
ABOUT TIME YOU SHOWED UP, DOC!
I'VE BEEN ITCHIN' FOR A **REMATCH!**
COME ON!
KRAK
COME ON, YOU SON OF A BITCH--
--BLEED!

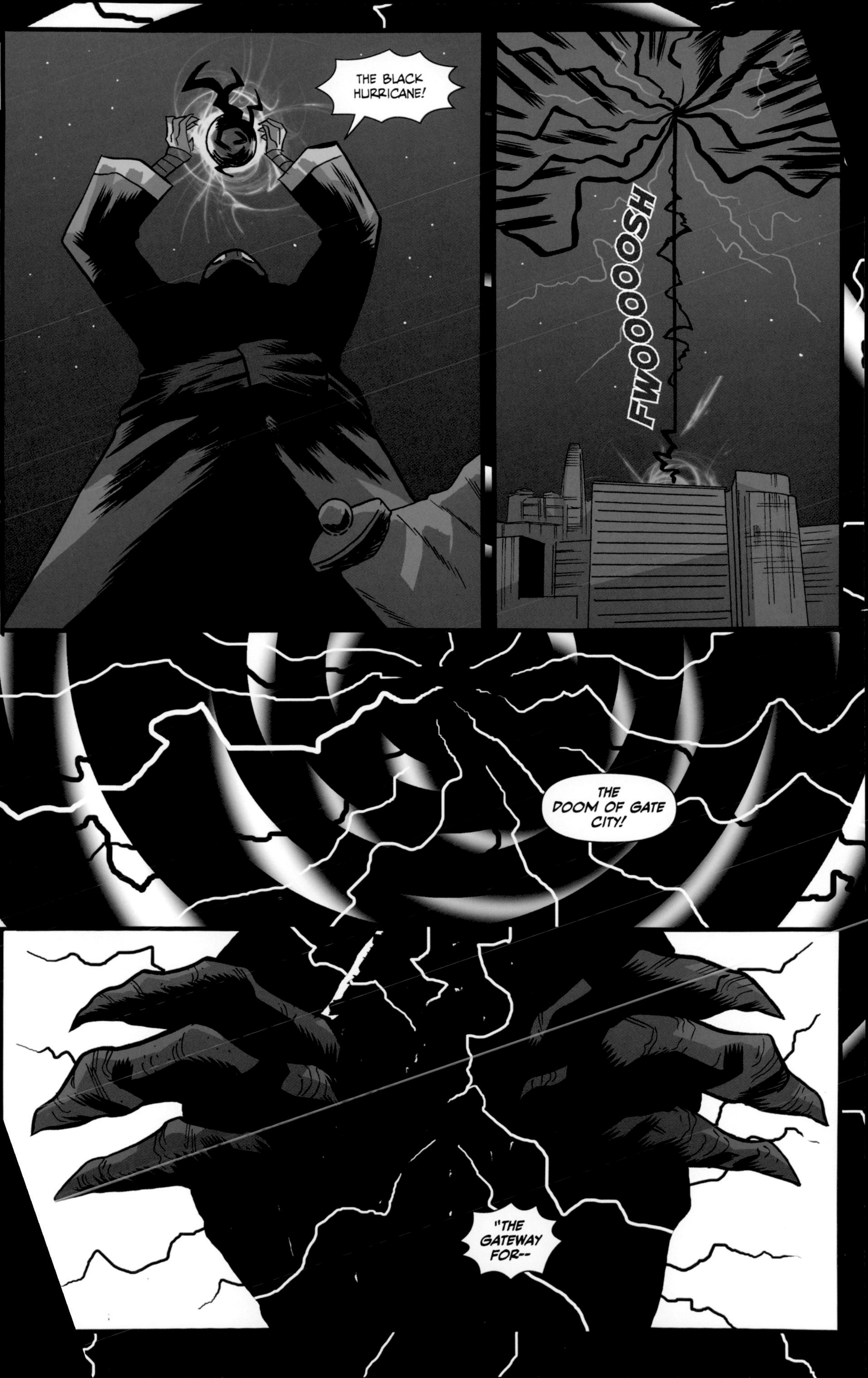
THE BLACK HURRICANE!
FWOOOOOOSH
THE DOOM OF GATE CITY!
"THE GATEWAY FOR--

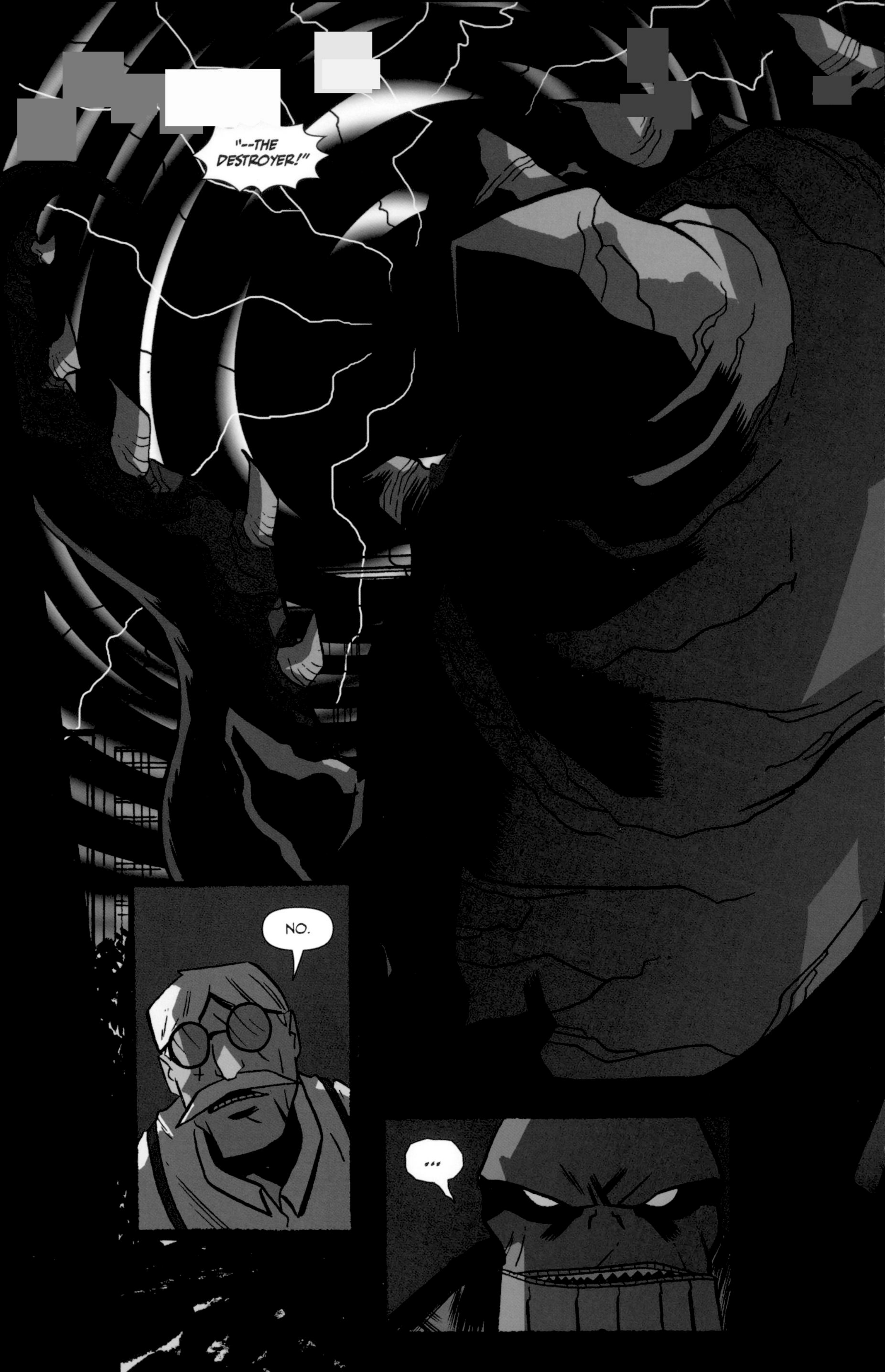
"--THE DESTROYER!"
NO.
...

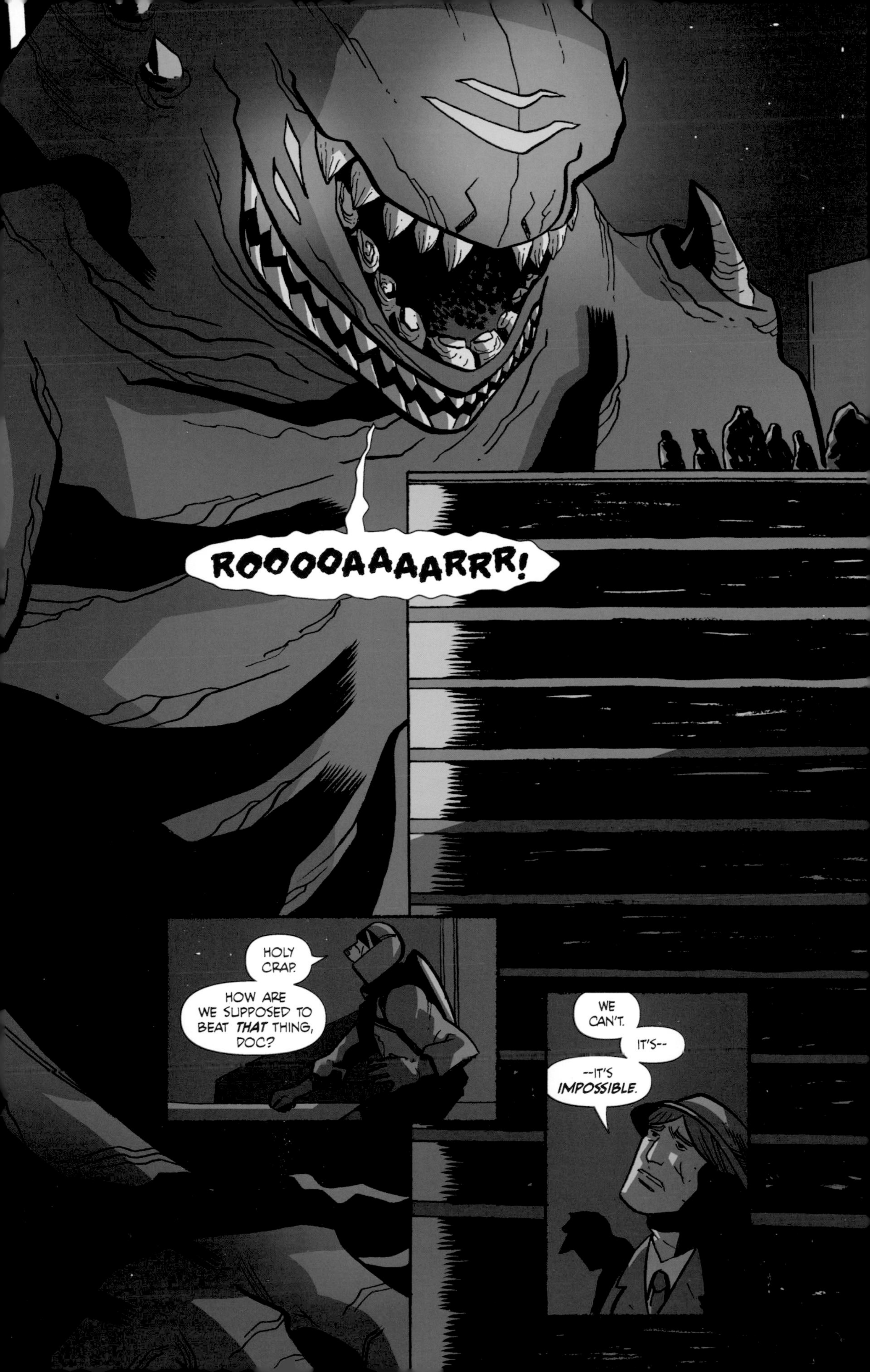
ROOOOAAAARRR!
HOLY CRAP.
HOW ARE WE SUPPOSED TO BEAT *THAT* THING, DOC?
WE CAN'T.
IT'S--
--IT'S *IMPOSSIBLE*.

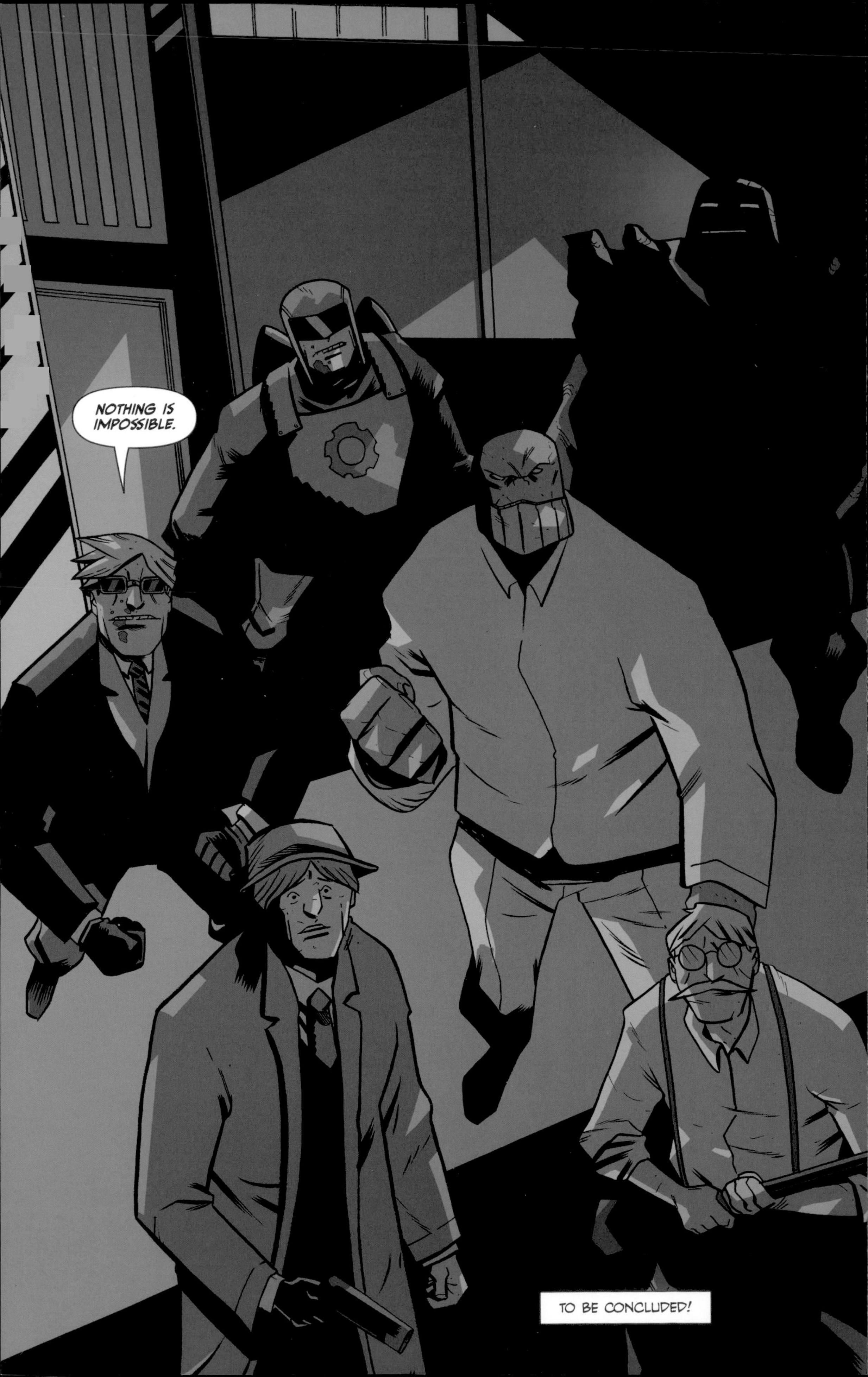
NOTHING IS IMPOSSIBLE.
TO BE CONCLUDED!

THE FATE OF ALL HEROES

SCRIPT BY **FABIAN RANGEL JR.**

ART BY **RYAN CODY**

LETTERS BY **EVELYN RANGEL**

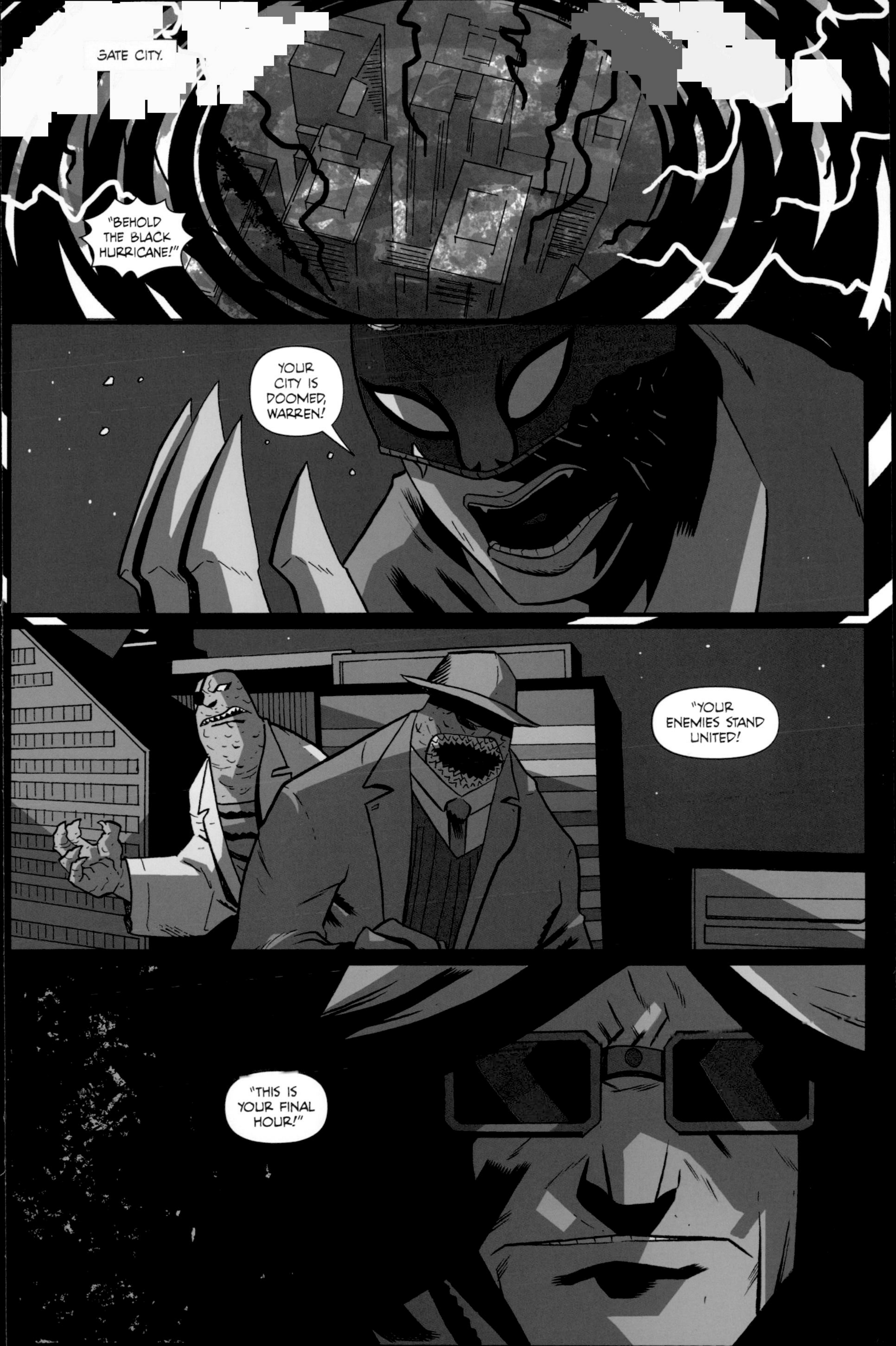
GATE CITY.
"BEHOLD THE BLACK HURRICANE!"
YOUR CITY IS DOOMED, WARREN!
"YOUR ENEMIES STAND UNITED!
"THIS IS YOUR FINAL HOUR!"

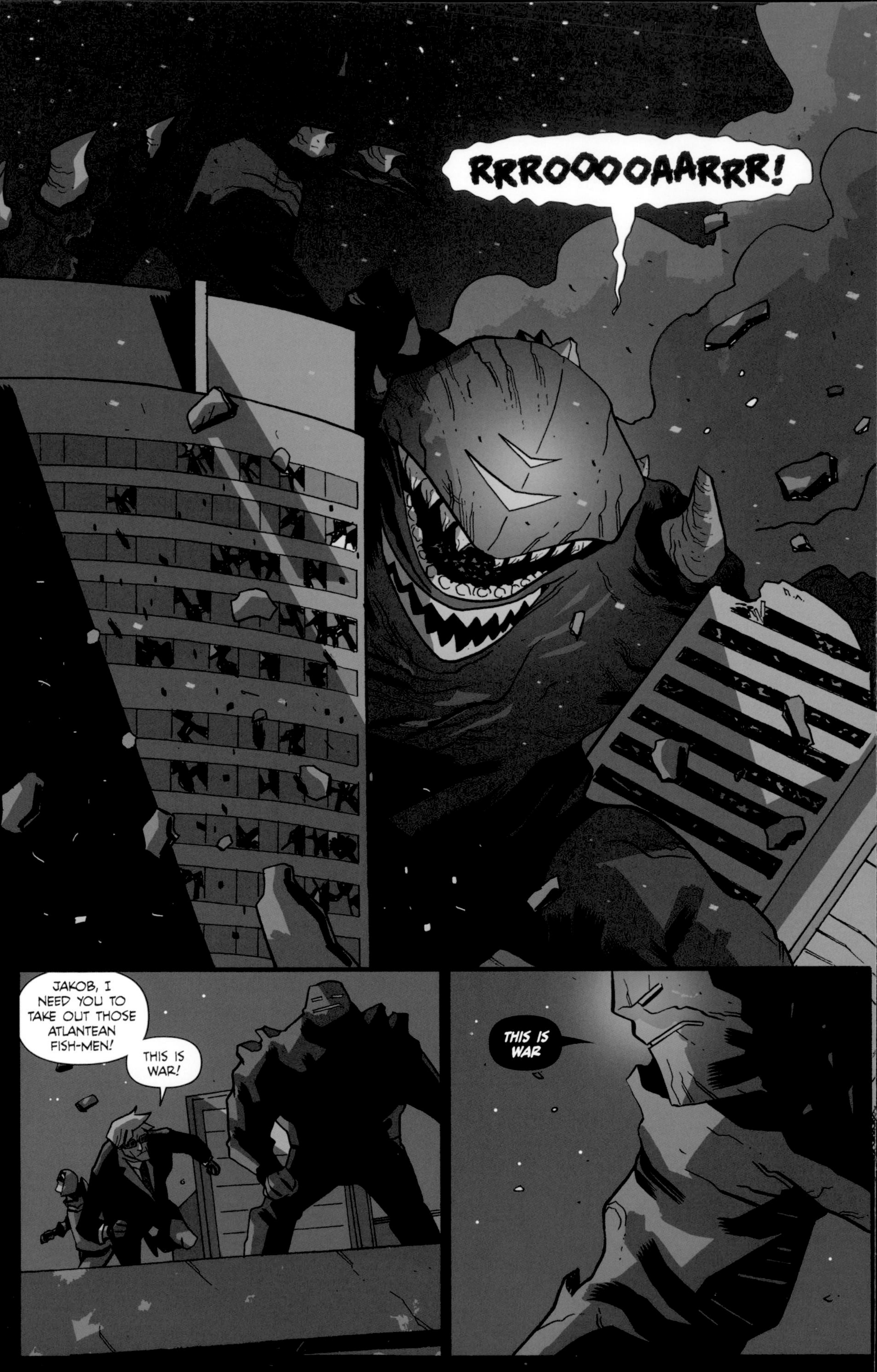
RRROOOOAARRR!
JAKOB, I NEED YOU TO TAKE OUT THOSE ATLANTEAN FISH-MEN!
THIS IS WAR!
THIS IS WAR

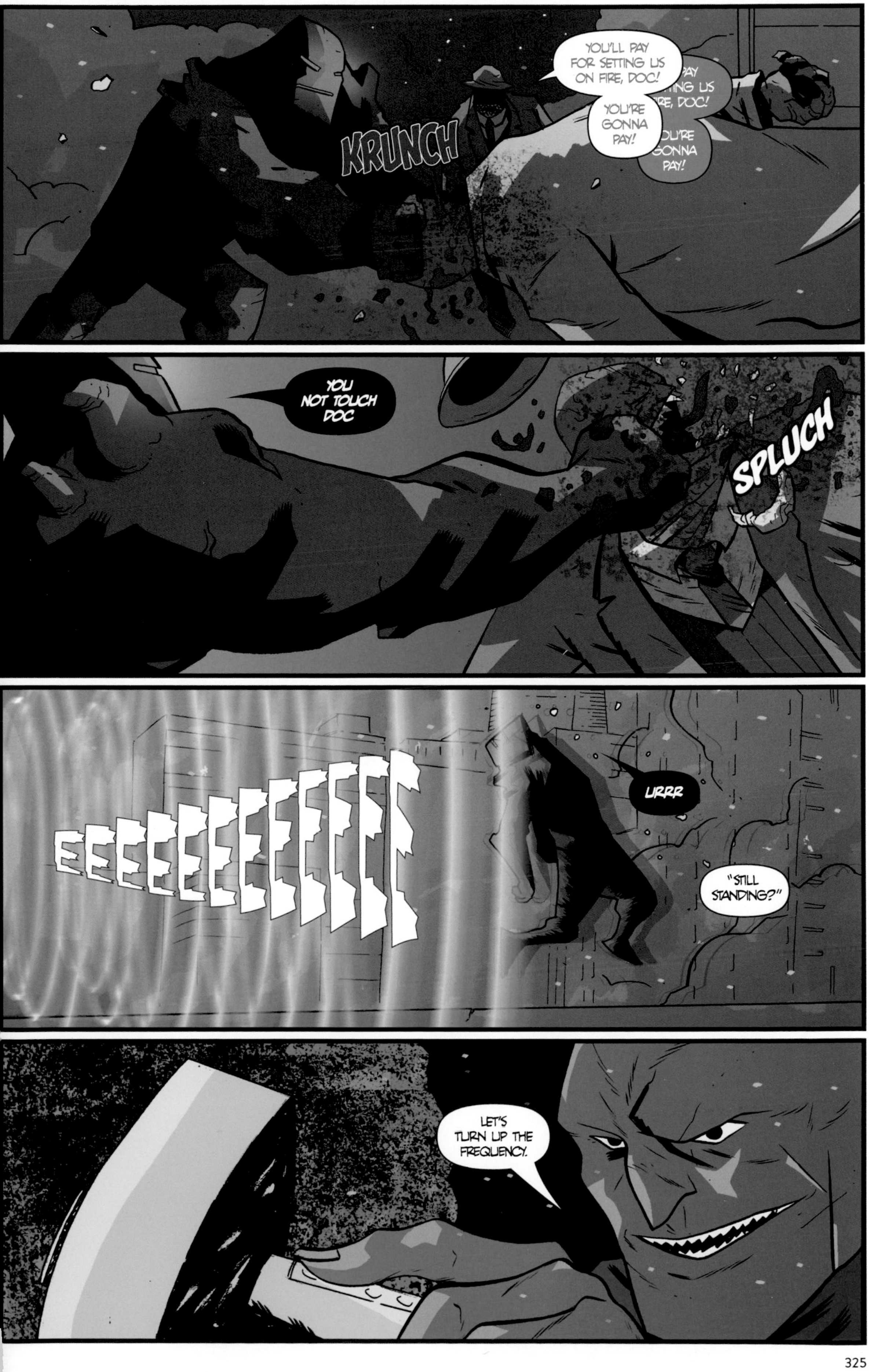
YOU'LL PAY FOR SETTING US ON FIRE, DOC!
YOU'RE GONNA PAY!
KRUNCH
YOU NOT TOUCH DOC
SPLUCH
URRR
"STILL STANDING?"
EEEEEEEEEEEE
LET'S TURN UP THE FREQUENCY.

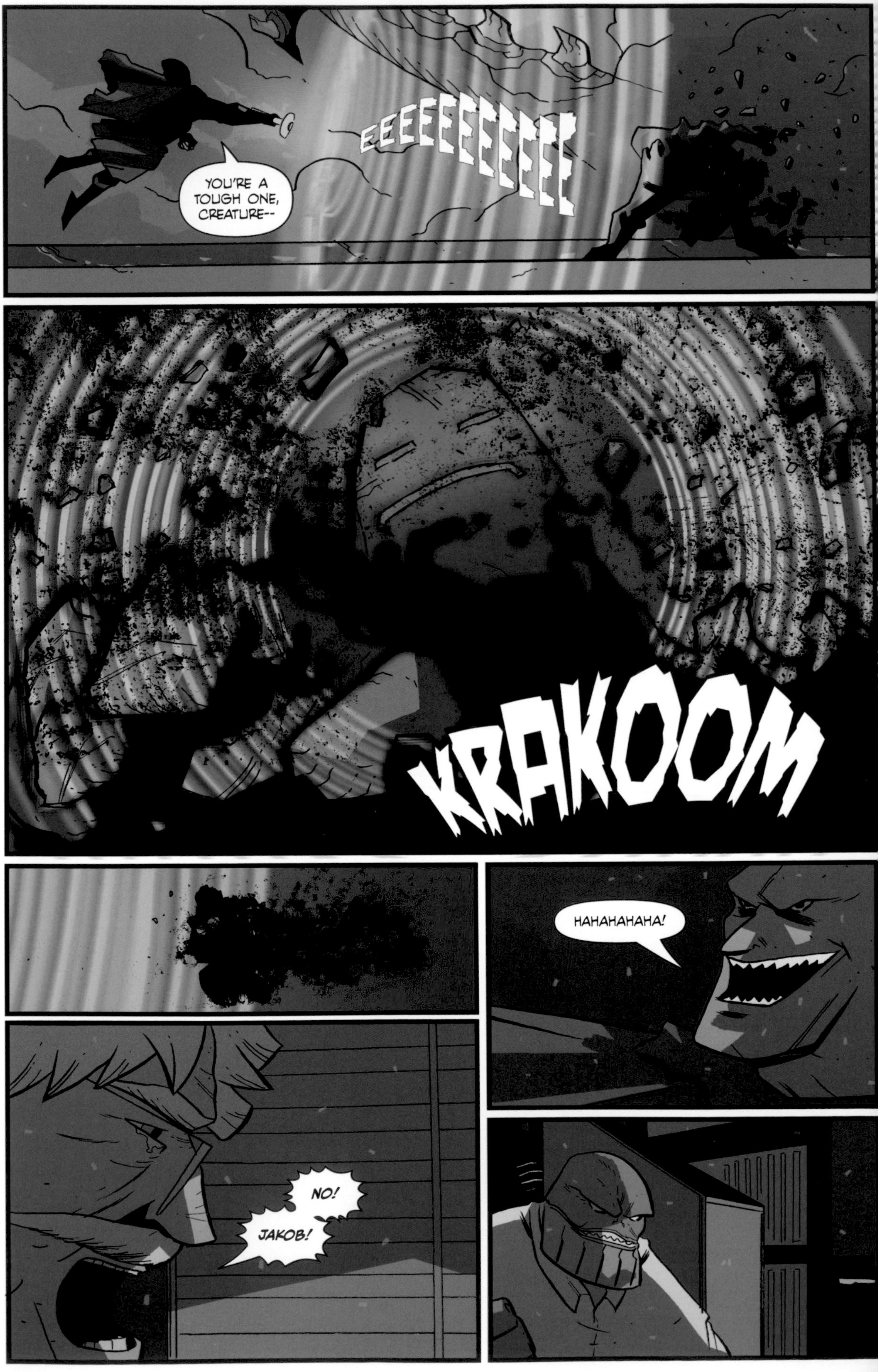
YOU'RE A TOUGH ONE, CREATURE--
EEEEEEEEEEEE
KRAKOOM
HAHAHAHAHA!
NO!
JAKOB!

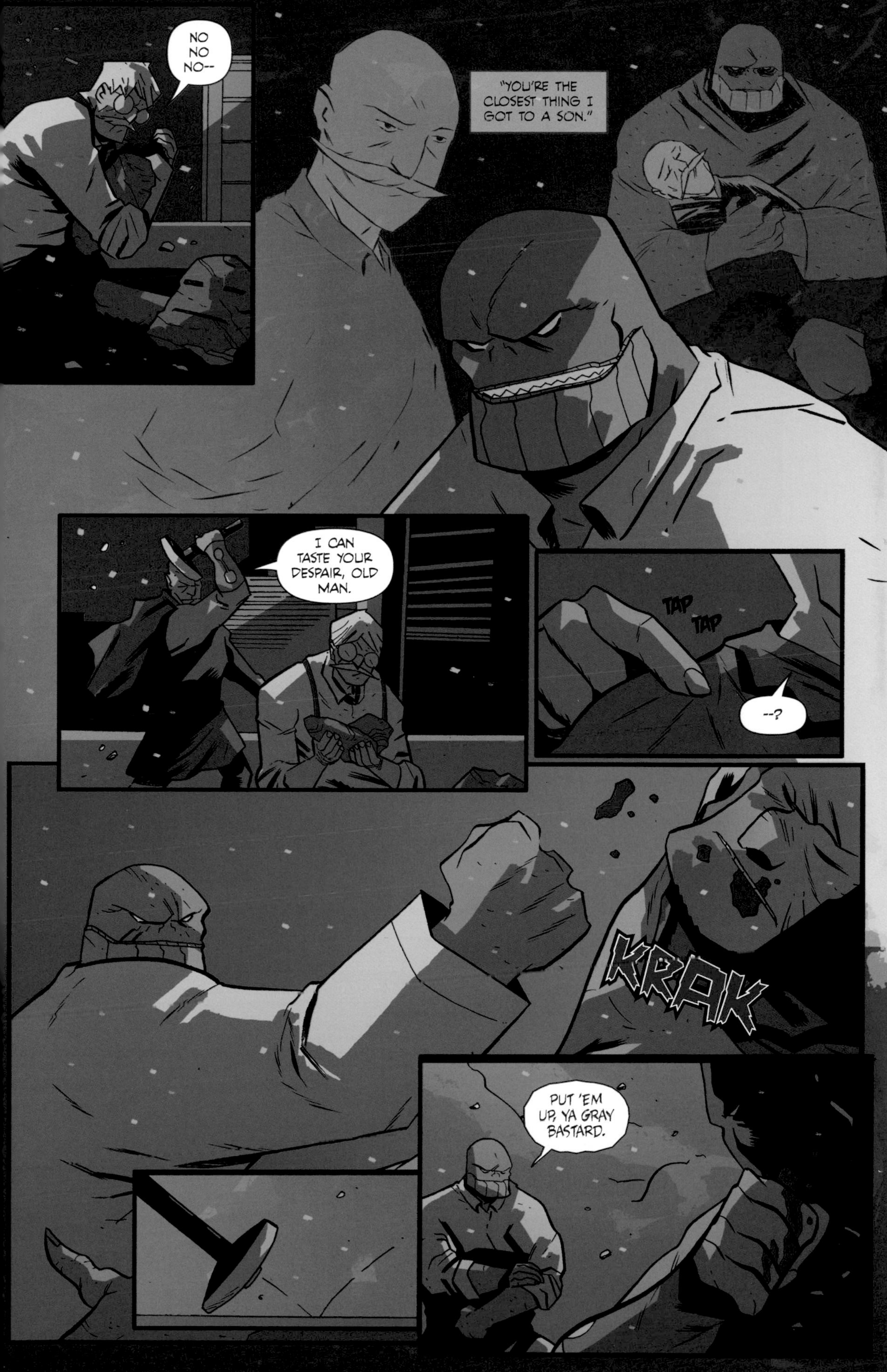
NO NO NO--
"YOU'RE THE CLOSEST THING I GOT TO A SON."
I CAN TASTE YOUR DESPAIR, OLD MAN.
TAP TAP
--?
KRAK
PUT 'EM UP, YA GRAY BASTARD.

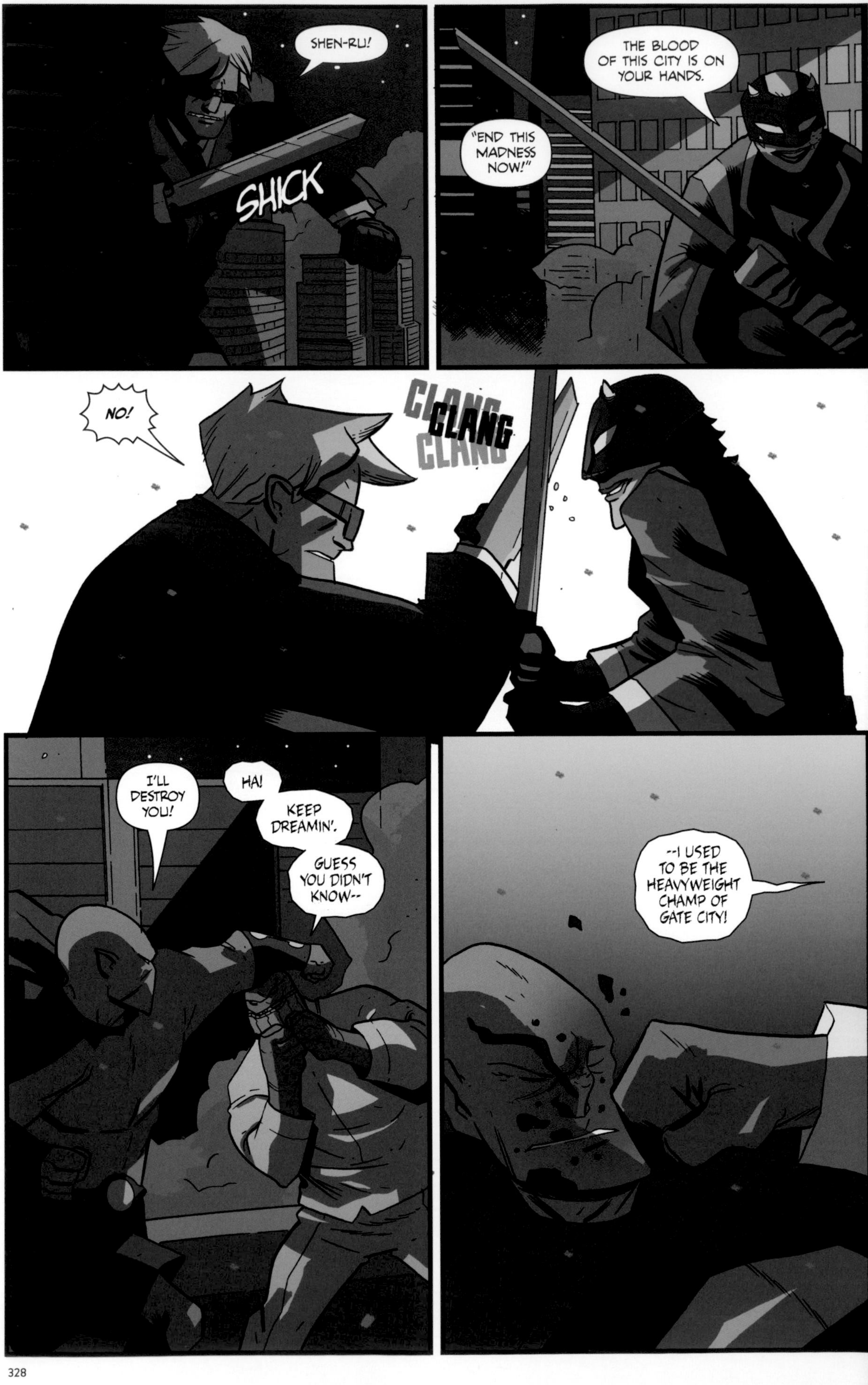
SHEN-RU!
SHICK
THE BLOOD OF THIS CITY IS ON YOUR HANDS.
"END THIS MADNESS NOW!"
NO!
CLANG CLANG CLANG
I'LL DESTROY YOU!
HA!
KEEP DREAMIN'.
GUESS YOU DIDN'T KNOW--
--I USED TO BE THE HEAVYWEIGHT CHAMP OF GATE CITY!

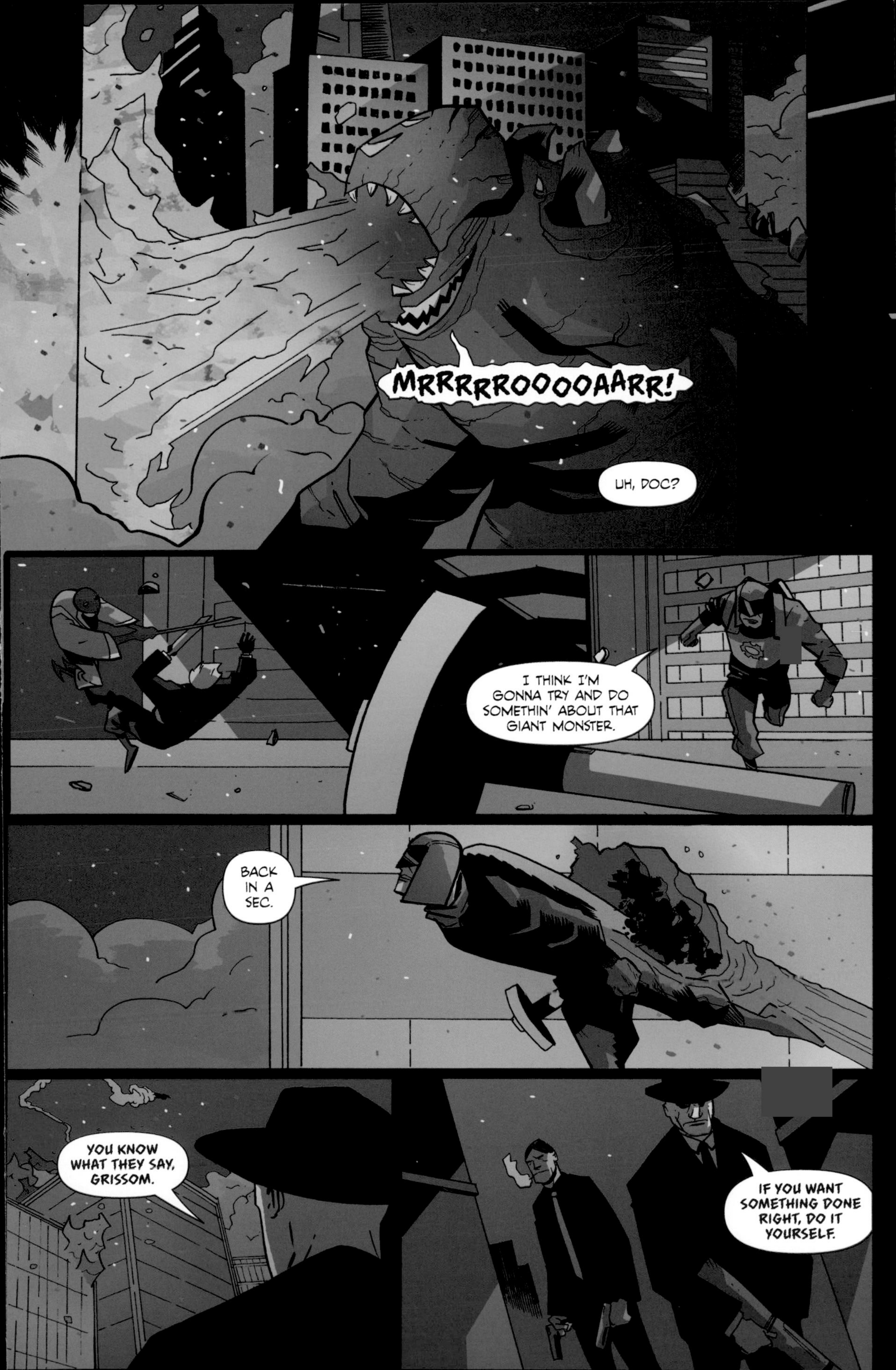
MRRRRROOOOAARR!
UH, DOC?
I THINK I'M GONNA TRY AND DO SOMETHIN' ABOUT THAT GIANT MONSTER.
BACK IN A SEC.
YOU KNOW WHAT THEY SAY, GRISSOM.
IF YOU WANT SOMETHING DONE RIGHT, DO IT YOURSELF.

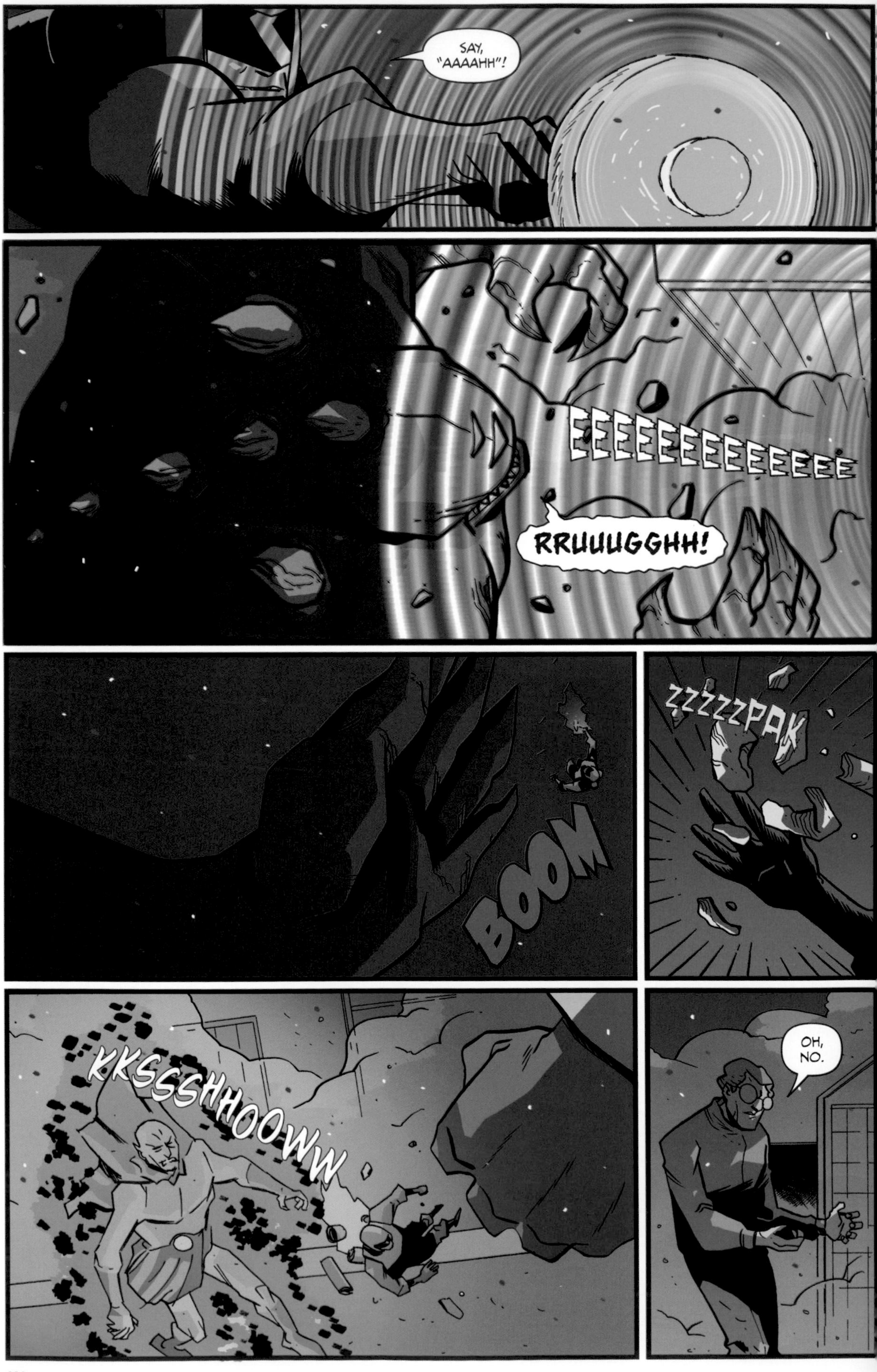
SAY, "AAAAHH"!
EEEEEEEEEEEEEE
RRUUUGGHH!
BOOM
ZZZZZPAK
KKSSSHHOOWW
OH, NO.

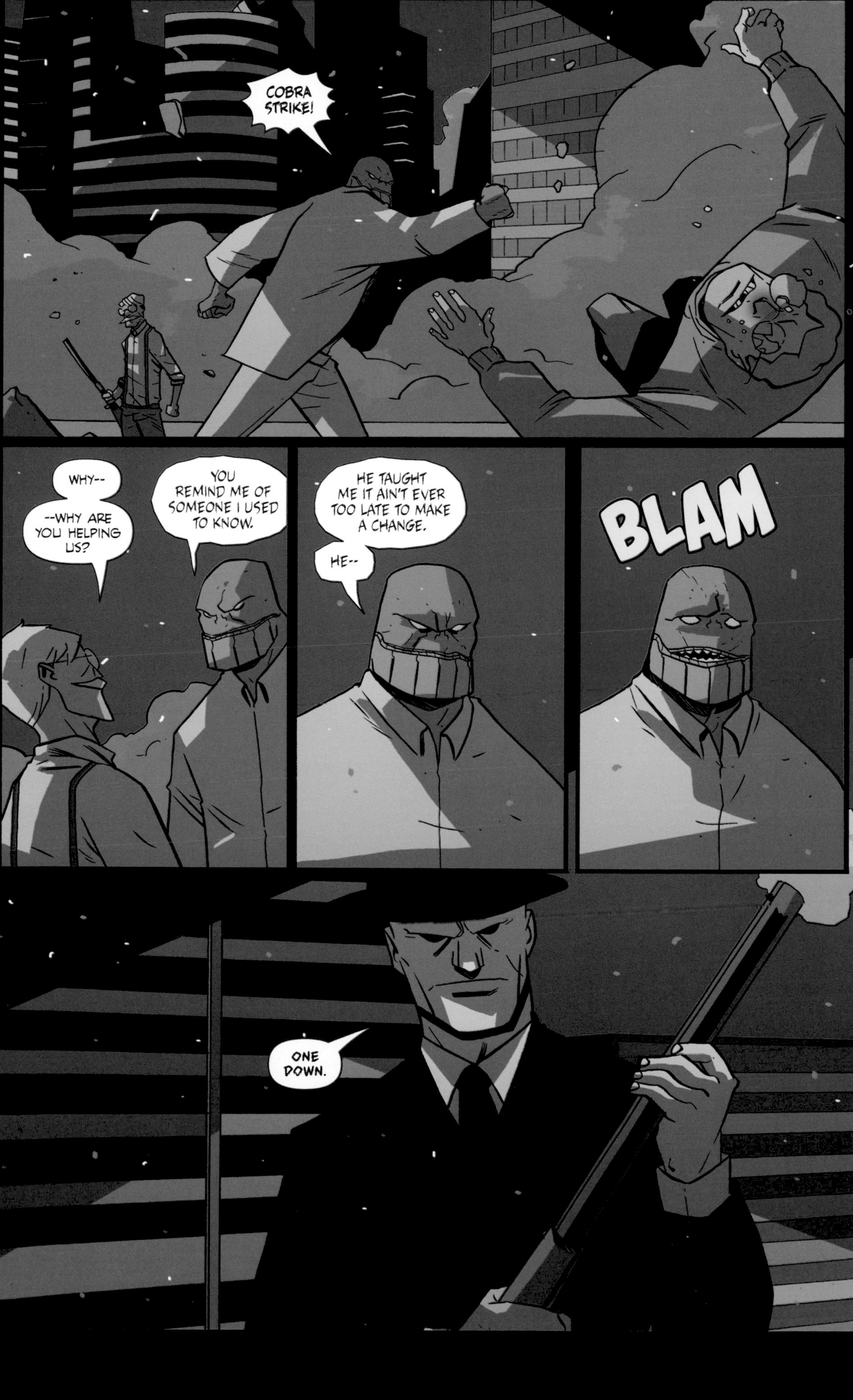
COBRA STRIKE!
WHY--
--WHY ARE YOU HELPING US?
YOU REMIND ME OF SOMEONE I USED TO KNOW.
HE TAUGHT ME IT AIN'T EVER TOO LATE TO MAKE A CHANGE.
HE--
BLAM
ONE DOWN.

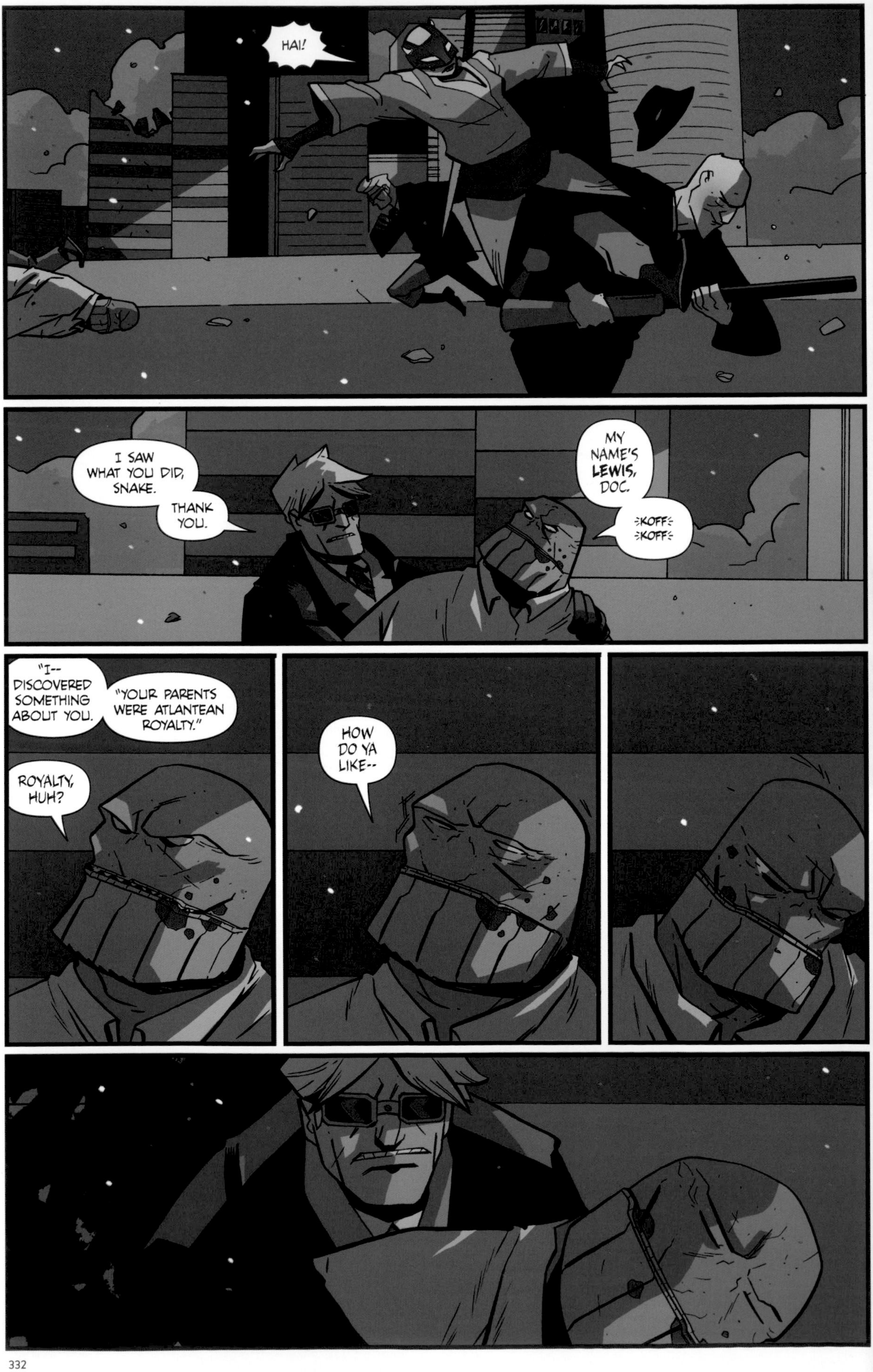
HAI!
I SAW WHAT YOU DID, SNAKE.
THANK YOU.
MY NAME'S **LEWIS,** DOC.
KOFF KOFF
"I-- DISCOVERED SOMETHING ABOUT YOU.
"YOUR PARENTS WERE ATLANTEAN ROYALTY."
ROYALTY, HUH?
HOW DO YA LIKE--

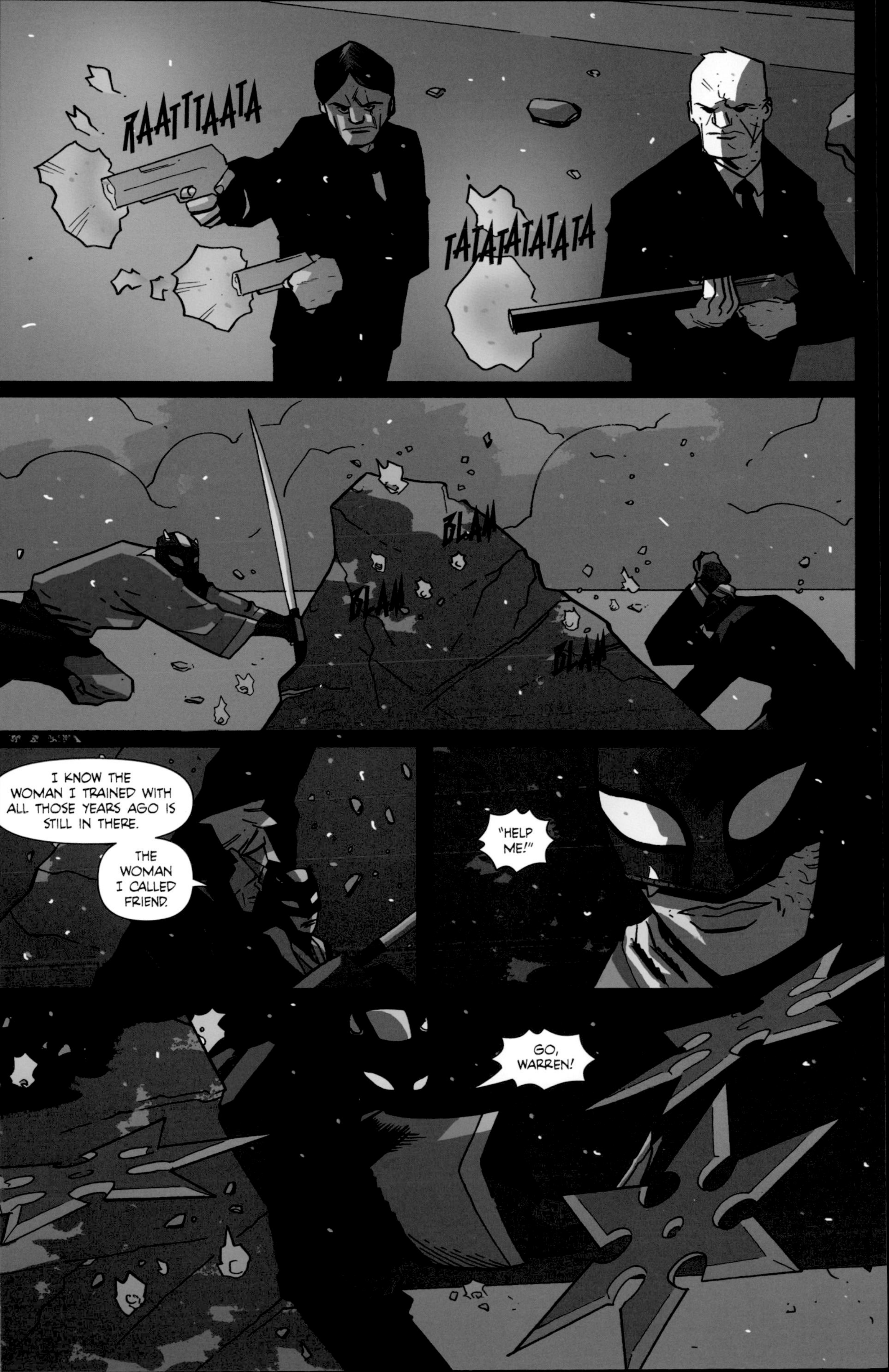
RAATTTAATA
TATATATATATA
BLAM
BLAM
BLAM
I KNOW THE WOMAN I TRAINED WITH ALL THOSE YEARS AGO IS STILL IN THERE.
THE WOMAN I CALLED FRIEND.
"HELP ME!"
GO, WARREN!

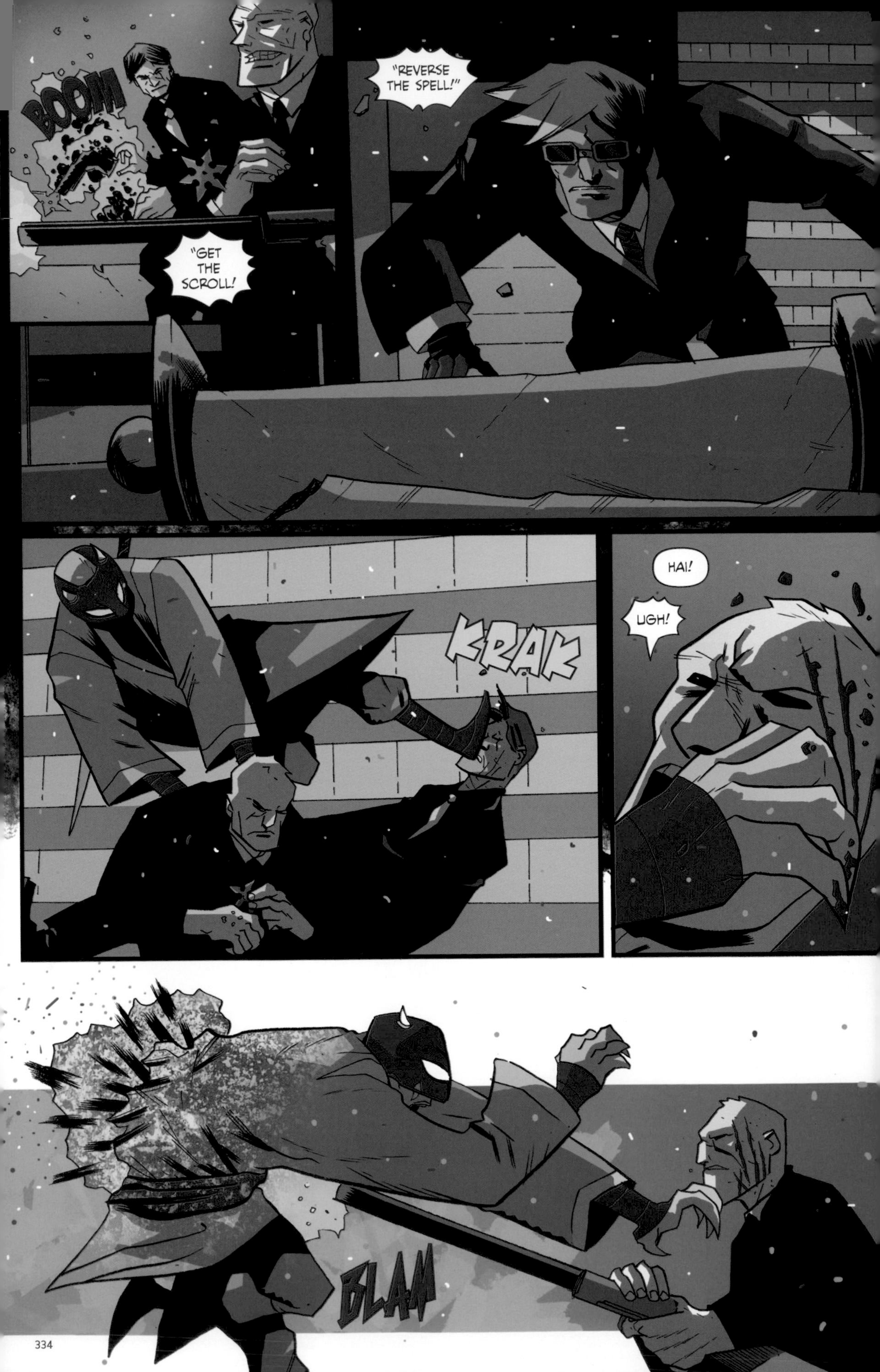
BOOM
"REVERSE THE SPELL!"
"GET THE SCROLL!
KRAK
HAI!
UGH!
BLAM

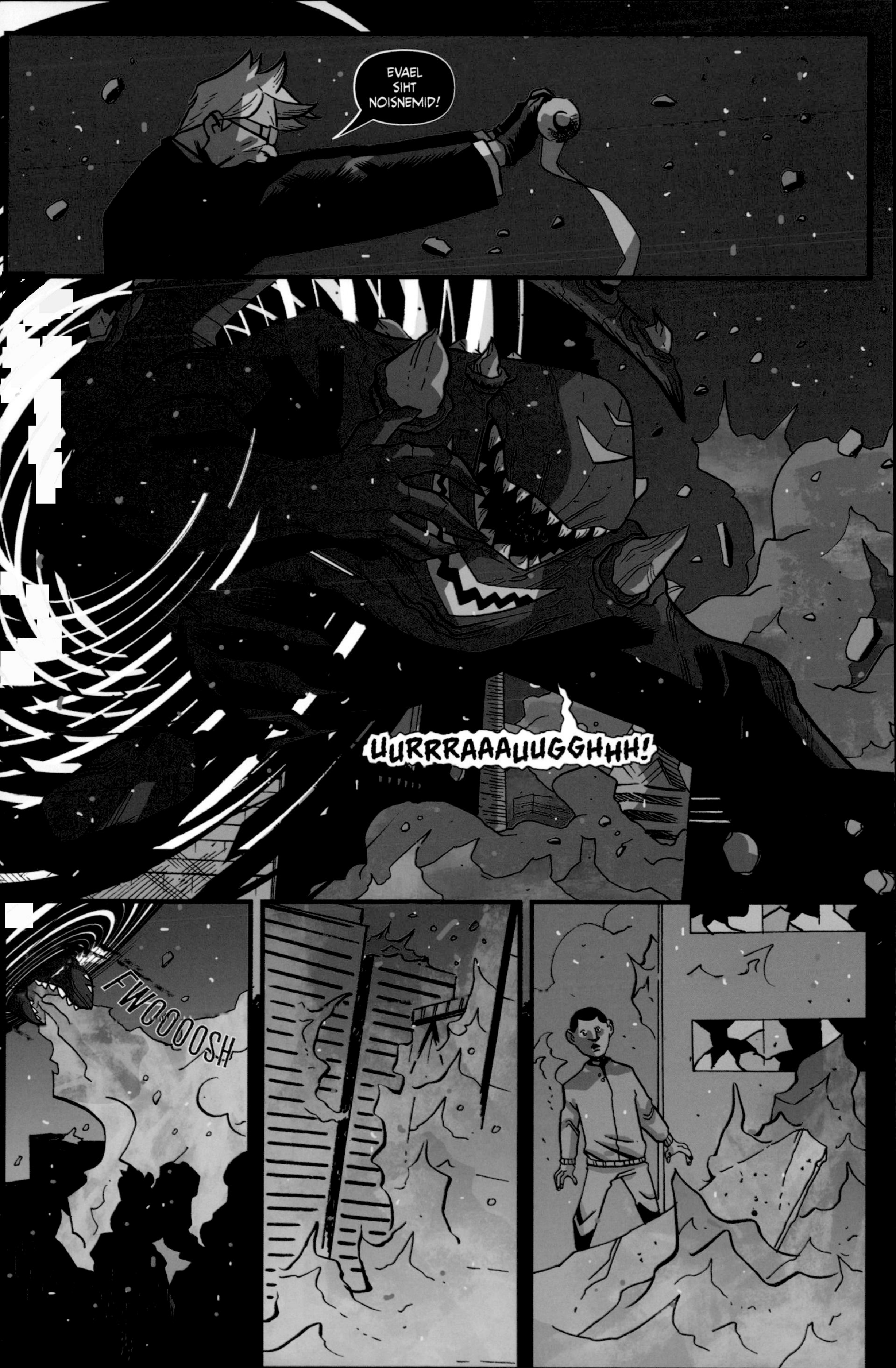
EVAEL SIHT NOISNEMID!
UURRRAAAUUGGHHH!
FWOOOOOSH

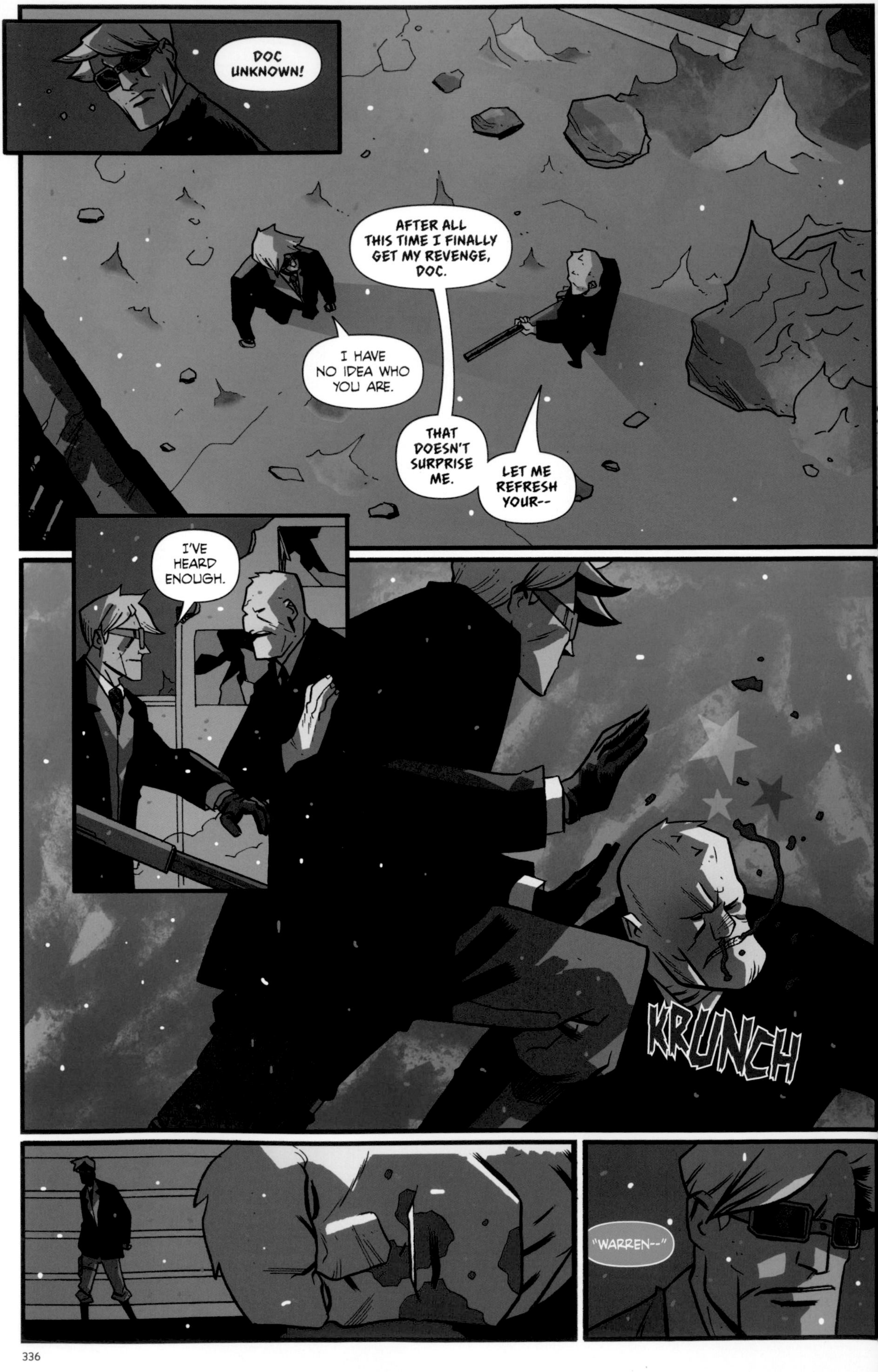
DOC UNKNOWN!
AFTER ALL THIS TIME I FINALLY GET MY REVENGE, DOC.
I HAVE NO IDEA WHO YOU ARE.
THAT DOESN'T SURPRISE ME.
LET ME REFRESH YOUR--
I'VE HEARD ENOUGH.
KRUNCH
"WARREN--"

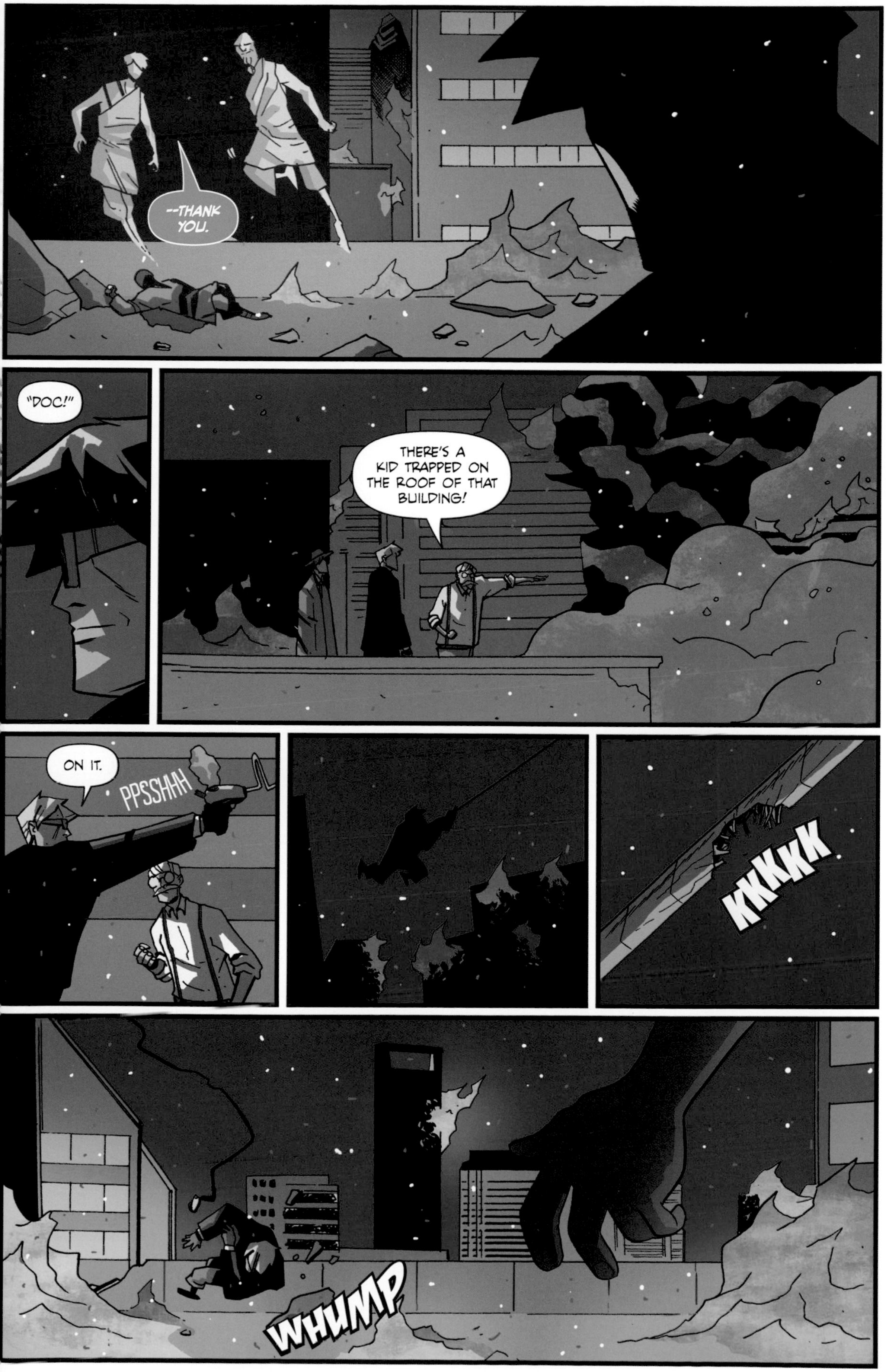
--THANK YOU.
"DOC!"
THERE'S A KID TRAPPED ON THE ROOF OF THAT BUILDING!
ON IT.
PPSSHHH
KKKKK
WHUMP

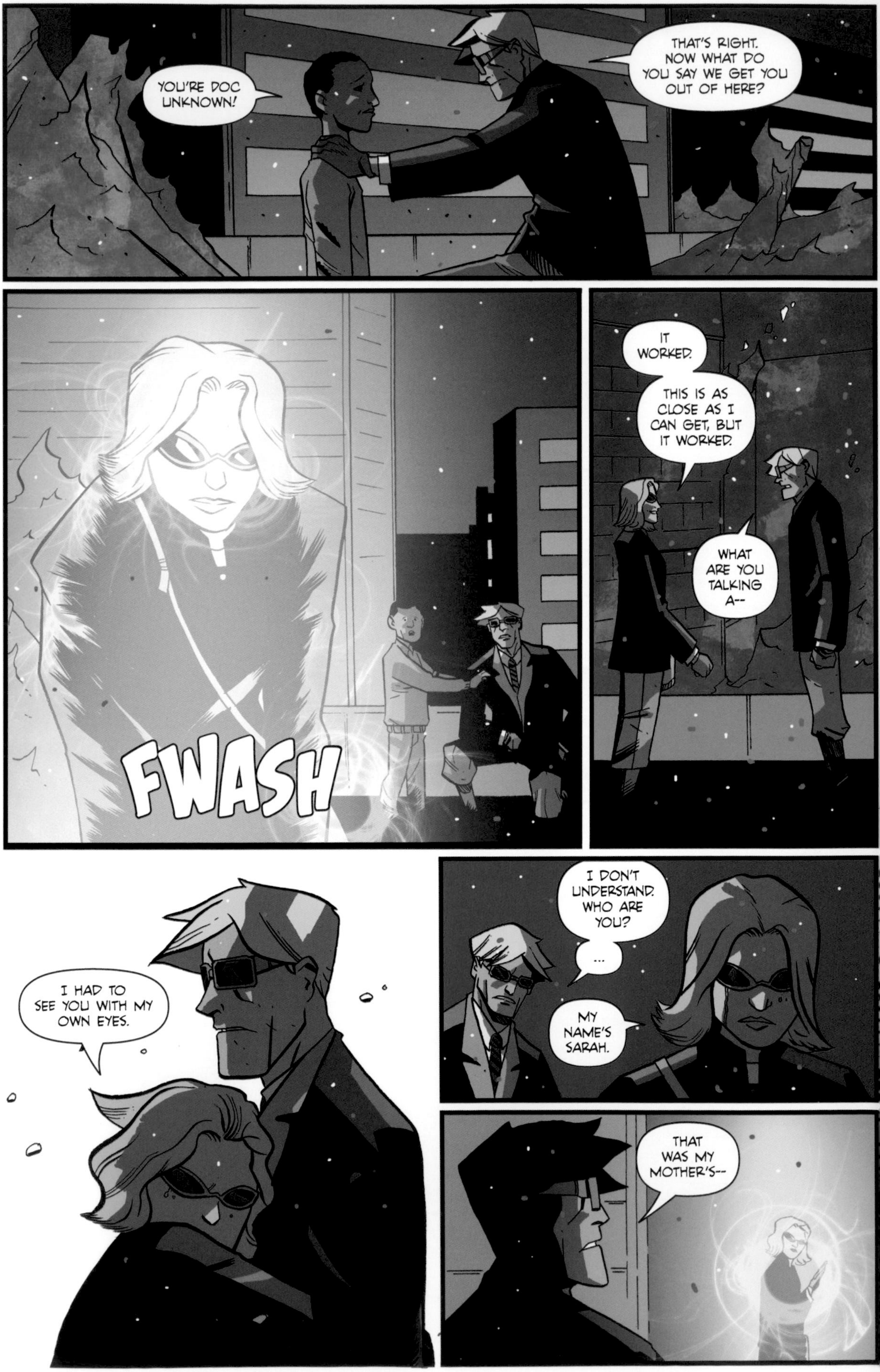
YOU'RE DOC UNKNOWN!
THAT'S RIGHT. NOW WHAT DO YOU SAY WE GET YOU OUT OF HERE?
FWASH
IT WORKED.
THIS IS AS CLOSE AS I CAN GET, BUT IT WORKED.
WHAT ARE YOU TALKING A--
I HAD TO SEE YOU WITH MY OWN EYES.
I DON'T UNDERSTAND. WHO ARE YOU?
...
MY NAME'S SARAH.
THAT WAS MY MOTHER'S--

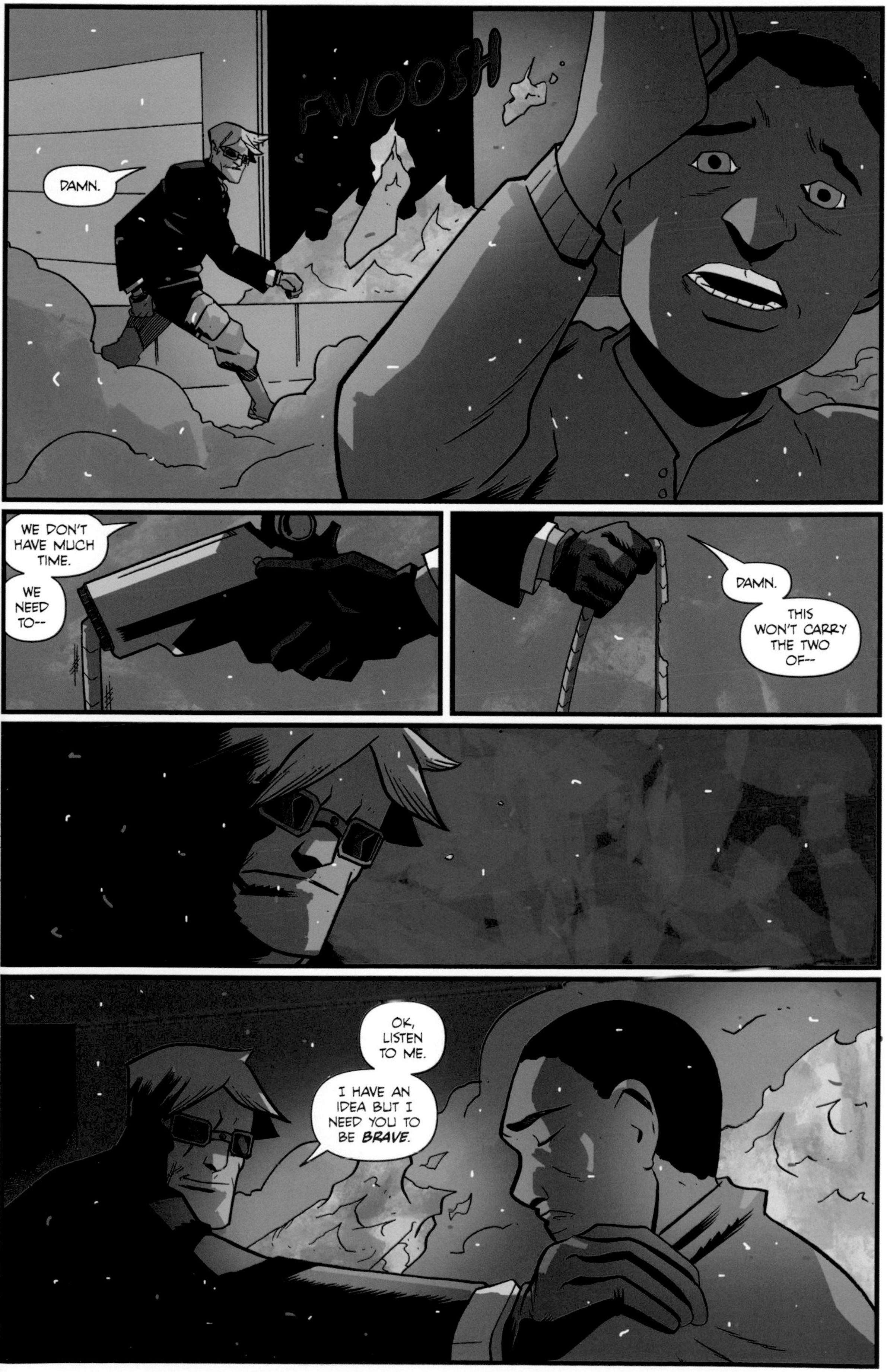
FWOOSH
DAMN.
WE DON'T HAVE MUCH TIME.
WE NEED TO--
DAMN.
THIS WON'T CARRY THE TWO OF--
OK, LISTEN TO ME.
I HAVE AN IDEA BUT I NEED YOU TO BE BRAVE.

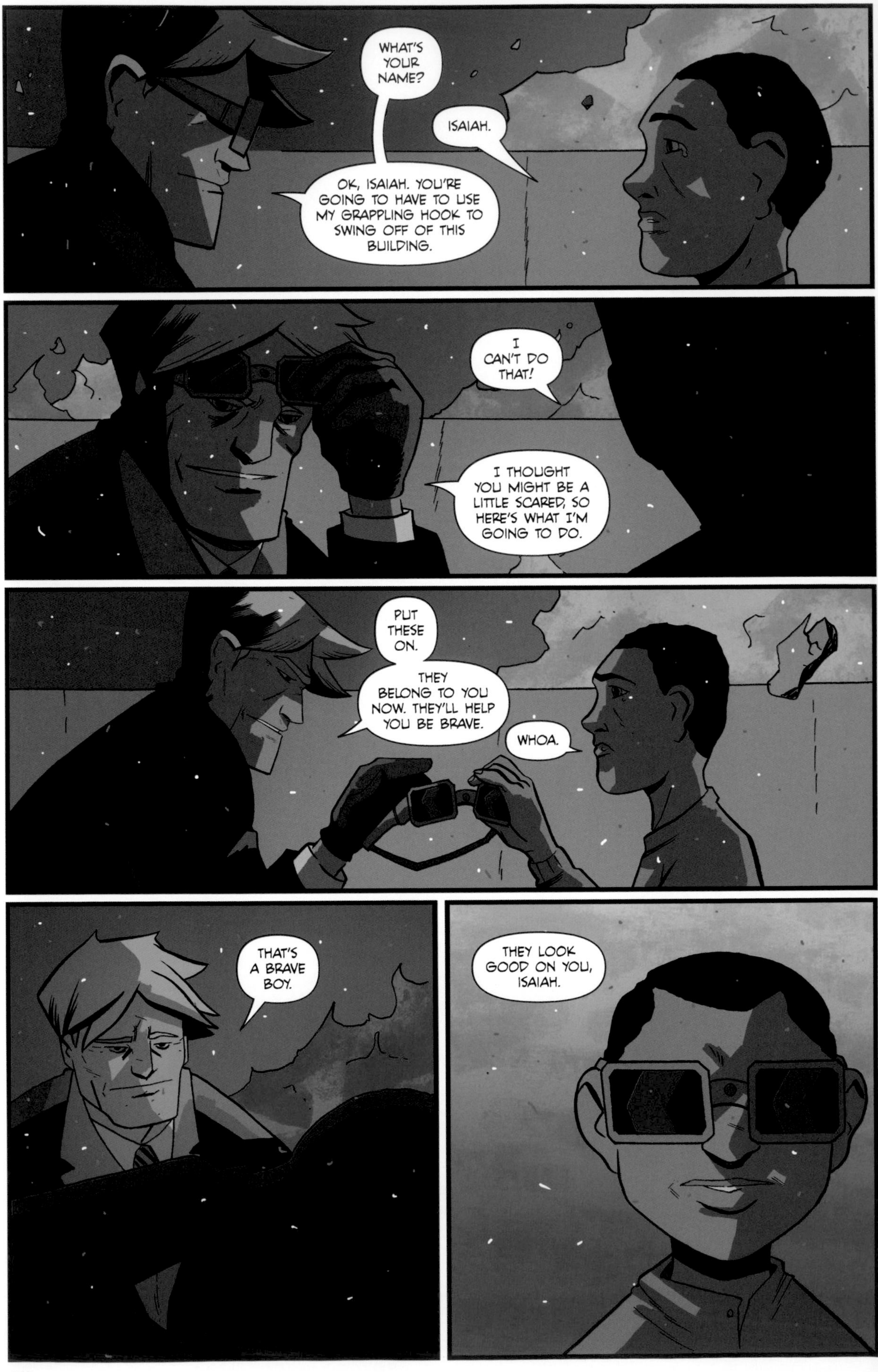
WHAT'S YOUR NAME?
ISAIAH.
OK, ISAIAH. YOU'RE GOING TO HAVE TO USE MY GRAPPLING HOOK TO SWING OFF OF THIS BUILDING.
I CAN'T DO THAT!
I THOUGHT YOU MIGHT BE A LITTLE SCARED, SO HERE'S WHAT I'M GOING TO DO.
PUT THESE ON.
THEY BELONG TO YOU NOW. THEY'LL HELP YOU BE BRAVE.
WHOA.
THAT'S A BRAVE BOY.
THEY LOOK GOOD ON YOU, ISAIAH.

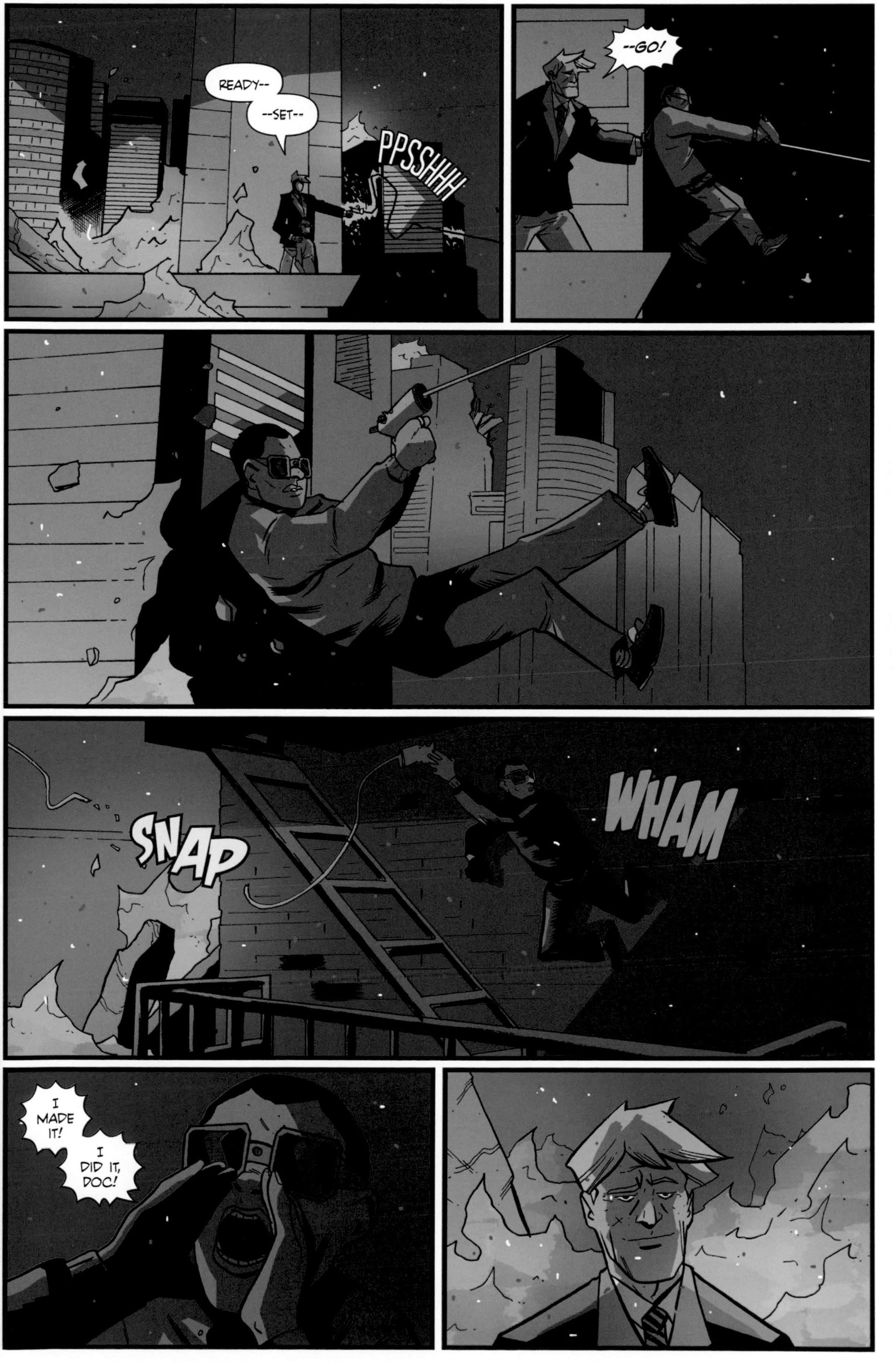
READY--
--SET--
PPSSHHH
--GO!
SNAP
WHAM
I MADE IT!
I DID IT, DOC!

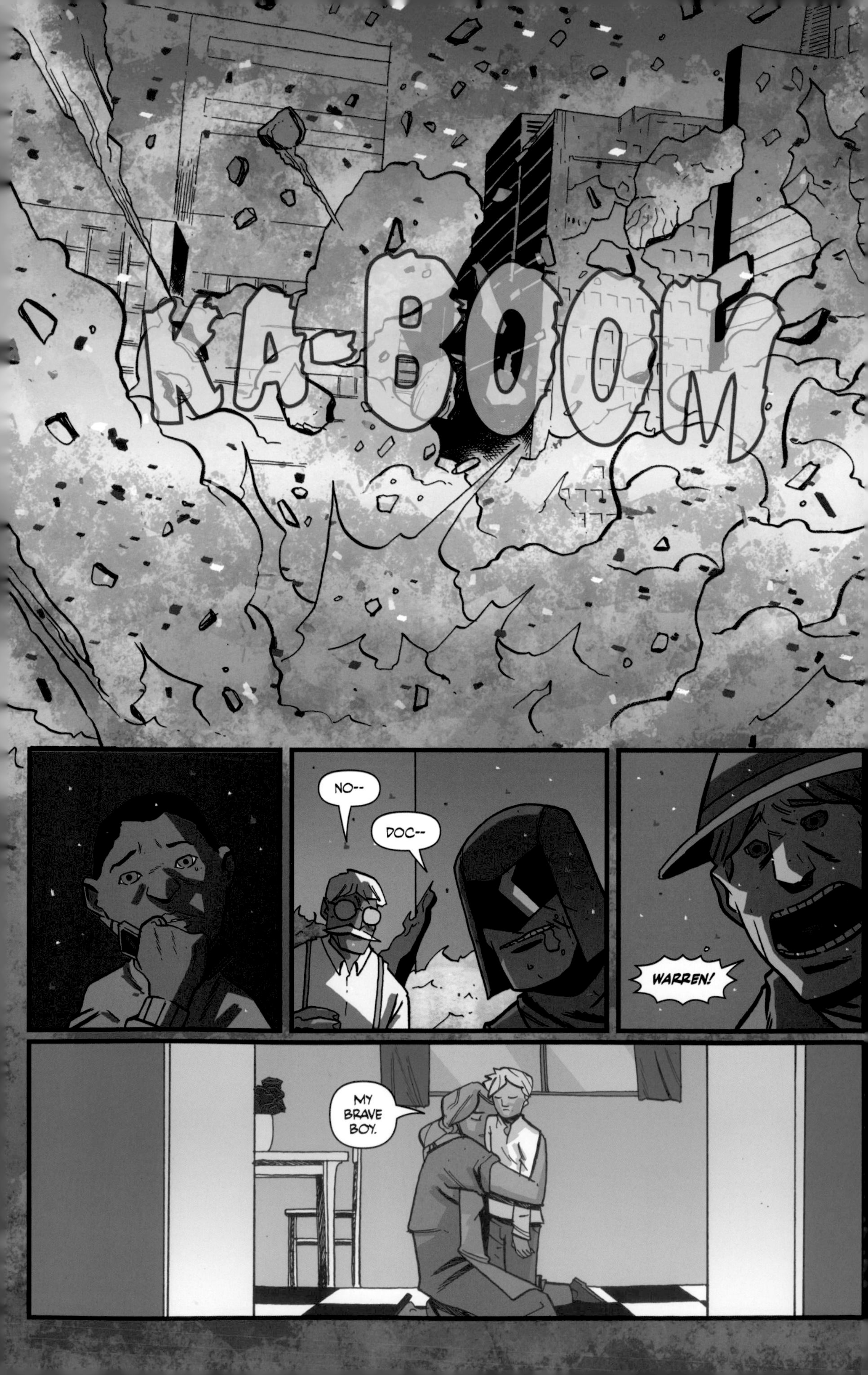
KA-BOOM
NO--
DOC--
WARREN!
MY BRAVE BOY.

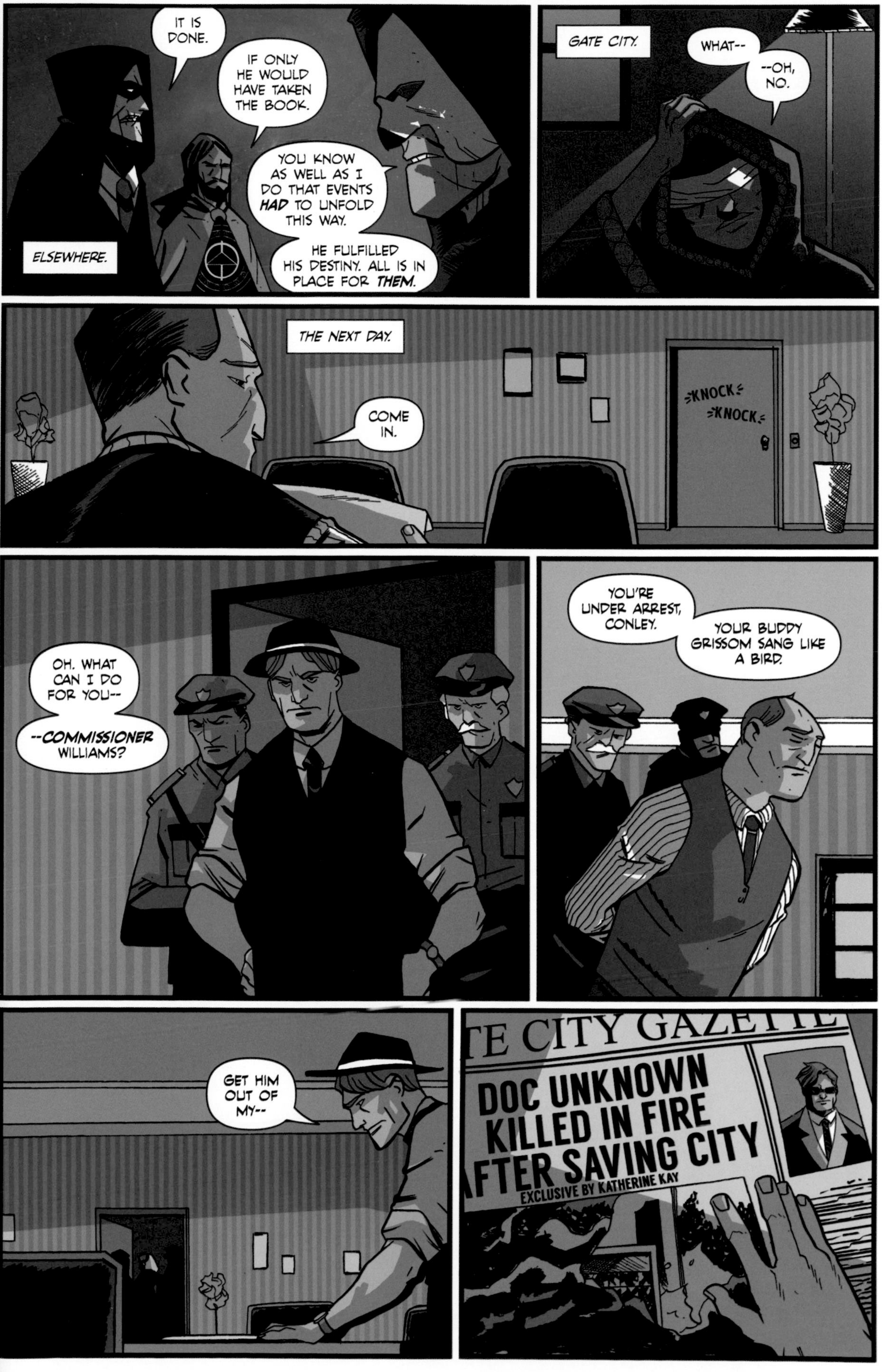
IT IS DONE.
IF ONLY HE WOULD HAVE TAKEN THE BOOK.
YOU KNOW AS WELL AS I DO THAT EVENTS HAD TO UNFOLD THIS WAY.
ELSEWHERE.
HE FULFILLED HIS DESTINY. ALL IS IN PLACE FOR THEM.
GATE CITY.
WHAT--
--OH, NO.
THE NEXT DAY.
COME IN.
KNOCK
KNOCK
OH. WHAT CAN I DO FOR YOU--
--COMMISSIONER WILLIAMS?
YOU'RE UNDER ARREST, CONLEY.
YOUR BUDDY GRISSOM SANG LIKE A BIRD.
GET HIM OUT OF MY--
TE CITY GAZETTE
DOC UNKNOWN KILLED IN FIRE AFTER SAVING CITY
EXCLUSIVE BY KATHERINE KAY

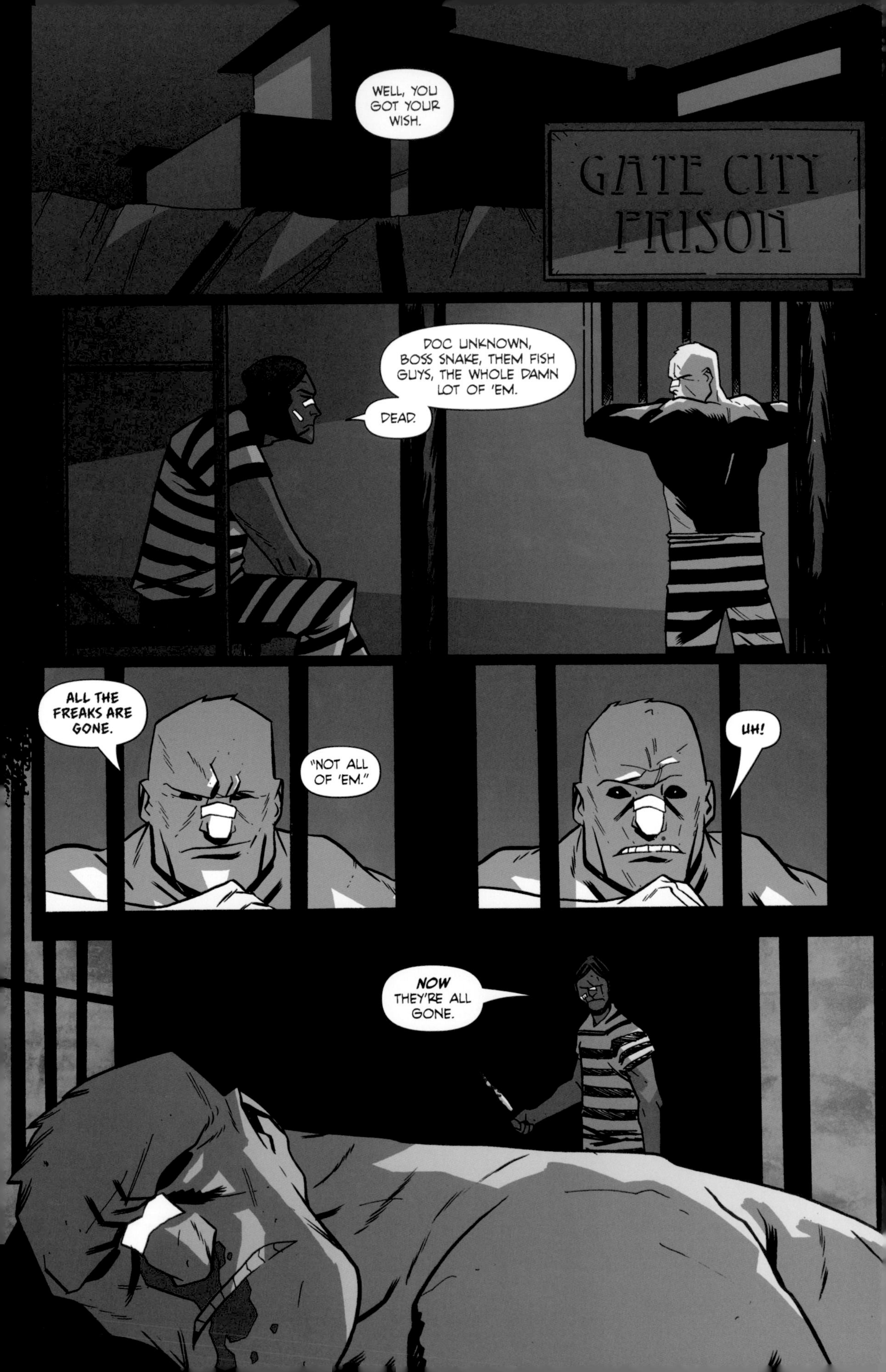
WELL, YOU GOT YOUR WISH.
GATE CITY PRISON
DOC UNKNOWN, BOSS SNAKE, THEM FISH GUYS, THE WHOLE DAMN LOT OF 'EM.
DEAD.
ALL THE FREAKS ARE GONE.
"NOT ALL OF 'EM."
UH!
NOW THEY'RE ALL GONE.

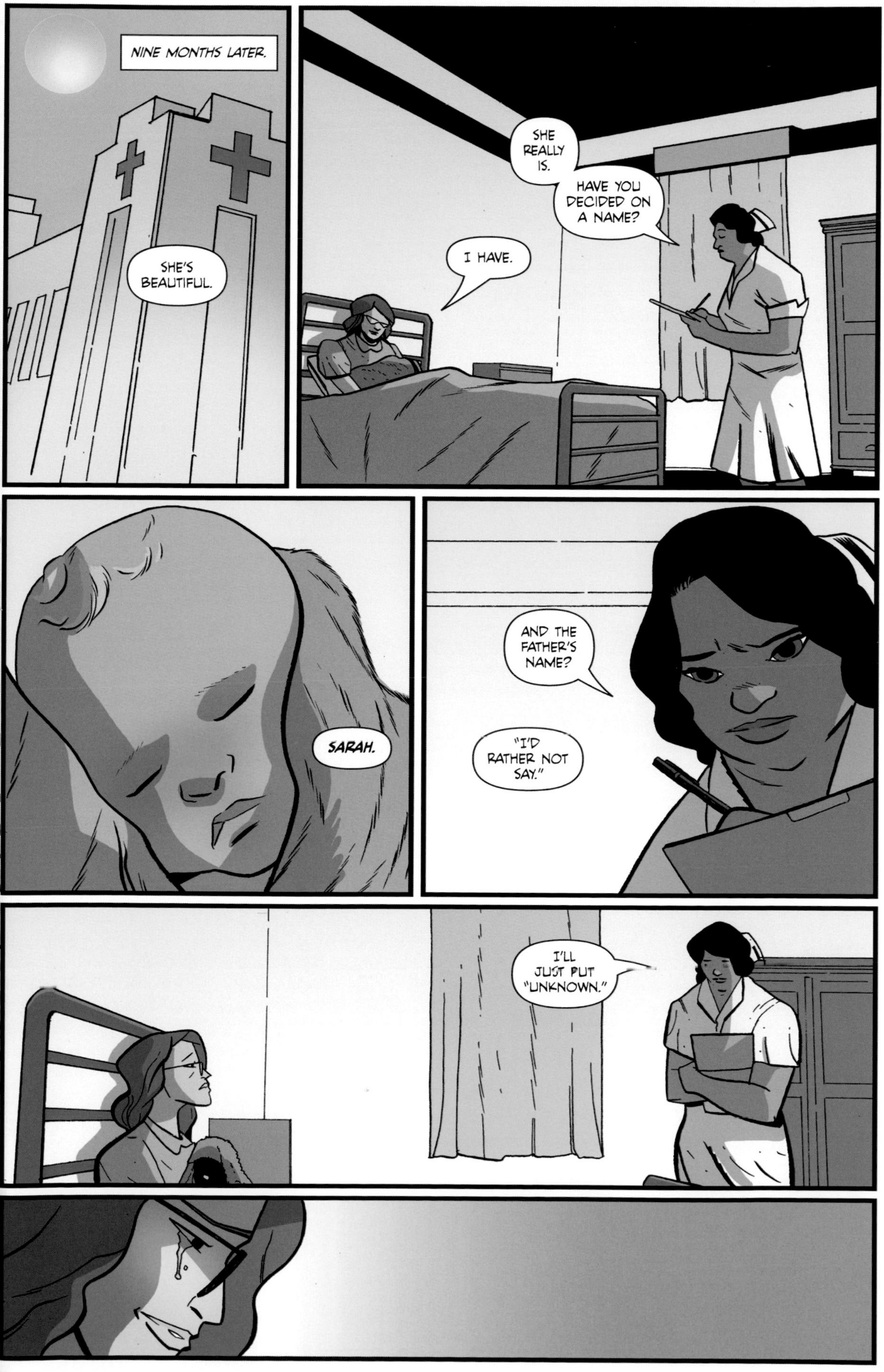
NINE MONTHS LATER.
SHE'S BEAUTIFUL.
SHE REALLY IS.
HAVE YOU DECIDED ON A NAME?
I HAVE.
SARAH.
AND THE FATHER'S NAME?
"I'D RATHER NOT SAY."
I'LL JUST PUT "UNKNOWN."

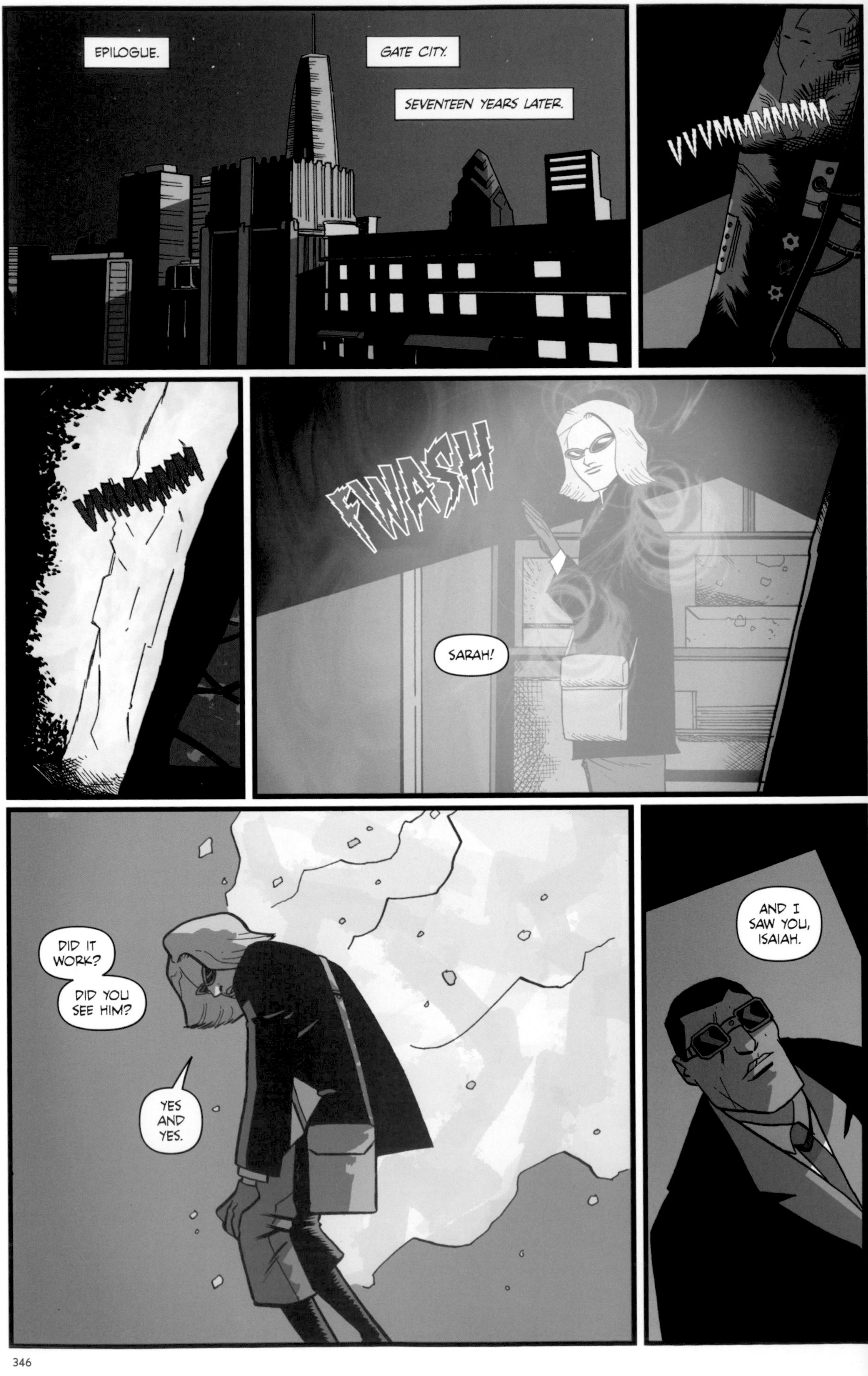
EPILOGUE.
GATE CITY.
SEVENTEEN YEARS LATER.
VVVMMMMMM
VVMMMMM
FWASH
SARAH!
DID IT WORK?
DID YOU SEE HIM?
YES AND YES.
AND I SAW YOU, ISAIAH.

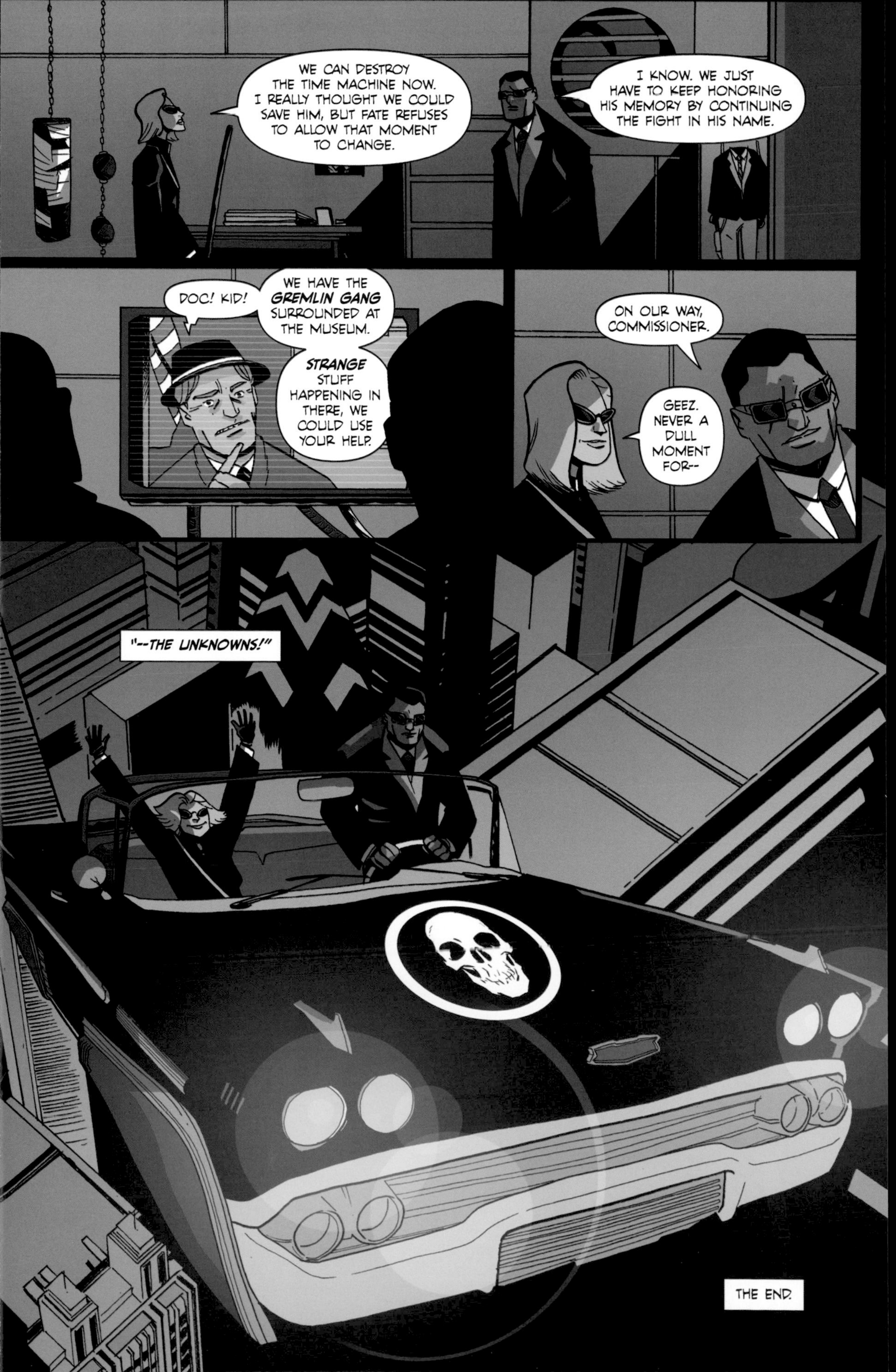
WE CAN DESTROY THE TIME MACHINE NOW. I REALLY THOUGHT WE COULD SAVE HIM, BUT FATE REFUSES TO ALLOW THAT MOMENT TO CHANGE.
I KNOW. WE JUST HAVE TO KEEP HONORING HIS MEMORY BY CONTINUING THE FIGHT IN HIS NAME.
DOC! KID!
WE HAVE THE ***GREMLIN GANG*** SURROUNDED AT THE MUSEUM.
STRANGE STUFF HAPPENING IN THERE, WE COULD USE YOUR HELP.
ON OUR WAY, COMMISSIONER.
GEEZ. NEVER A DULL MOMENT FOR--
"--*THE UNKNOWNS!*"
THE END.

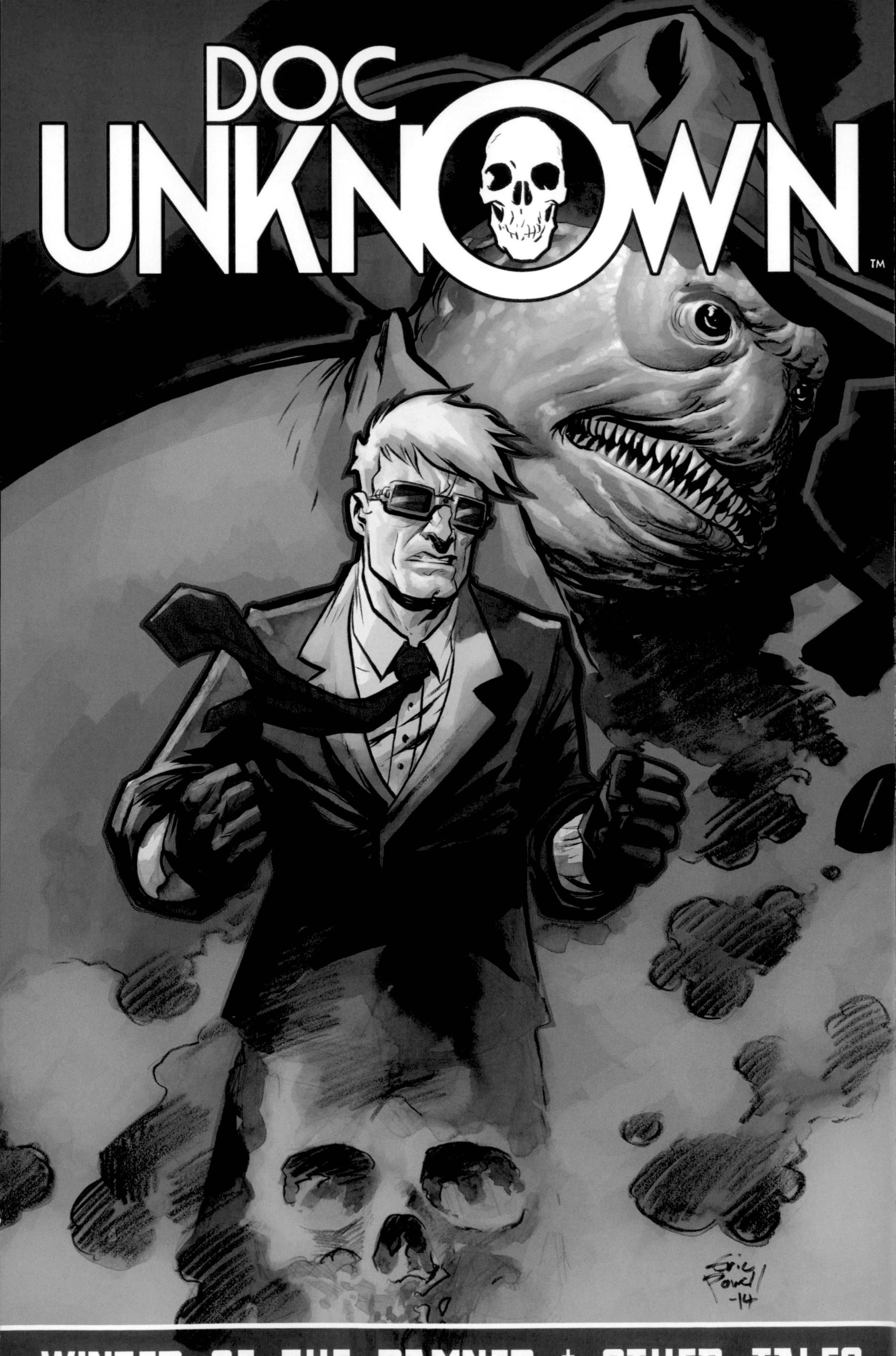
DOC
UNKNOWN
TM
Eric Powell -14

WINTER OF THE DAMNED & OTHER TALES

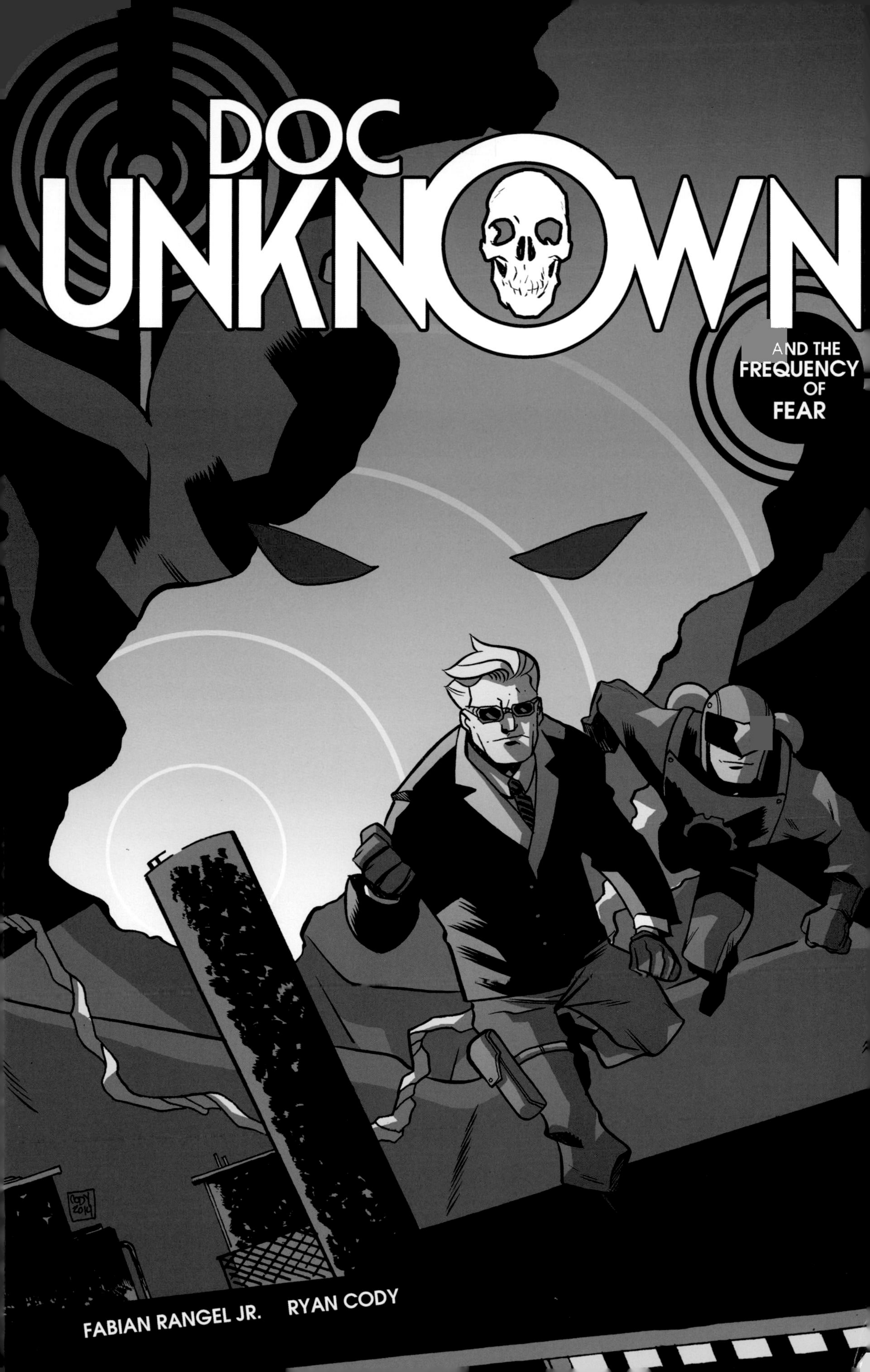
DOC UNKNOWN
AND THE FREQUENCY OF FEAR
CODY 2014
FABIAN RANGEL JR.
RYAN CODY

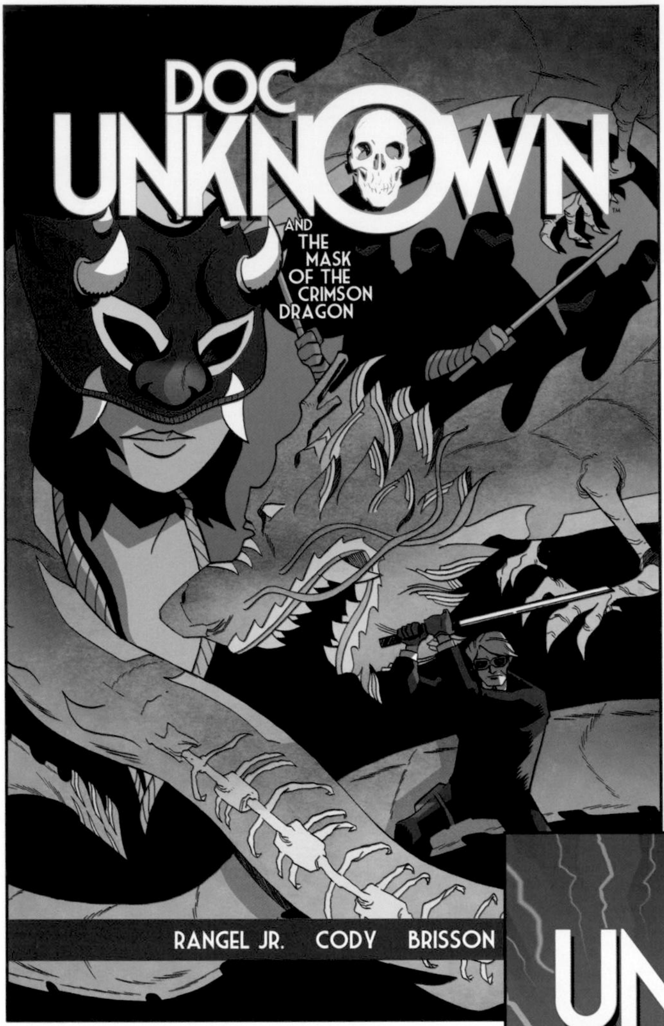
DOC
UNKNOWN
AND THE MASK OF THE CRIMSON DRAGON
RANGEL JR.
CODY
BRISSON

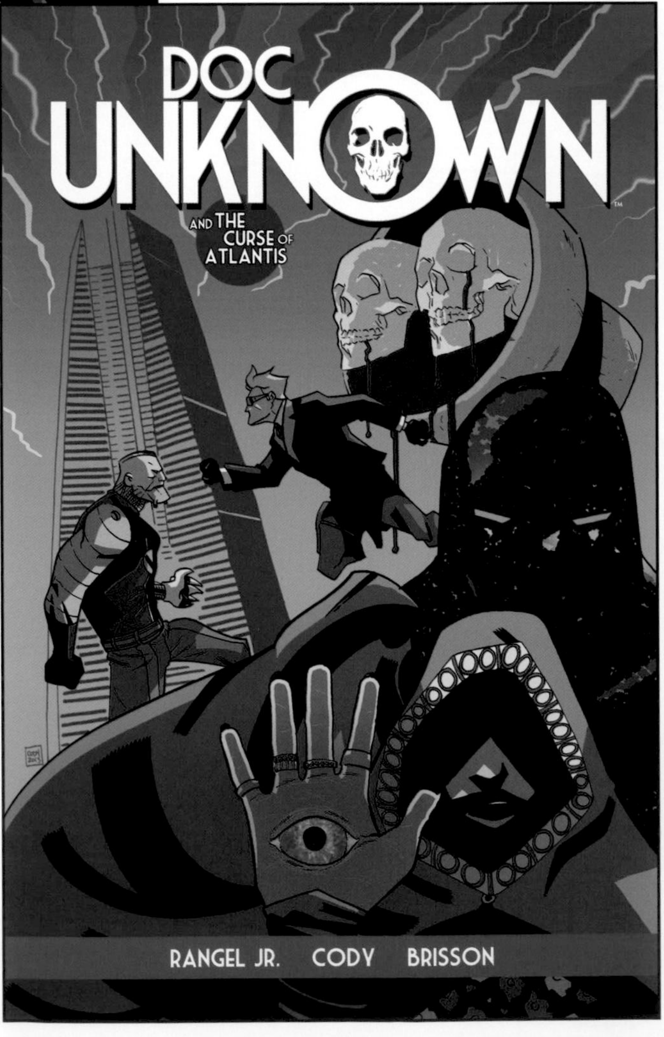
DOC
UNKNOWN
AND THE CURSE OF ATLANTIS
RANGEL JR.
CODY
BRISSON

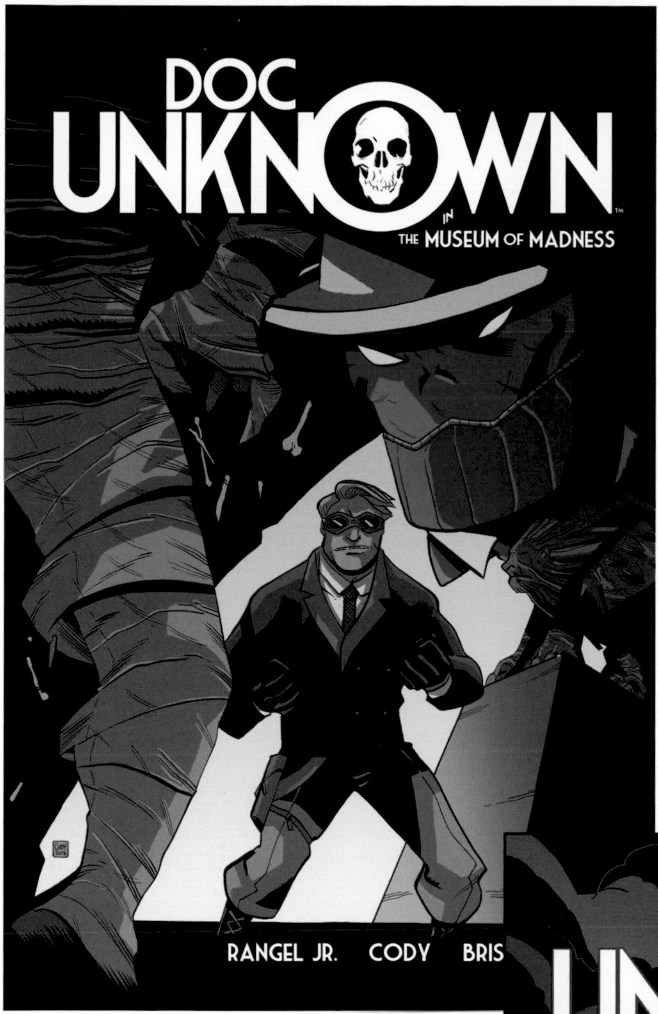
DOC
UNKNOWN™
IN
THE MUSEUM OF MADNESS
RANGEL JR.
CODY
BRIS

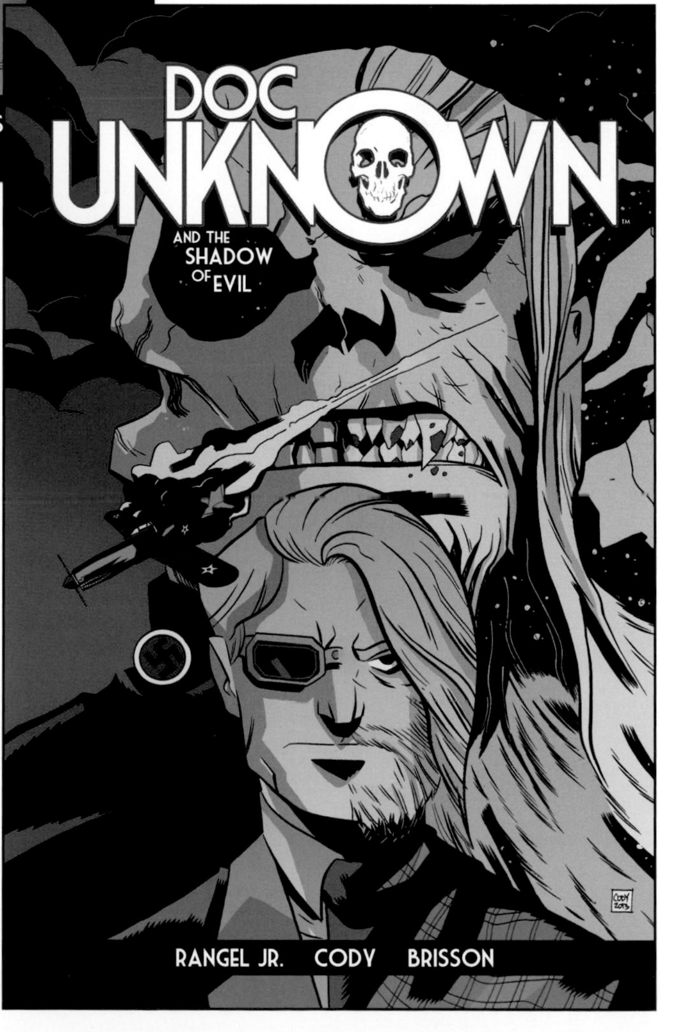
DOC
UNKNOWN™
AND THE
SHADOW
OF EVIL
CODY 2013
RANGEL JR.
CODY
BRISSON

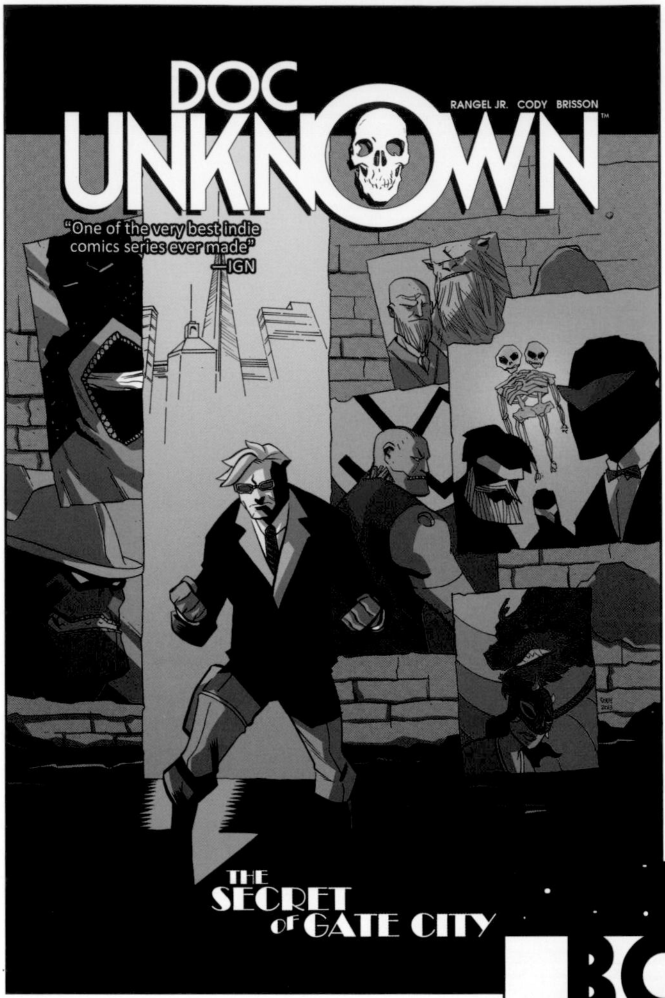
DOC UNKNOWN
RANGEL JR. CODY BRISSON
"One of the very best indie comics series ever made" —IGN
THE SECRET of GATE CITY

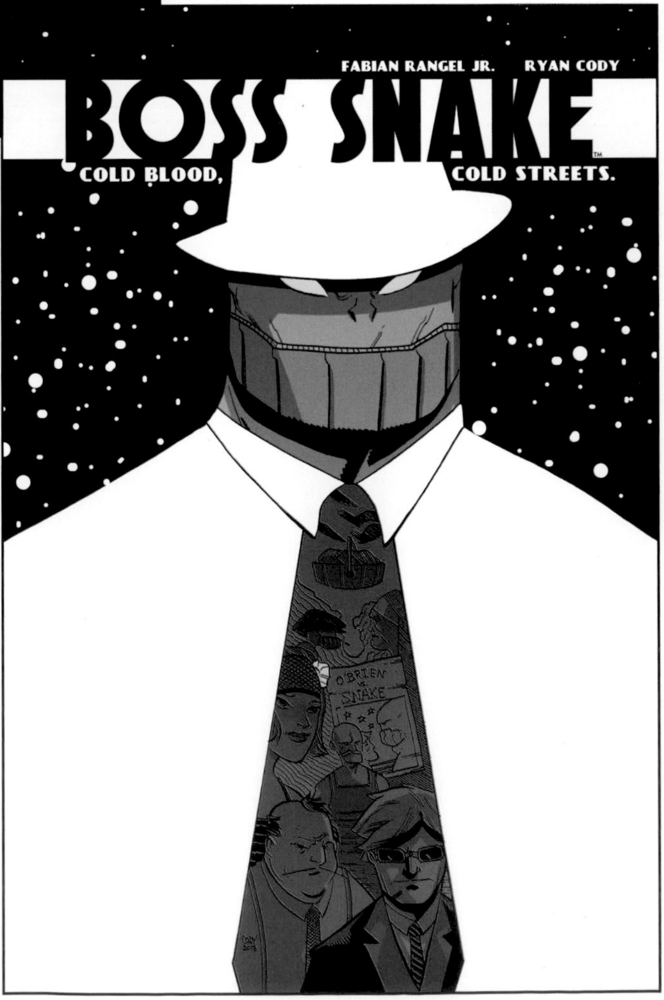
FABIAN RANGEL JR. RYAN CODY
BOSS SNAKE
COLD BLOOD, COLD STREETS.

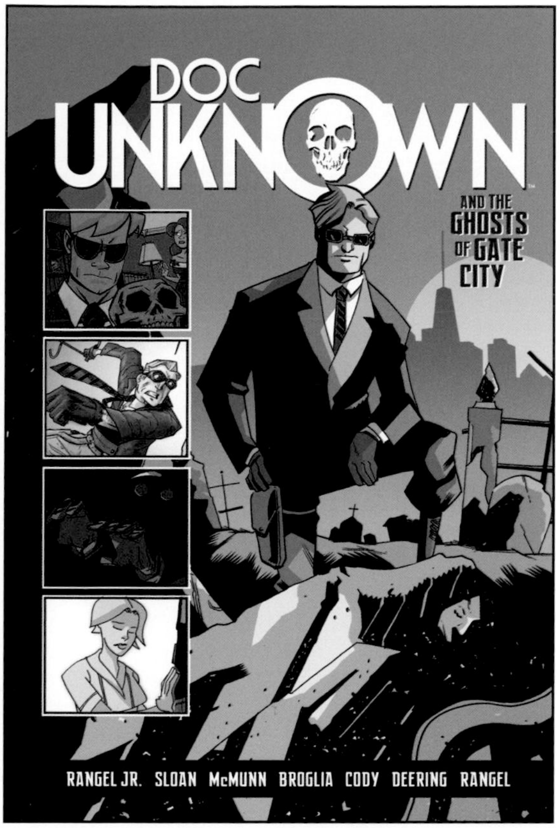
DOC
UNKNOWN
AND THE
GHOSTS
OF GATE
CITY
RANGEL JR. SLOAN McMUNN BROGLIA CODY DEERING RANGEL

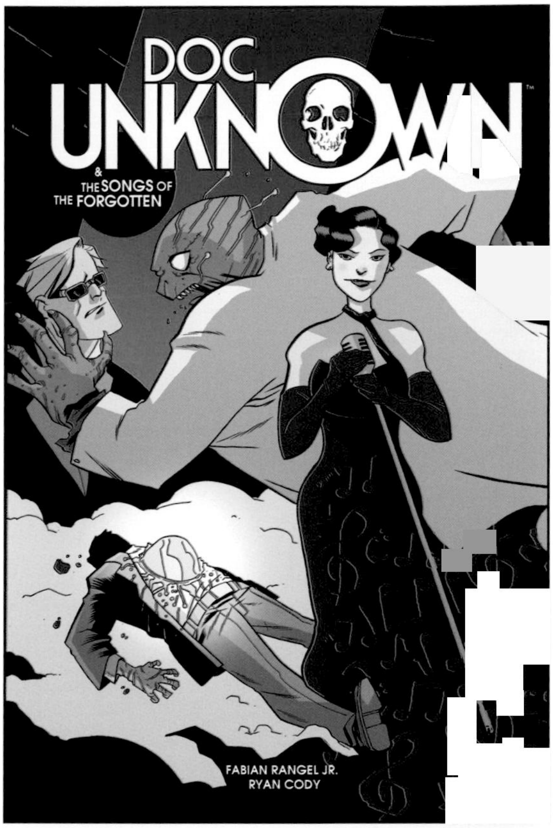
DOC
UNKNOWN
& THE SONGS OF
THE FORGOTTEN
FABIAN RANGEL JR.
RYAN CODY

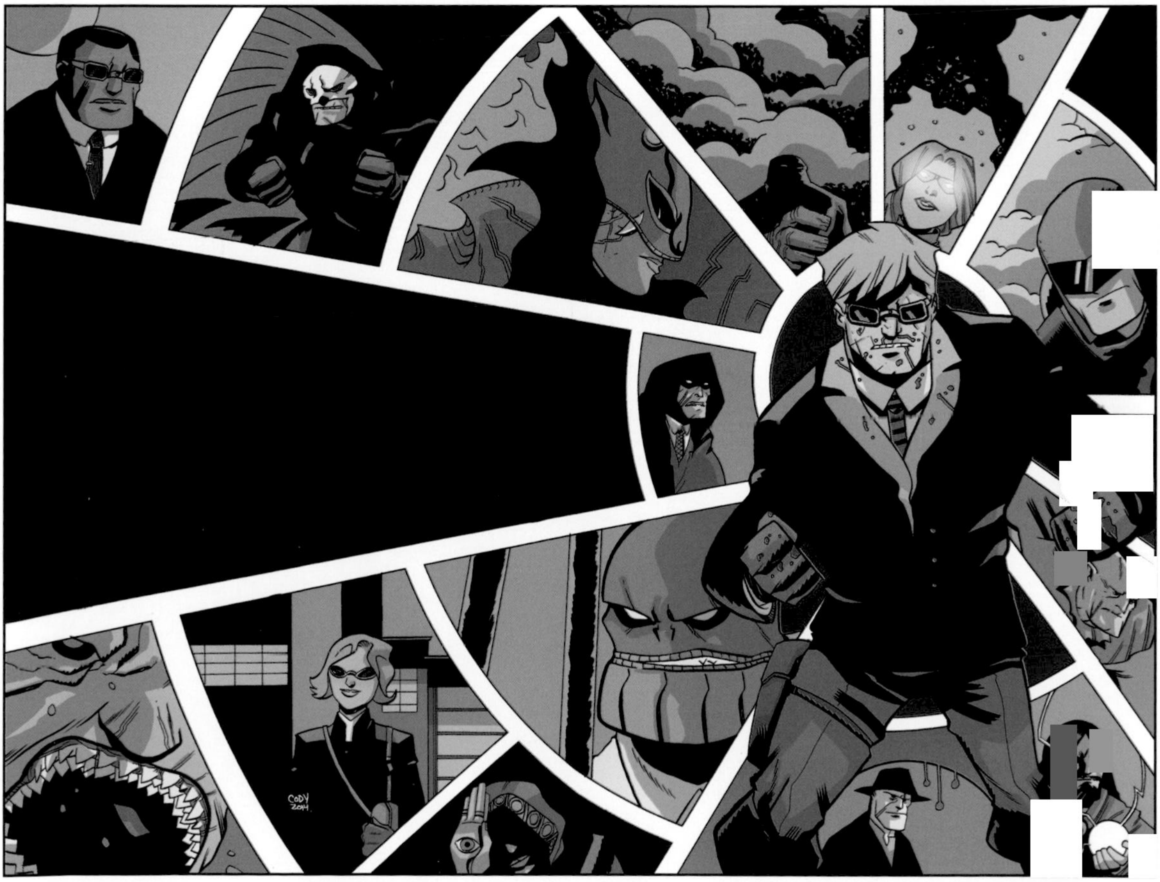
CODY
2014

ARTYOM TRAKHANOV

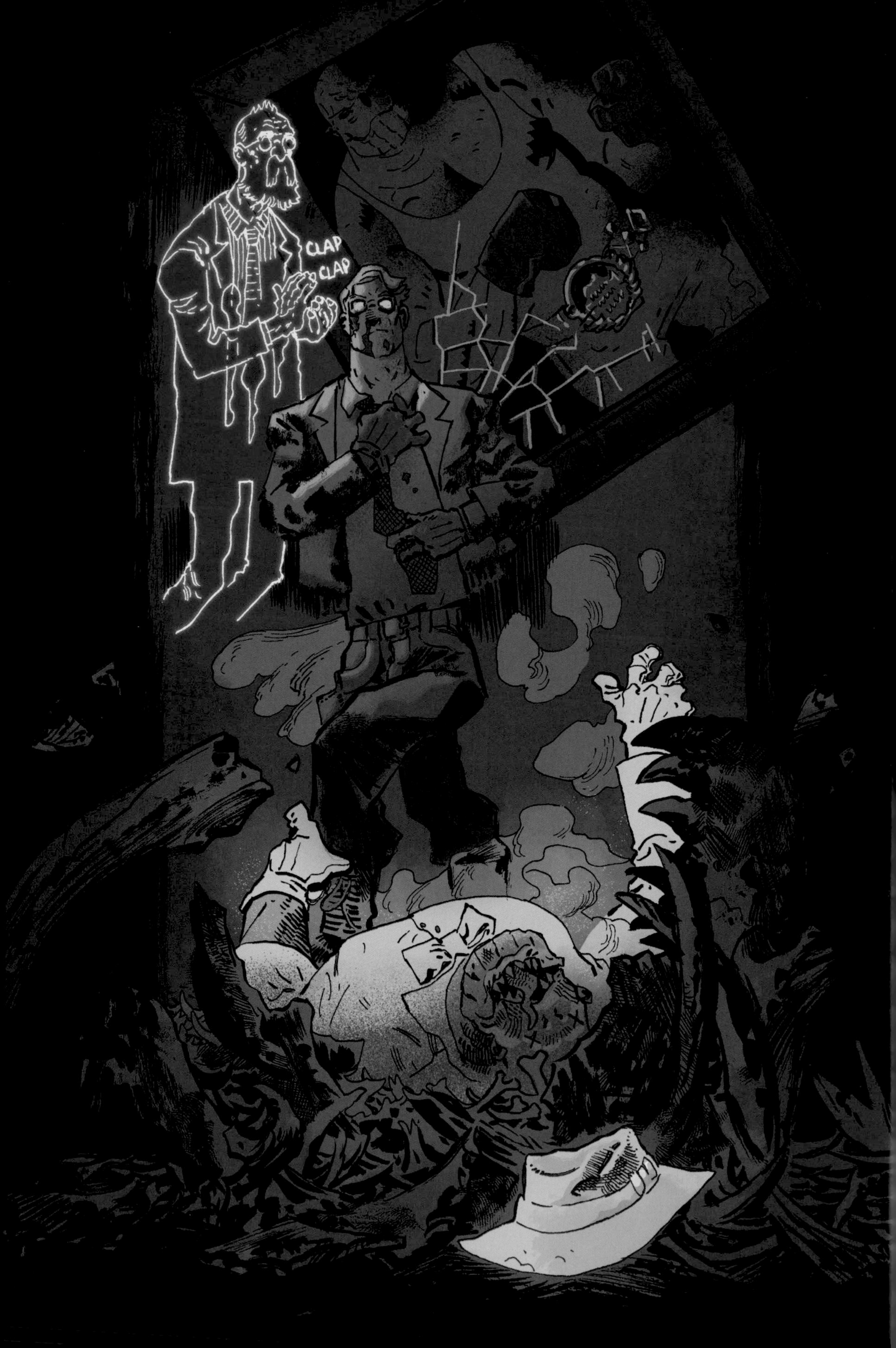
CLAP
CLAP

BELIEVE IN COMICS

JAMES HARREN

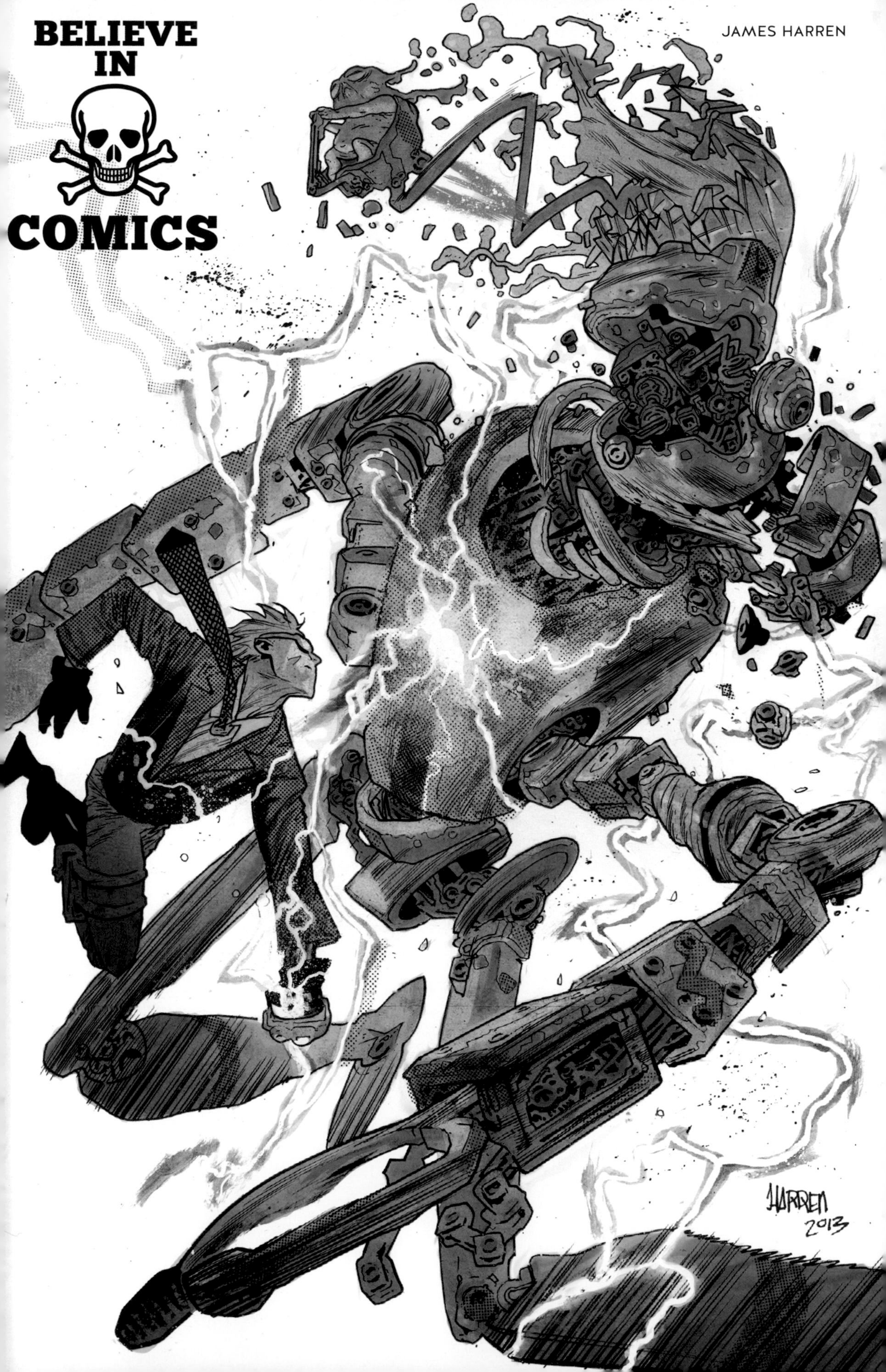
HARREN
2013

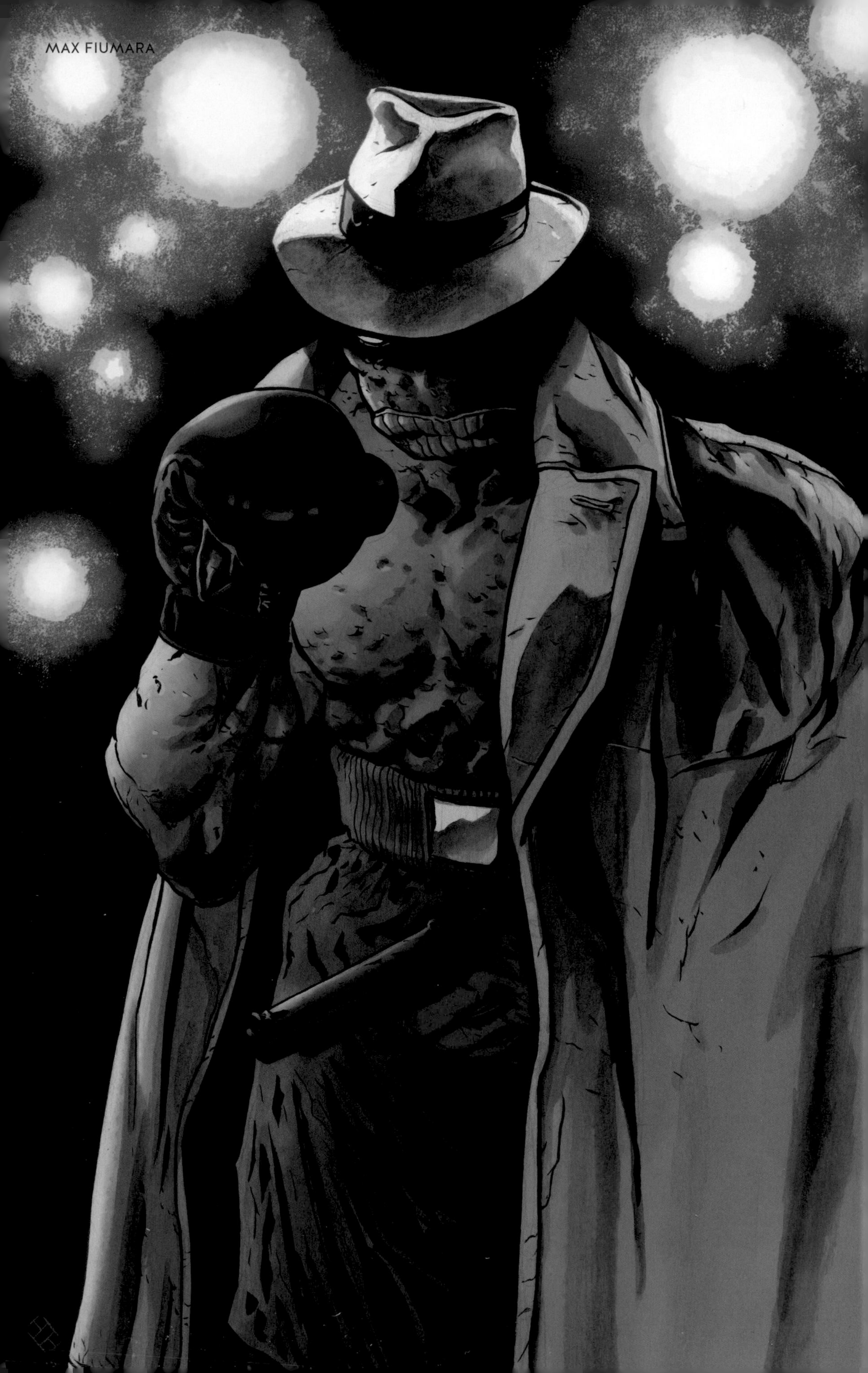

MAX FIUMARA

KELLY WILLIAMS

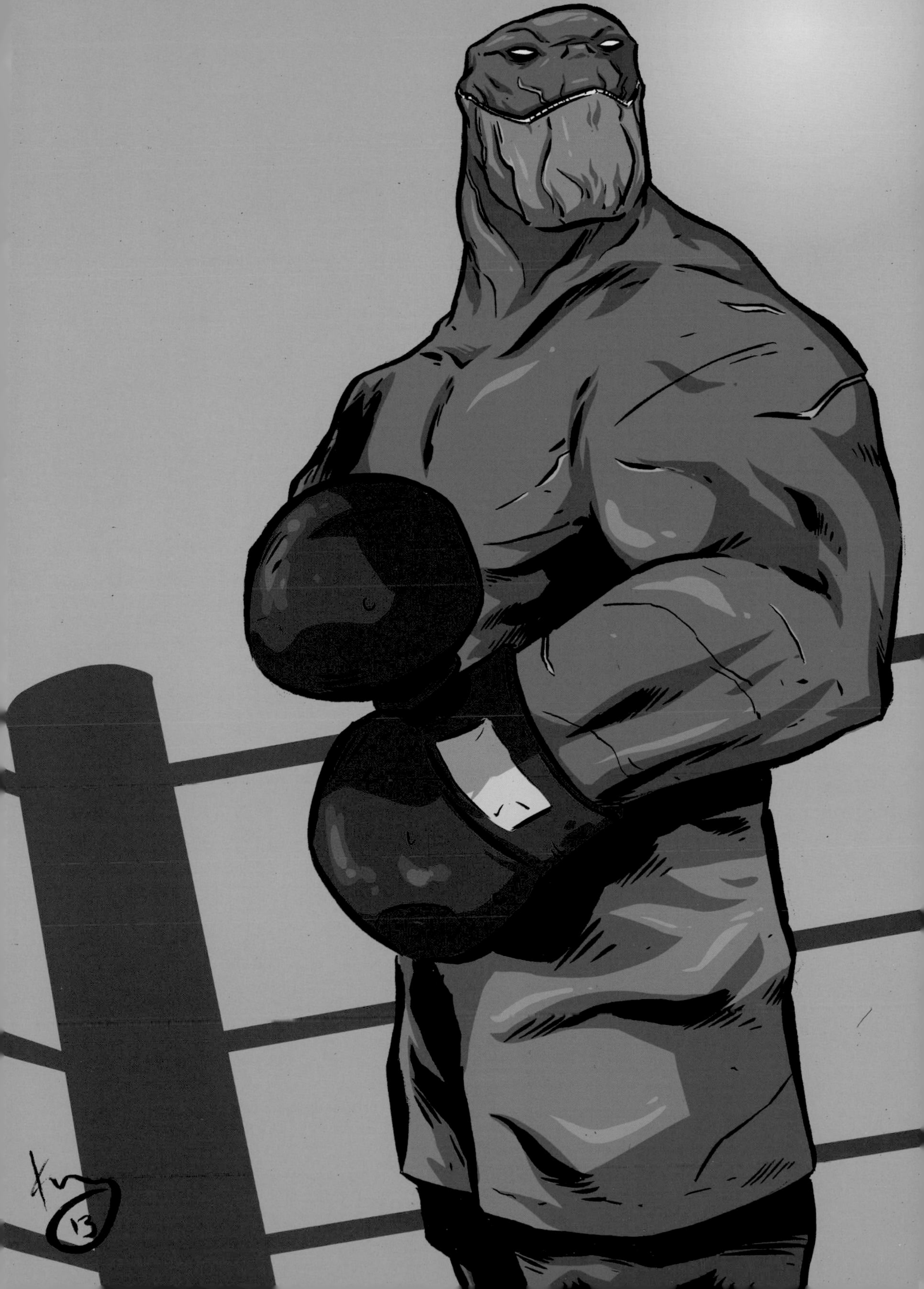

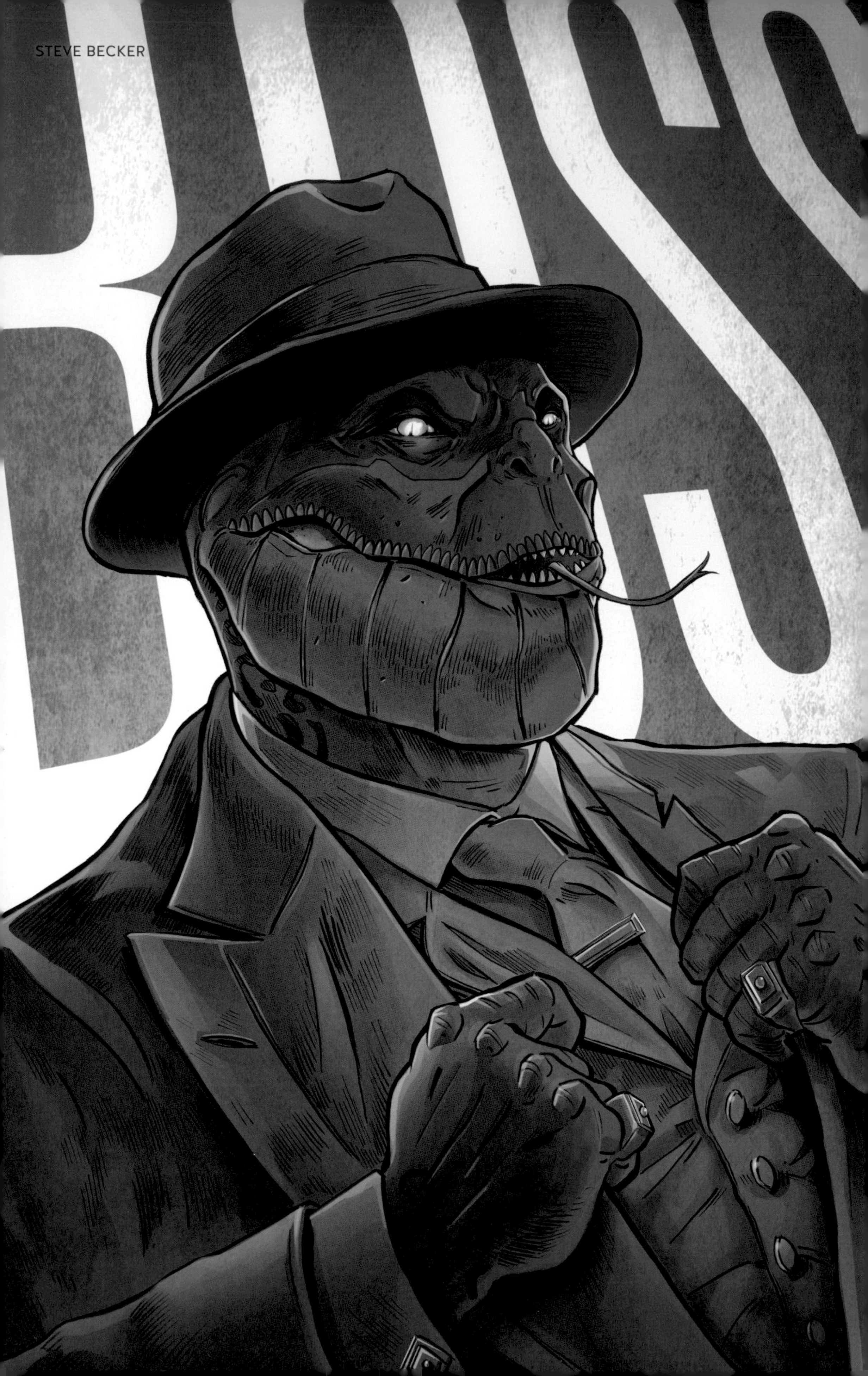
STEVE BECKER

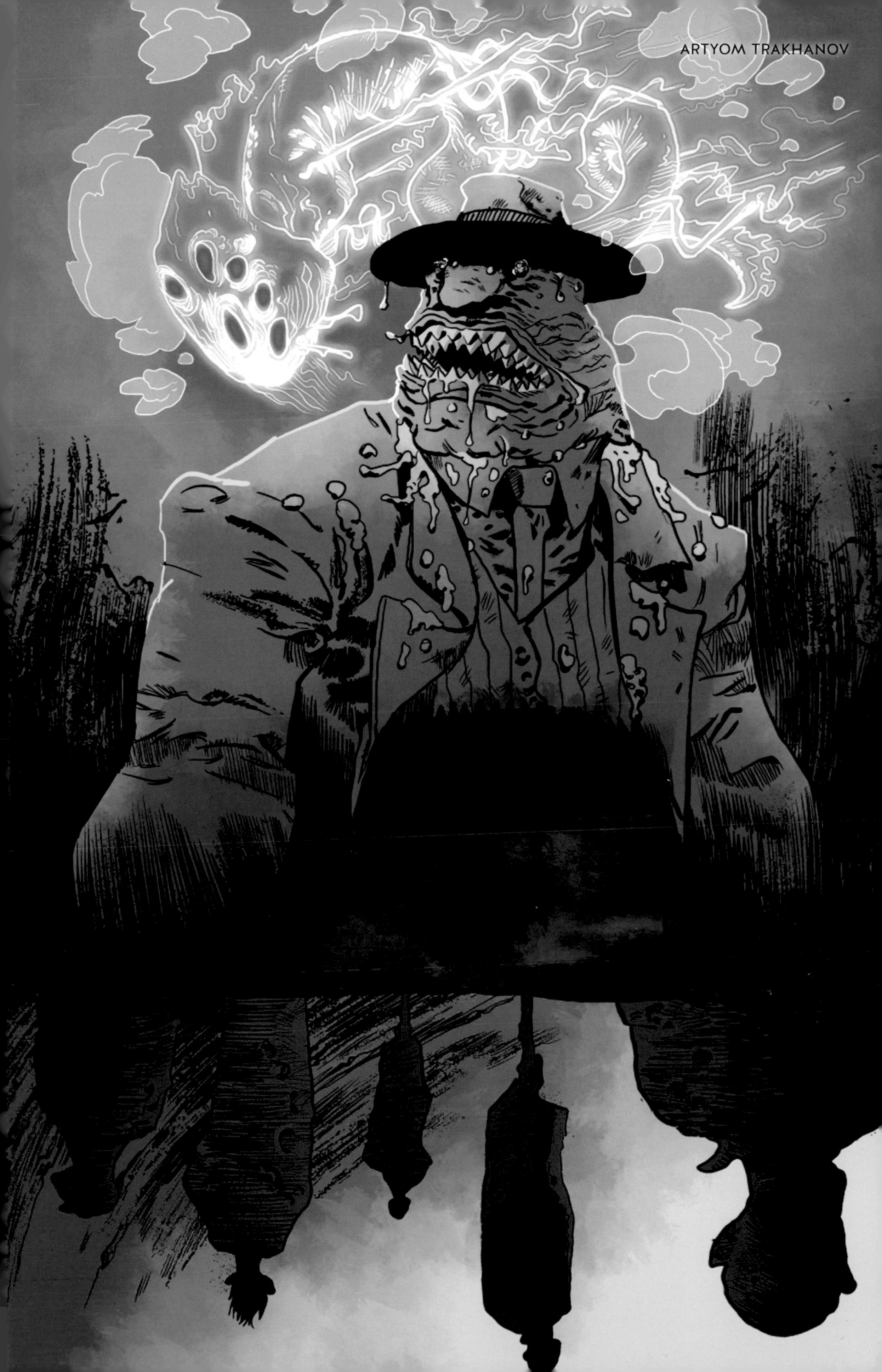
ARTYOM TRAKHANOV

SCOTT GODLEWSKI

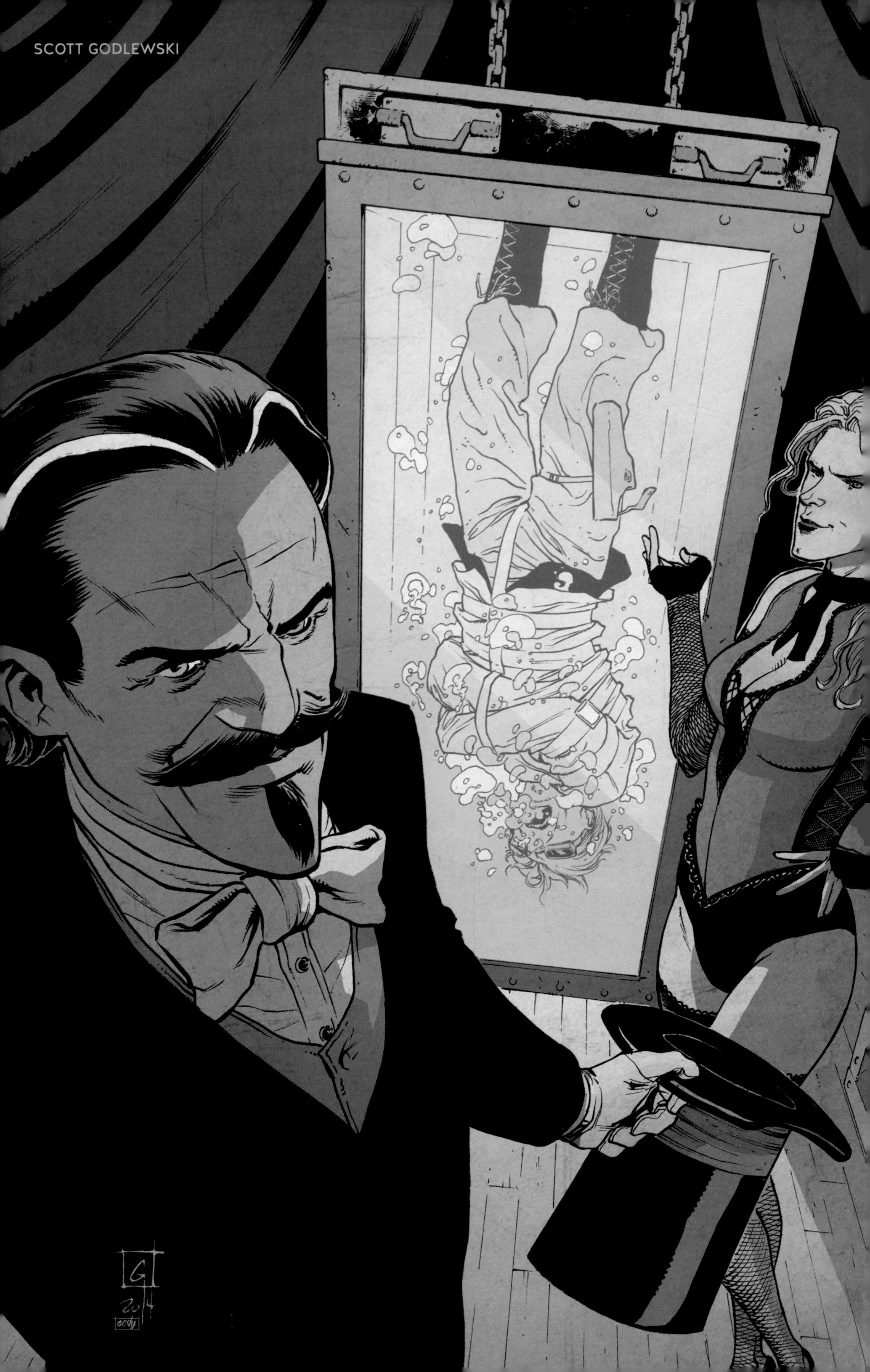
G
2014

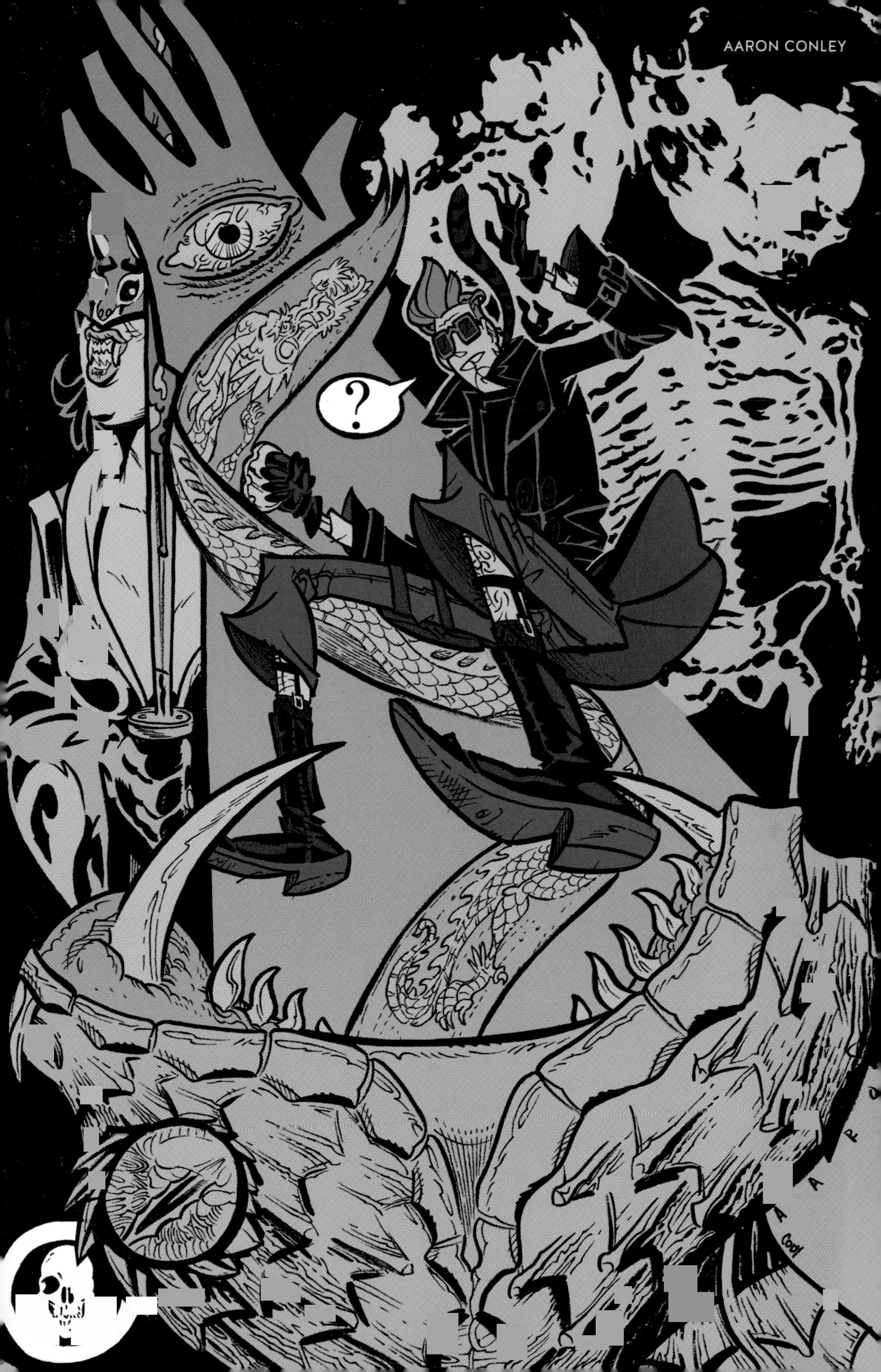
AARON CONLEY
?

JOHN BROGLIA

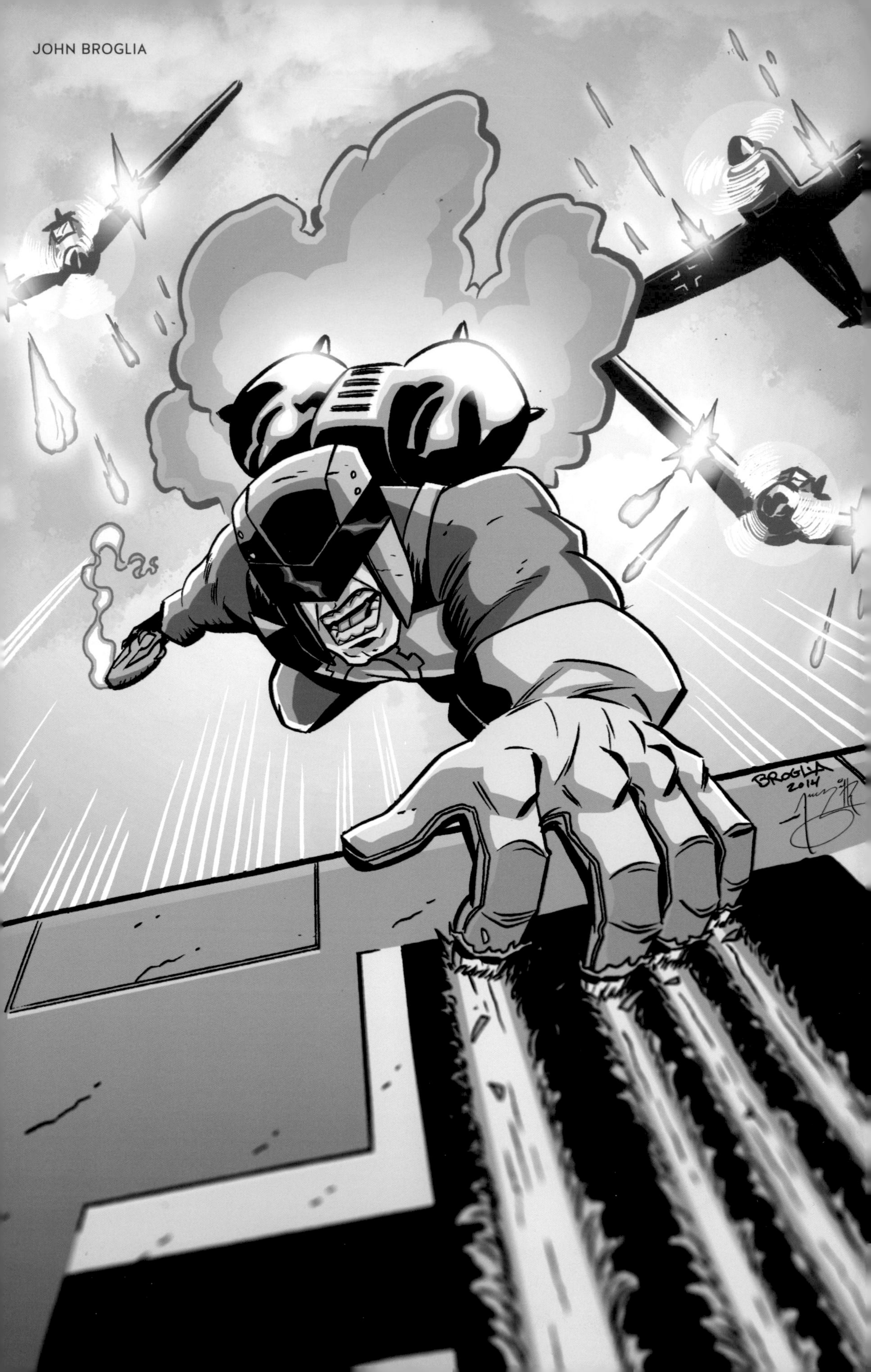
BROGLIA
2014

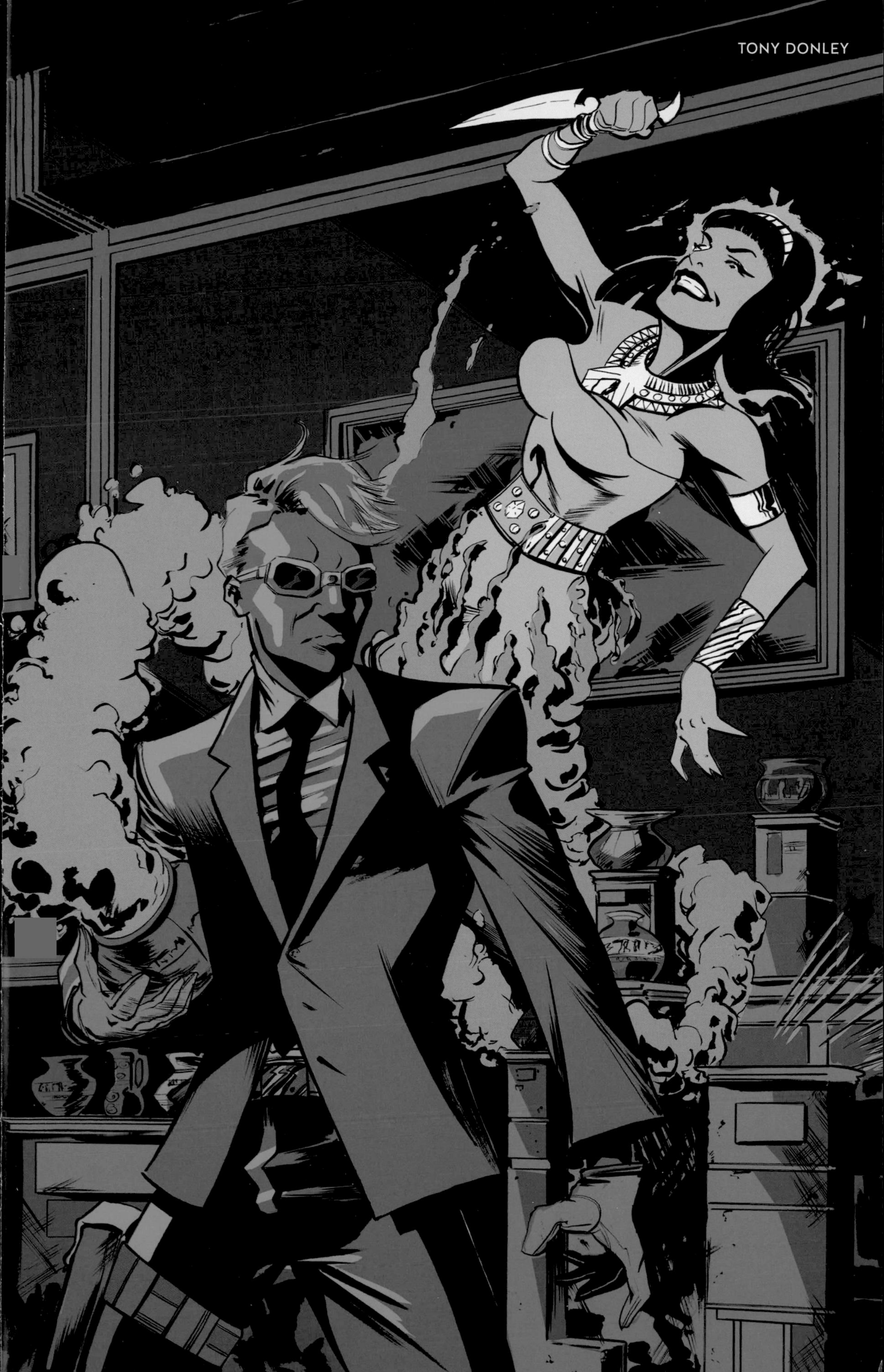
TONY DONLEY

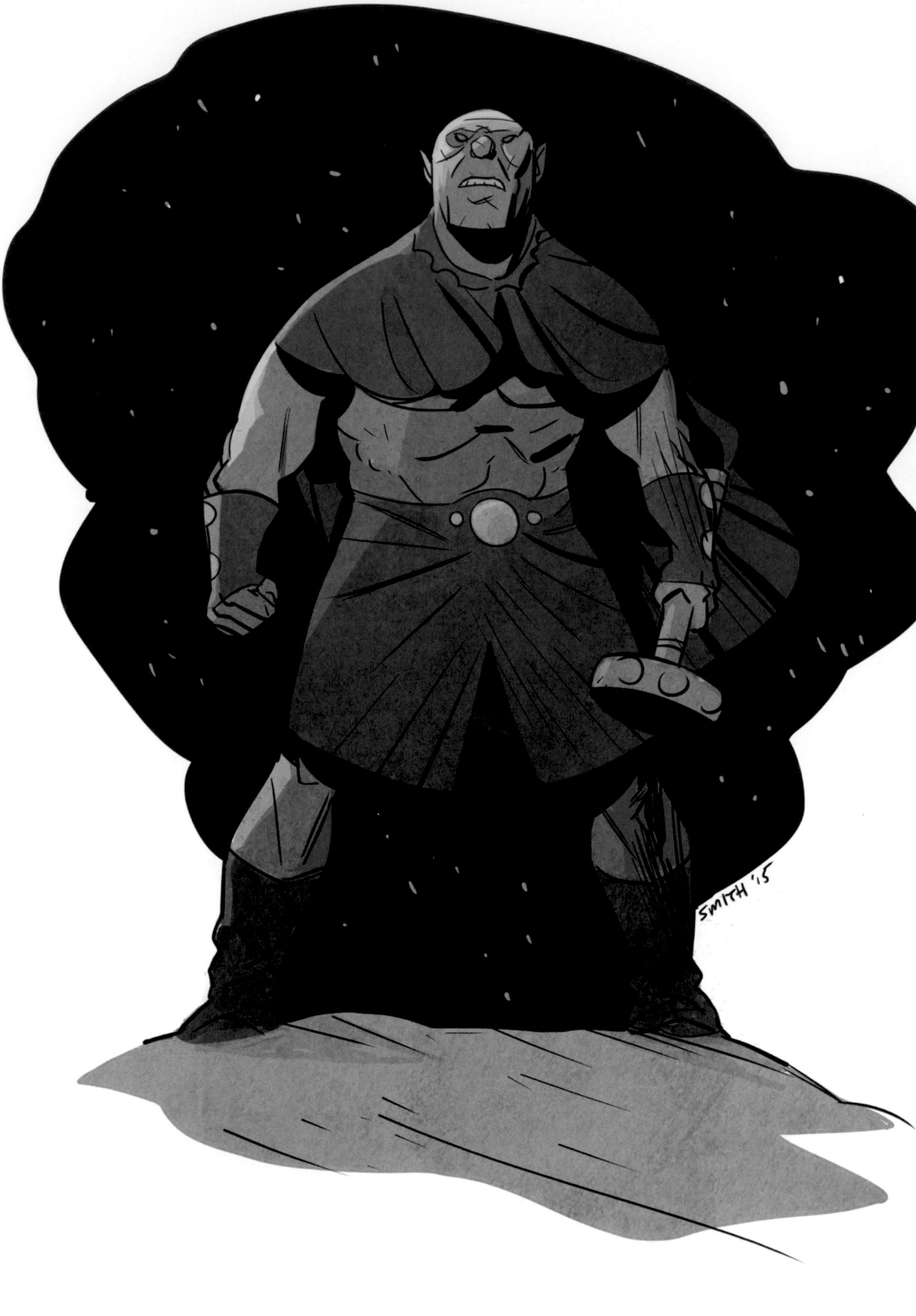
SMITH '15

LOGAN FAERBER

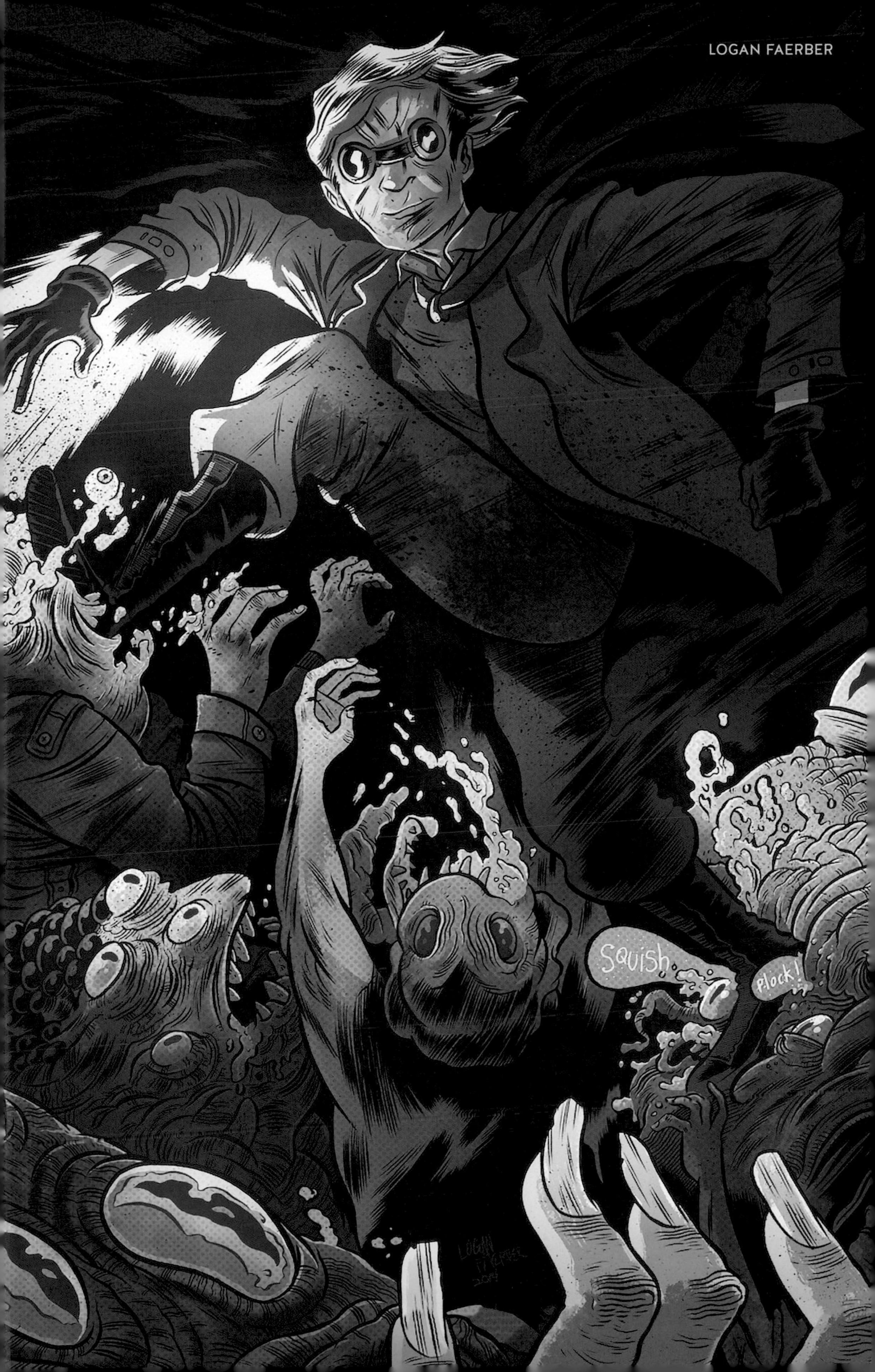
SQUISH
PLOCK!

MIKE MIGNOLA AND DAVE STEWART

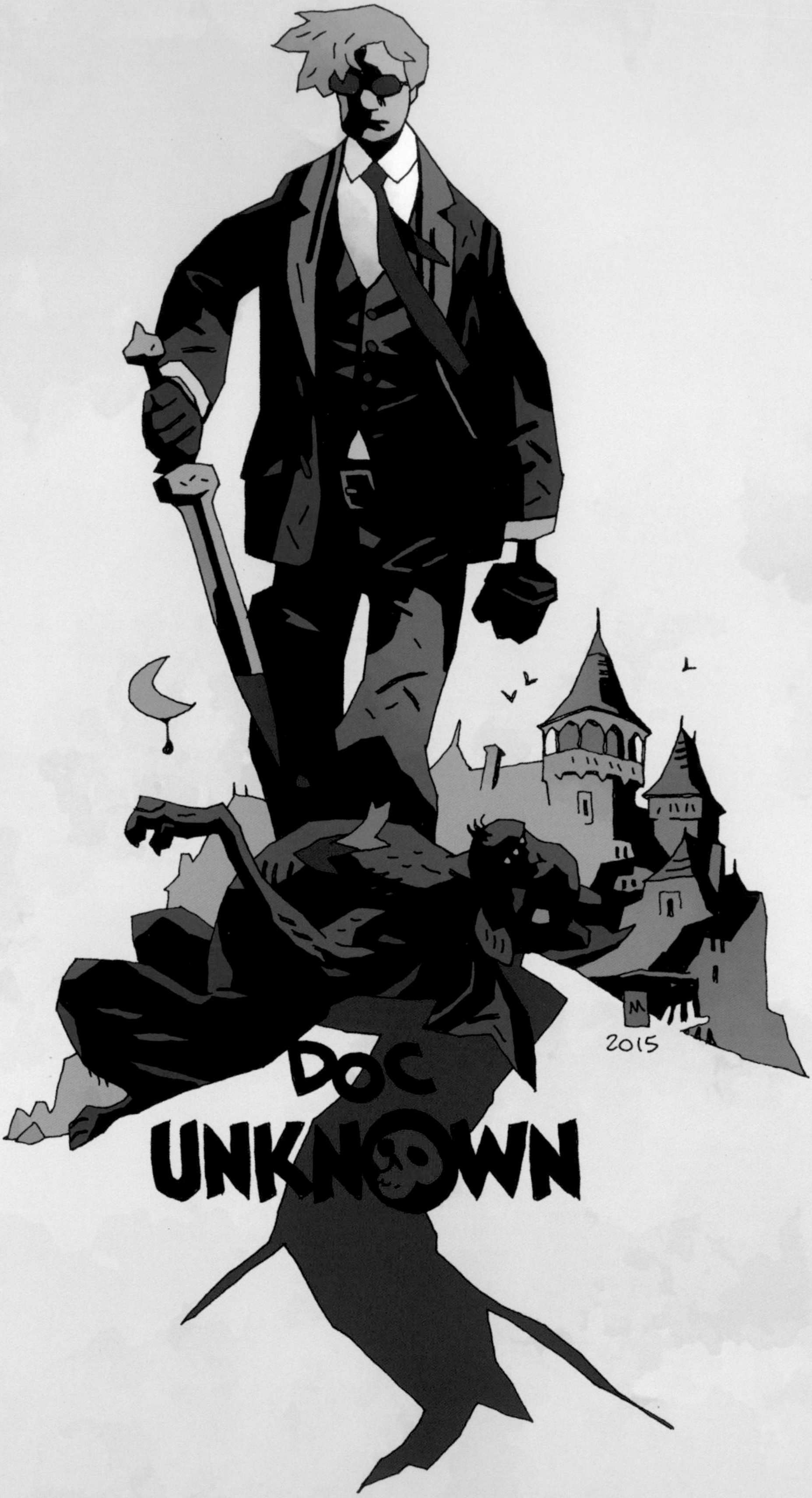
DOC
UNKNOWN
2015

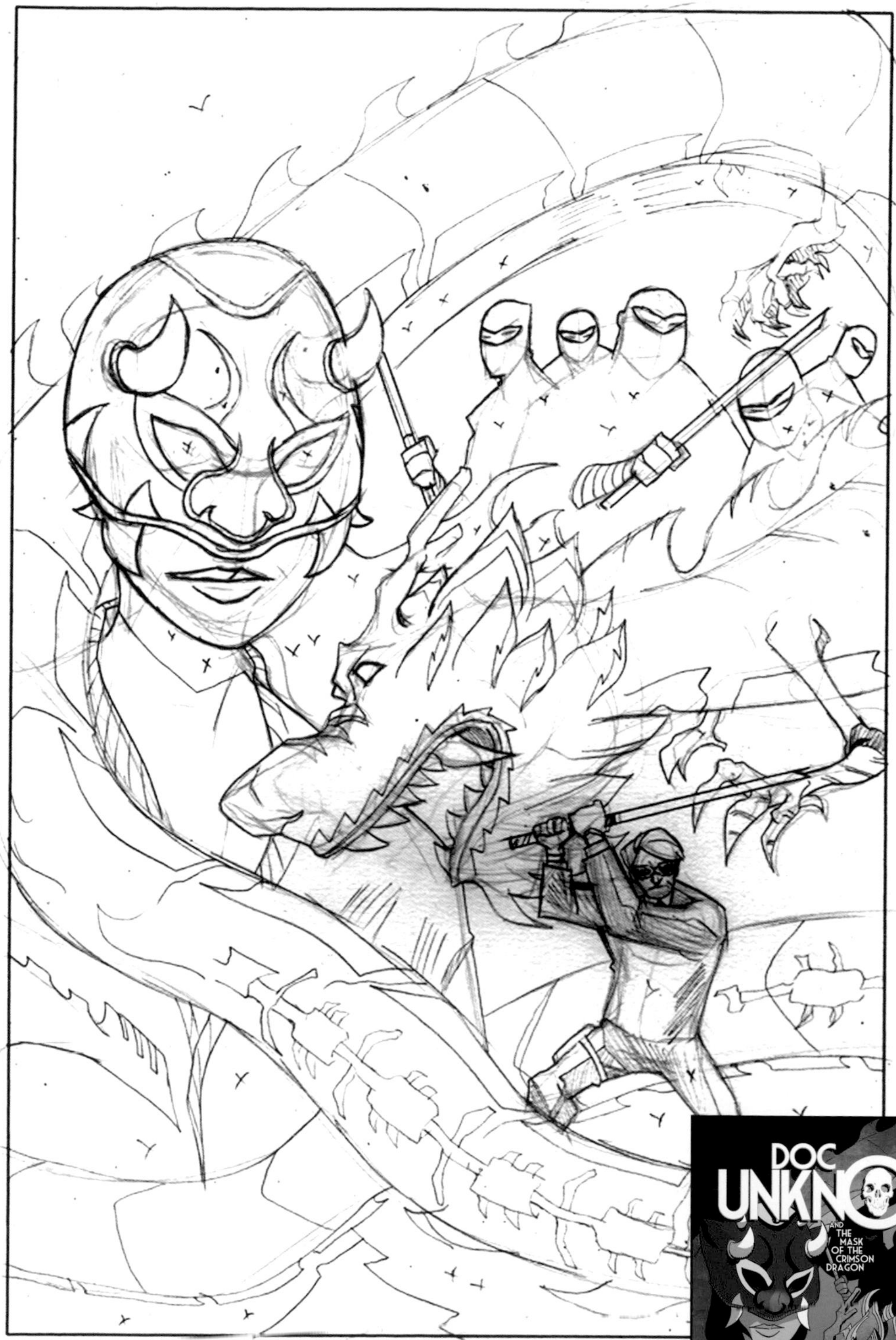

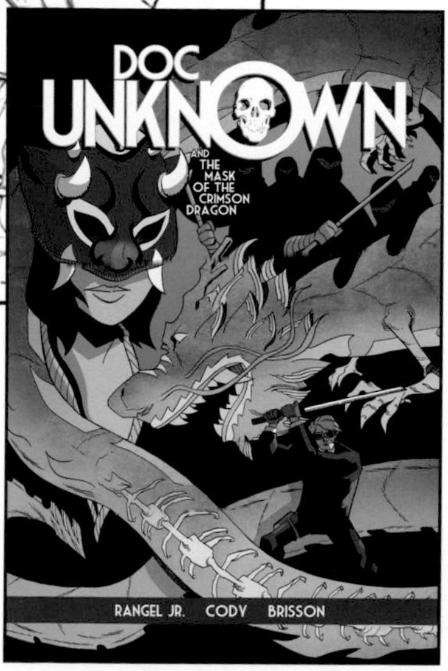
DOC UNKNOWN
AND THE MASK OF THE CRIMSON DRAGON
RANGEL JR. CODY BRISSON

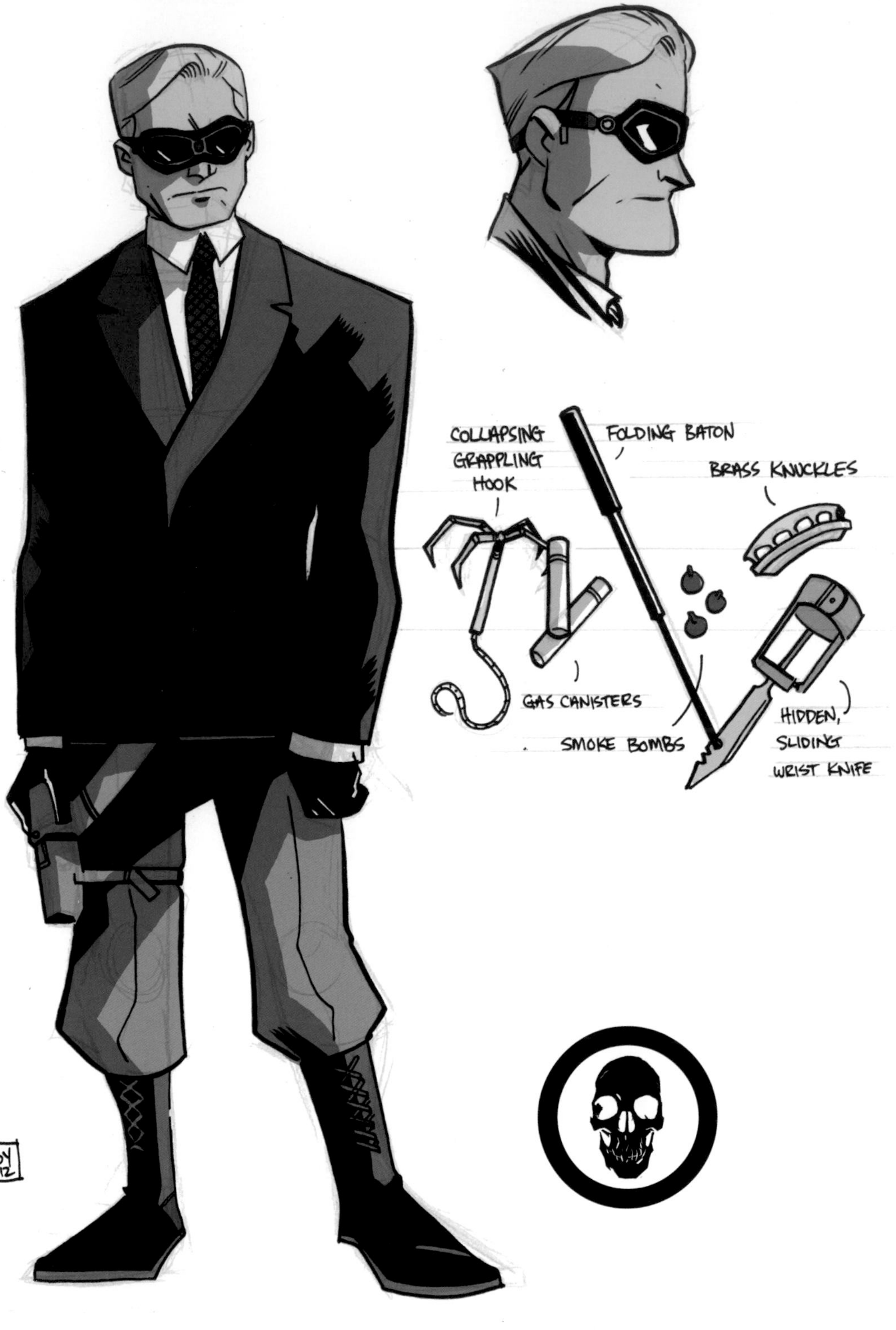
COLLAPSING GRAPPLING HOOK
FOLDING BATON
BRASS KNUCKLES
GAS CANISTERS
SMOKE BOMBS
HIDDEN, SLIDING WRIST KNIFE
CODY 2012

Original design for Doc Unknown. His design stayed pretty close to this through the series, with the exception of some changes to the goggles and holster.

—RYAN

It was in June of 2012 that I asked Ryan if he wanted to work on a new comic. I described it as "dark, pulp, noir, supernatural action stuff. Costumed mystery men, tough vigilantes, freakish crime bosses, and the four Ms: magic, monsters, murder, and mystery." Then in November we got rolling when he sent me this first character design. The guy still didn't have a name, but two days later I came up with "Doc Unknown," and the rest is history. After four years, three Kickstarters, and a lot of email, it's a dream come true to have this story collected as a hardcover with Dark Horse.

—FABIAN